HANDBOOK OF

Pediatric and Adolescent Obesity Treatment

HANDBOOK OF

Pediatric and Adolescent Obesity Treatment

EDITED BY

William T. O'Donohue

Brie A. Moore

Barbara J. Scott

Routledge
Taylor & Francis Group
New York   London

Routledge
Taylor & Francis Group
270 Madison Avenue
New York, NY 10016

Routledge
Taylor & Francis Group
2 Park Square
Milton Park, Abingdon
Oxon OX14 4RN

© 2008 by Taylor & Francis Group, LLC
Routledge is an imprint of Taylor & Francis Group, an Informa business

Printed in the United States of America on acid-free paper
10 9 8 7 6 5 4 3 2 1

International Standard Book Number-13: 978-0-415-95432-7 (Hardcover)

Library of Congress Cataloging-in-Publication Data

Handbook of pediatric and adolescent obesity treatment / [edited by] William T. O'Donohue, Brie A. Moore, and Barbara J. Scott.
    p. ; cm.
  Includes bibliographical references.
  ISBN-13: 978-0-415-95432-7
  ISBN-10: 0-415-95432-0
    1. Obesity in children--Treatment--Handbooks, manuals, etc. 2. Obesity in adolescence--Treatment--Handbooks, manuals, etc. I. O'Donohue, William T. II. Moore, Brie A. III. Scott, Barbara J.
    [DNLM: 1. Obesity--therapy. 2. Adolescent. 3. Child. 4. Nutritional Requirements. 5. Obesity--etiology. WD 210 H23675 2007]

RJ399.C6H34 2007
618.92'398--dc22   2007019101

Visit the Taylor & Francis Web site at
http://www.taylorandfrancis.com

and the Routledge Web site at
http://www.routledge.com

Contents

PART I Etiology, Diagnosis, and Sociocultural Considerations

PART II Toward a More Comprehensive Understanding: Relevant Process Variables

PART III Treatment Approaches: A Stepped Care Perspective

PART IV Nutritional Approaches

The Editors

William T. O'Donohue is a licensed clinical psychologist. He earned a doctorate in psychology from the State University of New York at Stony Brook and a master's degree in philosophy from Indiana University. He is a licensed clinical psychologist in Nevada and has been a full professor of clinical psychology at the University of Nevada, Reno since 1999. He is a member of the Association for the Advancement for Behavior Therapy and served on the board of directors. Since 1996 he has received more than $1,500,000 in federal grant monies from sources including the National Institute of Mental Health and the National Institute of Justice. He has edited more than 30 books, coauthored 3 books, and published more than 100 articles in scholarly journals.

Brie A. Moore is a doctoral student at the University of Reno and a psychology intern at the University of California, Los Angeles Semel Institute for Neuroscience and Human Behavior at the David Geffen School of Medicine. She has a master's degree in child development from the University of California, Davis and a master's degree in clinical psychology from the University of Nevada, Reno. For the past 10 years she has guided families in establishing new parenting behaviors that benefit their children's developmental, behavioral, and physical health. She is committed to the dissemination of cost-effective and empirically based treatments for pediatric obesity. With her coeditors, she has developed and evaluated, via a randomized clinical trial, an Internet-based pediatric obesity treatment called "Fit and Healthy Kids," which teaches children and families strategies for establishing and maintaining healthy lifestyles.

Barbara J. Scott is a registered dietitian and associate professor in the Department of Pediatrics at the University of Nevada School of Medicine. She has worked with children and families for more than 25 years and currently works with the Early Head Start Program and the Nevada Early Intervention Program, where helping children achieve their healthy weight is an important goal. She served as coinvestigator for a National Institutes of Health-funded study to examine the impact of family-based nutrition intervention on children's growth and eating habits. She is interested in providing information to health care professionals and parents regarding early feeding and parenting practices that help children develop lifelong enjoyment of healthy eating and the ability to evaluate and "filter" outside influences (such as TV advertising) on their food choices.

Contributors

Amanda M. Adams received her MA in psychology with an emphasis in behavior analysis from the University of Nevada, Reno, and her PhD from Florida State University. She is a Board Certified Behavior Analyst (BCBA) and is currently an assistant professor at California State University, Fresno, in the Department of Psychology. She is the director for the Behavior Analysis Program at Fresno State and the director of the Central California Autism Center at CSU, Fresno. Dr. Adams' areas of interest lie in the area of applied behavior analysis and the application of behavioral techniques to promote significant behavioral change. Specific research and applied interests have fallen into two areas: public health, especially increasing the level of physical activity in sedentary adults and children, and in the area of autism in early intervention for young children to improve rapid skill acquisition. Dr. Adams has published in several peer-reviewed journals and has been a speaker at regional and national conferences.

Mark A. Adams received his master's in psychology with an emphasis in developmental psychology from CSU, Fresno in 1992 and completed his doctorate in psychology with an emphasis in behavior analysis from the University of Nevada, Reno, in 2000. For over 15 years Dr. Adams has worked, trained, published, and presented in the areas of developmental disabilities, education, psychological theory and philosophy, and organizational behavior management. He is currently a clinical director and Northern Nevada director for B.E.S.T. Consulting Inc., serving children and young adults with autism spectrum and related disorders. He is also an adjunct faculty member in the Behavior Analysis departments at the University of Nevada, Reno, and CSU, Fresno.

Michael I. Axelrod is assistant professor of Clinical Services at Girls and Boys Town and is training director for the department's APA-accredited pre-doctoral psychology internship program. Dr. Axelrod's clinical and research interests include behavioral pediatrics, the assessment and treatment of ADHD, and the use of functional behavior assessment/analysis in residential care settings.

John E. Blundell holds the research chair of psychobiology and is founder and director of the Human Appetite Research Unit at the University of Leeds. He has been active in research on the mechanisms of appetite control for more than 20 years. During the 1980s he was instrumental in identifying a role for the neurotransmitter serotonin in appetite control. In 1990 he established a research unit for the study of energy balance and appetite control in the University of Leeds. John is currently a member of the UK Department of Health–Obesity Social Marketing Programme Expert Review Group. He is also chair of the Expert Group of the International Life Sciences Institute (Europe) Appetite Regulation Task Force. His research is funded by the Biotechnology and Biological Sciences Research Council, Medical Research Council, and industrial partners in the nutrition and pharmaceutical sectors. Current research projects include the characterization of individuals (phenotypes) susceptible or resistant to weight gain on high fat diets, the impact of physical activity on appetite control and weight regulation, and the role of CB1 receptors in appetite and body weight.

Emma Boyland studied molecular biology at the University of Liverpool from 1998 to 2001. She earned an MBA in 2002. In 2005 she received her master's in research methods from the School of Psychology and joined the Kissileff Laboratory as a full-time research assistant. During that time she was involved in a number of human experimental studies and clinical trials of potential weight control treatments. In 2006 she commenced her postgraduate studies on the effects of media exposure and product branding on children's caloric intake, food preferences, and habitual diet.

Caroline Braet is a professor in the Department of Developmental, Personality, and Social Psychology at Ghent University in Belgium. She also serves as the coordinator, supervisor, and a therapist at the Children's University Hospital at Ghent University where she provides childhood obesity consultations, the Ghent University Child Mental Health Center, and at de Haan, a residential care institution for severely obese children. Dr. Braet is interested in the developmental and clinical aspects of childhood therapy and the development and evaluation of programs for children. She received her PhD from the University of Ghent in 1993, with a specialization in the investigation of psychological aspects of childhood obesity. She is the author or co-author of over 100 scientific publications. She has conducted a number of research investigations, including studies evaluating binge-eating in obese children and adolescents, food-related thought suppression and cognitive processing in obese and normal-weight youngsters, and most recently, evaluations of structured parental guidance, impulsivity, and dysfunctional cognitions and core self-schemas related to overeating in obese children. Dr. Braet is a member of the Belgian Association for the Study of Obesity, the European Child Obesity Group, the Eating Disorder Research Society, and the European Association for Behavior Therapy. She has served on the editorial boards or as a reviewer for numerous scientific journals including the *Journal of Clinical Child & Adolescent Psychology*, *International Journal of Obesity*, *Obesity Research*, *Obesity Review*, *International Journal of Pediatric Obesity*, *JAMA Archives of Pediatrics*, *Child Development*, and the *Journal of Abnormal Psychology*.

Johnnie Sue Cooper is a nursing instructor at Holmes Community College in Grenada, Mississippi in the Associate Degree Nursing Program. She teaches clinical and didactic medical-surgical content, management, and coordinates both traditional and online pharmacology. Miss Cooper is a candidate for a PhD in nursing at the University of Mississippi Medical Center, where she also completed her BSN and MSN. She has served in numerous hospitals in Tennessee, Georgia, and Mississippi as a critical care and emergency department staff nurse. She has also worked since 2002 as a family nurse practitioner in occupational health as well as family practice. She currently practices at the Woodland Clinic in Woodland, Mississippi.

Sheila P. Davis is a native of Sumter, South Carolina and a 1975 graduate of the associate degree in nursing program at the University of South Carolina. She earned a BSN from the University of Alabama in Huntsville (UAH) in 1983 (magna cum laude), an MSN in cardiovascular nursing from the University of Alabama Birmingham (UAB) in 1984, and a PhD in nursing education from Georgia State University (GSU) in 1993. In nursing, Dr. Davis has served with distinction as staff nurse, charge nurse, float nurse, and critical care float in hospitals in South Carolina and Alabama. From 1984 to 1991, she was employed by UAB as an instructor, and later, assistant professor of nursing. At UAB, she initiated and coordinated the first State of Black Health Regional Conference and was awarded the Level III Faculty Recognition Award. From 1991 to 1995, she served as chair of the Department of Nursing at Oakwood College. She was awarded the Distinguished Service Award by Oakwood in 1995. Currently, she serves as assistant dean and director of the PhD in nursing program at the University of Mississippi Medical Center, deputy director of the Mississippi Institute for Improvement of Geographic and Minority Health Disparities, and is founder and editor of the *Online Journal of Health Ethics*.

Lisa K. Diewald is a research dietitian at the Center for Weight and Eating Disorders at University of Pennsylvania. She has a BS in food and nutrition sciences from Drexel University and an MS in health education from St. Joseph's University in Philadelphia. Her areas of expertise include the development, implementation, and evaluation of family and school based child obesity prevention and treatment programs.

Myles S. Faith is assistant professor of psychology in psychiatry at the University of Pennsylvania School of Medicine and is on the faculty at University of Pennsylvania's Center for Weight and Eating Disorders. Dr. Faith received his doctorate in clinical school psychology from Hofstra University in 1995. His research focuses on the development of child food preferences, eating styles, and body weight and the interplay of genetic and environmental influences on child eating patterns, parent-child feeding dynamics, and the measurement of child appetite and satiety. Dr. Faith and colleagues test interventions to help treat and/or prevent obesity in children. He holds multiple grants from the National Institutes of Health to study these issues and has authored numerous articles on these topics.

Zubaida Faridi is Assistant Director, Research and Operations at the Yale Prevention Research Center. She earned her MBBS from King Edward Medical College, Pakistan and her MPH from Southern Connecticut University. Dr. Faridi's research interests include community-based participatory research and diabetes prevention. She has managed several clinical trials at the Prevention Research Center and is also responsible for protocol development and establishing the research agenda at the center. Dr. Faridi is also an author of scientific papers, including the recent publication of an essay, "Community Participatory Research: Necessary Next Steps" in *Preventing Chronic Disease: Public Health Research, Practice, and Policy*, published by the National Center for Chronic Disease Prevention and Health Promotion, one of eight centers within the Centers for Disease Control and Prevention. Other publications of interest include, "Impediment Profiling for Smoking Cessation: application in the worksite," *American Journal of Health Promotion*.

John P. Foreyt is a professor in the Department of Medicine, the Department of Pediatrics, and the Department of Psychiatry and Behavioral Sciences at Baylor College of Medicine, Houston, Texas. He is the director of the DeBakey Heart Center's Behavioral Medicine Research Center, Department of Medicine. He earned his BS in psychology from the University of Wisconsin and his MS and PhD in clinical psychology in 1969 from Florida State University. He served on the faculty at Florida State University until 1974, when he moved to Baylor College of Medicine. He has served as a member of the National Task Force on the Prevention and Treatment of Obesity, National Institutes of Health; The Committee to Develop Criteria for Evaluating the Outcomes of Approaches to Prevent and Treat Obesity, Food and Nutrition Board, Institute of Medicine, National Academy of Sciences; and The Expert Panel on the Identification, Evaluation, and Treatment of Adults at High Risk for Cardiovascular Disease, National Institutes of Health, NHLBI. He is an honorary member of the American Dietetic Association and is currently a member of the editorial boards of *Obesity Research & Clinical Practice, American Journal of Lifestyle Medicine, Eating Disorders, American Journal of Health Behavior, American Journal of Health Promotion*, and *Diabetes, Obesity and Metabolism*. He is licensed to practice clinical psychology in Texas and maintains a private practice. Dr. Foreyt has published 17 books and more than 270 articles in the areas of diet modification, cardiovascular risk reduction, eating disorders, and obesity.

Fred Frankel is professor in the Department of Psychiatry and Biobehavioral Sciences at UCLA. Since 1982, Dr. Frankel has been the director of the UCLA Parent Training and Children's Friendship Program. His current research interests are in extending his studies of the effectiveness of Children's Friendship Training to community settings with different populations, including high-functioning autism, childhood obesity, ADHD, and fetal alcohol syndrome. These studies are based upon his published treatment manual, *Children's Friendship Training*. Dr. Frankel earned his PhD in psychology from the University of California at Irvine in 1971 and joined the UCLA faculty in 1972.

Trish Freed earned her BS in nutrition and her MPH from the University of Nevada, Reno, and completed her dietetic internship at the University of Virginia. Her professional experience includes positions as a cancer center dietitian, lead nutritionist for the Women's Health Initiative–University of Nevada site, co-founder and instructor of a university course on obesity, and most recently, project dietitian with Cooperative Extension to promote school gardens in low-income schools.

Patrick C. Friman is the director of clinical services at Girls and Boys Town and a clinical professor of pediatrics at the University of Nebraska School of Medicine. He has published more than 150 scientific articles and chapters and two books involving behavioral pediatrics and behavior disorders of childhood. Dr. Friman's research addresses the well-child gap between pediatrics and clinical psychology. The gap includes behavior problems that bedevil parents, are outside the core curriculum used to train pediatricians, and yet are not sufficiently serious to warrant a psychopathological interpretation. Dr. Friman is editor of the *Journal of Applied Behavior Analysis* and serves on the editorial boards of nine other scientific journals. He is a fellow in Divisions 25 (behavior analysis), 37 (Child, Youth, and Family Services), and 54 (pediatric psychology) of the American Psychological Association.

Lien Goossens is a PhD student at the Department of Developmental, Personality, and Social Psychology at Ghent University, Ghent, Belgium. Her research interests include the prevalence, characteristics, risk factors, and consequences of pathological eating behaviors, especially loss of control over eating and emotional eating, in overweight children and adolescents. She is (co-)author of some internationally published scientific articles within the domain of eating disorders and obesity. Her clinical experience includes several years of practice in the assessment and treatment of children and adolescents with eating disorders and obesity at the Ghent University Mental Health Centre.

Jason C. G. Halford is a chartered health psychologist with an interest in the expression of human appetite and the treatment of obesity, particularly the use of satiety enhancing foods and drugs for weight control. His undergraduate and postgraduate work was conducted at the University of Leeds with Professor John Blundell in the late 1980s and early 1990s. His research then focused on the role of serotonin in satiety and the use of feeding behavior to screen anti-obesity drugs. Some of this included early work on Sibutramine, its effect on satiety, and the neurochemical mechanisms which underpinned this effect. He set up a new human ingestive behavior laboratory at the University of Liverpool in 1999 to promote interdisciplinary research into obesity within the institution. Prior to that, he worked at Penn State University and the University of Central Lancashire. He has been involved in the behavioral assessment of potential anti-obesity drugs in preclinical models and humans ever since, including recent work on both Rimonabant and Sibutramine in clinical populations. Over the past 10 years his research has also focused on drug induced weight gain, the effects of nutrients and fiber on appetite and hormone release, the effects of stress on eating behavior, and on lean obese differences in the expression of appetite. More recently, he has focused on the effects of branding and food promotion on children's food preferences and diet. He is currently a reader in Appetite and Obesity at the University of Liverpool and director of the Human Ingestive Behaviour Laboratory. He is a committee member of the UK Association for the Study of Obesity (ASO).

Craig A. Johnston is a member of the faculty of Baylor's Department of Pediatrics. He obtained his doctorate degree in clinical child psychology from the University of Kansas. His research interests include translational research especially as it relates to childhood obesity. The program he is currently working on is a weight management intervention conducted with middle school Mexican-American children. This program focuses on promoting sustained behavior change in the areas of nutrition and lifestyle physical activity. For the past 3 years, participants enrolled in the study have shown statistically significant weight reduction compared with a control group.

Karen M. Kaphingst is deputy director for the Healthy Eating Research program of the Robert Wood Johnson Foundation. She is based in The Division of Epidemiology and Community Health at the University of Minnesota School of Public Health. Most recently she worked as a research assistant to Dr. Mary Story, researching issues related to childhood obesity. Prior to coming to the University of Minnesota, she was at the Center for Community-Based Research at the Dana-Farber Cancer Institute in Boston, where she worked as program coordinator for studies in a variety of content areas, including healthy weight, tobacco use, prostate cancer, and clinical trial recruitment. Other prior research experience includes working at the Education Development Center in Boston on a national study of high-risk alcohol use among college students. Ms. Kaphingst earned a BA in sociology from the University of St. Thomas and an MPH from the University of Minnesota School of Public Health.

David L. Katz is an associate professor (adjunct) of public health and director of the Prevention Research Center at the Yale University School of Medicine. He earned his BA from Dartmouth College, his MD from the Albert Einstein College of Medicine, and his MPH from the Yale University School of Public Health. A board-certified specialist in both internal medicine and preventive medicine, Dr. Katz has twice been recognized as one of America's Top Physicians in Preventive Medicine by the Consumers' Research Council of America. An expert in weight management, nutrition, and chronic disease prevention, he has served as an advisor on obesity control to the U.S. Secretary of Health, the Commissioner of the US FDA, the ministries of health in Canada and Israel, and the National Governors Association. Dr. Katz is the founder and director of the Integrative Medicine Center at Griffin Hospital in Derby, Connecticut, and the founder and president of Turn the Tide Foundation, Inc., a nonprofit foundation dedicated to reversing trends in obesity and related chronic disease. The author of nearly 100 scientific papers and chapters and 11 books, Dr. Katz is the nutrition columnist to *O* (the Oprah magazine), a syndicated health columnist for the *New York Times*, and has served as a medical contributor for ABC News.

Robert H. Lustig is professor of clinical pediatrics in the Division of Endocrinology at University of California, San Francisco. He is a neuroendocrinologist, with basic and clinical training relative to hypothalamic development, anatomy, and function. His research focuses on the regulation of energy balance by the central nervous system. He is currently investigating the contribution of biochemical, neural, hormonal, and genetic influences in the expression of the current obesity epidemic both in children and adults. Dr. Lustig graduated from MIT in 1976 and earned his MD from Cornell University Medical College in 1980. He completed his pediatric residency at St. Louis Children's Hospital in 1983 and his clinical fellowship at UCSF in 1984. He spent 6 years as a postdoctoral fellow and research associate in neuroendocrinology at The Rockefeller University. Dr. Lustig is the chairman of the Ad Hoc Obesity Task Force of the Lawson Wilkins Pediatric Endocrine Society, a member of the Obesity Task Force of The Endocrine Society, the Atherosclerosis, Hypertension and Obesity in Youth (AHOY) Committee of the American Heart Association, and the Steering Committee of the International Endocrine Alliance to Combat Obesity.

Ellen Moens is a PhD student at the department of Developmental, Personality, and Social Psychology at Ghent University, Ghent, Belgium. Her research interests include childhood obesity, especially the role of the family context and parental factors. She is (co-)author of some internationally published scientific articles within the domain of obesity and eating disorders. Her clinical experience includes several years of practice in the assessment and treatment of children and adolescents with obesity and eating disorders at the Ghent University Mental Health Centre.

Howard Rachlin earned his PhD in psychology at Harvard University in 1965. He is currently a research professor and an emeritus distinguished professor of Psychology at the State University of New York at Stony Brook. He has published more than 100 articles, written 6 books, including *Behavior and Mind* (Oxford University Press, 1994) and *The Science of Self-Control* (Harvard University Press, 2000), and edited two others. He has served on study sections for The National Institute of Health (NIH) and The National Science Foundation (NSF). He is on the editorial boards of 6 journals. His research (on choice, self-control, social cooperation, and experimental economics) has been continuously supported by grants from NIH and NSF including an NIH MERIT award. He has been elected Fellow at the American Psychological Society and the Society of Experimental Psychologists and has been the recipient of a James McKeen Cattell Fellowship (1975–1976) and an award for The Impact of Science on Application from the Society for the Advancement of Behavior Analysis (2005). He was a visiting scholar at the Russell Sage Foundation (1988–1989) and an invited speaker at the Nobel Symposium on Behavioral and Experimental Economics, Stockholm, Sweden (2001).

Jennifer L. Resetar is a postdoctoral fellow at the Girls and Boys Town Outpatient Behavioral Pediatrics and Family Services Clinic. She is a licensed mental health professional, board certified behavior analyst, and nationally certified school psychologist. She earned her doctoral degree in psychology from Louisiana State University. Her clinical and research interests include parent training, functional assessment, child and adolescent cognitive-behavior therapy, academic interventions, and applied behavior analysis.

Ellyn Satter pioneered the concepts of the feeding relationship and eating competence. She is the author of the division of responsibility in feeding. Her books, journal articles, consulting, and training have made her an internationally recognized authority on eating and feeding. Satter integrates her 40 years of experience in helping adults be more positive, organized, and nurturing in caring for themselves and their children. She emphasizes competency rather than deficiency: providing rather than depriving, and trust rather than control. Her theoretically grounded and clinically sound methods allow the individual's own capacity for effective and rewarding food behavior to evolve.

Madeleine Sigman-Grant is a maternal and child health and nutrition specialist and professor with the University of Nevada Cooperative Extension. Her primary areas of interest include nutrition guidelines for feeding children, as well as childhood obesity prevention and community lactation programs. She works with health professionals to understand and apply techniques to help facilitate behavior change in their target audiences and also works with families to help them facilitate behavior change in their food and physical activity choices. Dr. Sigman-Grant earned a BS in Nutritional Sciences (specialty: dietetics) from the University of California at Los Angeles (1966), completed a dietetic internship at the Veteran's Administration, West Los Angeles (1967), earned an MS in nutrition from Loma Linda University (1982) and a PhD in nutrition from the University of California at Davis (1988). She has been a public health nutritionist as well as a clinical, administrative, and community dietitian for almost 30 years. She was an associate professor at The Pennsylvania State University from 1989 to 1997. She is a member of the American Society of Nutrition, the American Dietetic Association, the Society for Nutrition Education, the FDA Food and Nutrition Advisory Committee, and the Partnership to Promote Healthy Eating and Active Living. Dr. Sigman-Grant is a frequent speaker at meetings and conferences for health professionals, academicians, and scientists as well as for consumers. Her publications have appeared in *JNEB*, *Pediatrics*, and the *Journal of the American Dietetic Association*. As an extension educator, she has published numerous consumer materials. She has served as a committee member of the Institute of Medicine and the American Academy of Pediatrics.

Meghan Sinton is a postdoctoral research scholar in the Department of Psychiatry at Washington University School of Medicine in Saint Louis, Missouri. Her research has focused on the developmental influences, including individual, family, peer, and cultural factors, associated with disordered eating and overweight in children and adolescents. She has a specific interest in elucidating the different etiological pathways associated with distinct forms of eating pathology and on examining how overweight is a risk factor for disordered eating. Dr. Sinton earned her PhD in human development and family studies from The Pennsylvania State University, University Park campus, in 2006.

Barbara Soetens is an academic lecturor, researcher, and research coordinator at the Department of Applied Psychology at the Lessius University College of the Catholic University of Leuven, Antwerp, Belgium. She earned her PhD in 2006 at Ghent University, Department of Developmental, Personality, and Social Psychology. Her primary research interests include thought suppression and attention bias in obese and normal-weight restrained and unrestrained eaters, emotional eating, precursors of dysfunctional eating patterns, and body image disorders. She is the (co-)author of several internationally published scientific articles within the domain of obesity and eating disorders and she has served as a reviewer for scientific journals, including *Appetite*. Her clinical experience includes several years of practice in the treatment of adolescents with eating disorders, body image disorders, and obesity, at the Ghent University Mental Health Centre.

Mary Story is a professor in the Division of Epidemiology and Community Health, School of Public Health, and an adjunct professor in the Department of Pediatrics, School of Medicine at the University of Minnesota. She is the director of the National Program Office for the Robert Wood Johnson Foundation Healthy Eating Research program. Dr. Story has her PhD in Nutrition and her interests are in the area of child and adolescent nutrition, and obesity prevention. Her research focuses on understanding the multiple factors related to eating behaviors of youth, and community- and school-based interventions for obesity prevention, healthy eating, and physical activity. She is currently on the editorial boards for the *Journal of the American Dietetic Association*, *Journal of Adolescent Health*, and *Nutrition Today*. She was a member of the Institute of Medicine Committee on Food Marketing and the Diets of Children and the Institute of Medicine Committee on Nutrition Standards for Foods in Schools.

Ann Tanghe has a master's degree in clinical psychology and is a behavioral therapist. Since 1990 she has worked at Zeepreventorium, a residential pediatric care center for chronically ill children in Belgium. In 1994 she started a project for the residential treatment of severely obese children. At that time the project was unique in Europe and around the world. Tanghe is coordinator-psychologist of a continuous population of 120 severely obese youngsters between 5 and 18 years old. There is a continuous waiting list of about 160 youngsters. Since 1994 she has collaborated with Professor Caroline Braet from the University of Ghent to evaluate and improve the treatment program. This scientific work is described in several publications of which Tanghe is co-author.

Chermaine Tyler is interested in pediatric obesity prevention. Her research has focused on assessing the effectiveness of community-based, multi-component physical activity and nutrition intervention for middle school aged children and adolescents. Her interventions involve behavioral approaches to weight management and stress the importance of balancing exercise and healthy nutrition in a family-based environment. These programs target both normal and overweight youth, especially those with a high risk of developing obesity and related disease (i.e., ethnic minority children and their families). Dr. Tyler's research addresses the importance of assessing social and emotional correlates of overweight in youth and how these factors relate to treatment outcomes.

Leen van Vlierberghe is a PhD student at the Department of Developmental, Personality, and Social Psychology at Ghent University, Ghent, Belgium. Her research is mainly concerned with cognitive theory on psychopathology, in youth in general and in obese youngsters in particular. She is co-author of several internationally published scientific articles within the domain of eating pathology and obesity. Her clinical experience includes several years of practice in assessment and treatment of children and adolescents with internalizing problem behavior at the Ghent University Child Mental Health Centre.

Denise E. Wilfley is professor of psychiatry, medicine, pediatrics, and psychology at Washington University in St. Louis, Missouri, where she also serves as director of the Weight Management and Eating Disorders Program at the Washington University School of Medicine. Dr. Wilfley has published over 100 original peer-reviewed articles, book chapters, and reviews, and her work has made substantial contributions to establishing the clinical significance of binge eating disorder, developing effective treatments for individuals suffering from eating disorders and obesity, and developing innovative and cost-effective methods for early intervention and prevention of eating disorders and obesity. Her research involves developing and evaluating treatment protocols (e.g., interpersonal psychotherapy) and the use of multi-method strategies (e.g., Internet-based, family-based, and group-based) in the context of clinical process and outcomes research.

Kashunda L. Williams is an assistant professor of school psychology at Texas A&M University–Commerce. She is a board certified behavior analyst and a nationally certified school psychologist. She earned her doctoral degree in psychology from Louisiana State University. Her research interests include academic and behavior consultation, applied behavior analysis, behavioral and academic intervention, and parent and school collaboration.

Elizabeth J. Zhe is a postdoctoral fellow at the Girls and Boys Town Outpatient Behavioral Pediatrics and Family Services Clinic. She is a licensed mental health professional and provisionally licensed psychologist. She earned her doctoral degree in school psychology from the University at Albany, State University of New York. Her clinical and research interests include school crisis prevention and intervention, child and adolescent cognitive-behavior therapy, parent training, behavioral and academic interventions, and pediatric obesity.

1

Overview

BRIE A. MOORE, WILLIAM T. O'DONOHUE, AND BARBARA J. SCOTT

We are now facing a new international problem: a growing number of children and adolescents who are overweight. The percentage of overweight children in the United States, ages 6 to 11 years old, has more than tripled in the last 30 years (National Center for Health Statistics, 2002). A dramatic increase in the incidence of obesity has been seen in both sexes and in children of all ages, with Mexican-American, African-American, and Native-American children disproportionately affected (Dietz, 2004). Childhood obesity is rapidly becoming a public health problem worldwide. According to the International Obesity Task Force report (2005), approximately one in five children in Europe is overweight, with a rapidly accelerating increase in prevalence (2% annually). Cross-national epidemiological studies suggest that the prevalence of obese and overweight individuals in Russia is between 6 and 10%, while the prevalence is less than 5% for children in China, with a relationship between obesity and socioeconomic status (SES) seen across countries (Wang, 2001). We are faced with the prospect that as other nations become richer they will also become less physically active, and traditional diets will be replaced with "westernized" processed, packaged diets resulting in excess calorie consumption and eventually childhood obesity. These unsettling trends have prompted public health researchers to call childhood obesity a crisis and a pandemic (Kimm & Obarzanek, 2002).

We decided to edit this book because the magnitude of this problem is escalating, because its consequences are quite serious, and because successful prevention and treatment have proven to be challenging. It is our wish to bring the field's leading scholars together into one compendium of the best current thinking and research regarding this problem. This book aims to emphasize several factors we feel are necessary for the highest standard of care in treatment delivery: 1) adopting public health and prevention strategies because of the scale of this problem; 2) adopting empirically validated treatment approaches from multiple disciplines including behavioral health, medicine, and nutrition; 3) recognizing unique developmental considerations; and 4) understanding fundamental process variables. In addition, we hope that this book will provide an impetus for professionals from a wide variety of disciplines to adopt a fully integrated approach to treatment—one that synthesizes biological, psychological, sociocultural, and public health perspectives—to effectively address this complex public health problem.

We also chose to edit this book because a review of the trends for both the rate of childhood obesity and what we believe are the most important causal factors indicates that this problem will get much worse before it gets better. We claim this not to be hyperbolic or alarmist but to call attention to this important problem. We know that obesity and overweight hurts children in many ways. The following chapters document how children's physical health is compromised, how their social functioning is hurt, how their self-esteem and experience of life is worsened, and how their longevity is shortened. In addition, this problem hurts others (e.g., parents worry, and health care costs associated with obesity-related disorders such as diabetes soar). This raises the question of why was this not much of a problem a few decades ago and why is it a growing problem now? Therefore, in this introductory chapter we will briefly examine some of the major trends we believe have caused and will continue to cause childhood obesity. These trends can be categorized into economic, technological, and psychobiological.

ECONOMIC TRENDS

According to the World Health Organization (WHO), for the first time in history the number of overfed people in the world has at least matched, if not surpassed, the number of hungry and malnourished individuals (Gardner & Halweil, 2000). Simultaneously, the world is becoming much richer. The per capita gross domestic products (GDPs) of many countries are increasing at a fairly healthy rate. This is not only true of the traditionally richer North American and European Union countries, but the recent trend is that it is also true of second world countries such as China and India. In general, this increased wealth is a good thing. Billions of people have less painful, more enjoyable, and longer existences. However, as economists teach us, there are tradeoffs.

The relationship between obesity and socioeconomic level is highly variable. In the United States, low socioeconomic groups are disproportionately affected (Dietz, 2004). However, in countries such as China and Russia, persons from higher SES groups are more likely to be overweight or obese. One hypothesis for rapid increase in the prevalence of childhood obesity internationally is that as individuals become richer they can afford more food. They also become marketing "targets" of the food industry and can be choosier about the types of food they consume. Individuals who were starving or malnourished are, as the world becomes richer, increasingly becoming well fed. In general, this is a good thing. However, an unfortunate psychobiological fact (see below) is that many individuals, when given the opportunity to choose the foods and activity levels that wealth provides, choose foods that are more fatty and sweet, and choose to become much more sedentary. Thus socioeconomic health may not translate into physical health in many cases. As the world becomes even richer (more individuals transitioning from subsistence existences as well as higher standards of living for individuals who have already made this transition), we predict that the problem of childhood obesity will increase.

China is an interesting case in point. China has approximately 20% of the world's population. Its GDP growth in 2005 was estimated to be 10.2% (compare that to a more than healthy rate for the United States of 3.2%). China's GDP has been doubling every 9 years (Fang & Meiyan, 2002). This change in wealth is particularly dramatic because during the 1960s and early 1970s famine and malnutrition were problems in China. It is estimated that 30 to 40 million people died in the famine produced by the Cultural Revolution (Becker, 1996).

In order to control population size, China instituted the now infamous one child policy. Because of societal values, the Chinese want this child to be a boy. It appears that this policy has had the unintended negative effect of producing a large number of overweight boys. A report from a recent Chinese newspaper states:

> Official statistics show that 10 percent of the children in China suffer from obesity and the number is increasing by 8 percent per year. Some 14.8 percent of boys in primary schools in China are obese, and some 13.2 percent of them are overweight, with the proportions for girls standing at 9 percent and 11 percent, respectively. Some 13.2 percent of children in northeast China are obese, the largest

proportion in the country, followed by 12.2 percent in east China and 10 percent in central and south China. In big cities like Beijing and Shanghai, there is an average of one obese child in every five. Taking less outdoor exercises and indulging in watching television and playing games at home are the main reasons behind the child obesity, said experts (www.worldpress.org/Africa/1961.cfm).

In addition, as China becomes more technologically advanced, cars are replacing bicycles, and factory jobs are replacing more physically demanding agricultural jobs. Thus China is making a transition that is following the development of Western countries. Although many advantages accrue with wealth and technology, inadvertently the Chinese environment also becomes obesogenic.

We spend some time focusing on China, not only because the 21st century has been predicted to be "China's century," but because some of the trends seen in this developing country will also be seen in other developing countries such as India, Russia, and Malaysia.

TECHNOLOGICAL TRENDS

Part of the reason the world is becoming richer is that technology makes workers more productive. An oxen-powered plow is more productive than a hoe; a small tractor is more productive than an oxen-powered plow; and a modern combine is more productive than a small tractor. But when washing machines replace hand washing, when cars replace bicycles, and when computer use replaces hard physical labor, fewer calories are expended. Thus a second piece of the obesity problem is seen when one unpacks the phrase "labor-saving devices." Much of our technological search is for labor-saving devices and better labor-saving devices (the move from a manual lawnmower to a self-propelled lawnmower to a riding lawnmower is such an example). But these change day-to-day experiences from activities involving large caloric expenditures (digging ditches by hand) to activities with relatively little caloric expenditures (digging ditches with a backhoe). Although this mostly affects adults, it also affects children in that the need for activity decreases with use of technology. In addition, some of these jobs were performed by children, making them more physically active (cutting lawns, helping around the farm, newspaper routes).

The second technological advance has been that we have entered the "information age." Many jobs now have nothing to do with physical labor (the assembly line is becoming extinct in the West) and more and more to do with developing, processing, and using information. People who work at information-based jobs expend very few calories. Children now spend large amounts of time in sedentary activities such as using the WorldWide Web, watching DVDs, listening to iPods®, and playing electronic games. Thus information technology, which will increase in power, scope, and reinforcing ability, will continue to promote low-calorie pursuits, which again will contribute to childhood obesity.

The third negative technological advance is the development of highly processed foods that are tasty to both children and adults. This includes the proliferation of fast food restaurants around the world (from McDonalds to Starbucks), as well as the development of microwavable foods so that the cost in time and effort to prepare food is minimized. The upside of this is that we can spend less time in meal preparation and more time in activities we generally value more, such as reading, being with family, working, etc. However, it makes any food urge more easy to fulfill, thus making food more accessible (and particularly calorie-dense foods) and contributing to childhood obesity.

PSYCHOBIOLOGICAL FACTORS

The economic and technical developments would not result in childhood obesity if we were not made as we are. Thus we also believe, roughly speaking, that human nature contributes to childhood obesity, and more accurately it is the interaction of human nature with these economic and technical trends that has produced so many obese children. We conjecture that human nature contributes to this problem in two main ways. First, changes in our external food environment are occuring at lightning speed, while our bodies continue to function essentially the same as those of our distant ancestors. As discussed throughout this text, we evolved in environments that were often characterized by food shortages. Thus we evolved to prefer high-calorie foods such as fats and sugars, as these kept us alive in food shortage environments. However, now we operate with these proclivities in increasingly food-rich environments. The unfortunate result is high rates of obesity. If we continue to base our diets primarily on the types and amounts of "invented" (flavored, shaped, colored, synthesized) food currently being thrust on us by the modern food industry, it is likely that rates of pediatric obesity will continue to rise. Second, we also evolved to conserve energy. Psychologists have studied optimal foraging theory and suggest that we seem to have genetic mechanisms that make us efficient food gatherers (i.e., we are good at making optimal tradeoffs between the calories required to gather food and the caloric value of the food we gather). Thus it is in some ways "unnatural" to expend energy for the sake of expending energy (as we do when we go to the gym or take a daily walk). However, in our modern technological environment we have to schedule in and commit to such energy-consuming workouts because our daily tasks no longer require much energy expenditure.

There may also be important changes in the family. There is a trend in many countries toward longer work hours. Parents may be interacting with children less and searching for technological babysitters. More research needs to be done regarding how lifestyle changes contribute to obesogenic environments for children.

OBESITY, PROGRESS, AND HUMAN FREEDOM

It might be tempting to look at these trends and respond that it should be the role of government to pass laws against or to tax certain foods, to mandate physical exercise, or to restrict or tax Game-boys® and iPods or anything else that interferes with exercise and health. However, such measures would also restrict freedom. A critical part of a free, open society is that individuals should be allowed considerable latitude in their "pursuit of happiness," even though such pursuits may harm them in the long run. We think it would be Orwellian for the government to be highly involved in these matters.

However, the argument for a government role is that usually freedom is restricted when behaviors have third-party effects. Thus someone can play their stereo as loud as they like when they live in a remote area and no one else can hear it, but when it affects other parties, such as in an apartment building, one has restrictions on the volume. Obesity leads to higher medical costs, and these medical costs can be borne by third parties, especially the government, through insurance programs like Medicaid and Medicare (and hence eventually taxpayers). However, the idea that individual "free" decisions are the primary cause of obesity, resulting in large social and health care costs, largely ignores the role of industry, marketing, and biology as causative influences. So, what does the government have the right to regulate? This is a difficult balancing act. What exactly would we do to a 200-pound, 8-year-old child who refuses or whose parents refuse to get him on an exercise program or have him eat more healthily? Are we willing to terminate his health insurance and then watch him suffer or die? We think not. However, this type of case illustrates the rub: How do we offer incentives and disincentives related to production and marketing of healthy foods, safe communities, healthy eating, and exercise in a way that does not restrict freedom and does not produce socially unacceptable outcomes such as children without health insurance?

TOWARD A SOLUTION

Health professionals can play a primary role in helping parents and children create a new paradigm (really returning to an older paradigm) and set a foundation for healthy eating through the following actions:

- Recognize and then break the food industry's stranglehold on our taste buds and pocketbooks.
- Reengage with the food system and food producers (not food processors) with lessons learned from the local food and slow food movements.
- Replace the majority of processed foods with fresh, basic, simple, tasty foods.
- Reprioritize our time and attention to include food preparation and family meals.

For many families, trying to decide what and how to eat well can seem overwhelming and confusing at times, with often conflicting advice coming from all directions. However, there are some simple basic ideas of sound nutrition that remain constant and that can be very helpful:

- Know what's in the food you eat: read labels and check ingredients.
- Follow rules of food safety.
- Base most of your diet on simple, fresh foods with about one-quarter of your plate including foods that provide good protein, one-quarter with foods that provide carbohydrates from whole grains, and the remaining one-half being covered with fruits and vegetables.
- Prepare most of your own foods: limit eating out to special occasions.
- Eat when you're hungry, stop when you're full.

Using a positive, "big picture" approach can help parents and children develop a comfortable and happy attitude about healthful eating. Food is meant to be both health enhancing and pleasurable—tasting good, fostering sociability, and providing for creativity in cooking and food combining. A realistic goal of treatment is to consume foods that are healthful and enjoyable. It is not realistic to ask or expect overweight children to adhere to a limited or restrictive diet of unappetizing, uninteresting food and then to declare noncompliance or treatment failure when they are unable to maintain this type of diet.

Sustainability, in the short and long terms, is key to achieving success in turning the tide of pediatric obesity. Short-term sustainable actions support overweight children in learning about and experiencing healthy eating that is satisfying and nourishing, and that allows them to achieve and maintain their healthy weight. Longer range sustainability recognizes that we are all (including future generations) ultimately dependent on maintaining the health of the food system through protecting the livelihoods of farmers and food producers, protecting the environment—the land, water, and air—and ensuring the safety of the food supply.

HANDBOOK OVERVIEW

This handbook aims to address a comprehensive spectrum of issues relevant to understanding the treatment of pediatric and adolescent obesity. Part I presents a thorough discussion of etiology, diagnoses, and sociocultural considerations.

First, to better understand this complex, multifactor phenomena, Emma Boyland, Jason C. G. Halford, and John Blundell, from the University of Leeds, England, present in Chapter 2 the psychobiological system approach to understanding the etiology and maintenance of pediatric and adolescent obesity. Dr. Blundell presents a description of the biological and psychological mechanisms that underlie control of feeding behavior. This chapter discusses how biological regulation and environmental adaptation interact to influence the physiology, conscious sensations, and actions of individuals, including physical activity, satiety signaling, and appetite control in children. The unique implications of this model for understanding pediatric and adolescent obesity are also discussed.

After a thorough assessment is completed, the issue of diagnostic clarification often arises. In Chapter 3, "Disordered Eating: Differential Diagnoses and Comorbidity," Barbara Soetens, Lien Goossens, Leen Van Vlierberghe, and Caroline Braet, from Ghent University, Belgium, aid the reader in the identification and diagnosis of disordered eating and facilitate an understanding of appropriate treatment formulation when comorbidities are present. Dr. Soetens and colleagues present a discussion of the clinical characteristics of eating disorders, the classification and diagnosis of eating disorders, atypical eating disorders (eating disorder not otherwise specified), and the measurement of eating disorder pathology. The authors provide the reader with a better understanding of binge eating, night eating syndrome, and the relationship between anxiety, depression, personality characteristics, and eating disorders often comorbid in pediatric and adolescent obesity.

To fully address case conceptualization and treatment formulation, cultural considerations must also be taken into account. In Chapter 4, "Culturally Sensitive Treatment of Pediatric and Adolescent Obesity," Sheila Davis and Johnnie Sue Cooper, from the University of Mississippi Medical Center, discuss the unique roles that ethnicity, culture, and socioeconomic status play in the pediatric and adolescent obesity epidemic. They discuss research on the cardiovascular risks present in ethnic minority children and present novel strategies, such as eliciting the assistance of ethnic minority nurses and faculty to educate and promote messages of health in indigenous communities. This chapter also addresses characteristics of minority populations that may impact their willingness and ability to access and benefit from typical treatment approaches. Lastly, the importance of aggressively targeting minority populations to adequately address the growing pediatric obesity epidemic is discussed.

In Chapter 5, "Anti-Fat Attitudes: A Barrier to Best Practice," Trish Freed reviews the current research exploring our implicit attitudes regarding the meaning of "being fat." Ms. Freed discusses the importance of assessing our value structure as we embark on the conceptualization of the pediatric obesity epidemic. She challenges the culturally derived link between thinness and health and questions the belief that health is a unanimously held cultural value. Rather than accepting weight as a valuable treatment target, this chapter presents a discussion of the ramifications of the "medicalization" of children who are overweight.

In Part II, relevant process variables are presented in order to facilitate a more thorough understanding of comprehensive pediatric and adolescent weight management. Experts in their fields address factors essential to successful treatment, such as the role of self-control, parent training and contingency management, stimulus control, social skills, and strength-based approaches.

In Chapter 6, "Contingency Management and Parent Training in the Treatment of Pediatric and Adolescent Obesity," Kashunda Williams, from Texas A&M University, and Elizabeth Zhe, Jennifer Resetar, Michael Axelrod, and Patrick Friman, from the Girls and Boys Town Behavioral Pediatrics and Family Services Clinic, discuss the importance of parent involvement, support, and skill development in effective treatment of pediatric and adolescent obesity. Many experts in the field hold that parenting skills are the foundation of successful interventions (Barlow & Dietz, 1998). The authors address the important role parents play in managing contingencies in the child's environment to promote healthy diet and activity behaviors. They present and discuss novel strategies for improving adherence and getting children to actively engage in health promotion behavior.

In Chapter 7, "Social Skills Training and the Treatment of Pediatric Overweight," Fred Frankel, from the UCLA Semel Institute, and Meghan Sinton and Denise Wilfley, from the Washington University School of Medicine, present new data exploring the importance of social skills training in the treatment of pediatric overweight. The authors discuss the reciprocal relationship between childhood obesity and impaired social functioning, including teasing, peer rejection, and low support for physical activity in social relationships. In addition, the authors present exciting new data suggesting that targeting social relationships, via Social Facilitation Maintenance (SFM) training, has a positive impact on weight loss and maintenance of weight loss, and may even positively augment the effects of weight loss treatment in children.

In Chapter 8, "Parent Feeding Practices and Child Overweight," Lisa Diewald and Myles Faith, director of the Weight and Eating Disorders Program at the University of Pennsylvania School of Medicine and Children's Hospital Philadelphia, discuss the essential role of parent feeding practices ily-based approaches, the gold standard of care. Limitations of this research and the importance of treatment acceptability and accessibility are discussed. In an effort to address the serious public health concern of pediatric and adolescent obesity, a stepped-care model that is mindful of cost and dissemination is presented.

In Chapter 15, "Behavioral Treatment of the Overweight Child and Families in Medical Settings," Amanda Adams and Mark Adams, from California State University at Fresno, discuss primary care approaches. Pediatric health care providers are often discouraged by the scope, magnitude, and refractory nature of pediatric obesity. In addition, health education provided in the primary care setting has not adequately addressed the current epidemic. The purpose of this chapter is to educate the reader about the effective implementation of behaviorally based obesity treatments in the pediatric primary care setting.

In Chapter 16, "School-Based Prevention of Child and Adolescent Obesity," Mary Story and Karen M. Kaphingst, from the School of Public Health at the University of Minnesota, Minneapolis, discuss the existing literature on the efficacy of school-based approaches. This chapter pays special attention to those studies that have produced the most promising results. The authors discuss the improvements that must be made to strengthen the effectiveness of the school-based approach. Approaches such as the adoption of greater school- and family-focused connections, more sensitive outcome measures, environmental approaches, and smaller scale and more innovative studies may increase the effectiveness of school-level interventions.

Lastly, in Chapter 17, "Public Health Approaches to the Control of Pediatric and Adolescent Obesity," Dr. David Katz, Professor of Public Health at Yale University, and Zubaida Faridi, from the Yale Prevention Research Center, present a treatment approach most commensurate with the scope of the current epidemic. This chapter provides readers with an overview of public health approaches aimed at the containment, control, and prevention of pediatric and adolescent obesity. This discussion of a public health approach will heighten the reader's awareness of the sociocultural factors that play a key role in the etiology and maintenance of pediatric and adolescent obesity and the opportunities present to positively impact the current epidemic.

In Part IV, nutritional approaches to pediatric and adolescent obesity treatment are discussed. In Chapter 18, "Nutrition Education Basics: Navigating the Food Environment," Madeline Sigman-Grant, from the University of Nevada–Reno Cooperative Extension, presents strategies for the practical application of nutrition guidelines. She discusses how practitioners working with children and families can assist them in navigating through an environment that promotes unhealthy eating and physical inactivity.

In Chapter 19, "The Satter Feeding Dynamics Model of Child Overweight Definition, Prevention, and Intervention," Ellyn Satter describes a family-based approach that incorporates recent literature to augment our understanding of parent-child feeding practices and childhood weight status. Satter's approach provides practitioners and families with an easily exportable model for employing behavioral strategies for weight management, while simultaneously considering the child's unique stage of development.

In Chapter 20, "Protecting Growth and Maintaining Optimal Nutrition," Barbara Scott, from the University of Nevada School of Medicine, discusses the importance of revisiting our ultimate goal of optimizing children's physical and mental health when determining appropriate treatment recommendations. This chapter provides basic guidance for what constitutes normal growth and good nutrition for children at different ages and offers practical examples, recommended readings, and useful references for practitioners and families.

in the development and maintenance of childhood feeding and weight disturbance. The authors present comprehensive modeling illustrative of the dynamic interchange that occurs between parents and children when weight issues are of concern. This chapter provides the reader with a comprehensive understanding of how altering maladaptive parent-child interactions can facilitate long-term health behavior changes.

In Chapter 9, "Ten Messages for Weight Control from Teleological Behaviorism," Howard Rachlin, from Stony Brook University, shares his considerable expertise in understanding self-control. For the first time, Dr. Rachlin extends his behavioral economic paradigm to the understanding of pediatric and adolescent obesity. This chapter provides the reader with new insights into the concept of self-control and the literature surrounding the reasons why and how individuals typically fail at self-regulation. The constructs of underregulation, misregulation, habit, willpower, ambivalence, and commitment are discussed.

Lastly, in Chapter 10, "Hedonic Approach to Pediatric and Adolescent Weight Management," Brie Moore and William O'Donohue discuss a novel way to address the problem of self-regulatory fatigue: a "hedonic" treatment approach. To minimize demands on the self-regulatory system, this chapter proposes that greater attention must be paid to the existing strengths in the child's, adolescent's, or family's repertoire. By capitalizing on these strengths, it is hypothesized that the result will be diminished resistance, strengthening of an existing behavioral repertoire, an increase in the overall capacity for self-regulation, and ultimately, better treatment outcomes. Together, these unique contributions represent a new approach to the conceptualization of pediatric weight management that integrates well-researched constructs to augment treatment outcomes.

In Part III, a wide range of approaches to pediatric and adolescent obesity treatment are presented. Our goal is to promote an individualized treatment approach that will best fit the identified child and family. These approaches are presented from most to least aggressive, in order to facilitate a progression of thought to a more public health-type model of the prevention and treatment of pediatric and adolescent obesity.

In Chapter 11, "Intensive Approaches to the Treatment of Pediatric and Adolescent Obesity," Robert Lustig, a leading endocrinologist in the Department of Medicine at the University of California, San Francisco, discusses the data supporting intensive pharmacological and surgical treatment of pediatric and adolescent obesity. This chapter presents a new understanding of pediatric obesity as a phenotype of many different pathologies rather than a discrete disease. This chapter discusses energy balance, highlighting the roles of leptin, insulin, and the autonomic nervous system. Dr. Lustig discusses the importance of expanding our understanding of those biological factors that play a key role in the etiology and maintenance of pediatric obesity.

In Chapter 12, "Inpatient Treatment of Severely Obese Children," Caroline Braet, Ann Tanghe, and Ellen Moens, from the University of Ghent and Zeepreventorium, Health Center de Haan in Belgium, discuss inpatient treatment of pediatric and adolescent obesity. Based on their clinical and research experience, the authors describe guidelines for organizing a multicomponent inpatient treatment program for severely overweight children. This chapter provides the reader with a greater understanding of the inclusion criteria for inpatient care, including considerations of the degree of overweight, family functioning, and medical comorbidity.

In Chapter 13, "Behavioral Approaches to Childhood Overweight Treatment," Craig Johnston, Chermaine Tyler, and John Foreyt, from the Department of Pediatrics–Nutrition, Baylor College of Medicine, Houston, Texas, discuss the efficacy of behaviorally based approaches in treating pediatric and adolescent obesity. To facilitate a better understanding of behavioral approaches, the authors provide a detailed description of specific techniques, including stimulus control, self-monitoring, contingency management, social support, modeling, and goal setting. In addition, the authors outline possible adjuncts to the behavioral treatment of pediatric overweight and indicate areas for future research.

In Chapter 14, Brie Moore and William O'Donohue present an overview of the empirically based treatment of pediatric obesity. This chapter focuses on data supporting the efficacy of fam-

REFERENCES

Barlow, S., & Dietz, W. (1998). Obesity evaluation and treatment: expert committee recommendations. *Pediatrics, 102*(3), e29.

Becker, J. *Hungry ghosts: Mao's secret famine.* New York: Henry Holt, 1996.

Dietz, W. H. (2004). Overweight in childhood and adolescence. *New England Journal of Medicine, 350*(9), 855–857.

Fang, C., & Meiyan, W. (2002). How fast and how far can China's GDP grow? *Economic Focus, 5*, 9–15.

Gardner, G., & Halweil, B. (2000). Overfed and underfed: the global epidemic of malnutrition (Peterson, J. A., ed.). Worldwatch Paper 150, pp. 5–67. Washington, DC: Worldwatch Institute; available at www.plantsforhunger.org/PDF/Overfed%20and%20Underfed.pdf.

International Obesity Task Force. (2005). EU platform on diet, physical activity, and health. London: International Association for the Study of Obesity; available at www.iotf.org/media/euobesity3.pdf.

Kimm, S. Y., & Obarzanek, E. (2002). Childhood obesity: a new pandemic of the new millennium. *Pediatrics, 110*(5), 1003–1007.

National Center for Health Statistics (1999–2002). Prevalence of overweight among children and adolescents: United States, 1999–2000. National Health and Nutrition Examination Survey (NHANES). Hyattsville, MD: National Center for Health Statistics; available at www.cdc.gov/nchs/products/pubs/pubd/hestats/overwght99.htm; accessed October 30, 2004.

Wang, Y. (2001). Cross-national comparison of childhood obesity: the epidemic and the relationship between obesity and socioeconomic status. *International Journal of Epidemiology, 30*, 1129–1136.

Part I
ETIOLOGY, DIAGNOSIS, AND SOCIOCULTURAL CONSIDERATIONS

Psychobiological Approach to the Prevention and Treatment of Pediatric and Adolescent Obesity

EMMA J. BOYLAND, JASON C. G. HALFORD,
AND JOHN E. BLUNDELL

A psychobiological approach is an orientation to human (and animal) phenomena that is different from a biological or sociological imperative. It is a way of interlinking various factors—from different domains—that contribute to energy balance and weight regulation.

The essence of a psychobiological approach is threefold. First, the psychobiological approach explains the interaction between biology and the environment in determining the expression of appetite, and therefore the likelihood of overconsumption leading to a positive energy balance and weight gain. The cause of increased consumption and weight gain is therefore not exclusively due to a biological determinant and, except in rare cases, cannot be sought in a reductionist philosophy.

Second, the psychobiological view must offer an explanation for the increase in mean body mass index (BMI) and obesity (the obesity epidemic) in most countries of the world over the last 20 years. How is the proposed existence of a weight regulatory system consistent with the demonstrated occurrence of an epidemic of massive weight gain?

Third, the psychobiological approach should account for the obvious facts of biological and psychological variability between individuals. It is fundamental to an understanding of the obesity epidemic that some individuals are more vulnerable to weight gain than others. This implies the existence of resistant and susceptible individuals. What are the processes that mediate susceptibility, and how is susceptibility characterized—genetically, physiologically, and behaviorally?

INTRODUCTION

A psychobiological approach to motivated behavior assumes an equal role of internal and external factors in determining subjective experience and behavior response. Environmental stimuli produce marked physiological changes, and these in turn initiate appropriate behavior. For both adults and children, a psychobiological approach to the prevention and treatment of obesity is based on our understanding of environmental and biological contributions to the expression of appetite and control of our feeding behavior. Our understanding of the physiological mechanisms underpinning appetite control has increased greatly over the last couple of decades. Despite this understanding, the obesity epidemic indicates that our biological mechanisms are not sufficiently robust to resist being overridden by environmental factors. However, it is noticeable that not everyone becomes obese or overweight. An appropriate working framework to understand this is to propose that environmental forces promote a general increase in energy intake and a decrease in energy expenditure, but the allelic variation across the population operates to determine the strength of the individual response. That is, the specific genetic makeup of each individual renders them more or less susceptible to weight gain in the face of this powerful environmental influence. This can be described as a "profile of genetic susceptibility" (Blundell et al., 2005). Indeed, a number of genes and allelic variations have already been identified as being involved in body weight gain and the development of obesity (Barsh, Farooqi, & O'Rahilly, 2000).

Our "obesogenic" environment contains potent factors able to readily overcome the biological processes that operate to maintain a healthy body weight (what is often called "energy homeostasis"). In such an environment, characterized by an abundance of accessible, highly palatable foods that are aggressively marketed, in addition to sedentary lifestyles, the psychological processes underpinning food preferences and food-seeking behavior are also capable of directing us into overconsumption and ultimately a state of obesity. This chapter provides an overview of the psychobiological system of appetite control, a crucial network for mediation of feeding behavior and body weight regulation (or dysregulation).

The concept of energy balance is key to understanding the processes involved in weight regulation (stability and instability). Based on the second law of thermodynamics, obesity can only develop if energy intake (diet) exceeds expenditure (metabolism and physical activity) over a prolonged period (Jebb, 1999). Thus energy intake > energy expenditure = positive energy balance and weight gain. This simple and universally accepted concept sometimes disguises the fact that energy balance is highly influenced by a complex interplay of genetic, metabolic, behavioral, and environmental factors, all of which are important components in the development of obesity, as they modulate the energy intake side of the equation. The way in which these factors exert their effect on energy consumption is partly due to their impact on our psychobiological mechanisms. However, currently little is known about the critical developmental periods that shape the psychobiology of appetite regulation. Do the demands of growth, development, and maturation cause the up-regulation or down-regulation of key energy regulatory systems, and what impact does this have on the individual liability to become obese?

THE NATURE OF THE PSYCHOBIOLOGICAL SYSTEM

The psychobiological system is an intricate network of interactions that govern the control of appetite. A large number of neurotransmitters, neuromodulators, pathways, and receptors are implicated in the processing of information relevant to appetite. It is helpful to conceptualize the flux of physiological and biochemical transactions that occur in the periphery, as they result in a pattern of behavioral events and associated motivational states important to the expression of appetite. For ease of understanding, it is beneficial to consider the system as consisting of three levels (Figure 2.1). The first level comprises psychological events (hunger perception, cravings, hedonic sensations) and behavioral operations (meals, snacks, energy and macronutrient intakes), the second level refers to peripheral physiological processes and metabolic events, and the third is the level of neurotransmitter activity in the brain (Blundell, 1991). Appetite is a combination of the events and processes occuring synchronously in all three levels.

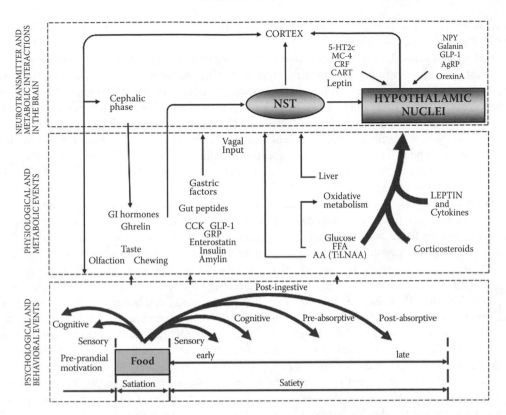

Figure 2.1 Diagram showing the expression of appetite as a relationship between three levels of operations: the behavior pattern, peripheral physiology and metabolism, and brain activity. PVN, paraventricular nucleus; NST, nuclease of the tractus solitarius; CCK, cholecystokinin; FFA, free fatty acids; T:LNAA, tryptophan: large neutral amino acids (see Blundell [1991] for a detailed diagram).

The three levels combine in a feedback loop, whereby behavior is triggered and guided initially by neural events. Each behavioral action then triggers a peripheral physiological response, which in turn is translated into further neurochemical activity in the brain via an integratory center (Kiess et al., 2006).

The first level incorporates all those events that stimulate eating or motivate an individual to seek food (a hunger "drive"), the behavioral actions that actually trigger an eating episode, and those processes immediately after termination of eating (referred to as postingestive events). This can be summed up as the "appetite cascade" (Blundell & Halford, 1994).

Hunger and Palatability

Hunger is regarded as the key internal factor triggering food intake. Traditionally hunger has been viewed as a homeostatic, deficit-driven internal drive to restore energy balance and maintain the body's supply of nutrients essential for growth, repair, and metabolism. However, in most humans who are not subjected to a scarcity of food, it is the anticipation of meal time, stimulation by food cues, or the craving for specific food items which seem to trigger intake, rather than deficit-driven hunger (Lowe & Levine, 2005). Nonetheless, while these are external, environmentally triggered feelings of hunger produce marked anticipatory physiological responses. Even prior to food reaching the mouth, there are potent physiological signals being generated by the mere sight or smell of food, or even learned contextual cues such as location and time of day (Rogers, 1999). These signals, produced in response to external stimuli exposure, comprise what is known as the cephalic phase of appetite. The cephalic response is expressed in numerous parts of the gastrointestinal tract and acts to anticipate food ingestion.

During and immediately after a meal, eating is controlled predominantly by afferent information, that is, both orosensory and postingestive effects of the food consumed. These influences can be considered as positive and negative feedback, respectively, whereby ingested food in the mouth contributes a stimulatory effect, whereas the entry of food into the stomach and the small intestine promotes primarily negative feedback (Blundell & Halford, 1994; Rogers, 1999). The positive feedback is essentially the stimulation of eating by eating (food consumption sustaining hunger) and can be affected by food palatability (Yeomans, 1996). While hunger is diminished with intake, the natural decline in hunger and the development of satiety is delayed if the palatability of food is increased.

What precisely determines which specific foods we find palatable is unclear. However, food preferences are both innate and learned. It is clear that children are born with innate preferences for certain flavors (e.g., sweet) and aversions to others (e.g., bitter). Moreover, these preferences and aversions change in intensity during early development. These can only serve to promote the intake of certain foods over others. It is notable that a number of studies have demonstrated that it is a preference for sweet and/or high-fat foods that characterizes obesity in both adults (Drewnowski, Kurth, & Rahaim, 1991; Mela & Sacchetti, 1991; Rissanen et al., 2002) and children, although the relationship between dietary fat and obesity is less clear in younger children (Gazzaniga & Burns, 1993; Halford et al., 2004; Maffeis, Pinelli, & Schutz, 1996; Obarzanek et al., 1994; Ortega et al., 1995). While the preferences are to some extent innate, data exist to demonstrate the critical role of exposure and learning in the development of appetite. It is far from clear whether some children are born with food preferences that make them more susceptible to obesity than others. However, the literature does suggest that early interventions can be used to modify infant food preferences. These may in turn prevent the development of obesity in childhood and adulthood.

Satiety and Satiation

It is important to note here the distinction between satiety and satiation. The term "satiety" represents simply the inhibition of hunger and further eating that occurs as a consequence of food ingestion. Satiation, however, refers to the processes that operate to terminate an eating episode. Clearly, therefore, satiation influences the volume of food consumed at a meal or a snack. Satiety and satiation provide both within-meal and between-meal controls of appetite. The level of control provided by these processes depends not only upon the properties of the food eaten and the act of ingestion itself, but also on both the quantity and quality of the food consumed. These aspects act to determine the time course of the resulting biological processes and the intensity of the signals involved. This relates to the concept of different types of food wielding different levels of satiating power, hence the importance of the diet's macronutrient content. Not all foods are equal in their impact on satiety. It is frequently argued that there is a hierarchy in the effect of macronutrients on satiety, with protein being the strongest (e.g., Blundell & Stubbs, 1999; Westerterp-Plantenga & Lejeune, 2005). The role of dietary fat in obesity will be discussed in more detail shortly, but first it is necessary to delve further into the specific role of neurochemical pathways in appetite regulation.

The physiological events triggered in response to the ingestion of food form the inhibitory processes that serve to both terminate eating episodes and temporarily prevent further eating. These processes, termed "satiety signals," are absolutely crucial to the action of appetite control mechanisms. Satiety signals include both the afferent, postingestive information and subsequent postabsorptive processes. A number of characteristics of ingested food are monitored, including taste (hedonics), energy density, and the proportion of macronutrients. The earliest indication of satiety comes from orosensory feedback, which is matched with our extensive experience of past consumption, allowing us to judge the satisfying properties of food items currently being consumed (Rogers, 1999). This means that satiety is, to some extent, learned or trained according to previous exposure.

It is self-evident that adults have consumed a far greater number of meals and a far wider range of differing food items than children. Whether this makes them better able to regulate their intake remains debatable. Other preabsorptive signals include gastric distension and preabsorption gut hormone release. Whether children differ in their endocrinological response to intestinal nutrients is unclear. However, the fact that they probably have considerably smaller gastric capacities has never been questioned.

Postabsorptive phase signals are generated when nutrients have been digested and have entered the circulation by passing through the intestinal wall. They provide an accurate reflection of the food consumed. Such products either travel to the peripheral tissues and organs to be metabolized further or alternatively can enter the brain directly in circulation. Whichever action is taken, these products act as another class of metabolic satiety signals. Digestion products or the agents responsible for their metabolism can enter the brain and bind to specific chemoreceptors, affect synthesis of neurotransmitters, or otherwise influence neuronal metabolism. Ultimately the brain receives some information about the metabolic state as a result of consuming food. The series of events following food consumption, coordinated by satiety signals, can be represented by the satiety cascade (Figure 2.2).

With regard to obesity, there is evidence that obese individuals may consume larger meals (Pearcey & De Castro, 2002), gain less satiating value from the foods they consume, and respond more strongly to the energy density of fat (Westerterp-Plantenga et al., 1998), or consume a diet

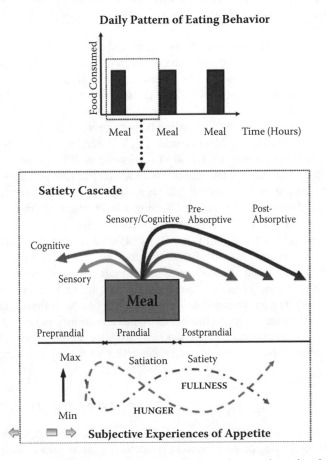

Figure 2.2 The satiety cascade illustrating the events that constitute satiety signals arising from food consumption.

high in energy density (fat and sugar) and low in fiber, which would produce less satiety (Rissanen et al., 2002). Thus, in adults, these data suggest that meals are large and differ in composition, attributes which the appetite system fails to correct for. It is interesting to note that children at the age of 3 years appear to regulate their intake well, irrespective of the portion sizes they are given (Rolls, Engell, & Birch, 2000). However, older children are more likely to overconsume when offered larger portions (Fisher, Rolls, & Birch, 2003; Rolls et al., 2000). These data collectively suggest that the satiety signaling system becomes less sensitive as development proceeds, allowing the environment to override these signals and stimulate overconsumption. This may be an example of the emergence of a thrifty genotype, or a thrifty phenotype (as described by Hales and Barker, 2001); the outcome is that with development appetite there is an emergence of dispositions that permit overconsumption.

One way in which the interaction of systems can lead to weight gain is through the overconsumption of dietary fats, and research in this area has led to the development of two terms, the "fat paradox" and "passive overconsumption." Passive overconsumption, or high-fat hyperphagia, refers to the following phenomenon. When an individual eats to a comfortable degree of fullness from a number of either high-fat or high-carbohydrate foods, that person will consume a much larger amount of energy from the high-fat foods. This is largely due to the high energy density of the high-fat foods, and hence why it is referred to as a passive rather than an active behavior, as the eater has no deliberate intent to overconsume. This does not mean, however, that biological mechanisms do not play a part in mediating this effect. The fat paradox describes the apparent contradiction between fat-induced satiety signals and the easy overconsumption of high-fat foods (Blundell et al., 1996).

Dietary fat is considered to be a potent environmental risk factor for obesity. It has also been found that fat has weak satiating power when compared to proteins or carbohydrates (Astrup et al., 1997). This could be because, while emulsified fat delivered to the intestine causes the prompt release of satiety signals, the time it takes consumed fat to get to the intestine in this form may allow its action to be diluted by other nutrients. In experimental situations, individuals do consume a majority of energy from high-fat foods, but often this is by consuming only a small amount of these foods (Blundell & Macdiarmid, 1997). Therefore it is probable that the satiety signals (including cholecystokinin [CCK]) are functioning well to cause meal termination, but that this system is overwhelmed by the rapidity with which the vast amounts of energy from the high-fat foods are arriving in the stomach. This is a clear example of a dietary (environmental) override of the physiological satiety system. To summarize, these characteristics—palatability and weak satiating power—lend themselves to overconsumption, including a loss of control over portion size (Bray, Paeratakul, & Popkin, 2004). As high-fat foods are highly energy dense, it is likely that persistent overconsumption of these foods would result in a positive energy balance and weight gain. It appears that the ability of individuals to compensate for previously eaten food is impaired when the foods eaten subsequently are high in fat (Bray et al., 2004; Speechly and Buffenstein, 2000). It would seem that most obese people do not possess a deficit in satiety per se, but rather their satiety systems are overwhelmed by highly palatable foods. There is no reason to assume that satiety systems function in a radically different way in children, nor that children are any more resistant than adults to the effect of highly palatable foods on human appetite.

THE SYSTEMS UNPINNING APPETITE REGULATION

The behavioral expression of appetite that results from both subjective sensations of hunger and a desire to eat is governed by a complex network of molecular processes and neural pathways. The central control of appetite occurs in the brain, but this control is guided by signals generated in the periphery to signal energy status.

Peripheral Signaling of Energy Status: Meal- and Adiposity-Derived Signals

There are two types of periphery signals: tonic and episodic. Tonic processes arise from tissue stores, in particular from adipose tissue, whereby the metabolic state of the adipose tissue provides what is thought to be a long-term signal that can act to drive feeding if energy reserves are low. Examples of these chemical signals include leptin, insulin, certain cytokines, and possibly amylin, visfatin, and adiponectin (Blundell, 2006). Episodic signals are predominantly generated by the gastrointestinal tract in response to each eating episode; therefore the levels rise and fall in synchronization with periodic acts of eating. Examples of such signals include CCK, peptide YY (PYY), glucagon-like peptide-1 (GLP-1), oxyntomodulin, amylin, and ghrelin. All these peripheral signals of energy status, whether tonic or episodic, alter neuronal activity within the brain, thus influencing feeding and energy intake. They can act in either an orexigenic (appetite-stimulating) or anorexigenic (appetite-inhibiting) manner via what has been referred to as the brain-gut axis (Chaudhri, Small, & Bloom, 2005). Some researchers argue that the appetite control system of the brain works to try to maintain a weight "set point" even when food supplies vary greatly (Arora & Anubhuti, 2006). It is clear, therefore, that central control of appetite is a crucial target for weight loss intervention strategies.

Cholecystokinin is an important endogenous peptide that is released postprandially from cells in the intestine and acts within the central nervous system (CNS) as a neurotransmitter. CCK has been confirmed as a hormone that mediates satiation and early phase satiety. The consumption of protein or fat triggers rapid CCK release locally and into the circulation and is thought to exert its effects on appetite via the CCK1R receptors located on the vagal afferent neurons (Arora & Anubhuti, 2006). Administration of CCK has been shown to suppress food intake by reducing meal size and duration (Kissileff et al., 1981). PYY is one of a family of structurally related peptides that also includes neuropeptide Y (NPY). PYY is released from the gastrointestinal tract postprandially in proportion to the calories ingested. Its truncated form PYY_{3-36} acts via the presynaptic Y2 receptor in the arcuate nucleus (ARC) (Chaudhri et al., 2005). In humans, infusion of PYY_{3-36} to mimic postmeal concentrations has been shown to reduce food intake by 30% (Batterham, as cited in Small & Bloom, 2004). It is thought to act by decreasing NPY release and exerting effects on the melanocortin system, although the specifics of this latter action are the subject of an ongoing debate. Ghrelin differs from the previous two examples of gut hormones in one distinct way, it acts to signal hunger. It is synthesized in the stomach in response to fasting, with levels rising sharply before meals and falling afterwards, and is therefore thought to be involved in meal initiation (Small & Bloom, 2004). Endogenous ghrelin has been found in several key regulatory areas of the hypothalamus, including the ARC (Chaudhri et al., 2005). Exogenous ghrelin has been shown to greatly stimulate feeding (Wren et al., 2000, 2001). However, since ghrelin levels are lower in obese than in lean individuals, it has been argued that ghrelin is not just an appetite stimulant, but that it plays a regulatory role in energy intake (Cummings, 2006).

As well as meal-by-meal signals, the body's energy stores have the potential to produce a powerful effect on the expression of appetite. In 1994, a landmark scientific event occurred. A mouse gene responsible for obesity was discovered and identified by Jeffrey M. Friedman and the team at Rockefeller University through the study of mutant mice (Zhang et al., 1994). In the ob/ob mouse, a single-base mutation leading to a nonfunctional leptin protein causes the mouse to demonstrate marked hyperphagia resulting in obesity. Leptin is a 16 kDa adipocyte-derived protein hormone that binds directly with a leptin receptor (Ob-R), a member of the cytokine receptor family (Venner et al., 2006). When the leptin receptor is activated, the appetite-regulating effects of leptin are initiated, mediated via orexigenic and anorectic neurons in the hypothalamus. It is thought that when peripheral leptin interacts with receptors on NPY and agouti-related peptide (AgRP) neurons, there is a suppression of NPY release and the antagonist AgRP produced by these neurons is reduced. However, rising levels of leptin also trigger the release of both α-MSH (melanocyte-stimulating hormone) and cocaine- and amphetamine-regulated transcript (CART). These interactions lead to reduced appetite (Venner et al., 2006). Circulating levels of leptin are known to be higher in obese than lean individuals, which is in keeping with the concept of leptin as a signal of the state of adipose tissue stores. However, this also indicates that high levels of leptin are not sufficient to defend the body against obesity. It is likely that a leptin-resistant state exists in most obese humans whereby there is a defect present in some aspect of the leptin-signaling cascade (Venner et al., 2006).

The potency of leptin's action on appetite can be seen in the leptin deficiency state (Montague et al., 1997). Individuals with a missense mutation in the leptin gene have no detectable circulating leptin and display a voracious appetite with a much weakened control over satiation and satiety, accompanied by a strong drive for food. The effects of leptin deficiency appear to be mediated entirely through effects on energy intake (appetite) and not through energy expenditure. Because of this dramatic action, it has been argued that leptin deficiency reflects the removal of "tonic" control over the orexigenic drive rather than the removal of a satiety signal (Blundell, Goodson, & Halford, 2001).

The Integration of Episodic and Tonic Signals: Central Appetite Circuits

The basal hypothalamus plays a crucial role in appetite regulation. This was first demonstrated by classical early experiments showing that damage to one region produces profound aphagia and weight loss, whereas damage to a neighboring region leads to marked hyperphagia and obesity (Rodgers et al., 2002). The ARC is one of the key areas of the hypothalamus, often referred to as the "feeding center." It is positioned partially outside the blood–brain barrier and is therefore able to be directly influenced by circulating factors (Small & Bloom, 2004). The ARC has a high density of neurons expressing receptors for gut hormones, enabling these hormones to modify neuropeptide release from two well-characterized populations of neurons within the ARC (Cone et al., 2001). One population of neurons coexpresses CART and proopiomelanocortin (POMC). These neurons inhibit appetite. The second neuron population coexpresses NPY and AgRP. These neurons stimulate appetite (Chaudhri et al., 2005). Another area of the hypothalamus vital to eating behavior is the paraventricular nucleus (PVN). Numerous neuronal pathways involved in appetite regulation converge in the PVN, including major projections from the ARC, orexins, POMC derivative α-MSH, and the appetite-stimulating peptide galanin (Arora & Anubhuti, 2006). It has been demonstrated that if genetic mutations disrupt these hypothalamic systems, the result is obesity in humans (Barsh et al., 2000).

As mentioned earlier, NPY is from the same family as PYY. NPY is one of the most abundant peptides in the hypothalamus and also one of the most potent orexigenic factors (Kalra & Kalra, 2004). The major site of expression of NPY is the ARC, within neurons that also project into a number of other hypothalamic regions, including the paraventricular nucleus. There is substantial evidence to suggest that activation of NPY can produce significant increases in food intake, and it is believed that both ghrelin and PYY_{3-36} exert at least some of their action on appetite via an interaction with NPY neurons (Blundell, 2006).

Formerly known as hypocretins, orexins are a class of hypothalamic neuropeptides known to increase food intake. Orexin A and orexin B act via two highly conserved G protein-coupled receptors termed orexin-1 and orexin-2 receptors (OX_1R and OX_2R). Orexin A has equal affinity for both receptors, whereas orexin B has an affinity for OX_2R ten times greater than that for OX_1R. OX_1R is expressed in numerous regions of the hypothalamus, including the ARC, while OX_2R is found mainly in the PVN (Arora & Anubhuti, 2006). There is significant evidence to suggest that orexin-A increases food intake by delaying the onset of the satiety sequence described earlier. Rodgers et al. (2002) describe the use of selective orexin-1 receptor antagonists (e.g., SB-334867) to suppress food intake and enhance the onset of satiety processes.

Table 2.1 Some Key Orexigenic and Anorexigenic Central and Peripheral Factors Involved in the Regulation of Energy and the Expression of Appetite

Orexigenic	Anorexigenic
Central	Serotonin (5-HT)
Neuropeptide Y (NPY)	Nor-adrenaline (NA)
Orexin A	α-Melanocyte-stimulating hormone (α-MSH)
Endocannabinoids	Cocaine- and amphetamine-regulated transcript (CART)
Endogenous opioids	Corticotropin-releasing factor (CRF)
Agouti-related peptide (AgRP)	Cholecystokinin (CCK)
Melanin-concentrating hormone	Glucagon-like peptide-1 (GLP-1)
Galanin	Enterostatin
Galanin-like peptides	Gastrin-releasing peptides (GRPs)
Peripheral	Somatostatin
Ghrelin	Satietin
	Neurotensin
	Apolipoprotein A-IV (apo A-IV)
	Oxyntomodulin
	Peptide YY3-36
	Pancreatic polypeptide (PP)
	Amylin
	Estradiol
	Leptin (ob protein)

Hedonic Systems

From a psychobiological point of view it is important to consider the fact that alongside the tonic and episodic processes that contribute to hunger and satiety, there are systems in the brain that are involved in determining the sensory pleasure derived from food. Given the role of palatability in food consumption, these hedonic systems may be critical to our understanding of the psychobiology of overconsumption. Positive energy balance leading to weight gain may result from an inappropriate sensitization of this hedonic network rather than disruptions in the biological appetite-regulating pathways governing satiety (Blundell & Finlayson, 2004). As mentioned previously, the current obesity epidemic shows that the energy homeostasis system cannot prevent weight gain. It seems likely that the potency of hedonic responses to highly palatable foods could overwhelm the physiological mechanisms, allowing overconsumption to occur. Signals of the hedonic system include glutamate, opioids, endocannabinoids, and dopamine pathways. While the mesolimbic system is thought to be the structural element of the hedonic system, the central processing is believed to be carried out in the nucleus accumbens region of the brain (Blundell, 2006).

As stated previously, dietary fat is considered to be a potent environmental risk factor for obesity. It is also well established that a high-fat diet is very palatable. The proportion of fat, in relation to other macronutrients, consumed in an individual's habitual diet is largely a result of food preferences (i.e., the selection of one item over others). Food preference and food selection can be causally linked to the current prevalence of overweight and obesity (Birch, 1999). Although certain aspects of food preference are innate—for example, the aversion to bitter taste and a predisposition to reject novel foods (neophobia)—it is generally agreed that most of our flavor preferences and associated dietary behaviors are learned (Birch, 1999; Brunstrom, 2005).

Food preferences in humans are thought to develop as a result of the postingestive consequences of eating a food (Sclafani, 1997). The occurrence of energy-yielding postingestive satiety signals following consumption of a certain food can lead to an association of that food's flavor with favorable sensations (another example of the interaction between biological mechanisms and environment). In contrast, if nausea is the consequence of eating a food, an aversion to that food type is likely to develop (Birch, 1999). As children have been shown to develop learned preferences for energy-dense foods over energy-dilute versions of the same foods, it is clear that food preferences, in addition to neophobia, can aversely affect dietary quality and lead to weight gain, particularly in children (Birch, 1999).

GENETICS, HEREDITY, AND INDIVIDUAL SUSCEPTIBILITY

Much of the discussion in this chapter has focused on ways in which the environment and internal molecular mechanisms interact. However, the internal molecular environment is determined by genes. Genetic factors determine each individual's response to environmental factors such as diet and exercise. The genetic element has been separated from other factors primarily through the study of twins. Monozygotic twins are genetically identical, and dizygotes share an average of 50% of their genes. Bouchard and Tremblay (1990) demonstrated that individuals have different genetic propensities toward the storage of excessive caloric intake as fat. After overfeeding pairs of monozygotic twins by 10%, it was observed that different sets of twins showed striking differences in the degree to which these calories were stored as fat, but that within the twin pairs, the tendency to increased adiposity was remarkably similar. This suggests that there is a genetic involvement in determining an individual's susceptibility to gain weight in a given environment (Farooqi, 2005). Furthermore, Mutch and Clément (2006) report that more than 240 genes have been identified by the Human Obesity Gene Map consortium which, when mutated or expressed as transgenes in mice, can act to modulate body weight and adiposity. However, there is little agreement over how much of the variation in BMI is due to genetic factors (Maes, Neale, & Eaves, 1997). Results from studies of twins have tended to indicate the highest heritability for body fatness, ranging from 50% to 90% (e.g., Allison et al., 1994; Bodurtha et al., 1990; Rasmussen et al., 2006), whereas estimates from family studies of parent-offspring and sibling correlations suggest heritabilities of 20% to 80% (Provencher et al., 2004; Stanforth et al., 2004), and those of adoption studies report the lowest values, in the range of 20% to 60% (Maes et al., 1997). The overriding message is that most authorities agree that genetic factors play a significant role in individual susceptibility to body weight gain, but the specific degree of genetic contribution to BMI is not yet known.

This chapter has emphasized the numerous ways in which obesity can result from environmental factors (e.g., the abundant availability of highly palatable, energy-dense foods) and factors relating to the foods themselves (e.g., high energy density, high fat content, and portion size). However, despite the obesogenic environment providing so many potent factors to encourage weight gain, some people remain lean. This suggests that in such an environment, some individuals have a susceptibility to gaining weight, whereas others do not. The most likely explanation for this phenomenon is the existence of some kind of psychobiological variability from person to person that affects their individual weight regulation. One widely adopted explanation is that of the "thrifty genotype" concept. This phrase was coined in 1962 by J. V. Neel, who noted that some organisms have highly advantageous survival mechanisms; specifically, adaptations that enable them to store fat in times of food plenty so that they are sufficiently prepared for times of food scarcity (Prentice, 2005). Thriftiness is said to take many forms, including metabolic (an "energy sparing, superefficient" metabolism), adipogenic (a propensity toward rapid weight gain), physiologic (the ability to switch off nonessential processes), gluttony (a tendency to gorge when food is available), sloth (a tendency to conserve energy through inactivity), or behavioral (hoarding, meanness, theft, etc.) (Prentice, 2005). Although many of these forms, brought about in part by evolution, may seem archaic, there is clearly still much relevance to the concepts of appetite and satiety in today's feeding environment.

The way in which a thrifty genotype could be expressed through appetite has been investigated in a large European study on the impact of high-fat diets. This was based on the identification of susceptible and resistant phenotypes (Blundell et al., 2005). Those individuals characterized as susceptible to weight gain on a habitual high-fat diet (compared with resistant individuals) show distinctive eating characteristics, including a reduction in the strength of fat-induced satiety; a weak degree of satiation (intrameal satiety), particularly to high-fat foods; the retained preference for fat in the postprandial period; and a high disinhibition score (general readiness to eat in response to environmental stimulation). This set of outcomes has shown that factors specific to individuals (endogenous variables) determine their response to a hedonically potent high-fat food environment. It is a good example of the psychobiological approach—an interaction between individual states and environmental features—which in turn determines the susceptibility or resistance to weight gain. The important message is that not all individuals respond in the same way.

Perhaps the most startling demonstration of the effect of genes on the psychobiology of appetite regulation is chromosomal or signal gene mutation disorders such as Prader-Willi syndrome (PWS) and congenital leptin deficiency. PWS is caused by a rearrangement of the paternal chromosome, either by partial deletion of a critical segment or a total deletion of the chromosome. The primary characteristic of the condition is marked hyperphagia, leading to obesity in a majority of cases. The precise mechanisms through which this appetite dysfunction occurs are still not fully elucidated, however, it is suspected that ghrelin may be involved, as it has been demonstrated that both children and adults with PWS have fasting plasma ghrelin levels that are 4.5-fold higher than in equally obese non-PWS controls (Cummings et al., 2002). Similarly, a rare mutation in the human leptin receptor gene was discovered in two severely obese cousins of Pakistani ancestry (Montague et al., 1997). Despite their acute obesity, the children both had virtually undetectable levels of serum leptin. This was found to be due to a mutation in the ob gene, which resulted in a truncated protein that was not secreted (Montague et al., 1997). These authors have since identified many more individuals with similar afflictions; notable characteristics include intense hyperphagia and little or no pubertal development (Farooqi, 2005). Therefore, genetic aberrations in a single key episodic or tonic psychobiological system can cause severe changes to appetite, feeding behavior, caloric intake, and adiposity in children, which if not corrected will persist into adulthood.

PREVENTION AND TREATMENT OPTIONS FOR OBESITY IN CHILDREN AND ADOLESCENTS

We have detailed the psychobiological processes critical to the expression of human appetite. Moreover, this chapter has also provided an overview of some of the numerous physiological and neurochemical mechanisms that underpin these processes. Vast strides have been made toward elucidating the complex and specific internal mechanisms presiding over our control of appetite. But how much of this knowledge can be used to develop effective prevention and treatment strategies for obesity treatment, specifically for children, is uncertain. The vast majority of the literature on treatment guidelines for pediatric obesity focus exclusively on lifestyle interventions (Berkel et al., 2005), due in part to the highly complex ethical and moral issues of providing more invasive treatments for children. Psychobiological interventions (i.e., those using current knowledge of our appetite regulation systems, and the psychological factors that influence them) have not been at the center of pediatric treatment strategies. However, there are a number of treatments for adult obesity which do influence appetite regulation that have also been used in children. With regard to children, much clinical research has focused on prevention.

Obesity Prevention

Preventing pediatric obesity is likely to be the only way in which the current obesity epidemic can be contained, yet the number of prevention strategies designed remains limited. In principle, all prevention is aimed at preventing the positive energy balance produced by excessive intake and inadequate expenditure of energy, which, left unchanged, produces excessive weight gain (i.e., that above normal development associated with increasing adiposity). However, it has been noted that a chronic mismatch exists between obesity prevalence and the knowledge base from which to inform preventative activity (Ells et al., 2005). For instance, the Cochrane review was only able to find seven randomized control trials with adequate long-term evaluations of their efficacy (Campbell, as cited in Ells et al., 2005). Even with these studies, the authors found it difficult to make many conclusions about what was the most effective approach due to the small sample sizes of children involved.

Dehghan, Akhtar-Danesh, and Merchant (2005) suggest some potential prevention strategies that could be targeted at the food sector, which, via changes in dietary intake, could allow the psychobiological system to regain control over appetite regulation. The ideas proposed include applying a small tax on high-volume foods of low nutritional value (e.g., soft drinks and snack foods), food labeling and nutrition "signposts" (e.g., logos for nutritious foods), and implementing standards for product formulation (Dehghan et al., 2005). It is put forward that food prices, for example, have a marked influence on food-buying behavior and therefore on nutrient intake. The authors believe that making it easier for consumers to identify healthier food choices will be a significant step toward tackling obesity (Dehghan et al., 2005).

Current governmental guidelines recommend that we consume at least five portions of fruits and vegetables per day, not including potatoes. Adjusting habitual diets to include a greater proportion of fruits and vegetables is an extremely beneficial step toward weight management. Not only are fruits and vegetables nutrient dense (i.e., they have high nutritive value relative to their energy content), but such foods have been shown to be protective against childhood overweight and associated health problems (Lin & Morrison, 2002; Ness et al., 2005). Moreover, their fiber content increases their satiating value. Numerous published intervention studies in the United States and United Kingdom have used the "5 A Day" message as the basis of their program, and systematic reviews suggest these are effective at increasing fruit and vegetable intake in children and adults (Ammerman et al., 2002). The long-term benefits of these programs in terms of the permanence of change in diet and reductions in future health risk, specifically later obesity, remain to be fully determined. However, with regard to obesity, increases in the number of fresh fruits and vegetables in children's diets are associated with a reduction in the intake of high-fat food items associated with obesity.

The problem remains that few of the interventions promoting the intake of fruits and vegetables are based on a scientific understanding on how children's food preferences develop. Often, by the time children attend school—the location of most prevention interventions—the child has already developed a robust set of food preferences. At this stage, food neophobia and picky eating can provide a barrier to effective change in those children whose food preferences leave them most at risk of weight gain.

Once children are obese, treatment options are generally limited to lifestyle changes that promote a reduction in energy intake and an increase in energy expenditure (diet and exercise). Again, reviews of the efficacy of weight loss treatments in children have found few studies worthy of inclusion. Also, of those that are included, evidence for a long-term impact on weight control is limited. More radical solutions used in adults, such as drugs and even surgery, are not normally considered as treatment options in children. However, it is these radical interventions that appear to produce the best results in adults.

Antiobesity drug therapy for adults is now widely accepted, although few medications are currently approved for use; notably sibutramine, orlistat (Molnár, 2005), and recently rimonabant (not in the United States) (Gobshtis, Ben-Shabat, & Fride, 2007). All of these reduce energy intake. Sibutramine and rimonabant act directly on the CNS mechanisms that underpin the homeostatic and hedonic aspects of appetite control (satiety and palatability), while orlistat blocks digestion of energy and may also influence food choice (Gobshtis et al., 2007; Halford, 2006a,b; Molnár, 2005).

Pharmacological treatment in young people has not been extensively studied, however, sibutramine and orlistat have been the subject of a few promising randomized control trials in adolescents (Berkowitz et al., 2003; Chanoine et al., 2005; Godoy-Matos et al., 2005).

With regard to sibutramine, in the Berkowitz et al. trial, 82 adolescents, age 13 to 17 years (BMI 32 to 44 kg/m^2), were randomized to treatment for 6 months with placebo or sibutramine (with behavioral therapy for all). Weight loss in the drug-treated group was 7.8 kg, with an 8.5% reduction in BMI, which was significantly higher than the placebo group, who showed a weight loss of 3.2 kg and a 4.0% reduction in BMI. When the placebo group was switched to treatment with sibutramine after the initial 6 months, there was an additional loss of 1.3 kg (Berkowitz et al., 2003). Godoy-Matos et al. (2005) studied 60 adolescents, age 14 to 17 years (BMI 30 to 45 kg/m^2), assigned to either sibutramine or placebo for 6 months of treatment. Patients assigned to the sibutramine group lost significantly more weight than the control group (10.3 kg vs 2.4 kg) and showed a significantly greater reduction in BMI (3.6 kg/m^2 vs 0.9 kg/m^2). However, as has been seen in studies with adults (Bray et al., 1996), 5 participants (6.1%) in the Berkowitz et al. study (2003) had marked and sustained increases in blood pressure (10 mmHg) that required discontinuation of the medication. In the Godoy-Matos et al. study (2005), sibutramine was reported to be well tolerated by the participants and no significant differences in cardiovascular parameters were found between placebo and treatment groups, although constipation was significantly increased in the treatment group. Both authors recommend that further controlled studies be done in children and adolescents before it can be concluded that sibutramine can be safely used in this age group (Berkowitz et al., 2003; Godoy-Matos et al., 2005).

With regard to orlistat, Chanoine et al. (2005) conducted a multicentered trial in 539 obese adolescents (age 12 to 16 years, BMI c^2 units above the 95th percentile). Participants were randomized to either a treatment group or a placebo control group, where they received a 120 mg dose of orlistat or placebo three times a day for 1 year (in addition to a mildly hypocaloric diet, exercise, and behavioral therapy). At the end of the study, BMI had decreased by 0.55 kg/m^2 with orlistat, but had increased by 0.31 kg/m^2 with placebo, a significant difference. The most common side effects found in the Chanoine et al. study were gastrointestinal (GI) tract related (e.g., fatty/oily stools and fecal urgency) and were more common in the orlistat group than the placebo group; however, these events were reported to be mild to moderate in intensity and may be related to the mechanism of action of the drug. Only one serious adverse event, symptomatic cholelithiasis that led to cholecystectomy in a 15-year-old girl treated with orlistat, was considered to be possibly related to the study medication (Chanoine et al., 2005). However, overall it was reported that orlistat did not raise any safety issues and the adverse event profiles (except GI tract events) were similar between orlistat and placebo groups (Chanoine et al., 2005).

Leptin has been shown to be a potent reducer of energy intake in rodents. Moreover, the absence of tonic inhibitory signals can cause dramatic effects on the expression of feeding behavior. For instance, individuals unable to produce the adipose tissue signal leptin (ob protein) are unable to control their food intake. However, most obese humans, including obese children, have higher levels of leptin relative to their lean counterparts (Venner et al., 2006). It is believed that a leptin-resistant state exists in most obese humans, as a consequence of either repeated exposure of the hypothalamus to the signal or a defect occuring within the leptin signaling cascade system (Arora & Anubhuti, 2006; Venner et al., 2006). Consequently, in humans, clinical trials have shown that administration of leptin has little effect on body weight in the obese (Hukshorn et al., 2002). However, Sinha & Caro (1998) have proposed that approximately 5% of the obese population have some degree of leptin deficiency/resistance that could benefit from leptin therapy. Moreover, the administration of recombinant leptin normalizes feeding behavior in children with leptin deficiency, reinstating the episodic operation of hunger and satiety (Farooqi et al., 2002).

For a long period of time, surgery has been considered to be a mechanical rather than a psychobiological intervention. However, it is now recognized that the fitting of a gastric lap band not only reduces intake but changes subjective experiences of appetite. Post-operation, patients report less hunger and feel more in control of their appetite (Lang, Hauser, Buddeberg, & Klaghofer, 2002). Similarly with gastric bypass, it has been suggested that the reasons for success could be more hormonal than mechanical. Malabsorption does prevent some energy from passing from the gut into the body. However, some authors have pointed out that this effect is transient in nature and cannot explain the permanent reduction in appetite patients report after the operation (Small & Bloom, 2004). Surgery appears to reduce circulating ghrelin levels and may also increase circulating PYY (shown in rat models). These changes would explain reductions in hunger after surgery and resulting sustained weight loss (Small & Bloom, 2004). It is extremely rare for bariatric surgery to be carried out on children or adolescents. Nevertheless, it has been suggested as appropriate for use in treating morbidly obese adolescents, those with a BMI above the 95th percentile for their age and sex, who have accompanying medical complications remediable through weight reduction (Cuttler, Whittaker, & Kodish, 2005). More recently, guidelines published by the UK National Institute for Clinical Excellence state that drug treatment is now recommended for children 12 years of age and older if there are physical or severe psychological comorbidities, and can be prescribed to children younger than 12 years of age in exceptional circumstances (i.e., severe life-threatening comorbidities). The report also states that while surgery is generally not recommended for children, it can be considered in exceptional circumstances (i.e., physical maturity, a particularly high BMI, significant weight-related disease, or a failure to respond to other treatments) (National Institute for Clinical Excellence, 2006).

FUTURE DIRECTIONS FOR RESEARCH

A psychobiological approach to the prevention and treatment of obesity in children stresses the need to understand the environmental and biological factors that promote obesity; in particular, how regulatory mechanisms of satiety are undermined and how food preferences develop. With regard to satiety, we are now aware of many of the mechanisms that underpin its operation. This enables us to devise treatments—nutritional or pharmacological—for obesity that reduce energy intake while not producing hunger. Regrettably, how much of this knowledge is used in current pediatric obesity treatment is unclear. With regard to prevention, it is clear that preferences for certain foods are critical. Early infancy has been identified by some authors as a critical period in the development of obesity (Dietz, 1994). For instance, both high and low birth weights are associated with an increased risk of childhood obesity (Ong & Dunger, 2004). Individual food preferences (i.e., what is liked and what is disliked) are the primary psychological drivers of actual food choice. These in turn determine the individual's habitual diet, impacting their future health. Food neophobia (unwillingness to eat novel foods) in children appears to be a powerful determinant of the child's food preferences. Evidence suggests that children's food preferences become stable as early as the age of 2 years (Birch, 1999). Prior to this age there appear to be three critical stages at which the young are exposed to different flavors and consequently develop the food preferences that will, in part, determine their food choices into adult life. Exposure of the child to a greater number of different foods during this critical period predicts acceptance of a greater range of foods later in childhood. Regrettably, there is very little evidence that scientific understanding of the development of food preferences is informing many childhood obesity prevention programs.

Even if we are able to produce psychobiological interventions, evaluating their efficacy against existing approaches may be difficult. There have been a number of reports and systematic reviews of intervention strategies to prevent obesity in children. Flodmark, Marcus, and Britton (2006) found only 24 controlled studies with appropriate follow-up measures to include in their analysis. Only eight of these produced a significant reduction in the development of obesity in children. Similarly, a 2004 report from the British Nutrition Foundation also commented on the limited number of intervention studies in children aimed at promoting positive food choices. In particular, the report stressed the lack of randomized control trials, poorly defined outcome measures, and the importance of robust and appropriate tools for assessing changes in food choice. With regard to obesity treatment, the same problems exist (Ells et al., 2005). Given that we are not sure how effective existing treatment interventions are, we are not yet in a position to judge if adding antiobesity drugs to these could produce any additional benefit. With regard to the pharmacological approach, Molnár (2005) proposed that, with strict guidelines, more double-blind, placebo-controlled trials should be utilized to investigate the treatment of obese adolescents with the same drugs that are being used in the long-term treatment of adult obesity. While adjunct drug therapy may produce additional benefits for the treatment of obese children, more data need to be collected about the safety and efficacy of drug therapy in children and adolescents before any firm conclusions can be made (Godoy-Matos et al., 2005).

REFERENCES

Allison, D. B., Heshka, S., Neale, M. C., & Heymsfield, S. B. (1994). Race effects in the genetics of adolescents' body mass index. *International Journal of Obesity, 18,* 363–368.

Ammerman, A. S., Lindquist, C. H., Lohr, K. N., Hersey, J. (2002). The efficacy of behavioural interventions to modify dietary fat and fruit and vegetable intake: a review of the evidence. *Preventative Medicine, 35,* 25–41.

Arora, S., & Anubhuti. (2006). Role of neuropeptides in appetite regulation and obesity—a review. *Neuropeptides, 40,* 375–401.

Astrup, A., Toubro, S., Raben, A., & Skov, A. R. (1997). The role of low-fat diet and fat substitutes in body weight management: what have we learned from clinical studies? *Journal of the American Dietetic Association, 97*(7 suppl. 1), S82–S98.

Barsh, G. S., Farooqi, I. S., & O'Rahilly, S. (2000). Genetics of body weight regulation. *Nature, 404,* 644–651.

Berkel, L. A., Carlos Poston, W. S., Reeves, R. S., & Foreyt, J. P. (2005). Behavioural interventions for obesity. *Journal of the American Dietetic Association, 105*(suppl.), S35–S43.

Berkowitz, R. I., Wadden, T. A., Tershakovec, A. M., & Cronquist, J. L. (2003). Behavior therapy and sibutramine for the treatment of adolescent obesity. *JAMA, 289,* 1805–1812.

Birch, L. L. (1999). Development of food preferences. *Annual Review of Nutrition, 19,* 41–62.

Blundell, J. E. (1991). Pharmacological approaches to appetite suppression. *Trends in Pharmacological Science, 12,* 147–157.

Blundell, J. E. (2006). Perspective on the central control of appetite. *Obesity, 14*(suppl.), 160S–163S.

Blundell, J. E., & Finlayson, G. (2004). Is susceptibility to weight gain characterised by homeostatic or hedonic risk factors for overconsumption? *Physiology & Behaviour, 82,* 21–25.

Blundell, J. E., Goodson, S., & Halford, J. C. G. (2001). Regulation of appetite: role of leptin in signalling systems for drive and satiety. *International Journal of Obesity, 25*(suppl. 1), S29–S34.

Blundell, J. E., & Halford, J. C. G. (1994). Regulation of nutrient supply: the brain and appetite control. *Proceedings of the Nutrition Society, 53,* 407–418.

Blundell, J. E., Lawton, C. L., Cotton, J. R., & Macdiarmid, J. I. (1996). Control of human appetite: implications for the intake of dietary fat. *Annual Review of Nutrition, 16,* 285–319.

Blundell, J. E., & Macdiarmid, J. I. (1997). Fat as a risk factor for overconsumption: satiation, satiety, and patterns of eating. *Journal of the American Dietetic Association, 97*(7 suppl. 1), S63–S69.

Blundell, J. E., & Stubbs, R. J. (1999). High and low carbohydrate and fat intakes: limits imposed by appetite and palatability and their implications for energy balance. *European Journal of Clinical Nutrition, 53*(suppl. 1), S148–S165.

Blundell, J. E., Stubbs, R. J., Golding, C., Croden, F., Alam, R., Whybrow, S., Le Noury, J., & Lawton, C. L. (2005). Resistance and susceptibility to weight gain: individual variability in response to a high-fat diet. *Physiology & Behaviour, 86,* 614–622.

Bodurtha, J. N., Mosteller, M., Hewitt, J. K., Nance, W. E., Eaves, L. J., Moskowitz, W. B., Katz, S., & Schieken, R. M. (1990). Familial resemblance of body weight and weight/height in 374 homes with adopted children. *Journal of Pediatrics, 91,* 555–558.

Bouchard, C., & Tremblay, A. (1990). Genetic effects in human energy expenditure components. *International Journal of Obesity and Related Metabolic Disorders, 14,* 49–58.

Bray, G. A., Paeratakul, S., & Popkin, B. M. (2004). Dietary fat and obesity: a review of animal, clinical and epidemiological studies. *Physiology & Behaviour, 83,* 549–555.

Bray, G. A., Ryan, D. H., Gordon, D., Heidingsfelder, S., Cerise, F., & Wilson, K. (1996). A double-blind randomized placebo-controlled trial of sibutramine. *Obesity Research, 4,* 263–270.

Brunstrom, J. M. (2005). Dietary learning in humans: directions for future research. *Physiology & Behaviour, 85,* 57–65.

Chanoine, J. P., Hampl, S., Jensen, C., Boldrin, M., & Hauptman, J. (2005). Effect of orlistat on weight and body composition in obese adolescents. *JAMA, 293,* 2873–2883.

Chaudhri, O. B., Small, C. J., & Bloom, S. R. (2005). The gastrointestinal tract and the regulation of appetite. *Drug Discovery Today: Disease Mechanisms, 2,* 289–294.

Cone, R. D., Cowley, M. A., Butler, A. A., Fan, W., Marks, D. L., & Low, M. J. (2001). The arcuate nucleus as a conduit for diverse signals relevant to energy homeostasis. *International Journal of Obesity and Related Metabolic Disorders, 25*(suppl. 5), S63–S67.

Cummings, D. E. (2006). Ghrelin and the short- and long-term regulation of appetite and body weight. *Physiology & Behaviour, 89,* 71–84.

Cummings, D. E., Clement, K., Purnell, J. Q., Vaisse, C., Foster, K. E., Frayo, R. S., Schwartz, M. W., Basdevant, A., & Weigle, D. S. (2002). Elevated plasma ghrelin levels in Prader-Willi syndrome. *Nature Medicine, 8,* 643–644.

Cuttler, L., Whittaker, J. L., & Kodish, E. D. (2005). The overweight adolescent: clinical and ethical issues in intensive treatments for pediatric obesity. *Journal of Pediatrics, 146,* 559–564.

Dehghan, M., Akhtar-Danesh, N., & Merchant, A. T. (2005). Childhood obesity, prevalence and prevention. *Nutrition Journal, 4,* 24–31.

Dietz, W. H. (1994). Critical periods in childhood for the development of obesity. *American Journal of Clinical Nutrition, 59,* 995–999.

Drewnowski, A., Kurth, C. L., & Rahaim, J. E. (1991). Taste preferences in human obesity—environmental and familial factors. *American Journal of Clinical Nutrition, 54,* 635–641.

Ells, L. J., Campbell, K., Lidstone, J., Kelly, S., Lang, R., & Summerbell, C. (2005). Prevention of childhood obesity. *Best Practice & Research: Clinical Endocrinology & Metabolism, 19,* 441–454.

Farooqi, I. S. (2005). Genetic and hereditary aspects of childhood obesity. *Best Practice and Research: Clinical Endocrinology & Metabolism, 19,* 359–374.

Farooqi, S. F., Matarese, G., Lord, G. M., Keogh, J. M., Lawrence, E., Agwu, C., et al. (2002). Beneficial effects of leptin on obesity, T cell hyporesponsiveness, and neuroendocrine/metabolic dysfunction of human congenital leptin deficiency. *The Journal of Clinical Investigation, 110*: 1093–1103.

Fisher, J. O., Rolls, B. J., & Birch, L. L. (2003). Children's bite size and intake of an entree are greater with large portions than with age-appropriate or self-selected portions. *American Journal of Clinical Nutrition, 77,* 1164–1170.

Flodmark, C. E., Marcus, C., & Britton, M. (2006). Interventions to prevent obesity in children and adolescents: a systematic literature review. *International Journal of Obesity and Related Metabolic Disorders, 30,* 579–589.

Gazzaniga, J. M., & Burns, T. M. (1993). Relationship between diet composition and body fatness, with adjustment for resting energy expenditure and physical activity. *American Journal of Clinical Nutrition, 58,* 21–28.

Gobshtis, N., Ben-Shabat, S., & Fride, E. (2007). Antidepressant-induced undesirable weight gain: prevention with rimonabant without interference with behavioural effectiveness. *European Journal of Pharmacology, 554*(2–3), 155–163.

Godoy-Matos, A., Carraro, L., Vieira, A., Oliveira, J., Guedes, E. P., Mattos, L., Rangel, C., Moreira, R. O., Coutinho, W., & Appolinario, J. C. (2005). Treatment of obese adolescents with sibutramine: a randomized, double-blind, controlled study. *Journal of Clinical Endocrinology & Metabolism, 90,* 1460–1465.

Hales, C. N., & Barker, D. J. P. (2001). The thrifty phenotype hypothesis. *British Medical Bulletin, 60,* 5–20.

Halford, J. C. G. (2006a). Obesity drugs in clinical development. *Current Opinion in Investigational Drugs, 7,* 312–318.

Halford, J. C. G. (2006b). Pharmacotherapy for obesity. *Appetite, 45,* 6–10.

Halford, J. C. G., Gillespie, J., Brown, V., Pontin, E. E., & Dovey, T. M. (2004). The effect of television (TV) food advertisements/commercials on food consumption in children. *Appetite, 42,* 221–225.

Hukshorn, C. J., Dielen, F. M., Burrman, W. A., Westerp-Plantenga, M. S., Campfield, L. A., & Saris, W. H. (2002). The effect of pegylated recombinant human leptin (PEG-OB) on weight loss and inflammatory status in obese subjects. *International Journal of Obesity and Related Metabolic Disorders, 26,* 504–509.

Jebb, S. A. (1999). Obesity: from molecules to man. *Proceedings of the Nutrition Society, 58,* 1–14.

Kalra, S. P., & Kalra, P. S. (2004). NPY and cohorts in regulating appetite, obesity and metabolic syndrome: beneficial effects of gene therapy. *Neuropeptides, 38,* 201–211.

Kiess, W., Blüher, S., Kapellen, T., Garten, A., Klammt, J., Kratzsch, J., & Körner, A. (2006). Physiology of obesity in childhood and adolescence. *Current Paediatrics, 16,* 123–131.

Kissileff, H. R., Pi-Sunyer, F. X., Thornton, J., & Smith, G. P. (1981). C-terminal octapeptide of cholecystokinin decreases food intake in man. *American Journal of Clinical Nutrition, 34,* 154–160.

Lang, T., Hauser, R., Buddeberg, C., & Klaghofer, R. (2002). Impact of gastric banding on eating behavior and weight. *Obesity Surgery, 12,* 100–107.

Lin, B. H., & Morrison, R. M. (2002). Higher fruit consumption linked with lower body mass index. *Food Reviews, 25,* 28–32.

Lowe, M., & Levine, A. S. (2005). Eating motives and the controversy over dieting: eating less than needed versus less than wanted. *Obesity Research, 13,* 797–806.

Maes, H. H. M., Neale, M. C., & Eaves, L. J. (1997). Genetic and environmental factors in relative body weight and human adiposity. *Behavior Genetics, 27,* 325–351.

Maffeis, C., Pinelli, L., & Schutz, Y. (1996). Fat intake and adiposity in 8 to 11 year old obese children. *International Journal of Obesity and Related Metabolic Disorders, 20,* 170–174.

Mela, D. J., & Sacchetti, D. A. (1991). Sensory preferences for fats—relationships with diet and body composition. *American Journal of Clinical Nutrition, 53,* 908–915.

Molnár, D. (2005). New drug policy in childhood obesity. *International Journal of Obesity and Related Metabolic Disorders, 29,* 562–565.

Montague, C. T., Farooqi, I. S., Whitehead, J. P., Soos, M. A., Rau, H., Wareham, N. J., Sewter, C. P., Digby, J. E., Mohammed, S. N., Hurst, J. A., Cheetham, C. H., Earley, A. R., Barnett, A. H., Prins, J. B., & O'Rahilly, S. (1997). Congenital leptin deficiency is associated with severe early-onset obesity in humans. *Nature, 387,* 903–908.

Mutch, D. M., & Clément, K. (2006). Genetics of human obesity. *Best Practice & Research: Clinical Endocrinology & Metabolism, 20,* 647–664.

Ness, A. R., Maynard, M., Frankel, S., Davey Smith, G., Frobisher, C., Leary, S. D., Emmett, P. M., & Gunnell, D. (2005). Diet in childhood and adult cardiovascular and all cause mortality: the Boyd Orr cohort. *Heart, 91,* 894–898.

National Institute for Clinical Excellence. (2006). *Obesity: guidance on the prevention, identification, assessment and management of overweight and obesity in adults and children.* NICE Clinical Guidelines 43. London: National Institute for Clinical Excellence.

Obarzanek, E., Schreiber, G. B., Crawford, P. B., Goldman, S. R., Barrier, P. M., Frederick, M. M., & Lakatos, E. (1994). Energy intake and physical activity in relation to indices of body fat: the National Heart Lunch and Blood Institute Growth and Health Study. *American Journal of Clinical Nutrition, 60,* 15–22.

Ong, K. K., & Dunger, D. B. (2004). Birth weight, infant growth and insulin resistance. *European Journal of Endocrinology, 151*(suppl. 3), u131–u139.

Ortega, R. M., Requejo, A. M., Andres, P., Lopez-Sobaler, A. M., Redondon, R., & Gonzalez-Fernandez, M. (1995). Relationship between diet composition and body fat mass in a group of Spanish adolescents. *British Journal of Nutrition, 74,* 765–773.

Pearcey, S. M., & De Castro, J. M. (2002). Food intake and meal patterns of weight-stable and weight-gaining persons. *American Journal of Clinical Nutrition, 76,* 107–112.

Prentice, A. M. (2005). Early influences on human energy regulation: thrifty genotypes and thrifty phenotypes. *Physiology & Behaviour, 86,* 640–645.

Provencher, V., Drapeau, V., Tremblay, A., Despres, J. P., Bouchard, C., & Lemieux, S. (2004). Eating behaviours, dietary profile and body composition according to dieting history in men and women of the Quebec Family Study. *British Journal of Nutrition, 91,* 997–1004.

Table 3.1 Diagnostic Criteria for AN

A.	Refusal to maintain body weight at or above a minimally normal weight for age and height (e.g., weight loss leading to maintenance of body weight less than 85% of that expected or failure to make expected weight gain during period of growth, leading to body weight less than 85% of that expected).
B.	Intense fear of gaining weight or becoming fat, even though underweight.
C.	Disturbance in the way in which one's body weight or shape is experienced, undue influence of body weight or shape on self-evaluation, or denial of the seriousness of the current low body weight.
D.	In postmenarchal females, amenorrhea (i.e., the absence of at least three consecutive menstrual cycles). A woman is considered to have amenorrhea if her periods occur only following hormone (e.g., estrogen) administration.

Slightly adapted from DSM-IV-TR (American Psychiatric Association, 2000).

the diagnostic criteria and differential aspects for Anorexia Nervosa, Bulimia Nervosa, and Binge Eating Disorder are discussed.

Anorexia Nervosa

Anorexia nervosa (AN) is derived from the Greek word *orexis* and literally denotes a "nervous loss of appetite." This term is misleading, however, since AN is not characterized by a loss of appetite, but rather reflects a willing suppression of appetite and a relentless pursuit of thinness. The core feature of AN is a refusal to maintain body weight at a minimally acceptable standard for age and height. This minimally acceptable standard is set at 85% of expected weight in the DSM-IV-TR. Obviously, given this diagnostic weight criterion, AN and obesity cannot co-occur. Consequently, we will highlight only the most important characteristics of AN in this chapter.

A second diagnostic criterion for AN is an intense fear of gaining weight, of becoming fat, and of losing self-control in eating. Hence AN not only involves not wanting to gain weight, but also not daring to gain weight, and even a sense of not deserving to eat.

A third characteristic of individuals with AN is a disturbance in the perception of their own body weight or shape, an undue influence of weight or shape evaluation on self-esteem, or a denial of the seriousness of their low body weight. These features often prevent individuals with AN from getting help, which is alarming since AN can be associated with medical complications such as cardiovascular malfunctions, fertility problems, and metabolic diseases, among others, with potentially devastating consequences (Mitchell & Crow, 2006). Mortality rates in AN range from 6% up to 20% (Crisp, Callender, Halek, & Hsu, 1992; Fichter, Quadflieg, & Hedlund, 2006).

A final diagnostic criterion for postmenarchal females is amenorrhea, which is the absence of at least three subsequent menstrual cycles. The diagnostic criteria of AN are summarized in Table 3.1.

The DSM-IV-TR further distinguishes two subtypes of AN: the binge eating/purging subtype and the restricting subtype. The former subtype is characterized by recurrent binges and the use of self-induced vomiting, laxatives, or diuretics to lose weight, whereas the latter subtype primarily involves restrictive eating or excessive exercising as weight-control behaviors. Crossover between the two subtypes is not uncommon (Eddy et al., 2002). The binge/purge subtype is generally characterized by more severe eating disorder-specific and non-specific psychopathology than the restricting subtype (Geist, Davis, & Heinmaa, 1998).

Bulimia Nervosa

Bulimia nervosa (BN) literally denotes "appetite of an ox" and is derived from the Greek words *bous* (head of cattle) and *limos* (hunger). A core feature of BN is the presence of recurrent episodes of binge eating, which involves the consumption of an excessive amount of food within a short time frame as well as a sense of loss of control while eating. This latter characteristic distinguishes binge eating from overeating, where no sense of loss of control is experienced (Fairburn & Cooper, 1993).

Table 3.2 Diagnostic Criteria for BN

A. Recurrent episodes of binge eating. An episode of binge eating is characterized by both of the following:
  1. Eating, in a discrete period of time (e.g., within any 2 hour period) an amount of food that is definitely larger than most people would eat during a similar period of time and under similar circumstances.
  2. A sense of a lack of control over eating during the episodes (e.g., a feeling that one cannot stop eating or control what or how much one is eating).
B. Recurrent inappropriate compensatory behavior in order to prevent weight gain, such as self-induced vomiting; misuse of laxatives, diuretics, enemas, or other medications; fasting; or excessive exercise.
C. The binge eating and inappropriate compensatory behaviors occur, on average, at least twice a week for 3 months.
D. Self-evaluation is unduly influenced by body shape and weight.
E. The disturbance does not occur exclusively during episodes of anorexia nervosa.

Slightly adapted from DSM-IV-TR (American Psychiatric Association, 2000).

Typically, high-calorie or "forbidden" foods are consumed during binge eating episodes and the total caloric intake can take on extreme proportions (up to 10,000 kcal for 1 binge eating episode) (Klein & Walsh, 2003).

A second characteristic of BN is the occurrence of inappropriate behaviors such as self-induced vomiting, laxative or diuretic abuse, fasting, and excessive exercising as a means of compensating for the recurrent binge eating episodes. In order to meet the DSM-IV-TR criteria for BN, both the binge eating episodes and the compensatory behaviors must occur, on average, at least twice a week for 3 months.

A third diagnostic characteristic of individuals with BN is that their self-esteem is overly influenced by their evaluation of body weight and shape. In other words, their self-esteem rises or falls with the subjective perception of their appearance.

Finally, a current diagnosis of AN is regarded as an exclusion criterion for BN. Hence the two diagnoses cannot co-occur, although alternating diagnoses (e.g., developing BN after an episode of AN, or vice versa) are possible. The differential diagnosis between the two disorders mostly relies on the weight criterion. Individuals with BN most often have a normal body weight, although some are overweight or slightly underweight. If the body weight is less than 85% of expected weight (for age and height) and amenorrhea is present, then a diagnosis of AN should be made (subtype binge eating/purging), otherwise a diagnosis of BN is more appropriate.

As was the case for AN, the DSM-IV-TR distinguishes two subtypes of BN: a purging and a non-purging subtype. The latter subtype typically employs fasting or excessive exercising as compensatory behaviors, whereas the first subtype utilizes self-induced vomiting and/or laxative abuse or abuse of diuretics to avoid weight gain. Like AN, BN can pose a serious physical threat, with vitamin deficiencies, kidney and liver malfunctions, and cardiovascular disturbances, among others, as potential medical complications (Mitchell & Crow, 2006). Table 3.2 provides an overview of the diagnostic criteria for BN according to the DSM-IV-TR.

Binge Eating Disorder

Binge Eating Disorder (BED) is included in the DSM-IV-TR under the category "eating disorders not otherwise specified" (EDNOS) and hence is currently not recognized as a distinct eating disorder. The EDNOS category includes eating disorders that do not meet all the criteria to obtain a full-blown diagnosis of AN or BN. Although the criteria for BED are currently still under research (Niego, Pratt, & Agras, 1997; Rieder & Ruderman, 2001; Wilfley, Schwartz, Spurrell, & Fairburn, 2000), it will be shown that this diagnostic category is of special relevance when working with obese patients.

BED bares a resemblance to BN since recurrent episodes of binge eating are a core feature of both disorders. Yet, in BED, these episodes of binge eating are not compensated by the inadequate behaviors that are typical of BN, which is an important differential aspect between the two disor-

Table 3.3 Diagnostic Research Criteria for BED

A. Recurrent episodes of binge eating. An episode of binge eating is characterized by both of the following:
    1. Eating, in a discrete period of time (e.g., within a 2 hour period), an amount of food that is definitely larger than most people would eat during a similar period of time under similar circumstances.
    2. A sense of a lack of control over eating during the episode (e.g., a feeling that one cannot stop eating or control what or how much one is eating).

B. Binge eating episodes are associated with at least three of the following:
    1. Eating much more rapidly than normal.
    2. Eating until feeling uncomfortably full.
    3. Eating large amounts of food when not feeling physically hungry.
    4. Eating alone because of being embarrassed by how much one is eating.
    5. Feeling disgusted with oneself, depressed, or guilty after overeating.

C. Marked distress regarding binge eating.

D. The binge eating occurs, on average, at least twice a week for 3 months.

E. The binge eating is not associated with the regular use of inappropriate compensatory behavior (e.g., purging, fasting, excessive exercise) and does not occur exclusively during the course of AN or BN.

Slightly adapted from DSM-IV-TR (American Psychiatric Association, 2000).

ders. Given the lack of compensatory behaviors in BED, individuals suffering from BED are often obese, although obesity is not a necessary diagnostic criterion (Fairburn et al., 1998; Greeno, Wing, & Marcus, 1999). Thus not every person with BED is obese and not every obese person suffers from BED. Nevertheless, since binge eating leads to a higher energy intake, it is quite logical that obese subjects with BED usually have a higher degree of obesity compared to obese subjects who do not suffer from BED (Hay, 1998; Hay & Fairburn, 1998; Marcus, Wing, & Lamparski, 1985).

In the DSM-IV-TR, only research criteria are proposed for determination of the diagnostic frequency threshold for binges. Future research should address whether the preferred frequency threshold counts the number of days on which binges occur or rather the number of episodes of binge eating (Wilfley, Pike, & Striegel-Moore, 1997). Further, the binges have to elicit marked distress, which may include concerns about weight and shape, and they have to be characterized by at least three of the features listed in Table 3.3. Both AN and BN are considered exclusion criteria, although again, alternating diagnoses are possible, especially between BN and BED (Fairburn & Harrison, 2003).

AN and BN disproportionately affect women, at a ratio of 10 to 20:1 (females:males) (Klein & Walsh, 2003). Unlike AN and BN, which occur predominantly in women, men appear to comprise a substantial proportion of the BED population. Estimates are that women are 1.5 times more likely to have BED than men (Spitzer et al., 1992, 1993).

ETIOLOGICAL MODELS

A Transdiagnostic Perspective on Eating Disorders

At the moment, the cognitive behavioral theory is the most prominent evidence-based theory of eating disorders. Although initially developed for BN (Fairburn, 1981), currently a so-called transdiagnostic perspective (Fairburn, Cooper, & Shafran, 2003) has been adopted. Since eating disorder patients seem to migrate between AN, BN, and EDNOS, it is assumed that common mechanisms are involved in the maintenance of all diagnostic eating disorder categories (Fairburn & Harrison, 2003). We will restrict our discussion of the transdiagnostic perspective to the elements that might be relevant for the comorbidity of obesity and eating disorders.

Central to the model of Fairburn and colleagues is a dysfunctional system for evaluating self-worth, namely in terms of eating habits, shape, and/or weight, and the ability to control them. The typical clinical features of eating disorders (extreme weight control, use of laxatives and diuretics,

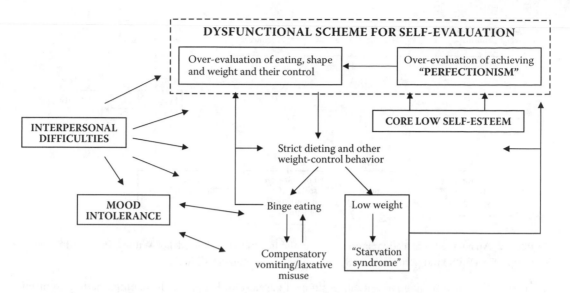

Figure 3.1 An adapted schematic representation of the transdiagnostic theory of the maintenance of bulimia nervosa. (Reprinted from Fairburn, C. G., Cooper, Z., & Shafran, R. (2003). Cognitive behaviour therapy for eating disorders. *Behaviour Research and Therapy, 41,* 509–528, with permission from Elsevier.)

etc.) are seen as a direct result of these concerns. Besides this "core psychopathology," the model elaborates on the origins of binge eating, which is seen as a result of patients' extreme dietary restraint. In line with the Restraint Model (Herman & Mack, 1975; Herman & Polivy, 1980), it is hypothesized that restrained eaters can lose control over eating under certain conditions, such as negative emotions, and develop binge episodes. Some patients subsequently compensate by vomiting or taking laxatives in the (false) belief that weight gain is thereby minimized. A third component in the model is the extreme self-criticalness of eating disorder patients. Finally, four additional maintaining mechanisms are formulated: severe perfectionism, core low self-esteem, difficulties in coping with intense mood states, and interpersonal problems. It is assumed that in some patients, one or more of these interact with the maintaining processes mentioned above, which might hamper effective treatment. A schematic representation of this transdiagnostic model of eating disorders is depicted in Figure 3.1.

The Integrated Model of Risk for BED

Wilfley and colleagues (1997) integrated two theoretical models of binge eating in order to provide a comprehensive risk model for BED in particular and eating disorders in general (see Figure 3.2). These models are the Restraint Model and the Interpersonal Vulnerability Model. The latter model is the theoretical framework behind the second leading evidence-based treatment protocol for eating disorders: Interpersonal Psychotherapy (Peterson & Mitchell, 1999). As such, the so-called Integrated Model of Risk more fully incorporates the range and complexity of risk factors supported by research and offers a better prediction of risk for binge eating than either model alone. The first branch of the integrated risk model, the Dietary Restraint Theory, is outlined above. The strength of the Restraint Model is that it highlights the potential role of body dissatisfaction and dieting in the development of binge eating, supported by various research findings (for a review and discussion, see Van Strien, 1997). The Restraint Model, however, falls short in addressing the question of why some individuals develop binge eating without having dietary restraint attitudes, and it does not account for interpersonal risk factors that may undermine self-esteem to a point where individuals become more susceptible to internalization of the harsh pressure of "ideal appearance." The second branch, the Interpersonal Vulnerability Model, postulates that disturbances in early child-

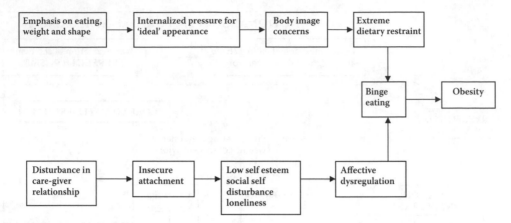

Figure 3.2 An adapted schematic representation of the Integrated Risk Model of Wilfley, Pike, and Striegel-Moore (1997). (With kind permission of Springer Science and Business Media.)

caretaker relationships (e.g., adoption, prolonged parent-child separation, unempathetic parenting style, parental psychopathology, and child physical or sexual abuse) may lie at the very heart of binge eating. According to the Interpersonal Vulnerability Model, these disturbances may first lead to insecure attachment, which in turn may lead to social self-disturbances, feelings of loneliness, and low self-esteem. These latter factors can cause affective dysregulation, which may trigger binge eating as a means of coping with the aversive emotional states. When left uncompensated, these recurrent binges can generate obesity.

The different steps of the Interpersonal Vulnerability Model are supported by various research findings (Taylor, Parker, Bagby, & Bourke, 1996; Telch & Agras, 1994; Villejo, Humphrey, & Kirschenbaum, 1997; Wonderlich, Connolly, & Stice, 2004). Generally, women with eating disorders are more commonly confronted with factors that may promote insecure attachment, such as adoption, parental psychopathology, and (sexual) abuse (Fairburn et al., 1998; Wilfley et al., 1997; Wonderlich et al., 2001). Sexual abuse in early childhood further appears to be particularly related to binge eating in later life (Wonderlich et al., 2001). A specific relationship between negative family influences and binge eating was also found in experimental research by Villejo and colleagues (1997). These findings clearly indicate a link between negative experiences in the early child-caregiver relationships and the development of eating pathology. More research is needed to address these issues, especially the interaction between the two pathways of the Interpersonal Vulnerability Model.

PREVALENCE OF BN AND BED IN OBESE CHILDREN AND ADOLESCENTS

In developmental psychopathology research, epidemiologists make frequent use of self-report questionnaires such as the adolescent version of the Questionnaire of Eating and Weight Patterns (QEWP-A) (Johnson, Grieve, Adams, & Sandy, 1999) and the Eating Disorders Examination Questionnaire (EDE-Q; Fairburn & Beglin, 1994), as these are quick, easy, and inexpensive to administer, score, and interpret. To estimate the prevalence of the disorder under study, the percentage of subjects exceeding a specified cutoff is reported. In this regard, Morgan et al. (2002) studied a sample of non-treatment-seeking overweight children (6 to 10 years old) and found that 5.3% of the participants met the criteria for BED. In a study by Decaluwé, Braet, and Fairburn (2003), 6% of the 126 referred youngsters (10 to 16 years old) in their sample reported binge eating episodes occuring frequently enough to justify a diagnosis of BED.

However, although self-report questionnaires are useful for screening purposes, structured clinical interviews are considered the "gold standard" to assess DSM-IV diagnoses (Costello, Egger, & Angold, 2005). Britz and colleagues (2000) administered the Munich Composite International Diagnostic Interview (U-CIDI; Wittchen et al., 1995) to 47 referred severely obese adolescents between the ages of 15 and 21. In this study, three obese adolescents (6.4%) fulfilled the DSM-IV criteria for BN, three (6.4%) received a BED diagnosis, and two (4.3%) were diagnosed with EDNOS. The most widely used clinical interview in the eating disorder literature is the Eating Disorder Examination (EDE; Fairburn & Cooper, 1993), which will be discussed in detail below. Decaluwé and Braet (2003) administered the modified version for children and adolescents (ChEDE; Bryant-Waugh, Cooper, Taylor, & Lask, 1996) in a sample of 196 obese youngsters (10 to 16 years old) seeking treatment for their obesity. These researchers found that only 1% of their sample met full DSM diagnostic criteria for BED and nobody received a BN diagnosis. Although studies on this topic are scarce, it seems reasonable to conclude that full-blown eating disorder diagnoses are not common in obese children and adolescents.

Most studies have focused on the prevalence of specific eating disorder symptoms; more specifically, on the occurrence of subclinical binge eating, defined as at least one episode of objective binge eating over the previous 3 months. First, questionnaire studies will be discussed. Severi, Verri, and Livieri (1993) reported that in a population of 52 referred obese youngsters (ages 13 to 19 years), 18% of the boys and 27% of the girls had binge eating problems. Berkowitz, Stallings, and Stunkard (1993) investigated a sample of treatment-seeking obese girls between the ages of 14 and 16 years and found that 30% of their sample reported binge eating. In the questionnaire study of Decaluwé et al. (2003), binge eating episodes were found in 36.5% of the participants. Morgan et al. (2002) demonstrated that 17.9% of their sample experienced binge eating. Using a clinical interview, Britz et al. (2000) detected binge eating episodes among 57% of the female and 35% of the male obese adolescents and young adults. With the ChEDE, Tanofsky-Kraff et al. (2004) found that in their sample of non-treatment-seeking overweight and normal weight children (6 to 13 years old), 9.3% reported binge eating episodes. Finally, in the Decaluwé and Braet study (2003), 18 of the 196 obese youngsters (9.2%) reported binge eating episodes. Outcome differences between studies can be attributed to the use of different measures and the inclusion of varying age groups. Moreover, studies focus on either referred or non-referred groups. Previous research in both adults and children has demonstrated that with regard to associated psychosocial aspects, obese individuals seeking treatment differ from those who do not seek treatment (Braet, Mervielde, & Vandereycken, 1997; Fitzgibbon, Stolley, & Kirschenbaum, 1993).

As mentioned in the introduction, childhood obesity is one of the risk factors for the later development of BN (Fairburn et al., 1997) and BED (Fairburn et al., 1998). It has also been associated with the development of AN (Fairburn, Cooper, Doll, & Welch, 1999). One possible reason for this may be that overweight children are taught a greater concern for weight, shape, and eating and a greater tendency toward dietary restraint than average weight children. These are key features of the specific psychopathology of eating disorders and have an important role in cognitive etiological models of AN and BN. Whether this has implications for practitioners in assessment and treatment is discussed below. When compared with normal weight children, non-referred overweight children (ages 6.1 to 13.8 years) report significantly more restraint, eating, shape, and weight concerns as measured with the ChEDE (Tanofsky-Kraff et al., 2004). Other researchers have also found that non-referred overweight girls (11 to 12 years old) have more concerns about weight, shape, and eating and attempt dietary restraint more often than non-overweight girls (Burrows & Cooper, 2002). Surprisingly few studies have focused on self-induced vomiting and diuretic or laxative misuse in obese or overweight youth. In the study by Decaluwé and Braet (2003), seven participants (3.6%) reported on the ChEDE making regular use of compensatory behavior such as self-induced vomiting, laxative or diuretic misuse, or intense exercising. In a large community sample, Neumark-Sztainer and Hannan (2000) demonstrated a strong positive association between body mass index

(BMI) on the one hand and dieting and unhealthy eating behaviors (purging) on the other hand, especially in girls.

In conclusion, although few children and adolescents seem to meet the full diagnostic criteria for BED or BN, subclinical binge eating appears to be a frequent behavior, especially in obese children and adolescents seeking treatment. Preliminary evidence suggests the presence of eating, shape, and weight concerns, compensatory behavior, and dietary restraint in at least some overweight youngsters.

DEVELOPMENTAL ASPECTS

In this section we will focus on developmental aspects that need to be considered when screening (obese) children and adolescents for disturbed eating behaviors. As outlined above, binge eating is defined as the consumption of a large quantity of food in a restricted period of time and associated with feelings of loss of control over eating (Fairburn & Wilson, 1993). More recently, however, research in children and adolescents has shown that the experience of loss of control over eating, as opposed to the amount of food that is eaten, is more salient for the identification of disordered eating behaviors (Marcus & Kalarchian, 2003; Morgan et al., 2002; Tanofsky-Kraff, Faden, Yanovski, Wilfley, & Yanovski, 2005; Tanofsky-Kraff et al., 2004). Especially in children and adolescents, there is a possibility that these subjects do experience loss of control over their eating, but that it is not accompanied by eating large amounts of food because they do not yet have access to large amounts. As such, they are not in a position to decide for themselves how much they eat and therefore their binges are considered to be limited in scope. Nevertheless, when these youngsters grow older, they acquire greater access to food and subsequently there is the possibility that former subjective binge episodes (binge episodes where loss of control is present but no objectively large amount of food has been eaten) evolve into objective binge eating episodes (binge episodes where loss of control is present and an objectively large amount of food has been eaten). Therefore we might question the use of the "objectively large amount" criterion in children and adolescents. Also, since children and adolescents are still "growing," it is hard to define certain norms regarding what amount is "normal" for a certain age and what amount is not.

Second, DSM-IV-TR research criteria of BED (American Psychiatric Association, 2000) require at least two binge eating episodes a week during the last 3 months. In other words, to meet the BED criteria, a child or adolescent has to report at least 24 binge eating episodes during the last 3 months. This rigid DSM-IV-TR criterion has already been modified by Fairburn and Cooper (in Fairburn & Wilson, 1993). These researchers state that there should have been at least 12 binge eating episodes over the past 3 months with no longer than a 2 week gap between them to make a diagnose of BED (or BN). Still, we might wonder if a child who, for example, reports 10 binge eating episodes over the last 3 months, and therefore cannot be "labeled" with a BED diagnosis (according to DSM and Oxford criteria), is maybe not all that different from a child who reports 12 binge eating episodes over the last 3 months? This question raises the whole categorical/dimensional classification discussion. Overall, it is important to state that, on the one hand, we do need some kind of classification system where distinct criteria are set to define a disorder and to foster communication, while on the other hand, and especially in younger populations, we should also make sure to include developmental aspects and we should avoid holding strictly to prescribed criteria or labels. The use of a more dimensional approach to classify psychopathology is indicated.

We can conclude that the DSM criteria for BED and BN that are used in adults are too stringent for use in younger populations. Not only does it seem important to apply the amount criterion in a more flexible way, but also the criterion regarding the frequency of binge episodes has to be handled carefully in children and adolescents.

Emerging evidence thus suggests that it may be appropriate to utilize broader, less stringent criteria to better characterize binge eating problems in younger children. Some investigators have pro-

Table 3.4 Provisional BED Research Criteria for Children

A. Recurrent episodes of binge eating. An episode of binge eating is characterized by both of the following:
  1. Food seeking in the absence of hunger (e.g., after a full meal).
  2. A sense of a lack of control over eating (e.g., "when I start to eat, I just can't stop").
B. Binge episodes are associated with one or more of the following:
  1. Food seeking in response to negative affect (e.g., sadness, boredom, restlessness).
  2. Food seeking as a reward.
  3. Sneaking or hiding food.
C. Symptoms persist over a period of 3 months.
D. Eating is not associated with the regular use of inappropriate compensatory behaviors (e.g., purging, fasting, excessive exercise) and does not occur exclusively during the course of AN or BN.

Source: Marcus & Kalarchian, 2003.

posed an alternate classification scheme for the diagnosis of eating disorders and eating problems in children that include developmentally appropriate criteria (Cooper, Watkins, Bryant-Waugh, & Lask, 2002; Lask & Bryant-Waugh, 1992; Nicholls, Chater, & Lask, 2000; Watkins & Lask, 2002). These criteria are known as the Great Ormond Street Criteria, and not only have better reliability (Nicholls et al., 2000) in younger children but also stimulate research on problematic eating in childhood. As discussed earlier, research has shown that clinically significant binge eating already occurs in younger (overweight) populations. However, these children often do not meet all the necessary criteria to obtain a BED diagnosis. Therefore Marcus and Kalarchian (2003) proposed modified criteria for BED in children younger than 14 years of age. These provisional BED criteria were selected to reflect extant research findings and to be broader than the DSM-IV-TR research criteria for BED. As demonstrated in Table 3.4, binge eating in children who are younger than 14 years of age is to a large extent characterized by physical and behavioral symptoms. Despite the low prevalence of full-blown eating disorder diagnoses, it is clear that disturbed eating already exists in (obese) children. The "full-blown" eating disorders predominantly develop during adolescence. Psychological reactions to the maturing body, changing peer relationships, and new life roles might play a part in the development of eating disorders (Klein & Walsh, 2003).

RELEVANCE OF STUDYING EATING DISORDER SYMPTOMS IN OBESE CHILDREN AND ADOLESCENTS

The high prevalence of eating disorder symptoms in referred obese youngsters raises concerns regarding assessment and treatment. Although it is beyond the scope of this chapter, it is noteworthy that treatment-seeking obese children and adolescents also demonstrate high rates of associated psychopathology other than eating disorders (Zametkin, Zoon, Klein, & Munson, 2004). In the study by Britz et al. (2000), lifetime diagnoses of mood disorders were found in 42.6% of the referred obese adolescents, anxiety disorders in 40.4%, and somatoform disorders in 14.9%. Taking into account the prevalence rates of eating disorders mentioned above, lifetime psychiatric diagnoses were obtained in 70.2% of the treatment seekers under study. Vila et al. (2004) interviewed 155 treatment-seeking obese youngsters between the ages of 5 and 17 years and obtained mental disorder diagnoses in 56.8% of the participants, anxiety disorders being most prominent. Note that these rates concern the prevalence of disorders and not merely of symptoms. It might be clear that a subgroup of treatment-seeking obese youngsters is characterized by severe associated psychopathology.

Youngsters presenting for treatment are those that suffer. To enhance the quality of life for these children and their families, their concerns should be addressed adequately. For youngsters with associated psychological disturbances, be it eating pathology or general psychopathology, it remains to be tested to what extent this can be attained by limited assessment procedures and highly standardized treatment programs. Moreover, clinicians are faced with a substantial percentage of dropout (Braet, Tanghe, Decaluwé, Moens, & Rosseel, 2004) and relapse (Epstein, Myers, Raynor, & Saelens, 1998; Wilson, 1994). It can be hypothesized that obesity treatment may be especially complicated in youngsters with associated problems. Research in adult samples, for example, suggests that obese "binge eaters" are more likely to drop out of treatment, lose less weight during treatment, and regain weight faster after treatment (Sherwood, Jeffery, & Wing, 1999). Unfortunately, treatment efficacy and psychiatric care in children with comorbid psychopathology are scarcely documented (Jelalian & Saelens, 1999; Zametkin et al., 2004). Finally, it is possible that disturbed eating behaviors in (obese) youngsters may eventually lead to full-blown eating disorders at later ages. No prospective longitudinal studies are available yet that investigate whether eating disorder symptoms predispose obese youngsters to develop an eating disorder in later life. In sum, those referred obese youngsters who report psychopathology in general and eating disorder symptoms in particular appear to be a vulnerable subgroup.

Since dieting is believed to have harmful side effects, as it is frequently implicated in the pathogenesis of eating disorders (Schmidt, 2002), one might argue that putting obese youngsters on a diet is not the way to go. However, in their review of treatment effect studies in overweight children, Butryn and Wadden (2005) demonstrate that professionally administered weight loss poses minimal risks of precipitating eating disorders. According to Stice, Cameron, Killen, Hayward, and Taylor (1999), the supervision and focus of replacing unhealthy eating and activity habits with healthy eating and activity behaviors may counter the increased risk of disordered eating observed in youngsters engaged in unsupervised efforts at weight control (see Epstein, Paluch, Saelens, Ernst, & Wilfley, 2001). It has also been recommended by Wilson (1994) that the harmful side effects of dieting may be prevented by setting a goal of weight management instead of weight loss, with a maximum of 10% weight loss allowed, and establishing a healthy lifestyle, which implies a more favorable prognosis with respect to the prevention of diseases.

In conclusion, when confronted with obese children and adolescents seeking treatment, a thorough screening of associated psychopathology, including eating disorder symptoms, is recommended. In case of comorbid psychological problems, we believe that treatment should focus not only on losing weight, but also on managing symptoms in order to prevent dropout, relapse, and, in the case of associated eating pathology, future eating disorders. Thus we suggest a two-track policy by simultaneously addressing the problem of being overweight and the comorbid psychopathology. However, certain conditions require more specific care that, in our opinion, cannot be provided within the framework of an obesity treatment program (e.g., psychosis, severe pervasive developmental disorder, suicidal ideations). If this is the case, we recommend referral to a specialist.

ASSESSMENT OF EATING DISORDER SYMPTOMS IN TREATMENT-SEEKING OBESE YOUNGSTERS

The previous section leads us to recommend screening of eating disorder symptoms in childhood obesity treatment. Measures of eating disorder-related psychopathology can commonly be administered to obese youngsters seeking treatment as well. In the following section, a non-exhaustive overview of relevant instruments is provided.

Eating Disorder Examination

The EDE (Fairburn & Cooper, 1993) is a standard semistructured investigator-based interview measuring the severity of the core psychopathology of eating disorders and generating an eating disorder diagnosis. The ChEDE is based on the adult EDE and was modified by experts in the field of eating disorders in children in collaboration with the authors of the original EDE (Bryant-Waugh et al., 1996). The ChEDE contains four subscales designed to provide a profile of individuals in terms of four major areas of eating disorder psychopathology: restraint, eating concern, shape concern, and weight concern. In addition, the ChEDE measures three forms of overeating: objective bulimic episodes, subjective bulimic episodes, and objective overeating episodes. The ChEDE also measures four methods of weight control: self-induced vomiting, laxative misuse, diuretic misuse, and intense exercising. Subscale items are scored on a 7-point rating scale. The higher the score on the scale, the greater the severity or presence of any given feature. There is a 28 day time frame for the subscales and the diagnostic features are assessed over a 3 month period. Recently, Watkins, Frampton, Lask, and Bryant-Waugh (2005) found that the alpha coefficients for the subscales varied between .80 and .91 and interrater reliability was high as well ($r = .91$ to 1.00). These researchers also made a comparison between children with AN, children with other clinical eating disturbances, and two age-matched control groups and concluded that the ChEDE was able to differentiate children with AN from children with other forms of clinical eating disturbances and control children. These results suggest that the ChEDE has sensitive discriminant validity.

Eating Disorder Examination Questionnaire

The Eating Disorder Examination Questionnaire (EDE-Q) (Fairburn & Beglin, 1994) is a self-report questionnaire that assesses the frequency of key eating disorder behaviors. The EDE-Q is the only self-report questionnaire that differentiates between the various forms of overeating and provides a determination of binge eating as defined in the DSM-IV-TR. The items of the EDE-Q are derived from the initial interview (EDE) (Fairburn & Cooper, 1993). Like the EDE, the EDE-Q contains four subscales (restraint, eating concern, shape concern, and weight concern) and also measures three forms of overeating (objective bulimic episodes, subjective bulimic episodes, and objective overeating episodes) and four methods of weight control (self-induced vomiting, laxative misuse, diuretic misuse, and intense exercising). The EDE-Q also uses the same 7-point rating scale as the EDE interview. The higher the score on the scale, the greater the severity or presence of any given feature. Like the EDE, the EDE-Q has a 28 day time frame for the subscales. Unlike the EDE, the diagnostic features are not assessed over a 3 month period, but over the same 28 day period.

Kalarchian, Wilson, Brolin, and Bradley (2000) and Grilo, Masheb, and Wilson (2001) suggest that the EDE-Q has utility for assessing objective binge episodes in obese bariatric surgery candidates and patients with BED. Luce and Crowther (1999) indicated that the subscales of the EDE-Q have excellent internal consistency (Cronbach's α ranged from .78 to .93) and test-retest reliability (Pearson's r ranged from .81 to .94). Reas, Grilo, and Masheb (2006) examined the reliability of the EDE-Q in patients with BED and concluded that the EDE-Q has utility for assessing the number of (objective) binge episodes and associated features of eating disorders in patients with BED. The EDE-Q also discriminates between obese binge eaters and obese non-binge eaters (Wilson, Nonas, & Rosenblum, 1993) and appears well-suited for use in prospective epidemiological studies (Mond, Hay, Rodgers, Owen, & Beumont, 2004). Future research is needed to investigate the reliability and validity of the EDE-Q in children.

The Dutch Eating Behavior Questionnaire

The Dutch Eating Behavior Questionnaire (DEBQ) is a 33-item self-report questionnaire consisting of three subscales referring to different eating styles, namely, external eating, emotional eating, and restrained eating. Items are formulated as specific eating behaviors to be rated at their frequency of occurrence on a 5-point Likert scale (1 = never, 2 = seldom, 3 = sometimes, 4 = often, 5 = very often). In addition, for some items there is a "not relevant" category. Each eating style corresponds with a major theory on the etiology of overeating. According to Schachter's externality theory of obesity (Schachter & Rodin, 1974), overweight people have not learned to recognize internal physiological cues of hunger and satiety and therefore are more inclined to rely on external food cues like the presence of (tasty) food, time of day, or smell and taste. As a consequence, presentation of food evokes an immediate reaction in obese people so that they eat in the absence of hunger and consume larger amounts than necessary to attain satiety, which might lead to a binge or overeating. In contrast, the concept of emotional eating stems from psychosomatic theory (Bruch, 1975, 1997; Ganley, 1989; Slochower, 1983), which considers overeating to be a reaction to emotional arousal, that is, a psychological conflict induces the overeating. Bruch (1975) based her observations on obese children and suggests that people with an emotional eating pattern have learned to label negative feelings as hunger. As a consequence, they develop the "habit" of overeating to numb negative feelings, reduce anxiety, or react against experiences of rejection (Ganley, 1989). The third theory, which explains overeating as a consequence of unsuccessful dieting, is the well-known Restraint Theory (Herman & Mack, 1975; Herman & Polivy, 1980), which was discussed above. In adult populations it has been demonstrated that the DEBQ is a reliable and valid instrument (Schlundt, 1995). Moreover, recent studies indicate the usefulness of the DEBQ in children and adolescents between the ages of 7 and 17 years (Braet, Tanghe, De Bode, Franckx, & Van Winckel, 2003; Braet et al., 2004; Edlund, Halvarsson, & Sjoden, 1996; Halvarsson & Sjoden, 1998; Hill, Draper, & Stack, 1994; Hill & Robinson, 1991; Lluch, Herbeth, Mejean, & Siest, 2000; Ricciardelli & McCabe, 2001; Wardle et al., 1992).

The Eating Disorder Inventory and the Eating Disorder Inventory II

The Eating Disorder Inventory (EDI) (Garner, Olmsted, & Polivy, 1985) is a self-report questionnaire that can be administered in youngsters age 11 years and older. Unlike the EDE, the EDI was not developed to diagnose eating disorders, but rather to assess psychological characteristics common in eating disorders. It is a widely used and accepted instrument, with translations in Dutch, French, German, Spanish, Swedish, and Chinese (Williamson, Anderson, Jackman, & Jackson, 1995). The EDI contains 64 items that form eight subscales. Five of these subscales tap general, personality-related characteristics of individuals with an eating disorder: Perfectionism, Ineffectiveness, Interpersonal Distrust, Interoceptive Awareness, and Maturity Fears. The remaining three subscales measure behavioral and attitudinal symptoms of eating disorders: Drive for Thinness, Bulimia, and Body Dissatisfaction. In 1991 Garner revised the original EDI by adding 27 items that form three additional scales: Social Insecurity, Asceticism, and Impulse Regulation. Subjects are asked to rate the items on a 6-point scale ranging from "never" to "always." In the Eating Disorder Inventory II (EDI-II), the most pathological response possible on an item earns a score of 6, while the least pathological response possible earns a score of 1.

In the original EDI, the most extreme eating disorder-like response is associated with a score of 3, the immediately adjacent response with a score of 2, and the next response with a score of 1. The three least pathological responses earn a score of 0. Total scores per subscale are obtained by summing all item scores for the scale in question.

Norms are available for both eating disordered patients and non-eating disordered males and females (adults and adolescents) (Garner, 1991; Shore & Porter, 1990). The internal consistency of the subscales is moderate to high (Cronbach's α ranges between .65 and .93, with the exception of Asceticism (.40) in non-clinical samples) (see Garner, 1991; Williamson et al., 1995). Test-retest reliability of the original EDI subscales has been found to be satisfactory, especially with shorter time periods between the first and the second administration (see Williamson et al., 1995). Test-retest correlations at 1 year follow-up ranged from .41 to .75 (Crowther, Lilly, Crawford, Shepherd, & Oliver, 1990). Most of the research on the validity of the EDI has been conducted with the original eight subscales and results were generally supportive. Significant positive correlations were found between subscales of the EDI and scores on the Eating Attitude Test (EAT) (Garner, Olmsted, Bohr, & Garfinkel, 1982) and the Restraint Scale (RS) (Herman & Mack, 1975), demonstrating the concurrent validity of the EDI. Predictive and discriminant validity were also found to be satisfying (Williamson et al., 1995).

The Children's Eating Attitude Test

The Children's Eating Attitude Test (ChEAT) (Maloney, McGuire, & Daniels, 1988) is the children's version of the EAT (Garner & Garfinkel, 1979). It is a self-report questionnaire designed to evaluate thoughts, symptoms, attitudes, and behaviors related to eating disorders, especially AN, such as food preoccupation, body image, vomiting and laxative abuse, dieting, slow eating, clandestine eating, and perceived social pressure to gain weight. The questionnaire can be administered to children as young as 8 years of age. The reading level of the EAT is fifth grade, so for children 11 years of age and older, it is recommended that the adult version be used. The ChEAT consists of 26 items, answered using a 6-point rating scale ranging from "never" to "always." Items are scored as 3 for the most extreme "pathological" response, the immediate adjacent response is scored 2, and the next response is scored 1. The three least "pathological" responses are scored 0. The ChEAT total score is the summation of all item scores. A total score of 20 or greater is indicative of severely disturbed eating attitudes and behaviors, but not necessarily a diagnosis of AN. As such, the ChEAT can best be regarded as a screening instrument for eating pathology.

The psychometric properties of the ChEAT are promising, with studies showing adequate reliability and validity (Maloney et al., 1988; Markovic, Votava-Raic, & Nikolic, 1998; Shariff & Yasin, 2005). In a sample of 88 overweight and normal weight children, Tanofsky-Kraff et al. (2003) found ChEAT global scores to be significantly related to ChEDE total scores, whereas specific items assessing guilt in relation to eating and preoccupation with food were not related. The authors therefore conclude that self-report questionnaires such as the ChEAT are useful sources for general information regarding eating pathology in children, but since they do not accurately reflect all the results of a structured interview such as the ChEDE, the latter should not be discarded when assessing eating pathology.

CONCLUSION

According to McDermott and Jaffa (2005), individuals with obesity are increasingly seen as the domain of eating disorder clinicians and researchers, given the similarity and the common overlap between the two conditions. From what has been discussed above, their statement is not surprising. Research has shown that childhood obesity is a risk factor for the development of eating disorders (especially BN and BED) in adulthood. Nevertheless, this chapter also clearly indicates that in childhood and adolescence, obesity and eating disorders can become intertwined. Overweight children show greater concern with weight, shape, and eating and greater tendency to dietary restraint than average weight children. Moreover, research has shown that specific eating disorder symptoms such as compensatory behavior, loss of control over eating, and binge eating are also prevalent among referred and non-referred obese youngsters. These are all key features of the specific psychopathology of eating disorders and have an important role in cognitive etiological models of AN and BN. However, only a few of these obese youngsters seem to meet the full (and stringent) diagnostic (DSM-IV-TR) criteria for BED or BN. Therefore it has been suggested that broader and more developmentally appropriate criteria should be utilized to better characterize binge eating and BED in younger populations. The substantial prevalence of eating disorder symptoms that have been found in referred obese youngsters also has some important clinical implications. First of all, it is recommended that obese children and adolescents be screened for eating pathology. Both clinical interview and self-report measures can be used. Second, if eating pathology has been detected in a referred obese child or adolescent, it is important to extend the standard obesity treatment program by including interventions that specifically target the disordered eating behaviors or conditions.

We conclude with some recommendations for future research. First, prospective longitudinal studies are needed to investigate if the endorsement of eating disorder symptoms predisposes obese youngsters to develop an eating disorder in late adolescence or in adulthood. Furthermore, clinicians and theorists would benefit from the development of a comprehensive etiological model on eating pathology in childhood obesity. The generation of broader and more developmentally appropriate criteria to characterize binge eating and BED in pediatric samples should be continued. Finally, further research can be conducted, in child and adolescent populations, on the psychometric properties of the assessment methods discussed above. Age- and gender-specific norms for obese and normal weight youngsters should be provided.

REFERENCES

American Psychiatric Association. (2000). *Diagnostic and statistical manual of mental disorders* (4th ed.), Text Revision. Washington, DC: American Psychiatric Association.

Berkowitz, R., Stallings, V. A., & Stunkard, A. J. (1993). Binge-eating disorder in obese adolescent girls. *Annals of the New York Academy of Sciences, 699,* 200–206.

Braet, C., Mervielde, I., & Vandereycken, W. (1997). Psychological aspects of childhood obesity: a controlled study in a clinical and nonclinical sample. *Journal of Pediatric Psychology, 22,* 59–71.

Braet, C., Tanghe, A., De Bode, P., Franckx, H., & Van Winckel, M. (2003). Inpatient treatment of obese children: a multicomponent programme without stringent calorie restriction. *European Journal of Pediatrics, 162,* 391–396.

Braet, C., Tanghe, A., Decaluwé, V., Moens, E., & Rosseel, Y. (2004). Inpatient treatment for children with obesity: weight loss, psychological well-being, and eating behavior. *Journal of Pediatric Psychology, 29,* 519–529.

Britz, B., Siegfried, W., Ziegler, A., Lamertz, C., Herpertz-Dahlmann, B. M., Remschmidt, H., Wittchen, H.-U., & Hebebrand, J. (2000). Rates of psychiatric disorders in a clinical study group of adolescents with extreme obesity and in obese adolescents ascertained via a population based study. *International Journal of Obesity, 24,* 1707–1714.

Bruch, H. (1975). Obesity and anorexia nervosa—psychosocial aspects. *Australian and New Zealand Journal of Psychiatry, 9,* 159–161.

Bruch, H. (1997). Obesity in childhood and personality development (reprinted from *American Journal of Orthopsychiatry, 11,* 467–473, 1941). *Obesity Research, 5,* 157–161.

Bryant-Waugh, R. J., Cooper, P. J., Taylor, C. L., & Lask, B. D. (1996). The use of the eating disorder examination with children: a pilot study. *International Journal of Eating Disorders, 19,* 391–397.

Burrows, A., & Cooper, M. (2002). Possible risk factors in the development of eating disorders in overweight pre-adolescent girls. *International Journal of Obesity, 26,* 1268–1273.

Butryn, M. L., & Wadden, T. A. (2005). Treatment of overweight in children and adolescents: does dieting increase the risk of eating disorders? *International Journal of Eating Disorders, 37,* 285–293.

Cooper, P. J., Watkins, B., Bryant-Waugh, R., & Lask, B. (2002). The nosological status of early onset anorexia nervosa. *Psychological Medicine, 32,* 873–880.

Costello, E. J., Egger, H., & Angold, A. (2005). 10-year research update review: the epidemiology of child and adolescent psychiatric disorders: I. Methods and public health burden. *Journal of the American Academy of Child and Adolescent Psychiatry, 44,* 972–986.

Crisp, A. H., Callender, J. S., Halek, C., & Hsu, L. K. G. (1992). Long-term mortality in anorexia nervosa—a 20-year follow-up of the St. George and Aberdeen cohorts. *British Journal of Psychiatry, 161,* 104–107.

Crowther, J. H., Lilly, R. S., Crawford, P. A., Shepherd, K. L., & Oliver, L. L. (1990). The stability of the Eating Disorder Inventory. Paper presented at the annual meeting of the American Psychological Association, Boston.

Decaluwé, V., & Braet, C. (2003). Prevalence of binge-eating disorder in obese children and adolescents seeking weight-loss treatment. *International Journal of Obesity, 27,* 404–409.

Decaluwé, V., Braet, C., & Fairburn, C. G. (2003). Binge eating in obese children and adolescents. *International Journal of Eating Disorders, 33,* 78–84.

Eddy, K. T., Keel, P. K., Dorer, D. J., Delinsky, S. S., Franko, D. L., & Herzog, D. B. (2002). Longitudinal comparison of anorexia nervosa subtypes. *International Journal of Eating Disorders, 31,* 191–201.

Edlund, B., Halvarsson, K., & Sjoden, P. O. (1996). Eating behaviours, and attitudes to eating, dieting, and body image in 7-year-old Swedish girls. *European Eating Disorders Review, 4,* 40–53.

Epstein, L. H., Myers, M. D., Raynor, H. A., & Saelens, B. E. (1998). Treatment of pediatric obesity. *Pediatrics, 101,* 554–570.

Epstein, L. H., Paluch, R. A., Saelens, B. E., Ernst, M. M., & Wilfley, D. E. (2001). Changes in eating disorder symptoms with pediatric obesity treatment. *Journal of Pediatrics, 139,* 58–65.

Fairburn, C. (1981). A cognitive behavioral approach to the treatment of bulimia. *Psychological Medicine, 11,* 707–711.

Fairburn, C. G. (2001). Atypical eating disorders. In C. G. Fairburn & K. D. Brownell (Eds.), *Eating disorders and obesity: a comprehensive textbook* (2nd ed.). New York: Guilford Press.

Fairburn, C. G., & Beglin, S. J. (1994). Assessment of eating disorders: interview or self-report questionnaire? *International Journal of Eating Disorders, 16,* 363–370.

Fairburn, C. G., & Cooper, Z. (1993). The eating disorder examination. In C. G. Fairburn & T. Wilson (Eds.), *Binge eating: nature, assessment and treatment* (12th ed., pp. 317–331). New York: Guilford Press.

Fairburn, C. G., Cooper, Z., Doll, H. A., & Welch, S. L. (1999). Risk factors for anorexia nervosa: three integrated case-control comparisons. *Archives of General Psychiatry, 56,* 468–476.

Fairburn, C. G., Cooper, Z., & Shafran, R. (2003). Cognitive behaviour therapy for eating disorders: a "transdiagnostic" theory and treatment. *Behaviour Research and Therapy, 41,* 509–528.

Fairburn, C. G., Doll, H. A., Welch, S. L., Hay, P. J., Davies, B. A., & O'Connor, M. E. (1998). Risk factors for binge eating disorder: a community-based, case-control study. *Archives of General Psychiatry, 55,* 425–432.

Fairburn, C. G., & Harrison, P. J. (2003). Eating disorders. *Lancet, 361,* 407–416.

Fairburn, C. G., Welch, S. L., Doll, H. A., Davies, B. A., & O'Connor, M. E. (1997). Risk factors for bulimia nervosa: a community-based case-control study. *Archives of General Psychiatry, 54,* 509–517.

Fairburn, C. G., & Wilson, G. T. (1993). *Binge eating: nature, assessment and treatment* (12th ed.). New York: Guilford Press.

Fichter, M. M., Quadflieg, N., & Hedlund, S. (2006). Twelve-year course and outcome predictors of anorexia nervosa. *International Journal of Eating Disorders, 39,* 87–100.

Fitzgibbon, M. L., Stolley, M. R., & Kirschenbaum, D. S. (1993). Obese people who seek treatment have different characteristics than those who do not seek treatment. *Health Psychology, 12,* 342–345.

Ganley, R. M. (1989). Emotion and eating in obesity: a review of the literature. *International Journal of Eating Disorders, 8,* 343–361.

Garner, D. M. (1991). *Eating disorder inventory-2 manual.* Odessa, FL: Psychological Assessment Resources, Inc.

Garner, D. M., & Garfinkel, P. E. (1979). The eating attitudes test: an index of the symptoms of anorexia nervosa. *Psychological Medicine, 9,* 273–279.

Garner, D. M., Olmsted, M. P., Bohr, Y., & Garfinkel, P. E. (1982). The eating attitudes test: psychometric features and clinical correlates. *Psychological Medicine, 12,* 871–878.

Garner, D. M., Olmsted, M. P., & Polivy, J. (1985). Eating disorder inventory. *Psychopharmacology Bulletin, 21,* 1009–1010.

Geist, R., Davis, R., & Heinmaa, M. (1998). Binge/purge symptoms and comorbidity in adolescents with eating disorders. *Canadian Journal of Psychiatry, 43,* 507–512.

Greeno, C. G., Wing, R. R., & Marcus, M. D. (1999). How many donuts is a "binge?" Women with BED eat more but do not have more restrictive standards than weight-matched non-BED women. *Addictive Behaviors, 24,* 299–303.

Grilo, C. M., Masheb, R. M., & Wilson, G. T. (2001). A comparison of different methods for assessing the features of eating disorders in patients with binge eating disorder. *Journal of Consulting and Clinical Psychology, 69,* 317–322.

Halvarsson, K., & Sjoden, P. O. (1998). Psychometric properties of the Dutch Eating Behaviour Questionnaire (DEBQ) among 9–10-year-old Swedish girls. *European Eating Disorders Review, 6,* 115–125.

Hay, P. (1998). The epidemiology of eating disorder behaviors: an Australian community-based survey. *International Journal of Eating Disorders, 23,* 371–382.

Hay, P., & Fairburn, C. (1998). The validity of the DSM-IV scheme for classifying bulimic eating disorders. *International Journal of Eating Disorders, 23,* 7–15.

Herman, C. P., & Mack, D. (1975). Restrained and unrestrained eating. *Journal of Personality, 43,* 647–660.

Herman, C. P., & Polivy, J. (1980). Restrained eating. In A. Stunkard (Ed.), *Obesity.* Philadelphia, PA: Saunders.

Hill, A. J., Draper, E., & Stack, J. (1994). A weight on children's minds: body shape dissatisfactions at 9 years old. *International Journal of Obesity, 18,* 383–389.

Hill, A. J., & Robinson, A. (1991). Dieting concerns have a functional effect on the behavior of 9-year-old girls. *British Journal of Clinical Psychology, 30,* 265–267.

Jelalian, E., & Saelens, B. E. (1999). Empirically supported treatments in pediatric psychology: pediatric obesity. *Journal of Pediatric Psychology, 24,* 223–248.

Johnson, W. G., Grieve, F. G., Adams, C. D., & Sandy, J. (1999). Measuring binge eating in adolescents: adolescent and parent versions of the Questionnaire of Eating and Weight Patterns. *International Journal of Eating Disorders, 26,* 301–314.

Kalarchian, M. A., Wilson, G. T., Brolin, R. E., & Bradley, L. (2000). Assessment of eating disorders in bariatric surgery candidates: self-report questionnaire versus interview. *International Journal of Eating Disorders, 28,* 465–469.

Klein, D. A., & Walsh, B. T. (2003). Eating disorders. *International Review of Psychiatry, 15,* 205–216.

Lask, B., & Bryant-Waugh, R. (1992). Early-onset anorexia nervosa and related eating disorders. *Journal of Child Psychology and Psychiatry and Allied Disciplines, 33,* 281–300.

Lluch, A., Herbeth, B., Mejean, L., & Siest, G. (2000). Dietary intakes, eating style and overweight in the Stanislas family study. *International Journal of Obesity, 24,* 1493–1499.

Luce, K. H., & Crowther, J. H. (1999). The reliability of the Eating Disorder Examination-Self-Report Questionnaire Version (EDE-Q). *International Journal of Eating Disorders, 25,* 349–351.

Maloney, M. J., McGuire, J. B., & Daniels, S. R. (1988). Reliability testing of a children's version of the Eating Attitude Test. *Journal of the American Academy of Child and Adolescent Psychiatry, 27,* 541–543.

Marcus, M. D., & Kalarchian, M. A. (2003). Binge eating in children and adolescents. *International Journal of Eating Disorders, 34*(suppl.), S47–S57.

Marcus, M. D., Wing, R. R., & Lamparski, D. M. (1985). Binge eating and dietary restraint in obese patients. *Addictive Behaviors, 10,* 163–168.

Markovic, J., Votava-Raic, A., & Nikolic, S. (1998). Study of eating attitudes and body image perception in the preadolescent age. *Collegium Antropologicum, 22,* 221–232.

McDermott, B. M., & Jaffa, T. (2005). Eating disorders in children and adolescents: an update. *Current Opinion in Psychiatry, 18,* 407–410.

Mitchell, J. E., & Crow, S. (2006). Medical complications of anorexia nervosa and bulimia nervosa. *Current Opinion in Psychiatry, 19,* 438–443.

Mond, J. M., Hay, P. J., Rodgers, B., Owen, C., & Beumont, R. J. V. (2004). Validity of the Eating Disorder Examination Questionnaire (EDE-Q) in screening for eating disorders in community samples. *Behaviour Research and Therapy, 42,* 551–567.

Morgan, C. M., Yanovski, S. Z., Nguyen, T. T., McDuffie, J., Sebring, N. G., Jorge, M. R., Keil, M., & Yanovski, J. A. (2002). Loss of control over eating, adiposity, and psychopathology in overweight children. *International Journal of Eating Disorders, 31,* 430–441.

Neumark-Sztainer, D., & Hannan, P. J. (2000). Weight-related behaviors among adolescent girls and boys: results from a national survey. *Archives of Pediatrics and Adolescent Medicine, 154,* 569–577.

Nicholls, D., Chater, R., & Lask, B. (2000). Children into DSM don't go: a comparison of classification systems for eating disorders in childhood and early adolescence. *International Journal of Eating Disorders, 28,* 317–324.

Niego, S. H., Pratt, E. M., & Agras, W. S. (1997). Subjective or objective binge: Is the distinction valid? *International Journal of Eating Disorders, 22,* 291–298.

Peterson, C. B., & Mitchell, J. E. (1999). Psychosocial and pharmacological treatment of eating disorders: a review of research findings. *Journal of Clinical Psychology, 55,* 685–697.

Reas, D. L., Grilo, C. M., & Masheb, R. M. (2006). Reliability of the Eating Disorder Examination-Questionnaire in patients with binge eating disorder. *Behaviour Research and Therapy, 44,* 43–51.

Ricciardelli, L. A., & McCabe, M. P. (2001). Children's body image concerns and eating disturbance: a review of the literature. *Clinical Psychology Review, 21,* 325–344.

Rieder, S., & Ruderman, A. (2001). Cognitive factors associated with binge and purge eating behaviors: the interaction of body dissatisfaction and body image importance. *Cognitive Therapy and Research, 25,* 801–812.

Schachter, S., & Rodin, J. (1974). *Obese humans and rats (complex human behavior).* New York: John Wiley & Sons.

Schlundt, D. G. (1995). Assessment of specific eating behaviors and eating style. In D. B. Allison (Ed.), *Handbook of assessment methods for eating behaviors and weight-related problems: measures, theory, and research* (pp. 241–302). Thousand Oaks, CA: Sage.

Schmidt, U. (2002). Risk factors for eating disorders. In C. Fairburn & K. Brownell (Eds.), *Eating disorders and obesity: a comprehensive handbook* (pp. 247–252). New York: Guilford Press.

Severi, F., Verri, A., & Livieri, C. (1993). Eating behavior and psychological profile in childhood obesity. *Advances in the Biosciences, 90,* 329–336.

Shariff, Z. M., & Yasin, Z. M. (2005). Correlates of children's eating attitude test scores among primary school children. *Perceptual and Motor Skills, 100,* 463–472.

Sherwood, N. E., Jeffery, R. W., & Wing, R. R. (1999). Binge status as a predictor of weight loss treatment outcome. *International Journal of Obesity, 23,* 485–493.

Shore, R. A., & Porter, J. E. (1990). Normative and reliability data for 11-year-olds to 18-year-olds on the Eating Disorder Inventory. *International Journal of Eating Disorders, 9,* 201–207.

Slochower, J. A. (1983). *Excessive eating: the role of emotions and environment.* New York: Human Science Press.

Spitzer, R. L., Devlin, M., Walsh, B. T., Hasin, D., Wing, R., Marcus, M., Stunkard, A., Wadden, T. A., Agras, W. S., Mitchell, J., & Nonas, C. (1992). Binge eating disorder: a multisite field trial of the diagnostic criteria. *International Journal of Eating Disorders, 11,* 191–203.

Spitzer, R. L., Yanovski, S., Wadden, T., Wing, R., Marcus, M. D., Stunkard, A., Devlin, M., Mitchell, J., & Hasin, D. (1993). Binge eating disorder: its further validation in a multisite study. *International Journal of Eating Disorders, 13,* 137–153.

Stice, E., Cameron, R. P., Killen, J. D., Hayward, C., & Taylor, C. B. (1999). Naturalistic weight-reduction efforts prospectively predict growth in relative weight and onset of obesity among female adolescents. *Journal of Consulting and Clinical Psychology, 67,* 967–974.

Tanofsky-Kraff, M., Faden, D., Yanovski, S. Z., Wilfley, D. E., & Yanovski, J. A. (2005). The perceived onset of dieting and loss of control eating behaviors in overweight children. *International Journal of Eating Disorders, 38,* 112–122.

Tanofsky-Kraff, M., Morgan, C. M., Yanovski, S. Z., Marmarosh, C., Wilfley, D. E., & Yanovski, J. A. (2003). Comparison of assessments of children's eating-disordered behaviors by interview and questionnaire. *International Journal of Eating Disorders, 33,* 213–224.

Tanofsky-Kraff, M., Yanovski, S. Z., Wilfley, D. E., Marmarosh, C., Morgan, C. M., & Yanovski, J. A. (2004). Eating-disordered behaviors, body fat, and psychopathology in overweight and normal-weight children. *Journal of Consulting and Clinical Psychology, 72,* 53–61.

Taylor, G. J., Parker, J. D. A., Bagby, R. M., & Bourke, M. P. (1996). Relationships between alexithymia and psychological characteristics associated with eating disorders. *Journal of Psychosomatic Research, 41,* 561–568.

Telch, C. F., & Agras, W. S. (1994). Obesity, binge-eating and psychopathology: are they related. *International Journal of Eating Disorders, 15,* 53–61.

Van Strien, T. (1997). Are most dieters unsuccessful? An alternative interpretation of the confounding of success and failure in the measurement of restraint. *European Journal of Psychological Assessment, 13,* 186–194.

Vila, G., Zipper, E., Dabbas, M., Bertrand, C., Robert, J. J., Ricour, C., Mouren-Simeoni, M. C. (2004). Mental disorders in obese children and adolescents. *Psychosomatic Medicine, 66,* 387–394.

Villejo, R. E., Humphrey, L. L., & Kirschenbaum, D. S. (1997). Affect and self-regulation in binge eaters: effects of activating family images. *International Journal of Eating Disorders, 21,* 237–249.

Wardle, J., Marsland, L., Sheikh, Y., Quinn, M., Fedoroff, I., & Ogden, J. (1992). Eating style and eating behavior in adolescents. *Appetite, 18,* 167–183.

Watkins, B., Frampton, I., Lask, B., & Bryant-Waugh, R. (2005). Reliability and validity of the child version of the eating disorder examination: a preliminary investigation. *International Journal of Eating Disorders, 38,* 183–187.

Watkins, B., & Lask, B. (2002). Eating disorders in school-aged children. *Child and Adolescent Psychiatric Clinics of North America, 11,* 185–199.

Wilfley, D. E., Pike, K. M., & Striegel-Moore, R. H. (1997). Toward an integrated model of risk for binge eating disorder. *Journal of Gender, Culture, and Health, 2,* 1–31.

Wilfley, D. E., Schwartz, M. B., Spurrell, E. B., & Fairburn, C. G. (2000). Using the eating disorder examination to identify the specific psychopathology of binge eating disorder. *International Journal of Eating Disorders, 27,* 259–269.

Williamson, D. A., Anderson, D. A., Jackman, L. P., & Jackson, S. R. (1995). Assessment of eating disordered thoughts, feelings and behaviours. In D. B. Allison (Ed.), *Handbook of assessment methods for eating behaviours and weight-related problems: measures, theory and research* (pp. 347–386). Thousand Oaks, CA: Sage Publications.

Wilson, G. T. (1994). Behavioral treatment of childhood obesity: theoretical and practical implications. *Health Psychology, 13,* 371–372.

Wilson, G. T., Nonas, C. A., & Rosenblum, G. D. (1993). Assessment of binge eating in obese patients. *International Journal of Eating Disorders, 13,* 25–33.

Wittchen, H. U., Beloch, E., Garczynski, E., Holly, A., Lachner, G., & Perkonigg, A. (1995). *Münchener Composite International Diagnostic Interview (M-CIDI),* version 2.2. Munich: Max Planck Institut für Psychiatrie.

Wonderlich, S. A., Connolly, K. M., & Stice, E. (2004). Impulsivity as a risk factor for eating disorder behavior: assessment implications with adolescents. *International Journal of Eating Disorders, 36,* 172–182.

Wonderlich, S. A., Crosby, R. D., Mitchel, J. E., Thompson, K. M., Redlin, J., Demuth, G., Smyth, J., & Haseltine, B. (2001). Eating disturbance and sexual trauma in childhood and adulthood. *International Journal of Eating Disorders, 30,* 401–412.

Zametkin, A. J., Zoon, C. K., Klein, H. W., & Munson, S. (2004). Psychiatric aspects of child and adolescent obesity: a review of the past 10 years. *Journal of the American Academy of Child and Adolescent Psychiatry, 43,* 134–150.

4

Culturally Sensitive Treatment of Pediatric and Adolescent Obesity

SHEILA P. DAVIS AND JOHNNIE SUE COOPER

CHILDHOOD OBESITY

National agencies continue to monitor obesity and overweight in children, revealing steady increases. According to the National Center for Health Statistics (Centers for Disease Control, 2006b), the prevalence of overweight children increased from 4% (1963 to 1970) to 15.8% (1999 to 2002). Among boys, the prevalence increased from 11.6% (1988 to 1994) to 16.9% (1999 to 2002). The prevalence among girls increased from 11% to 14.7% for the same time period. The prevalence of overweight for non-Hispanic black (19.8 %) and Mexican American (21.8%) children was greater than in non-Hispanic white children (13.5%) (1999 to 2002). Research revealed that children who become overweight by age 8 years are more severely obese as adults (Freedman, Kahn, Dietz, Srinivasan, & Berenson, 2001). Also, type 2 diabetes has increased significantly among children and adolescents as weights have increased. It is estimated that one in three Caucasian children born in 2000 and beyond will develop diabetes in their lifetime and that one in two African American and Mexican American children born during this time period will develop diabetes if the obesity epidemic is not curbed (Venkat-Narayan, Boyle, Thompson, Sorensen, & Williamson, 2003). The earliest indicators of heart disease and atherosclerosis begin early in childhood and there is an association between atherosclerosis, high blood pressure, high cholesterol levels, and poor dietary habits (Kavey et al., 2003). Because of these adverse health outcomes, there is a need to stress prevention and treatment of obesity. In order to adequately address obesity in a culturally appropriate manner, one must be cognizant of the effects of sociocultural and environmental impacts on this phenomenon.

Table 4.1 Health Risks Associated with Childhood and Adolescent Obesity

Type 2 diabetes
Cardiovascular disease
Metabolic syndrome
Dyslipidemia
Polycystic ovarian syndrome
Psychological
Pulmonary hypertension
Gastrointestinal
Neurological
Orthopedic
Advanced maturation
Renal

Source: Vargas (2006).

ADOLESCENT OBESITY

Obesity that begins in adolescence is likely to persist into adulthood (Whitaker, Wright, Pepe, Seidel, & Dietz, 1997). A recent study indicates that there is a 17.5% increase in obesity among adults who were also overweight during adolescence (Hughes, Areghan, & Knight, 2005). According to the Surgeon General's report (2002), the prevalence of adolescent obesity has nearly tripled over the past two decades.

Estimates from the Centers for Disease Control and Prevention (CDC) show that between 1979 and 1999, rates of obesity-related hospital discharge diagnosis and cost tripled among children 6 to 17 years of age (Vargas, 2006). It is also known that obesity among adolescents accounts for 50% of the cases of juvenile hypertension (see Table 4.1 for specific health risks associated with adolescent obesity). In particular, Vargas (2006) emphasizes risk factors for type 2 diabetes in youth, including belonging to an ethnic minority population and having had some exposure to diabetes before birth (in utero).

Quality of life issues for adolescents who are overweight or at risk for becoming overweight are also extremely important factors to consider. It is noted in the literature that adolescents who are overweight are more likely to suffer from low self-esteem and experience difficulty in peer relationships (Pearce, Boergers & Prinstein, 2002). Overweight teens are likely to become overweight adults, and there is a higher incidence of depression in adults who are overweight. Furthermore, morbidly obese adolescents have a greater incidence of depression and also report a low health-related quality of life (Zeller, Roehrig, Avani, Daniels, & Inge, 2006). Clearly, the physiological and emotional benefits for early prevention and treatment of obesity are great.

Adolescent Obesity in Ethnic Minority Groups

A review by Jimenez-Cruz, Bacardi-Gascon, and Spindler (2003) of selected studies on the prevalence of overweight and obesity in America Indians from 1981 to 1998 revealed that 29% of Navajo and 40.4% of Pueblo Indian children 9 to 13 years of age had a body mass index (BMI) over the 85th percentile. The CDC (2003) reported that African American and Hispanic children and adolescents are disproportionately affected by this problem, with 21.5% and 21.8%, respectively, classified as overweight compared to 12.3% of non-Hispanic white children. Further, non-Hispanic black and Mexican American adolescents experienced the greatest increase in prevalence between surveys undertaken in 1988–1994 and 1999–2000, an increase of more than 10% (Kibbe & Offner, 2003). Findings of the National Heart, Lung, and Blood Institute (NHLBI), as reported in Kibbe and Offner (2003), revealed that by age 9, the prevalence of overweight was one-third higher in black girls

(31%) versus white girls (22%). They concluded that while parental socioeconomic status (SES) is associated inversely with childhood obesity among white children, among African American and Hispanic populations, childhood obesity does not seem to be linked significantly with parental income or education. Concurrent correlations are also observed between SES and obesity among African American and Hispanic adults (Gordon-Larsen, Adair, & Popkin, 2003; Winkleby, Kraemer, Ahn, & Varady, 1998).

ETHNIC VARIATIONS IN OBESITY/OVERWEIGHT

As of 2006, the CDC reports that more than nine million young people are considered overweight. Further, the CDC (2006a,b) notes that non-Hispanic black girls (ages 12 to 19 years) were disproportionately affected in 2003–2004, with 25.4% classified as overweight, an almost doubling (from 13.2%) in prevalence from 1988–1994. The prevalence for non-Hispanic white girls more than doubled from 1988–1994 (7.4% to 15.4%) and the prevalence for Mexican American girls increased from 9.2% to 14.1% in 2003–2004. The same rate was not observed for boys (ages 12 to 19 years). The prevalence of overweight in non-Hispanic white boys increased from 11.6% to 19.1% from 1988–1994 to 2003–2004, higher than that observed among non-Hispanic black boys (10.7% to 18.5%) and Mexican American boys (14.1% to 18.3%).

Results from the NHLBI Growth and Health Study (NGHS), conducted in a biracial sample of children, revealed that the prevalence of overweight at age 9 years was one-third higher in black girls (31%) than white girls (22%). Further, the rates of overweight and obesity doubled in both groups over the 10 years between ages 9–10 years and 18–19 years. Interestingly, while researchers determined an inverse relationship with childhood obesity and income/education among Caucasian children, the same was not true for African American and Hispanic populations. For the latter groups, researchers concluded that parental income and education did not seem to be significantly linked to obesity (Kibbe & Offner, 2003).

The Department of Health and Human Services (DHHS) reported that findings from studies (Troiano & Flegal, 1998) reveal race/ethnicity and SES are collinear and their effects on the prevalence of childhood obesity cannot be determined individually. They conclude that prevalence rates are often inconsistent as a result of separating out confounding variables. Furthermore, they state that the relationship between race/ethnicity, SES, and childhood obesity may result from a number of underlying causes, including, but not limited to, less healthy eating patterns (e.g., eating fewer fruits and vegetables, more saturated fats), engaging in less physical activity, more sedentary behavior, and cultural attitudes about body weight. The DHHS reports and the present authors agree that the above-mentioned factors tend to co-occur and are likely to contribute jointly to ethnic differentials in increased risk of obesity in children (Department of Health and Human Services, 2006d). The nutritional data in Table 4.2 and Table 4.3 further explain unhealthy eating patterns as derived from selected studies. Although the data are not racially or ethnically characterized, we believe this should be considered by practitioners in treatment modalities.

SOCIAL CULTURAL INDICES OF OBESITY

Young and Nestle (2002) suggest that expanding portion sizes have contributed greatly to the obesity epidemic. Researchers have obtained information about current portions from manufacturers or from direct weighing. Their results reveal that food portions have increased in size and now exceed federal standards. Portion sizes began to increase in the 1970s, rose sharply in the 1980s, and have persisted in parallel with increasing body sizes. With the exception of sliced white bread, Young and Nestle found that all of the commonly available food portions exceeded, sometimes greatly, U.S. Department of Agriculture (USDA) standard portion sizes. The largest of these excesses over

Table 4.3 Eating Behaviors of Young People

Less than 40% of children and adolescents in the United States meet the U.S. dietary guidelines for saturated fat.	U.S. Department of Agriculture (1998). Continuing survey of food intake by individuals, 1994–96. Washington, DC: U.S. Department of Agriculture.
Eighty percent of high school students do not eat fruits and vegetables at the recommended five servings per day.	Centers for Disease Control (2006). Youth risk behavior surveillance—United States, 2005. *Morbidity and Mortality Weekly Report*, 55(SS-5), 1–108.
Only 30% of children age 2 to 17 meet the USDA's dietary recommendation for fiber.	Lin, B., Guthrie, J., & Frazao, E. (2001). American children's diets not making the grade. *Food Review*, 24(2), 8–17.
Eighty-five percent of adolescent females do not consume enough calcium.	U.S. Department of Health and Human Services (2004). Bone health and osteoporosis: a report of the Surgeon General. Rockville, MD: Department of Health and Human Services, Office of the Surgeon General.
Calcium intake has decreased 36% among adolescent females.	Cavadini, C., Siega-Riz, A., & Popkin, B. (2000). U.S. adolescent food intake trends from 1965 to 1996. *Archives of Disease in Childhood*, 83, 18–24.
Daily soft drink consumption almost doubled among adolescent females and tripled among adolescent males.	U.S. Department of Agriculture (1998). Continuing survey of food intake by individuals, 1994–96. Washington, DC: U.S. Department of Agriculture.
To lose weight, many high school students report unhealthy methods. One nationwide study revealed that during the month prior to the survey, 12.3% of students went without food for 24 hours or more, 4.5% had vomited or taken laxatives, and 6.3% had taken diet pills, powders, or liquids without a doctor's advice.	Centers for Disease Control (2006). Youth risk behavior surveillance—United States, 2005. *Morbidity and Mortality Weekly Report*, 55(SS-5), 1–108.

Source: National Center for Chronic Disease Prevention and Health Promotion. Healthy youth. Atlanta, GA: Centers for Disease Control. Available at www.cdc.gov/HealthyYouth/nutrition/facts.htm.

USDA standards (700%) occurred in the cookie category, but cooked pasta, muffins, steaks, and bagels exceeded USDA standards by 480%, 333%, 224%, and 195%, respectively.

Bray, Nielson, and Popkin (2004) examined the increased use of high fructose corn syrup (HFCS) in beverages and the obesity epidemic. Consumption of HFCS increased more than 1000% between 1970 and 2000, far exceeding the changes in intake of any food or food group. HFCS represents greater than 40% of caloric sweeteners added to foods and beverages, and is the sole caloric sweetener in soft drinks in the United States. Conservative estimates of the consumption of HFCS indicate a daily average of 132 kcal for all Americans 2 years of age and older, and the top 20% of consumers of caloric sweeteners ingest 316 kcal/day from HFCS. The digestion, absorption, and metabolism of fructose differ from that of glucose in that fructose does not stimulate insulin secretion or enhance leptin (regulator of food intake), thus caloric overconsumption may be enhanced. Hence fructose is strongly implicated in the obesity epidemic. Nearly one-fourth of adolescents drink more than 26 oz/day of soft drinks, which provides at least 300 kcal, approximately 12% to 15% of their daily caloric need. Furthermore, students in schools that provide access to soft drinks and snack foods are less likely to consume fruits, juice, milk, and vegetables than students who do not have access (Cullen, Ash, Warneke, & deMoor, 2002; Fried & Nestle, 2004).

Giammattei, Blix, Marshak, Wollitzer, & Pettitt's (2003) work lends support to the influence of HFCS and the occurrence of obesity. They sampled 319 sixth- and seventh-grade students in California to determine the prevalence of lifestyle parameters associated with obesity. The analysis revealed that increased levels of television viewing and soda intake are associated with a higher prevalence of overweight and obesity among sixth and seventh graders. Latinos spent more time

Table 4.2 Selected Nutritional Trends as Derived from Studies that Used the USDA's Nationwide Food Consumption Survey and the Continuing Survey of Food Intakes by Individuals

Children are getting more of their food away from home. Energy intake from away-from-home food sources increased from 20% to 32% from 1977–1978 to 1994–1996.	Lin, B., Guthrie, J., & Frazao, E. (1999). Quality of children's diets at and away from home: 1994–96. *Food Review*, 22, 2–10.
Daily total energy intake did not significantly increase for children ages 6 to 11, but did increase for adolescent girls and boys ages 12 to 19 (by 113 and 243 kcal), respectively.	Enns, C., Mickle, S., & Goldman, J. (2002). Trends in food and nutrient intakes by children in the United States. *Family Economics and Nutrition Review*, 14(2), 56–58.
Daily total energy intake that children derived from energy-dense (high-calorie) snacks increased by approximately 121 kcal between 1977 and 1996.	Jahns, L., Siega-Riz, A., & Popkin, B. (2001). The increasing prevalence of snacking from 1977–1996. *Journal of Pediatrics*, 138, 493–498.
There has been a decline in breakfast consumption, especially for children of working mothers.	Department of Health and Human Services. (2006d). Childhood obesity. Washington, DC: Department of Health and Human Services. Available at http://aspe.hhs.gov/health/reports/child_obesity/.
Portion sizes increased between 1977 and 1996. Average portion sizes increased for salty snacks from 1.0 to 1.6 oz and for soft drinks from 12.2 oz to 19.9 oz.	Nielsen, S., & Popkin, B. (2003). Patterns and trends in food portion sizes, 1977–1998. *JAMA*, 289, 450–453.
Only 21% of young people eat the recommended five or more servings of fruits and vegetables each day. Nearly half of all vegetable servings are fried potatoes.	Centers for Disease Control and Prevention (2004). Physical activity and good nutrition essential elements to preventing chronic disease and obesity. Atlanta, GA: Centers for Disease Control. Available at www.cdc.gov/nccdphp/publications/aag/dnpa.htm.
Soda consumption increased dramatically in the early to mid-1990s. Thirty-two percent of adolescent girls and 52% of adolescent boys consume three or more 8 oz servings of soda per day. Soft drink consumption for adolescent boys has nearly tripled, from 7 to 22 oz per day. Children as young as 7 months are consuming soda.	Gleason, P., & Suitor, C. (2001). Children's diets in the mid-1990s: dietary intake and its relationship with school meal participation. Report CN-01-CDI. Washington, DC: U.S. Department of Agriculture.

Source: U.S. Department of Health and Human Services. Childhood Obesity. Available at http://aspe.hhs.gov/health/reports/child_obesity/.

watching television and consumed more soft drinks than did non-Hispanic white or Asian students, hence they had higher levels of overweight and obesity. Cullen, Ash, Warneke, and deMoor's (2002) study of the intake of soft drinks, fruit flavored beverages, and fruits and vegetables by children in grades 4 through 6 in Texas ($n = 504$) supported the disproportionate intake of soft drinks and other sweetened beverages by ethnic and minority children. Mexican American children reported the highest soft drink consumption, and African American children reported the highest fruit flavored drink consumption. The researchers also found a negative relationship between sweetened drink consumption and consumption of fruits and vegetables.

Another correlate to overweight and obesity that one must consider is the lack of physical activity in the schools. Children now spend an average of 25% of their time in front of the television and computer (Neisner, Histon, Goeldner, & Moon, 2003; Robinson, Kiernan, Matheson, & Haydel, 2001). Fiscal crises in schools have led to cuts in physical education programs. In 2005 only 35.8% of youth nationwide met the current recommended levels of physical activity (Centers for Disease Control, 2006c). Also, only 33% of youth nationwide attended physical education (PE) classes daily (Centers for Disease Control, 2006c). More than half (64.2% and 67%, respectively) did not meet current recommended levels of physical activity and did not attend PE classes on a daily basis. A second factor, although not inclusive of environmental factors, is that community designs are often not supportive of physical activity, with an absence of sidewalks, unleashed animals, and other safety concerns (Sallis, Bauman, & Pratt, 1998). Third, LaPoint's (2003) work on the commercial environments created by social marketing directed toward ethnic minority children demands consumer activism to promote more prosocial behavior in media venues. Marketers often produce advertisements where low-nutrition foods are cross-marketed with other products such as fashion, music videos, movies, and toys with the use of ethnic celebrities and models and other elements of ethnic culture. These influences are deemed toxic for children and families (Alleyne & LaPoint, 2004).

PROFILE OF MISSISSIPPI: NUMBER ONE IN THE NATION FOR OBESITY

To illustrate the sociocultural factors that are unique to Mississippi, the state which has consistently been ranked as number one in the nation in terms of obesity, consider the story of Mr. Deke, as told by the *Washington Post* editor, Michael Leahy (2004), and the documentary done by the *Guardian*. Mr. Leahy interviewed Mr. David (Deke) Baskin of Oxford, Mississippi in 2004.

> Mr. Baskin, age 52, 5 feet and 296 pounds, has a BMI of 43.7. He is ambulatory, but not fit to walk more than a few steps. At 52, he is an ill man who views his plight as a consequence in no small part to all his "good" eating. Good eating consists of Boston butt roasts and slabs of pork ribs and green beans cooked in ham fat. "Damn, those beans are good, man," Deke says. Hush yer mouth, a praise often applied to "good eating," means that no praise is necessary because the food is so superb that compliments are gratuitous; that it should just be eaten. Although Deke has had diabetes for 10 years, suffers from lupus and gout, is in a motorized scooter, and has heart problems, he says, "I'd go crazy if I didn't get some of my food." Deke concludes the interview with these remarks: "There is this chain place called Church's Chicken down here that just makes me gotta have their fried chicken. The world's hard, you know, man? Stressful. And then somebody says, 'This food is gonna make you feel good, and everybody's tryin' it. Why aren't you tryin' it? Gotta try it!' And you can try it, you know? You can't do that with some things. It costs a lot, too much, to get some things, you know, like a new house, new car, vacations. But you can get food. You can get all the Church's fried chicken you want."

The *Guardian* (2002) did a documentary of residents in Chunky (actual name), Mississippi and other parts of the Delta region of Mississippi where mechanization has replaced the once more labor-intensive agricultural jobs. Food items they found which were "particularly Mississippian" included fried catfish, crawfish, shrimp, oysters, fried tomatoes, and fried dill pickles, plus sweet iced tea ("the house wine of the south"). A colloquial expression is that your tea can never be too sweet. In Mississippi, the *Guardian* reported that even churches add to the obesity epidemic because there are regular socials where food is always present and southern manners dictate that you eat the food so as not to offend anyone. Even funerals are occasions to eat heartily. "There are casseroles, and people put in cream of chicken soup, lots of Velveeta cheese, bacon, etc." Dr. Alan Penman, a former epidemiologist with the Mississippi Department of Health, told reporters that he prefers not to use the word epidemic as it relates to the obesity problem in Mississippi and the nation because an epidemic normally refers to a condition that is transient. Rather, Penman says, "What we have here are normal adaptations to the kind of environment we now live in. It's Darwinian. Everyone is at risk, if not actually affected, because we have created what some people have called an obesogenic environment." Further, Penman states that Mississippi is a "public health disaster unfolding right before our eyes." In Mississippi, black women age 45 to 54 are the worst affected by this environment; 56% of them are obese.

CULTURAL ATTITUDES TOWARD OBESITY

Currently 77% of black women are in the overweight or obese category (defined as a BMI of 25 kg/m²) and 50% are considered obese (a BMI of 30 kg/m²). Further, according to Kumanyika (2005), the severity of obesity among black women is also greater than average when judged by the 15% who have a BMI of 40 kg/m² or greater, as well as compared to white women when considering SES factors such as income and education. Not only is obesity confined to black women, as demonstrated in the aforementioned NHLBI research, it is also apparent in younger African Americans and does not appear to differ along socioeconomic lines. Kumanyika (2005) offers the following perspective regarding possible attitudes among some black women related to obesity:

> Emphasizing weight issues within African American communities, in which nearly 80% of women would be targeted as overweight or obese, would raise the potential for harmful effects on self-esteem. Attitudes among African Americans and other populations with a history of economic stress and deprivation include some that equate being heavier with being healthier relative to thin people. Thin people may be seen as wasting away due to illness or addictions, leading to attitudes that are less negative about excess weight than in the mainstream. (p. 6)

From an ethical perspective as it relates to the preponderance of African Americans who are affected by overweight/obesity, the question Kumanyika (2005) poses is: Is obesity really a high priority in the face of other health disparities?

> Those of us in the nutrition, physical activity, and obesity fields must face the question of whether, for the overall good of the black community, for example, some of the resources devoted to obesity would be more appropriately placed elsewhere. Take data on women's health, for example. While it is true that heart disease, stroke, and diabetes—all of which are obesity related—are the leading causes of death for black women and affect large numbers of black women, the more dramatic disparities relative to white women are in conditions that threaten black women in their prime: this risk of developing acquired immunodeficiency syndrome (AIDS) (incidence ratio of about 20 to 1 for blacks vs whites), maternal mortality, or homicide (both with a ratio of about 4 to 1 for blacks vs whites) (NWLC, 2004). The black-white gap in infant mortality, with a ratio of about 2 to 1, also persists as a continuing reminder of the ethnic differences in life chances from conception onward. There is no obvious answer as to the question of which of these problems is the most important. They are all important. (p. 5)

Focus group studies by Davis et al. (submitted) of African American parents of obese children (95th percentile for BMI) revealed that parents (all of whom were obese) tended to explain the child's obesity away by stating that the child had big bones, took after his or her parents, or it was caused by their DNA. Of interest, when parents were told of the health consequences associated with obesity, parents began to spontaneously discuss strategies for helping the child lose weight. These preliminary findings suggest that when ethnic minority parents are educated about the health consequences of their child's weight status in a manner understandable to them, it may lead to more meaningful involvement of the parents in weight management of their children.

Using a rural population in a southern city, Davis et al. (2003) used the revised Cardiovascular Risk Reduction in Children (CRRIC) survey (see Appendix) to collect data regarding cardiovascular risk behaviors in 113 ethnic minority children ranging from 8 to 13 years of age. The majority of the children (99%) were African American and lived in single-parent homes (66%). The weight of the female parent/guardian ranged from 68 lb to 400 lb. Results revealed that 46% of the boys and 46% of the girls had BMIs at or above the 85th percentile. Fitness profile results revealed that only 11% of the children were classified as fit, 84% were classified as fair, and 5% were deemed unfit. Regarding family perception of the child's weight, 67% of the parents/guardians described their

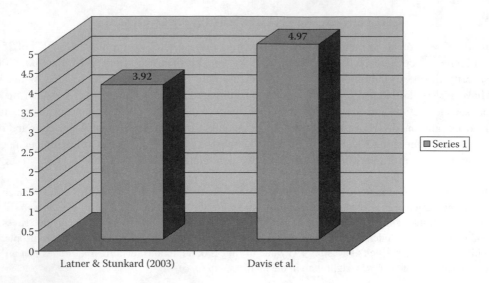

Figure 4.1 Levels of stigma and weight in Caucasian and African-American samples.

child's weight as normal, while 2% perceived their children to be "a lot overweight." The remaining 31% perceived their child as simply overweight (22%) or underweight (9%). In her presentation at the Pediatric Academic Societies annual meeting, *Washington Post* writer Sandra Boodman (2006) reported that a recent study of 194 Latina mothers in California revealed that 44% had children who were overweight by age 3, but three-quarters thought their children were of normal weight.

Consistent with results of the focus group session of African American parents of obese children conducted by Davis et al. (submitted), attitudes and perceptions of the child's weight status by ethnic parents were that this was not an acute problem. When viewed in light of Kumanyika's (2005) proposition that in ethnic populations with a history of economic deprivation, being heavier in weight was a more desirable attribute than being thin, this may explain the different perceptions and seemingly greater acceptance of ethnic parents regarding overweight and obesity. Stigma studies of obesity among African American children suggest confirmatory evidence that heavier weights are much more tolerated among this group than in other culture groups. Davis et al. (submitted) studied the stigma against African American children among a predominantly African American sample of college students. Figure 4.1 illustrates the results. The predominantly African American sample of college students displayed a significantly lower level of stigma compared to the predominantly white sample (Latner and Stunkard, 2003).

Do parents perceive their children as overweight when they indeed are? Baughcum, Burklow, Deeks, Powers, and Whitaker (1998) performed a focus group study of low-income mothers and found that mothers believed that heavier infants were healthier, that their infants were not getting enough to eat and required the introduction of solid foods at ages earlier than recommended, and that it was appropriate to use foods to illicit good behavior from the children. In a study of Women, Infants, and Children (WIC) program mothers with preschoolers at risk for overweight, mothers did not assess a child's weight status by the charted weight and height used by health care providers, but rather were more likely to see weight as a problem only if peers teased the child about his or her weight or if the child became inactive (Jain et al., 2001).

The Davis et al. (2002) study of African American children in rural and urban Mississippi also lends support to the phenomenon of perception of a child's weight by parents. In these studies, although 39% to 49% of both boys and girls were at the 85th or higher percentile for BMI, only 13% of the parents perceived their child as overweight. In a subsequent focus group study of parents whose children were at the 95th or higher percentile, their responses to the question, "What are some of the reasons you think that your child may be a little overweight?" indicated a lack of perception of the causes or the health risks associated with obesity. Caregivers blamed genetics, DNA, and family predisposition for their child's weight status. They also intimated that they were comfortable that their children would grow out of their obesity. However, the researchers noted a decided change in attitude and mood in the group when the health consequences of obesity were discussed. The general response was that they were unaware that children could get adult diseases like diabetes (Davis, Davis, Beal, & Ballard, 2005).

According to an Office of Communications (Ofcom, London; n.d.) document, parents in the United Kingdom are not aware of their obese children and the situation they may be in. Some choose to ignore this reality. The parents' and the children's attitudes appear accepting; most claim they are happy and have high self-esteem. Knowledge about healthy eating is limited and eating fresh fruits and vegetables is of little importance. Also, less motivation about health is noted and food choice is driven by marketing, convenience, and price. Of note, minorities do not support a change in food advertisements to children (available at www.ofcom.org.uk/research/tv/reports/food_ads).

TREATMENT CONSIDERATIONS OF CHILDHOOD AND ADOLESCENT OVERWEIGHT AND OBESITY

As reported by *Washington Post* editor Sandra Boodman (2006), some doctors call it "the other f-word"—a problem they see daily but are in many cases reluctant to address. Yet, as obesity, now at epidemic levels, continues to spread at a record pace and take its toll on young and old, it demands a decided response. To add to this urgency, Boodman reports that at the Children's National Medical Center in Washington, DC, where 38% of patients are obese, physicians say that in recent years they treated a 9-year-old who suffered a heart attack. The affected child's BMI was 52. This BMI in adult terms is equivalent to a 5-foot 6-inch person who weighs 322 pounds!

Breaking the Ice

Kumanyika (2005) sheds some light on why ethnic minorities may not be as concerned about their weight (77% of black women are overweight or obese) or that of their children. This may be especially noteworthy, she claims, when health practitioners weigh the risks of damage to the patient's self-image by calling attention to their body weight. Kumanyika asserts that populations with a history of oppression have, of necessity, honed their ability to be self-accepting to a fine art in order to survive, buffering mistreatment and derogatory images from outside the community. The example given is the idea exposed in oppressed people that the majority may not love us, but we can love ourselves, regardless. Further, attitudes among African Americans and other populations with a history of economic stress and deprivation include some that equate being heavier with being healthier relative to thin people. In other words, personal acquiescence is a survival skill in oppressed people.

Concurrently, Crawford et al. (2004) looked at attitudes of Latina women regarding their children's weight and concluded that among this group: (1) thinness was troublesome to immigrant Latinas, who associated it with malnutrition and disease and had difficulty perceiving being overweight as a threat to their child's health, (2) mothers consistently rated being part of a loving, attentive family as the most important value when it came to raising happy children, and (3) the women expressed fear of allowing their children to play unattended at nearby parks and regretted that they did not have time to accompany them.

Use of a relativistic approach is favored by Kumanyika (2005) in therapeutic interactions with ethnic groups. With this approach, health practitioners formulate weight control programs and interventions in the context of the cultural perspectives in African American communities, under the assumption that these cultural perspectives are not only valid, but also dominant considerations for achieving salience and effectiveness of programs that address eating behaviors and physical activity lifestyles. The opposite approach to the relativistic approach is the cultural imposition approach. This approach is described by Kumanyika as ignoring the cultural bearings on one's lifestyle and thereby supplanting the ethnic culture with the mores and values of the dominant culture. She concludes that there may be some hope for a blending of these two approaches in the obesity epidemic.

Charity Begins at Home: The Role of Parents. Given the impact of the home environment as evidenced by parental influences, we believe that it is important for practitioners to consider the home environment in treatment modalities. The American Academy of Pediatrics (2003) warns that for children less than 3 years old, parental obesity is a stronger predictor of obesity in adulthood than the child's weight status and that parental food choices influence children. Further, they contend having a television in a child's bedroom serves as a strong predictor of overweight in children as young as preschool. Cullen, Ash, Warneke, and deMoor's (2002) study of 504 multiethnic children revealed that students whose parents had a high school education or less drank more soft drinks and total sweetened beverages. They determined that Mexican American children (grades 4 through 6 in parochial school) had the highest soft drink intake and that African American children had the highest sweetened beverage intake. Among these groups, 51% of the daily intake consisted of sweetened beverages. Mustillo's (2003) study of 991 non-Hispanic white children residing in the Great Smoky Mountains confirmed that children with chronic obesity were twice as likely to come from families where one or both parents had less than an 11th-grade education.

Strauss and Knight (1999) also noted a significant relationship between the home environment and development of obesity in children. Slyper (2004) reviewed studies of the causes and consequences of the pediatric obesity epidemic and concluded that the prime cause of obesity is not decreased physical activity, albeit physical activity does impact the regulation of body weight. Rather, Slyper asserts that the intake of high-glycemic carbohydrates, leading to postprandial hyperinsulinemia and excess weight gain, is what is increasing in children. Regarding fat intake in children, when eaten in excess, this may lead to obesity in predisposed individuals. Nesbitt et al. (2004) reviewed the literature on overweight as a risk factor in children with a focus on ethnicity and reported that lower income families are at higher risk for obesity. Associated factors with this phenomenon included sweetened beverages, large portion sizes, and meal structure. They affirmed that academic performance and family support are important in weight loss in these families. Golan, Weizman, and Fainaru (1999) studied 60 obese children (ages 6 to 11 years) and determined that when parents are the sole agents of change, children are more successful in losing weight and that parents themselves receive benefits from changing their eating and activity patterns. This study supports family centered treatment for childhood obesity.

A study of Canadian children by Williams (2004) indicated that the prevalence of overweight children in Canada between the ages of 7 and 13 years was 23% to 36%. This rate has doubled since 1981. Risk factors for childhood obesity in this group included parental obesity and maternal smoking during pregnancy. In addition, Williams contends that when overweight children enter school, they are at greater risk of being overweight and obese through their school years and into adulthood. Boney, Verma, Tucker, and Vohr (2005) affirm that the metabolic syndrome begins in childhood and that associated variables are birth weight, maternal obesity, and gestational diabetes. Parker (2004) shares data from the Act 1220 legislation of Arkansas. In essence, schools were mandated to measure every public school student's BMI and report this to parents. They discovered that 38% of the children are overweight or at risk of becoming overweight. Hispanic males and African American girls had higher rates of overweight than other racial/ethnic groups. In a study of 101 girls (mean age 8.5 years) and their biological parents, Treuth, Butte, Ellis, Martin, and Comuzzie (2001) discovered that the girls' body composition was significantly related to both parents' body composition.

Birch, Fisher, and Grimm-Thomas (1996) affirm that parents' child-feeding practices shape children's food preferences and that these preferences in turn affect the percent of energy from fat in a child's diet. Common food inducement practices of parents may have the opposite effect from those intended. In essence, having children eat a nutritious food (vegetable) in order to obtain a non-nutritious food (cookie) tends to decrease the child's preference for the nutritious food. Robinson, Kiernan, Matheson, and Haydel's (2001) research lends support to findings that parental control over children's eating may not have the intended effect. The inability of children to self-regulate food intake has been identified as one causal factor in adult obesity. For example, 3- to 5-year-old children whose mothers were more controlling of their food intake showed higher rates of eating, less ability to self-regulate energy intake, and increased adiposity (Birch, 1999; Birch & Davidson, 2001; Drucker, Hammer, Agras, & Bryson, 1999; Fisher & Birch, 1999; Johnson & Birch, 1994). Further, children whose food intake was restricted exhibited behaviors similar to those associated with severe scarcity of food, such as scavenging and stealing of food (Ikeda, 1995).

To summarize, researchers are in agreement that parental influences must be considered in the causes, consequences, and treatment of childhood obesity. Studies confirm a significant correlation between parents' BMI and the child's BMI. Parental practices of permitting a television in the child's room, child feeding (too restrictive or too lax), food choices, and promotion of outdoor physical activity have been observed to impact the weight status of the child. Culture also seems to impact on the child's weight status. Hispanic and African American children's higher intake of soft drinks, sweetened beverages, and other high-glycemic carbohydrates may have some, yet to be investigated, cultural innuendoes. While major health care organizations present a message of admonition for parents to serve as roles models and to create an active environment for children, one must ask to what extent do parents feel as if they have the capacity or self-efficacy to create a healthy home environment for their child? This question is currently being investigated by Cooper (2006). And to what extent do these parents really understand the physiology and consequences of childhood obesity? A pilot research study by Davis (2004) suggested that parents' attitudes toward the causes and consequences of their child's obesity appeared to change as the physiological consequences were discussed with them. This phenomenon needs further exploration.

Charity Spreads Abroad: The School Environment

Story, Kaphingst, and French (2006) report that more than 95% of American youth ages 5 to 17 are enrolled in school and that no other institution has as much continuous and intensive contact with children during their first two decades of life. Specifically, they suggest that schools can promote good nutrition, physical activity, and healthy weights among children through healthful school meals and foods, physical education programs and recess, classroom health education, and school health services.

A comprehensive listing of effective prevention and treatment options prepared for the National Institute for Health Care Management Foundation Forum can be accessed in Kibbe and Offner (2003). This issue paper reports studies of diverse youth populations by Stanford researchers that encourage health care providers to attempt to slow or halt weight gain in pediatric patients who are at risk for overweight. This will allow the patient to "grow into" his or her body weight. Key interventions include identifying overweight and at risk for overweight children and adolescents, intervening early, and goal setting. Some other interventions for prevention focus on parental involvement, including parent education about critical behavior areas (e.g., praise behavior, no food as reward, establish meal and snack times, parents provide children with options then children decide, be a role model, and be consistent), increasing physical activity levels, decreasing caloric intake, and eliminating tobacco use.

Treatment by Health Care Professionals

Caprio (2006) suggests that, at present, pediatricians are woefully unprepared to effectively address the obesity epidemic in children. Caprio states that effective obesity treatment programs combining a dietary component, behavioral modification, physical activity, and parental involvement have been carried out in academic centers, but these have not carried over to primary pediatric care centers. Although strides are being made in the medical community to close this gap, a major shift in pediatric care that builds on findings from academic medical centers regarding structured intervention programs is warranted. Building on the research and strategies of others, Caprio lists the following specific considerations for health care professionals in their treatment of childhood obesity (Table 4.4). Family history and assessment, and dietary components of treatment should be considered the areas where the most ethnic and cultural diversity will be evident. Ethnic diets and diseases with higher prevalence among ethnic minorities (e.g., sickle cell disease among African Americans) should be considered and understood by the practitioner interested in administering culturally sensitive treatment.

Table 4.4 Considerations for Health Care Professionals Treating Childhood Obesity

Pediatricians and others treating children	A comprehensive medical examination, complete with assessment of nutrition, physical activity, and behaviors linked to obesity. Appraisal of the degree of obesity and associated metabolic complications
Family history and assessment	Document family history of parental obesity, gestational diabetes, dyslipedemia, cardiovascular disease, and history of diabetes. Include history of medication usage (glucocorticoids and antipsychotic medications may influence weight). A detailed nutritional history should include quality and portion size of meals, when and where the child eats, levels of satiety with meals, etc. Continual assessment and tracking of child's BMI and assessment for obesity-related diseases such as type 2 diabetes, signs of insulin insensitivity, or hypertension. It is suggested that laboratory tests should include a fasting lipid profile, a liver function test, and fasting glucose and insulin levels. Refer patients with obesity-related diseases such as type 2 diabetes, hypertension, polycystic ovarian syndrome, dyslipedemia, nonalcoholic steatohepatitis, and sleep apnea to appropriate specialists such as a pediatric endocrinologist, cardiologist, gastroenterologist, or pulmonologist.
Dietary components of treatment	Mild restriction of calories such as the Traffic Light Diet. Severely restricted diets such as high-protein diets should be implemented under strict medical supervision. Until more information is available regarding the effects of low-carbohydrate diets on insulin resistance and their long-term effects on weight and metabolic health, they should not be used in children. Emerging data suggest restricting carbohydrate or other sugary drinks from the diet.
Role of physical activity	Physical activity is critical to obesity treatment. Exercise in the absence of dietary modification has not been found to significantly affect weight. There are currently no evidence-based guidelines by which to design exercise programs for obese children. Reduce sedentary behaviors such as television viewing.
Pharmacologic approaches in pediatrics	Few studies and guidelines exist for medication use in treating obesity in children. The newest medication treatments are aimed at reducing metabolic complications associated with obesity by targeting insulin resistance. Sibutramine (Meridia), an appetite suppressant, for weight loss and maintenance in combination with reduced calorie intake has been approved for adolescents older than 16 years. Orlistat (Xenical), which decreases nutrient absorption by cutting intestinal fat absorption by up to 30%, has been approved for use in children older than 12 years. Metfomin targets insulin resistance and may have a duel effect by preventing further weight gain and thereby improving the associated metabolic complications.
Surgical approaches	At present, surgery is only used to treat adult obesity when patients are severely obese (BMI greater than 40) or a BMI greater than 30 with accompanying obesity-related complications.

Source: Caprio (2006).

Considerations for Weight Management in Ethnic Minority Children

Unlike the usually reported sense of high self-worth demonstrated by many African American girls, Orenstein (1994) suggests that Hispanic girls in general may experience lower self-esteem and more depression than other ethnic groups. Factors thought to contribute to this are prejudice and discrimination based on ethnicity, language, and social status. In addition, media that target Latinas, inclusive of Hispanic television and magazines, are increasingly reinforcing thinness as beauty. Related to this phenomenon, Hispanic high school students are found to have rates of bulimia comparable to those of whites and to use laxatives for weight reduction more frequently than girls from other racial groups. Strategies suggested by the DHHS Office on Women's Health (2006b) addressing eating disorders among Latina children and adolescents include:

1. Conduct media literacy activities that critique the images of thinness as beauty in television, magazines, and advertisements targeting girls.
2. Incorporate culturally appropriate materials, curricula, and interventions. The DHHS Office on Women's Health (2006c) lists numerous publications of this type in "Resources for School Personnel: Education Materials." Some materials listed include curricular support materials such as Folkers and Engelmann's *Taking Charge of My Mind and Body: A Girl's Guide to Outsmarting Alcohol, Drugs, Smoking, and Eating Problems* and Ikeda and Naworski's *Am I Fat? Helping Young Children Accept Differences in Body Size*; individual reading materials including Judy Bloom's *Blubber* and *Tales of a Fourth Grade Nothing*; classroom reading materials like Cherie Bennet's *Life in the Fat Lane* and Lisa F. Hall's *Perk! The Story of a Teenager With Bulimia*; and videotapes such as "Self-Image: The Fantasy, The Reality," "Body Talk," and "NCAA: Nutrition and Eating Disorders."
3. Refer girls committed to achieving a healthy weight to appropriate health care professionals (e.g., dietitians, nutritionists, physicians, nurse practitioners, or school nurses specializing in pediatric or adolescent weight management) for information on effective weight management strategies. These programs are often covered by health insurance programs (Caprio, 2006).
4. Help girls understand the impact of culture on body image and weight control.
5. Provide families with copies of the information sheet "Jóvenes Latinas" (Department of Health and Human Services, 2006a). "Jóvenes Latinas" highlights findings from recent studies about disordered eating and eating disorders among Latina girls. It also provides suggestions for promoting positive body image and health behaviors among middle-school Hispanic students.
6. Be aware that Hispanic families may be reluctant to seek help from experts outside of their culture. Some examples of how to improve this situation are for more health care providers to improve their foreign language skills to bridge the language barrier, work to address both the mental health and physical health aspects of obesity and eating disorders, and participation from clinics in community health education projects, especially in areas of diversity.
7. Facilitate access and understanding for Hispanic families in the health care system.
8. As noted in "Targeting Interventions for Ethnic Minority and Low-Income Populations," Kumanyika and Grier (2006) posit many considerations in addressing obesity in these population groups (see Table 4.5). We believe these social, economic, and environmental factors should be considered and incorporated into treatment modalities.

Table 4.5 Considerations in Addressing Obesity in Ethnic Populations

Obesity prevalence	Obesity prevalence has increased for all ethnic groups, but has increased at disproportionately higher rates for African Americans and Mexican American children. Among Native American children, an Indian Health Service study estimated obesity prevalence at 22% for boys and 18% for girls based on data for more than 12,000 five- to seventeen-year-old American Indian children in North and South Dakota, Iowa, and Nebraska. Obesity prevalence was reported as 26.8% for boys and 30.5% for girls based on data for 1704 elementary school American Indian children in Arizona, New Mexico, and South Dakota.
Low SES children	Low SES children are at excess risk of obesity regardless of ethnicity. Ethnic differences in pediatric obesity appear at lower income levels. Generally, among white children, obesity typically declines as income and parental education increase.
Health effects of childhood obesity on minority and low-income populations	Ethnic minority and low-income children appear to be at greater risk of developing obesity-related health problems such as type 2 diabetes, precursors of cardiovascular disease, and sleep-disordered breathing.
Media and marketing	Low-income and ethnic minority youth appear to be disproportionately exposed to marketing activities. African Americans and Hispanics spend considerably more time watching television and movies and playing video games than white youth. As such, these groups are more exposed to food advertising, which can influence food selection practices.
Food access and availability	Minority and low-income communities have fewer than average supermarkets and convenience stores that stock fresh fruits and vegetables and other "healthy" foods. In addition, African American and low-income neighborhoods also have many fast food restaurants.
Built environment	The physical design and quality of the neighborhood impacts where and how often children and adolescents engage in physical activity. Other factors to consider in low-income communities are family work schedules, discretionary time, money, and car ownership.
School settings	While schools offer a tremendous opportunity to improve children's nutrition, increase physical activity, and prevent obesity, schools in the inner city or low-income communities are restrained by lack of funds.
Home environment	Minority and low-income households have a higher percentage of female-headed households, lower parental education, and higher rates of teenage parenting. All these factors are thought to profoundly impact the home environment, contributing to obesity in adults and children.

Source: Kumanyika and Grier (2006).

SUMMARY

To begin the work of applying culturally sensitive treatment methods in the treatment of childhood and adolescent obesity, sociocultural/environmental indices of obesity were examined. During the past several decades there has been a tremendous increase in portion sizes and an exponential increase in the use of high fructose corn syrup. The lifestyle of Mr. Deke, an obese African American in Mississippi, a state that has consistently led the nation in obesity prevalence, was reviewed. Although he experienced health challenges consistent with the metabolic syndrome, Mr. Deke provided a perspective on the role of culture in eating behaviors. In most measures, ethnic variations of overweight and obesity in children and adults reveal that African Americans, Mexican Americans, and Native Americans experience a disproportionate share of weight challenges. Selected nutritional trends reveal disappointing results for ethnic minority children and adolescents. For instance, in these groups, soft drink consumption is nearly twice that of white children, and as a whole, only about 21% ate the recommended amount of fruits and vegetables. Presently nearly 77% of black women experience overweight or obesity. Kumanyika (2005) poses the difficult question of how does one single out the obesity issue in this population group when there are so many other equally demanding challenges. To date, the infant mortality rate for black infants remains twice that of white infants. This is just one of the myriad challenges.

Health care practitioners say that to speak to parents about obesity in their children is tantamount to using the other f-word (fat). These dialogues are difficult and many health care practitioners avoid the topic altogether in the patient-provider setting. Health care practitioners should focus on dialogues that educate and encourage families about diets and lifestyles and how small changes (e.g., switching from sugary drinks to water or exchanging 30 minutes of television time for walking four to five days per week) can make large differences in caloric balance. In examining the role of parents, it was noted that parental modeling and body size, condoning attitudes about their children's weight status, parental skills, etc., all impacted upon the weight of children. Of note were the more accepting attitudes of ethnic parents regarding their children's weight status. In fact, certain ethnic groups such as African Americans and Hispanics had a preference for heavier weights in children. This was especially true if the family had experienced a period of deprivation.

Caprio (2006) provides a synopsis of current treatment options for children and adolescents, inclusive of the use of medication. She cautions providers to, first and foremost, seek a lifestyle intervention in treating adolescents prior to prescribing medication. In targeting interventions specifically for ethnic minority and low-income populations, one is admonished to consider the influence of the media and marketing. Ethnic minority and low-income groups watch more media and therefore are exposed to a greater number of food advertisements. Another factor to consider is environment. Generally in ethnic minority and low-income communities, there are more concerns about neighborhood safety. Schools have the potential to positively impact the nutrition and physical activity of children, but a lack of financial resources may prohibit utilization of programs developed to promote health.

CONCLUSIONS AND RECOMMENDATIONS

As heath care practitioners, we must not be afraid to open the dialogue with obese, overweight, or at-risk patients and their family members no matter what their ethnic or cultural background. It is our responsibility to say, "I am concerned about your child's weight." Without question, unless decided efforts and sweeping reforms are implemented in an expeditious manner to counteract the effects of the obesity epidemic, we will all bear the burden. One out of every three white children and one out of every two ethnic minority children born in 2000 and beyond will become diabetic unless the epidemic is halted (CDC, 2003). In terms of loss of lives, productivity, services, etc., this is beyond our imagination. Readers are asked to consider the following recommendations from the *Online Journal of Health Ethics* (Davis, 2004):

> Children are not city planners who design communities without sidewalks, walking trails, or neighborhood supermarkets that carry fresh fruits and vegetables. Our children do not make decisions regarding the need to "supersize" ice cream, soft drinks, burgers, fries, and other things marketed to them as "must have" foods. The children are not making the decisions that physical activity is not as important as the mastery of math, science, or language skills. Children cannot be made to carry the weight of adult planning and decision making. My challenge is for us to give serious dialogue to this dilemma.

Specific policy-oriented government remedies for the obesity epidemic suggested by the author include, but are not limited to:

1. Require physical education classes for all children in grades one to eight, and at least two units of physical education classes for all high school students.

2. Mandate nutrition instruction for all children in grades one to eight and at least one unit of nutrition for all high school students.
3. Place parks, walking trails, bike trails, etc., in accessible areas when possible. Make these priorities when planning new communities.
4. Regulate and limit target marketing to young children of low-nutritive foods (high sugar and high fat).
5. Have yearly citywide, community oriented, mass marketing health campaigns that emphasize physical activity, a reduction in sedentary behavior, and the eating of healthy foods.
6. Establish government programs (local, state, federal) to supplement prices for fruits, vegetables, whole grains, bottled water, etc., to greatly reduce the price of these commodities.
7. Have citywide Olympic-like events that emphasize physical activity across all age groups.
8. Establish a reward mechanism to recognize restaurants and fast food establishments that offer high-nutritive food choices.
9. Provide tax breaks and other financial incentives to industries that reward and contribute to health-promoting behaviors of employees (exercise trails, weight rooms, health foods, etc).
10. Regularly highlight in the public press and other media success stories of people who have sustained weight loss using practical, economical means that are amenable to the public.
11. Provide financial incentives and advertisements to malls and other public areas that are designed as indoor walking trails and fitness centers.
12. Fully fund K–12 educational institutions so that they will not be dependent on revenue from vending machines to supplement classroom instruction.
13. Treat obesity like the life-threatening epidemic it is. Keep the issue in the public press.

Obesity reduction and prevention remedies for families include:

1. Set healthy examples as parents and caregivers. Children model home behaviors to a great extent.
2. Sit together as a family to eat meals without the distraction of television viewing.
3. Encourage water drinking among family members. Have special water bottles for each family member.
4. Plan a family physical activity calendar of events:
   Walks
   Picnics in the park with playing
   Ball playing
   Skating
   Bicycling
   Other
5. Minimize the amount of and access to low-nutritive snacks in the home.
6. Plan ahead for events involving food (church potlucks, social events, etc).
7. Balance sedentary behaviors with physical activity (set limits on television watching, computer use, and other sedentary behaviors).
8. Resist the urge to place the family or an overweight family member on a diet unless directed to do so by a health care professional. Rather, focus on healthy lifestyle changes. Keep the focus on improving health as opposed to losing weight.
9. Give unconditional love and acceptance to all family members regardless of body size. Overweight children, and even some adults, are subjected to an immense amount of teasing and bullying. Home must become a safe place for them.
10. Cook and teach your children to prepare simple, healthy meals.
11. Keep an abundant amount of healthy snacks at home (fresh fruits and vegetables).
12. Become an advocate for school-based physical activity programs (Davis, 2004).

REFERENCES

Alleyne, S., & La Point, V. (2004). Obesity among black adolescent girls. *Genetic, Psychological and Cultural Influences, 30*(3), 344–365.

American Academy of Pediatrics. (2003). Prevention of pediatric overweight and obesity. *Pediatrics, 112*(2), 424–430.

Baughcum, A., Burklow, K., Deeks, C., Powers, S., & Whitaker, R. (1998). Maternal feeding practices and childhood obesity: a focus group study of low-income mothers. *Archives of Pediatric Adolescent Medicine, 152,* 1010–1014.

Bennet, C. (1999). *Life in the fat lane.* New York: Random House.

Birch, L. (1999). Children's preferences for high-fat foods. *Nutrition Review, 50,* 249–255.

Birch, L., & Davidson, K. (2001). Family environmental factors influencing the developing behavioral controls of food intake and childhood overweight. *Pediatric Clinics of North America, 48*(4), 893–907.

Birch, L., Fisher, J., & Grimm-Thomas, K. (1996). The development of children's eating habits. In H. L. Meiselman (Ed.), *Food choice, acceptance, and consumption.* Glasgow, Scotland: Blackie.

Blume, J. (1986). *Blubber.* New York: Bantam Doubleday.

Blume, J. (2003). *Tales of a fourth grade nothing.* New York: Penguin.

Boney, C., Verma, A., Tucker, R., & Vhor, B. (2005). Metabolic syndrome in childhood: association with birthweight, maternal obesity, and gestational diabetes mellitus. *Pediatrics, 115,* 290–296.

Boodman, S. (2006). Who are you calling fat? For fear of parents' reactions—and other reasons—many pediatricians ignore the biggest problem that weighs on young patients." *Washington Post,* July 18, 2006; F1.

Bray, G., Nielson, S., & Popkin, B. (2004). Consumption of high-fructose corn syrup in beverages may play a role in the epidemic of obesity. *American Journal of Clinical Nutrition, 79*(4), 537–543.

Caprio, S. (2006). Treating child obesity and associated medical conditions. *The Future of Children: Childhood Obesity, 16,* 209–224.

Centers for Disease Control (2003). CDC makes dire diabetes prediction for US children. Atlanta, GA: Centers for Disease Control. Available at www.mhanet.org/i4a/pages/headlinedetails.cfm?id=425&archive=1.

Centers for Disease Control (2006a). Childhood overweight. Atlanta, GA: Centers for Disease Control. Available at www.cdc.gov/nccdphp/dnpa/obesity/childhood/index.htm.

Centers for Disease Control (2006b). Overweight prevalence. Atlanta, GA: Centers for Disease Control. Available at www.cdc.gov/nccdphp/dnpa/obesity/childhood/prevalence.htm

Centers for Disease Control (2006c). Youth risk behavior surveillance—United States, 2005. *Morbidity and Mortality Weekly Report, 55*(SS-5), 1–108. Available at www.cdc.gov/mmwr/PDF/SS/SS5505.pdf.

Cooper, J. (2006). Development and testing of self efficacy of parental ability to influence child health behavior scale. Unpublished manuscript.

Crawford, P., Gosliner, W., Anderson, C., Strude, P., Becerra-Jones, Y., Samuels, S., Carroll, A., & Ritchie, L. (2004). Counseling Latino mothers of preschool children about weight issues: suggestions for a new framework. *Journal of American Dietetic Association, 104*(3), 387–394.

Cullen, K., Ash, D., Warneke, C., & deMoor, C. (2002). Intake of soft drinks, fruit-flavored beverages, and fruits and vegetables by children in grades 4 through 6. *American Journal of Public Health, 92*(9), 1475–1477.

Davis, M., Davis, S., Williams, L., Adbelrahman, L., Futch, T., Okeke, O., Young, L., & Davis, S. (Submitted). Stigmatization of obese children across race and gender.

Davis, S. (2004). Remedies for the obesity epidemic: Can we afford them? Do we want them? *Online Journal of Health Ethics, 1*(1), 1–4.

Davis, S., Arthur, C., Davis, M., Goldberg, D., Moll, G., & Davis, G. (2002). Assessing cardiovascular risk in children. The Jackson Mississippi CRRIC Study. *Journal of Cultural Diversity, 9*(3), 66–71.

Davis, S., Bienemey, C., Ellis, J., Ferdinand, D., Loustalot, F., Trabeaux, S., & Webb, S. (2003). A descriptive analysis of CRRIC II results: cardiovascular risks of African-American children in Mississippi. *Journal of Cultural Diversity, 10*(3), 84–90.

Davis, S., Davis, M., Beal, R., & Ballard, P. (2005). When I jump, I feel the earth move under my feet: experiences of African American children who are overweight. Poster session presented at the 19th annual meeting of the Southern Nursing Research Society, Atlanta, GA.

Davis, S., Davis, M., Moll, G., Davis, G., Goodwin, E., & Nick, T. (2002). CRRIC health survey [research survey]. Jackson, MS: Author.

Department of Health and Human Services. (2006a). BodyWise. Jóvenes Latinas. Eating disorders information sheet. Washington, DC: Department of Health and Human Services, Office on Women's Health. Available at www.womenshealth.gov/bodyimage/bodywise/bp/latinas.pdf.

Department of Health and Human Services. (2006b). BodyWise. Latina girls. Eating disorders information sheet. Washington, DC: Department of Health and Human Services, Office on Women's Health. Available at www.womenshealth.gov/bodyimage/bodywise/uf/LatinaGirls.pdf.

Department of Health and Human Services. (2006c). BodyWise. Resources for school personnel: education materials. Eating disorders information sheet. Washington, DC: Department of Health and Human Services, Office on Women's Health. Available at www.womenshealth.gov/bodyimage/bodywise/bp/Resources-materials.pdf.

Department of Health and Human Services. (2006d). Childhood obesity. Washington, DC: Department of Health and Human Services. Available at http://aspe.hhs.gov/health/reports/child_obesity/.

Drucker, R., Hammer, L., Agras, W., & Bryson, S. (1999). Can mothers influence their child's eating behavior. *Journal of Developmental and Behavioral Pediatrics, 20,* 88–92.

Fisher, J., & Birch, L. (1999). Restricting access to foods and children's eating. *Appetite, 32,* 405–419.

Folkers, G., & Engelmann, J. (1997). *Taking charge of my mind and body: a girl's guide to outsmarting alcohol, drugs, smoking, and eating problems.* Minneapolis, MN: Free Spirit.

Freedman, D., Kahn, L., Dietz, W., Srinivasan, S., & Berenson, G., (2001). Relationship of childhood obesity to coronary heart disease risk factors in adulthood: The Bogalusa Heart Study. *Pediatrics, 108*(3), 712–718.

Fried, E., & Nestle, M. (2004). The growing political movement against soft drinks in schools. *JAMA, 288*(17), 2181.

Giammattei, J., Blix, G., Marshak, H., Wollitzer, A., & Pettitt, D. (2003). Television watching and soft drink consumption: associations with obesity in 11- to 13-year-old school children. *Archives of Pediatric and Adolescent Medicine, 157,* 882–886.

Golan, M., Weizman, A., & Fainaru, M. (1999). Impact of treatment for childhood obesity on parental risk factors for cardiovascular disease. *Preventive Medicine, 29,* 519–526.

Gordon-Larsen, P., Adair, L., & Popkin, B. (2003). The relationship between ethnicity, socioeconomic factors and overweight in US adolescents. *Obesity Research, 11,* 121–129.

Guardian (2002). Land of the fat. Available at www.guardian.co.uk/g2/story/0,3604,708373,00.html.

Hall, L. F. (1997). *Perk! The story of a teenager with bulimia.* Carlsbad, CA: Gurze Books.

Hughes, G., Areghan, G., & Knight, B. (2005). Obesity and the African-American in Mississippi: an overview. *Southern Medical Journal, 98*(1), 72–78.

Ikeda, J. (1995). Promoting size acceptance for children. *Healthy Weight Journal, 9,* 108–109.

Ikeda, J., & Naworski, P. (1992). *Am I fat? Helping young children accept differences in body size.* Santa Cruz, CA: ETR Associates.

Jain, A., Sherman, S., Chamberlain, L., Carter, Y., Powers, S., & Whitaker, R. (2001). Why don't low-income mothers worry about their preschoolers being overweight? *Pediatrics, 107,* 1138–1146.

Jimenez-Cruz, A., Bacardi-Gascon, M., & Spindler, A. (2003). Obesity and hunger among Mexican-Indian migrant children on the US-Mexico border. *International Journal of Obesity, 27,* 740–747.

Johnson, S., & Birch, L. (1994). Parent's and children's adiposity and eating style. *Pediatrics, 94,* 653–661.

Kavey, R., Daniels, S., Lauer, R., Atkins, D., Hayman, L., & Taubert, K., (2003). American Heart Association guidelines for primary prevention of atherosclerosis cardiovascular disease beginning in childhood. *Journal of Pediatrics, 142*(4), 368–372.

Kibbe, D., & Offner, R. (2003). Childhood obesity—advancing effective prevention and treatment: an overview for health professionals. Issue paper. Washington, DC: National Institute for Health Care Management Foundation.

Kumanyika, S. (2005). Obesity, health disparities, and prevention paradigms: hard questions and hard choices. *Prevention of Chronic Disease* [serial online], 2(4). Available at www.cdc.gov/pcd/issues/2005/oct/05_0025.htm.

Kumanyika, S., & Grier, S. (2006). Targeting interventions for ethnic minority and low-income populations. *The Future of Children: Childhood Obesity, 16,* 187–207.

La Point, V., (2003). Commercialism in lives of children of color: change, challenges, and confrontation. *Journal of Negro Education, 70,* 357–370.

Latner, J., & Stunkard, A. (2003). Getting worse: the stigmatization of obese children. *Obesity Research, 11,* 452–456.

Leahy, M. (2004). The weight. *Washington Post,* July 18, 2004; W.14.

Liburd, L, Anderson, L., Edgar, T., & Jack, L. (1999). Body size and body shape: perceptions of black women with diabetes. *Diabetes Education, 25*(3), 382–388.

Mustillo, S. (2003). Special report. Pediatric and adolescent obesity: chronic obesity linked to psychopathology in youth. *Brown University Child and Adolescent Behavior Letter,* April 25, 2003.

Neisner, J., Histon, T., Goeldner, J., & Moon, C. (2003). Prevention and treatment of overweight and obesity: toward a roadmap for advocacy and action. *Permanente Journal, 7*(4), 6–8. Available at http://xnet.kp.org/permanentejournal/fall03/update.pdf.

Nesbitt, S., Ashaye, M., Stettler, N., Sorof, J., Goran, M., Parekh, R., & Falkner, B. (2004). Overweight as a risk factor in children. *Ethnicity and Disease, 14,* 94–110.

Orenstein, P. (1994). *Schoolgirls: young women, self-esteem, and the confidence gap.* New York: Doubleday.

Parker, S. (2004). Arkansas provides startling evidence of childhood obesity epidemic. *Advances, 4,* 9. Available at www.rwjf.org/files/publications/newsletter/Advances4_2004.pdf.

Pearce, M., Boergers, J., Prinstein, M. (2002). Adolescent obesity, overt and relational peer victimization and romantic relationship. *Obesity Research, 10,* 386–393.

Robinson, I., Kiernan, M., Matheson, D., & Haydel, K. (2001). Is parental control over children's eating associated with childhood obesity? Results form a population-based sample of third graders. *Obesity Research, 9,* 306–312.

Sallis, J., Bauman, A., & Pratt, M. (1998). Environmental and policy interventions to promote physical activity. *American Journal of Preventive Medicine, 15,* 379–397.

Slyper, A. (2004). The pediatric obesity epidemic: causes and controversies. *Journal of Clinical Epidemiology and Metabolism, 89,* 2540–2547.

Story, M., Kaphingst, K. M., and French, S. (2006). The role of schools in obesity prevention. *The Future of Children: Childhood Obesity, 16,* 109–142.

Strauss, C., & Knight, J. (1999). Influence of the home environment on the development of obesity in children. *Pediatrics, 103*(6), 1–8.

Surgeon General. (2002). Surgeon General's call to action to prevent and decrease overweight and obesity. Washington, DC: Department of Health and Human Services. Available at www.surgeongeneral.gov/topics/obesity/calltoaction/fact_adolescents.htm.

Treuth, M., Butte, N., Ellis, K., Martin, R., & Comuzzie, A. (2001). Familiar resemblance in body composition in prepubertal girls and their biological parents. *American Journal of Clinical Nutrition, 74,* 529–533.

Troiano, R. P. & Flegal, K.M. (1998). Overweight children and adolescents: Description, epidemiology, and demographics. *Pediatrics, 10* (3), 497–504.

Vargas, I. (2006). Treatment of childhood and adolescent obesity and PCOS. Available at http://cumc.columbia.edu/dept/ihn/courses/documents/Vargas.pdf.

Venkat-Narayn, K., Boyle, J., Thompson, T., Sorensen, S., & Williamson, D. (2003). Lifetime risk for diabetes mellitus in the United States. *JAMA, 290,* 1884–1890.

Whitaker, R., Wright, J., Pepe, M., Seidel, K., & Dietz, W. (1997). Predicting obesity in young adulthood from childhood and parental obesity. *New England Journal of Medicine, 337,* 869–873.

Williams, J. (2004). Early childhood obesity: a call for early surveillance and preventive measures [electronic version]. *Canadian Medical Association Journal, 171*(3), 1–5.

Winkleby, M., Kraemer, H., Ahn, D., & Varady, A. (1998). Ethnic and socioeconomic differences in cardiovascular disease risk factors: findings for women from the Third National Health and Nutrition Examination Survey, 1988–1994. *JAMA, 280,* 356–362.

Young, L., & Nestle, M. (2002). The contribution of expanding portion sizes to the US obesity epidemic. *American Journal of Public Health, 92,* 246–249.

Zeller, M., Roehrig, H., Avani, M., Daniels, S., & Inge, T. (2006). Adolescents seeking bariatric surgery: an examination of health-related quality of life and depressive symptoms. *Pediatrics, 117,* 1133–1161.

APPENDIX

_____

ID#   **CRRIC FAMILY HEALTH HISTORY©**

Cardiovascular Risk Reduction in Children Survey

Cardiovascular Risk Reduction in Children

Directions: Please check and/or write in the answer that best describes your response. Do not place your name or your child's name on the form. All responses to this survey are kept as private information.

1. Child's sex:
   ☐ female
   ☐ male
2. Child's birthday:
   _____month
   _____day
   _____year
3. Child's race/ethnicity:
   _____
*4. In the past 12 months, did your child get exercise or physical activity at least three times through any of the following organizations?
   ☐ Public park or recreation
   ☐ Church or other place or worship
   ☐ Sports teams or leagues
   ☐ YMCA, YWCA, or similar organization
   ☐ Health club, private spa, or private lessons
   ☐ Cub Scouts, Brownies, or other scouts
   ☐ Other _____
   ☐ None
*5. How many days a week does your child's class participate in physical activity?
   ☐ 1 day per week
   ☐ 2 days per week
   ☐ 3 days per week
   ☐ 4 days per week
   ☐ 5 days per week
   ☐ None
6. Family structure that child has lived in for most of his/her life (check only one)?
   ☐ Single-parent home
   ☐ Home with both parents
   ☐ With relative other than parents
   ☐ Foster care home
*7. How much time does your child spend watching television or playing computer/video games on a typical school day:
   ☐ 1 hour or less
   ☐ 2 hours
   ☐ 3 hours
   ☐ 4 hours

☐ 5 hours
☐ 6 hours
☐ None

*8. How much time does your child spend watching television or playing computer/video games on a typical weekend day:
   ☐ 1 hour or less
   ☐ 2 hours
   ☐ 3 hours
   ☐ 4 hours
   ☐ 5 hours
   ☐ 6 hours
   ☐ None

9. Educational level of primary caregiver of child:
   ☐ 1–8 years
   ☐ 9–12 years
   ☐ Some college preparation
   ☐ College graduate
   ☐ Post college

10. Age of birth father at time of child's birth (if known):
    _____ years

11. Age of birth mother at time of child's birth:

    _____

12. How many people smoke cigarettes in the home where your child lives?

    _____

13. Please place a check by all conditions that these relatives of the child have (if known):

    M = mother, F = father, B/S = brother/sister, G = grandparent

	M	F	B/S	G
Sickle cell anemia	☐	☐	☐	☐
Renal dialysis	☐	☐	☐	☐
Obesity (overweight)	☐	☐	☐	☐
Sudden death (illness)	☐	☐	☐	☐
High blood pressure	☐	☐	☐	☐
Blindness	☐	☐	☐	☐
Diabetes	☐	☐	☐	☐
Amputation	☐	☐	☐	☐
Heart attack before age 55	☐	☐	☐	☐
Stroke before age 55	☐	☐	☐	☐

14. Total yearly income of household (this includes all earned income and government assisted income):
    ☐ Less than $5,000/yr
    ☐ $5,001–$15,000
    ☐ $15,001–$25,000
    ☐ $25,001–$35,000
    ☐ $35,001–$45,000

☐ $45,001–$55,000
☐ More than $55,000/yr

15. Check all the health problems that your child has:
    ☐ Sickle cell anemia
    ☐ Obesity/overweight
    ☐ Asthma
    ☐ High blood pressure
    ☐ Diabetes
    ☐ Other (specify)_____
    ☐ No health problems

16. Length of time child breastfed:
    ☐ 1 month or less
    ☐ 2–3 months
    ☐ 4–6 months
    ☐ 6–12 months
    ☐ More than 1 year
    ☐ Did not breast feed

17. How often does your child eat at a fast food restaurant (e.g., McDonalds, Burger King, etc.)?
    ☐ Less than twice per month
    ☐ 1–2 times per week
    ☐ 3–4 times per week
    ☐ More than 4 times per week
    ☐ Never

*18. Compared to other adults of the same age, how physically active is the mother or female guardian of the child:
    ☐ A lot more physically active than most
    ☐ A little more physically active than most
    ☐ Average, same as most
    ☐ A lot less physically active than most
    ☐ Does not apply

19. Compared to other adults of the same age, how physically active is the father or male guardian of the child:
    ☐ A lot more physically active than most
    ☐ A little more physically active than most
    ☐ Average, same as most
    ☐ A lot less physically active than most
    ☐ Does not apply

20. Age of child when table food first given:
    ☐ 1 month or less
    ☐ 2–3 months
    ☐ 4–6 months
    ☐ 6–8 months
    ☐ 8–12 months
    ☐ More than 1 year

21. How often does your child go outside to play while at home:
    ☐ Daily
    ☐ Several times a week
    ☐ Several times a month
    ☐ Less than once per month

☐ Less than twice per year
☐ Never

22. Please check all the sites that are within one to two miles of your home:
   ☐ Parks
   ☐ Biking/walking trails
   ☐ Baseball field
   ☐ Recreation center
   ☐ Soccer field
   ☐ Basketball court
   ☐ Other (specify)_____

23. How often does your child go to the grocery store with you to buy groceries?
   ☐ Each time that I go
   ☐ Most of the time
   ☐ About half the time
   ☐ About one time out of four or less
   ☐ Never

24. How often does your child have the following (circle the number that best describes your response):
   0 = never
   1 = three (3) or fewer times per week
   2 = four (4) or more times per week

Whole milk	0	1	2
Eggs	0	1	2
Red meat (beef, pork, lamb)	0	1	2
Corn chips, potato chips, etc.	0	1	2
Fried foods	0	1	2

25. Child's average soft drink intake (12 oz serving size): How many sodas?
   _____ per day
   _____ per week

26. Child's average daily water intake (serving size 8 oz): How many servings (glasses) of water?
   _____ per day

27. Child's average intake of fruit per day: How many servings of fruit?
   _____ per day

28. Child's daily intake of vegetables: How many servings of vegetables?
   _____ per day

29. How often does your family participate in social/religious activities outside of your home?
   ☐ Once a week or more often
   ☐ Once a month or more often
   ☐ Six or more times per year
   ☐ Once a year or less
   ☐ Never

30. What is the approximate weight and height of female parent or guardian of child?
   Weight _____
   Height _____

31. What is the approximate weight and height of male parent or guardian of child?
   Weight _____
   Height _____

32. How would you describe your child's weight?
    ☐ Underweight
    ☐ A lot underweight
    ☐ Normal weight
    ☐ Overweight
    ☐ A lot overweight

33. What is the approximate weight and height of your child?
    Weight _____
    Height _____

34. Is your child in a Special Education program?
    No
    Yes
    If yes, why_____

STOP HERE! Thank You!

*Questions 4, 5, 7, 8, and 18 were used per permission of the National Children and Youth Fitness Study II. The remaining questions are the property of the CRRIC Committee.

CRRIC Committee in alphabetical order: Chris Arthur, PhD, CHES, Tracilia Brown, MSN, RN, Gary Davis, MD, Melvin Davis, PhD, Sheila Davis, PhD, RN**, Terry Doddato, EdD, RN, CRNA, Elizabeth Goodwin, MSN, FNP, Dena Goldberg, PhD, RD, Beatrice Jackson, RN, Kathy Kolar, PhD, RN, George Moll, MD, PhD, Ladonna Northington, DNS, RN, William Replogle, PhD*, Nick Todd, PhD, and Robin Wilkerson, PhD, RN

**Committee chair
*Consultant on instrument

Revised 11/30/04

Parents and guardians, do not write on this page.

For Administrative Purposes Only
CRRIC Staff

ID# _____ _____ _____ _____ _____

Height _____in inches

Weight _____in pounds

BMI _____

Left arm blood pressure   Right arm blood pressure
1_____   1_____
2_____   2_____
3_____   3_____
4 _____ average left arm   4_____ average right arm

Average of right and left arm blood pressures _____

Cholesterol_____

Glucose _____

Total score on CRRIC Family Health History _____

Antifat Attitudes
A Barrier to Best Practice

TRISH FREED

INTRODUCTION

Treatment of pediatric overweight may be dangerous to children. Our society has placed the responsibility of reversing the "pediatric obesity epidemic" on health professionals. We are reminded daily by the media of the urgency of our mission. We are so busy implementing strategies to save the health of society's children that examining the consequences of our beliefs seems indulgent. As we continue our standard practices, the danger to children remains. This danger lies in our actions that stem from our antifat attitudes and the value we place on health.

Much of the attention generated by the current focus on fatness is aimed toward modifying the physical body in order to improve health, regardless of the success of various methods or the psychological suffering from social discrimination (Brownell, Puhl, Schwartz, & Rudd, 2005). Proponents of the categorization of fatness as a disease cite destigmatization as one of the consequences, therefore removing moral connotations (O'Brien, Dixon, & Brown, 2004). Labeling fatness as a disease can result in the benign approval of medical interventions, however ineffective, to modify what is seen as deviance in the name of health. America's weight experts hold value-laden views regarding medicine when they link thinness to health (Tong, 2004). One of the outcomes of an association of thinness and health is a cultural acceptance of antifat attitudes.

In Western culture, the fat body exists in transformation only, since the idea of being "permanently fat" is unacceptable (Harjunen, 2003, p. 3). Even with the low rates of successful weight loss, our society seldom questions the ethics of continued promotion of such programs (Rich & Evans, 2005). Instead of questioning the recommendation of weight loss, the conclusion sections of journal articles call for better programs and more effective behavioral change skills. This tunnel vision of health professionals can be attributed to their medicine-based training—they are "trained to (not) see in particular ways" (Aphramor, 2005, p. 315). To exemplify this "not seeing," the assumption that health is valued equally by all people is widespread yet mistaken. When an individual appears not to value health as we do, our judgment soon follows. We value health so much that it can be seen as a popular religion in which the crusade is against fat. To challenge the majority-held convictions about fat would be considered "blasphemous" (Monaghan, 2005, p. 304).

Our antifat attitudes and belief that health is everyone's highest value may result in a legion of well-meaning health professionals battling pediatric overweight with little effectiveness. In this chapter, I define antifat attitudes and present theories about the origins and development of these attitudes; review studies of antifat attitudes in pediatric samples; present the idea of health as a value we do not all equally share; discuss the pros and cons of the Health at Every Size paradigm; consider whether attitudes lead to behavior by reviewing relevant literature on racism; and provide links to learn more.

ANTIFAT ATTITUDES

The term "antifat attitude" is used in this chapter to encompass the prejudice, bias, belief, phobia, negative thoughts, and stigma held about the concept of fatness and demonstrated toward people whose bodies are perceived by others as too large. The term "attitude" is specified because the literature on attitudes reflects the richest source of information on the subject. According to modern uses of the words, stigma and stigmatization refer to "an invisible sign of disapproval that permits insiders to draw a line around 'outsiders' in order to demarcate the limits of inclusion in any group" (Falk, 2001, p. 17).

Obvious examples of antifat attitudes toward adults are common: television shows in which fat people compete to lose weight in order to be declared a winner; our conviction that fat people's lives would improve if they would simply eat less and exercise more. Not so obvious examples are also common: the lack of eye contact; the knowledge of being the largest person in the room while being invisible at the same time; being considered lazy. Children experience antifat attitudes by being teased about their size or abilities, being chosen last for teams, and being judged as not worthy of friendship.

Antifat attitudes are held and expressed toward fatness as a health condition, as well as the fat individual (Teachman & Brownell, 2001). Fat is a battle, a tide to be stemmed, and an epidemic with which we are at war. It is wrong to be fat in Western society because being fat is viewed as unhealthy, uncomfortable, and unattractive. As health professionals, we may confuse our concern about health issues associated with fatness with our stigmatization of fat people, "Obese people are not discriminated against because they are medically compromised. They are stigmatized because their obesity is viewed as a reflection of poor character" (Schwartz & Puhl, 2003, p. 64). When we experience antifat thoughts in the presence of a fat person, it is not because we feel sorry for the fat person and want the individual to experience good health, it is because we are repulsed by them.

Antifat attitudes can be measured in two ways: explicitly and implicitly. An example of an explicit measure is a questionnaire that asks us direct questions about fat people and allows us to tap into and respond with our conscious attitudes. An implicit measure, on the other hand, measures our decisions after we have been exposed to a certain stimulus or measures the associations we make with words or images. Implicit measures are timed, and we are instructed to work as quickly and accurately as possible. Under such time pressure, the decisions or associations we make reveal our unconscious attitudes. Implicit attitudes are introspectively unidentified, but on an unconscious level are held (Greenwald & Banaji, 1995). While most people do not explicitly admit to disparaging fat people, an assessment of implicit attitudes reveals that most people do hold strong antifat attitudes.

Health professionals have been found to hold antifat attitudes. At an obesity conference, antifat attitudes were assessed both explicitly and implicitly in attendees (physicians, dietitians, pharmacologists, researchers, epidemiologists, psychologists, nurses, and other clinicians [$n = 389$]). The belief that fat people are bad, lazy, stupid, and worthless in relation to thin people was significantly held overall by conference attendees whether assessed explicitly or implicitly. Health providers' antifat attitudes could lead to fat peoples' discomfort in the health care setting, which could in turn lead to health care avoidance (Schwartz, Chambliss, Brownell, Blair, & Billington, 2003).

Other studies support these findings: 67% of family practice physicians ($n = 318$) believe that their fat patients lack self-control and 39% believe them to be lazy (Price, Desmond, Krol, Snyder,

& O'Connell, 1987). Medical and nursing students (n = 28 and 102, respectively) felt repulsed at the sight of obese people and labeled them as unhealthy (Petrich, 2000). Physical educators (n = 105) reported antifat attitudes, negative expectations of performance and ability, and a strong endorsement of personal responsibility for weight toward fat youth (Greenleaf & Weiller, 2005). A study of exercise science students (n = 246) found similar antifat attitudes and weight blame held toward fat people (Chambliss, Finley, & Blair, 2004). A sample of 298 dietetic students and registered dietitians also reported holding antifat attitudes (Oberrieder, Walker, Monroe, & Adeyanjum, 1995). One study revealed that dietitians (n = 152) held less negative attitudes toward being fat themselves than they did toward clients (McArthur & Ross, 1997).

Many of us have not examined the presence, prevalence, and strength of our antifat attitudes, and our repulsion is most likely an implicit, or unconscious, reaction. Considering the influences of our attitudes may be helpful in increasing our awareness of antifat attitudes.

There is a history of holding and expressing antifat attitudes. A panel of the 12th-century Japanese illnesses scrolls depicts a fat woman representing greed and selfishness—both of which are disparaged in the Buddhist belief of the era. In 15th-century Europe, Hieronymus Bosch linked fatness to gluttony in the portrayal of *The Seven Deadly Sins and the Four Last Things*, none of which could be hidden from the eyes of God (Stunkard, LaFleur, & Wadden, 1998).

The discussion presented here, although not specific to children, is relevant when we consider the milieu in which we raise children. Antifat attitudes have been attributed to several influences: our sociocultural climate, attribution theory and just world belief, and the controllability of weight. Each influence will be discussed briefly.

Culturally we develop a preference for the thin body by the following influences: the pervasiveness of the thin woman as the ideal in all media formats (Tiggemann, 2002); how major health organizations and media present fatness (Rich & Evans, 2005); and how book publishers, food producers, and the pharmaceutical and insurance industries endorse fatness as unhealthy and malleable (Rogge et al., 2004). Fat people are subject to the same cultural and societal norms as everyone else, and they have also been found to hold antifat attitudes (Crandall, 1994; Crandall et al., 2001; Crocker, Cornwell, & Major, 1993; Latner et al., 2005; Lewis, Cash, Jacobi, & Bubb-Lewis, 1997; Puhl & Brownell, 2003; Wang, Brownell, & Wadden, 2004).

Our antifat attitudes have been attributed to our belief that fatness is caused by self-indulgence, gluttony, and laziness (Brink, 1994; DeJong, 1980; Rogge et al. 2004). Attribution theory, when applied to antifat attitudes, is expressed as the search for explanations to determine the cause of fatness. Our conclusions then form impressions and expectations of the fat person. To draw these conclusions we are required to endorse the just world belief (Puhl & Brownell, 2003). The just world belief is our "strong desire or need to believe that the world is an orderly, predictable, and just place, where people get what they deserve" (Andre & Velasques, 1990, p. 2). The relationship between the Just World scale and the Antifat Attitudes (AFA) scale was assessed in a study of college men and women (n = 190). There was a correlation between just world beliefs and two of the subscales of the AFA (dislike [of fat people]: r =.47, $p < .005$; and willpower [lacking in fat people:] r =.48, $p < .005$) (Crandall, 1994).

A belief that weight is controllable also influences our attitudes toward fat people. A study tested the relationship between college students' (n = 59) belief in weight controllability and antifat attitudes. After participants viewed a before-and-after photo advertisement from a national commercial diet company, they indicated that weight is more easily controllable than students who viewed only the before or the after photo (Geier, Schwartz, & Brownell, 2003).

The attribution theory was used in a study of children (n = 42) ages 4 to 6 years to explain their antifat attitudes. The authors found that attributions for control of body size were related to negative adjective ratings for the chubby figure in the drawing (Musher-Eizenman, Holub, Miller, Goldstein, & Edwards-Leeper, 2004).

PERSONAL RESPONSIBILITY IDEOLOGY

While the influences briefly discussed above all may contribute to the formation of antifat attitudes, they are but components of the prevailing ideology in Western society: the idea that we are personally responsible for our health. The personal responsibility ideology hails from the Protestant work ethic, a code of morals based on the principles of thrift, discipline, necessity of hard work, perfection, the goodness of labor, and individualism. The relationship between the Protestant Ethic Value scale and the Antifat Attitudes scale was assessed in a study of college men and women ($n = 288$). There was a correlation between Protestant ethic endorsement and two subscales of the AFA (dislike [of fat people]: $r = .29$, $p < .005$; and willpower [lacking in fat people]: $r = .32$, $p < .005$) (Crandall, 1994). This work ethic is a value deeply ingrained in many Americans. Health professionals may find it hard to believe that the ethics and values of religious leaders and philosophers, specifically John Calvin and the Mayflower-era Puritan English immigrants, could have withstood the changes of the past 400 years, but Falk (2001) asserts that is the case—these ethics have left "lasting impressions on innumerable generations" (p. 334).

Falk (2001) states that the Protestant ethic and individualism are the core values in today's American society, and that "behavior in the United States is judged by assuming we are all responsible for our own actions, social standing and achievements, or lack thereof" (p. 333). "The Protestant ethic ... is universal in the Western world so that hard work, frugality, and the virtue of anglomorality is explicitly or implicitly preached everywhere in the United States" (p. 209). The moral underpinnings of the personal responsibility culture are described by Leichter (2003). In a frank description, Leichter concluded that toward the end of 20th century America, good health was synonymous with a life lived virtuously. Paralleling the Christian Right are the

> self-appointed moral elite who extorted others to follow low-fat, high-fiber diets, not to smoke, to exercise regularly, to consume alcohol only in moderation, to practice yoga, and to drink at least eight glasses of designer-label water per day...Such a priestly class establishes rituals relating to personal habits involving food and drink, sexual relations, personal hygiene and grooming, clothing, birth and death...[H]ighly detailed rituals and elaborate paraphernalia associated with the late 20th century wellness movement in the United States serve much the same social purpose as did biblical dietary and sexual prescriptions and proscriptions that were less public health measures than rules for defining the path to spiritual salvation. (Leichter (2003, pp. 620–621)

Minkler (1999) defined the criticisms of the ideology as an "overriding emphasis on personal responsibility [that] blames the victim, by ignoring the social context in which individual decision making and health-related action takes place" (p. 126). Guttman and Ressler (2001) questioned the ethics of health professionals who would "add to an individual's suffering by implying they are at fault for their suffering" (p. 122).

The idea that "healthy" people carry the economic burden of fat people is often heard, however, many less than perfect human beings or people with other chronic conditions that result in costly problems for society are being created every day (i.e., children born with severe antisocial behaviors, oppositional-defiance disorders, different attention deficits, and "horrible" genetic diseases). Rarely are the parents of these children blamed and held financially responsible. In addition, a woman who develops breast cancer is not abhorred as are fat people (Banja, 2004; Barron & Hollingsworth Lear, 1989).

Closely linked to the personal responsibility ideology is our implicit belief that health is our highest value. The idea of heath as a value is so embedded in our society that it is referred to as common sense (Cribb & Duncan, 2002). "As long as I have my health" is the oft-uttered declaration of what we value.

It is socially desirable to value health (Shelton Smith & Wallston, 1992). Health professionals, especially those who hold health as the highest value, may turn into moral crusaders, labeling those who appear less than biologically fit as deviants. Our claim that health is the highest value is true as long as we all agree. If we relentlessly promote health as the highest good without consideration of other viewpoints, we are in danger of alienating those we wish to reach.

When an individual's highest value differs from health (i.e., spirituality, world peace), we may assume that the individual does not value health as much as we. Hicks (1970, in Shelton Smith and Wallston, 1992) described another viewpoint we might consider in this case. Instead of categorizing the person as deviant, we could consider that the individual values health just as much as we do—*and* that this individual places a higher importance on spirituality or world peace than we do.

Antifat attitudes, regardless of their basis or origins, are expressed by very young children. Fat people ($n = 140$) reported antifat comments from children as the most frequently experienced stigmatizing experience (Myers & Rosen, 1999). Brink (1994) asserted that "children learn early to make comments about the obese...the most common being that the obese are 'fat and ugly'" (p. 292).

ANTIFAT ATTITUDES AND CHILDREN

Cramer and Steinwert (1998) conducted a study using the youngest sample—preschoolers age 3 ($n = 30$) and 5 ($n = 83$) years—to test a new method for assessing antifat attitudes. Brief stories were read to children, followed by the showing of two figures—one "chubby" and one "thin." Size stigma was measured in four different ways, and overwhelmingly the chubby figure was seen as (1) being mean, (2) having unfavorable characteristics and an undesirable self-image, and (3) being undesirable as a playmate. We cannot underestimate the young age at which our children are indoctrinated to our culture's repulsion of fat.

A study of 9-year-old white girls ($n = 178$) and their mothers and fathers was completed to determine the characteristics that are associated with antifat attitudes. A body mass index (BMI) reflective of obesity was noted in 14% of the girls, 28% of the mothers, and 31% of the fathers. The Fat Stereotypes Questionnaire data showed a significant tendency to attribute negative characteristics (i.e., have difficulty making friends, are lazy, have few friends, is bad to be fat) to fat people rather than thin people by all participants. These findings did not differ in relation to participants' BMI, and the girls' antifat attitudes were not related to the attitudes of their parents. Girls reported greater fat stereotypes when they perceived that both their mothers and their peers placed a greater importance on being slim (Davison & Birch, 2004).

The landmark study of antifat attitudes was conducted with six sets of children ages 10 to 11 ($n = 540$ total) from diverse ethnic and social backgrounds from three geographic locations: New York, Montana, and California. The children were asked to look at drawings of children who had the presence or absence of different visible disabilities: (1) a child with no visible disability, (2) a child with crutches, (3) a child in a wheelchair, (4) a child with the left hand missing, (5) a child with a facial disfigurement, and (6) a fat child. The children were then asked to tell the researcher which child they liked best. When the most liked drawing was removed the question was asked again until a rank order for all six drawings was obtained. The authors hypothesized all children who participated would rank the drawings in the same way, and the rank would match the above-ordered description of the drawings—the child with no visible disability being most preferred and the fat child being least preferred. Both hypotheses were strongly supported by the findings. Every group ranked the drawings of children exactly the same: the child with no visible disability was most preferred and the fat child was least preferred. The authors speculated on the reasons why the children reacted in such a uniform way: (1) children with disabilities which limit physical activity will be liked least; (2) children with a disability farther away from the face will be liked more; (3) and children have a preference for the familiar. Even in the early 1960s, mass media was thought to influence attitudes, and the authors concluded that the children may have been influenced by mass media, with its stereotypes of physical beauty as good and physical ugliness as evil (Richardson, Goodman, Hastorf, & Dornbusch (1961).

Since research on antifat attitudes is in its infancy, we can refer to the literature on racism to learn how our attitudes affect our behavior and approaches to decreasing our antifat attitudes.

FATISM AND RACISM

Research on antifat attitudes has been preceded by years of research on racism. Social norms, anti-discriminatory laws, and an increasing appreciation of cultural diversity in Western societies have led to the unacceptability of expressing racist attitudes or behaviors (Rutland, Cameron, Milne, & McGeorge, 2005). Crandall (1994) states that antifat attitudes are at the stage that racism was 50 years ago: "overt, expressible, and widely held" (p. 891). To test this statement, college student ($n =$ 1147) scores for the Modern Racism scale and the Antifat Attitude subscale "dislike [of fat people]" were grouped and compared. Students were more than three times more likely to have a score of zero (indicating that social norms and egalitarian values were exerting their influence) on the Modern Racism scale than on the Dislike subscale. The magnitude of acceptability of antifat attitudes is not subject to the same normative pressure (i.e., social desirability) as racism.

The executive function (i.e., cognitive processes) of white college students ($n = 50$) with high levels of racial prejudice was significantly impaired after an interaction with a black study partner in comparison to a white partner (Richeson & Shelton, 2003). In this study, participants' attitudes were measured both explicitly and implicitly. Executive function was assessed using the Stroop task, a computerized test in which participants respond to stimuli about words and colors as quickly as possible. Study videotapes were analyzed and participants with higher levels of implicit prejudice were more likely to control their behavior (i.e., body movement, hand movement, looking around the room) than those with lower levels of prejudice. The more participants controlled their behavior, the worse they performed on the Stroop task. Holding racist attitudes led to behaviors which in turn affected how well the participants' paid attention to the task. An additional study of female college students ($n = 40$) determined that the demands of self-regulatory behaviors, not participant distraction, were responsible for the decreased executive function (Richeson & Trawalter, 2005).

Increasing the amount and kind of contact we have with members of an outgroup is one way to learn about others. Recent literature on racism may renew interest in studying the effects of contact on attitudes. Two studies were conducted using a measure of implicit attitudes about race. The first study assessed negative attitudes held by white college students ($n = 70$) with or without self-defined close black friends; the second assessed negative attitudes held by white students ($n = 96$) with or without Hispanic friends. In both studies, although most students exhibited an implicit negative bias, the levels were significantly lower in those participants reporting friendships. The authors speculated that the difference between these findings and those of other studies may be explained as the difference in contact type. Friendships are usually classified as positive contact, and other types of contact (i.e., providing health care) may be considerably less positive (Aberson, Shoemaker, & Tomolillo, 2004).

A study was conducted to determine how a romantic partnership influenced racist attitudes. Electrical shocks were used to create a fear association to black and white faces in black and white participants. Once the fear association was made, the shocks ceased while the participants continued to view the faces. By measuring the skin conductance response (SCR), the authors discovered that viewing faces of the participant's own race after the shocks ended led to an end in SCR. However, when the participants viewed faces of the other race after the shocks ceased, they continued to show a significant SCR. The authors found that the only variable to significantly moderate the fear association of the shocks was the number of interracial romantic partners reported by the participant. The authors speculated that the sociocultural learning of the qualities of other races was the primary explanation for the persistence of stereotypes and suggested that developing relationships may weaken such responses (Olsson, Ebert, Banaji, & Phelps, 2005).

Amygdala responses to black and white male faces were investigated in college women (n = 42). Students performed a lexical decision test on a computer while inside a functional magnetic resonance imaging (fMRI) scanner. The test was designed so that participants would have to make one of three decisions: search the face for dots, categorize the face according to age, or indicate if they thought the person would enjoy the vegetable that was shown immediately before the face. When amygdala activity was assessed, a significant difference in the responses to black and white faces was discovered only when categorizing faces by age. The authors noted that simply searching a face failed to produce a stereotypical response, and considering the faces as individuals who may or may not enjoy a certain vegetable allowed participants to focus on traits deeper than stereotypes. The authors concluded that participants were able to change the social context in which they viewed previously stereotyped faces and the change resulted in measurable differences in brain activity and test reaction time (Wheeler & Fiske, 2005).

Although these studies on racism may or may not show equivocal results in the study of antifat attitudes, they do show promise in furthering our understanding of how our thoughts and attitudes are formed, how they affect our brain function, and how they might be reduced. Future research could examine the potentially protective factors of considering people as more than a face (i.e. vegetable enjoyment), having fat friends, and having a fat romantic partner.

WHAT WE CAN DO

Given the current cultural norms, being fat is equal to being bad. Challenging these norms is to risk being viewed as deviant. Despite this risk, we need to begin a discussion about the ethical implications and consequences of continuing the war on obesity when the methods available may be seen as neither effective nor valuable to our clients. With obesity diagnosed at epidemic levels, antifat attitudes will persist and there is ample opportunity for these attitudes to be behaviorally expressed. As health professionals, we have a responsibility to show concern and respect for others, and this concern should be grounded in a deeper understanding of our values and credible evidence, not in the myth of stereotypes.

The assumption that health is the highest value held by everyone is wrong. We can be more effective with those we serve when we are willing to acknowledge the differing levels of importance others may place on health as a value. The expression "meeting clients where they are" can be applied to our clients' value of health. One way of learning our clients' values is to ask the reasons for seeking our services and the outcome goal they desire. Setting treatment goals suitable for a distance runner when a client's goal is to walk around the block is but one example of our disconnect. Drury and Louis (2002) urge health care professionals to become aware of their antifat attitudes, to provide the same level of care as they would to a not-fat person, and to recognize that nonjudgmental care is central to client follow-up. Health promotion is fraught with ethical concerns (Buchanan, 2000; Cribb & Duncan, 2002; Guttman & Ressler, 2001; Guttman & Salmon, 2004), and in our enthusiasm for motivating behavior change in others we must not forget to act with the same level of compassion and respect we wish for ourselves.

If we want to change our implicit repulsion of fat people, we must combat the insidious moral assumptions that are responsible for the formation of our antifat attitudes (Blaine, DiBlasi, & Connor, 2002).

- If we can't let go of the idea that being fat is unhealthy, perhaps we can consider health in a more expanded perspective: Lance Armstrong cites the day he was diagnosed with cancer as the day he started to live (*Livestrong Newsletter*, 2006).
- If we can't help but think fat people must lose weight or lead shorter lives, perhaps we can remember that we cannot effectively prevent every life from being cut short: by violence,

suicide, war, or genetics. In addition, there are people for whom a long life may not be as highly valued as we assume.

- If a fat person wants to lose weight, there are many paths to take; we need to respect his or her values.
- If we find fat people to be ugly, then we can acknowledge the judgments we feel and the value we place on aesthetics. A close inspection of the assumptions we have about others may leave us feeling shocked by how much power we have given to the forces that shape our attitudes.

We can choose to become more aware of how sociocultural influences shape our thoughts and actions. We can acknowledge the burden the personal responsibility ideology places on all of us. We can identify our antifat thoughts when they occur and notice where these thoughts lead. Once identified, we can strive to change our antifat attitudes. When considering this, research shows that thinking positive thoughts about fat people instead of attempting to suppress negative thoughts is significantly more effective in reducing antifat attitudes (Akalis, Nannapaneni, & Banaji, 2006).

Imagine a world where different body sizes are not condemned. Can we tolerate fat people? Even accept them? Negative attitudes start at repulsion and lessen to pity, tolerance, and then broaden to acceptance. Acceptance can be seen as more negative than positive in its assumption that there is something negative that requires "acceptance." Positive attitudes begin with support and expand into admiration, appreciation, and nurturance (Riddle, 1985, in O'Bear, 1990).

Researchers who reported antifat attitudes held by health professionals called for education to raise awareness of these attitudes and the causes of fatness (Chambliss et al., 2004; Greenleaf & Weiller, 2005; Oberrieder et al. 1995; Petrich, 2000; Price et al., 1987). We could start with very young children, since antifat attitudes have been shown to exist at an early age. Cramer & Steinwert (1998) suggest that curricula for preschoolers could be designed to discuss the differences among people, including size, and books and television programs targeted toward preschoolers could include "overweight characters who are heroes, not villains, who are glamorous, not ugly" (p. 450). Portraying fat characters in mainstream educational materials and media images—as with people of different ethnic backgrounds—could promote an appreciation of different body sizes (Cramer and Steinwert, 1998).

RESOURCES

- Personal Values Card Sort; available at casaa.unm.edu/inst/Personal%20Values%20Card%20Sort.pdf. To clarify your values, print, cut, and sort cards into the following categories: very important to me, important to me, not important to me. This activity can be done with groups (Miller, C'de Baca, Matthews, & Wilbourne, 2001).
- To determine if you hold antifat attitudes, take the online implicit attitude test on weight, found at Harvard's Project Implicit Web site (https://implicit.harvard.edu/implicit/). The weight test assesses the user's preference for fat people or thin people.

REFERENCES

Aberson, C. L., Shoemaker, C., & Tomolillo, C. (2004). Implicit bias and contact: the role of interethnic friendships. *Journal of Social Psychology, 144,* 335–347.

Ajzen, I. (1991). The theory of planned behavior. *Organizational Behavior and Human Decision Processes*, *50,* 179–211.

Akalis, S., Nannapaneni, J., & Banaji, M. (2006). Do-it-yourself mental makeovers: how self-generated thoughts shift implicit attitudes. Poster. Society for Personality and Social Psychology Annual Conference, Palm Springs, CA, January 27, 2006. Available at www.wjh.harvard.edu/~akalis/spsp2006.pdf.

Andre, C., & Velasquez, M. (1990). The just world theory. *Issues in Ethics, 3.* Available at www.scu.edu/ethics/publications/iie/v3n2/justworld.html.

Aphramor, L. (2005). Is a weight-centered health framework salutogenic? Some thoughts on unhinging certain dietary ideologies. *Social Theory and Health, 3,* 315–340.

Barron, N., & Hollingsworth Lear, B. (1989). Ample opportunity for fat women. *Women and Therapy, 8,* 79–92.

Bessenoff, G. R., & Sherman, J. W. (2000). Automatic and controlled components of prejudice toward fat people: evaluation versus stereotype activation. *Social Cognition, 18,* 329–353.

Blaine, B., DiBlasi, D. M., & Connor, J. M. (2002). The effect of weight loss on perceptions of weight controllability: implications for prejudice against overweight people. *Journal of Biobehavioral Research, 7,* 44–56.

Brink, P. J. (1994). Stigma and obesity. *Clinical Nursing Research, 3,* 291–293.

Brownell, K. D., Puhl, R. M., Schwartz, M. B., & Rudd, L. (Eds.). (2005). *Weight bias: nature, consequences and remedies.* New York: Guilford Press.

Buchanan, D. R. (2000). *An ethic for health promotion: rethinking the sources of human well-being.* New York: Oxford University Press.

Chambliss, H. O. Finley, C. E., & Blair, S. N. (2004). Attitudes toward obese individuals among exercise science students. *Medicine and Science in Sports and Exercise, 36,* 468–474.

Cramer, P., & Steinwert, T. (1998). Thin is good, fat is bad: How early does it begin? *Journal of Applied Developmental Psychology, 19,* 429–451.

Crandall, C. S. (1994). Prejudice against fat people: Ideology and self-interest. *Journal of Personality and Social Psychology, 66,* 882–894.

Crandall, C. S., D'Anello, S., Sakalli, N., Lazarus, E., Nejtardt, G. W., & Feather, N. T. (2001). The attribution-value model of prejudice: anti-fat attitudes in six nations. *Personality and Social Psychology Bulletin, 27,* 30–37.

Cribb, A., & Duncan, P. (2002). *Health promotion and professional ethics.* Malden, MA: Blackwell Science.

Crocker, J., Cornwell, B., & Major B. (1993). The stigma of overweight: affective consequences of attributional ambiguity. *Journal of Personality and Social Psychology, 64,* 60–70.

Davison, K. K., & Birch, L. L. (2004). Predictors of fat stereotypes among 9-year-old girls and their parents. *Obesity Research, 12,* 86–94.

Drury, C. A., & Louis, M. (2002). Exploring the association between body weight, stigma of obesity, and health care avoidance. *Journal of American Academy of Nurse Practitioners, 14,* 554–561.

Falk, G. (2001). *Stigma: how we treat outsiders.* Amherst, NY: Prometheus Books.

Greenleaf, C., & Weiller, K. (2005). Perceptions of youth obesity among physical educators. *Social Psychology of Education, 8,* 407–423.

Greenwald, A. G., & Banaji, M. R. (1995). Implicit social cognition: attitudes, self-esteem and stereotypes. *Psychological Review, 102,* 4–27.

Guttman, N., & Ressler, W. H. (2001). On being responsible: ethical issues and appeals to personal responsibility in health campaigns. *Journal of Health Communication, 6,* 117–136.

Guttman, N., & Salmon, C. T. (2004). Guilt, fear, stigma and knowledge gaps: ethical issues in public health communication interventions. *Bioethics, 18,* 531–552.

Hebl, M. R., & Mannix, L. M. (2003). The weight of obesity in evaluating others: a mere proximity effect. *Personality and Social Psychology Bulletin, 29,* 28–38.

Harjunen, H. (2003). Obesity as a liminal and marginalized experience. Paper presented at the Second Global Conference of Making Sense of Health, Illness, and Disease. St. Hilda's College, Oxford, UK. Available at www.inter-disciplinary.net/mso/hid/hid2/hid03s7a.htm

Irving, L. M. (2000). Promoting size acceptance in elementary school children: the EDAP puppet program. *Eating Disorders, 8,* 221–232.

Jonas. S. (2002). A healthy approach to the "health at any size" movement. *Healthy Weight Journal, 16*(3), 45–48.

Latner, J. D., & Stunkard, A. J. (2003). Getting worse: the stigmatization of obese children. *Obesity Research, 11,* 452–456.

Leichter, H. M. (2003). "Evil habits" and "personal choices": assigning responsibility for health in the 20th century. *Milbank Quarterly, 81,* 603–626.

Lewis, R. J., Cash, T. F., Jacobi, L., & Bubb-Lewis, C. (1997). Prejudice toward fat people: the development and validation of the antifat attitudes test. *Obesity Research, 5,* 297–307.

Livestrong Newsletter (2006). Nike 10//2 and Lance. *Livestrong Newsletter, June.* Available at www.livestrong. org/site/apps/nl/content2.asp?c=khLXK1PxHmF&b=2661937&ct=3755079.

McArthur, L. H., & Ross, J. K. (1997). Attitudes of registered dietitians toward personal overweight and overweight clients. *Journal of the American Dietetic Association, 97,* 63–66.

Miller, W. R., C'de Baca, J., Matthews, D. B., & Wilbourne, P. L. (2001). Personal values card sort. Available at http://casaa.unm.edu/inst/Personal%20Values%20Card%20Sort.pdf.

Minkler, M. (1999). Personal responsibility for health? A review of the arguments and the evidence at century's end. *Health Education and Behavior, 26,* 121–140.

Monaghan, L. F. (2005). Discussion piece: a critical take on the obesity debate. *Social Theory & Health, 3,* 302–314.

Musher-Eizenman, D. R., Holub, S. C., Miller, A. B., Goldstein, S. E., & Edwards-Leeper, L. (2004). Body size stigmatization in preschool children: the role of control attributions. *Journal of Pediatric Psychology, 29,* 6213–6220.

Myers, A., & Rosen J. C. (1999). Obesity stigmatization and coping: relation to mental health symptoms, body image, and self-esteem. *International Journal of Obesity Related Metabolic Disorders, 23,* 221–230.

Oberrieder, H., Walker, R., Monroe, D., & Adeyanjum, M. (1995). Attitude of dietetics students and registered dietitians toward obesity. *Journal of the American Dietetic Association, 95,* 914–916.

O'Brien, P. E., Dixon, J. B., & Brown, W. (2004). Obesity is a surgical disease: overview of obesity and bariatric surgery. *ANZ Journal of Surgery, 74,* 200–204.

Olsson, A., Ebert, J. P., Banaji, M. R., & Phelps, E. A. (2005). The role of social groups in the persistence of learned fear. *Science, 309,* 785–787.

Petrich, B. E. A. (2000). Medical and nursing students' perceptions of obesity. *Journal of Addictions Nursing, 12,* 3–16.

Price, J. H., Desmond, S. M., Krol, R. A., Snyder, F. F., & O'Connell, J. K. (1987). Family practice physicians' beliefs, attitudes, and practices regarding obesity. *American Journal of Preventive Medicine, 3,* 339–451.

Puhl, R., & Brownell, K. D. (2003). Psychosocial origins of obesity stigma: toward changing a powerful and pervasive bias. *Obesity Reviews, 4,* 213–227.

Rich, E., & Evans, J. (2005). "Fat ethics"—the obesity discourse and body politics. *Social Theory and Health, 3,* 341–358.

Richardson, S. A. (1971). Research report: handicap, appearance and stigma. *Social Sciences and Medicine, 5,* 621–628.

Richardson, S. A., Goodman, N., Hastorf, A. H., & Dornbusch, S. M. (1961). Cultural uniformity in reaction to physical disabilities. *American Sociological Review, 26,* 241–247.

Richeson, J. A., & Shelton, J. N. (2003). When prejudice does not pay: effects of interracial contact on executive function. *Psychological Science, 14,* 287–290.

Richeson, J. A., & Trawalter, S. (2005). Why do interracial interactions impair executive function? A resource depletion account. *Journal of Personality and Social Psychology, 88,* 934–947.

Robison, J. (2001). First do no harm. Evolution of the new paradigm: health at every size. Lesson D: new paradigm: origins & major foci. References. Available at www.jonrobison.net/FDNH/INDEX.HTM.

Robison, J. (2003a). Bringing the "war on obesity" to our children." *Healthy Weight Journal, 2,* 17.

Robison, J. (2003b). Health at every size: Antidote for the "obesity epidemic." *Healthy Weight Journal, 17*(1), 4–7.

Rutland, A., Cameron, L., Milne, A., & McGeorge, P. (2005). Social norms and self-presentation: Children's implicit and explicit intergroup attitudes. *Child Development, 76,* 451-466.

Schwartz, M. B., Chambliss, H. O., Brownell, K. D., Blair, S. N., & Billington, C. (2003). Weight bias among health professionals specializing in obesity. *Obesity Research, 11,* 1033–1039.

Schwartz, M. B., & Puhl, R. (2003). Childhood obesity: a societal problem to solve. *Obesity Reviews, 4,* 57–71.

Shelton Smith, M., & Wallston, K. A. (1992). How to measure the value of health. *Health Education Research, 7,* 129–135.

Stunkard, A. J., LaFleur, W. R., & Wadden, T. A. (1998). Stigmatization of obesity in medieval times: Asia and Europe. *International Journal of Obesity Related Metabolic Disorders, 22,* 1141–1144.

Teachman, B. A., & Brownell, K. D. (2001). Implicit anti-fat bias among health professionals: Is anyone immune? *International Journal of Obesity, 25,* 1525–1531.

Tiggemann, M. (2002). Media influences on body image development. In T. F. Cash & T. Pruzinsky (Eds.). *Body image: a handbook of theory, research and clinical practice.* (pp. 91–98). New York: Guilford Press.

Tong, R. (2004). Taking on "big fat": the relative risks and benefits of the war against obesity. In M. Boylan (Ed.). *Public health policy and ethics* (pp. 39–58). Netherlands: Kluwer Academic.

Wang, S. S., Brownell, K. D., & Wadden, T. A. (2004). The influence of stigma of obesity on overweight individuals. *International Journal of Obesity, 28,* 1333–1337.

Wheeler, M. E., & Fiske, S. T. (2005). Controlling racial prejudice: social-cognitive goals affect amygdala and stereotype activation. *Psychological Science, 16,* 56–63.

Part II

TOWARD A MORE COMPREHENSIVE UNDERSTANDING: RELEVANT PROCESS VARIABLES

6

The Role of Contingency Management and Parent Training in the Treatment of Pediatric and Adolescent Obesity

KASHUNDA L. WILLIAMS, ELIZABETH J. ZHE,
JENNIFER L. RESETAR, MICHAEL I. AXELROD,
AND PATRICK C. FRIMAN

National health data estimate that approximately 30% of youth in the United States are overweight while approximately 15% are considered obese (Ogden, Flegal, Carroll, & Johnson, 2002). Perhaps more concerning is the fact that prevalence rates have increased rapidly over the last three decades. The prevalence of obesity in childhood and adolescence has gone from approximately 4% to almost 16% over the last 25 years (Ogden et al., 2002). The negative effects of pediatric and adolescent obesity are far reaching. Childhood obesity has been linked to significant medical problems, including high blood pressure, diabetes mellitus, coronary heart disease, colorectal cancer, sleep apnea, asthma, and orthopedic complications (Stice, Shaw, & Marti, 2006). Negative psychosocial effects include weight-related teasing, social rejection, negative body image, and depression.

Coinciding with the rise of this public health dilemma, attention and research efforts focused on the prevention and intervention of pediatric and adolescent obesity have expanded. While a range of prevention and treatment programs exist, there is well-established literature providing empirical support for the use of multidimensional family-based behavioral programming in the treatment of childhood obesity (Jelalian & Saelens, 1999). This chapter directs the audience to two components of such programs, parent training and contingency management, which have empirical support within the behavioral and child psychology literatures, as well as the literature on pediatric obesity treatment.

This chapter begins with a brief overview of contingency management and related behavioral components. Next, developmental considerations in the use of contingency management to treat pediatric and adolescent obesity are considered. Third, practical applications and recommendations for practitioners working with children and families within medical and mental health clinics are provided. Finally, future research directions are discussed.

Definition of Contingency Management. There is considerable literature on contingency management and a comprehensive critique of the literature is beyond the scope of this chapter. Instead, this chapter will cover elements of the contingency management literature that have direct relevance for parent training programs aimed at the treatment of obesity. In general, contingency management has been used to treat a wide range of childhood behavior problems (i.e., Kazdin, 1986; Martens, Witt, Daly, & Vollmer, 1999), and research specific to pediatric obesity indicates that reinforcement systems for weight loss are important components of a comprehensive treatment protocol (Epstein, Wing, Koeske, & Valoski, 1987).

A contingency describes the relationship between a behavior and environmental circumstances that influence the future probability of that behavior. More specifically, a contingency is a unit consisting of the antecedent(s), the target behavior, and the consequence(s) that all interact to influence the probability of the target behavior occuring. Contingency management, an application of B. F. Skinner's operant theory (1971), focuses on decreasing maladaptive behaviors and increasing adaptive behaviors through systematically manipulating contingencies. Contingency management programs utilize two basic operant principles: reinforcement (i.e., a process by which the future probability of a behavior is increased) and punishment (i.e., a process by which the future probability of a behavior is decreased).

Contingency management programs are designed to produce changes in behavior by specifying conditions under which events or materials that have presumed reinforcing functions can be accessed. Often cited examples of contingency management programs include employment responsibilities and corresponding incentives and school-based academic or behavior plans. Successful utilization of contingency management has been reported with individuals across a wide age range (Epstein, Valoski, Koeske, & Wing, 1986; Tingstrom, Sterling-Turner, & Wilczynski, 2006) and levels of skill (i.e., cognitive or behavioral; Minor, Minor, & Williams, 1983). Some of the more frequent behavioral applications that utilize contingency management are token economies, behavior contracting, and self-monitoring with reinforcement. These applications can be used alone or in combination to modify behavior.

Token Economies

Token economies involve an exchange context in which individuals earn tokens for performing target behaviors. Earned tokens are later exchanged for items or privileges. In some designs, the occurrence of undesirable behaviors results in the removal of tokens, often referred to as "response cost" (Witt & Elliott, 1982). Token economies typically have three components: specific behaviors to be rewarded, a medium of exchange (i.e., the token), and preferred activities or items that can be purchased with the tokens (Upper, Lochman, & Aveni, 1977). These components, together with well-defined rules (e.g., general procedures, ratio for exchange, and consistent implementation), comprise a token economy system. Designed to increase desirable behavior and decrease undesirable behavior, token economy systems have been used widely across populations and behaviors in treatment, rehabilitation, education, and community settings (Kazdin, 1986).

Behavior Contracting

Behavior contracts, often referred to as contingency contracts, are an agreement that involves a reward or a response cost system. Contracts call for specifically defining the desired behavior, its required level of performance, and any rewards that will be given for failing to attain, attaining, or exceeding the performance level (Martens et al., 1999). Behavior contracts are usually the product of collaborative efforts in which all parties (i.e., consultant, consultee, and client) are responsible for establishing the contingencies for earning rewards. In addition, the contract is typically in written form and copies are given to all parties involved. Research on behavior contracting suggests that it is effective in altering behavior across a broad range of ages (e.g., early childhood through geriatrics) and can be implemented with individuals or groups (Rutherford & Nelson, 1995).

Self-Monitoring

Self-monitoring refers to a multistage process of observing one's own behavior for the purpose of identifying the occurrence or nonoccurrence of a specified target response (Heward, 1987; Mace, Belfiore, & Hutchinson, 2001). Self-monitoring involves two steps. First, the individual must discriminate the occurrence of a target response. Second, the individual self-records some dimension of the target response (Mace et al., 2001). Self-monitoring combined with rewards is often recommended for children and adolescents as an incentive for increased monitoring as well as behavior change (Reid, Trout, & Schartz, 2005). Practitioners can select to reward performance (i.e., behavior change), accuracy of self-recording, or both.

Parental Role and Training

There is empirical support for using parent training as one dimension of multifaceted obesity treatment programs (Epstein et al., 1986; Israel, Guile, Baker, & Silverman, 1994). At the center of most behavioral parent training programs, including those used to treat and prevent childhood obesity, is an emphasis on teaching parents' skills that will enable them to alter the antecedent and consequence events that elicit, evoke, and maintain problematic child behavior (Skinner, 1953). When implementing a contingency management plan that is purely home-based, parents can be responsible for part or all of the following: identifying target behaviors, creating a contingency contract, implementing contingency management procedures by providing consequences based on a child's performance, monitoring the child's progress, and evaluating program effectiveness. In order to successfully implement strategies taught within parent training programs and contingency management plans, a practitioner typically provides parents with training.

Several instructional techniques have been used to teach skills to parents, including manualized treatments (O'Dell et al., 1982), modeling (Flanagan, Adamns, & Forehand, 1979; O'Dell et al., 1982), role playing (Flanagan et al., 1979), performance feedback (Budd, Green, & Baer, 1976), modeling plus manualized treatment (O'Dell et al., 1982), and modeling plus discussion (Webster-Stratton, 1981). Both individual and group formats for parent training have been found to be effective (Barkley, 1987). Group parent training curricula often have an educational focus and include a variety of instructional techniques (e.g., lectures, modeling, and discussion) designed to enhance parents' knowledge, attitudes, and skills (Dangel & Polster, 1988). The parent training literature indicates that didactic instruction, in combination with modeling, role playing, and feedback, can be used to provide effective training in the management of child behavior (Anderson & Kratochwill, 1988). An alternative to didactic instruction is competency-based parent training. In this approach, emphasis is placed on what an individual can do as a result of completing a program of training. During competency-based parent training, parents must demonstrate skill mastery in order to complete training.

In sum, contingency management applications have been found to be effective in treating child behavior problems, including pediatric obesity (i.e., Epstein et al., 1986, 1987; Epstein, Wing, Koeske, & Valoski et al., 1985; Epstein, Wing, Woodall, et al., 1985; Kazdin, 1986). Token economies, behavior contracts, and self-monitoring plus rewards have all been used as components of programs designed to treat pediatric obesity (Epstein, 1990; Epstein, 2003; Saelens & McGrath, 2003). Typically, multidimensional pediatric obesity treatment programs provide parents with training in behavior modification and contingency management techniques similar to those listed above (Epstein et al., 1986; Israel et al., 1994).

DEVELOPMENTAL CONSIDERATIONS

When treating any childhood behavior problem, practitioners must consider how treatment will be affected by development. For example, self-monitoring interventions should be developed with the child's age and developmental level in mind. Language ability and self-awareness are particularly important developmental domains that are often considered necessary for the successful implementation of a self-monitoring intervention (Kauffman, 2001). Consideration of age and developmental level appears critical in the prevention and treatment of child and adolescent obesity. Research on obesity treatment and prevention programs has most often targeted adults, and these programs have only recently been applied to children and adolescents. In a recent meta-analysis, Stice et al. (2006) found that obesity prevention programs were most effective for adolescents and concluded that, in theory, adolescents are better able to understand intervention methods and have more control over food and physical activity options than younger children. Not surprisingly, the meta-analysis also found that prevention programs with a high degree of parent involvement produced the greatest effects for children. The involvement of parents in child obesity and weight loss treatment programs has been associated with significantly higher percentages of weight loss when compared to treatment programs targeting children as the direct change agent (e.g., Epstein et al., 1987). While there is less research on the treatment of adolescent populations, there is evidence suggesting teenagers are better able to independently manage their weight loss (e.g., Weiss, 1977).

Infancy, Preschool, and Early Childhood (Birth to Age 8 Years)

The majority of the research with infants and young children has focused on prevention and early intervention. Limited research exists regarding contingency-based weight programs for children between birth and age 8 years (Epstein, 1990; Jelalian & Saelens, 1999). This is surprising given that habits, including habits associated with eating and physical activity, are formed at an early age (Berkowitz & Stunkard, 2002; Friman & Christophersen, 1986; Israel & Zimand, 1989). It is also true that as an obese child's age increases, so does the likelihood that his or her obesity will persist and the probability of remission decreases (Dietz, 1983). Furthermore, children who have at least one obese parent are at a greater risk for becoming obese themselves (Berkowitz & Stunkard, 2002).

Parent involvement is particularly relevant with infants and young children, as both typically have a limited ability to discern healthy food choices from unhealthy food choices and select food based on its nutritional value. As a result, they require external guidance and controls in order to manage their weight-related behaviors. Parents can be highly influential over a child's dietary habits and activity level (Friman & Christophersen, 1986; Harris & Ferrari, 1983). For example, parents should avoid using feedings in order to calm or quiet infants who have just been fed and are clearly no longer hungry, as it can lead to increased preference for that food or increased food intake (Berkowitz & Stunkard, 2002; Birch, Zimmerman, & Hind, 1980; Friman & Christophersen, 1986). In these situations, it would be most prudent to utilize social rewards. In addition, parents can allow space and time for infants to move about and encourage toddlers and preschoolers to engage in physical activity and avoid spending an excessive amount of time watching television (Neumann, 1983). To form healthy eating habits in early childhood, parents can also provide rewards for fewer bites and more chews per minute (Drabman, Hammer, & Jarvie, 1977). Finally, parents exert control as direct change agents by serving as the primary model of healthy eating and exercise habits for their children (Harris & Ferrari, 1983).

Two exemplar studies have investigated the effectiveness of contingency management methods for treating obesity in children younger than age 8 years. In 1985, Epstein, Wing, Woodall, et al., compared a family-based behavioral treatment to a health education control condition for addressing obesity in children ages 5 to 8 years. The treatment condition resulted in significantly greater weight loss. The second study was conducted by Epstein et al. (1986) and again evaluated a family-based behavioral treatment program, which involved exercise, diet, and child contingency management.

The participants were children ages 1 to 6 years. The study found the program significantly reduced calorie intake as well as relative body weight. In addition, the density of all recommended daily nutrients (except for fat) increased.

Late Childhood and Preadolescence (Ages 8 to 12 Years)

A common component of preadolescent development is the emergence of independence. Children between the ages of 8 and 12 years typically work to become more autonomous in their day-to-day functioning and, as a result, unhealthy habits might begin to develop. Late childhood is characterized by a transitional stage in which parents maintain general supervisory control over their children, while children begin establishing minute-to-minute control (Papalia & Olds, 1996). This becomes important in the development of interventions, particularly contingency management interventions. The utility of contingency-based weight management interventions with children between ages 8 and 12 years has been highlighted by a number of studies that have found behavioral treatments to be superior to no treatment, wait list, and education-only conditions (i.e., Epstein & Wing, 1987; Jelalian & Saelens, 1999). For example, Epstein, Wing, Steranchak, Dickson, and Michelson (1980) found a behavior modification condition that manipulated contingencies associated with eating and activity produced significant weight loss as compared to an education-only condition for participants ages 6 to 12 years. This study allowed the children day-to-day control over eating and physical activity, while parents maintained control over the larger contingencies within the environment by providing rewards for weight loss.

While behavior modification has been successful in obesity programs with older children and preadolescents, the degree to which parental involvement is required to produce adequate levels of change is less clear (Epstein, 2003; Epstein & Wing, 1987; Israel, Stolmaker, Sharp, Silverman, & Simon, 1984; Jelalian & Saelens, 1999). Studies have compared the following levels of parental involvement for older children: parent and child both as targets, parent as a facilitator or primary change agent and child as target, and child alone as target. Generally, short-term program outcomes have not been found to differ based on the level of parental involvement. It should be noted, however, that the most significant long-term decreases in weight loss reported with older children and preadolescents were accomplished with a program that required a high level of parent participation (Jelalian & Saelens, 1999). This finding is not surprising given that treatment protocols focusing on changing a child's daily routine are more productive when parents are involved (Papalia & Olds, 1996).

Well-established treatments for pediatric obesity with older children and preadolescents typically target both eating behavior and physical activity (Jelalian & Saelens, 1999). Programs that combine both diet and exercise components have been found to produce more significant gains than those that only target diet (Epstein & Wing, 1987). Changes in diet and exercise can be established through the use of behavior modification techniques. Interventions designed to address dietary changes with older children and preadolescents often involve education, goal setting, and behavioral contracting (Jelalian & Saelens, 1999). Furthermore, overall increased activity may be identified as a target behavior and rewards provided contingent on child activity. For example, rewards could be earned for participation in individual physical activity as well as organized recreation groups with less time spent watching television (Neumann, 1983).

Adolescence (Ages 12 to 18 Years)

Adolescence is described as a developmental transition between childhood and adulthood, and involves momentous changes in multiple developmental domains (e.g., cognitive, emotional, physical, and social). In fact, adolescence may be the most extreme transition period across the life span, as it involves changes in almost every feature of individual development, resulting in perhaps one of the most critical developmental periods (Papalia & Olds, 1996). In adolescence, the consequences of obesity are far reaching and have an impact on a multitude of physical and psychological variables. For example, overweight adolescents are at risk for developing chronic health conditions in adulthood, and there appears to be a significant relationship between adolescent obesity and poor psychological adjustment (Papalia & Olds, 1996). There is hope, however, as research on obesity prevention and intervention indicates that adolescents respond better to treatment than children (Stice et al., 2006). Stice et al. (2006) cite developmental factors as one possible reason for the discrepancy. They hypothesize that adolescents might be better able to understand ideas and skills presented in treatment. Furthermore, adolescents can be more autonomous than children and consequently have more control over their food choices and activity routines.

Despite the fact that adolescents might understand a treatment protocol or have a high degree of autonomy in food selection, research on treatment protocols for adolescent obesity often includes a parental dimension that involves contingency management. The primary difference between the uses of contingency management for children versus adolescents involves the degree to which parents are a part of treatment, and differing levels of parent involvement have been recommended (Brownell, Kelman, & Stunkard, 1983; Coates, Killen, & Slinkard, 1982; Wadden et al., 1990). Brownell et al. (1983) compared the effectiveness of a behavioral treatment implemented under three different conditions: separate adolescent and parent participation, conjoint adolescent and parent participation, and adolescent alone. Their findings suggest that separate participation is superior to conjoint participation or having the adolescent participate alone. While this makes intuitive sense given the need for autonomy during adolescence (Holmbeck, Greenley, & Franks, 2003) and the importance parental involvement plays in behavioral treatments, this finding was not replicated with a sample of African American females (Wadden et al., 1990). A study by Coates, Killen, and Slinkard (1982) also failed to find any differences in effectiveness between an adolescent alone condition and separate adolescent and parent participation.

Several studies have suggested that parental involvement is not a necessary component of contingency management in the treatment of obesity in adolescence. Coates, Jeffery, Slinkard, Killen, & Danaher (1982) found that adolescents benefited from self-delivered rewards related to daily weight loss. Weiss (1977) compared five separate conditions: no treatment, stimulus control, diet plus stimulus control, diet education, and diet education plus reward for dieting. Results suggested that the conditions involving stimulus control produced significantly more weight loss maintained at 1 year follow-up. The two studies described above provide evidence suggesting adolescents can be autonomous in managing contingencies related to their own weight loss. As children enter into adolescence, independence becomes increasingly more important, and these studies offer examples of ways to address obesity issues while taking into account the developmental needs of the adolescent (Holmbeck et al., 2003). Because of the differential findings across studies regarding the level of parental involvement needed in the application of contingency management procedures, further research is needed before empirically based recommendations are made. It would make sense, however, for practitioners to base their recommendations on the degree to which the adolescent is willing to participate in the required behavior change. Less willing participants might be more appropriate candidates for an obesity treatment program that involves contingency management carried out by a parent or caregiver.

PRACTICAL APPLICATIONS OF CONTINGENCY MANAGEMENT

There is strong empirical support for the use of multidimensional family-based behavioral programming in the treatment of pediatric obesity (Epstein, Valoski, Wing, & McCurley, 1994; Jelalian & Saelens, 1999). These programs typically promote contingency management procedures in the management of diet and exercise. Research on these programs has found them to be superior to education-only treatments when examining long-term maintenance. As a result, family-based behavioral intervention programs for the treatment of pediatric obesity have been labeled efficacious (Jelalian & Saelens, 1999).

Parent Training in Pediatric Obesity Treatment

Parental participation in treatment is critical to the success of many pediatric obesity intervention and prevention programs. Research has suggested that parental involvement in child weight loss programs is associated with higher percentages of child weight loss during treatment and with long-term treatment adherence (Golan, Weizman, Apter, & Menahem, 1998; Wrotniak, Epstein, Paluch, & Roemmich, 2005). Parental involvement often involves the manipulation of contingencies necessary to change a child's behavior, yet parents also play a role in heightening children's long-term treatment success through modeling appropriate weight loss practices (Epstein, Valoski, et al., 1994) and engaging in a parenting style characterized by acceptance as opposed to rejection (Stein, Epstein, Raynor, Kilanowski, & Palnuch, 2005).

Parent training is often viewed as a vital component in the behavioral treatment of pediatric obesity (Barlow & Dietz, 1998). Several studies have suggested that the use of parent training in behaviorally based pediatric obesity treatment can result in short-term (i.e., 8 weeks to 2 years) weight loss (e.g., Epstein, McKenzie, Valoski, Klein, & Wing, 1994; Israel, Stolmaker, & Andrian, 1985; Stein et al., 2005). Additional support exists for the long-term (i.e., 5 to 10 years) effectiveness of multidimensional family-based behavioral pediatric obesity treatment programs that include parental education on behavior modification principles (Epstein, McCurley, Wing, & Valoski, 1990; Epstein et al., 1987; Epstein, Valoski, et al., 1994).

Parent training in most pediatric obesity programs involves education on strategies to enhance a child's adherence to a specified weight loss program and attainment of specified weight loss goals. Education often occurs through therapist-parent discussions, didactic training, and homework assignments (Israel et al., 1994). Commonly taught strategies include identifying problem behaviors, using social reinforcement through verbal praise, using effective discipline through planned ignoring and time-out procedures, using behavioral modification strategies (e.g., contingency management systems), and planning and implementing a treatment program (Epstein, Wing, Keoske, Andrasik, & Ossip, 1981; Israel et al., 1994; Wrotniak et al., 2005). Parent training and education also involves teaching parents about the influence their own diet has on their child's diet and how to model a healthy lifestyle (Epstein et al., 1981; Wrotniak et al., 2005). Formats for parent training typically include family sessions, parent group sessions, and therapist-directed phone contact (e.g., Israel et al., 1985; Stein et al., 2005). The frequency and length of sessions and time devoted to parent training varies in the literature, but there is generally a high degree of contact between the therapist and parent at the beginning of treatment (e.g., weekly) that is gradually reduced over time (e.g., monthly). As expected, research suggests that increased frequency of parent-therapist contact is an important factor in the successful treatment of pediatric obesity (e.g., Senediak & Spence, 1985). Practitioners, however, should be aware that research on child and adolescent obesity prevention programs has found that prevention efforts are most effective when shorter in duration (Stice et al., 2006). Such a finding might indicate that interventions long in duration are less appealing because they require more time, effort, and involvement.

The Role of Practitioners in Training Parents in Contingency Management

Contingency management is often a core component of pediatric obesity behavior modification programming and has been used to achieve both short- and long-term childhood weight loss (e.g., Aragona, Cassady, & Drabman, 1975; Epstein, Valoski, et al., 1994; Wrotniak et al., 2005). The majority of research evaluating contingency management in the treatment of childhood obesity is based on multicomponent programs. As a result, little is known about the effects of contingency management alone on pediatric and adolescent obesity treatment outcomes. However, research suggests a direct relationship between contingency management alone and short-term reductions in body fat percentages (De Luca & Holborn, 1990). In the promotion of childhood weight loss, research also suggests that contingency management can be an integral tool when used both in isolation and in combination with other behaviorally based treatment modalities; however, research examining the specific effects of contingency management systems is needed.

The effectiveness of contingency management in the treatment of childhood obesity depends upon a multitude of factors. For example, the effectiveness of contingency management can be maximized by integrating contingencies for the weight loss goals of both children and parents versus contingencies for a child alone or parent alone (Epstein et al., 1987, 1990). Successful outcomes also appear to depend upon identifying appropriate target behaviors (e.g., diet and exercise) and reinforcing activities and tangibles, as well as applying contingencies through behavioral contracts (e.g., Epstein, McKenzie, et al., 1994), token economies (e.g., Epstein et al., 1986), and self-monitoring (e.g., Epstein, Wing, Keoske, Ossip, & Beck, 1982).

Identifying Target Behaviors for Contingency Management

The first step in setting up an effective contingency management system is identifying the target behavior for change. Results can be maximized through the use of contingency management systems that target changes in diet management and lifestyle exercise activities (e.g., taking the stairs instead of the elevator) (Epstein et al., 1990; Epstein, Valoski, et al., 1994). While exercise is essential for childhood weight loss, exercise alone can fail to yield successful treatment outcomes when exercise involves aerobic exercise or calisthenics instead of lifestyle exercise (Epstein, Valoski, et al., 1994). Over the past 25 years, Epstein et al. (1981) have validated the use of the "Traffic Light Diet," which applies simple contingencies to diet modification. This diet program involves recording the intake of low-fat, nutritionally dense foods ("green foods") versus unhealthy foods that are high in calories ("yellow foods" and "red foods"), along with rewarding the child's change in eating habits or weight loss (Epstein et al., 1981). Contingencies linked to both the "Traffic Light Diet" alone and in combination with exercise have resulted in short-term weight loss (Epstein, Wing, Koeske, & Valoski, 1984). Therefore it should be beneficial for practitioners to help families develop contingencies that involve target behaviors related to both food intake and nonsedentary activity.

In general, there is a range of variables that can be used as part of a contingency management system for weight management. Contingencies can involve attendance at appointments or sessions (e.g., Aragona et al., 1975); changes in food preferences (Birch et al., 1980); slowing the rate of eating and drinking (Epstein, Parker, McCoy, & McGee, 1976); preplanning of meals and exercise (Kirschenbaum, Harris, & Tomarken, 1984); increased engagement in physical activity and decreased engagement in preferred sedentary activities, such as video games and television (e.g., Epstein, Saelens, Myers, & Vito, 1997; Epstein, Smith, Vara, & Rodefer, 1991); and mastery of weight management skills and goal attainment (e.g., Epstein, McKenzie, et al., 1994). Caution should be taken to exclude the use of daily weight loss as a variable in contingency management, as such a focus can be inappropriate for children and meta-analytic research suggests that treatment programs focusing on weight control or maintenance lead to better outcomes (Stice et al., 2006). A primary role for practitioners is to guide families in identifying target behaviors and corresponding contingencies that best fit an individual child's or family's treatment needs and goals.

Identifying Reinforcing Stimuli for Use in Contingency Management

The next step in contingency management is building parental understanding and competence in the identification and administration of reinforcing events or objects. Parents should be educated on the importance of avoiding the use of food as a reward or the removal of food as punishment within weight loss contingencies (Jelalian & Mehlenbeck, 2003). Practitioners need to emphasize to parents the significance of identifying motivators other than food to reward children and all family members for goal attainment related to weight loss management and other life celebrations (e.g., holidays, job promotions). Furthermore, caution should be taken when using the removal of exercise as a reward or the addition of exercise as punishment. Finally, contingencies involving positive reinforcement have resulted in short-term weight loss (Aragona et al., 1975) and should be implemented prior to inclusion of a response cost procedure.

To create an effective contingency management plan, it is also important that parents be taught to assess their children's preferences for tangibles or activities and utilize these preferred items to reinforce a behavior. Assessment can be conducted through observation or the use of Likert rating scales, where children can rate their preference of activities or tangibles (Epstein et al., 1991). Offering rewards for obtaining daily goals has been found to be more effective than offering reinforcement for weekly goals (Coates, Jeffery, et al., 1982). Educating parents on the use of less preferred or smaller rewards, such as tokens that can later be redeemed for a larger highly preferred reward, and inexpensive tangibles or activities is also essential to establishing contingency management systems (Epstein, Paluch, Kilanowski, & Raynor, 2004).

Behavior Contracts

After target behaviors and possible reinforcing tangibles and activities have been identified, a behavior contract can be created. Behavior contracts have been widely used within empirically supported multifaceted behavioral weight management programs (e.g., Epstein et al., 2004; Epstein, McKenzie, et al., 1994; Epstein et al., 1980). Behavior contracts have been applied to the child alone (e.g., Epstein et al., 2004), parent alone (Aragona et al., 1975), and the parent and child together (e.g., Epstein et al., 1980). At the child level, contracts can include a plan for short- and long-term goals, as well as an integration of reinforcing objects and events (Epstein et al., 2004). Parental contracts can involve short- and long-term goals or be focused on the weight loss and goal attainment of both the parent and child. Family-based contracts can also target treatment integrity issues, including attendance at scheduled appointments, adherence to a specified diet plan, and compliance with an exercise program.

Practitioners should help the parent and child develop a behavioral contract that specifies straightforward and understandable contingencies (Cooper, Heron, & Heward, 1987). Parents will likely benefit from learning how to describe the task or specified target behavior presented within the contract in a clear, observable, and objective manner. This involves (1) who will be completing the task or behavior, (2) who will be obtaining a reward and providing the reward, (3) what the task is and how well it must be completed before a reward is earned, (4) what the reward is and how much of it can be earned, and (5) the time frame of completing the task and obtaining the reward. A task record should include self-monitoring of both the behavior and reward/goal attainment. Behavior contracts can be utilized for many components of weight management. For example, a system can be established that allows a child to earn token rewards for eating a specified number of fruits and vegetables per day, and when he or she accumulates a specified number of token rewards, those tokens can be redeemed for a reinforcing object or event.

Token Economy

Token economies involve three basic components: (1) clearly stated behaviors to be reinforced, (2) procedures for administering reinforcing stimuli (tokens) when the target behavior occurs, and (3) rules that are devised to govern the exchange of tokens for reinforcing objects or events (O'Leary & Drabman, 1971). Based on the information obtained in the above steps, the practitioner can help parents develop a token economy system with rules directed at the selected target behaviors and identified reinforcing tangibles or activities. The behavior contract can serve to implement the rules governing the token economy. Practitioners should assist parents in specifying the conditions under which tokens are earned or lost, should response cost procedures be used for inappropriate behaviors. Tokens can consist of monetary rewards, points, checkmarks, stickers, play money, tickets, poker chips, stars, or any other object that is preferable to the child. Tokens should also be easy to dispense and track.

Token economy systems have been utilized as components of highly effective pediatric obesity programs (e.g., De Luca & Holborn, 1990; Epstein et al., 1986). Points, lottery tickets, and monetary rewards have been included in the application of token economies at the child and parent level (Aragona et al., 1975; Epstein et al., 1997; Epstein, McKenzie, et al., 1994). For example, Epstein et al. (1997) created a token economy system in which children earned points for every minute they did not spend in high-preference sedentary activities and lost points for participation in such activities. The study concluded that the combination of reinforcement and punishment within a token economy system resulted in increased physical activity and decreased engagement in preferred sedentary activity.

Self-Monitoring

Once a behavioral contract has been developed and a token economy put in place, the practitioner should consider what type of monitoring the family will most benefit from. Child- and parent-directed monitoring systems are key aspects of contingency management and are often recommended in behavior management programs. Child-directed self-monitoring has been linked to both successful treatment adherence and short- and long-term weight loss (Israel, Silverman, & Solotar, 1988; Saelens & McGrath, 2003; Wrotniak et al., 2005). Child self-monitoring alone has also been shown to be effective in the short-term maintenance of weight loss goals (Cohen, Gelfand, Dodd, Jensen, & Turner, 1980).

Several successful weight management programs have included instruction on self-monitoring of weight loss; physical activity; type of food eaten, with caloric intake and nutritional information; food portions; and bite sizes (e.g., Cohen et al., 1980; Duffy & Spence, 1993; Epstein et al., 1982). Parents are often asked to self-monitor components of their own weight loss and eating patterns in addition to those of their child (Epstein et al., 1987, 1990). Parents have also self-monitored their implementation of behavioral techniques or parenting skills, such as positive reinforcing statements and stimulus control changes made to their home environment (e.g., removing unhealthy foods from the home) (Epstein, McKenzie, et al., 1994).

Practitioners can help families develop self-monitoring records through education and ongoing data collection. Elements of an educational discussion on the implementation of a self-monitoring intervention should include (1) identifying and defining the specific behavior to be monitored, (2) indicating how the behavior will be self-monitored and checked for accuracy, (3) choosing implementation procedures involving rewards and response costs, (4) implementing the procedures, and (5) evaluating the self-management plan (Heward, 1987). A faded matching technique should be considered to help youth acquire the skill of self-monitoring and reach a higher level of self-regulatory diet and exercise patterns. This technique involves rewarding the child for accurately recording the target behavior based on a match with the parent's monitoring record. Parental involvement in the monitoring of accuracy fades as the child becomes more independent in the completion of the self-monitoring procedures.

Ensuring Treatment Integrity

Treatment integrity and adherence is critical to the success of any weight loss management program. Within pediatric obesity treatment programs, parents become the primary source of ensuring treatment integrity and adherence (Golan et al., 1998; Wrotniak et al., 2005). Research on parental involvement in obesity treatment programs suggests high levels of parental engagement are associated with lower attrition rates and more thorough compliance with treatment protocols (Golan et al., 1998). Changes in parental lifestyle and parenting habits have also predicted child adherence to treatment components. Parental contracts are one means of maintaining parental involvement and facilitating parental behavioral changes. For example, Aragona et al. (1975) used a parental behavior contract involving a response cost procedure in order to promote treatment adherence. Within this contingency management system, parents lost previously deposited money for missing weekly meetings, failing to complete treatment charts and graphs, and when their child missed weekly weight loss goals. Joint contract systems might also be considered, given the importance of involving both parent and child in the weight management program. Such systems involve writing reciprocal contracts and receiving reinforcement when both parties master treatment skills and meet weight loss goals (e.g., Epstein, McKenzie, et al., 1994).

FUTURE DIRECTIONS

Many opportunities exist for researchers to explore the relationship between aspects of parent training and contingency management within the context of pediatric obesity treatment. For example, parent training needs to be examined further to determine how it relates to effectiveness, adherence, and generalization of treatment. Furthermore, the relationship between a youth's developmental level and the effectiveness of varying contingency management applications should be examined. In addition, researchers need to examine the most effective and efficient form of parental involvement when considering contingency management in treatment programs. Finally, treatment integrity issues should be addressed in order to increase the effectiveness of these interventions.

Although existing research supports the use of parent training in the treatment of pediatric obesity, more research is needed examining the long-term effects of such programs. It is also critical to examine the effectiveness of particular components of multidimensional family-based behavioral programming utilized in the treatment of pediatric obesity. Further research is needed to investigate whether children of parents that have undergone training benefit more from a contingency management intervention than parents without direct training. It is unclear how specific forms of parent training (i.e., education versus role play) effect overall child weight loss. Similarly, there has been very little research examining the most appropriate amount of direct parent training in contingency management (Epstein, Roemmich, & Raynor, 2001; Jelalian & Mehlenbeck, 2003), as well as whether contingency management adds to behavioral obesity treatments by ensuring generalization across situations and behaviors (Israel, 1990). Reviews have noted that strong correlations exist between obesity and behavior problems in children (Israel, 1990), however, it is unknown whether behavioral treatments for obesity that include parent training in contingency management produce changes in both weight and unrelated behavior problems.

Israel et al. (1984) suggest that there might be a relationship between the effectiveness of the type of parental involvement and the age of the child. Future studies should specifically examine how a child's age and developmental level relate to the effectiveness of different parental roles in obesity treatment. As the majority of the outpatient clinic pediatric obesity research has been conducted on children ages 8 to 12 years, more research is needed with both younger and older age groups to definitively determine their level of benefit from parent training and involvement (Epstein, 2003; Jelalian & Saelens, 1999). In particular, research with adolescents remains mixed as to how parental involvement effects treatment outcomes (Jelalian & Saelens, 1999).

More research on prevention and early intervention with infants and young children is needed. These primary interventions are essential in order to address the growing obesity problem in youth (Epstein, 1990; Jelalian & Saelens, 1999). It appears essential that weight management issues be considered earlier within the developmental course, given that the prognosis is poor for children with early onset obesity (Dietz, 1983). Specific interventions, target populations, and the most appropriate modes of dissemination should be examined further.

Future obesity research with adolescents should consider their developmental needs for autonomy and affiliation with peers (Holmbeck et al., 2003). It may be that adolescents will respond more favorably to contingency management treatments that utilize parents in a helper role versus a participant role (Israel et al., 1984). It is also possible that contingencies in adolescent obesity treatment may be enhanced through peer involvement. Researchers should examine the differential effects of parent versus peer involvement (Jelalian & Mehlenbeck, 2002).

Treatment integrity and adherence is perhaps the most critical variable in producing successful outcomes for children and adolescents with significant weight problems. Surprisingly, few studies have considered parent and child adherence components. Although Wrotniak et al. (2005) attempted to address this issue by measuring adherence through a self-report questionnaire, future studies need to examine treatment integrity of contingency management procedures using more reliable methods, including direct observation and collection of permanent products.

CONCLUSION

Child and adolescent obesity is growing at an alarming rate, and effective prevention and treatment programs are needed to curb these trends. Parent training and contingency management are likely to be components of a comprehensive treatment program given their empirical base within the behavioral and child psychology literatures as well as the literature on pediatric obesity treatment. Training parents to effectively manage their child's problems can be a powerful way to change behavior, as parents typically control the reinforcing contingencies within a child's environment (Shriver, 1998). In most parent training contexts, parents are instructed to manipulate contingencies, reward appropriate behavior, and punish inappropriate behavior. Parents are also taught to use behavioral contracts, token economies, and child-directed self-monitoring procedures. Within child and adolescent obesity treatment programs, parent training and contingency management strategies have been found to contribute to participants' weight loss and adherence to intervention protocols. Contingency management procedures have also increased compliance with exercise regimens and decreased sedentary activity. While research has provided direction regarding pediatric obesity treatment, more studies are needed before the effectiveness of particular intervention components is fully understood. Furthermore, studies are needed that investigate the effects parent training and contingency management have on long-term outcomes. Finally, issues pertaining to child development need to be considered when building prevention and intervention programs, and future research should examine the role of development in pediatric obesity and pediatric obesity treatment.

REFERENCES

Anderson, T., & Kratochwill, T. *(1988)*. Dissemination of behavioral procedures in the schools: issues in training. In J. C. Witt & S. N. Elliott (Eds.), *Handbook of behavior therapy in education* (pp. 217–244). New York: Plenum Press.

Aragona, J., Cassady, J., & Drabman, R. S. (1975). Treating overweight children through parental training and contingency contracting. *Journal of Applied Behavioral Analysis, 8,* 269–278.

Barkley, R. A. (1987). *Defiant children: a clinician's manual for parent training.* New York: Guilford Press.

Barlow, S. E., & Dietz, W. H. (1998.) Obesity evaluation and treatment: expert committee recommendations. *Pediatrics, 102,* 626–639.

Berkowitz, R. I., & Stunkard, A. J. (2002). Development of childhood obesity. In T. A. Wadden & A. J. Stunkard (Eds.), *Handbook of obesity treatment* (pp. 515–531). New York: Guilford Press.

Birch, L. L., Zimmerman, S. I., & Hind, H. (1980). The influence of social-affective context on the formation of children's food preferences. *Child Development, 51,* 856–861.

Brownell, K. D., Kelman, J. H., & Stunkard, A. J. (1983). Treatment of obese children with and without their mothers: changes in weight and blood pressure. *Pediatrics, 71,* 515–523.

Budd, K. S., Green, D. R., & Baer, D. M. (1976). An analysis of multiple misplaced parental social contingencies. *Journal of Applied Behavior Analysis, 9,* 459–470.

Coates, T. J., Jeffery, R. W., Slinkard, L. A., Killen, J. D., & Danaher, B. G. (1982). Frequency of contact and monetary reward in weight loss, lipid change, and blood pressure reduction with adolescents. *Behavior Therapy, 13,* 175–185.

Coates, T. J., Killen, J. D., & Slinkard, L. A. (1982). Parent participation in a treatment program for overweight adolescents. *International Journal of Eating Disorders, 1,* 37–48.

Cohen, E. A., Gelfand, D. M., Dodd, D. K., Jensen, J., & Turner, C. (1980). Self-control practices associated with weight loss maintenance in children and adolescents. *Behavior Therapy, 11,* 26–37.

Cooper, J. O., Heron, T. E., & Heward, W. L. (Eds.). (1987). *Applied behavioral analysis.* Upper Saddle River, NJ: Prentice-Hall.

Dangel, R. F., & Polster, R. A. (1988). *Teaching child management skills.* Elmsford, NY: Pergamon Press.

De Luca, R. V., & Holborn, S. W. (1990). Effects of fixed-interval and fixed-ratio schedules of token reinforcement on exercise with obese and nonobese boys. *Psychological Record, 40,* 67–83.

Dietz, W. H., Jr. (1983). Childhood obesity: susceptibility, causes, and management. *Journal of Pediatrics, 103,* 676–686.

Duffy, G., & Spence, S. H. (1993). The effectiveness of cognitive self-management as an adjunct to a behavioral intervention for childhood obesity: a research note. *Journal of Child Psychology and Psychiatry, 34,* 1043–1050.

Drabman, R. S., Hammer, D., & Jarvie, G. J. (1977). Eating styles of obese and nonobese black and white children in a naturalistic setting. *Addictive Behavior, 2,* 83–86.

Epstein, L. H. (1990). Behavioral treatment of obesity. In N. T. Adler & E. M. Stricker (Eds.), *Handbook of behavioral neurobiology: Vol. 1. Neurobiology of food and food intake* (pp. 61–73). New York: Plenum Press.

Epstein, L. H. (2003). Development of evidence-based treatments for pediatric obesity. In A. E. Kazdin & J. R. Weisz (Eds.), *Evidence-based psychotherapies for children and adolescents* (pp. 374–388). New York: Guilford Press.

Epstein, L. H., McCurley, J., Wing, R. R., & Valoski, A. (1990). Five-year follow-up of family-based behavioral treatments for childhood obesity. *Journal of Consulting and Clinical Psychology, 58,* 661–664.

Epstein, L. H., McKenzie, S. J., Valoski, A., Klein, K. R., & Wing, R. R. (1994). Effects of mastery criteria and contingent reinforcement for family-based child weight control. *Addictive Behaviors, 19,* 135–145.

Epstein, L. H., Paluch, R. A., Kilanowski, C. K., & Raynor, H. A. (2004). The effect of reinforcement or stimulus control to reduce sedentary behavior in the treatment of pediatric obesity. *Health Psychology, 22,* 371–380.

Epstein, L. H., Parker, L., McCoy, J. F., & McGee, G. (1976). Descriptive analysis of eating regulation in obese and nonobese children. *Journal of Applied Behavior Analysis, 9,* 407–415.

Epstein, L. H., Roemmich, J. N., & Raynor, H. A. (2001). Behavioral therapy in the treatment of pediatric obesity. *Pediatric Clinics of North America, 48,* 981–993.

Epstein, L. H., Saelens, B. E., Myers, M. D., & Vito, D. (1997). Effects of decreasing sedentary behaviors on activity choice in obese children. *Health Psychology, 16,* 107–113.

Epstein, L. H., Smith, J. A., Vara, L. S., & Rodefer, J. S. (1991). Behavioral economic analysis of activity choice in obese children. *Health Psychology, 10,* 311–316.

Epstein, L. H., Valoski, A., Koeske, R., & Wing, R. R. (1986). Family-based behavioral weight control in obese young children. *Journal of the American Dietetic Association, 86,* 481–484.

Epstein, L. H., Valoski, A., Wing, R. R., & McCurley, J. (1994). Ten-year outcomes of behavioral family-based treatments for childhood obesity. *Health Psychology, 13,* 373–383.

Epstein, L. H., & Wing, R. R. (1987). Behavioral treatment of childhood obesity. *Psychological Bulletin, 101,* 331–342.

Epstein, L. H., Wing, R. R., Koeske, R., Andrasik, F., & Ossip, D. J. (1981). Child and parent weight loss in family-based behavior modification programs. *Journal of Consulting and Clinical Psychology, 49,* 674–685.

Epstein, L. H., Wing, R. R., Keoske, R., Ossip, D. J., & Beck, S. (1982). A comparison of lifestyle change and programmed aerobic exercise on weight and fitness changes in obese children. *Behavior Therapy, 13,* 651–665.

Epstein, L. H., Wing, R. R., Koeske, R., & Valoski, A. (1984). Effects of diet plus exercise on weight change in parents and children. *Journal of Consulting and Clinical Psychology, 52,* 429–437.

Epstein, L. H., Wing, R. R., Koeske, R., & Valoski, A. (1985). Effect of parent weight on weight loss in obese children. *Journal of Consulting and Clinical Psychology, 54,* 400–401.

Epstein, L. H., Wing, R. R., Koeske, R., & Valoski, A. (1987). Long-term effects of family-based treatment of childhood obesity. *Journal of Consulting and Clinical Psychology, 55,* 91–95.

Epstein, L. H., Wing, R. R., Steranchak, L., Dickson, B., & Michelson, J. (1980). Comparison of family-based behavior modification and nutrition education for childhood obesity. *Journal of Pediatric Psychology, 5,* 25–35.

Epstein, L. H., Wing, R. R., Woodall, K., Penner, B. C., Kress, M. J., & Koeske, R. (1985). Effects of family-based behavioral treatment on obese 5- to 8-year-old children. *Behavior Therapy, 16,* 205–212.

Flanagan, S., Adamns, H. E., & Forehand, R. (1979). A comparison of four instructional techniques for teaching parents to use time-out. *Behavior Therapy, 10,* 94–102.

Friman, P. C., & Christophersen, E. R. (1986). Biobehavioral prevention in primary care. In N. A. Krasnegor, J. D. Araseth, & M. F. Cataldo (Eds.), *Child health behavior: a behavioral pediatrics perspective* (pp. 254–280). New York: John Wiley & Sons.

Golan, M., Weizman, A., Apter, A., & Menahem, F. (1998). Parents as the exclusive agents of change in the treatment of childhood obesity. *American Journal of Clinical Nutrition, 67,* 1130–1135.

Harris, S. L., & Ferrari, M. (1983). Developmental factors in child behavior therapy. *Behavior Therapy, 14,* 54–72.

Heward, W. L. (1980). A formula for individualizing initial criteria for reinforcement. *Exceptional Teacher, 1,* 7.

Heward, W. L. (1987). Self management. In J. O. Cooper, T. E. Heron, & W. L. Heward (Eds.), *Applied behavioral analysis* (pp. 515–549). Upper Saddle River, NJ: Prentice-Hall.

Holmbeck, G. H., Greenley, R. N., & Franks, E. A. (2003). Developmental issues and considerations in research and practice. In A. E. Kazdin & J. R. Weisz (Eds.), *Evidence-based psychotherapies for children and adolescents* (pp. 21–41). New York: Guilford Press.

Israel, A. C. (1990). Childhood obesity. In A. S. Bellack, M. Hersen, & A. E. Kazdin (Eds.), *International handbook of behavior modification and therapy* (pp. 819-830). New York: Plenum Press.

Israel, A. C., Guile, C. A., Baker, J. E., & Silverman, W. K. (1994). An evaluation of enhanced self-regulation training in the treatment of childhood obesity. *Journal of Pediatric Psychology, 19,* 737–749.

Israel, A. C., Silverman, W. K., & Solotar, L. C. (1988). The relationship between adherence and weight loss in a behavioral treatment program for overweight children. *Behavior Therapy, 19,* 25–33.

Israel, A. C., Stolmaker, L., & Andrian, C. A. G. (1985). The effects of training parents in general child management skills on a behavioral weight loss program for children. *Behavior Therapy, 16,* 169–180.

Israel, A. C., Stolmaker, L., Sharp, J. P., Silverman, W. K., & Simon, L. G. (1984). An evaluation of two methods of parental involvement in treating obese children. *Behavior Therapy, 15,* 266–272.

Israel, A. C., & Zimand, E. (1989). Obesity. In M. Hersen (Ed.), *Innovations in child behavior therapy* (pp. 306–323). New York: Springer.

Jelalian, E., & Mehlenbeck, R. (2002). Peer-enhanced weight management treatment for overweight adolescents: some preliminary findings. *Journal of Clinical Psychology in Medical Settings, 9,* 15–23.

Jelalian, E., & Mehlenbeck, R. (2003). Pediatric obesity. In M. C. Roberts (Ed.), *Handbook of pediatric psychology* (pp. 529–543). New York: Guilford Press.

Jelalian, E., & Saelens, B. E. (1999). Empirically supported treatments in pediatric psychology: pediatric obesity. *Journal of Pediatric Psychology, 24,* 223–248.

Kauffman, J. M. (2001). *Characteristics of emotional and behavioral disorders of children and youth* (7th ed.). Upper Saddle River, NJ: Prentice-Hall.

Kazdin, A. E. (1986). *Treatment of antisocial behaviour in children and adolescents.* Homewood, IL: Dorsey.

Kirschenbaum, D. S., Harris, E. S., Tomarken, A. J. (1984). Effects of parental involvement in behavioral weight loss therapy for preadolescents. *Behavior Therapy, 15,* 485–500.

Mace, F. C., Belfiore, P. J., & Hutchinson, J. M. (2001). Operant theory and research on self-regulation. In B. Zimmerman & D. Schunk (Eds.), *Learning and academic achievement: theoretical perspective* (pp. 39–65). Mahwah, NJ: Lawrence Erlbaum.

Martens, B. K., Witt, J. C., Daly, E. J., & Vollmer, T. R. (1999). Behavior analysis: theory and practice in educational settings. In C. R. Reynolds & T. R. Gutkin (Eds.), *The handbook of school psychology* (pp. 638–663). New York: John Wiley & Sons.

Minor, S. W., Minor, J. W., & Williams, P. P. (1983). A participant modeling procedure to train parents of developmentally disabled infants. *Journal of Psychology, 115,* 107–111.

Neumann, C. G. (1983). Obesity in childhood. In M. D. Levine, W. B. Carey, A. C. Crocker, & R. T. Gross (Eds.), *Developmental-behavioral pediatrics* (pp. 536–551). Philadelphia: W. B. Saunders.

O'Dell, S. L., O'Quin, J. A., Alford, B. A., O'Brian, A. L., Bradlyn, A. S., & Giebenhain, J. E. (1982). Predicting the acquisition of parenting skills via four training methods. *Behavior Therapy, 13,* 194–208.

Ogden, C. L., Flegal, K. M., Carroll, M. D., & Johnson, C. L. (2002). Prevalence and trends in overweight among US children and adolescents, 1999–2000. *JAMA, 288,* 1728–1732.

O'Leary, K. D., & Drabman, R. (1971). Token reinforcement in the classroom: a review. *Psychological Bulletin, 75,* 379–398.

Papalia, D. E., & Olds, S. W. (1996). *A child's world: infancy through adolescence* (7th ed.). New York: McGraw Hill.

Reid, R., Trout, A., & Schartz, M. (2005). Self-regulation interventions for children with attention deficit/hyperactivity disorder. *Exceptional Children, 71,* 361–377.

Rutherford, R. B., & Nelson, C. M. (1995). Management of violent and aggressive behavior in the schools. *Focus on Exceptional Children, 27,* 1–15.

Saelens, B. E. & McGrath, A. M. (2003). Self-monitoring and adolescent weight control efficacy. *Children's Health Care, 32,* 137–152.

Senediak, C., & Spence, S. H. (1985). Rapid versus gradual scheduling of therapeutic contact in a family based behavioural weight control programme for children. *Behavioral Psychotherapy, 13,* 265–287.

Shriver, M. D. (1998). Teaching parenting skills. In W. T. Steuart & F. M. Gresham (Eds.), *Handbook of child behavior therapy* (pp. 165–182). New York: Plenum Press.

Skinner, B. F. (1953) *Science and human behavior.* New York: Macmillan.

Skinner, B.F. (1971). *Beyond freedom and dignity.* New York: Knopf.

Stein, R. I., Epstein, L. H., Raynor, H. A., Kilanowski, C. K., & Paluch, R. A. (2005). The influence of parenting change on pediatric weight control. *Obesity Research, 13,* 1749–1755.

Stice, E., Shaw, H., & Marti, C. N. (2006). A meta-analytic review of obesity prevention programs for children and adolescents: the skinny on interventions that work. *Psychological Bulletin, 132,* 667–691.

Tingstrom, D. H., Sterling-Turner, H. E., & Wilczynski, S. M. (2006). The good behavior game: 1969–2002. *Behavior Modification, 30,* 225–253.

Upper, D., Lochman, J. E., & Aveni, C. A. (1977). Using contingency contracting to modify the problematic behaviors of foster home residents. *Behavior Modification, 1,* 405–416.

Wadden, T. A., Stunkard, A. J., Rich, L., Rubin, C. J., Sweidel, G., & McKinney, S. (1990). Obesity in black adolescent girls: a controlled clinical trial of treatment by diet, behavior modification, and parental support. *Pediatrics, 85,* 345–352.

Weiss, A. R. (1977). A behavioral approach to the treatment of adolescent obesity. *Behavior Therapy, 8,* 720–726.

Webster-Stratton, C. (1981). Modification of mothers' behaviors and attitudes through a videotape modeling group discussion program. *Behavior Therapy,* 12(5), 634–642.

Witt, J. C., & Elliott, S. N. (1982). The response cost lottery: a time efficient and effective classroom intervention. *School Psychology Review, 20,* 155–161.

Wrotniak, B. H., Epstein, L. H., Paluch, R. A., & Roemmich, J. N. (2005). The relationship between parent and child self-reported adherence and weight loss. *Obesity Research, 13,* 1089–1096.

7

Social Skills Training and the Treatment of Pediatric Overweight

FRED FRANKEL, MEGHAN SINTON, AND DENISE WILFLEY

It is well established that overweight is associated with a series of health complications and psychological impairment. Of additional concern is that overweight is associated with specific deficits within the social domain. Though often considered secondary to the comorbid physical complications, these psychosocial complications may be one of the more salient consequences associated with childhood overweight (Hayden-Wade et al., 2005; Kolotkin et al., 2006; Zeller, Saelens, Roehrig, Kirk, & Daniels, 2004). Indeed, overweight youth report not only increased physical health problems but also greater psychological and social consequences in comparison to their nonoverweight peers (Koplan, Liverman, & Kraak, 2005).

The first part of this chapter reviews evidence indicating that overweight youth experience specific barriers within the social domain that negatively influence weight loss and maintenance of weight loss. This review highlights the relevance of social skills treatment for child and adolescent overweight and discusses the application of social skills treatment to overweight in youth. Although such treatment represents a novel approach in addressing child and adolescent overweight, recent studies, as described in the latter part of the chapter, suggest that such treatments are a promising approach to reducing overweight in youth.

SOCIAL CONTEXT OF OVERWEIGHT STATUS

Because of the higher rates of physical health and psychosocial problems associated with overweight, it is not surprising that overweight children and adolescents in general report poorer quality of life than nonoverweight children and adolescents. One study found quality of life scores for children and adolescents who were severely overweight to be significantly lower when compared to nonoverweight youth (67.0 versus 83.0 out of 100; Schwimmer, Burwinkle & Varni, 2003). Overweight children also report lower self-ratings of social acceptance, physical appearance, and global self-worth (Davison & Birch, 2002; Kimm et al., 1997; Manus & Killeen, 1995). Poor feelings of self-worth and social acceptance may impact feelings of loneliness and depression. Though several factors contribute to the greater psychological burden among overweight youth, experiences with teasing and peer rejection, as well as the general nature of friendships in children and adolescents, have specific implications for understanding the social relationships and environments that are associated with childhood overweight.

Teasing

The psychological burden for overweight children is significant, as they are stigmatized and marginalized. Young children describe silhouettes of an overweight child as "lazy," "dirty," "stupid," "cheats," and "liars," ranking overweight children as those they would least like to have as friends (e.g., Goldfield & Chrisler, 1995; Staffieri, 1967). Peer biases against overweight children increase their risk for psychological victimization, and these experiences appear to have implications for how overweight children evaluate themselves and approach their social world. Overweight youth are more likely to experience weight-related teasing as compared to their nonoverweight peers (Haines & Neumark-Sztainer, 2006; Hayden-Wade et al., 2005; Janssen et al., 2005; Neumark-Sztainer et al., 2002; Shapiro, Baumeister, & Kessler, 1991). One study found that 78% of overweight children reported having been teased or criticized about their appearance, compared to 37.2% of nonoverweight children (Hayden-Wade et. al., 2005). Among those who were teased about their appearance, overweight children were more likely to have been teased about weight-related aspects of their appearance and also report more frequent and enduring experiences with teasing (Hayden-Wade et al., 2005). The effects of teasing are quite persistent. Wilfley, Grilo, and Brownell (1994) found in a clinical sample of overweight females that the frequency of being teased about weight and size while growing up was negatively correlated with evaluation of their own appearance and positively correlated with body dissatisfaction during adulthood.

These findings are of relevance to this chapter because, as children age, factors such as appearance and weight are associated with social standing (e.g., popularity). Therefore being teased or stigmatized about weight and appearance has specific implications for the social interactions and relationships of overweight children. Perhaps because of the burden of enduring stigmatization, rejection, and teasing, obese children are at increased risk for social problems (Banis et al., 1988; Israel & Shapiro, 1985; Myers, Raynor, & Epstein, 1998). Indeed, Hayden-Wade et al. (2005) report that the emotional impact of teasing experiences was associated with greater loneliness, suggesting that chronic teasing increases the risk for social isolation in overweight youth.

Further, the effects of teasing have a negative effect on body image and physical activity. Shape and weight concerns and body dissatisfaction are associated with increased adiposity among pre-adolescent girls (Striegel-Moore et al., 1995) and appear to be elevated in overweight children and adolescents relative to their nonoverweight peers (Burrows & Cooper, 2002; Haines & Neumark-Sztainer, 2006; Neumark-Sztainer et al., 2002). Such concerns decrease the likelihood of engaging in physical activity (Neumark-Sztainer, Paxton, Hannan, Haines, & Story, 2006), which in turn increases the risk for weight gain. Similarly, a fear of being teased may discourage overweight children from trying new physical activities, from joining other peers engaged in such activities, or from persisting with new activities (Zabinski, Saelens, Stein, Hayden-Wade, & Wilfley, 2003); such experienced or perceived barriers to physical activity clearly impact the risk for overweight. In a study of middle school children, verbal teasing by peers during physical activity was significantly associated with less reported high-intensity physical activity, less reported physical activity, and less enjoyment of sports (Pietrobelli, Leone, Heymsfield, & Faith, 1998). It is clear that overweight children may benefit from being taught effective strategies to cope with teasing and how to select playmates who are less likely to tease them. Success in handling teasing may increase self-esteem and also promote more risk taking in terms of beginning and maintaining a more physically active lifestyle.

Peer Rejection

Clearly, experiences such as teasing may decrease the likelihood that overweight youth participate in social activities, leading to feelings of loneliness and isolation as well as decreased physical activity.

Children who are rejected by their peers also experience fewer opportunities for social interaction such that an examination of the impact of peer rejection on overweight youth may further illustrate how the social environment of overweight youth differs from their nonoverweight peers.

Starting in second grade, the school acquaintanceship network becomes especially valuable. This is for two reasons: First, status within this network determines the company that children keep in public places, such as the schoolyard. Second, such status may promote or hinder the development of best friends. Consequently, rejection from this network has a severe emotional toll (East & Rook, 1992). Of concern is that a substantial segment of overweight children appear to be at risk for experiencing such rejection: Children rank obese children as those they would least like to have as friends (Goldfield & Chrisler, 1995; Latner & Stunkard, 2003; Staffieri, 1967). Consequently, between 11% and 49% of overweight children have problems making or keeping friends (Epstein, Klein, & Wisniewski, 1994; Epstein, Myers, & Anderson, 1996; Epstein, Wisniewski, & Weng, 1994), so that overweight children report being more socially isolated than their normal-weight peers (Phillips & Hill, 1997). Peer status appears to be trans-situational, applying not only during school but after school as well. One recent study found that overweight children were rated as significantly more rejected and isolated than nonoverweight children within an after-school program (Mahoney, Lord, & Carryl, 2005). Parents also report that overweight children are at increased risk for peer problems in their neighborhoods (e.g., Epstein, Klein, & Wisniewski, 1994). Therefore, many overweight children appear to experience rejection across a number of daily environments, including school, after-school, and neighborhood contexts.

The combination of peer rejection and teasing may force overweight children to seek the solitude of home activities that focus on television, video watching, video game playing, and snacking ("screen time"; Robinson, 1999), which maintains their overweight status (Andersen, Crespo, Bartlett, Cheskin, & Pratt, 1998, Crespo et al., 2001; Dietz & Gortmaker, 2001; Gortmaker et al., 1996; Saelens et al., 2002), rather than participating in after-school programs, which have been found to be negatively related to overweight (Elkins, Cohen, Koralewicz & Taylor, 2004; Mahoney et al., 2005). Therefore interventions that improve peer status may make it easier for the substantial numbers of overweight children who are rejected by their peer group to participate in after-school activities (which tend to promote physical activity) while decreasing their screen time.

The Nature of Best Friendships

Within children's social networks, best friends are especially important. Having a best friend may be of great psychological significance in terms of responses to stressful events, self-esteem, potential for depression (Buhrmester, 1990; Parker & Asher, 1993), and loneliness (Bagwell Newcomb, & Bukowski, 1998; Parker & Asher, 1993). Best friends are synonymous with social support for the overweight child for better or worse.

The available evidence suggests that physical activity and weight management views tend to be shared by one's close friends (Gibbs, 1986; Levine, Smolak, Moodey, Shuman, & Hessen, 1994; Paxton, Schutz, Wertheim, & Muir, 1999). Inactive teenagers tend to have friends who are also inactive (Allison, 1996; Allison & Adlaf, 1997).

However, best friends may be mobilized to support weight reduction and maintenance interventions. Peer participation in and encouragement of physical activity are related to both children's and adolescents' higher rates of physical activity (Brown, Frankel, & Fennell, 1989; Greendorfer & Lewko, 1978; Wold & Anderssen, 1992). One study of children 10 to 14 years old showed that support from friends was most strongly related to physical activity, and it was due mainly to friends being present during periods of physical activity (Duncan, Duncan, & Stryker, 2005). Further, social connectedness (i.e., being more satisfied with one's social network) among both children and adolescents is positively correlated with the amount of their physical activity (Page, Frey, Talbert, & Falk, 1992) and healthy dietary practices (Schwarzer, Jerusalem, & Kleine, 1990). Data from Epstein, Valoski, Wing, and McCurley (1994) indicate that after pediatric obesity treatment, those who had maintained weight loss at a 10-year follow-up are more likely to participate in physical activity with their college roommates and to receive reinforcement for physical activity from their roommates. Therefore consideration of the best friendship network must play a key role in weight maintenance strategies. This can be accomplished therapeutically through parent management of the overweight child's play dates.

Play dates are central to the formation of best friendships, and parents are especially important in promoting play dates. A series of studies (Ladd & Golter, 1988; Ladd & Hart, 1991; Ladd, Profilet, & Hart, 1992) suggest that parents who facilitate contact between their children and their peers have children with a wider range of playmates and more consistent play partners. Children of parents who arranged peer contacts had a greater number of playmates and more frequent play companions outside of school than children of parents who were less active in initiating peer contacts.

Thus structuring play dates may help the social context of overweight children in three ways: (1) by involving the parent in helping the child develop and maintain friendships that will increase self-esteem and body image, (2) by decreasing screen time and promoting enjoyable physical activities with close friends, and (3) by providing supportive company on the school playground. The parent and overweight child should collaborate in the search for potential friends with more physically active interests. Parents should supervise play dates in order to ensure the integration of physical activity on a play date and the reduction or elimination of screen time.

SOCIAL SKILLS TRAINING: CRITICAL FEATURES FOR EFFECTIVENESS

Clearly, overweight youth are at increased risk for specific psychosocial deficits. These deficits influence their psychological health and reduce their ability to lose weight or maintain weight loss. Thus it has become increasingly important to develop practical but innovative treatments for overweight that address these broad social influences.

Indeed, recent findings suggest that targeting social relationships has a positive impact on weight loss and maintenance of weight loss. For example, Epstein, Klein, and Wisniewski (1994) reported that obesity treatment effects were enhanced with family and friends' support for eating and physical activity Wing and Jeffrey (1999) reported that weight control participants who brought friends with them to behavioral treatment were more likely to maintain their weight loss at the 6-month follow-up. Similarly, social support predicts exercise adherence in adults (Oka, King, & Young, 1995). Friends can provide two types of social support: emotional support, such as making the physical activity experience more pleasant, and instrumental support, such as helping to ensure that the child engages in physical activity regularly.

Increasing physical activity and decreasing sedentary behavior are among the most promising interventions to reduce the prevalence of overweight (Anderson et al., 1998; Troiano & Flegal, 1998). Epstein, Paluch, Kilanowski, and Raynor (2004) reported that increasing physical activity was equivalent to decreasing targeted sedentary behaviors (including television viewing) in a 2-year follow-up of a weight control program for 8- to 12-year-old children. These authors point out however that "[c]hildren without access to enjoyable physical activities may not increase their activity when targeted sedentary behaviors are decreased, but rather switch over to other sedentary behaviors" (Epstein et al., 2004, p. 225). As will be shown below, the company of friends may make many types of physical activity more enjoyable.

Social Facilitation Maintenance Treatment

In one of the few intervention studies that considered social context in weight maintenance, Wilfley et al. (in press) treated a group of 150 overweight children who were 20% to 100% overweight with a 5-month behavioral family-based weight loss program. Following this initial phase of treatment, subjects were randomly assigned to one of three conditions: behavioral skills maintenance (BSM), social facilitation maintenance (SFM), and a no-treatment control condition (NTC). As highlighted

Table 7.1 Common and Distinctive Features of the BSM and SFM Treatments

Description of Maintenance Treatment	Behavior Skills Maintenance	Social Facilitation Maintenance
Weight maintenance skills training	X	
Parental positive reinforcement of meeting weekly eating and physical activity goals	X	
Motivation enhancement techniques	X	
Coping skills and relapse prevention training	X	
Engineering of supportive peer environment		X
Parental positive reinforcement of peer-related activities involving healthy eating and exercise		X
Promotion of positive body image		X
Development of effective coping responses for eating- and weight-related teasing and criticism		X
Written weight maintenance plan, consistent with treatment-specific foci, provided at termination	X	X

in Table 7.1, BSM utilizes cognitive behavioral strategies that emphasize self-regulation behaviors and relapse-prevention strategies relevant to weight-loss maintenance while SFM is based on broader ecological tenets that emphasize the importance of the developmentally relevant social contexts (e.g., peer support) for assisting with weight maintenance behaviors.

Of note, findings from Wilfley et al. (in press) indicate short-term effects for both BSM and SFM relative to a no-treatment control but long-term effects relative to no-treatment control for SFM only. Therefore targeting the social domain appears to influence the immediate and long-term maintenance of weight loss. Overall, the findings suggest that SFM may augment the effects of weight loss treatment in children such that long-term weight maintenance may be enhanced by attending to the increased role of social support in weight-maintenance (e.g., enlisting peer support for physical activity and healthy eating, coping with teasing). Findings also indicate that children were amenable to treatments with a social focus and that socially based weight maintenance treatments may target constructs uniquely relevant to the needs of overweight children. However, future studies examining the underlying mechanisms by which SFM achieved its effects are warranted.

Wilfley et al.'s (in press) findings also point to the need to examine the impact of children's level of social problems and/or social skills on successful weight maintenance. In their study, child baseline levels of social problems had significant long-term moderation effects on weight change findings over the two-year course of the study. Children who had a low level of social problems and received SFM had better maintenance of weight loss over the course of the 2-year study in comparison to all other children. Overweight children with functional best friend and peer networks may have been able to utilize interventions that focus on enhancing social support, whereas children with elevated social problems may first work on building these networks and may need additional social skills training so that social support treatments can enhance weight loss maintenance. The segment of overweight children with higher levels of social problems may benefit from a combination of social skills training to develop a supportive peer group and social facilitation techniques to mold this network to maintain weight reduction. Future directions to enhance the long-term efficacy of SFM for such children also include an examination of the role of treatment duration and/or dose as either longer treatment or more frequent treatment sessions may improve long-term maintenance of weight-loss in this subset of children.

Children's Friendship Training

As evidenced by the work from Wilfley et al. (in press), social skills interventions may hold great promise for overweight children. However, meta-analyses of the social skills intervention literature

Table 7.2 Social Skills Training Components, Their Functions, and Potential Application to Weight Control Maintenance

Social Skills Treatment Component	Social Function	Promoting Weight Maintenance	Preventing Weight Regain
Information exchange conversations	Finding common interests upon which to base friendships	Finding physical activities that others also like	Avoiding sedentary behaviors as play activities
Peer group entry	Meeting other children through play	Meeting children who play physically active games at the right skill level	Making friends with peers who provide positive support for physical activity
Effective responses to teasing	Improving reputation among peers	Increasing confidence in entering physical activities	Discriminating teasing from informational feedback
Structuring the play date	Making best friends	Verifying peer choices to promote physical activity; directly promoting physical activity	Parents monitor play date to ensure less sedentary behavior

(Quinn, Kavale, Mathur, Rutherford, & Forness, 1999) suggest that most social skills training programs do not produce large, socially meaningful, long-term, or generalized changes in social competence. In contrast, children's friendship training (CFT) (Frankel & Myatt, 2003) has been shown to be effective for children with autism-spectrum disorders (Frankel & Myatt, 2007), attention deficit hyperactivity disorder (ADHD), oppositional defiant disorder (Frankel, 2005; Frankel, Myatt, & Cantwell, 1995; Frankel, Myatt, Cantwell, & Feinberg, 1997), and children with fetal alcohol spectrum disorders (Frankel, Paley, Marquart, & O'Connor, 2006; O'Connor et al., 2006). Key features of CFT that differentiate it from most social skills programs are (1) incorporating parents as an integral part of the intervention, (2) including homework assignments as part of the treatment sessions, (3) teaching socially valid skills, and (4) structuring play dates to be maximally effective in promoting best friendships. Each of these features is discussed with specific relevance to overweight children who are rejected by peers. Table 7.2 lists the key components of CFT and their potential application to weight control maintenance. A comprehensive description of the manualized intervention can be found in Frankel and Myatt (2003).

Incorporating Parents as an Integral Part of the Intervention. In CFT, children and parents attend separate, but concurrent sessions that are 60 minutes in length and meet weekly for 12 weeks. Parents are assigned homework to do with their child between sessions and are fully informed about the purpose and goals of the homework. Discussion of potential barriers to implementation is encouraged when the homework is presented. Homework assigned in the previous session is first on the agenda for the next session, again focusing on how the homework was accomplished and problem solving with parents over any additional barriers to implementation.

Including Homework Assignments as Part of Treatment Sessions
Six features of the intervention facilitate the performance of the homework: (1) The date and time and other party to the assignment is prearranged between the parent and child before they leave the session, (2) The parent's role is clearly delineated and described in handouts, (3) Children and parents are accountable for their parts of the homework assignments, since they recount the results of the assignment at the beginning of the next session, (4) The assignments are easier at first and gradually become more difficult, (5) High compliance for the easier assignments, together with pressure from the group, sets an expectation for homework compliance.

Teaching Socially Valid Skills

Socially valid skills are defined as those that discriminate socially successful from unsuccessful children. Teaching these skills facilitates generalization by helping children to attend to key situations in their social world and noticing that when they perform these skills they are more successful. Critical child and parent behaviors that have been shown to discriminate accepted children from rejected children include:

1. Information exchange with peers, which leads to common-ground activities (Black & Hazen, 1990; Coie & Kupersmidt, 1983; Dodge, 1983; Garvey, 1984). Socially successful children are able to find others who have interests similar to theirs. They do this through their initial conversations with peers where they discuss likes and dislikes. In the case of overweight children, these conversations should also include preferences of physical activities. When a child finds another who likes the same activities then they should do the activity together on a more regular and frequent basis.

2. Peer entry into a group of children already at play (Gelb & Jacobson, 1988). Entry into a group of children already at play is one of the most common and easiest ways for young children to make new friends. The initial stage is the most important, as it involves observing the other children at play and judging whether they are nice children, who may be fun to play with, and who are at the same skill level as the child thinking about joining them. It is just as important for the overweight child to walk away from peers who don't fit these criteria as to join those who do. The overweight child may attempt to join others at play who are significantly faster and more proficient at sports and be turned down because of this. Alternatively, they may be discouraged from joining any peers, not knowing whom to select. Parents should encourage children to look for others who match their physical competence.

3. Successful responses to teasing which employ humor or assertion (Kochenderfer & Ladd, 1997; Perry, Williard, & Perry, 1990). In teaching effective responses to teasing, it is important for the child to differentiate teasing from informational feedback. For instance, the statement "you stink" may be a tease if it has no basis in reality (and intended only to get the victim upset), or it may indicate poor personal hygiene or entry into the wrong game where the peers are much more competent than the overweight child. Parents must help the overweight child deal with teasing by helping them practice humorous comebacks to teases, remediate the poor personal hygiene, or select peers at the same competence level. Teaching effective responses to teasing may inoculate the overweight child so that he or she may persist in the face of teasing.

Structuring Play Dates

The goal of avoiding conflict with best friends discriminates children with more versus fewer best friends (Fonzi, Schneider, Tani, & Tomada, 1997; Rose & Asher, 1999). Parents are integral to implementing this skill (Frankel, 1996). Parents should not be a formal part of the play date, but should intervene in conflicts (Lollis & Ross, 1987, cited in Ladd, 1992).

Immediately before the time of the play date, the parent's jobs are to remind the child of the rules of a good host and to exclude media viewing (watching television, playing electronic games, and computers) and encourage a mix of activities that includes physical activity. Parent monitoring of play dates ensures that playmates have been selected well and that the play date itself involves an adequate amount of physical activity and minimal screen time.

CONCLUSION

Overweight youth are more likely to encounter a constellation of factors, such as teasing, peer rejection, and low support for physical activity, that place them at increased risk for problems in social relationships. These factors then lead to weight gain or reduce the efficacy of weight loss treatment. Social problems may contribute to weight gain and decrease exposure to physical activity opportunities such that a reciprocal cycle of weight gain and social problems is set in motion. Clearly, continued examination of the social development and problems associated with this population is merited.

In addition, the application of ecological treatment approaches to childhood overweight appears a relevant and warranted area for future research. Socially based treatments for overweight appear appropriate for a range of children. Children with low levels of social problems appear to benefit from learning how to apply specific social skills to weight maintenance (e.g., making play dates more physically active) (Wilfley et al., in press), while children with higher levels of social problems may profit from more general social skills training that over time teaches children to apply social skills to achieve weight-loss maintenance. Although additional research is needed to elaborate on the promise of social skills training in the treatment of childhood overweight, such innovative treatments are needed to address the rising rates of obesity in children.

REFERENCES

Allison, K. R. (1996). Predictors of inactivity: an analysis of the Ontario Health Survey. *Canadian Journal of Public Health, 87,* 354–358.

Allison, K. R., & Adlaf, E. M. (1997). Age and sex differences in physical inactivity among Ontario teenagers. *Canadian Journal of Public Health, 88,* 177–180.

Andersen, R., Crespo, C., Bartlett, S., Cheskin, L., & Pratt, M. (1998). Relationship of physical activity and TV watching with body weight and level of fatness among children: results from the Third National Health and Nutrition Examination Survey. *JAMA, 279,* 938–942.

Bagwell, C. L., Newcomb, A. F., & Bukowski, W. M. (1998). Preadolescent friendship and peer rejection as predictors of adult adjustment. *Child Development, 69,* 140–153.

Banis, H. T., Varni, J. W., Wallander, J. L., Korsch, B. M., Jay, S. M., et al. (1988). Psychological and social adjustment of obese children and their families. *Child: Care, Health, and Development, 14*(3), 157–173.

Black, B., & Hazen, N. L. (1990). Social status and patterns of communication in acquainted and unacquainted preschool children. *Developmental Psychology, 26,* 379–387.

Brown, B. A., Frankel, B. G., & Fennell, M. P. (1989). Hugs or shrugs: parental and peer influence on continuity of involvement in sport by female adolescents. *Sex Roles, 20*(7–8), 397–412.

Buhrmester, D. (1990). Intimacy of friendship, interpersonal competence, and adjustment during preadolescence and adolescence. *Child Development, 6,* 1101–1111.

Burrows, A., & Cooper, M. (2002).Possible risk factors in the development of eating disorders in overweight pre-adolescent girls. *International Journal of Obesity and Related Metabolic Disorders, 26*(9), 1268–1273.

Coie, J. D., & Kupersmidt, J. B. (1983). A behavioral analysis of emerging social status. *Child Development, 54,* 1400–1416.

Crespo, C. J., Smit, E., Troyano, R. P., Bartlet, S. J., Macera, C. A., & Andersen, R. E. (2001). Television watching, energy intake, and obesity in US children: results from the Third National Health and Nutrition Examination Survey, 1988–1994. *Archives of Pediatric and Adolescent Medicine, 155,* 360–365.

Davison, K. K., & Birch, L. L. (2002). Processes linking weight status and self-concept among girls from ages 5 to 7 years. *Developmental Psychology, 38,* 735–758.

Dietz, W. H., & Gortmaker, S. L. (2001). Preventing obesity in children and adolescents. *Annual Review of Public Health, 22,* 337–353.

Dodge, K. A. (1983). Behavioral antecedents of peer social rejection and isolation. *Child Development, 54,* 1386–1399.

Duncan, S. C., Duncan, T. E., & Stryker, L. A. (2005). Sources and types of social support in youth physical activity. *Health Psychology, 24,* 3–10.

East, P. L., & Rook, K. S. (1992). Compensatory patterns of support among children's peer relationships: a test using school friends, nonschool friends, and siblings. *Developmental Psychology, 28,* 163–172.

Elkins, W. L., Cohen, D. A., Koralewicz, L. M., & Taylor, S. N. (2004). After school activities overweight, and obesity among inner city youth. *Journal of Adolescence, 27,* 181–189.

Epstein, L. H., Klein, K. R., & Wisniewski, L. (1994). Child and parent factors that influence psychological problems in obese children. *International Journal of Eating Disorders, 15,* 151–158.

Epstein, L. H., Myers, M. D., & Anderson, K. (1996). The association of maternal psychopathology and family socioeconomic status with psychological problems in obese children. *Obesity Research, 4,* 65–74.

Epstein, L. H., Paluch, R. A., Kilanowski, C. K., & Raynor, H. A. (2004). The effect of reinforcement or stimulus control to reduce sedentary behavior in the treatment of pediatric obesity. *Health Psychology, 23,* 371–380.

Epstein, L. H., Valoski, A. M., Wing, R. R., & McCurley, J. J. (1994). Ten-year outcomes of behavioral family-based treatment of childhood obesity. *Health Psychology, 13,* 373–383.

Epstein, L. H., Wisniewski, L., & Weng, R. (1994). Child and parent psychological problems influence child weight control. *Obesity Research, 2,* 509–515.

Fonzi, A., Schneider, B. H., Tani, F., & Tomada, G. (1997). Predicting children's friendship status from their dyadic interaction in structured situations of potential conflict. *Child Development, 68,* 496–506.

Frankel, F. (1996). *Good friends are hard to find: help your child find, make, and keep friends.* Los Angeles: Perspective Publishing.

Frankel, F. (2005). Parent-assisted children's friendship training. In E. D. Hibbs & P. S. Jensen (Eds.), *Psychosocial treatments for child and adolescent disorders: empirically based approaches* (2nd ed.) (pp. 693–715). Washington, D.C.: American Psychological Association.

Frankel, F., & Myatt, R. (2003). *Children's friendship training.* New York: Brunner-Routledge.

Frankel, F., & Myatt, R. (2007). Parent-assisted friendship training for children with autism spectrum disorders: Effects associated with psychotropic medication. *Child Psychiatry and Human Development, 4,* 337–346.

Frankel, F., Myatt, R., & Cantwell, D. P. (1995). Training outpatient boys to conform with the social ecology of popular peers: effects on parent and teacher ratings. *Journal of Clinical Child Psychology, 24,* 300–310.

Frankel, F., Myatt, R., Cantwell, D. P., & Feinberg, D. T. (1997). Parent assisted children's social skills training: effects on children with and without attention-deficit hyperactivity disorder. *Journal of the Academy of Child and Adolescent Psychiatry, 36,* 1056–1064.

Frankel, F., Paley, B., Marquart, R., & O'Connor, M. J. (2006). Stimulants, neuroleptics and children's friendship training in children with fetal alcohol spectrum disorders. *Journal of Child and Adolescent Psychopharmacology, 16,* 777–789.

Garvey, C. (1984). *Children's talk.* Cambridge, MA: Harvard University Press.

Gelb, R., & Jacobson, J. L. (1988). Popular and unpopular children's interactions during cooperative and competitive peer group activities. *Journal of Abnormal Child Psychology, 16,* 247–261.

Gibbs, R. E. (1986). Social factors in exaggerating eating behavior among high school students. *International Journal of Eating Disorders, 5,* 1103–1107.

Goldfield, A., & Chrisler, J. C. (1995). Body stereotyping and stigmatization of obese persons by first graders. *Perceptual and Motor Skills, 81,* 909–910.

Gortmaker, S., Must, A., Sobol, A., Peterson, K. I., Colditz, G., & Dietz, W. (1996). TV viewing as a cause of increasing obesity among children in the United States, 1986–1990. *Archives of Pediatric and Adolescent Medicine, 150,* 356–362.

Greendorfer, S. L., & Lewko, J. H. (1978). Role of family members in sport socialization of children. *Research Quarterly, 49*(2), 146–152.

Haines, J., & Neumark-Sztainer, D. (2006). Prevention of obesity and eating disorders: a consideration of shared risk factors. *Health Education Research, 21,* 770–782.

Hayden-Wade, H. A., Stein, R. I., Ghaderi, A., Saelens, B. E., Zabinski, M. F., & Wilfley, D. E. (2005). Prevalence, characteristics, and correlates of teasing experiences among overweight children vs. non-overweight peers. *Obesity Research, 13,* 1381–1392.

Israel, A. C., & Shapiro, L. S. (1985). Behavior problems of obese children enrolling in a weight reduction program. *Journal of Pediatric Psychology, 10*(4), 449–460.

Janssen, I., Craig, W. M., Boyce, W. F., & Pickett, W. (2004). Associations between overweight and obesity with bullying behaviors in school-aged children. *Pediatrics, 113*(4), 1187–1194.

Kimm, S. Y., Barton, B. A., Berhane, K., Ross, J. W., Payne, G. H., & Schreiber, G. B. (1997). Self-esteem and adiposity in black and white girls: the NHLBI Growth and Health Study. *Annals of Epidemiology, 7,* 550–560.

Kochenderfer, B. J., & Ladd, G. W. (1997). Victimized children's responses to peers' aggression: behaviors associated with reduced versus continued victimization. *Development and Psychopathology, 9,* 59–73.

Kolotkin, R. L., Zeller, M., Modi, A. C., Samsa, G. P., Quinlan, N. P., Yanovski, J. A., Bell, S. K., Maahs, D. M., de Serna, D. G., & Roehrig, H. R. (2006). Assessing weight-related quality of life in adolescents. *Obesity, 14,* 448–457.

Koplan, J. P., Liverman, C. T., & Kraak, V. A. (Eds.). (2005). *Preventing childhood obesity: health in the balance.* Washington, D.C.: National Academies Press. Available at www.nap.edu/catalog/11015.html.

Ladd, G. W. (1992). Themes and theories: perspectives on processes in family-peer relationships. In R. D. Parke & G. W. Ladd (Eds.), *Family-peer relationships: modes of linkages* (pp. 3–34). Hillsdale, NJ: Lawrence Erlbaum.

Ladd, G. W., & Golter, B. S. (1988). Parents' management of preschoolers peer relations: Is it related to children's social competence? *Developmental Psychology, 24,* 109–117.

Ladd, G. W., & Hart, C. H. (1991). Parents' management of peer relations: patterns associated with social competence. Paper presented at the 11th meeting of the International Society of Behavioral Development, Minneapolis, MN.

Ladd, G. W., Profilet, S. M., & Hart, C. H. (1992). Parents' management of children's peer relations: facilitating and supervising children's activities in the peer culture. In R. D. Parke & G. W. Ladd (Eds.), *Family-peer relationships: modes of linkages* (pp. 215–253). Hillsdale, NJ: Lawrence Erlbaum.

Latner, J. D., & Stunkard, A. J. (2003). Getting worse: the stigmatization of obese children. *Obesity Research, 11,* 452–456.

Levine, M. P., Smolak, L., Moodey, A. F., Shuman, M. D., & Hessen, L. D. (1994). Normative developmental challenges and dieting and eating disturbances among middle school girls. *International Journal of Eating Disorders, 15,* 11–20.

Mahoney, J. L., Lord, H., & Carryl, E. (2005). Afterschool program participation and the development of child obesity and peer acceptance. *Applied Developmental Science, 9,* 202–215.

Manus, H. E., & Killeen, M. R. (1995). Maintenance of self-esteem by obese children. *Journal of Child and Adolescent Psychiatric Nursing, 8,* 17–27.

Myers, M. D., Raynor, H. A., & Epstein, L. H. (1998). Predictors of child psychological changes during family-based treatment for obesity. *Archives of Pediatric and Adolescent Medicine, 152*(9), 855–861.

Neumark-Sztainer, D., Falkner, N., Story, M., Perry, C., Hannan, P. J., & Mulert, S. (2002). Weight-teasing among adolescents: correlations with weight status and disordered eating behaviors. *International Journal of Obesity and Related Metabolic Disorders, 26,* 123–131.

Neumark-Sztainer, D., Paxton, S. J., Hannan, P. J., Haines, J., & Story, M. (2006). Does body satisfaction matter? Five-year longitudinal associations between body satisfaction and health behaviors in adolescent females and males. *Journal of Adolescent Health, 39,* 244–251.

O'Connor, M. J., Frankel, F., Paley, B., Schonfeld, A. M., Carpenter, E. M., Laugeson, E. A., & Marquardt, R. (2006). A controlled social skills training for children with fetal alcohol spectrum disorders. *Journal of Consulting and Clinical Psychology, 74,* 639–648.

Oka, R. K., King, A. C., & Young, D. R. (1995). Sources of social support as predictors of exercise adherence in women and men ages 50 to 65 years. *Women's Health, 1,* 161–175.

Page, R. M., Frey, J., Talbert, R., & Falk, C. (1992). Children's feelings of loneliness and social dissatisfaction: relationship to measures of physical fitness and activity. *Journal of Teaching in Physical Education, 11,* 211–219.

Parker, J. G., & Asher, S. R. (1993). Friendship and friendship quality in middle childhood: links with peer group acceptance and feelings of loneliness and social dissatisfaction. *Developmental Psychology, 29,* 611–621.

Paxton, S. J., Schutz, H. K., Wertheim, E. H., & Muir, S. L. (1999). Friendship clique and peer influences on body image concerns, dietary restraint, extreme weight-loss behaviors, and binge eating in adolescent girls. *Journal of Abnormal Behavior, 108,* 255–266.

Perry, D. G., Williard, J. C., & Perry, L. C. (1990). Peer perceptions of the consequences that victimized children provide aggressors. *Child Development, 61,* 1310–1325.

Phillips, R. G., & Hill A. J. (1997). Fat, plain, but not friendless: Self-esteem and peer acceptance of obese pre-adolescent girls. *International Journal of Obesity and Related Metabolic Disorders*, *22*(4), 287–293.

Pietrobelli, A., Leone, M. A., Heymsfield, S. B., & Faith, M. S. (1998). *Association of physical-activity-teasing with reported activity and activity attitudes in pediatric sample.* Paper presented at the Eighth International Congress on Obesity, Paris, France.

Quinn, M. M., Kavale, K. A., Mathur, S. R., Rutherford, R. B., Jr., & Forness, S. R. (1999). A meta-analysis of social skill interventions for students with emotional or behavioral disorders. *Journal of Emotional and Behavioral Disorders, 7,* 54–64.

Robinson, T. N. (1999). Reducing children's television viewing to prevent obesity: a randomized controlled trial. *JAMA, 282,* 1561–1567.

Rose, A. J., & Asher, S. R. (1999). Children's goals and strategies in response to conflicts within a friendship. *Developmental Psychology, 35,* 69–79.

Saelens, B. E., Sallis, J. F., Nader, P. R., Broyles, S. L., Berry, C. C., & Taras, H. L. (2002). Home environmental influences on children's television watching from early to middle childhood. *Journal of Developmental and Behavioral Pediatrics, 23,* 127–132.

Schwarzer, R., Jerusalem, M., & Kleine, D. (1990). Predicting adolescent health complaints by personality and behaviors. *Psychology and Health, 4,* 233–244.

Schwimmer, J. B., Burwinkle, T. M., & Varni, J. W. (2003). Health-related quality of life of severely obese children and adolescents. *JAMA, 289,* 1813–1819.

Shapiro, J. P., Baumeister, R. E., & Kessler, J. W. (1991). A three-component model of children's teasing: aggression, humor, and ambiguity. *Journal of Social & Clinical Psychology, 10,* 459–472.

Staffieri, J. R. (1967). A study of social stereotype of body image in children. *Journal of Personality and Social Psychology, 7,* 101–104.

Striegel-Moore, R. H., Schreiber, G. B., Pike, K. M., Wilfley, D. E., & Rodin, J. (1995). Drive for thinness in black and white preadolescent girls. *International Journal of Eating Disorders, 18,* 59–69.

Troiano, R. P., & Flegal, K. M. (1998). Overweight children and adolescents: description, epidemiology, and demographics. *Pediatrics, 101*(suppl.), 497-504.

Wilfley, D. E., Grilo, C. M., & Brownell, K. D. (1994). Exercise and regulation of body weight. In M. M. Shangold (Ed.), *Women and exercise: physiology and sports medicine* (pp. 27–59). Philadelphia: F. A. Davis.

Wilfley, D. E., Stein, R. I., Saelens B. E., Mockus, D. S, Matt G. E., Hayden-Wade, H. A., Welch, R. R., Schectman, K. B., Thompson, P. A., Epstein, L. H. (in press). The efficacy of maintenance treatment approaches for childhood overweight. *Journal of the American Medical Association.*

Wing, R. R., & Jeffrey, R. W. (1999). Benefits of recruiting participants with friends and increasing social support for weight loss and maintenance. *Journal of Consulting and Clinical Psychology, 67,* 132–138.

Wold, B., & Anderssen, N. (1992). Health promotion aspects of family and peer influences on sport participation. *International Journal of Sport Psychology, 23,* 343–359.

Zabinski, M. F., Saelens, B. E., Stein, R. I., Hayden-Wade, H. A., & Wilfley, D. E. (2003). Overweight children's barriers to and support for physical activity. *Obesity Research, 11,* 238–246.

Zeller, M. H., Saelens, B. E., Roehrig, H., Kirk, S., & Daniels, S. R. (2004). Psychological adjustment of obese youth presenting for weight management treatment. *Obesity Research, 12,* 1576–1586.

8

Parent Feeding Practices and Child Overweight

LISA K. DIEWALD AND MYLES S. FAITH

INTRODUCTION AND CONCEPTUAL MODEL

The dramatic and pervasive increase in childhood overweight in the United States represents a daunting public health concern of impressive magnitude and scope. Currently 10% of 2- to 5-year-old children in the United States and 15% of children ages 6 to 19 years are overweight, representing a doubling over the past 30 years (Collins, Johnson, & Krebs, 2004; Hedley et al., 2004). This trend is especially challenging given the high likelihood of childhood overweight persisting into adulthood and the associated medical, psychological, social, and economic implications (Guo & Chumlea, 1999; Must et al., 1999). In one study, infants who were overweight during the first year of life (greater than the 95th percentile of weight for length) were three times more likely to be overweight during the preschool years compared to children who were not overweight as infants (Mei, Grummer-Strwan, & Scanlon, 2003). A child who is overweight at 3 to 6 years of age has a 50% chance of being an obese adult, and the risk increases to 80% if a child remains overweight at age 15 to 17 years (Fox, Pac, Devaney, & Jankowski, 2004; Whitaker, Wright, Pepe, Seidel, & Dietz, 1997).

This global childhood overweight epidemic requires novel prevention and treatment interventions, yet the complex nature of this public health crisis makes management difficult for individuals and families. The ongoing interplay of genetic, environmental, and familial influences represents a challenge in identifying causal mechanisms for childhood obesity and subsequently in prescribing effective prevention and treatment. Current research suggests that obesity occurs due to a complex pattern of genetic and environmental interactions, with heritability estimates as high as 90% in some studies (Faith et al., 1999; Jacobson & Rowe, 1998; Maes, Neale, & Eaves, 1997). Despite the important role of genetics, children are living in an ever-changing environment in which food is plentiful and readily available, portions are large, and family meal time is limited. These factors make it difficult for many parents to recognize and implement healthy feeding strategies with their children, which can make prevention difficult. Despite the obstacles, given the extensive parent-child feeding interactions that occur during the early years of life, it is important to identify how the family home environment and parent feeding practices can impact on child overweight.

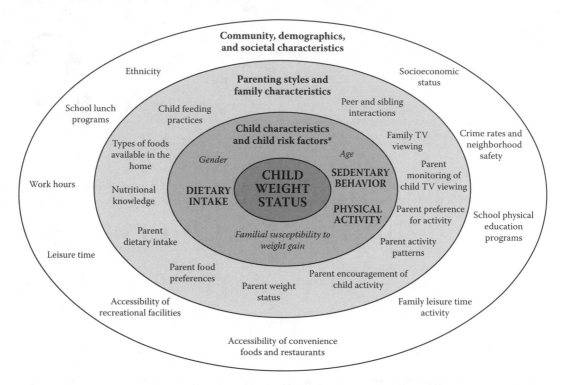

Figure 8.1 Ecological model of predictors of childhood overweight. Child risk factors (shown in uppercase lettering) refer to child behaviors associated with the development of overweight. Characteristics of the child (shown in italic lettering) interact with child risk factors and contextual factors to influence the development of overweight. (Used by permission. Source: Davison, K. K., & Birch, L. L. (2001). Childhood overweight: a contextual model and recommendations for future research. *Obesity Reviews*, 2, 159–171.)

According to Davison and Birch (2001), the ecological systems theory may effectively summarize the many influences that shape the development of overweight (Davison & Birch, 2001). Using this theory, childhood overweight occurs as a result of a host of variables that exert varying levels of influence on the child's eating and activity habits during different periods of life (see Figure 8.1). This multilevel system illustrates that a child's own characteristics, such as dietary intake, inactivity patterns, and predisposition to weight gain, significantly affect obesity risk. Community and societal factors, represented by the outermost concentric circle, influence the young child as well. Despite these broader social factors, the young child is embedded within the family system and therefore is dependent upon parental control in multiple areas, including food access and selections, and intergenerational transmission of attitudes, knowledge, and beliefs about food and physical activity. The family environment is proposed to exert the strongest impact on the young child's developing dietary habits and lifestyle practices, be bidirectional in nature (with parents and children influencing each other mutually), and to play an early and ongoing role in establishing a child's risk of overweight (Davison & Birch, 2001; Stang, Rehorst, & Golicic, 2004).

PARENTAL OBESITY AND RISK OF CHILD OVERWEIGHT

While obesity risk in children is substantially increased when at least one parent is obese, isolating the cause for this familial aggregation is difficult (Whitaker et al., 1997). Parental obesity more than doubles the risk of adult obesity among both obese and nonobese children under the age of 10 years. The risk of obesity in 10- to 14-year-olds with at least one obese parent is 79%, as compared to only 8% for 1- to 2-year-olds with no obese parents. Before age 3 years, parental obesity is a stronger predictor for adult obesity than the child's weight status, highlighting the strong genetic link (Whitaker et al., 1997). Other studies confirm that parental overweight is the most potent indicator of a child's future obesity risk (Agras, Hammer, McNicholas, & Kramer, 2004; Agras et al., 1987). This strong correlation between parental obesity status and child obesity risk may be due to parental eating behaviors, as well as feeding styles and practices that impact on child eating and body weight (Wardle et al., 2002). The early family environment can contribute to eating patterns that promote childhood overweight, as discussed in the following sections.

EATING PATTERN DEVELOPMENT

During infancy, parents are the primary gatekeeper for food access, selection, and availability, and also serve as a child's first models and instructors on eating and activity behaviors. Dietary and physical activity patterns develop within the context of the family environment and thus parent-child feeding interactions can have a significant impact on future dietary and lifestyle practices (Zeller & Stephen, 2004). In most cases, the mother assumes the primary responsibility for feeding, beginning at birth and continuing through the early school years. These early interactions may have a dramatic effect on long-term eating patterns, potentially impacting a child's preferences at especially sensitive and formative periods of life.

Even very early dietary experiences and interactions surrounding food appear to shape a child's later eating patterns and affirm the importance of healthy parental feeding practices in molding early eating habits. For example, infants and young children tend to be "neophobic," that is, they easily reject new foods (Birch & Marlin, 1982; Birch, McPhee, Shoba, Pirok, & Steinberg, 1987). Yet often when offered new foods, toddlers are more likely to accept the food when it is offered by a parent rather than a stranger (Harper & Sanders, 1975). Repeated exposure to new foods by parents is often necessary to promote acceptance in children, with an estimated 5 to 10 exposures needed before a child will accept the food (Birch et al., 1987; Birch & Fisher, 1998; Sullivan & Birch, 1994). Other research has demonstrated that the earliest parental feeding practice, breast-feeding, is associated with positive feeding outcomes, such as delayed introduction of solid foods, greater fruit intake, and avoidance of sugar-sweetened beverages, practices all consistent with overweight prevention (Hendricks, Briefel, Novak, & Ziegler, 2006). Moreover, breast-fed infants have been shown to be more tolerant and accepting of new foods than formula-fed infants (Capretta, Petersik, & Steward, 1975; Sullivan & Birch, 1994). Not all data support these conclusions, however. Parsons, Power, Logan, and Summerbell (1999) found no consistent association between the method of feeding, length of breast-feeding, solid food introduction, and early calorie intake and subsequent obesity risk up to 7 years of age. In sum, while results are sometimes inconsistent, the current body of evidence suggests that, even early in life, parents play a large role in eating pattern development.

PARENTS AS ROLE MODELS

Observational learning, or role modeling, can have a powerful effect on the development of childhood food preferences and selections. Research demonstrates a reliable association between the eating habits of children and eating habits of parents, suggesting the influence of parental role modeling (Birch & Fisher, 1998). For instance, the degree to which fruits and vegetables are made accessible to children may have a significant impact on shaping childhood preferences (Cullen et al., 2003). Parents consuming a diet rich in fruits and vegetables and low in fat had daughters who exhibited similar dietary patterns (Fisher, Mitchell, Smiciklas-Wright, & Birch, 2002). Alternatively, poor parental modeling may have detrimental effects on children's early dietary habits. In a study of 106 children whose parents consumed a diet rich in saturated fat, the children also developed a high fat diet over time (Oliveria et al, 1992). Moreover, mothers' soft drink and milk consumption predicted daughters' intake of these beverages (Birch & Davison, 2001). Repeated exposure by parents/caregivers to energy-dense foods may strengthen a child's preference for these foods, since consumption of high fat foods may be associated with satiety prompts (Kern, McPhee, Fisher, Johnson, & Birch, 1993; Johnson, McPhee, & Birch, 1993; Sclafani, 1995). Role modeling of a healthy diet is a key component of family behavior modification for childhood obesity. When a pleasant meal environment, shared family meals, and adult role modeling occurred in concert with adequate access to nutritional foods, overweight children's dietary quality was improved (Golan & Grow, 2004; Gillman, Rifas-Shiman, & Frazier, 2000; Stanek, Abbott, & Cramer, 1990; Swarr & Richards, 1996). Parents modeling healthier eating habits often adopt improved dietary habits as well (Haire-Joshu & Nanney, 2002; Tibbs, Haire-Joshu, & Schechtman, 2001).

The nature and extent of parental control during childhood may vary, with older children receiving less direct efforts by parents to influence their eating habits than younger children. Still, it remains clear that parents can exert a significant influence on a child's dietary practices as well as lifestyle-related issues such as physical activity, sedentary habits, and overall body satisfaction through role modeling (Spruijt-Metz, Li, Cohen, Birch, & Goran, 2006).

PARENTAL FEEDING PRACTICES AND CHILD SELF-REGULATION OF ENERGY INTAKE

Children seem to be born with an ability to self-regulate intake to meet energy requirements for healthy growth (Haire-Joshu & Nanney, 2002; Birch, 1999). Infants as young as 6 weeks of age have demonstrated the ability to regulate energy intake independent of parental control (Forman, 1993). As children develop, however, this natural ability to self-regulate may be diminished in some children as internal controls for hunger and satiety are replaced with external cues and prompts (Haire-Joshu & Nanney, 2002; Birch, Johnson, Peterson, & Schulte, 1991). Rolls, Engell, and Birch (2000) discovered that 2- to 3-year-old children consumed the same quantity of a main course item regardless of whether the portion size was regular or large, yet when 4- to 6-year-olds were offered the same choices, they consumed an average of 60% more when the portion size was doubled. The gradual loss of the natural self-regulatory mechanisms guiding a child's energy intake may promote an increase in a child's obesity risk over time, yet the factors precipitating this disruption are not well understood and require additional investigation.

Parent-child communications regarding food selection, preferences, and consumption are instrumental in molding eating patterns in children (Haire-Joshu & Nanney, 2002; Johnson & Birch, 1994). Well-meaning parents may utilize a number of different feeding strategies in an effort promote healthy eating patterns in their children, including modulating food selections, portion sizes, meal timing, frequency, and the social context in which foods are served and consumed (Birch, Fisher, & Davison, 2003). They may knowingly or unknowingly incorporate practices such as instrumental feeding (the use of food as a reward or punishment), emotional feeding (the use of food to calm an infant or child), or restrictive feeding, provide social interactions during feeding, encourage foods they perceive as "healthy," and otherwise control the feeding experience (Faith & Kerns, 2005). These feeding practices may have unintended and counterproductive effects on the child's long-term eating habits and weight status by interfering with self-regulation of energy intake, increasing the desire for "forbidden" foods, or promoting disinhibited eating or eating in the absence of hunger (Fisher & Birch, 2002; Fisher & Birch, 1999).

One study examined changes in child food preferences subsequent to imposing restrictions on their food choices and found that 40% of parents believed that eliminating or forbidding "junk" foods would result in a lessened preference for that food (Casey & Rozin, 1989). However, some research has suggested the opposite effect. Restrictive feeding practices, in which energy-dense foods are limited or eliminated in a child's diet, were associated with an increased preference for and overconsumption of those foods when they are freely accessible to the child (Birch, Zimmerman, & Hind, 1980; Fisher & Birch, 1999; Hill & Peters, 1998). This practice may be especially detrimental to girls (Johnson & Birch, 1994). Dietary restraint employed with 5- to 7-year-old girls has been associated with an increase in eating in the absence of hunger, negative self-evaluations, restrained eating, lower self-concept, and overweight in young girls (Carper, Orlet Fisher, & Birch, 2000; Davison & Krahnstoever, 2001; Fisher & Birch, 2000; Spruijt-Metz et al., 2002). In a study of girls 5 to 9 years of age, girls with mothers reporting the highest level of maternal dietary restriction at age 5 years experienced the greatest degree of eating in the absence of hunger (EAH) at 9 years of age when compared with girls whose mothers reported a lower level of restriction. All girls who were overweight or normal weight at baseline experienced increases in EAH over time; however, those girls who were the most overweight at the start of the study experienced the greatest levels of overeating by 9 years of age (Fisher & Birch, 2002).

Despite some inconclusive findings, parent feeding practices that impose excessive restrictions on child food choices and focus on external cues may disrupt the natural self-regulatory mechanisms. This may diminish the child's ability to adjust energy intake to meet needs, and as reviewed in the next section, may impact on child body weight (Birch, Fisher, & Davison, 2003; Harper & Sanders, 1975).

PARENTAL RESTRICTION AND CHILD WEIGHT

While parenting feeding practices may alter a child's preferences and intake, research on the effects of these practices on weight status is inconclusive. In one review of all feeding domains, the strongest correlate of child weight status was feeding restriction, although results were inconsistent (Faith et al., 2004). In a study of 57 families, parental overcontrol of a child's intake was associated with excess child weight gain, but only among children who were born at risk for overweight (Faith et al., 2004). Restriction or excessive feeding control may hamper the development of healthy eating habits, condition the child to respond to external cues, and strengthen the child's preferences for restricted foods (Faith & Kerns, 2005). These findings suggest that restrictive feeding practices that are maintained over an extended period of time may lead to excess child weight gain, triggering an increase in parental concern and maintenance of restrictive feeding practices, as illustrated in Figure 8.2.

Parental restriction has been associated with excess weight gain in infants as young as 6 months, suggesting that even very early control-based feeding practices may be counterproductive. Farrow and Blissett (2006) reported further rapid weight gain in infants already showing early rapid weight gain and further low weight gain in infants already showing early slow weight gain among mothers practicing restrictive feeding (Farrow & Blissett, 2006). In another multiethnic cohort, rapid infant weight gain was associated with increased risk of child overweight at 4 years of age, independent of potential confounders such as socioeconomic status, highlighting the importance of early identification and correction of problematic parental feeding strategies (Dennison, Edmunds, Stratton, & Pruzek, 2006).

Despite these findings, results are not conclusive, as some studies have failed to find an association between parental feeding restriction and child weight status. Robinson, Kiernan, Matheson, and Haydel (2001) conducted a population-based study of 792 ethnically diverse third graders and found only a weak association between parental control and weight, and that was only observed in girls (Robinson, Kiernan, Matheson, & Haydel, 2001). Parental control was not associated with overweight in boys, and those parents reporting a higher degree of control had children with less overweight (Baughcum et al., 2001). While unexpected, these results may reflect in part the diminishing parental control over food consumption and choices during the school-age years relative to preschool years. Among another diverse group of 1000 mothers of infants and preschoolers, no specific parental feeding behaviors were associated with an increase in risk of childhood overweight.

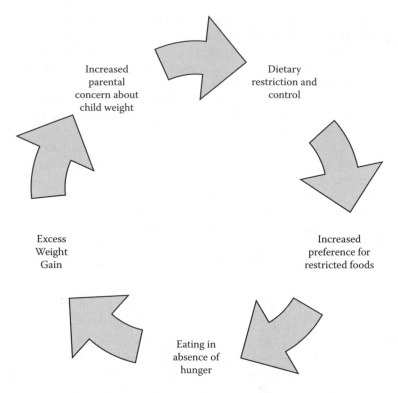

Figure 8.2 Proposed relationship between parental food restriction and excess child weight gain.

In a study comparing parenting practices within 214 families of same-sex twins (half with parental obesity and half without), parents differed on the level of dietary control exerted on their children. In contrast to other studies, obese parents were more likely to impose less rather than more control over the feeding process. These findings suggest that a lack of parental control over food intake, rather than restriction, may be a contributing factor in the weight status of some children (Wardle et al., 2002). These findings underscore the importance of exercising caution in making assumptions regarding parental restriction and causal effects on child weight status.

RELATIONSHIP BETWEEN PARENTAL PERCEPTIONS AND BELIEFS ABOUT CHILD WEIGHT STATUS AND PARENTAL FEEDING STYLES

Costanzo and Woody (1985) introduced the principle of "domain-specific parenting," proposing that parenting practices depend upon parental concerns about and perceptions of child weight status and obesity risk (Costanzo & Woody, 1985). That is, parental feeding practices are partially elicited by child weight status and adiposity, a finding that has been supported in the literature (Faith & Kerns, 2005; Fisher & Birch, 1999; Spruijt-Metz et al., 2006). For example, in a study of 197 mother-daughter pairs, initial maternal restriction of the daughter's dietary intake was precipitated by the daughter's increase in body weight (Birch & Fisher, 2000). Within the same group, one-third of the girls reported moderate levels of dietary restraint and 75% experienced some measure of disinhibited eating in the presence of palatable foods (Carper et al., 2000; Fisher & Birch, 2000).

Maternal perception of child weight status may not always be consistent with national growth charts or practitioner advice. In a focus group of primarily African American mothers of preschool children, participants reported a strong distrust of the growth charts as a tool for identifying overweight in children and preferred to rely instead on other informal criteria, such as the child's ability to maintain activity and the level of teasing (Jain et al., 2001). Moreover, in a survey of 83 parents of overweight and normal weight children, only 10.5% of parents of overweight children perceived their child as overweight (Etelson et al., 2003). Baughcum, Chamberlin, Deeks, Powers, and Whitaker (2000) and determined that only one in five parents of overweight children identified their child as overweight. Even when perception of weight status was consistent with accepted norms, some parents of obesity-prone children regarded body weight as a predetermined characteristic that was not amenable to change. These mothers also reported that implementing controls on a child's intake was emotionally difficult regardless of weight status (Jain et al., 2001).

A parent's own self-imposed dietary restriction may be linked to feeding practices (Tiggemann, 2004). In a study of 89 parents of 5- to 8-year-old boys and girls, maternal pressure to control their child's weight was higher for girls than it was for boys and was associated with the mother's own dietary restraint practices. This suggests an intergenerational transmission of food attitudes. Parents, particularly mothers, who were most preoccupied with their own weight, appeared to more stringently control their child's weight and eating habits by limiting access to high calorie snack foods or by encouraging weight loss (Birch & Fisher, 1995; Francis & Birch, 2005; Tiggemann & Lowes, 2002).

A mother's preoccupation with her own weight may influence her feeding practices and the weight-related attitudes, beliefs, and eating habits of her daughters. In one study, girls as young as 6 years of age expressed a desire to be thinner, and their level of body dissatisfaction was closely related to their perception of their mother's dissatisfaction (Lowes & Tiggemann, 2003). In children ages 9 to 11 years, girls responded to encouragement from their mothers to lose weight by curtailing their eating (Francis & Birch, 2005). Although attempts by mothers to restrict food access and encourage weight loss in their daughters were most often predicted by a mother's own preoccupation with weight and diet, only encouragement to lose weight was associated with daughters' restrained eating behavior.

Finally, maternal disinhibited eating (the tendency to eat in response to external food cues) is associated with the child's propensity to eat in the absence of hunger, as well as elevated body fat (Cutting, Fisher, Grimm Thomas, & Birch, 1999). This again illustrates how a mother's eating practices and attitudes may impact on a child's eating practices and body weight.

PARENTAL NEGLECT

Parental neglect during childhood, defined as a lack of parental support and poor hygiene, was a strong predictor of adult obesity in a large-scale epidemiological study. In a study of 756 children, ages 9 to 10 years, parental support had a significant effect on a child's future risk of obesity; specifically, poorly groomed children were nearly 10 times more likely to become overweight as young adults than those who were clean and well groomed. This finding was true when controlling for childhood body mass index (BMI), gender, and family structure, and this association was far stronger than parental occupation or level of education in predicting future obesity risk (Lissau, 1994).

DIETARY COMPOSITION

The Feeding Infants and Toddlers Study (FITS), the first nationwide survey analyzing the dietary composition and nutrient intakes of more than 3000 children ages 4 to 24 months, reported that the dietary intake in this sample was excessive in sweets and sugar-sweetened beverages, and inadequate in fruits and vegetables. This indirectly reveals feeding practices in this age range that are a concern (Fox, Pac, Devaney, & Jankowski, 2004). The average portion sizes for infants and toddlers exceeded the Child and Adult Care Food Program (CACFP) guidelines for 50% to 90% of the children. Beyond 8 months, nearly all infants/toddlers consumed at least one type of sweet dessert or sugar-sweetened beverage daily, and french fried potatoes were among the top vegetables consumed by 9- to 11-month-olds (Devaney, Ziegler, Pac, Karwe, & Barr, 2004; Fox, Reidy, Karwe, & Ziegler, 2006).

Interestingly, while the overweight prevalence has increased among children and teens, energy intake from snacks has also increased to 20% of total calories, and 93% of youth report snacking on a daily basis (Adair & Popkin, 2005). There is also concern that the current level of fat intake among children (33.5%) remains above recommendations (Troiano, Briefel, Carroll, & Bialostosky, 2000). When analyzing weight change data for 146 children over a 3 year period, Klesges et al. (1992) found that fat consumption was associated with a greater change in child BMI. In a similar study, Lee, Mitchell, Smiciklas-Wright, and Birch (2001) found that children consuming more than 30% of their calories from fat experienced larger gains in BMI and fat skin-fold measurements than children consuming less than 30% of their calories from fat (Lee, Mitchell, Smickiklas, Wright, & Birch, 2001). While a direct cause has not been firmly established, eating habits likely play a role in promoting undesired weight gain in children (Birch & Davison, 2001).

ETHNICITY AND CULTURAL CONSIDERATIONS

Ethnic, cultural, and socioeconomic factors may play a role in the development of parental feeding practices, yet the specific role is not well understood. In one population-based study, mothers of white children reported allowing more food choice than Hispanic or African American mothers (Faith et al., 2003). In another study, white mothers reported less monitoring of child eating, restrictions, pressure to eat, or weight concern than African American mothers (Spruijt-Metz et al., 2002). In one of the first studies analyzing the relationship between weight concern, restrictive feeding behaviors, and changes in total fat mass between different ethnic groups, both African American and Caucasian parents' concern for their child's weight was directly related to the total fat mass in the child. White parents of heavier children implemented more restrictive practices in response to their concern about their child's weight compared to African American parents (Spruijt-Metz et al., 2006). While both groups of children gained weight, total fat mass increases over time were less for Caucasian children than for African American children. Additional formative research is necessary to reveal dimensions of parental feeding practices that are relevant in ethnically and socioeconomically diverse groups.

RECOMMENDATIONS

The data reviewed in this chapter reveal how parental feeding practices and eating behaviors can influence a child's early eating habits and potentially affect his or her future obesity risk. Successful interventions to prevent and treat childhood overweight should be aimed at early identification of problematic eating behaviors and feeding practices within the family system. Healthy parent-child interactions during feeding not only represent an important component of the bonding process, but may impact on the development of early eating patterns as well. While research remains inconclusive, evidence thus far underscores the importance of striving for a balance between excess parental control, with concomitant dietary restriction, and too little control, where, in the absence of role modeling and boundaries, the child may select foods that exceed energy needs.

One way to effectively address childhood eating issues is to strive for a reciprocal feeding relationship in which parents and children assume different responsibilities in the feeding process. This concept, "division of responsibility," advocates a clear division of responsibility between parents and children, in which parents assume the responsibility for what foods are available in the home and when these foods are offered and provide an atmosphere conducive to a relaxed and pleasant eating experience (Satter, 1995). Foods and meals provided in the home should be planned in accordance with established nutritional guidelines for variety, moderation, and balance, ensuring exposure to ample fruits, vegetables, whole grains, low-fat milk and dairy, and lean meats and meat alternatives

Table 8.1 Parental Feeding Practice Recommendations

Feeding Dimension	Recommendation
Dietary Quality	Provide a variety of foods from all food groups, emphasizing fruits, vegetables, lean meats, low-fat dairy products and whole grain breads and cereals.
	Avoid categorizing foods as "good" or "bad."
	Frequent exposure to new foods at home.
	Make healthy snacks available and accessible to the child.
Child Choice	Empower the child with a choice of foods, structuring selections to be healthy options.
	Offer repeated exposures to nutritious food selections to increase acceptance and familiarity.
Parent Feeding Practices	Avoid use of food to calm, bribe, reward, or punish a child.
	Model healthy eating and activity behaviors.
	Establish consistent meal and snack times.
	Limit food eating locations in the home to the kitchen and dining room.
	Establish television viewing budget of 2 hours per day or less.
	Allow the child a choice in "spending" his or her television viewing budget.
	Maintain a pleasant atmosphere at meal times.
	Avoid pressuring a child to eat a food or finish a meal.
	Promote family meals whenever possible.
	Remove the television from the child's bedroom.
	Promote fruit and vegetable intake as an alternative to dietary restriction.
	Improve access to healthy foods in the home.

(USDA, 2005). Children are responsible for choosing foods to taste and the quantity of food consumed. According to Ellyn Satter (1995), optimal feeding relationships and habits develop when this division of responsibility is accepted and respected by both parties. Failure to do so may lead to distorted eating habits and attitudes, which in some children may continue into adulthood. By providing an eating environment that allows for flexibility and autonomy in food and portion selection, within the realm of nutritious selections, an appropriate division of responsibility is maintained. Recommendations such as those listed in Table 8.1 may be helpful in promoting healthy parental feeding practices in the home. Interventions that facilitate positive parent-child interactions are likely to engender healthy eating habits in the early years, setting the stage for healthier lifelong eating styles. However, controlled studies are needed to test the long-term effects of such practices.

Efforts should also focus on preserving energy intake self-regulation through hunger/satiety awareness training and practice. Parental practices such as withholding food as a punishment, using food to calm a child, or pressuring a child to eat should be discouraged. Such feeding practices may disrupt natural self-regulation tendencies and promote responsiveness to external rather than internal hunger/satiety cues (Johnson & Birch, 1994; Rolls, Engell, & Birch, 2000). Indeed, research suggests that even young children have the capacity to report hunger/fullness sensations when introduced to simple satiety scaling measures (Faith, Kermanshah, & Kissileff, 2002). Some intervention studies have even demonstrated that a child's ability to respond to internal hunger/satiety prompts may be improved following a 6 week training program (Johnson, 2000).

In an effort to promote early identification of children at risk for overweight, clinicians routinely measure child BMI and assess changes over time. Additional screenings during routine office visits may be instrumental in uncovering potential problems that may interfere with the development of healthy eating patterns. Inquiring about maternal feeding practices and level of concern regarding weight or eating status may be helpful in the early identification of unhealthy parental feeding practices. Parental concern about child food preferences, weight status, and eating habits might be addressed with anticipatory guidance on normal childhood growth patterns to prevent unnecessary feeding pressure or restrictions (Collins, Johnson, & Krebs, 2004). In addition, parents should be counseled on appropriate child development transitions, including changes in food preferences,

Hedley AA, Ogden CL, Johnson CL, Carroll MD, Curtin LR, Flegal KM. Prevalence of overweight and obesity among US children, adolescents, and adults, 1999-2002. *JAMA*. 2004;291:2847–2850.

Hendricks K, Briefel R, Novak T, Ziegler P. Maternal and child characteristics associated with infant and toddler feeding practices. *J Am Diet Assoc*. 2006;106:S135–148.

Hill JO, Peters JC. Environmental contributions to the obesity epidemic. *Science*. 1998;280:1371–1374.

Jacobson KC, Rowe DC. Genetic and shared environmental influences on adolescent BMI: Interactions with race and sex. *Behav Genet*. 1998;28:265–278.

Jain A, Sherman SN, Chamberlin LA, Carter Y, Powers SW, Whitaker RC. Why don't low-income mothers worry about their preschoolers being overweight? *Pediatrics*. 2001;107:1138–1146.

Johnson S, Birch LL. Parents' adiposity and eating style. *Pediatrics*. 1994;94:653–661.

Johnson S, McPhee L, Birch LL. Conditioned preferences: Young children prefer flavors associated with high dietary fat. *Physiol Behav*. 1993;54:71–76.

Johnson SL. Improving preschoolers' self-regulation of energy intake. *Pediatrics*. 2000;106:1429–1435.

Kern DL, McPhee L, Fisher JO, Johnson SL, Birch LL. The postingestive consequences of fat condition preferences for flavors associated with high dietary fat. *Physiol Behav*. 1993;54:71–76.

Klesges RC, Haddock CK, Stein RJ, Klesges LM, Eck LH, Hanson CL. Relationship between psychosocial functioning and body fat in preschool children: A longitudinal investigation. *J Consult Clin Psycho*. 1992;60:793–796.

Lee Y, Mitchell DCRD, Smiciklas Wright H, Birch LL. Diet quality, nutrient intake, weight status, and feeding environments of girls meeting or exceeding recommendations for total dietary fat of the American Academy of Pediatrics. *Pediatrics*. 2001;107:e95.

Lissau I, Sorensen TIA. Parental neglect during childhood and increased risk of obesity in young adulthood. *Lancet*. 1994;343:324–327.

Lowes J, Tiggemann M. Body dissatisfaction, dieting awareness and the impact of parental influence in young children. *Br J Health Psychol*. 2003;8:135–147.

Maes HH, Neale MC, Eaves LJ. Genetic and environmental factors in relative body weight and human adiposity. *Behav Genet*. 1997;27:325–351.

Mei Z, Grummer-Strawn LM, Scanlon KS. Does overweight in infancy persist through the preschool years? An analysis of CDC pediatric nutrition surveillance system data. *Soz Praventivmed*. 2003;48:161–167.

Must A, Spadano J, Coakley EH, Field AE, Colditz G, Dietz WH. The disease burden associated with overweight and obesity. *JAMA*. 1999;282:1523–1529.

Oliveria, S.A et al. Parent-child relationships in nutrient intake: The framingham children's study. *Am J Clin Nutr*. 1992;56:593–598.

Parsons TJ, Power C, Logan S, Summerbell CD. Childhood predictors of adult obesity: A systematic review. *Int J Obes Relat Metab Disord*. 1999; 23: S1–107.

Robinson TN, Kiernan M, Matheson DM, Haydel KF. Is parental control over children's eating associated with childhood obesity? Results from a population-based sample of third graders. *Obes Res*. 2001;9:306–312.

Rolls BJ, Engell D, Birch LL. Serving portion size influences 5-year-old but not 3-year-old children's food intakes. *J Am Diet Assoc*. 2000;100:232-234.

Sclafani A. How food preferences are learned: Laboratory animal models. *Proc Nutr Soc*. 1995;54:419–427.

Spruijt-Metz D, Li C, L., Cohen E, Birch LL, Goran MI. Longitudinal influence of mother's child-feeding practices on adiposity. *J Pediatr*. 2006;148:314–320.

Spruijt-Metz D, Lindquist CH, Birch LL, Fisher JO, Goran MI. Relation between mothers' child-feeding practices and children's adiposity. *Am J Clin Nutr*. 2002;75:581–586.

Stanek K, Abbott D, Cramer S. Diet quality and the eating environment. *J Am Diet Assoc*. 1990;90:1582–1584.

Stang J, Rehorst J, Golicic M. Parental feeding practices and risk of childhood overweight in girls: Implications for dietetics practice. *J Am Diet Assoc*. 2004;104:1076–1079.

Sullivan SA, Birch LL. Infant dietary experience and acceptance of solid foods. *Pediatrics*. 1994;93:271–277.

Swarr AE, Richards MH. Longitudinal effects of adolescent girl's pubertal development, perceptions of pubertal timing, and parental reactions on eating problems. *Dev Psychol*. 1996;32:636–646.

Tibbs T, Haire-Joshu D, Schechtman KB. The relationship between parental modeling, eating patterns, and dietary intake among African American parents. *J Am Diet Assoc*. 2001:535–541.

Tiggemann M, Lowes J. Predictors of maternal control over children's eating behaviour. *Appetite.* 2002;39:1–7.

Tiggemann M. Dietary restraint and self-esteem as predictors of weight gain over an 8-year time period. *Eat behav.* 2004;5:251–259.

Troiano RP, Briefel RR, Carroll MD, Bialostosky K. Energy and fat intakes of children and adolescents in the united states: Data from the national health and nutrition examination surveys. *Am J Clin Nutr.* 2000;72:1343S–1353.

USDA. My Pyramid Dietary Guidance System. 2005. Available from: www.mypyramid.gov/professionals/index.html. Accessed 1/31/07.

Wardle J, Sanderson S, Guthrie CA, Rapoport L, Plomin R. Parental feeding style and the inter-generational transmission of obesity risk. *Obes Res.* 2002;10:453–462.

Whitaker RC, Wright JA, Pepe MS, Seidel KD, Dietz WH. Predicting obesity in young adulthood from childhood and parental obesity. *N Engl J Med.* 1997;337:869–873.

Zeller, Meg D, Stephen. The obesity epidemic: Family matters *Pediatr.* 2004;145:3–4.

9

Ten Messages for Weight Control from Teleological Behaviorism

HOWARD RACHLIN

TELEOLOGICAL BEHAVIORISM

This introductory section attempts to justify my own theoretical approach—teleological behaviorism (Rachlin, 1994). It may be skipped by readers interested primarily in practical issues.

Teleological behaviorism differs from most forms of behaviorism in that it uses mental terms as scientific concepts. But it is truly behavioristic in that it defines those terms as patterns of overt behavior—patterns extended in time.

Imagine you see a snippet of film that shows a man swinging a hammer. But what is he actually doing? Now consider the following alternatives. He is

- swinging a hammer
- hammering a nail
- joining one piece of wood to another
- building a floor
- building a house
- providing shelter for his family
- supporting his family
- being a good husband and father
- being a good person

All of these may be valid descriptions of his behavior. Based on the snippet of film you saw, all you can say is that he is swinging the hammer. He might have been swinging it at someone's head. But if you said, "He's just swinging the hammer," someone else who saw more of the film might reasonably say, "Yes, he's doing that, but what he's really doing is hammering a nail." A third person who saw still more of the film might then correct the second in a similar way: "Yes, he's hammering a nail, but what he's really doing is building a floor." And so forth until we get to an observer who has sat through a film of this man's entire life and can make the final judgment: "He's being a good person."

The important point is that all of the descriptions are equally valid descriptions of the man's behavior. As you go down the list, more and more context is incorporated into the description, but that context is always behavioral. The final observer need not look into the man's heart as long as he has looked at the complete film of the man's life. Then the observer can say, "He's a good man," without fear of contradiction—regardless of the state of the man's heart. The validity of any of the above descriptions may be settled by moving the camera back or showing more film—earlier and later.

You might say that there's a difference between the man who intentionally swings a hammer and the man who accidentally swings a hammer—even though the two men are behaving in the same way. And, you might add, the difference lies inside them. While it is true that something inside of people must mediate behavioral differences, the difference between intention and accident is behavioral. The difference between a man purposely swinging a hammer and a man accidentally swinging a hammer can be resolved not by looking inside him, but by looking at more of his behavior. A man accidentally swinging a hammer will not be hammering a nail or building a floor.

The teleological behaviorist studies patterns of behavior. The question of why I am writing this chapter cannot be broken up into the question of why I am writing this sentence, why I am writing the next sentence, and so forth. Rather, you have to look at why I am writing the chapter as a whole—extrinsic social reinforcers as well as the intrinsic value of the activity itself. If I had to decide whether to write each sentence individually I'd have writer's block—since there is no reinforcement for writing each sentence individually. Correspondingly, in the area of weight control, there is no reinforcement for each act of food refusal. It is sometimes said that the reinforcement for such acts is delayed. But if a child refuses a single candy bar tonight she will not wake up 3 weeks from today suddenly a slimmer, healthier, happier person. A single act of self-control is not reinforced—now or ever, internally or externally. Reinforcement of acts such as refusing a candy bar is to be found not in particular acts themselves but in the value of a pattern of acts strung out over time. This value may be extrinsic to the pattern—like social approval—or intrinsic in the pattern itself.

The following very loosely organized guidelines come from this teleological viewpoint. I call them "messages" rather than prescriptions because, as a former engineer, I believe that practice has much more to tell theory than theory has to tell practice. If the reader is a behavior therapist looking for ways to improve her practice she may be familiar with most of the following—although the language will be more mentalistic than she may be used to. Teleological behaviorism accepts mental terms such as perception, imagination, and even willpower, although it defines those terms strictly as patterns of overt behavior (see Rachlin, 1994). The difference between a person with strong willpower and a person with weak willpower lies not inside them, but in their behavior—temporally extended into the past and the future as well. Thus willpower is a concept much like probability. The only sure way to know if a coin is honest is to toss it over and over again and see if the relative frequency of heads approaches 50%. But no matter how many times you toss it, future tosses may contradict your conclusion. The same may be said for willpower as well as other mental terms. Their validity as applied to a given act (a given candy bar refusal, for instance) does not depend on the existence of internal events at that moment in time (a lighting up of some place in the brain, for instance), but on external, observable events spread out over time.

MESSAGE 1: ECONOMICS AND REINFORCEMENT: THE JOYS OF OBESITY

Teleological behaviorism and economic theory of individual behavior (microeconomic theory) are really the same theory. The reinforcement contingencies of behavioral theory correspond to the constraints (prices and budgets) of economic theory. Both specify relationships between behavior and consequences. The behavioral concept of reinforcement maximization corresponds to utility maximization in economic theory (Kagel, Battalio, & Green, 1995). For example, a ratio schedule of reinforcement specifies the number of responses required for the delivery of a reinforcer. In economic terms, the price of the commodity is a ratio requirement. Economic theory predicts how much of a commodity will be bought as the price of that commodity increases or decreases by assuming that utility, in terms of the amount obtained (a positive function) and price paid (a negative function), is maximized. Similarly, behavioral analysis attempts to determine how behavior varies as a function of the reinforcement contingencies. Reinforcement maximization (together with minimizing the response output) is a way of predicting such variation.

How does the concept of self-control fit into microeconomics? Economic theory assumes that people behave so as to maximize utility under any given set of constraints (prices and budgets in economic language—reinforcement contingencies in behavioral language). Often, behavior that maximizes utility in the relatively short run does not maximize utility in the relatively long run. A child who overeats maximizes utility in the short run (in terms of immediate pleasure), but not in the long run (in terms of health and social acceptance and possibly even school performance). This is the outcome regardless of whether such overeating is caused mainly by genetic or environmental factors (an issue about which the present chapter takes no stand).

The economic question, "What is maximized?" corresponds to the behavioral question, "What are the reinforcers?" Just as all acts, no matter how irrational they may seem, must, according to the economist, maximize utility over some time span (Stigler & Becker, 1977), so all acts, no matter how irrational they seem, must, according to the behaviorist, be reinforced (or themselves be high-valued reinforcers). Let us consider then what reinforces overeating. What are the joys of obesity?

The short-term reinforcers of overeating—the taste of food and the reduction of hunger, the immediate satisfactions—are so clear and distinct that they tend to blind us to the long-term advantages of obesity as a lifestyle. What might they be? First, are there physical tasks that cannot be performed? If mowing the lawn becomes a major undertaking, then someone else in the family is likely to be mowing the lawn. Inactivity or sloth is a venal sin and disapproved of strongly, especially in Western societies. But a thin, able-bodied teenager sitting around all day watching television will be perceived as more socially hostile than an obese teenager doing the same thing. For obese people of any age, along with the social disapproval comes a certain measure of social accommodation. An obese person essentially carries a sign saying, "I was wounded in the war against temptation." By implication, so might you be. And just as the able-bodied accommodate the disabled, they also accommodate the obese. The loss of that accommodation may be felt if and when weight is brought under control.

A second source of reinforcement stems from the very social disability that obesity causes. Nearly every teenager is nervous about going to a dance. But there are usually sufficient social forces to overcome that obstacle. For an obese teenager, however, such countervailing forces may be relaxed, the dance missed, and the evening spent watching television—to the understanding and relief of everyone concerned. Related to social factors are sexual ones. The obese teenager, boy or girl, is less of a threat to other teenagers of the same sex and therefore may find it easier than would a nonobese teenager to develop secure and lasting same-sex friendships.

The medium-term and long-term joys of obesity described above are those that come to the mind of a nonclinician. Clinicians working with obesity can undoubtedly think of many more. Therefore weight control programs need to acknowledge the long-term benefits of obesity as well as the short-term ones. Of course, regardless of how numerous the joys of obesity may be, they are dwarfed by the long-term benefits (such as greater social acceptance and better health) attendant upon reduction and maintenance of normal weight.

MESSAGE 2: WEIGHT CONTROL IS MORE IMPORTANT THAN WEIGHT REDUCTION

There is a natural tendency among pigeons, rats, and people to increase behavioral variability when things are not going well. This tendency serves us well in most real-life situations—as it has served our ancestors (otherwise we wouldn't have it). When a rat has been trained to press a lever for food and then food is withheld (extinction), the rat starts to press faster and harder before giving up and trying other responses. As long as the food was coming, the rat would have found a favorite way to press the lever—usually the most efficient way. But once the food stops coming, the rat starts banging the lever down, pressing it sideways, lifting it, and gnawing at it. If the lever is large, the rat presses it in different places. The rat is behaving as I do when a soda machine swallows my money and fails to produce a soda. I bang on it, kick it, and curse at it.

The general term for such a strategy, built into all of us, is "win-stay, lose-shift." As long as things go well, keep doing what you were doing; as soon as things start going badly, increase the variability of your behavior by trying something else. This is nothing but a Darwinian evolutionary model applied to the behavior of an individual. Reinforcement determines which of our behaviors survive and which are extinguished. But in order for reinforcement to work, behavior has to vary. That is, the animal's behavior has to come into contact with the contingencies. When things start going badly for us we help reinforcement to do its work by increasing behavioral variability.

And so it goes with weight control. Eating is a necessity. If things start going badly in life, as they inevitably do for all of us at some time, or some previous source of excitement or comfort dries up for some reason, our natural tendency—like the rat's tendency to press the lever faster—is to increase the rate of other normally satisfying activities. When it seems as if all our friends have deserted us, it also seems as if food remains our friend, and we increase variability by increasing our rate of eating. But food, in our modern Western society, is not always a friend. In the long run it can harm us. So we must learn to counteract this natural tendency and control our intake. This means not just reducing food intake, but also reducing its variability. The governing rule of any weight control program therefore should be "weight control, not weight reduction." For growing children, whose baseline weight is constantly increasing, the problem is compounded; variability must be reduced not around a fixed baseline, but around a continuously increasing one. Weight reduction for obese children may be not only impractical, but also undesirable. For them, weight control becomes doubly important.

MESSAGE 3: MONITORING IS AN EFFECTIVE PART OF WEIGHT CONTROL

Counting calories is difficult and time consuming. A life of counting every single calorie consumed would be grim indeed. That is certainly not what I am suggesting here. Nevertheless, counting calories is a skill that should be in everyone's armamentarium—to be taken out and used when necessary. It would be similarly grim to spend your life checking the addition on every restaurant bill, every store receipt, every bank statement. Yet being able to do so is a necessary skill. The fact that counting calories is difficult is why it should be learned before, not during or after, losing weight. If children, before any kind of weight reduction plan is instituted, are thoroughly trained and tested to the point where they can accurately estimate the number of calories in a given portion of food, it will be relatively easy for them to lose weight afterwards. This is a skill that will prove useful for the rest of their lives—as important as brushing their teeth. Calorie counting, as well as nutrition, should be part of the school curricula for all children. It should become second nature for them to gain a feeling for the calories in whatever food they eat. In addition, obese children should be trained to record calories consumed on a hand calculator or in a notebook and keep track of their weight. Again, it makes sense that calorie counting be thoroughly learned before any attempt at weight reduction is instituted.

This is not to say that calories are the only factor in weight control. Other factors, especially exercise, are also important. But their importance (as regards weight control) can be folded into calorie consumption. A child who exercises a lot will maintain a given weight at a higher calorie level than will a child who exercises a little. But both children can learn to maintain their weights solely by controlling calorie intake. The onerous aspect of calorie counting is its currently invariable association with calorie restriction. When these two activities are disassociated, learning to count calories is no more onerous than learning to tell time. Moreover, the soft-commitment weight reduction method that I will propose later (see Message 9) does not involve imposition of calorie restrictions by adults (or by anyone other than the child herself). If a child increases or decreases her exercise level over several months, the adjustments necessary for weight control will become clear as time passes. Precise programs that attempt to micromanage calorie intake by subtracting calories burned through exercise on a daily basis are too difficult for children; indeed, once the novelty wears off, they become too difficult for adults to maintain. Moreover, such programs encourage attempts to compensate for overeating by overexercising.

MESSAGE 4: MAINTAIN WEIGHT BEFORE REDUCING WEIGHT

Let us assume that the obese child is now a whiz at calorie counting. Should a weight reduction program be instituted now? No, not yet. Before learning to reduce her weight the obese child should be taught to maintain her weight. For adults, maintenance means reduction of variability around their current weight; for growing children, maintenance means reduction of variability around an increasing baseline.

It may seem as if I have gotten things backwards here. How can you maintain weight if you haven't lost it? Weight reduction and weight maintenance constitute a sequence like a chain schedule of reinforcement. Usually it is a good idea to begin training with such schedules with the final link first. If you want to train your dog to fetch your slippers and then drop them in front of you, you should first train him to drop them, and only after he has learned that, to fetch them. Once a dog has learned to drop the slippers in front of you (rather than play tug of war with you) it will be much easier to teach him to retrieve them from under the bed. Similarly, after a child has learned to maintain his weight within a given range, it will be much easier for him to reduce his weight and then maintain it within the new range than it would be if he had to learn to maintain his weight only after he had reduced it. I would even go so far as to (tentatively) recommend that a weight loss program penalize dieters who lose weight during the initial maintenance period. The goal, at this stage, is to learn to count calories and to reduce variability—to keep weight at baseline level—not to lose it.

Recent research with both human and nonhuman subjects (Neuringer, 2004) has found that when reduction in variability of behavior is reinforced, variability decreases. An obese person will find it much easier to learn techniques to reduce variability before she reduces her weight than if she waits until she first loses 20 pounds. In other words, she should first try to learn to maintain her weight at its current value and only then try to reduce it and finally to maintain it at its reduced value. The problem with losing weight first and then trying to maintain it is that the point where a dieter has just reached her goal is the most vulnerable point of weight control. Unless the dieter, as she was losing weight, was consuming just the right amount of calories to maintain her weight at its current lower level, she will have to eat more so as to stop losing weight, but not so much more as to gain weight. If, at this vulnerable point, she has already developed maintenance skills, she can more easily apply them now.

This is the point where fad diets fail. Programs that prepackage meals are good for losing weight. They take all the responsibility for controlling intake off the dieter's shoulders. But they teach him no long-term skills for weight control. They are like crutches for a broken leg without a physical therapy program to develop muscle strength. As soon as the crutches are taken away, he falls down; his muscles have atrophied. The same goes for fad diets that restrict the dieter to just one or two kinds of food. When the dieter abandons them, they abandon him, and leave him without the skills necessary to keep his weight under control.

MESSAGE 5: WEIGHT MAINTENANCE IS A LIFETIME PROJECT

It would be better to say that good health is a lifetime project and that weight maintenance is an essential part of good health. The plentiful availability of food in our society, together with our inheritance of eating patterns appropriate for the environment of scarcity faced by our ancestors, imposes problems for all of us. But for almost all of us the gains of civilization are well worth the costs. To paraphrase a recent *New Yorker* cartoon, one Neanderthal man says to the other, "Our water is unpolluted, our air is clean, we eat only organic vegetables, and free-ranging meat. How come we all die at the age of 30?" Like dental hygiene, bathing regularly, eating with knives and forks, and the hundreds of other adjustments we must make to civilized society (including control of rage), weight maintenance is something we need to do. But like many of our other adjustments to civilization, once it's learned we do not need to be concentrating on it all the time. As the old advertisement for a stick-shift Volkswagen said: "After a while it becomes automatic."

Once calorie and weight monitoring have been thoroughly learned, weight reduction may begin. Weight reduction works best if it is carried out under conditions as similar as possible to those of weight maintenance. After weight has been reduced, a second maintenance period has to begin at the lower weight. Habits learned during the initial maintenance period need to be maintained during reduction and then transferred to the new, lower weight, maintenance period. And then those habits must essentially be kept for the rest of the child's life. Therefore any period of weight reduction needs to be as similar as possible in all respects to the maintenance periods between which it is sandwiched. Otherwise, painfully acquired maintenance habits will be lost. That is another reason why crash diets do not work in the long run. Dieting, which must be a lifetime process, becomes a special occasion; rapid weight reduction habits, usually drastic in nature and not maintainable in the long run, must then be unlearned at the same time as new habits are acquired for long-term maintenance.

Weight control is a dynamic process. Once weight is reduced, it does not automatically stay where it is. If weight is lost too fast, the dieter is likely to overshoot her natural resting point and keep bouncing around like a car without shock absorbers (the "yo-yo" effect). Finally, after her weight settles at a new resting point, she will still have to painfully relearn all of her maintenance habits. She will be like a driver who steers only by turning the wheel violently in one direction or the other.

It takes months, perhaps years, for the body as well as behavior to adjust comfortably to a lower weight. Moreover, in a child's later life, there will be many bumps—exceptions where weight mainte-nance will be abandoned—weddings, celebrations, and so forth. On the other side of the ledger, there will be tragic occasions—deaths, divorces—when the value of controlling weight will be dwarfed by other concerns. Those are the times when relapses will occur. If a boy learns a program for losing a few pounds as a teenager, he will easily be able to put that program back into place. But if the only skill he has learned is how to lose 20 lb in 7 days (by adopting a crash diet), then he will be tempted to wait until his weight has climbed to dangerous levels before trying to lose the excess weight.

MESSAGE 6: HABITS, BOTH BAD AND GOOD, ARE SITUATION BOUND

Heroin addiction was very common among American soldiers in Vietnam (Robins, 1974). When the war ended, officials became concerned that the returning soldiers would bring their habits home with them. But that did not happen. Most of the soldiers were able to slough off their addiction along with their uniforms—no violent withdrawal effects, no deep anguish. Why? Because hormonal effects within the bodies of the soldiers as well as overt behavior caused by contingencies of reinforcement are strongly controlled by environmental context. And the contexts provided by army life in Vietnam and family life in the United States could not have been more different: in one case, living without family like an animal in the jungle; in the other, living with family in a civilized society.

In the area of weight control, it is common for people who cannot control their eating under normal conditions to easily control it on religious fast days such as Yom Kippur, Lent, or Ramadan. The special conditions of the holiday isolate it from the rest of life. The selection pressure of reinforcement on behavior may differ in different situations and allow the habits of the isolated situation to develop differently from those of everyday life—just as the flora and fauna of an isolated group of islands may evolve differently from those on the mainland.

In weight control, this specificity of reinforcement to its (discriminative) stimulus situation is both a disadvantage and an advantage. It is a disadvantage in that the one set of contingencies we carry around with us from one environment to another are those within our own bodies; sooner or later you get hungry wherever you are. Unless a teenager goes to Timbuktu for summer vacation, junk food will be plentiful. Bad habits (reinforced in the short run) may then carry over or evolve anew in those situations.

On the other hand, the stimulus specificity of habit development allows a person to get rid of a bad habit in one situation at a time. Divide and conquer. The differing stimulus conditions across two situations constitute a wall (permeable though it may be) between habits. Nevertheless, a bad habit—overeating, for example—may develop in both situations. You cannot just assume that if you succeeded in arranging your life so that you manage to stop desiring chocolate-covered almonds when you enter a movie theater, you will not feel a sudden desire for a hot dog and a beer at the ball park. Some situations are especially conducive to overeating—the movie theater and the ballpark being two of them. The distinct situations in any dieter's life have to be tackled one at a time and bad eating habits corralled to specific places and times (say, only weddings and bar mitzvahs) where they will do no harm.

MESSAGE 7: CONTROLLING TWO HABITS AT A TIME

According to Premack's (1965) reinforcement theory, the effect of a reinforcement contingency depends on behavior without that contingency present. Suppose, with a lever and a dish of milk freely available, a rat spends 1 minute pressing the lever for every 5 minutes drinking the milk. That is, the rat's ratio of lever pressing to milk drinking is 1:5 when both activities are freely available. You now arrange a reinforcement contingency: the milk (the reinforcer) is no longer freely available; if the rat presses the lever for 1 minute, it will be able to drink milk for only 1 minute. This imposes a new ratio of 1:1 between time spent lever pressing and time spent drinking milk. The result of this new arrangement is that the rat will press the lever more than it did before (lever pressing is reinforced), but the rat will also drink less milk than it did before. The reinforcement contingency causes the lower valued activity to increase in rate, but it also causes the higher valued activity to decrease in rate. This fact can be used in self-control. In general, if there is a pair of activities, one of which you want to decrease and the other of which you want to increase, you may accomplish both by establishing a new pattern. Less of the activity you want to decrease should be made contingent on more of the activity you want to increase.

Suppose that between-meal eating is the activity to be decreased. What activity needs to be increased? Let us say this is homework. It would then be possible to simultaneously reinforce doing homework and decrease between-meal eating by making less eating (than was previously done) contingent on doing more homework (than was previously done). Obviously such a program would require careful planning and monitoring. If it were strictly implemented, it could be an effective way to decrease a bad habit and increase a good one at the same time. However, such an approach would require monitoring and control of behavior from the outside, by parents and teachers. This would be difficult to implement, especially as the child grows older and is out of the house for extended periods. It may seem as if the reciprocal contingencies could be self-imposed by the child. But self-reinforcement and self-punishment work, when they do work, not directly, but by increasing the salience of behavior—as a form of self-monitoring. (Think of slapping your own hand when you start to reach for the refrigerator door. This doesn't punish opening the refrigerator door, it just underlines the fact that you are about to take something to eat.) Strict monitoring and restriction of two behaviors simultaneously may be too difficult for adults, let alone children. Another method of weight reduction is needed and will be proposed in Message 9.

MESSAGE 8: THE INTERACTION OF NEGATIVE AND POSITIVE ADDICTIONS

The economists Stigler and Becker (1977) distinguish between negative and positive addictions. Negative addictions are the ones we usually identify as addictive—smoking cigarettes, drinking alcohol, taking heroin or cocaine, overeating to obesity. The thing that makes negative addictions negative is that they are generally bad for you. Beyond a certain point, the more you drink, take heroin, overeat, etc., the worse your health gets, the more you get teased by other children, the worse your social life gets, the worse your school performance gets. The crucial theoretical property of negative addictions, however, is that as their rate increases, tolerance builds up. An amount of heroin that would kill a nonaddict is barely enough to satisfy the craving of a heroin addict. The defining property of a negative addiction is the higher its rate, the less satisfaction is obtained from (the less the value of) the marginal unit of consumption.

Positive addictions, on the other hand, are activities that many people spend a lot of time doing but are not usually identified as addictions—physical exercise, social activity, reading serious literature, listening to classical music, stamp collecting, doing crossword puzzles. The thing that makes positive addictions positive is that they are generally considered to be good for you—or at least not bad. For behavior theory, however, the crucial property of positive addictions is opposite to tolerance. The more you do them, the more satisfying they become. Positive addictions all involve a practice effect. The defining property of a positive addiction is opposite to that of a negative addiction: the higher its rate, the more satisfaction is obtained from (the more the value of) the marginal unit of consumption.

As a person engages in more social activities—goes to more parties, for instance—the more enjoyment she tends to get from each one. As she collects more stamps, the more fun stamp collecting becomes. Some positive addictions may not be good for us beyond a certain point. In fact, unless they go beyond that point, we do not usually identify them as addictions. Playing computer games, for example, is technically a positive addiction: as the player gains skill she comes to enjoy the game more; as she plays less frequently she loses skill and enjoys the game less. Even exercise and social activity may reach a point where we call them addictive. For our purposes, however, negative and positive addictions are defined not by whether they are bad or good for us generally, but whether they are characterized by tolerance or practice—that is, whether a unit of an act decreases or increases in value as its rate increases.

Activities may be both negatively and positively addictive at the same time. As a boy learns the skills that make some sport (basketball, for example) enjoyable, he may develop a tolerance for the immediate euphoric effects (the rush) of physical exercise per se. The two effects may then work together to addict the child to basketball. Such an addiction may be harmless or even beneficial, as it crowds out overeating. But if it also crowds out activities such as doing homework or learning social skills (other than passing the ball), it may become harmful. Any activity, no matter how beneficial, may be overdone.

Now imagine a boy, Billy, existing in a world where the only activities available are positive and negative addictions. In a sense this scenario is realistic, since very few of the things we do remain constant in value as we increase their rate beyond a certain point. To make the illustration still simpler, let us represent the group of negative addictions by a single one—**overeating**—and the group of positive addictions by a single one—**exercise**. (To remind the reader that these examples stand for a whole class of activities, they are printed in bold type.) Billy's world is so constrained that, during his waking hours, when he's not **eating,** he's **exercising,** and when he's not **exercising**, he's **eating**; if he spends 90% of his time **eating,** he must spend 10% **exercising**; if he spends 60% of his time **exercising**, he must spend 40% **eating**.

Now let us set up a self-control problem for Billy—a modified version of Herrnstein and Prelec's (1992) primrose path. Let us arbitrarily suppose that in the long run the healthiest, happiest ratio of **eating** to **exercise** for Billy is 20:80. **Eating** beyond that point is unhealthy. As the ratio of **eating** to **exercise** increases further and further from that point, the pleasure he used to take in both activities decreases and Billy becomes less and less healthy and happy. However, at every point along the road, from 20:80 to 50:50 to 100:0, the marginal value of **eating** (the value of the very next unit of it) is higher than the marginal value of **exercise**. At any given moment Billy would rather eat a candy bar than go out and play basketball. This immediate preference applies all of the time, whatever the overall ratio.

As Billy's **eating** rate increases, the value of each unit of food decreases. To keep the total value of **eating** at a high level, Billy has to **eat** more and more. If he **eats** more and more, he will be **exercising** less and less (because by hypothesis **eating** and **exercise** occupy all his waking hours). As he **exercises** less and less, the value of each unit of **exercise** decreases because of the practice effect; the less time he spends playing basketball, the worse his fitness and skill, the more effortful and the less fun playing basketball becomes. Thus the more Billy **eats**, the worse both **eating** and **exercise** become. This concept is hard to grasp, so at the risk of belaboring the point, let me repeat it in another way. **Eating** and **exercise** have opposite properties in that the more **eating** you do, the less you enjoy each unit of **eating**, but the more **exercising** you do, the more you enjoy each unit of **exercise**. So if Billy is **eating** more and **exercising** less, he is enjoying both activities less. But because the enjoyment he gets from **eating** always remains above that of **exercise**, Billy continues to choose **eating** over **exercise**. Meanwhile, not only does his long-term health and happiness decrease, but the immediate pleasures he gets from both **eating** and **exercise** decrease as well—going down in parallel. This sort of dilemma appears in many real-life situations not usually thought of as self-control. For example, a baseball pitcher has two pitches, a fastball and a changeup. Regardless of the percentage of fastballs he throws, the fastball is always a better pitch than the changeup. If the pitcher is concerned only with this very pitch, he will always throw fastballs. Yet, he should still sometimes throw changeups. Why? Because, the changeup increases the effectiveness of his fastball in the future. As his percentage of changeups increases (up to a very limited point), batters must watch out for them and cannot comfortably expect fastballs. Therefore, by throwing his changeup, his fastball will be more effective. (For the same reason, a poker player should occasionally be caught bluffing.)

You may well ask, if this theory is true, why aren't we all addicts? If the marginal unit of the negative addiction is always higher than that of the positive addiction, how can positive addictions gain a foothold in competition with negative addictions? The answer is that as we mature we learn not to choose the highest valued momentary option and to choose on the basis of our longer term benefits. Billy's problem is essentially a cognitive or perceptual one. He needs to see his options as ratios of activities over an extended period—a more abstract kind of choice—rather than as individual actions. To some extent we all must make such abstractions all the time. Otherwise we would never get out of bed in the morning. But, as beneficial options become more and more abstract and spread out over time, they become harder and harder to identify. Eating a healthy diet is one of these. In the next message I propose a method for weight control based on the concept of increasing the time period of the consequences of choices and making choices more abstract.

MESSAGE 9: A SOFT-COMMITMENT PROGRAM FOR WEIGHT REDUCTION

In general, commitment devices and strategies are ways of ensuring that choices are based on abstract patterns of behavior rather than on particular individual actions. If Billy could ignore his momentary preference between one bite of food and one bit of exercise and instead choose among ratios of food to exercise over the next week or month, he would exercise much more frequently. With regard to weight control, many crash diets work temporarily to reduce weight because they require simple, easily perceptible eating patterns. But it may be possible to use what I call "soft commitment" (Siegel & Rachlin, 1996) in weight control.

In this weight reduction procedure, a child or adolescent (let us call her Betty), previously trained in monitoring and maintenance, eats freely 1 day each week. She may eat a lot, she may eat a little, just as she desires. But on each of the next 6 days she is obliged to eat the very same number of calories—no more and no less—as on the first day. Each Twinkie eaten on day 1 would thus entrain six more Twinkies or their equivalent over the next 6 days. Such a restriction keeps the responsibility on Betty to choose her own behavioral pattern over the course of the first day of each week and also compels her to perceive and record that pattern. This gives heavy weight to choices on the first day. It focuses attention on eating and monitoring and provides an exemplar for eating over the rest of the week. Betty's commitment to keep to the same number of calories each day is a soft commitment in that obedience is not compelled. The advantage of such a commitment procedure is that Betty sets her own consumption pattern, not by imposition from an adult in authority, but by her own behavior. She knows she can keep to the chosen number of calories because she has already kept to it on the first day. And if Betty should be uncomfortable with her self-imposed eating pattern, but sticks to it anyway, she will get an opportunity to set a new pattern next week. Moreover, such a method uses previously learned monitoring skills and blends in smoothly with initial and subsequent maintenance programs. After a relapse, it can easily be reinstituted. In theory, therefore, this program should be effective in weight reduction not only for children old enough to learn calorie counting, but for anyone.

MESSAGE 10: ECONOMIC SUBSTITUTABILITY

The classic examples of economically substitutable commodities are Coke and Pepsi. The more Coke you drink, the less Pepsi you are going to buy, and vice versa. Increasing the price of Coke (while keeping the price of Pepsi constant) will increase consumption of Pepsi. The opposite of substitutability is complementarity. Examples of economically complementary commodities are beer and pretzels. Increasing the price of beer (while keeping the price of pretzels constant) will decrease consumption of pretzels (because people will buy less beer and don't need as many pretzels to go with the beer).

Consumption of Coke and Pepsi, or beer and pretzels, may or may not be harmful. But suppose there were, among generally beneficial positive addictions, some activity that substituted for a generally harmful negative addiction. Just as, over a wide range, negative addictions become more immediately valuable the less you do them (you build up an appetite for them), so positive addictions become more immediately valuable the more you do them (you become better at them with practice). If a positive addiction were an economic substitute for a negative addiction, anything that increased the rate of the positive addiction would also decrease the rate of the negative addiction (the more Pepsi you drink, the less Coke you will drink).

Are there positive addictions that substitute for negative addictions? Surprisingly, there are. Considerable evidence exists that, in adults, social activity substitutes for cigarette smoking and heroin and cocaine consumption. For example, training in social skills is the single most effective treatment for addiction to cigarettes, cocaine, heroin, and alcohol (Green & Kagel, 1996).

I am not aware of corresponding studies in childhood or adolescent weight control, but it would be surprising if training in social skills did not prove to be substitutable for overeating as well as for other addictions. Another likely candidate for a substitute for overeating is exercise. That is, the activities of overeating and exercising may satisfy some common basic need. (What that need may be is of less interest to the behaviorist than the economic substitutability itself.) The effectiveness of exercise in weight control may not be so much in the calories exercising consumes as in its economic substitutability for overeating.

Exercise has the further advantage over social activity as a substitute for eating in that our social system does not impose a degree of complementarity on exercise and eating. It is easy—in fact almost necessary—to eat while socializing in our society, but difficult to eat while swimming, riding a bicycle, or playing basketball (although I have known it to be done). This constitutes some theoretical support for the common wisdom that an exercise program should be an important part of any weight control program—especially one for children or adolescents. But if the effectiveness of exercise lies more in its substitutability for eating than directly in calorie reduction, then there is a reason to include training in other positive addictions (music appreciation, playing a musical instrument, reading serious literature, collecting stamps or baseball cards, playing chess or computer games) as well as social skills as part of weight control programs. But it is important to remember that any activity may be harmful if it crowds out all of the others. Weight control cannot be treated in isolation.

CONCLUSION

The relation between theory and practice is probably closer in behavioral psychology than it is in any other psychological field. Still, a wide gap remains. Since practice has more to tell theory than theory has to tell practice, it would be presumptuous for an experimentalist and theorist to try to tell clinicians how to design a weight control program. Nevertheless, some practical problems, especially those involving self control, are tied at various points to current behavior theory (Rachlin, 2000). This article brings together ten such connecting strands (economics and reinforcement, weight control versus weight reduction, monitoring, maintenance versus reduction, maintenance duration, the stimulus boundedness of habits, behavior patterning to control two habits at once, negative versus positive addictions, and soft commitment). They are not intended as prescriptions, not even strong suggestions, for clinical practice. They are rather just messages from an experimenter and theorist of a particular kind (a teleological behaviorist) that may prove useful to clinicians dealing with problems of weight control in children and adolescents.

ACKNOWLEDGMENT

This chapter was prepared with the assistance of a grant from the National Institutes of Health.

REFERENCES

Green, L., & Kagel, J. H. (1996). *Advances in behavioral economics. Vol. 3: Substance use and abuse.* Norwood, NJ: Ablex Publishing.
Herrnstein, R. J., & Prelec, D. (1992). A theory of addiction. In G. Loewenstein & J. Elster (Eds.), *Choice over time* (pp. 331–360). New York: Russell Sage.

Kagel, J. H., Battalio, R. C., & Green, L. (1995). *Economic choice theory: an experimental analysis of animal behavior.* New York: Cambridge University Press.

Neuringer, A. (2004). Reinforced variability in animals and people. *American Psychologist, 59,* 891–906.

Premack, D. (1965). Reinforcement theory. In D. Levine (Ed.), *Nebraska symposium on motivation* (pp. 123–179). Lincoln: University of Nebraska Press.

Rachlin, H. (1994). *Behavior and mind: the roots of modern psychology.* New York: Oxford University Press.

Rachlin, H. (2000). *The science of self-control.* Cambridge, MA: Harvard University Press.

Robins, L. (1974). The Vietnam drug user returns. Final Report. Special Action Office Monograph, Series A, Number 2, May 1974. Washington D.C.: U.S. Government Printing Office.

Siegel, E., & Rachlin, H. (1996). Soft commitment: self-control achieved by response persistence. *Journal of the Experimental Analysis of Behavior, 64,* 117–128.

Stigler, G. J., & Becker, G. S. (1977). De gustibus non est disputandum. *American Economic Review, 67,* 76–90.

10

Hedonic Approach to Pediatric and Adolescent Weight Management

BRIE A. MOORE AND WILLIAM T. O'DONOHUE

Throughout history, children and adults alike have indulged in reinforcing sedentary activities and consumed calorie- and fat-laden foods. As recently as three decades ago it was unheard of to limit the amount or type of food a child could eat. Yet the issue of overweight in children and adolescents is historically rare. One hypothesis for this seeming contradiction is that children were engaged in a greater variety of pleasurable, hedonic, and highly reinforcing activities.

According to early Greek philosophers, hedonism was the belief that pleasure was the greatest good and highest aspiration of mankind (Bunnin & Tsui-James, 2002). From a behavioral perspective, any behavior that is reinforced by its pleasurable consequences may be considered hedonic (Foxall, 1999). Reinforcement is the contingency of a higher valued activity over a less preferred activity (Premack, 1965). The term hedonic, as used here, describes items and activities that are liked and have high reinforcing values relative to many available alternatives. Behavioral science has found that when presented with a choice, we often act in ways to maximize pleasurable consequences and reduce behavioral costs (Hernstein, Rachlin, & Laibson, 1997), with a bias toward short-term, immediate reinforcers (Rachlin et al., 1976). When considering the challenge of child and adolescent weight management, it becomes evident that the current environment is filled with a myriad of discriminative stimuli for engaging in reinforcing, pleasure-seeking behaviors. When children are presented with unlimited access to potent reinforcing stimuli, such as mocha almond fudge ice cream or an X Box 360, they predictably choose these alternatives at higher rates. Easy access to a variety of such items characterizes the current obesogenic environment.

To date, in order to challenge this toxic environment (Horgen & Brownell, 2002), the majority of weight management efforts have focused on breaking the connections between discriminative stimuli and problematic lifestyle behaviors through education and contingency management (Epstein et al., 2007). For example, parents are often encouraged to discourage mindless munching on high-calorie snacks by removing chips, candy, and ice cream from the house. This, of course, is sound advice. There is, however, another half of the equation that must be addressed for successful long-term weight management. Effective weight management depends not only on breaking the connection between discriminative stimuli and unhealthy lifestyle behaviors, but also establishing connections between discriminative stimuli and health-promoting behaviors (Rachlin, 2004). That is, how do we create environments that elicit reinforcing healthy behaviors?

Establishing new connections between discriminative stimuli and healthy behaviors can be most easily established by capitalizing on our tendency to seek out and frequently engage in activities that have the greatest reinforcing value. Researchers have adopted various theoretical models to address this issue. Through the theoretical lens of behavioral economics, this chapter proposes one strategy for establishing the connections necessary for health promotion—a hedonic approach to child and family weight management.

BEHAVIORAL ECONOMICS, UTILITY, AND HEDONISM

According to behavioral economic theory, choice can be empirically determined by taking into account the perceived utility (i.e., costs and benefits) of an activity. Beyond the rational calculation of utility, this theory holds that our behavior is largely controlled by the time horizon within which we consider the consequences of our actions. Consequences are less powerful, or discounted, the more distal they are (Rachlin et al., 1981). For example, while in the cookie section of the local grocers, we are able to fully consider the costs and benefits of the many alternatives while at the store. We ignore, however, the more distal consequences, such as the possible weight gain or health effects that could occur after the selection has been made. Similarly, educational efforts that seek to create connections between health knowledge and lifestyle choices may have limited efficacy because of our tendency to overweight benefits that are immediately available, specific, clearly definable, or precisely measurable (such as the tastiness of the cookies) and underweight benefits, like better health, that are delayed, not clearly definable, nor precisely measurable (Rachlin, 2004).

Whereas certain immediate choices may be detrimental to the future local utility of other factors, such as in the example above, other activities can have positive effects on future utility. In particular, the utility of activities that involve the learning of skills tends to increase the more the activity is performed (Rachlin, 2004). The relative costs of performing these activities decreases as new skills are acquired and the activity elicits greater enjoyment. Recreational sports, such as skiing, tennis, and golf, are just a few examples of such activities.

Given the limited time horizons of children (i.e., inability to consider long-term consequences) and the tendency to maximize local utility (Hernstein & Vaughaun, 1980; Rachlin et al., 1981), intervention efforts that focus on maximizing distal utility by maximizing local utility may hold considerable promise. Said differently, behavior directed to particular ends can also achieve abstract ends—by accident. By engaging in pleasurable, "inherently" reinforcing or valued activities now (a concrete target), children establish the first link in a chain of behavioral patterns that will enable them to reap long-term health benefits. For example, the child who dances vigorously to her favorite music or runs as fast as he can to "tag" his friend unknowingly works toward the abstract goal of improved health. Furthermore, as these health promotion behaviors become habits, they create the behavioral momentum necessary to generally make daily choices that are consistent with this implicit, long-term goal. This implementation of the hedonic principle deemphasizes weight management and capitalizes on an existing strength in the child's behavioral repertoire—having fun!

EMPIRICAL SUPPORT FOR HEDONIC APPROACHES

Our tendency to allocate behavioral resources in such a way that pleasure is maximized also can be seen as an asset in the design and implementation of family-based weight management programs. In the empirically based treatment of pediatric and adolescent overweight, there is a dearth of outcome studies that conceptualize the positive clinical implications of the hedonic appetite. A Medline database search using the terms "child," "adolescent," "hedonic," "overweight," and "obesity" produced 13 results. When the limits (1) English, (2) randomized controlled trial/clinical trial, and (3) age 0–18 were applied, two studies were found, with only one of these relevant to pediatric obesity (the other relevant to pain tolerance). However, several policy statements, review articles, and data from the larger body of literature concerned with childhood obesity treatment provide support for a hedonic approach to weight management and are reviewed below.

Palatability and the Relative Reinforcing Value of Food

Palatability is often defined as the sensory properties of food, such as smell, taste, and texture, which comprise a perceived level of pleasure attained from eating that food. Research on the etiology and maintenance of overweight has underscored the relationship between palatability and a "hedonic response." This response is characterized by our tendency, regardless of physiological need, to respond to the discriminative stimulus of highly palatable food with short-term overconsumption. Over time, this response ultimately leads to weight gain and has been demonstrated in both animal (Sclafani, 2004) and human models (Blundell & Finlayson, 2004). In the presence of a variety of high-calorie, palatable foods, satiation of the hedonic appetite is prolonged and more calories are generally consumed (Raynor & Epstein, 2001).

Studies have found that children who are overweight demonstrate stronger preferences for energy-dense foods (Wardle, Guthrie, Sanderson, Birch, & Plomin, 2001). For example, Smith and Epstein, 1991 found that before participation in a behavioral weight control program, ratings of high-fat and high-sugar foods were higher for children who were overweight than for children whose weight was within normal limits. Wardle et al. (2001) demonstrated similar results in their sample. In contrast, a randomized controlled trial investigating food preferences among 101 lean (girls' mean body mass index [BMI] = 20.94 ± 1.93) and overweight (girls' mean BMI = 28.71 ± 1.55) 13-year-olds found no differences between children in preferences for higher fat, higher sugar, or more energy-dense foods as measured by a face valid hedonic Likert scale (Perl, Mandic, Primorac, Klapec, & Perl, 1998). In fact, lean children demonstrated greater liking of sweets, meat, and cereals than children in the overweight group, with normal weight boys preferring meat and sweets more than lean girls. Similar results have been found in other studies conducted with lean and obese adults (Cox et al., 1998). A considerable body of research conducted by Leann Birch and colleagues cautions that children's food preferences are largely shaped by exposure to certain foods in the family environment (Savage, Fisher, & Birch, 2007). In fact, children presented with fruits and vegetables over 8 to 10 exposures later choose these items at higher rates (Birch & Fisher, 2000). Thus reported preferences may be a better reflection of experience than actual liking.

Researchers have explored the contextual factors that elicit the choice of healthy foods in children who are overweight and in adults whose weight is within the normal range. In an investigation examining the relative reinforcing values of snack foods, healthy foods, and sedentary behaviors, normal weight college students reported equal hedonic ratings for preferred snack foods and preferred alternative reinforcers, yet worked twice as hard for access to preferred snack foods (Goldfield & Epstein, 2002). Using a computerized behavioral choice task paradigm, these researchers found that increasing behavioral costs for snack foods decreased snack food consumption while increasing the choice of healthier food and nonfood alternatives. Thus, by limiting access to preferred reinforcers and providing easy access to alternative reinforcers, participants' choices shifted to the more readily available options.

Based on this research, a number of intervention strategies have been proposed for the prevention and treatment of obesity. Strategies such as keeping high-fat snack foods out of the house and making fruits, vegetables, and nonfood alternatives easily available are common in behavioral weight control. In addition, reducing the variety of high-calorie foods offered while increasing the variety in healthy foods such as fruits and vegetables may be effective in the prevention and treatment of obesity (Raynor & Epstein, 2001). Together, treatment strategies should target maximizing hedonic satisfaction by creating environments where the cost of accessing highly reinforcing alternatives is low.

Activity Preference

Play is an integral part of child development. Research has shown that physically active play is also a cornerstone in successful long-term weight control for the overweight child (Epstein et al., 2000b). Physically active play has been demonstrated to have a high hedonic value in preadolescent children (Sherwood, Story, Neumark-Sztainer, Adkins, & Davis, 2003). In a survey study of the activity preferences of 96 eight- to ten-year-old normal and overweight African American girls (mean BMI = 19.2 ± 4.3), large majorities of the sample expressed strong interest in unstructured outdoor activities such as water play (94%), biking (85%), jumping rope (81%), skating (79%), and playing tag, chase, hopscotch, and at the playground (79%). Based on these findings, the researchers concluded that if given the opportunity to engage in pleasurable active pursuits, children may be more likely to substitute these activities for sedentary activities such as television viewing (Sherwood et al., 2003).

Increasing the availability of active play opportunities may not be enough for substitution to occur. For many children who are overweight, physical activity may be less reinforcing than sedentary alternatives (Epstein, Smith, Vara, & Rodefer, 1991). To address this challenge, researchers have examined the contextual factors that prompt children who are overweight to choose physically active alternatives to reinforcing sedentary behaviors. In a study of the substitutability of physically active behavior for sedentary activities, 26 overweight (BMI = 28.0 ± 4.3) and 32 nonoverweight (BMI = 18.9 ± 2.1) 8- to 16-year-old children participated in a baseline phase, and then two consecutive treatment phases in which targeted sedentary activities were first increased, then decreased (Epstein, Roemmich, Paluch, & Raynor, 2005). Children recorded the time and duration of sedentary behaviors in a monitoring log. Physical activity was measured on two weekdays and one weekend day using an accelerometer. Results indicated that the children with greater BMI scores were more likely to reduce physical activity when sedentary behaviors were increased. Moreover, youth with low levels of activity at baseline were more likely to show larger increases in physical activity when sedentary behaviors were decreased (Epstein et al., 2005). The results of this study indicate that reductions in sedentary activity may lead overweight children to spontaneously increase physical activity.

These findings are consistent with the results of previous studies (Epstein, Valoski, Wing, & McCurley, 1994). Children participating in a 4-month, family-based behavioral obesity treatment were randomized to one of three groups who received differential reinforcement for (1) increasing physical activity, (2) reducing sedentary activity, or (3) doing both. After treatment, children for whom reducing sedentary behavior was reinforced demonstrated greater changes in percent overweight than children for whom increases in physical activity were reinforced. Moreover, these children demonstrated a higher level of preference for physical activities than children for whom physical activity was reinforced. These results were maintained at 1-year follow-up. Together, these studies illustrate that establishing environmental contingencies that promote substitution of physically active play for sedentary play may prove to be an effective strategy for promoting the active lifestyle necessary for successful long-term weight control.

Reducing access to sedentary activity may be particularly challenging for families and children who are overweight. This effective approach can be complemented by an unstructured, hedonic approach to lifestyle physical activity. A lifestyle approach to physical activity promotes enjoyment and choice and sets the stage for the development of habits that can function to maintain reductions in weight status. To promote energy expenditure in children and families, researchers have compared unstructured and structured exercise programs. Early studies conducted by Epstein et al. (1982, 1985) investigated the structure and intensity of the exercise component of a family-based behavioral weight control program. In one study, participants were assigned to one of four groups: (1) aerobic exercise plus the Traffic Light Diet (described below), (2) aerobic exercise only,

(3) lifestyle exercise programs plus the Traffic Light Diet, or (4) lifestyle exercise only. Lifestyle exercise included unstructured activities of varying intensity, such as walking or biking to school or doing household chores. Programmed exercise was conducted in one bout of moderate to vigorous intensity aerobic activity. The groups that participated in lifestyle physical activity programs with and without the Traffic Light Diet demonstrated greater reductions in overweight at a 17 month follow-up than the aerobic exercise groups. These findings are consistent with longitudinal data showing maintenance of treatment gains at 5- and 10-year follow-up evaluations (Epstein et al., 1990; Epstein et al., 1994). Together, these studies suggest that promotion of an unstructured approach to physical activity promotes long-term changes in activity levels that can be incorporated into the child's and family's lifestyle.

These results highlight the importance of providing various opportunities for pleasurable and unstructured active play. Like substitutability in food choice, for children who are overweight, increasing the cost of sedentary activity (i.e., reducing access) may function as a prompt to sample the physical activities that are available in their environment. With increased skill development, the relative costs of performing these activities may decrease substantially and the reinforcing value of activity may increase as it comes to elicit greater enjoyment (Rachlin, 2004). With this shift in allocation of costs and benefits, children may be more likely to adopt active habits in the short-term which will serve to create the behavioral momentum necessary to make daily choices that promote long-term improvements in health.

General Support in Pediatric Behavioral Weight Control

To date, a number of behavioral weight management programs have adopted this general approach to diet. Most notably so, over the past 25 years, Epstein et al. (2007) have conducted a series of empirical investigations of the Traffic Light Diet. The Traffic Light Diet is a family-based, behavioral weight control program. According to the Traffic Light Diet, rather than restricting any one type of food, energy balance across food groups is promoted with an overall calorie goal of 900 to 1200 kcal/day. Foods are classified as red, yellow, or green based on their nutrient density. Red foods consist of high-fat and high-sugar foods, such as chips and candy, and should be eaten in limited quantities. Yellow foods are foods that should be eaten primarily at meals, such as lean meats. Green foods, consisting primarily of vegetables, can be eaten in unlimited quantities. Thus consumption of energy-dense foods is restricted and promoted in the lowest calorie foods.

A series of randomized controlled trials have investigated the efficacy of the Traffic Light Diet as compared to no treatment (Epstein, Wing, Koeske, & Valoski, 1984), problem-solving (Epstein, Paluch, Gordy, Saelens, & Ernst, 2000a; Epstein, Paluch, Saelens, Ernst, & Wifley, 2001); and treatment as usual (Epstein et al., 1985). At the 10-year follow-up, children who received the Traffic Light Diet demonstrated sustained reductions in their percentage of overweight as compared to controls (Epstein et al., 1994). Comprehensive reviews of these and other studies involving a behavioral approach to pediatric weight management are available in other chapters of this book.

Behavioral weight management programs readily endorse the presentation of a variety of healthy foods and moderation in energy-dense foods. However, these programs are less likely to explicitly endorse a hedonistic approach based on palatability, child involvement, and collaborative choice. In the past decade, a number of policy statements have been released by prominent organizations that are concerned about the growing pediatric and adolescent obesity epidemic. Consistent across these recommendations is an emphasis on implementing strategies for weight control and health promotion that can be maintained long term as part of a healthy lifestyle.

Expert Recommendations. In line with a hedonic approach, the American Academy of Pediatrics Expert Committee on Obesity Evaluation and Treatment recommended the provision of pleasurable choices for food and play (Barlow & Dietz, 1998). Similarly, the American Dietetic Association (Nicklas & Johnson, 2004) holds that children should "enjoy food" (p. 660). To this end, practitioners and parents are advised to ask children which of two enjoyable options they would prefer (e.g., playing outside or going to the park; an apple or popcorn) and to avoid encouraging structured exercises, such as aerobics or treadmills (as children often find these activities boring or punitive). "When children can choose, they are less likely to view the alternative they select as unattractive" (Barlow & Dietz, 1998, p. 8). Together, these policy statements support a collaborative effort between parents and children to choose options that are both pleasant and healthy.

IMPLICATIONS FOR FUTURE RESEARCH

As the reviewed studies suggest, a hedonic approach to the treatment of pediatric and adolescent overweight may prove a viable strategy for long-term weight management; however, this approach is not without its limitations. As discussed above, behavioral economic theory holds that individuals seek to maximize benefits and minimize costs (Rachlin, 2004). When strategically aligned, local utility can function to complement future utility. Playing soccer now can improve a child's health in the long term (assuming this is not an isolated event, but rather an opportunity to nurture an enjoyment for physical activity).

Future research is needed to examine the relative efficacy of a hedonic approach when combined with existing treatment strategies. Does this approach contribute substantially to existing methodologies in promoting treatment engagement, reducing resistance, increasing adherence, and augmenting outcomes? Can this approach promote treatment readiness and facilitate movement through the stages of change? Research is also needed to examine the contextual factors necessary to elicit behaviors that are consistent with health promotion across varied populations of children who are overweight. In particular, strategies to encourage alternative behaviors are needed to overcome a history of failure in weight control programs. This research should address barriers to adherence for both parents and children. Many existing techniques are difficult for families to employ. It is the aim of the present approach to reduce this perceived level of difficulty. Future investigations should explore the acceptability of this approach, as attrition is a serious problem in the empirically based treatment of pediatric obesity. Lastly, the hedonic approach to weight control may have implications within a stepped care model of prevention. Educational efforts that prompt children and families to increase their involvement in pleasurable physical activities and their consumption of preferred, healthy foods may prove to be successful and cost-effective preventive approaches. Further research is needed in this area as well.

PRACTICAL IMPLICATIONS

Indeed, the current environment is filled with opportunities for pleasure-seeking behaviors. Just as the environment can serve as a prompt for engaging in sedentary behaviors and consumption patterns that may be detrimental to long-term health, it can also function to prompt the development of healthy habits.

As mentioned above, several limitations to this approach do exist. Practitioners and parents should adopt this hedonic principle, rather than a prescriptive list, as an overarching philosophy to inform decision-making practices. That is, those interested in altering behavior should elicit the child's active collaboration in determining preferred weight management strategies, with few restrictions placed on appropriate choices. Parents may be surprised to learn that their child is interested in yoga, dance, gymnastics, martial arts, or trying foods from various cultures.

Making new choices can be daunting for children and families. To encourage success, children may benefit from first being introduced to new activities in a supportive, noncompetitive environment and at a slow pace. Indeed, enrolling a child who has no experience with soccer in a fast-paced club full of seasoned players may be intimidating and may only function to discourage future attempts at physical activity. However, getting a group of neighborhood kids together at a local park may be a more welcoming setting for skill building, socialization, and gradual cardiovascular conditioning. With increased involvement and choice, children may be more apt to engage in new activities. Readers interested in resources for selecting age- and ability-appropriate activities are encouraged to access the guidelines from the Centers for Disease Control and Prevention for school and community activity programs (1997) and the Surgeon General's (1996) report on physical activity.

Similar to adopting new active pursuits, parents should be advised to plan the introduction to new foods thoughtfully. Consistent with a hedonic approach, three main principles apply here: (1) solicit child input and collaboration (looking at recipes, at the store, and in meal preparation), (2) consider the palatability of foods, and (3) focus on the nutritional quality of foods over quantity.

Increased involvement in food selection and preparation has been found to be a viable strategy for encouraging consumption of a variety of foods (Barlow & Dietz, 1998). Children who are typically characterized as "picky eaters" often enjoy trying new foods that they have prepared. Interested readers can find various quick, easy, inexpensive, and creative strategies in children's cookbooks and activity books such as *365 Activities for Food, Fitness and Fun* (Sweet & Jacobson, 2001).

In addition to increasing child involvement, introducing highly palatable new foods may reinforce the general class of behaviors associated with trying new foods and dissuade children and families from perpetuating the notion that healthy foods cannot taste good. However, it is not uncommon for children who are overweight to have had little experience eating a wide variety of foods—especially fruits and vegetables. Because food preferences are learned through repeated exposure, these foods may initially be viewed as unpalatable. Therefore parents should be encouraged to persist in offering a variety of healthy foods to encourage the development of a "taste" for healthier alternatives.

Lastly, health promotion and weight reduction strategies should focus on increasing the nutritional quality of foods consumed rather than a reduction in caloric intake. The overall goal of pediatric weight management is to slow the rate of weight gain as the child grows (Barlow & Dietz, 1998). Efforts to restrict the amount or types of foods children eat is positively associated with increased weight status (Birch & Fisher, 2000; Birch & Fisher, 1999). When adopting a hedonic approach to weight management, children should be offered a variety of healthy foods that they enjoy and should be encouraged to eat based on hunger and satiety levels rather than on caloric prescriptions.

Overall, adopting a hedonic approach to child weight management is consistent with lifestyle approaches reviewed here that underscore variety and moderation. The hedonic principle aims to make it pleasurable for children and families to adopt healthier lifestyle habits while preserving opportunities to engage in pleasurable activities not commonly associated with weight management. This moderate lifestyle approach aims to reduce the relative reinforcing values of commonly targeted and restricted foods and activities. Moreover, in the service of long-term behavior change, this approach seeks to make a wide range of pleasurable behaviors available for enjoyment of the child and family.

REFERENCES

Barlow, S., & Dietz, W. (1998). Obesity evaluation and treatment: expert committee recommendations. *Pediatrics, 102*(3), e29.

Birch, L. L., & J. O. Fisher (2000). Mothers' child-feeding practices influence daughters' eating and weight. *American Journal of Clinical Nutrition, 71,* 1054–1061.

Blundell, J. E., & Finlayson, G. (2004). Is susceptibility to weight gain characterized by homeostatic or hedonic risk factors for overconsumption? *Physiology and Behavior, 82*(1), 21–25.

Bunnin, N., & E. Tsui-James (2002). Glossary of philosophical terms. In *The Blackwell Companion to Philosophy*, 2nd ed. Cambridge: Cambridge University Press. Accessed from http://www.filosofia.net/materiales/rec/glosaen.htm.

Centers for Disease Control and Prevention (1997). Guidelines for school and community programs to promote lifelong physical activity among young people. *Morbidity and Mortality Weekly Report, 46*, 1–36.

Cox, D. N., van Galen, M., Hedderley, D., Perry, L., Moore, P. B., & Mela, D. J. (1998). Sensory and hedonic judgments of common foods by lean consumers and consumers with obesity. *Obesity Research, 6*, 438–447.

Epstein, L. H., McCurley, J., Wing, R. R., & Valoski, A. (1990). Five-year follow-up of family-based behavioral treatments for childhood obesity. *Journal of Consulting and Clinical Psychology, 58*(5), 661–664.

Epstein, L. H., Paluch, R. A., Saelens, B. E., Ernst, M. M. & Wilfley, D. E. (2001). Changes in eating disorder symptoms with pediatric obesity treatment. *Journal of Pediatrics, 139*(1):58–65.

Epstein, L. H., Roemmich, J. N., Paluch, R. A., & Raynor, H. A. (2005). Physical activity as a substitute for sedentary behavior in youth. *Annals of Behavioral Medicine, 29*, 200–209.

Epstein, L. H., Smith, J. A., Vara, L. S., & Rodefer, J. S. (1991). Behavioral economic analysis of activity choice in obese children. *Health Psychology, 10*, 311–316.

Epstein, L. H., Valoski, A., Wing, R. R., & McCurley, J. (1994). Ten-year outcomes of behavioral family-based treatment for childhood obesity. *Health Psychology, 13*, 373-383.

Epstein, L. H., Paluch, R. A., Gordy, C. C., Saelens, B. E., & Ernst, M. M. (2000a). Problem solving in the treatment of childhood obesity. *Journal of Consulting and Clinical Psychology, 68*(4), 717–721.

Epstein, L. H., Paluch, R. A., Gordy, C. C., & Dorn, J. (2000b). Decreasing sedentary behaviors in treating pediatric obesity. *Archives of Pediatric and Adolescent Medicine, 154*(3), 2202–2226.

Epstein, L. H., Paluch, R. A., Roemmich, J. N., & Beecher, M. D. (2007). Family-based obesity treatment, then and now: twenty-five years of pediatric obesity treatment. *Health Psychology, 26*(4), 381–391.

Epstein, L. H., Wing, R. R., Koeske, R., Ossip, D., & Beck, S. (1982). A comparison of lifestyle change and programmed aerobic exercise on weight and fitness change in obese children. *Behavior Therapy, 13*, 651–665.

Epstein, L. H., Wing, R. R., Koeske, R., & Valoski, A. (1985). A comparison of lifestyle exercise, aerobic exercise, and calisthenics on weight loss in obese children. *Behavior Therapy, 16*, 345–356.

Epstein, L. H., Wing, R. R., Koeske, R., & Valoski, A. (1984). Effects of diet plus exercise on weight change in parents and children. *Journal of Consulting and Clinical Psychology, 52*(3), 429–437.

Fisher, J. O., & Birch, L. L. (1999). Restricting access to foods and children's eating. *Apptetite, 32*, 405–419.

Foxall, G. R. (1999). The behavioral perspective model: Consensiblity and consensuality. *European Journal of Marketing, 33*(5/6), 570–597.

Goldfield, G. S., & Epstein, L. H. (2002). Can fruits and vegetable and activities substitute for snack foods? *Health Psychology, 21*, 299–303.

Hernstein, R. J., Rachlin, H., & D. Liabson (1997). *The Matching Law: Papers in Psychology and Economics.* Rachlin, H., & Laibson, D (Eds.). Cambridge: Harvard University Press.

Hernstein, R. J., & Vaughn, W. (1980). Melioration and behavioral allocation. In *Limits to action: The allocation of behavior*, Staddon, J. E. R. (Ed.), pp. 143–176. New York: Academic Press.

Horgen, K. B., & Brownell, K. D. (2002). Confronting the toxic environment: Environmental, public health actions in a world crisis, In *Handbook of obesity treatment*, T. A. Wadden, & A. J. Stunkard (Eds.), pp. 95–106. New York: Guilford Press.

Logue, A. W. (1995). *Self-control: waiting for tomorrow for what you want today.* Englewood Cliffs, NJ: Prentice Hall.

Nicklas, T. & Johnson, R. Position of the American Dietetic Association: dietary guidance for healthy children ages 2 to 11 years. *Journal of the American Dietetic Association, 104*, 660–677.

Perl, M. A., Mandic, M. L., Primorac, L., Klapec, T., & Perl, A. (1998). Adolescent acceptance of different foods by obesity status and sex. *Physiology and Behavior, 65*, 241–245.

Premack, D. (1965). Reinforcement theory. In *Nebraska Symposium on Motivation*, D. Levine (Ed.), Lincoln: University of Nebraska Press.

Rachlin, H. (2004). *The science of self-control.* Cambridge, MA: Harvard University Press.

Raynor, H. A., & Epstein, L. H. (2001). Dietary variety, energy regulation, and obesity. *Psychological Bulletin, 127*, 325–341.

Rachlin, H. (1981). Maximization theory in behavioral psychology. *Behavioral and Brain Sciences, 4,* 371–417.

Rachlin, H., Green, L., Kagel, J. H., & Battalio, R. C. (1976). Economic demand theory and psychological studies of choice. In *The psychology of learning and motivation*, Vol. 10, G. H. Bower (Ed.), pp. 129–154. New York: Academic Press.

Savage, J. S., Fisher, J. O., & L. L. Birch (2007). Parental influence on eating behavior: Conception to adolescence. *Journal of Law, Medicine, and Ethics, 35*(1), 22–34.

Sclafani, A. (2004). Oral and postoral determinants of food reward. *Physiology and Behavior, 81,* 773–779.

Sherwood, N. E., Story, M., Neumark-Sztainer, D., Adkins, S., & Davis, M. (2003). Development and implementation of a visual card-sorting technique for assessing food and activity preferences and patterns in African-American girls. *Journal of the American Dietetic Association, 103,* 1473–1479.

Smith, J. A., & Epstein, L. H. (1991). Behavioral economic analysis of food choice in obese children. *Appetite, 17*(2), 91–95.

Surgeon General. (1996). *Physical activity and health: a report of the surgeon general.* Washington, D.C.: Department of Health and Human Services.

Wardle, J., Guthrie, C., Sanderson, S., Birch, L., & Plomin, R. (2001). Food and activity preferences in children of lean and obese parents. *International Journal of Obesity Related Metabolic Disorders, 25,* 971–977.

Part III

TREATMENT APPROACHES: A STEPPED CARE PERSPECTIVE

11

Intensive Approaches to the Treatment of Pediatric and Adolescent Obesity

ROBERT H. LUSTIG

INTRODUCTION

Lifestyle modification (diet and exercise) is and remains the cornerstone of pediatric obesity therapy; nonetheless, the number of studies that demonstrate efficacy in the clinical realm are exceedingly few (Center for Weight and Health, 2001). It has been suggested that "intensive therapy," including pharmacotherapy, be reserved for 2- to 7-year-old children with a body mass index (BMI) greater than or equal to the 95th percentile with secondary complications (e.g., hypertension, dyslipidemia, insulin resistance, sleep apnea), children older than 7 years of age with a BMI between the 85th and 95th percentiles with secondary complications, and children older than 7 years of age with a BMI greater than the 95th percentile, regardless of complications (Barlow & Dietz, 1998; Cuttler, Whittaker, & Kodish, 2005; Speiser et al., 2005; Yanovski, 2001). Unfortunately the percentage of children who meet these criteria is increasing with each successive year, making prevention the highest priority, with safe and effective pediatric pharmacotherapy and surgery a close second.

This chapter is written with the working assumption that a formal 6- to 12-month period of psychodynamic, cognitive, or family therapy has been attempted and has not been effective. The standard uninformed provider response is that such patients and families are noncompliant; after all, if obesity is just a matter of eating too much and exercising too little, then changing the behavior should change the weight, right? In fact, such an approach to obesity therapy ignores the numerous medical syndromes and pathophysiologic mechanisms that have been elaborated over the past decade with the discovery of leptin (see below).

In fact, obesity is not a behavior; it is not even a disease (as that would assume a common pathophysiology). Indeed, obesity is a phenotype of many different pathologies, listed in Table 11.1, that adversely affect the negative feedback energy balance pathway, resulting in an increased storage of energy in adipose tissue due to increased lipogenesis, decreased lipolysis, or both. In some cases, these various processes can promote an obligate and primary weight gain (see below), and

Table 11.1 Classification of Childhood Obesity Disorders

Leptin Resistance

Most common; also accounts for diet-induced obesity

Monogenetic Disorders of the Energy Balance Pathway

Leptin deficiency
Leptin receptor deficiency
POMC mutation (red hair, adrenal insufficiency)
Prohormone convertase-1 deficiency
MC_3R mutation
MC_4R mutation
SIM1 mutation

Genetic Disorders (Mental Retardation Prominent)

Prader-Willi syndrome
    Short stature
    Hypogonadism
    Hypotonia
    Ghrelin overproduction
Bardet-Biedl syndrome
    Retinitis pigmentosa
    Polydactyly
    Hypogonadism
TrkB mutation
    Hypotonia
    Impaired short-term memory
    Decreased nociception
Borjeson-Forssman-Lehmann syndrome
    Microcephaly
    Large ears
    Hypogonadism
Carpenter syndrome
    Variable craniosynostosis
    Brachdactyly, polydacytly, syndactyly
    Congenital heart disease
    Hypogonadism
Cohen syndrome
    Persistent hypotonia
    Microcephaly
    Maxillary hypoplasia
    Prominent incisors
Alstrom syndrome
    Hypogonadism
    Short stature
    Neurosensory deficits

"Classical" Endocrine Disorders (Short Stature/Growth Failure Prominent)

Hypothyroidism
    Primary
    Central

Table 11.1 Classification of Childhood Obesity Disorders (Continued)

Cushing's syndrome (adrenal hypercorticism)
    Adrenal adenoma/carcinoma
    Adrenal micronodular hyperplasia
    Pituitary ACTH-secreting tumor
    Ectopic ACTH-secreting tumor
    Exogenous glucocorticoid administration
Growth hormone deficiency
Pseudohypoparathyroidism 1a
    Maternal transmission (AHO + multihormone resistance)
    Paternal transmission (pseudopseudohypoparathyroidism, AHO only)

Insulin Dynamic Disorders

    Hypothalamic obesity (insulin hypersecretion)
    Primary insulin resistance

increased energy intake and decreased energy expenditure may secondarily result. The key to successful therapy is accurate diagnosis. Unfortunately our diagnostic armamentarium is not yet fully developed, so matching treatment to diagnosis is still uncertain. This chapter attempts to provide a paradigm and framework for diagnosis and intensive treatment of different etiologies of dysfunctional energy balance.

LEPTIN, INSULIN, THE AUTONOMIC NERVOUS SYSTEM, AND ENERGY BALANCE

First, we must understand how our body normally regulates energy balance (Figure 11.1) (Lustig, 2001). This is also covered in Chapter 2. Our energy intake versus expenditure is normally regulated very tightly (within 0.15% per year) by the hormone leptin. Leptin is a 167 amino acid hormone produced by adipocytes; it transmits the primary long-term signal of energy depletion/repletion to the ventromedial hypothalamus (VMH) (Lustig, 2006). On transducing this leptin signal, the VMH does two things. First, the VMH increases the activity of the sympathetic nervous system (SNS) (Mark, Rahmouni, Correia, & Haynes, 2003). The SNS regulates energy balance by

- Innervating the hypothalamus and appetite centers in the medulla to reduce appetite
- Increasing thyroid-stimulating hormone (TSH) secretion to increase thyroid hormone release and energy expenditure
- Innervating skeletal muscles to increase energy expenditure, by stimulating the production of ATP for muscle contractility, and also by increasing uncoupling proteins within the mitochondria, which increases heat loss from muscle
- Innervating β_3-adrenergic receptors in white adipose tissue to increase lipolysis

The magnitude of energy expenditure also has a salutary effect on one's quality of life; those factors that reduce resting energy expenditure (REE) (e.g., hypothyroidism) reduce quality of life, while those factors that increase REE (e.g., caffeine) increase quality of life (at least acutely).

Second, the VMH reduces the activity of the vagus nerve, which serves essentially the opposite role of the SNS in the regulation of energy balance, as it promotes energy storage (Lustig, 2006). Inhibition of the vagus nerve

- Speeds the heart rate, increasing myocardial oxygen consumption
- Slows peristalsis and energy substrate absorption in the intestine
- Reduces insulin secretion (Lustig, 2003) to reduce energy clearance into adipocytes
- Reduces adipose tissue insulin sensitivity to prevent energy accumulation in fat (Kreier et al., 2002)

Every person has a "personal leptin threshold" above which the brain interprets a state of energy sufficiency. Thus the leptin-replete state is characterized by increased physical activity, decreased appetite, and increased feelings of well-being.

The Starvation Response

Conversely, in conditions of leptin depletion, such as in the "starvation response," the VMH, of necessity, decreases SNS tone (to conserve energy) (Aronne, Mackintosh, Rosenbaum, Leibel, &

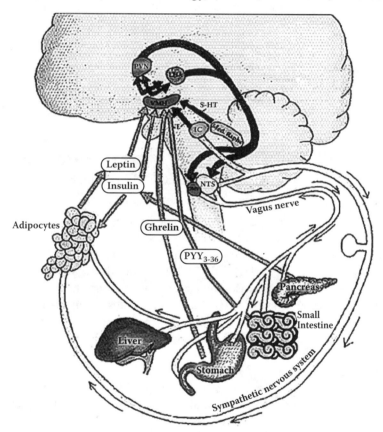

Figure 11.1 The negative feedback pathway of energy balance. Afferent (gray), central (black), and efferent (white) pathways are delineated. The hormones insulin, leptin, ghrelin, and peptide $YY_{(3-36)}$ (PYY_{3-36}) provide afferent information to the ventromedial hypothalamus (VMH) regarding short-term energy metabolism and energy sufficiency. From there, the VMH elicits anorexigenic and orexigenic signals to the melanocortin-4 receptor in the paraventricular nucleus (PVN) and lateral hypothalamic area (LHA). These lead to efferent output via the locus coeruleus (LC), which activates the sympathetic nervous system, causing the adipocyte to undergo lipolysis, or via the dorsal motor nucleus of the vagus (DMV), which activates the vagus nerve to store energy, both by increasing pancreatic insulin secretion and (in rodents) by increasing adipose tissue sensitivity to insulin. (From Lustig, 2006. Reprinted with permission from Nature Publishing Group.)

Hirsch, 1995; Leibel, Rosenbaum, & Hirsch, 1995), with resultant decreases in REE, activity, and well-being, and increases vagal tone to increase appetite and insulin release in order to store more energy in adipose tissue (Lustig, 2003). In the energy-replete state, humans burn energy at 50 kcal/kg fat-free mass. However, in the starvation state, this is reduced to 40 to 42 kcal/kg fat-free mass (Leibel et al., 1995). In other words, starvation results in a 20% increased efficiency of energy utilization in an attempt to conserve energy (Rosenbaum et al., 2003). The result of the starvation response is an increase in plasma leptin to restore the periphery, and the brain, to a state of leptin repletion (Flier, 1998; Lustig, 2006).

The prototype of leptin depletion in humans is mutation of the leptin gene, resulting in leptin deficiency, which manifests as severe early morbid obesity. Approximately 11 such patients have been described, who manifested hyperphagia from birth, with obesity documentable as early as 6 months of age. The lack of leptin induces the starvation response in the form of reduced REE, lack of pubertal progression, and defective immunity (Farooqi et al., 2002). The hyperinsulinemia due to vagal overactivity and insulin resistance cross reacts with the insulin-like growth factor 1 (IGF-1) receptor to increase growth rate and bone age. The diagnosis is made by unmeasurable serum leptin levels. However, daily injections of recombinant leptin restore leptin signaling to the VMH, with reduction in hyperphagia, increased REE, resolution of obesity, induction of puberty, and improvement in immune function (Farooqi et al., 2002).

Obesity Is the Same Process in the Central Nervous System as Starvation

On first thought this sounds ludicrous, but in fact, it actually makes a lot of sense. If you examine the constitutional symptoms of obese and starved individuals, they are very similar. Both are associated with fatigue, malaise, inactivity, often with an inability to motivate, and depression. The reason is the inability of the VMH to transduce the leptin signal: in starvation, because there is inadequacy of leptin, and in obesity, because there is resistance to leptin. Furthermore, serum leptin concentrations drop precipitously during periods of short-term fasting (within 12 hr), declining faster than body fat stores (Keim, Stern, & Havel, 1998), which would account for the recidivism of obesity; the VMH is interpreting a declining leptin signal similar to starvation, which then promotes increased energy intake and decreased energy expenditure.

Leptin Resistance

Most obese children have high leptin levels, but do not have genetic mutations, manifesting what is commonly referred to as "leptin resistance." The response to most weight loss regimens is to plateau rapidly due to the rapid decrease in peripheral leptin levels below one's personal "leptin threshold" (Rosenbaum et al., 1997). The leptin decrease causes the VMH to sense a reduction in peripheral energy stores, which modulates a decrease in REE to conserve energy, analogous to the starvation response (see above) (Leibel et al., 1995), but occuring at elevated leptin levels. Leptin resistance prevents exogenous leptin administration from promoting weight loss in obese adults (Heymsfield et al., 1999).

Insulin Is an Endogenous Leptin Antagonist

Two clinical paradigms have been shown to improve leptin sensitivity. In response to weight loss after marked food restriction, exogenous administration of leptin can increase REE back to baseline and permit further weight loss (Rosenbaum, Murphy, Heymsfield, Matthews, & Leibel, 2002), suggesting that the weight loss itself improves leptin sensitivity. Second, suppression of insulin correlates with improvement in leptin sensitivity and promotes weight loss (Lustig, Sen, Soberman, & Velasquez-Mieyer, 2004), suggesting that hyperinsulinemia and leptin resistance are the same phenomenon (Lustig, 2006). The reason for insulin antagonizing leptin action is the mechanism behind weight gain common to both puberty and pregnancy. If leptin signaling were not modulable, the weight accrual for reproductive competency during puberty and pregnancy would be compromised.

Therefore reversible antagonism of leptin action is in the best interest of survival of the species. Since insulin promotes energy deposition into fat, it makes sense that it should be the central blocker of leptin as well. Indeed, both puberty and pregnancy are hyperinsulinemic and insulin-resistant states (Li, Ji, Wang, & Hu, 2005), with requisite increases in insulin levels. In both, leptin levels increase acutely, and then when adulthood is reached or postpartum, insulin levels decrease, weight stabilizes or is lost, and leptin returns to baseline (McLachlan, O'Neal, Jenkins, & Alford, 2006). However, in maladaptive conditions when insulin rises chronically, leptin signaling is impeded, and obesity worsens. Indeed, insulin reduction strategies can be effective in promoting weight loss in children with hyperinsulinemia by improving leptin sensitivity (Lustig et al., 2006b).

Although many contend that hyperinsulinemia is a result of obesity, numerous lines of evidence point to the conclusion that hyperinsulinemia may in fact be a cause of obesity (Lustig, 2006; Odeleye, de Courten, Pettitt, & Ravussin, 1997; Sims, 1996). There are two forms of hyperinsulinemia in children: (1) fasting hyperinsulinemia due to defective hepatic and muscle insulin signal transduction, what we commonly call "insulin resistance" (Caprio & Tamborlane, 1999; Michael et al., 2000; Rothman et al., 1995); and (2) glucose-stimulated hyperinsulinemia, also called "insulin hypersecretion," which occurs due to neural dysregulation of the β-cell, often seen in subjects with hypothalamic obesity due to central nervous system (CNS) insult (Bray, Inoue, & Nishizawa, 1981; Lustig, 2002) (see below). These are endocrine conditions that are modulable with endocrine therapies. Thus insulin reduction should be a primary goal of intensive therapy for obesity.

PHARMACOTHERAPY FOR CHILDHOOD OBESITY

Indications for Pharmacotherapy

Pharmacologic therapies in children must currently be considered adjuncts to standard lifestyle modification. At present, several limitations preclude physicians from early implementation of drug therapies for the treatment of childhood obesity, including (1) the youngest child for whom any obesity pharmacotherapy is currently U.S. Food and Drug Administration (FDA)-approved is 10 years; (2) the long-term use of pharmacological intervention has rarely proven to be more efficacious than behavior modification; (3) there exist a limited number of well-controlled studies of safe and effective pharmacological intervention in obese children; (4) the relative risk for the development of adverse events in children must be weighed against the long-term potential for improvement of morbidity and mortality, which is difficult to estimate in children; and (5) targeting the pathology is still in its infancy. Also, we cannot forget that many drugs used for the treatment of adult obesity have resulted in unforeseen complications which resulted either in the drug's restriction (thyroid hormone, amphetamine) or recall (e.g., dinitrophenol, fenfluramine, dexfenfluramine, phenylpropanolamine, ephedra) (Abenhaim et al., 1996; Bray & Greenway, 1999; Jick et al., 1998; Morgan & Funderburk, 1992; Weintraub, 1985; Yanovski & Yanovski, 2002). Despite these concerns, the negative health impact of childhood obesity may justify long-term medication to control its progression.

In the current pharmacopoeia of childhood obesity, both nonspecific and specific strategies based on mechanisms of action within the energy balance negative feedback system are employed (Table 11.2). Currently the approaches are suppression of caloric intake, limitation of the availability or absorption of nutrients, and insulin suppression or sensitization.

Nontargeted Therapies (FDA Approved)

Reduction of Energy Intake: Sibutramine

Numerous anorexiant drugs have been used to treat obesity in adults. These drugs alter neurotransmission within the VMH in order to reduce caloric intake. Only sibutramine (Bray & Greenway, 1999) is approved for children as young as 16 years. Sibutramine is a nonselective reuptake

Table 11.2 Medications for the Treatment of Obesity[a]

Drug	Dosage	Efficacy	Side Effects	Monitoring and Contraindications
Sibutramine (reduction of food intake) Not FDA approved for less than 16 years of age	5–15 mg by mouth once a day	RCT: Wt –4.6 kg, BMI –4.5%, WC –5.4 cm over placebo at 6 months; RCT: Wt –8.1 kg, BMI –2.5 kg/m² over placebo at 6 months	Tachycardia, hypertension, palpitations, insomnia, anxiety, nervousness, depression, diaphoresis	Monitor heart rate and blood pressure Do not use with other drugs, MAO inhibitors
Orlistat (inhibition of intestinal absorption) Not FDA approved for less than 12 years of age.	120 mg by mouth three times a day	Open-label: Wt –5.4 kg, BMI –2.0 kg/m² at 6 months; RCT: Wt –2.6 kg, BMI –0.85, WC –2.7 cm over placebo at 12 months	Borborygmi, flatus, abdominal cramps, fecal incontinence, oily spotting, vitamin malabsorption	Monitor 25OHD3 levels MVI supplementation is strongly recommended A lower dose preparation has been approved for over-the-counter sale
Metformin (insulin sensitization) Not FDA approved for treatment of obesity Approved for 10 years of age and older for type 2 diabetes mellitus	250–1000 mg by mouth twice a day	RCT: BMI z-score –0.35 SD versus placebo at 6 months; RCT: Wt –2.7% versus placebo at 6 months; Post hoc analysis: efficacy dependent on degree of insulin resistance; BMI z-score –0.23 SD in first 4 months, –0.12 SD in next year	Nausea, flatulence, bloating, diarrhea; usually resolves Lactic acidosis not yet reported in children	Do not use in renal failure or with intravenous contrast MVI supplementation is strongly recommended
Octreotide (insulin suppression) Not FDA approved for treatment of obesity Otherwise 18 years of age or older	5–15 µg/kg/day subcutaneously three times a day	Open-label: Wt –4.8 kg, BMI –2.0 kg/m² in 6 monthsRCT: –7.6 kg, BMI –2.5 kg/m² over placebo at 6 months; Post hoc analysis: BMI z-score –0.70 SD in 6 months, dependent on insulin secretion and sensitivity	Gallstones, diarrhea, edema, abdominal cramps, nausea, bloating, reduction in thyroxine concentrations	Monitor fasting glucose, FT4, HbA1c Useful only for hypothalamic obesity Ursodiol coadministration strongly recommended
Leptin (suppression of starvation response) Not approved by FDA	Titration of dose to serum levels, subcutaneously	Anecdotal case reports only	Local reactions	Useful only in leptin deficiency

Continued

Table 11.2 Medications for the Treatment of Obesity[a] (Continued)

Drug	Dosage	Efficacy	Side Effects	Monitoring and Contraindications
Topiramate (CNS channel opener) Not FDA approved for treatment of obesity	96–256 mg by mouth four times a day	RCT: Wt –8.0% over placebo at 6 months	Paresthesia, difficulty with concentration/attention, depression, difficulty with memory, language problems, nervousness, psychomotor slowing	No pediatric data
Growth hormone (lipolytic agent) Not FDA approved for treatment of obesity	1–3 mg/m^2 subcutaneously four times a day	Decreases in percentage of body fat, with increases in absolute lean body mass	Edema, carpal tunnel syndrome, death in patients with preexisting obstructive sleep apnea	Recommended only in Prader-Willi syndrome primarily to increase height velocity It also decreases fat mass, but should only be used after screening to rule out obstructive sleep apnea Must closely monitor pulmonary function, glucose, HbA1c
Rimonabant (endocannabinoid antagonist) Denied approval by FDA Only available in Europe	20 mg by mouth four times a day	RCT: Wt –4.8 kg over placebo at 12 months	Depression, nausea, vomiting, diarrhea, dizziness, headache, anxiety	40% dropout rate No pediatric data

Note: RCT, randomized controlled trial; MVI, multivitamins; WC, waist circumference; Wt, weight; BMI, body mass index (wt/ht^2).

[a] Should be considered only after an unsuccessful 6- to 12-month trial of lifestyle intervention. All drugs effective only when combined with appropriate lifestyle intervention.

inhibitor of serotonin and norepinephrine, but also blocks dopamine reuptake (Bray et al., 1999; Ryan, Kaiser, & Bray, 1995). Sibutramine effectively inhibits caloric intake (Heal et al., 1992) and also stimulates thermogenesis in rats, although data on humans are contradictory (Hansen, Toubro, Stock, MacDonald, & Astrup, 1998; Seagle, Bessesen, & Hill, 1998).

In adolescents, three randomized controlled trials (RCTs) document the safety and efficacy of sibutramine:

- Eighty-two adolescents (13 to 17 years old, BMI 32 to 44 kg/m^2) underwent a double-blind, placebo-controlled trial for 6 months in addition to a family-based behavioral weight control program (Berkowitz, Wadden, Tershakovec, & Cronquist, 2003). The 43 subjects randomized to sibutramine experienced a change in weight of –7.8 ± 6.3 kg versus –3.2 ± 6.1 kg for placebo (P = .001), a change in BMI of –8.5 ± 6.8% versus –4.0 ± 5.4% (P = .001), and a change in waist circumference of –8.2 ± 6.9 cm versus –2.8 ± 5.6 cm (P < .001). However, as expected, the weight loss plateaued by the fourth month. Those treated with sibutramine open-label for a full year lost a total of 7.0 ± 9.3 kg. Sibutramine treatment also improved high-density lipoprotein (HDL) levels by 7.6 ± 17.7% ($P = 0.001$) and reduced fasting insulin by 20.2 ± 42.7% ($P < 0.001$). The large standard deviations in all efficacy parameters demonstrate the variability in clinical response. Forty percent experienced tachycardia, of which 12% required discontinuation.

- Sixty obese adolescents underwent a 6-month, double-blind, placebo-controlled trial of sibutramine without behavioral intervention (Godoy-Matos et al., 2005). Those treated with sibutramine versus placebo exhibited a weight change of −10.3 kg versus +2.4 kg and a BMI change of −3.6 kg/m^2 versus −0.9 kg/m^2 at month 16 ($P < .001$). Triglycerides fell in the sibutramine-treated group by a mean of 38.5 mg/dl ($P < .05$), although fasting insulin was unchanged. Side effects were uncommon, and included dry mouth and constipation, but hypertension was not seen.

- A total of 498 obese adolescents (Berkowitz et al., 2006) enrolled in a 12-month RCT of behavior therapy plus sibutramine or placebo. Those treated with sibutramine versus placebo exhibited a weight change of −6.7% versus +1.2% and a BMI change of −3.1 kg/m^2 versus −0.3 kg/m^2 at month 12 ($P < .001$). Lipids, fasting insulin, and insulin sensitivity were all improved ($P < .001$). Tachycardia was more frequent with sibutramine therapy (12.5%), but did not require discontinuation. Adverse events were not different.

The tolerability and side effects of sibutramine are similar to those of adults (James et al., 2000). Sibutramine can cause vasoconstriction and an increase in heart rate and blood pressure that persists even after significant weight loss (Bray & Greenway, 1999). Other adverse reactions include dry mouth, headache, insomnia, anxiety, nervousness, depression, somnolence or drowsiness, edema, palpitations, diaphoresis, xerostomia, constipation, dizziness, paresthesia, mydriasis, and nausea, which occur in approximately 5% to 10% of children. Sibutramine cannot be administered in conjunction with monoamine oxidase inhibitors or selective serotonin reuptake inhibitors (Yanovski, 2001; Yanovski & Yanovski, 2002). Sibutramine is currently licensed in the United States for use in patients 16 years of age and older, and it is expected to be used as an adjunct to behavioral modification. The FDA has extended the interval of treatment to 2 years (James et al., 2000).

Reduction of Energy Absorption: Orlistat. This drug is a modified bacterial product that specifically inhibits intestinal lipase and can reduce fat and cholesterol absorption by approximately 30% in subjects eating a 30% fat diet (Mittendorfer, Ostlund, Patterson, & Klein, 2001). Orlistat irreversibly binds to the active site of the lipase, preventing intraluminal deacylation of triglycerides, resulting in a 16 g/day increase in fecal fat excretion (Guerciolini, Radu-Radulescu, Boldrin, Dallas, & Moore, 2001). Orlistat does not inhibit other intestinal enzymes. It has minimal absorption and exerts no effect on systemic lipases (Reitman, Castro-Cabezas, de Bruin, & Erkelens, 1994; Zhi et al., 1994). Although there have been several open-label trials of orlistat in adolescents, only two RCTs have been published.

- A total of 534 obese adolescents received behavioral therapy plus orlistat or placebo for 1 year (Chanoine, Hampl, Jensen, Boldrin, & Hauptman, 2005). Orlistat resulted in a change in weight and BMI of +0.5 kg and −0.55 kg/m^2, as opposed to +3.1 kg and +0.3 kg/m^2 in the placebo group ($P = .001$). Waist circumference decreased by 2.7 cm in the orlistat-treated group and did not change in the placebo group. Other secondary efficacy variables, such as lipids, were not improved. In this study there was a 33% dropout rate and a 50% adverse event rate, primarily restricted to gastrointestinal distress, diarrhea, steatorrhea, and fecal accidents.

- Forty adolescents received lifestyle recommendations plus orlistat or placebo (Maahs et al., 2006). Although the decrease in BMI within the orlistat group (−1.3 ± 1.6 kg/m^2; $P =$

.04) and within the placebo group (-0.8 ± 3.0 kg/m^2; $P = .02$) was statistically significant from zero, the difference between the two groups was not significant ($P = .39$).

The side effects with orlistat are predictable from its mechanism of action on intestinal lipase (Yanovski & Yanovski, 2002). Orlistat appears to be well tolerated in adults, with the principal complaints being borborygmi, flatus, and abdominal cramps. The most troubling side effects are fecal incontinence, oily spotting, and flatus with discharge, which are highly aversive in the pediatric population. Orlistat does not affect the pharmacokinetic properties of most other pharmaceutical agents. Absorption of vitamins A and E and β-carotene may be slightly reduced, and this may require vitamin therapy in a small number of patients. In one study (McDuffie, Calis, Booth, Uwaifo, & Yanovski, 2002), vitamin D supplementation was required in 18% of subjects despite the prescription of a daily multivitamin containing vitamin D, although in the company-sponsored study, effects on vitamin levels were minor (Chanoine et al., 2005). Orlistat must be taken with each meal, which reduces its attractiveness in children, who are in school during lunchtime. Orlistat is currently approved for treatment of children as young as 12 years. An over-the-counter lower dose preparation recently obtained FDA approval and is available now.

Targeted Therapies (Not FDA Approved)

Improvement of Insulin Resistance: Metformin

Metformin is a bisubstituted, short-chain hydrophilic guanidine derivative used for the treatment of children and adults with type 2 diabetes mellitus (T2DM) (Davidson & Peters, 1997; DeFronzo & Goodman, 1995; Jones, Arslanian, Peterokova, Park, & Tomlinson, 2002; Stumvoll, Nurjhan, Perriello, Dailey, & Gerich, 1995). Metformin also decreases fasting hyperinsulinemia and prevents T2DM (Diabetes Prevention Program Research Group, 2002) and promotes weight loss in some obese individuals (Lee & Morley, 1998; Mogul, Peterson, Weinstein, Zhang, & Southren, 2001) by improving hepatic and muscle insulin sensitivity. Metformin has little effect on energy expenditure (Stumvoll et al., 1995). Although some believe that metformin promotes weight loss through a primary anorectic effect (as initial side effects of nausea and gastrointestinal distress acutely limit caloric intake) (Paolisso et al., 1998), most believe that the decline in caloric intake observed with metformin is related to its enhancement of glucose clearance, through reduction of hepatic glucose output, and reduction in fasting hyperinsulinemia (Bailey & Turner, 1996; Lenhard et al., 1997). Metformin improves hepatic insulin resistance by inducing hepatic adenosine 5′-monophosphate (AMP) kinase (Zhou et al., 2001), which reduces hepatic gluconeogenesis, therefore pancreatic insulin secretion and peripheral insulin levels decrease. Metformin also restores phosphatidylinositol 3 (PI3) kinase and AMP kinase activity in muscle cells, improving muscle insulin sensitivity (Kumar & Dey, 2002). Another possible mechanism of metformin action is through stimulation of glucagon-like peptide 1 (GLP-1) (Kiefer & Habener, 1999; Mannucci et al., 2001), which may inhibit food intake through central actions on the VMH (Drucker, 2005).

Thus far, two RCTs and an observational prediction study in children and adolescents have been conducted.

- Twenty-nine obese adolescents with a family history of T2DM (Freemark & Bursey, 2001) were treated with metformin versus placebo, without lifestyle intervention. Metformin treatment demonstrated a significant reduction of BMI z-score of 0.1 in 6 months, which was a 3.6% reduction relative to placebo, along with significant reductions of plasma leptin and fasting glucose (-9.8 mg/dl) and insulin (-12 μU/ml), even in the absence of dietary intervention.
- Twenty-four obese adolescents (Kay et al., 2001) combined a low-calorie diet plus metformin or placebo for 10 weeks. The metformin patients exhibited a weight loss of 6.5%

compared with 3.8% with placebo ($P < .01$). Metformin also decreased plasma leptin, insulin, glucose, cholesterol, and thyroglobulin concentrations ($P < .001$).

- Examination of the open-label responses to metformin in a multivariate analysis demonstrated two predictors for efficacy: race (Caucasian > African American) and a poorer degree of insulin resistance prior to therapy (Lustig et al., 2006b).

Metformin has also been used off-label for treatment of polycystic ovarian syndrome and nonalcoholic steatohepatitis, with varying degrees of success (Ibanez, Valls, Potau, Marcos, & de Zegher, 2000; Jamieson, 2002; Marchesini et al., 2001; Pasquali et al., 2000; Schwimmer, Middleton, Deutsch, & Lavine, 2005; Velasquez, Mendoza, Hamer, Sosa, & Glueck, 1994). One particular use for metformin may be to combat the weight gain observed in children taking the atypical antipsychotics olanzapine, risperidone, quetiapine, and valproate (Morrison, Cottingham, & Barton, 2002). However, cessation of metformin therapy leads to rebound hyperinsulinemia and rapid weight gain, which may negate any beneficial effects seen during the medication window.

Side effects with metformin include nausea, flatulence, bloating, and diarrhea at initiation of therapy, which appears to be self-limited and resolves within 3 to 4 weeks. Approximately 5% of pediatric patients discontinue metformin therapy because of the severity of the side effects. The most feared complication of metformin in adults is lactic acidosis, which is estimated to occur at a rate of 3 per 100,000 patient-exposure years, primarily in patients with contraindications to the use of metformin; however, no documented cases in children have been reported. Metformin increases the urinary excretion of vitamins B_1 and B_6, which are important in the tricarboxylic acid cycle and which may hasten the lactic acidosis (Centers for Disease Control, 1997). Vitamin B_{12} deficiency has also been reported in as many as 9% of adult subjects using metformin. Therefore prophylactic multivitamin supplementation is recommended with metformin use. Contraindications to metformin use include renal insufficiency, congestive heart failure or pulmonary insufficiency, acute liver disease, and alcohol use sufficient to cause acute hepatic toxicity. Metformin also should be withheld when patients are hospitalized with any condition that may cause decreased systemic perfusion or when use of contrast agents is anticipated (Bailey & Turner, 1996). It should be noted that metformin is FDA approved for treatment of T2DM in children, but is unlikely to be approved for childhood obesity or insulin resistance because of the short exclusivity interval afforded the makers of metformin by the FDA upon its introduction to the United States in 1996.

Suppression of Insulin Hypersecretion: Octreotide

It is well known that bilateral electrolytic lesions or deafferentation of the VMH in rats leads to intractable weight gain (Berthoud & Jeanrenaud, 1979; Bray et al., 1981; Jeanrenaud, 1985; Rohner-Jeanrenaud & Jeanrenaud, 1980; Satoh et al., 1997), even upon food restriction (Bray & Nishizawa, 1978). In humans, hypothalamic damage, due to either CNS tumor, surgery, radiation, or trauma, can alter both the afferent and efferent pathways of energy balance and lead to severe and intractable weight gain (Bray, 1984; Daousi, Dunn, Foy, MacFarlane, & Pinkney, 2005). In this syndrome of "hypothalamic obesity," hypothalamic insult confers an "organic leptin resistance" as the VMH senses starvation (Satoh et al., 1997; Thornton, Cheung, Clifton, & Steiner, 1997), therefore energy intake is high and expenditure is low (Harz, Muller, Waldeck, Pudel, & Roth, 2003). Children with hypothalamic obesity exhibit weight gain, even in response to forced caloric restriction (Bray & Gallagher, 1975), secondary to (1) overactivation of the vagus, which promotes an obligate insulin hypersecretion and energy storage; and (2) defective activation of the SNS, which retards lipolysis and energy expenditure (Lustig, 2002, 2003). Insulin hypersecretion with normal insulin sensitivity is noted on oral glucose tolerance testing in these children (Preeyasombat, Bacchetti, Lazar, & Lustig, 2005). This same phenomenon of insulin hypersecretion has also been documented in a subset of obese adults without CNS damage (Velasquez-Mieyer et al., 2003).

The voltage-gated calcium channel of the β-cell is coupled to a somatostatin ($SSTR_5$) receptor (Hsu, Xiang, Rajan, Kunze, & Boyd, 1991; Mitra et al., 1999). Octreotide binds to this receptor, which limits the opening of this calcium channel, and reduces influx of calcium into the β-cell, which reduces calmodulin activation and vesicle exocytosis, and acutely decreases the magnitude of insulin response to glucose (Bertoli et al., 1998; Lustig, 2003), resulting in weight loss or stabilization. Two RCTs and an observational prediction study using octreotide for obesity have been performed.

- Eighteen children (ages 8 to 18 years) with obesity due to CNS insult (brain tumor or cranial irradiation) (Lustig et al., 2003) receiving octreotide versus placebo for 6 months demonstrated weight ($+1.6 \pm 0.6$ kg versus $+9.2 \pm 1.5$ kg; $P < .001$) and BMI stabilization (-0.2 ± 0.2 kg/m^2 versus $+2.3 \pm 0.5$ kg/m^2; $P < .001$), suppression of insulin response ($P < .001$), increased physical activity by report ($P = .03$), and improved quality of life, which correlated with the degree of insulin suppression ($P = .041$).
- A total of 172 obese adults without CNS insulin insult received octreotide long-acting release (LAR) in a dose-finding trial for 6 months, without lifestyle intervention (Lustig et al., 2006a). Those receiving 40 mg or 60 mg octreotide LAR intramuscularly once a month experienced a weight change of -1.98% and -1.87%, and decreases in BMI of 0.73 kg/m^2 and 0.79 kg/m^2, respectively ($P < .001$). Post hoc analysis revealed a 3.5% to 3.8% weight loss at month 6 in the two higher dose groups among Caucasian patients demonstrating insulin hypersecretion.
- Lastly, an examination of BMI responses to octreotide in pediatric hypothalamic obesity in a multivariate analysis ($n = 24$) demonstrated that insulin hypersecretion with concomitant retention of insulin sensitivity prior to therapy augured for success (Lustig et al., 2006b).

Octreotide is usually well tolerated. The most common side effects include diarrhea, abdominal cramps, nausea, and bloating, which are self-limited and usually resolve in 3 to 4 weeks (Krentz, MacDonald, & Schade, 1994; Lamberts, Van Der Lely, De Herder, & Hofland, 1996). Other adverse events include gallstones (which are preventable by coadministration of ursodiol), edema, development of sterile abscesses at the injection sites, B_{12} deficiency, suppression of growth hormone and TSH secretion, and mild hyperglycemia, especially in those with severe insulin resistance (Tauber, Harris, & Rochiccioli, 1994). At present, octreotide offers a promising approach for the treatment of insulin hypersecretion as seen in hypothalamic obesity, but it is not FDA approved. The use of octreotide in obese children with acute glucose-stimulated insulin hypersecretion without cranial pathology has not yet been evaluated.

Other Targeted Therapies

Leptin. Mutations of the leptin gene in humans recapitulate the phenotype of the ob/ob leptin-deficient mouse (Montague et al., 1997). Approximately 11 such patients have been described who manifest hyperphagia from birth, with obesity documentable as early as 6 months of age. Leptin deficiency induces the starvation response (Farooqi et al., 2002), with increased energy intake and decreased REE. The diagnosis is made by unmeasurable serum leptin levels (it should be pointed out that while many clinical specialty laboratories perform this test, many insurance companies will not reimburse for it). In children with leptin deficiency, leptin therapy results in extraordinary loss of weight and fat mass (Farooqi et al., 1999; Gibson et al., 2004), along with reduction in hyperphagia, resolution of obesity, induction of puberty, and improvement in immunity (Farooqi et al., 2002). Although leptin administration in adults did not prove effective by itself due to leptin resistance (Heymsfield et al., 1999), leptin may serve as an adjunct in combination with other medications after leptin sensitivity is ameliorated through weight loss (Rosenbaum et al., 2002; Shi et al., 2002).

Growth Hormone. Growth hormone (GH) fosters anabolism and lipolysis. GH therapy has been shown to increase REE, promote linear growth, increase muscle mass, and decrease the percent body fat in Prader-Willi syndrome (Carrel et al., 2002, 2004). It has also been shown to decrease the percent body fat in children with GH deficiency (Kaplowitz, Rundle, & Blethen, 1998) due to its effect on lipoprotein lipase (Simsolo, Ezzat, Ong, Saghizadeh, & Kern, 1995). However, it is unclear whether these reductions in percent body fat are primary effects on the adipose tissue compartment or are due to the increase in lean body mass. Obesity results in a state of functional GH insufficiency, which can be ameliorated through weight loss (Williams et al., 1984). GH therapy also improves the lipid profile in GH-deficient adults (Jorgensen et al., 1994). Currently the role of GH therapy in the treatment of nonsyndromic childhood obesity is unclear. In addition, GH therapy costs from $5,000 to $40,000 annually, depending on the patient's weight.

The Future of Pediatric Obesity Pharmacotherapy

In response to the relative lack of efficacy of lifestyle interventions, the ever-expanding knowledge of the physiology of energy balance, and particularly as a business decision, most pharmaceutical companies have launched obesity research programs. The following agents are currently in human study; however, use of any of these new agents in children will depend on proof of safe and efficacious experience in adults.

Oxyntomodulin is an analog of PYY(3-36) that has been shown in a 4-week RCT in adults to reduce energy intake and weight (Wynne et al., 2005). Topiramate is a novel anticonvulsant that blocks voltage-dependent sodium channels, enhances the activity of the $GABA_A$ receptor, and antagonizes a glutamate receptor other than the N-methyl-D-aspartate (NMDA) receptor (Teter, Early, & Gibbs, 2000). Topiramate promotes weight loss in a dose-dependent fashion (Wilkes, Nelson, Osborne, Demarest, & Olefsky, 2005). A recent RCT in adults demonstrated a 9.1% weight loss in those subjects taking 192 mg/day of topiramate, along with significant improvements in blood pressure, waist circumference, and fasting glucose and insulin (Wilding, Van Gaal, Rissanen, Vercruysse, & Fitchet, 2004). However, almost 33% of the subjects dropped out due to adverse events, which included paresthesia, somnolence, anorexia, fatigue, nervousness, decreased concentration, difficulty with memory, and aggression. There are currently no studies of topiramate in childhood obesity. Rimonabant is an endocannabinoid receptor-1 antagonist that reduces the reinforcement and reward properties of drugs of dependence at the level of the nucleus accumbens (LeFoll & Goldberg, 2005). It also extinguishes the reward properties of food. A 1-year RCT in adults demonstrated a 6.6 ± 7.2 kg weight loss ($P < .001$), 6.5 ± 7.4 cm reduction in waist circumference ($P < .001$), and improvement in lipid profile (Van Gaal, Rissanen, Scheen, Ziegler, & Rossner, 2005). Side effects included depressed mood, nausea, vomiting, diarrhea, dizziness, headache, and anxiety in 20% of subjects, but did not lead to discontinuation of the drug. Rimonabant is approved in Europe, but the FDA recently denied its introduction into the United States, due to its side-effect profile.

BARIATRIC SURGERY FOR PEDIATRIC OBESITY

Indications for Surgery

Conventional treatment of childhood obesity has proven to be time consuming, difficult, frustrating, and expensive. Although numerous short-term successes have been noted, long-term weight reductions are modest, and recidivism is the rule. In adolescents who have almost completed growth, and with extreme and morbid obesity that may be life threatening, surgical therapy may be indicated in extreme and defined circumstances (Inge et al., 2004; Strauss, 2002). However, in comparison to adults, stricter and more conservative criteria must be applied to adolescents due to the fact that not all obese adolescents will become obese adults (Whitaker, Wright, Pepe, Seidel, & Dietz, 1997); the slightly improved rate of lifestyle and pharmacotherapeutic efficacy; the longer time interval before comorbidities become life threatening; and their inability to give legal consent.

Therefore it is virtually impossible to perform RCT surgical studies in children. The efficacy of any given approach will continue to be suspect and different procedures cannot be compared head to head. For all these reasons, an expert panel with representation from the American Pediatric Surgical Association and the American Academy of Pediatrics (Inge et al., 2004) suggests that bariatric surgery in adolescence could be justified in situations when obesity-related comorbid conditions threaten the child's health. They provided stringent recommendations that bariatric surgery be limited to those adolescents with a BMI greater than 40 kg/m² with the presence of severe comorbidity, or a BMI greater than 50 kg/m² with less severe comorbidity.

Special consideration should be taken to avoid bariatric surgery at very late stages of obesity, when the presence of obesity-related comorbidities and the inaccessibility of imaging (most magnetic resonance imaging [MRI] scanners have a weight limit of 450 lb) may affect surgery outcome. Indeed, a review of eight retrospective studies in adolescents found that bariatric surgery in adolescents can promote durable weight loss in most patients, but there appears to be a significant complication and mortality rate, although this may improve with increased surgical experience (Apovian et al., 2005). Therefore guidance is needed to determine the ideal circumstances under which the balance of risk versus benefit favors health preservation and reversion of complications with the lowest risk of morbidity and mortality from the procedure.

Bariatric Procedures

Bariatric procedures for weight loss can be divided into malabsorptive, restrictive, and combination procedures. Purely malabsorptive procedures aim to decrease the functional length or efficiency of the intestinal mucosa through anatomic rearrangement of the intestine. These procedures include jejunoileal bypass and biliopancreatic diversion with duodenal switch. Because of the high morbidity and mortality of these procedures, they cannot be recommended in children and will not be discussed further. The restrictive procedures reduce stomach volume to decrease the volume of food ingested. They include the bariatric intragastric balloon (BIB) and laparoscopic adjustable gastric band (LAGB). The Roux-en-Y gastric bypass (RYGB) is a combination procedure (Mun, Blackburn, & Matthews, 2001).

Restrictive: Endoscopically Placed Bariatric Intragastric Balloon

One or more water-filled balloons are placed within the stomach to induce a sense of fullness. The BIB may be a short-term alternative for weight loss in patients with severe obesity complications requiring weight loss before a more definitive surgery (Doldi et al., 2000). In children there is very limited and conflicting data regarding the efficacy of BIB. One report of 82 subjects ages 12 to 73 years (Hodson et al., 2001) documents a mean weight loss of 15%, with the majority during the first month. Adverse events include early gastric intolerance (48 hr) in 3.6%, balloon valve leakage in 3.6%, and rare anaerobic colonization of the intragastric mucosa. Conversely, a study of five morbidly obese adolescents whose weights were 148% to 293% above ideal for height showed that the use of a BIB was not effective in decreasing weight (Vandenplas, Bollen, de Langhe, Vandemaele, & DeSchepper, 1999); in fact, 6 months after BIB insertion, the percent overweight in all five had increased significantly. At present, more research is needed to elucidate whether the BIB is a suitable technique for the treatment of childhood obesity, especially in those children with high immediate operative risk whose morbidity may be lessened after definitive surgical treatment.

Restrictive: Laparoscopic Adjustable Gastric Banding

Laparoscopic adjustable gastric banding utilizes a prosthetic band to encircle and compartmentalize the proximal stomach into a small pouch and a large remnant (Mun et al., 2001). The theoretical advantage of this technique is decreased risk of staple line dehiscence. The more recent introduction of a new laparoscopic approach and the use of an adjustable band (allowing the stomach size to change) make this procedure more attractive. Finally, this procedure is reversible, or can be modified into the RYGB at a later date. Results vary widely in adults, with most exhibiting benefit (20% to 30% excess weight lost in the first year). Several small studies support the safety and efficacy of LAGB in morbidly obese adolescents. In one study of 11 morbidly obese adolescents (ages 11 to 17 years), LABG resulted in decreased mean BMI from 46.6 kg/m^2 to 32.1 kg/m^2 at a mean follow-up of 23 months, with improved comorbidities. No patient experienced operative or late complications (Abu-Abeid, Gavert, Klausner, & Szold, 2003). In another study following LAGB, BMI in seven adolescents (ages 12 to 19 years) fell from a preoperative median of 44.7 kg/m^2 to 30.2 kg/m^2 at 24 months, which corresponded to a 59.3% loss of excess weight (Dolan, Creighton, Hopkins, & Fielding, 2003). In a 3-year follow-up study of 41 adolescents, BMI was reduced from 42 ± 8 kg/m^2 to 29 ± 6 kg/m^2, with an excess weight loss of 70% (Fielding & Duncombe, 2005). Again, complications were minor. Although this procedure is considered safer than RYGB, it has not yet been approved by the FDA for use in adolescents, although several studies now support its use.

Combination: Roux-en-Y Gastric Bypass

Roux-en-Y gastric bypass involves dividing the stomach to create a small (15 to 30 ml) stomach pouch into which a segment of jejunum approximately 15 to 60 cm inferior to the ligament of Treitz is inserted, while the proximal portion of the jejunum that drains the bypassed lower stomach and duodenum is reanastomosed 75 to 150 cm inferior to the gastrojejunostomy (Mun et al., 2001). This procedure combines the restrictive nature of gastrectomy with the consequences of dumping physiology as a negative conditioning response when high-calorie liquid meals are ingested. In addition, RYGB is associated with a decline in the circulating level of ghrelin, which may be responsible in part for the decrease in hunger associated with this procedure (Cummings et al., 2002).

Roux-en-Y gastric bypass appears to result in significant early weight reduction in adults (Mun et al., 2001; Sjostrom, Peltonen, & Sjostrom, 2002; Sjostrom, 2002); however, long-term studies demonstrate weight regain in many patients (Shah, Simha, & Garg, 2006). Limited data are available regarding the efficacy of these surgical procedures to induce weight loss in severely obese children and adolescents, and most of these are case series from individual surgeons or institutions (Yanovski, 2001). A case review of 10 severely obese adolescents (BMI 52.5 ± 10.0 kg/m^2) who underwent RYGB were followed for a mean of 69 months (range 8 to 144 months) (Strauss, Bradley, & Brolin, 2001). In this series, weight loss was significant in 9 of 10 adolescents and was maintained as long as 10 years. The average weight loss was 53.6 ± 25.6 kg, which represents approximately 59% excess weight loss. Weight loss was also associated with improvement of associated comorbidities, including sleep apnea and hypertension. Finally, a large retrospective series of 33 obese adolescents (Sugerman et al., 2003) ages 15 to 17 years, BMI 52 ± 11 kg/m^2 (range 38 to 91 kg/m^2) with obesity comorbidities, followed these subjects up to 14 years after bariatric surgery, mostly RYGB. There were surgical complications in 13, which were treated. There were two sudden deaths, and five of the subjects regained their weight. However, the majority experienced significant weight loss with resolution of their comorbidities and improvement in quality of life. Adolescents participating in a multicenter study reported by the Pediatric Bariatric Study Group experienced excellent weight loss after laparoscopic RYGB, with a mean BMI change from 58 kg/m^2 to 35.8 kg/m^2 at 1 year (Lawson et al., 2006). Gastrojejunostomy stenosis (21 patients) requiring endoscopic balloon dilation and internal hernia (14 patients) requiring either laparoscopic or open reduction were the most common complications. This procedure appears to be safe and effective when candidates are carefully selected and the bariatric surgeon has advanced laparoscopic skills.

The most common reported complications of RYGB include iron-deficiency anemia (50%), transient folate deficiency (30%), and events requiring surgical intervention (40%: cholecystectomy in 20%, small bowel obstruction in 10%, and incisional hernia in 10%) (Mun et al., 2001). Because most of the stomach and duodenum is bypassed in this procedure, there is an increased risk for deficiencies in vitamin B_{12}, iron, calcium, and thiamine. Although beriberi has been reported in teenagers after RYGB (Towbin et al., 2004), compliance with daily supplementation and regular monitoring of patients can prevent such nutritional deficiencies.

Who Should Perform Bariatric Surgery In Children

Surgical outcomes in adults vary widely between surgeons and institutions (Breaux, 1995; Greenstein & Rabner, 1995; Mason et al., 1995). Furthermore, there is a very clear learning curve, as the morbidity of bariatric surgery varies inversely with the number of procedures performed (Nguyen et al., 2004). Also, since RCTs in adolescents are unlikely, the only method to validate and refine the use of these procedures will come from following patients carefully and long term. Lastly, the increased risk of readmission after bariatric surgery in adults (Zingmond, McGory, & Ko, 2005) argues for close and careful follow-up and monitoring in adolescents. Therefore it is essential that bariatric surgery in adolescents be performed in regionalized pediatric academic centers with programs equipped to handle the data acquisition, long-term follow-up, and multidisciplinary nature of these difficult patients (Inge et al., 2004). It is also necessary to secure an appropriate payer for reimbursement, as these procedures can cost anywhere from $15,000 to $40,000 just for the surgery, let alone the pre-op evaluation, any complications, and the long-term follow-up. Several insurance companies have agreed to pay for these procedures (e.g., Kaiser Permanente), as they realize that the payout for resultant morbidity will ultimately dwarf the cost of the surgery.

A multidisciplinary team with medical, surgical, nutritional, and psychological expertise should carefully select adolescents who are well informed and motivated as potential candidates for LAGB or RYGB. Attention to the principles of growth, development, and compliance is essential to avoid adverse physical, cognitive, and psychosocial outcomes following bariatric surgery (Inge et al., 2004). It must be clear to the subject and the parent that bariatric surgery is in fact an adjunct to a sincere commitment to lifestyle rather than a "magic bullet." Indeed, evidence of recidivism in adults after RYGB is now commonplace.

Subjects and families must be well informed as to the risks and complications of such surgery. The medical team will require endocrine, gastrointestinal, cardiac, pulmonary, and otolaryngologic support. Prophylactic tracheostomy is rarely required to maintain airway patency and to allow for resolution of the hypercapnia prior to surgery (Ray & Senders, 2001). Adolescents undergoing bariatric surgery require lifelong medical and nutritional surveillance postoperatively (Strauss, 2002). Extensive counseling, education, and support are required both before and after bariatric surgery; indeed, patients left on their own tend to regain weight over time. Indeed, studies in adults document an increased risk of hospitalization after RYGB due to difficulties from the procedure (Zingmond et al., 2005). Monitoring of long-term weight maintenance, improvements in cardiovascular morbidity, and longevity are all necessary to determine the cost-effectiveness of bariatric surgery in the pediatric population.

REFERENCES

Abenhaim, L., Moride, Y., Brenot, F., Rich, S., Benichou, J., Kurz, X., Higenbottam, T., Oakley, C., Wouters, E., Aubier, M., Simonneau, G., & Bégaud, B., for the International Primary Pulmonary Hypertension Study Group. (1996). Appetite-suppressant drugs and risk of primary pulmonary hypertension. International pulmonary hypertension study group. *New England Journal of Medicine, 335,* 609–616.

Abu-Abeid, S., Gavert, N., Klausner, J. M., & Szold, A. (2003). Bariatric surgery in adolescence. *Journal of Pediatric Surgery, 38,* 1379–1382.

Apovian, C. M., Baker, C., Ludwig, D. S., Hoppin, A. G., Hsu, G., Lenders, C., Pratt, J. S. A., Forse, R. A., O'Brien, A., & Tarnoff, M. (2005). Best practice guidelines in pediatric/adolescent weight loss surgery. *Obesity Research, 13,* 274–282.

Aronne, L. J., Mackintosh, R., Rosenbaum, M., Leibel, R. L., & Hirsch, J. (1995). Autonomic nervous system activity in weight gain and weight loss. *American Journal of Physiology, 269,* R222–R225.

Bailey, C. J., & Turner, R. C. (1996). Metformin. *New England Journal of Medicine, 334,* 574–579.

Barlow, S. E., & Dietz, W. H. (1998). Obesity evaluation and treatment: expert committee recommendations. The Maternal and Child Health Bureau, Health Resources and Services Administration and the Department of Health and Human Services. *Pediatrics, 102,* e29.

Berkowitz, R. I., Fujioka, K., Daniels, S. R., Hoppin, A., G., Owen, S., Perry, A. C., Sothern, M. S., Renz, C. L., Pirner, M. A., Walch, J. K., Jasinsky, O., Hewkin, A. C., Blakesley, V. A., & Sibutramine Adolescent Study Group. (2006). Effects of sibutramine treatment in obese adolescents: a randomized trial. *Annals of Internal Medicine, 145,* 81–90.

Berkowitz, R. I., Wadden, T. A., Tershakovec, A. M., & Cronquist, J. L. (2003). Behavior therapy and sibutramine for the treatment of adolescent obesity: a randomized controlled trial. *JAMA, 289,* 1805–1812.

Berthoud, H. R., & Jeanrenaud, B. (1979). Acute hyperinsulinemia and its reversal by vagotomy following lesions of the ventromedial hypothalamus in anesthetized rats. *Endocrinology, 105,* 146–151.

Bertoli, A., Magnaterra, R., Borboni, P., Marini, M. A., Barini, A., Fusco, A., & Bollea, M. R. (1998). Dose-dependent effect of octreotide on insulin secretion after OGTT in obesity. *Hormone Research, 49,* 17–21.

Bray, G. A. (1984). Syndromes of hypothalamic obesity in man. *Pediatric Annals, 13,* 525–536.

Bray, G. A., Blackburn, G. L., Ferguson, J. M., Greenway, F. L., Jain, A. K., Mendel, C. M., Mendels, J., Ryan, D. H., Schwartz, S. L., Scheinbaum, M. L., & Seaton, T. B. (1999). Sibutramine produces dose-related weight loss. *Obesity Research, 7,* 189–198.

Bray, G. A., & Gallagher, T. F. (1975). Manifestations of hypothalamic obesity in man: a comprehensive investigation of eight patients and a review of the literature. *Medicine, 54,* 301–333.

Bray, G. A., & Greenway, F. L. (1999). Current and potential drugs for treatment of obesity. *Endocrine Reviews, 20,* 805–875.

Bray, G. A., Inoue, S., & Nishizawa, Y. (1981). Hypothalamic obesity. *Diabetologia, 20,* 366–377.

Bray, G. A., & Nishizawa, Y. (1978). Ventromedial hypothalamus modulates fat mobilization during fasting. *Nature, 274,* 900–902.

Breaux, C. W. (1995). Obesity surgery in children. *Obesity Surgery, 5,* 279–284.

Caprio, S., & Tamborlane, W. V. (1999). Metabolic impact of obesity in childhood. *Endocrinology and Metabolism Clinics of North America, 28,* 731–747.

Carrel, A. L., Moerchen, V., Myers, S. E., Bekx, M. T., Whitman, B. Y., & Allen, D. B. (2004). Growth hormone improves mobility and body composition in infants and toddlers with Prader-Willi syndrome. *Journal of Pediatrics, 145,* 744–749.

Carrel, A. L., Myers, S. E., Whitman, B. Y., & Allen, D. B. (2002). Benefits of long-term GH therapy in Prader-Willi syndrome: a 4-year study. *Journal of Clinical Endocrinology and Metabolism, 87,* 1581–1585.

Center for Weight and Health. (2001). *Pediatric overweight: a review of the literature.* Berkeley: University of California. Available at www.cnr.berkeley.edu/cwh/PDFs/Full_COPI_secure.pdf.

Centers for Disease Control. (1997). Lactic acidosis traced to thiamine deficiency related to nationwide shortage of multivitamins for total parenteral nutrition. *MMWR Morbidity and Mortality Weekly Report, 46(23),* 523-528.

Chanoine, J. P., Hampl, S., Jensen, C., Boldrin, M., & Hauptman, J. (2005). Effects of orlistat on weight and body composition in obese adolescents: a randomized controlled trial. *JAMA, 293,* 2873–2883.

Cummings, D. E., Weigle, D. S., Frayo, R. S., Breen, P. A., Ma, M. K., Dellinger, E. P., & Purnell, J. Q. (2002). Plasma ghrelin levels after diet-induced weight loss or gastric bypass surgery. *New England Journal of Medicine, 346,* 1623–1630.

Cuttler, L., Whittaker, J. L., & Kodish, E. D. (2005). The overweight adolescent: clinical and ethical issues in intensive treatments for pediatric obesity. *Journal of Pediatrics, 146,* 559–564.

Daousi, C., Dunn, A. J., Foy, P. M., MacFarlane, I. A., & Pinkney, J. H. (2005). Endocrine and neuroanatomic predictors of weight gain and obesity in adult patients with hypothalamic damage. *American Journal of Medicine, 118,* 45–50.

Davidson, M. B., & Peters, A. L. (1997). An overview of metformin in the treatment of type 2 diabetes mellitus. *American Journal of Medicine, 102,* 99–110.

DeFronzo, R. A., & Goodman, A. M. (1995). Efficacy of metformin in patients with non-insulin-dependent diabetes mellitus. *New England Journal of Medicine, 333,* 541–549.

Diabetes Prevention Program Research Group. (2002). Reduction in the incidence of type 2 diabetes with lifestyle intervention or metformin. *New England Journal of Medicine, 346,* 393–403.

Dolan, K., Creighton, L., Hopkins, G., & Fielding, G. (2003). Laparoscopic gastric banding in morbidly obese adolescents. *Obesity Surgery, 13,* 101–104.

Doldi, S. B., Micheletto, G., di Prisco, F., Zappa, M. A., Lattuada, E., & Reitano, M. (2000). Intragastric balloon in obese patients. *Obesity Surgery, 10,* 578–581.

Drucker, D. J. (2005). Biologic actions and therapeutic potential of the proglucagon-derived peptides. *Nature Clinical Practice Endocrinology & Metabolism, 1,* 22–31.

Farooqi, I. S., Jebb, S. A., Langmack, G., Lawrence, E., Cheetham, C. H., Prentice, A. M., Hughes, I. A., McCamish, M. A., & O'Rahilly, S. (1999). Effects of recombinant leptin therapy in a child with congenital leptin deficiency. *New England Journal of Medicine, 341,* 879–884.

Farooqi, I. S., Matarese, G., Lord, G. M., Keogh, J. M., Lawrence, E., Agwu, C., Sanna, V., Jebb, S. A., Perna, F., Fontana, S., Lechler, R. I., DePaoli, A. M., & O'Rahilly, S. (2002). Beneficial effects of leptin on obesity, T cell hyporesponsiveness, and neuroendocrine/metabolic dysfunction of human congenital leptin deficiency. *Journal of Clinical Investigation, 110,* 1093–1103.

Fielding, G. A., & Duncombe, J. E. (2005). Laparoscopic adjustable gastric banding in severely obese adolescents. *Surgery for Obesity and Related Diseases, 1,* 399–405.

Flier, J. S. (1998). What's in a name? In search of leptin's physiologic role. *Journal of Clinical Endocrinology and Metabolism, 83,* 1407–1413.

Freemark, M., & Bursey, D. (2001). The effects of metformin on body mass index and glucose tolerance in obese adolescents with fasting hyperinsulinemia and a family history of type 2 diabetes. *Pediatrics, 107,* e55.

Gibson, W. T., Farooqi, I. S., Moreau, M., DePaoli, A. M., Lawrence, E., O'Rahilly, S., & Trussell, R. A. (2004). Congenital leptin deficiency due to homozygosity for the Δ133G mutation: report of another case and evaluation of response to four years of leptin therapy. *Journal of Clinical Endocrinology and Metabolism, 89,* 4821–4826.

Godoy-Matos, A., Carraro, L., Vieira, A., Oliveira, J., Guedes, E. P., Mattos, L., Rangel, C., Moreira, R. O., Coutinho, W., & Appolinario, J. C. (2005). Treatment of obese adolescents with sibutramine: a randomized, double-blind, controlled study. *Journal of Clinical Endocrinology and Metabolism, 90,* 1460–1465.

Greenstein, R. J., & Rabner, J. G. (1995). Is adolescent gastric-restrictive anti-obesity surgery warranted? *Obesity Surgery, 5,* 138–144.

Guerciolini, R., Radu-Radulescu, L., Boldrin, M., Dallas, J., & Moore, R. (2001). Comparative evaluation of fecal fat excretion induced by orlistat and chitosan. *Obesity Research, 9,* 364–367.

Hansen, D. L., Toubro, S., Stock, M. J., MacDonald, I. A., & Astrup, A. (1998). Thermogenic effects of sibutramine in humans. *American Journal of Clinical Nutrition, 68,* 1180–1186.

Harz, K. J., Muller, H. L., Waldeck, E., Pudel, V., & Roth, C. (2003). Obesity in patients with craniopharyngioma: assessment of food intake and movement counts indicating physical activity. *Journal of Clinical Endocrinology and Metabolism, 88,* 5227–5231.

Heal, D. J., Frankland, A. T., Gosden, J., Hutchins, L. J., Prow, M. R., Luscombe, G. P., & Buckett, W. R. (1992). A comparison of the effects of sibutramine hydrochloride, bupropion and methamphetamine on dopaminergic function: evidence that dopamine is not a pharmacological target for sibutramine. *Psychopharmacology, 107,* 303–309.

Heymsfield, S. B., Greenberg, A. S., Fujioka, K., Dixon, R. M., Kushner, R., Hunt, T., Lubina, J. A., Patane, J., Self, B., Hunt, P., & McCamish, M. (1999). Recombinant leptin for weight loss in obese and lean adults: a randomized, controlled, dose-escalation trial. *JAMA, 282,* 1568–1575.

Hodson, R. M., Zacharoulis, D., Goutzmani, E., Slee, P., Wood, S., & Wedgwood, K. R. (2001). Management of obesity with the new gastric balloon. *Obesity Surgery, 11,* 327–329.

Hsu, W. H., Xiang, H. D., Rajan, A. S., Kunze, D. L., & Boyd, A. E. (1991). Somatostatin inhibits insulin secretion by a G-protein-mediated decrease in Ca^{2+} entry through voltage-dependent Ca^{2+} channels in the beta cell. *Journal of Biological Chemistry, 266,* 837–843.

Ibanez, L., Valls, C., Potau, N., Marcos, M. V., & de Zegher, F. (2000). Sensitization to insulin in adolescent girls to normalize hirsutism, hyperandrogenism, oligomenorrhea, dyslipidemia, and hyperinsulinism after precocious adrenarche. *Journal of Clinical Endocrinology and Metabolism, 85,* 3526–3530.

Inge, T. H., Krebs, N. F., Garcia, V. F., Skelton, J. A., Guice, K. S., Strauss, R. S., Albanese, C. T., Brandt, M. L., Hammer, L. D., Harmon, C. M., Kane, T. D., Klish, W. J., Oldham, K. T., Rudolph, C. D., Helmrath, M. A. Donovan, E., & Daniels, S. R. (2004). Bariatric surgery for overweight adolescents: concerns and recommendations. *Pediatrics, 114,* 217–223.

James, W. P. T., Astrup, A., Finer, N., Hilsted, J., Kopelman, P., Rössner, S., Saris, W. H., & Van Gaal, L. F. (2000). Effect of sibutramine on weight maintenance after weight loss: a randomized trial. *Lancet, 356,* 2119–2125.

Jamieson, M. A. (2002). The use of metformin in adolescents with polycystic ovary syndrome: for and against. *Journal of Pediatric and Adolescent Gynecology, 15,* 109–114.

Jeanrenaud, B. (1985). An hypothesis on the aetiology of obesity: dysfunction of the central nervous system as a primary cause. *Diabetologia, 28,* 502–513.

Jick, H., Vasilakis, C., Weinrauch, L. A., Meier, C. R., Jick, S. S., & Derby, L. E. (1998). A population-based study of appetite-suppressant drugs and the risk of cardiac valve regurgitation. *New England Journal of Medicine, 339,* 719–724.

Jones, K. L., Arslanian, S., Peterokova, V. A., Park, J. S., & Tomlinson, M. J. (2002). Effect of metformin in pediatric patients with type 2 diabetes. *Diabetes Care, 25,* 89–94.

Jorgensen, J. O., Pedersen, S. B., Borglum, J., Moller, N., Schmitz, O., Christiansen, J. S., & Richelsen, B. (1994). Fuel metabolism, energy expenditure, and thyroid function in growth hormone-treated obese women: a double-blind, placebo-controlled study. *Metabolism, 43,* 872–877.

Kaplowitz, P. B., Rundle, A. C., & Blethen, S. L. (1998). Weight relative to height before and during growth hormone therapy in prepubertal children. *Hormone and Metabolism Research, 30,* 565–569.

Kay, J. P., Alemzadeh, R., Langley, G., D'Angelo, L., Smith, P., & Holshouser, S. (2001). Beneficial effects of metformin in normoglycemic morbidly obese adolescents. *Metabolism, 50,* 1457–1461.

Keim, N. L., Stern, J. S., & Havel, P. J. (1998). Relation between circulating leptin concentrations and appetite during a prolonged, moderate energy deficit in women. *American Journal of Clinical Nutrition, 68,* 794–801.

Kiefer, T. J., & Habener, J. F. (1999). The glucagon-like peptides. *Endocrine Reviews, 20,* 876–913.

Kreier, F., Fliers, E., Voshol, P. J., Van Eden, C. G., Havekes, L. M., Kalsbeek, A., Van Heijningen, C. L., Sluiter, A. A., Mettenleiter, T. C., Romijn, J. A., Sauerwein, H. P., & Buijs, R. M. (2002). Selective parasympathetic innervation of subcutaneous and intra-abdominal fat-functional implications. *Journal of Clinical Investigation, 110,* 1243–1250.

Krentz, A. J., MacDonald, L. M., & Schade, D. S. (1994). Octreotide: a long-acting inhibitor of endogenous hormone secretion for human metabolic investigations. *Metabolism, 43,* 24–31.

Kumar, N., & Dey, C. S. (2002). Metformin enhances insulin signalling in insulin-dependent and -independent pathways in insulin resistant muscle cells. *British Journal of Pharmacology, 137,* 329–336.

Lamberts, S. W. J., Van Der Lely, A. J., De Herder, W. W., & Hofland, L. J. (1996). Drug therapy: octreotide. *New England Journal of Medicine, 334,* 246–254.

Lawson, M. L., Kirk, S., Mitchell, T., Chen, M. K., Loux, T. J., Daniels, S. R., & Inge, T. (2006). One-year outcomes of Roux-en-Y gastric bypass for morbidly obese adolescents: a multicenter study from the pediatric bariatric study group. *Pediatric Surgery, 41,* 137–143.

Lee, A., & Morley, J. E. (1998). Metformin decreases food-consumption and induces weight-loss in subjects with obesity with type-ii non-insulin-dependent diabetes. *Obesity Research, 6,* 47–53.

LeFoll, B., & Goldberg, S. R. (2005). Cannabinoid CB1 receptor antagonists as promising new medications for drug dependence. *Journal of Pharmacology and Experimental Therapeutics, 312,* 875–883.

Leibel, R. L., Rosenbaum, M., & Hirsch, J. (1995). Changes in energy expenditure resulting from altered body weight. *New England Journal of Medicine, 332,* 621–628.

Lenhard, J. M., Kliewer, S. A., Paulik, M. A., Plunket, K. D., Lehmann, J. M., & Weiel, J. E. (1997). Effects of troglitazone and metformin on glucose and lipid metabolism: alterations of two distinct molecular pathways. *Biochemical Pharmacology, 54,* 801–808.

Li, H. J., Ji, C. Y., Wang, W., & Hu, Y. H. (2005). A twin study for serum leptin, soluble leptin receptor, and free insulin-like growth factor-1 in pubertal females. *Journal of Clinical Endocrinology and Metabolism, 90,* 3659–3664.

Lustig, R. H. (2001). The neuroendocrinology of childhood obesity. *Pediatric Clinics of North America, 48,* 909–930.

Lustig, R. H. (2002). Hypothalamic obesity: the sixth cranial endocrinopathy. *Endocrinologist, 12,* 210–217.

Lustig, R. H. (2003). Autonomic dysfunction of the β-cell and the pathogenesis of obesity. *Reviews of Endocrine and Metabolic Disease, 4,* 23–32.

Lustig, R. H. (2006). Childhood obesity: behavioral aberration or biochemical drive? Reinterpreting the first law of thermodynamics. *Nature Clinical Practice Endocrinology & Metabolism, 2,* 447–458.

Lustig, R. H., Greenway, F., Velasquez-Mieyer, P., Heimberger, D., Schumacher, D., Smith, D., Smith, W., Soler, N., Warsi, G., Berg, W., Maloney, J., Benedetto, J., Zhu, W., & Hohneker, J. (2006a). A multicenter, randomized, double-blind, placebo-controlled, dose-finding trial of a long-acting formulation of octreotide in promoting weight loss in obese adults with insulin hypersecretion. *International Journal of Obesity (London), 30,* 331–341.

Lustig, R. H., Hinds, P. S., Ringwald-Smith, K., Christensen, R. K., Kaste, S. C., Schreiber, R. E., Rai, S. N., Lensing, S. Y., Wu, S., & Xiong, X. (2003). Octreotide therapy of pediatric hypothalamic obesity: a double-blind, placebo-controlled trial. *Journal of Clinical Endocrinology and Metabolism, 88,* 2586–2592.

Lustig, R. H., Mietus-Snyder, M. L., Bacchetti, P., Lazar, A. A., Velasquez-Mieyer, P. A., & Christensen, M. L. (2006b). Insulin dynamics predict BMI and z-score response to insulin suppression or sensitization pharmacotherapy in obese children. *Journal of Pediatrics, 148,* 23–29.

Lustig, R. H., Sen, S., Soberman, J. E., & Velasquez-Mieyer, P. A. (2004). Obesity, leptin resistance, and the effects of insulin suppression. *International Journal of Obesity, 28,* 1344–1348.

Maahs, D., de Serna, D. G., Kolotkin, R. L., Ralston, S., Sandate, J., Qualls, C., Schade, D. S. (2006). Randomized, double-blind, placebo-controlled trial of orlistat for weight loss in adolescents. *Endocrine Practice, 12,* 18–28.

Mannucci, E., Ognibene, A., Cemasco, F., Bardini, G., Mencucci, A., Pierazzuoli, E., Ciani, S., Messeri, G., & Rotella, C. M. (2001). Effect of metformin on glucagon-like peptide-1 (GLP-1) and leptin levels in obese nondiabetic subjects. *Diabetes Care, 24,* 489–494.

Marchesini, G., Brizi, M., Bianchi, G., Tomassetti, S., Zoli, M., & Melchionda, N. (2001). Metformin in non-alcoholic steatohepatitis. *Lancet, 358,* 893–894.

Mark, A. L., Rahmouni, K., Correia, M., & Haynes, W. G. (2003). A leptin-sympathetic-leptin feedback loop: potential implications for regulation of arterial pressure and body fat. *Acta Physiologica Scandinavica, 177,* 345–349.

Mason, E. E., Scott, D. H., Doherty, C., Dullen, J. J., Rodriguez, E. M., Maher, J. W., & Soper, R. T. (1995). Vertical banded gastroplasty in the severely obese under age twenty-one. *Obesity Surgery, 5,* 23–33.

McDuffie, J. R., Calis, K. A., Booth, S. L., Uwaifo, G. I., & Yanovski, J. A. (2002). Effects of orlistat on fat-soluble vitamins in obese adolescents. *Pharmacotherapy, 22,* 814–822.

McLachlan, K. A., O'Neal, D., Jenkins, A., & Alford, F. P. (2006). Do adiponectin, TNFalpha, leptin and CRP relate to insulin resistance in pregnancy? Studies in women with and without gestational diabetes, during and after pregnancy. *Diabetes/Metabolism Research and Reviews, 22,* 131–138.

Michael, M. D., Kulkarni, R. N., Postic, C., Previs, S. F., Shulman, G. I., Magnuson, M. A., & Kahn, C. R. (2000). Loss of insulin signaling in hepatocytes leads to severe insulin resistance and progressive hepatic dysfunction. *Molecular Cell, 6,* 87–97.

Mitra, S. W., Mezey, E., Hunyady, B., Chamberlain, L., Hayes, E., Foor, F., Wang, Y., Schonbrunn, A., & Schaeffer, J. M. (1999). Colocalization of somatostatin receptor sst5 and insulin in rat pancreatic β-cells. *Endocrinology, 140,* 3790–3796.

Mittendorfer, B., Ostlund, R. J., Patterson, B., & Klein, S. Z. (2001). Orlistat inhibits dietary cholesterol absorption. *Obesity Research, 9,* 599–604.

Mogul, H. R., Peterson, S. J., Weinstein, B. I., Zhang, S., & Southren, A. L. (2001). Metformin and carbohydrate-modified diet, a novel obesity treatment protocol: preliminary findings from a case series of nondiabetic women with midlife weight gain and hyperinsulinemia. *Heart Disease, 3,* 285–292.

Montague, C. T., Farooqi, I. S., Whitehead, J. P., Soos, M. A., Rau, H., Wareham, N. J., Sewter, C. P., Digby, J. E., Mohammed, S. N., Hurst, J. A., Cheetham, C. H., Earley, A. R., Barnett, A. H., Prins, J. B., & O'Rahilly, S. (1997). Congenital leptin deficiency is associated with severe early-onset obesity in humans. *Nature, 387,* 903–908.

Morgan, J. P., & Funderburk, F. R. (1992). Phenylpropanolamine and blood pressure: a review of prospective studies. *American Journal of Clinical Nutrition, 55,* 206S–210S.

Morrison, J. A., Cottingham, E. M., & Barton, B. A. (2002). Metformin for weight loss in pediatric patients taking psychotropic drugs. *American Journal of Psychiatry, 159,* 655–657.

Mun, E. C., Blackburn, G. L., & Matthews, J. B. (2001). Current status of medical and surgical therapy for obesity. *Gastroenterology, 120,* 669–681.

Nguyen, N. T., Paya, M., Stevens, M., Mavandadi, S., Zainabadi, K., & Wilson, S. E. (2004). The relationship between hospital volume and outcome in bariatric surgery at academic medical centers. *Annals of Surgery, 240,* 586–594.

Odeleye, O. E., de Courten, M., Pettitt, D. J., & Ravussin, E. (1997). Fasting hyperinsulinemia is a predictor of increased body weight gain and obesity in Pima indian children. *Diabetes, 46,* 1341–1345.

Paolisso, G., Amato, L., Eccellente, R., Gambardella, A., Tagliamonte, M. R., Varricchio, G., Carella, C., Giugliano, D., & D'Onofrio, F. (1998). Effect of metformin on food intake in obese subjects. *European Journal of Clinical Investigation, 28,* 441–446.

Pasquali, R., Gambineri, A., Biscotti, D., Vicennatti, V., Gagliardi, L., Colitta, D., Fiorini, S., Cognigni, G. E., Filicori, M., & Morselli-Labate, A. M. (2000). Effect of long-term treatment with metformin added to hypocaloric diet on body composition, fat distribution, and androgen and insulin levels in abdominally obese women with and without the polycystic ovary syndrome. *Journal of Clinical Endocrinology and Metabolism, 85,* 2767–2774.

Preeyasombat, C., Bacchetti, P., Lazar, A. A., & Lustig, R. H. (2005). Racial and etiopathologic dichotomies in insulin secretion and resistance in obese children. *Journal of Pediatrics, 146,* 474–481.

Ray, R. M., & Senders, C. W. (2001). Airway management in the obese child. *Pediatric Clinics of North America, 48,* 1055–1063.

Reitman, J. B., Castro-Cabezas, M., de Bruin, T. W., & Erkelens, D. W. (1994). Relationship between improved postprandial lipemia and low-density lipoprotein metabolism during treatment with tetrahydrolipstatin, a pancreatic lipase inhibitor. *Metabolism, 43,* 293–298.

Rohner-Jeanrenaud, F., & Jeanrenaud, B. (1980). Consequences of ventromedial hypothalamic lesions upon insulin and glucagon secretion by subsequently isolated perfused pancreases in the rat. *Journal of Clinical Investigation, 65,* 902–910.

Rosenbaum, M., Murphy, E. M., Heymsfield, S. B., Matthews, D. E., & Leibel, R. L. (2002). Low dose leptin administration reverses effects of sustained weight reduction on energy expenditure and circulating concentrations of thyroid hormones. *Journal of Clinical Endocrinology and Metabolism, 87,* 2391–2394.

Rosenbaum, M., Nicolson, M., Hirsch, J., Murphy, E., Chu, F., & Leibel, R. L. (1997). Effects of weight change on plasma leptin concentrations and energy expenditure. *Journal of Clinical Endocrinology and Metabolism, 82,* 3647–3564.

Rosenbaum, M., Vandenborne, K., Goldsmith, R., Simoneau, J. A., Heymsfield, S. B., Joanisse, D. R., Hirsch, J., Murphy, E., Matthews, D., Segal, K. R., & Leibel, R. L. (2003). Effects of experimental weight perturbation on skeletal muscle work efficiency in human subjects. *American Journal of Physiology. Regulatory, Integrative and Comparative Physiology, 285,* R183–R192.

Rothman, D. L., Magnusson, I., Cline, G., Gerard, D., Kahn, C. R., Shulman, R. G., & Shulman, G. I. (1995). Decreased muscle glucose transport/phosphorylation is an early defect in the pathogenesis of non-insulin-dependent diabetes mellitus. *Proceedings of the National Academy of Sciences USA, 92,* 983–987.

Ryan, D. H., Kaiser, P., & Bray, G. A. (1995). Sibutramine: a novel new agent for obesity treatment. *Obesity Research, 3,* S553–S559.

Satoh, N., Ogawa, Y., Katsura, G., Tsuji, T., Masuzaki, H., Hiraoka, J., Okazaki, T., Tamaki, M., Hayase, M., Yoshimasa, Y., Nishi, S., Hosoda, K., & Nakao, K. (1997). Pathophysiological significance of the *obese* gene product, leptin in ventromedial hypothalamus (VMH)-lesioned rats: evidence for loss of its satiety effect in VMH-lesioned rats. *Endocrinology, 138,* 947–954.

Schwimmer, J. B., Middleton, M. S., Deutsch, R., & Lavine, J. E. (2005). A phase 2 clinical trial of metformin as a treatment for non-diabetic paediatric non-alcoholic steatohepatitis. *Alimentary Pharmacology & Therapeutics, 21,* 871–879.

Seagle, H. M., Bessesen, D. H., & Hill, J. O. (1998). Effects of sibutramine on resting metabolic rate and weight loss in overweight women. *Obesity Research, 6,* 115–121.

Shah, M., Simha, V., & Garg, A. (2006). Review: long-term impact of bariatric surgery on body weight, comorbidities, and nutritional status . *Journal of Clinical Endocrinology and Metabolism, 91,* 4223–4231.

Shi, Z. Q., Chinookoswong, N., Wang, J. L., Korach, E., Lebel, C., DePaoli, A., et al. (2002). Additive effects of leptin and oral anti-obesity drugs in treating diet-induced obesity in rats. *Diabetes, 51*(suppl. 2), 1707.

Sims, E. A. H. (1996). Insulin resistance is a result, not a cause of obesity: Socratic debate: the con side. In A. Angel, H. Anderson, C. Bouchard, D. Lau, L. Leiter, & R. Mendelson (Eds.), *Progress in obesity research* (pp. 587–592). London: Libbey.

Simsolo, R. B., Ezzat, S., Ong, J. M., Saghizadeh, M., & Kern, P. A. (1995). Effects of acromegaly treatment and growth hormone on adipose tissue lipoprotein lipase. *Journal of Clinical Endocrinology and Metabolism, 80,* 3233–3238.

Sjostrom, C. D., Peltonen, M., & Sjostrom, L. (2002). Effects of 2 and 10 years weight loss retention on cardiovascular risk factors. *International Journal of Obesity, 26*(suppl. 1), S231.

Sjostrom, L. (2002). Surgical outcomes from the SOS study. *International Journal of Obesity, 26*(suppl. 1), 825.

Speiser, P. W., Rudolf, M. C. J., Anhalt, H., Camacho-Hubner, C., Chiarelli, F., Eliakim, A., Freemark, M., Gruters, A., Hershkovitz, E., Iughetti, L., Krude, H., Latzer, Y., Lustig, R. H., Pescovitz, O. H., Pinhas-Hamiel, O., Rogol, A. D., Shalitin, S., Sultan, C., Stein, D., Vardi, P., Werther, G. A., Zadik, Z., Zuckerman-Levin, N., & Hochberg, Z., on behalf of the Obesity Consensus Working Group. (2005). Consensus statement: childhood obesity. *Journal of Clinical Endocrinology and Metabolism, 90,* 1871–1887.

Strauss, R. (2002). Perspectives on childhood obesity. *Current Gastroenterological Reports, 4,* 244–250.

Strauss, R. S., Bradley, L. J., & Brolin, R. E. (2001). Gastric bypass surgery in adolescents with morbid obesity. *Journal of Pediatrics, 138,* 499–504.

Stumvoll, M., Nurjhan, N., Perriello, G., Dailey, G., & Gerich, J. E. (1995). Metabolic effects of metformin in non-insulin-dependent diabetes mellitus. *New England Journal of Medicine, 333,* 550–554.

Sugerman, H. J., Sugerman, E. L., DeMaria, E. J., Kellum, J. M., Kennedy, C., Mowery, Y., & Wolfe, L. G. (2003). Bariatric surgery for severely obese adolescents. *Journal of Gastrointestinal Surgery 7,* 102–108.

Tauber, M. T., Harris, A. G., & Rochiccioli, P. (1994). Clinical use of the long-acting somatostatin analog octreotide in pediatrics. *European Journal of Pediatrics, 153,* 304–310.

Teter, C. J., Early, J. J., & Gibbs, C. M. (2000). Treatment of affective disorder and obesity with topiramate. *Annals of Pharmacotherapy, 34,* 1262–1265.

Thornton, J. E., Cheung, C. C., Clifton, D. K., & Steiner, R. A. (1997). Regulation of hypothalamic proopiomelanocortin mRNA by leptin in ob/ob mice. *Endocrinology, 138,* 5063–5066.

Towbin, S., Inge, T. H., Garcia, V. F., Roehrig, H. R., Clements, R. H., Harmon, C. M., & Daniels, S. R. (2004). Beriberi after gastric bypass surgery in adolescence. *Journal of Pediatrics, 145,* 263–267.

Van Gaal, L. F., Rissanen, A. M., Scheen, A. J., Ziegler, O., & Rossner, S. (2005). Effects of the cannabinoid-1 receptor blocker rimonabant on weight reduction and cardiovascular risk factors in overweight patients: 1-year experience from the RIO-Europe study. *Lancet, 365,* 1389–1397.

Vandenplas, Y., Bollen, P., de Langhe, K., Vandemaele, L., & DeSchepper, J. (1999). Intragastric balloons in adolescents with morbid obesity. *European Journal of Gastroenterology and Hepatology, 11,* 243–245.

Velasquez, E. M., Mendoza, S., Hamer, T., Sosa, F., & Glueck, C. J. (1994). Metformin therapy in polycystic ovarian syndrome reduces hyperinsulinemia, insulin resistance, hyperandrogenemia, and systolic blood pressure, while facilitating normal menses and pregnancy. *Metabolism, 43,* 647–654.

Velasquez-Mieyer, P. A., Cowan, P. A., Buffington, C. K., Arheart, K. L., Cowan, G. S. M., Connelly, B. E., Spencer, K. A., & Lustig, R. H. (2003). Suppression of insulin secretion promotes weight loss and alters macronutrient preference in a subset of obese adults. *International Journal of Obesity, 27,* 219–226.

Weintraub, M. (1985). Phenylpropanolamine as an anorexiant agent in weight control: a review of published and unpublished studies. In J. P. Morgan, D. V. Kagan, & J. S. Bordy (Eds.), *Phenylpropanolamine: risks, benefits, and controversies* (pp. 53–79). New York: Praeger.

Whitaker, R. C., Wright, J. A., Pepe, M. S., Seidel, K. D., & Dietz, W. H. (1997). Predicting obesity in young adulthood from childhood and parental obesity. *New England Journal of Medicine, 337,* 869–873.

Wilding, J., Van Gaal, L., Rissanen, A., Vercruysse, F., & Fitchet, M. (2004). A randomized double-blind placebo-controlled study of the long-term efficacy and safety of topiramate in the treatment of obese subjects. *International Journal of Obesity, 28,* 1399–1410.

Wilkes, J. J., Nelson, E., Osborne, M., Demarest, K. T., & Olefsky, J. M. (2005). Topiramate is an insulin-sensitizing compound in vivo with direct effects on adipocytes in female ZDF rats. *American Journal of Physiology Endocrinology and Metabolism, 288,* E617–E624.

Williams, T., Berelowitz, M., Joffe, S. N., Thorner, M. O., Rivier, J., Vale, W., & Frohman, L. A. (1984). Impaired growth hormone responses to growth hormone-releasing factor in obesity: a pituitary defect reversed with weight reduction. *New England Journal of Medicine, 311,* 1403–1407.

Wynne, K., Park, A. J., Small, C. J., Patterson, M., Ellis, S. M., Murphy, K. G., Wren, A. M., Frost, G. S., Meeran, K., Ghatei, M. A., & Bloom, S. R. (2005). Subcutaneous oxyntomodulin reduces body weight in overweight and obese subjects: a double-blind, randomized, controlled trial. *Diabetes, 54,* 2390–2395.

Yanovski, J. A. (2001). Intensive therapies for pediatric obesity. *Pediatric Clinics of North America, 48,* 1041–1053.

Yanovski, S. Z., & Yanovski, J. A. (2002). Drug therapy: obesity. *New England Journal of Medicine, 346,* 591–602.

Zhi, J., Melia, A. T., Guercioloni, R., Chung, J., Kinberg, J., Hauptman, J. B., & Patel, I. H. (1994). Retrospective population-based analysis of the dose-response (fecal fat excretion) relationship of orlistat in normal and obese volunteers. *Clinical Pharmacology and Therapeutics, 56,* 82–85.

Zhou, G., Myers, R., Li, Y., Chen, Y., Shen, X., Fenyk-Melody, J., Wu, M., Ventre, J., Doebber, T., Fujii, N., Musi, N., Hirshman, M. F., Goodyear, L. J., & Moller, D. E. (2001). Role of AMP-activated protein kinase in mechanism of metformin action. *Journal of Clinical Investigation, 108,* 1167–1174.

Zingmond, D. S., McGory, M. L., & Ko, C. Y. (2005). Hospitalization before and after gastric bypass surgery. *JAMA, 294,* (15), 1918–1924.

12

Inpatient Treatment of Severely Obese Children

CAROLINE BRAET, ANN TANGHE, AND ELLEN MOENS

INTRODUCTION

Most children with obesity continue to be overweight into adulthood (Whitaker, Wright, Pepe, Seidel, & Dietz, 1997). A considerable body of evidence is now available demonstrating that continued obesity leads to serious health problems (Dietz, 1998; Mossberg, 1989). Unfortunately, actions to reduce problems of overweight have met with failure. While adult obesity is known to be resistant to treatment (Wilson, 1994), intervention programs for children are producing promising results for some children, but not for all (Braet & Van Winckel, 2000; Epstein, Valoski, Wing, & McCurley, 1990, 1994; Nuutinen & Knip, 1992). Although a 10% reduction in weight is associated with reduced health risks in adults (Wilson, 1994), the maximum weight loss reached by the child obesity treatment programs is disappointingly low for severely obese children. Furthermore, not all children benefit from this approach. In the study of Epstein et al. (1994), one-third of the sample failed to reduce their obese status.

Attempts to treat severely obese children are rare (Jelalian & Saelens, 1999; Rössner, 1998). Five reports were published on bariatric procedures in adolescents that were at least 100% over their ideal body weight (for a review, see Marcus, 2004a). The quality of the reports as well as the follow-up time varied considerably. The results were promising, but careful medical and psychological examination was lacking. Moreover, the authors reported negative side effects like gallstones and anemia. In one study, two deaths were reported. In one of the first studies on jejunoileal bypass in adolescents ages 11 to 22 years (Silber, Randolph, & Robbins, 1986), 3 of the 11 patients died. Although significant weight loss was maintained in the eight survivors, side effects and complications such as diarrhea and electrolyte disturbances continue to develop. Age was a significant factor in this study, with older patients doing better. Two patients had a miscarriage, probably related to iron deficiency anemia and hypoproteinemia. Furthermore, Marcus (2004a) admits that there are many ethical problems involved if bariatric surgery is considered for childhood obesity because it is an extensive operation with life-long consequences and careful follow-up for an indefinite time. Moreover, bariatric surgery does not encourage healthy eating habits, so it is questionable whether it promotes a healthy lifestyle, and there are questions about whether it provides a decrease in the cardiovascular risks associated with severe obesity. Therefore the U.S. Preventive Services Task Force (2006) recently stated that, at the moment, no acceptable quality evidence is available for children and adolescents to advise surgical approaches for reducing overweight.

Drug treatments for young obese adolescents are also not advisable (Epstein, Myers, Raynor, & Saelens, 1998). It is still unknown whether antiobesity agents are safe and functional. This has to be evaluated in double-blind, placebo-controlled clinical trials, and the lack of such studies in children and adolescents is noteworthy (Marcus, 2004b).

In their proposal of possible treatment options for severely obese adults, Brownell and Wadden (1991) suggest a stepped care treatment decision scheme based on the degree of overweight. In their scheme, approaches or programs are ranked according to cost, intrusiveness, side effects, risk, and other factors used to make a cost-effectiveness judgment. The least expensive and least distressing treatments are the first level of intervention, with more aggressive programs reserved for the most severely overweight. According to level 1 (5% to 20% overweight), self-help groups and commercial programs are the approaches that would be relevant to the individual. People in level 2 (20% to 40% overweight) will probably not respond to a self-directed program and might need something more intensive, such as behavioral programs. An inpatient program is recommended for obese people with medical complications (40% to 100% overweight) (levels 3 and 4) or morbidly obese people (more than 100% overweight) (levels 4 and 5). Obese children with comorbid medical conditions would be ideal candidates for inpatient programs, as they need both treatment and close monitoring. However, in stark contrast to other chronic diseases, few centers for inpatient treatment of obese children exist. As the World Health Organization (WHO) (1998) points out, only a few countries have a comprehensive range of services capable of providing the level of care required to effectively manage obese patients.

At times, inpatient treatment is justified not only because of the insufficient effect of current outpatient treatments for some children, but also because of the need to treat children from less supportive families. Although potential disadvantages of inpatient treatments need to be recognized, such as the cost and intrusiveness, intensive inpatient programs have the advantage of offering children with obesity an environment with more opportunities to acquire a healthy lifestyle. This can offer the child a good start before returning to their family environment.

Furthermore, the psychological burden for overweight children is significant and can lead to emotional problems and social isolation (Braet, Mervielde, & Vandereycken, 1997; Rössner, 1998). Research has shown that once they become young adults, obese people tend to receive less higher education, earn less money, and marry to a lesser extent (Gortmaker, Must, Perrin, Sobol, & Dietz, 1993). Also, after experiencing outpatient treatment failures, it is reasonable to assume that these children will suffer from frustration and feelings of incompetence. So, from a psychological point of view, it is advisable for specific groups of overweight children and adolescents to be offered specific services.

Initial experiences with long-term inpatient treatment for morbidly obese children have been reported by Boeck et al. (1993). The authors developed a program of weight management within a 44 bed rehabilitation facility designed for long stays. In their study, the children had a mean age of 14 years (range 9.5 to 17.5 years) and an average body mass index (BMI) of 47.5 on admission. The duration of the residential stay ranged from 1 to 21 months (mean duration 8 months). Program components were (1) individualized exercise, (2) a behavior modification program, (3) eating cafeteria style with other (nonobese) patients, (4) weekly weigh-in, and (5) nutrition group sessions. Twenty-one patients participated in the study and nine of them left early. The results presented thus far are preliminary, but suggest a moderate positive outcome. The mean weight loss was equivalent to a decrease in BMI of 11 (range of decrease 2.3 to 37.6). However, nearly all the patients still had a BMI in the morbidly obese range at the time of discharge. In the case of planned discharge, the physiological consequences of their obesity were reversed. The mean BMI at the time of discharge was 36.6 (range 26.9 to 59.0). A few other studies have reported on inpatient treatment for children with obesity (Braet, Van Winckel, Tanghe, de Bode, & Franckx, 2003; Fenning and Fenning, 2006; Gately, Cooke, Butterly, Mackreth, & Carroll, 2000; Torigoe et al., 1997; Wabitsch et al., 1996).

The inpatient treatment of six obese children was reported by Torigoe et al. (1997). The treatment program was located in a pediatric hospital and consisted of strict dietary therapy and therapeutic exercise. The program was evaluated using the intra-abdominal visceral fat to subcutaneous fat ratio (V:S ratio) and found that the V:S ratio of the inpatient group decreased significantly during weight loss. Although the results were promising, replication in a larger sample of obese children should be studied to test the findings. Also, Fenning and Fenning (2006) report the progress of three complicated cases of obesity using inpatient treatment in a medical psychiatric unit with a multidisciplinary program. The adolescents were 14, 15, and 17 years old. One patient (BMI = 64) lost 40 kg during 6 months of hospitalization, and she continued to maintain her weight 4 years after discharge. A 15-year-old girl (BMI = 48) was treated for 3 months and was then treated as an outpatient after a 10% weight reduction. At the 3-year follow-up she weighed 90 kg (BMI = 33). The case report of the third child (age 14 years, BMI = 43) revealed no weight evolution, but progress on medical parameters. This patient was referred because of severe sleep apnea. The program incorporated the six elements recommended by the Expert Committee on obesity evaluation: (1) close monitoring of the medical condition, (2) moderate caloric restriction to induce a modest weight reduction of 5 to 10%, (3) intensive family intervention, (4) individual behavioral and cognitive therapy, (5) physical activity education, and (6) gradual community involvement. Unfortunately, although case reports are promising, replication in larger sample of obese children should be studied before firm conclusions and recommendations can be formulated.

Wabitsch et al. (1996) describe a 6-week intervention in a pediatric hospital consisting of dietary restriction and exercise therapy (1 to 2 hr/day) for 73 girls with a mean age of 15 years (range 13 to 19 years) and an average BMI of 31.1. The BMI was reduced by 3 (corresponding with a weight loss of 8 kg). Moreover, cardiovascular risk factors (e.g., blood pressure, total and low-density lipoprotein [LDL] cholesterol levels) decreased significantly as well. Although this study is well-designed, it does not include a long-term follow-up.

Gately et al. (2000) reported an 8-week residential summer weight loss camp for obese youngsters ages 10 to 15 years. The BMI at baseline ranged from 20.2 and 67.6 (mean BMI = 32.7). The camp program utilized (1) structured fun-based physical activities, (2) moderate dietary restrictions, and (3) behavior modification. After the camp, weight loss was equivalent to a decrease in BMI of 4 (range of decrease in BMI 0.6 to 10.6). After the camp, however, there was an increase in BMI. A 10-month follow-up collected in 53% of the sample revealed stable findings, with a mean BMI of 30.1, and compared to baseline, a mean decease in BMI of 2.6, but with considerable variations in responses. Follow-up shows that 26% of the subjects continued to reduce their BMI during the follow-up (while 74% regained some weight) and 83% had a lower BMI than when they enrolled in the camp program 1 year before.

Given the urgent need for treatment options for severely obese children, our group developed an inpatient treatment program for obese children and adolescents. Braet et al. (2003, 2004) evaluated the effects of a 10-month inpatient treatment program implemented as a nondiet, healthy lifestyle approach in a rehabilitation center. The program is conducted at a recognized medical pediatric center that specializes in the treatment of children with chronic diseases (such as asthma) and has a specialized boarding school. Twice a month the children return home for the weekend. The other two weekends and half of the school holidays they stay in the center. The treatment was carried out with the help of one dietician, one psychologist, one social worker, one medical doctor, one physiotherapist, and six group leaders for 30 patients. It was supervised by two behavior therapists and two medical doctors. A pre-/post-within-subjects design was employed to evaluate treatment outcome, including a 2-year follow-up. Children ($N = 122$) ranged in age from 7 to 17 years (mean 12.7 years) with a mean BMI of 32.5, expressed as a percentage of overweight (mean = 77.4%). The results of this program will be discussed in detail below.

To conclude, the interventions vary in their approach, but most of them were multidisciplinary and include a physical activity program (conventional approaches like exercise prescriptions based on fixed intensity, duration, and frequency, as well as fun-based sports), dietary interventions (strict dietary restrictions limited to 1400 kcal/day as well as eating traditional cafeteria style or a nondiet, healthy lifestyle approach), and behavioral components (using diaries, self-control strategies, contracts). Unfortunately the studies do not always describe strict admission criteria and limit their reports on the procedures and methods used, which makes it difficult to compare. Moreover, follow-up results in a representative sample were available for just one study. Our own experience, contrasted against available scientific literature, inspired us to describe some guidelines for organizing a multicomponent inpatient treatment program for severely overweight children.

ADMISSION CRITERIA

Brownell and Wadden (1991) suggest evaluating different client factors before referral to an intensive treatment program. An individual's degree of overweight is usually the determining factor when recommending an inpatient treatment. The overweight had to be "severe" (e.g., a BMI greater than the 97th percentile for age and gender) in the presence of obesity-related medical complications such as metabolic complications. It is recommended that the adjusted BMI index ([actual BMI/percentile 50 of BMI for age] × 100) be calculated. An index up to 20% refers to normal weight, an index between 20% and 40% refers to overweight in the 85th to 95th percentile, an index of 40% or higher refers to obesity (greater than the 95th percentile), an index of 60% or higher refers to severe obesity (greater than the 97th percentile). Body composition, dieting history, eating patterns, and degree of dysphoria need to be considered as well. For children and adolescents who were morbidly obese (more than 100% of ideal body weight), inpatient treatment is always a worthwhile treatment option because of concomitant major medical conditions (Silber et al., 1986).

It is advisable to determine if the patients have already been treated as part of an outpatient treatment program, as well as the reason for the outpatient treatment failure. Any inpatient treatment program needs to establish eligibility criteria prior to enrollment and decide whether mentally retarded children, nonmotivated children, children with psychological comorbid problems such as depression, or children from less supportive families will be included. We will now discuss these criteria.

Data from several studies indicate that the participation of at least one supportive parent in the treatment of childhood obesity is optimal for best outcomes. Involvement of one of the parents is therefore recommended to provide continued support during the time periods the child spends at home. This is especially important for younger children. Mentally retarded children can apply for an inpatient care treatment program as long as their mental age fits in the age range considered. In cases where children suffer from Prader-Willi syndrome or other primary obesity syndromes, a specific approach and specific services for this subgroup are necessary. It is our experience that obese children applying for inpatient treatment have more learning disabilities and find themselves in special needs education to a higher degree. This is of importance when selecting an appropriate school program, as well as a treatment program. Patients were also required to show sufficient sense of motivation to take part in the treatment course. A motivational interview, usually assessed by a psychologist, can be helpful in determining if the child is motivated enough and how the motivation can be enhanced. A rule of thumb here is that the child has to decide by him- or herself that he or she really wants this treatment. As such, it is advisable that the child (and the parents) be given sufficient time for reflection prior to enrolling.

Whether children with comorbid psychological problems should be excluded is not easy to decide. There is still substantial disagreement on the association of obesity and psychopathology because of contradictory findings in research on this topic. As yet, the *Diagnostic and Statistical Manual of Mental Disorders* (4th edition–text revision) (DSM-IV-TR) (American Psychiatric Association, 2000) does not include obesity because no consistent association has been found with a psychological or behavioral syndrome. However, some studies exist that suggest an increased comorbidity of psychopathology such as depression in obese adolescents (Vila et al., 2004). One could hypothesize that treatment might be especially complicated in these obese youngsters with comorbid psycho-pathology. However, it is unclear how the comorbid psychopathology is causally related with the obesity. Prospective research designs are needed, including pretreatment assessment of psychiatric disorders with clinical interviews and successive monitoring of accomplishment and maintenance of treatment goals. In a 2-year follow-up study (Braet, Tanghe, Decaluwé, Moens, & Rosseel, 2004), a significant decrease in general psychopathology, as measured by the Child Behavior Checklist (Achenbach & Edelbrock, 1983), was found in obese children with maintenance of posttreatment gains. So, it is still unclear if psychopathology needs to serve as an exclusion criterion.

Children less than 12 years of age are treated differently from adolescents. Although both can profit from an inpatient approach, homogeneous groups are recommended. In cases where inpatient services are limited, centers are advised to formulate age-related inclusion/exclusion criteria. These criteria can be based on staff expertise or age-related treatment facilities.

TREATMENT INGREDIENTS

Treatment Goals

The goals of an inpatient treatment program are (1) to induce a change in lifestyle, (2) to effect a sig-nificant improvement in the patient's medical condition, and (3) to reduce body weight. The weight criterion for discharge has to be well defined (e.g., adjusted BMI of less than 140%). Increased physical activity over long-term periods, cognitive behavioral techniques, and dietary change are seen as important strategies effective in attaining these goals in children (Epstein et al., 1990). The program needs to be protocolized and supervised.

Physical Activity

In order to learn a healthy lifestyle, moderate aerobic exercise is recommended every day. The chil-dren should be motivated to exercise 2 hr/day or more. Further, an individual exercise program for each child is needed, which can include swimming, cycling on an exercise bike, jogging, abdominal exercises, yoga, dancing, and ball sports. Obviously this requires centers to have the necessary sports facilities to enable patients to engage in individual exercise as well as group sports activities. In order to enhance participation, the children need to be encouraged to make their own choices in planning their program. This means giving children the opportunity to find out which activities they enjoy doing as well as which exercises they are capable of doing (see Moore and O'Donohue, Chap-ter 10 in this volume). However, to date there is little evidence to suggest that such an exercise inter-vention, independent of dietary changes, is likely to result in a considerable reduction in children's overweight. More likely, physical exercise contributes to the effects of treatment by enhancing the effects of dietary changes and by promoting physical fitness (Roberts, 2005).

Diet

In order to affect the energy balance, a reduction in energy intake is recommended (Epstein et al., 1990). Energy restriction in children is a debatable issue and is not recommended in outpatient treat-ment. Although aggressive diets may have a place in the treatment of selected patients, it remains unclear whether these diets induce the long-lasting weight changes that are necessary for the proper treatment of pediatric obesity (Zametkin, Zoon, Klein, & Munson, 2004). When treating obese children, one also needs to be careful not to develop the type of dietary restraint that is seen as a risk factor in developing eating disorders (Garner & Wooley, 1991). Because obese children are still growing, very low-calorie diets are questionable (Epstein et al., 1998) and probably not necessary (Barlow & Dietz, 1998; Braet, 1999). In contrast, moderate caloric restriction increases patient adherence and can serve as an example of a healthy lifestyle. Therefore residential centers need to work out and put in place a purposeful diet. Learning to eat healthy food and developing healthy eating habits, as recommended by public health centers, are seen as important treatment goals. At each meal, the drinking of water and the eating of vegetables and other high-fiber and low-fat foods has to be encouraged, while the consumption of soft drinks and calorie dense foods has to be limited. As recommend by the Expert Committee on obesity evaluation and treatment (Barlow & Dietz, 1998), the following standard diet is recommended. Children should have three meals a day (breakfast, lunch, and dinner) and two to three between-meal snacks. Total intake per day should be no more than 1400 to 1600 kcal. Each meal should consist of all necessary components as described by the U.S. Department of Agriculture (www.healthierus.gov/dietaryguidelines/), with, depending on the age and gender of the child, at least 100 g protein/day (26% to 33% of the total energy), 294 g carbohydrates (53% to 56% of the total energy), and 39 g fat (14% to 18% of the total energy). Snacks and calorie dense food, such as pancakes, french fries, etc., are permitted as part of the diet, be it in limited amounts.

Psychological Interventions

If enhancing physical activity levels and changing dietary habits are considered the ultimate goals of the treatment, strong complementary components of behavior therapy are needed (Jelalian & Saelens, 1999). In most successful outpatient treatment programs for obese children, it is hypothesized that cognitive behavioral modification techniques are responsible for the results (Braet & Van Winckel, 2000; Epstein et al., 1990). Common behavior modification components are self-monitoring, stimulus control strategies, problem solving, and contingency management. It appears necessary to implement them in every treatment program (Jelalian & Saelens, 1999). In a residential program, however, minor changes (e.g., homework) are necessary, but nevertheless, this psychological approach is seen as an important framework for developing an inpatient treatment program for obese children.

As part of the treatment program, we recommend a 12-week cognitive behavioral treatment (CBT) program with small groups, followed by weekly individual problem-solving-based booster sessions. The CBT program contains the following themes. The sessions in a first phase focus on explaining the importance of daily aerobic exercise and the principles of healthy eating habits. Gradually, throughout the sessions, children learn about the energy balance as a model, providing them with an understanding of the mechanism of obesity. In each session they learn new principles on how to adopt a healthy lifestyle. In order to achieve lifestyle changes, in the second phase children learn self-regulation skills such as self-observation, self-instructions (e.g., "stop and think"), self-evaluation, and self-reward (Duffy & Spence, 1993). Modeling, contracts, and behavioral rehearsal can be used to train self-regulation skills. The use of contracts outlining the next week's steps to be complied with in terms of daily aerobic exercise and healthy eating habits is highly recommended. A problem-solving approach can be introduced as part of the program to teach children to cope with different high-risk situations (e.g., feeling alone) and relapse moments (e.g., feeling hungry). Also, the children need to learn to make a personal plan about handling unhealthy food and favorite meals (e.g., planning them once in the month or asking Mom to prepare them, but a very small portion). Together with the therapist, they can learn to evaluate their plans and use problem-solving steps if they find themselves faced with difficult situations. Motivation can be enhanced by adopting a child-friendly stance with respect to developmental demands. This implies that each session should include activities such as cooking, exercise, and playing and be supported by a child-friendly workbook using pictures to illustrate the goals, the principles, and each new step in adopting a new lifestyle. As part of this evaluation process, therapists must provide a very high degree of positive feedback.

Afterward, preferably before returning home, a relapse prevention program should be put in place. In three weekly group sessions, therapists sit down with the children and summarize what they have learned, looking ahead about how to implement this into their daily routines and trying to identify the kinds of problems they may face.

Finally, if children suffer from comorbid psychopathology, individual treatment by psychologists is needed as well. The topics of these sessions are variable and depend on the child's problems. It is our experience that most of these children lack age-related social skills. This can be addressed by staging supplementary individual or group sessions.

Organization of Daily Activities

Because obese children are not ill, it is recommended that they go to school during their stay at the residential center. Not only does this help provide structure to their days, but returning to school is often one of the goals for these youngsters. Indeed, a substantial number of the children suffer from low school competence because of learning disabilities, social isolation, or other reasons, and some of them even drop out of school. So positive experiences with school, attuned to their needs, will enhance their psychological sense of well-being. While some may attend a school located near the center, Boeck et al. (1993) suggest visits to the local school combined with inpatient care before and after school time.

Outside school hours, daily structured group activities are necessary for all children (football, basket ball, walks, creative moments, dancing, etc.). One research group organized weight-loss programs during summer camps (Gately et al., 2000) in which the primary focus was on sports and amusement. However, large variations in responses and subsequent outcomes were found when the children returned to their home environment.

Parental Involvement

Interaction with the parents is not easy to organize as part of an inpatient treatment program. Inpatient treatment services need to think about ways of working with the parents. Group parent training meetings are seen as a worthwhile component of inpatient care because parent management techniques are easier to teach in a group setting. Any involvement of parents in an inpatient treatment program should include the following components:

- Education. Parents should be taught the importance of acquiring and maintaining healthy behaviors as well as learning to question their own (unhealthy) eating habits. Leaflets can be handed out with information on how to prepare healthy food, how to organize shopping habits, and how to limit the child's and family's television viewing time.
- Mediation. Parents should be asked to help their child in adopting a new lifestyle and in controlling negative stimuli. In addition, parents need to be involved in evaluating the contracts discussed earlier. Parent management techniques can be taught which can help parents to educate their child in observing the recommendations set out previously.
- Problem solving. When problems arise (e.g., how to implement the program on the weekends and during the holidays), together with the therapist, parents can learn to adopt a problem-solving approach.
- Family therapy. The lack of control over food may be part of a general lack of self-regulation skills of the child. Indeed, delaying the fulfillment of one's needs, dealing with frustrations, and resistance against food persuaders are self-regulation skills that are gradually acquired through education and learning. Within this context, overeating may be considered a behavioral deficit; that is, the child may not have learned good eating habits. In such cases, treatment for overweight also implies working on parenting skills. Thus, family-based treatment programs should include discussions about adequate amounts of parental control, rules, and restrictions, including giving children sufficient guidelines on how to implement their own choices and responsibilities.
- Return to the family environment. Gradually the child and his or her parents have to learn to implement the new habits in their normal living environment. When the child returns

home (on weekends, during the holidays, or for a 1-week tryout), there are opportunities to evaluate the problems that confront them. Judicious follow-up is equally advisable. After the child is discharged at the end of the treatment, follow-up sessions can be organized for the youngsters and their parents, focusing on instances of relapse and discussing their expectations regarding their weight. Frequent follow-up contacts by phone can also help the child maintain their new lifestyle.

Staff

Inpatient treatment can only be implemented when a team of specialists is available: psychologists with expertise in behavioral and family therapy, medical doctors, dieticians, social workers, physiotherapists, and group leaders. It should be recognized that other nonspecific treatment variables, such as the role of social support, can be as important in inpatient programs as the techniques used. In the case of obesity, we observed negative stereotypes and myths regarding obesity, even by caregivers, which is why it is advisable that these specialists be made to face up to their own attitudes toward obese children and to be trained in how to cope with their own attitudes and preconceptions.

COMORBIDITY ISSUES

Based on findings obtained with reliable standardized interviews and self-report questionnaires, it seems justified to conclude that psychiatric disorders are highly prevalent in obese children and adolescents seeking inpatient treatment (Zametkin, Zoon, Klein, & Munson, 2004). This finding confirms the idea of heterogeneity in clinical samples of obese youngsters and thus parallels the findings in the adult obesity literature: some individuals suffer from severe psychological problems, but others do not. Therefore a differentiation between children with and without comorbid psychiatric disorders seems essential. On an individual level, explanations on the origins of the coexistence of obesity and psychopathology might be very diverse. It is a challenge to treatment centers to untangle the relationship between obesity, family characteristics, and psychopathology for each obese youngster. Inpatient settings allow for 24-hr assessment of the child's behavior. When needed, psychiatric care can be provided, based on a thorough assessment, in addition to the standard obesity treatment program.

To obtain an overall picture, it would seem particularly relevant in obese youngsters to include an assessment of any eating disorders. Binge eating is frequently observed in obese adults seeking treatment (Marcus, Wing, & Hopkins, 1988) and in adolescents with obesity (Decaluwé, Braet, & Fairburn, 2003). However, no weight control programs that are successful in reducing symptoms of disordered eating exist for childhood obesity (Epstein, Paluch, Saelens, Ernst, & Wilfley, 2001). Thus it is reasonable to assume that as long as current treatment programs for obesity fail to address binge eating, relapse will occur. Since the literature on coping strategies and binge eating offers different treatment options for adult binge eaters, it is recommended that coping strategies be added to manage binge eating. These interventions can be seen as extensions of the standard CBT and can improve the maintenance of weight loss after treatment. According to a cue exposure treatment, it is hypothesized that parallel to the addiction model, the craving and excessive food intake of binge eaters is cue controlled. The model predicts that if binge eating is not treated with cue exposure and response prevention, no reduction in binge eating is to be expected. Six pilot studies on cue exposure suggest good results (Jansen, 1998). According to Fairburn and Wilson (1993), dysfunctional cognitions are the core symptoms of binge eating. Because a standard CBT does not specifically target the automatic thoughts of binge eaters, cognitive therapy is viewed as a necessary intervention for those with binge eating problems. As described by Braet et al. (2004), both protocols have been evaluated positively in the treatment of childhood obesity.

CHILDREN VERSUS ADOLESCENTS

Working with adolescents can be quite challenging, and very rewarding. In contrast with obese children, adolescents in residential care often consider themselves as abnormal compared with their peers because of their overweight. One of the first assignments of any team is to "normalize" these youngsters and to make them understand that although they may have had a hard time so far, ultimately they need to achieve the same developmental tasks as their normal-weight peers (i.e., being successful at school, having friends, developing a sense of self-worth and self-confidence, managing to create some distance between them and their parents). Obese adolescents should not exclude themselves from these tasks. Special attention should be given to self-worth programs and training social competences.

Especially when working with adolescents, we have to consider the development of each youngster individually. The development of an identity as well as future perspectives should be stimulated by all therapists. The development of this identity is only possible in a secure environment with a clear set of rules and structures in which all therapists are empathic, but directive and positive, in the face of each positive change (however minimal) they observe in the obese adolescent. Special attention needs to be paid to sexual and relational identity. As a result of social isolation, most obese adolescents are delayed in their developmental tasks, and severe dysfunctions are seen with regard to how to relate to the other gender.

Another important issue is not to give up. Obese adolescents have often failed in the past. They display a "learned helplessness attitude" and they show only minor persistence when faced with new failures or challenges (e.g., sports). In residential care, one of the first things they have to learn is efforts are only valuable if maintained. One of the basic rules is, "You can do it." This is only possible with support from all the people involved: staff members as well as parents. We recommend starting out by setting small goals that need to be achieved (e.g., taking responsibility for his or her own room, or losing at least 1 kg every 2 weeks). Particularly during leisure time, obese adolescents can be coached to reach personal goals. Group leaders can help them deal with leisure time and gradually stimulate adolescents to assume responsibility for themselves. After several mastery experiences, group leaders can coach adolescents when making personal decisions that enhance reintegration into normal life (e.g., starting sports in a club outside the center). Once a covenant is reached that they agree to, adolescents are encouraged to continue their efforts. It is important for them to learn that once an individual choice is made, they have to go for it. Furthermore, they learn when problems arise; they have to use a problem-solving approach, thereby identifying the barriers and evaluating or trying out different solutions instead of giving up.

EVALUATION

Assessment

In order to evaluate treatment progress, participants need to be weighed and measured regularly during their stay at the center (at least once a week). Close monitoring of the child's medical condition is recommended. Furthermore, psychological instruments can be used to assess eating psychopathology and psychological well-being. Measurements need to be administered at baseline and at the end of the treatment.

The issue of medical comorbidity is of particular interest. Evaluation of medical conditions such as hypertension, respiratory problems, diabetes, and sleep apnea is extremely important. At the start of treatment, a medical checkup should consist of a complete personal and family history, a thorough clinical examination, and blood tests. Establishing a growth curve marking the history of the obesity is helpful in determining possible underlying problems. An increase in growth accompanying the development of obesity is expected. If, on the contrary, growth slows down while obesity develops, an underlying endocrinological disorder should be excluded (e.g., hypothyroidism or Cushing's syndrome). Respiratory problems such as bronchial hyperactivity and asthma are not uncommon. The family history should focus on diabetes and premature cardiovascular morbidity/mortality. Clinical examination includes careful examination of the skin (intertrigo is a common problem). Blood pressure should be monitored. Orthopedic problems such as genua valga, hyperlordosis, hip problems, and foot problems are common and can hinder physical exercises. Patients should be screened for insulin resistance (morning insulin and glucose), disorders in lipid metabolism (high-density lipoprotein [HDL] and LDL cholesterol, triglycerides), elevated transaminases (possible sign of non-alcoholic steatohepatitis [NASH]), and hyperuricemia.

Most of the medical problems mentioned here are secondary to the underlying obesity. Diagnosing them does not alter the primary goal of treatment: loosing weight and enhancing physical fitness (Roberts & Barnard, 2005). Some associated medical problems, such as frank hypertension and diabetes, require individually adapted drug treatment. A detailed description of this treatment is outside the scope of this chapter. Respiratory obstructive problems are appropriately treated by inhalation therapy and should not restrict physical activity. Orthopedic problems require an individual approach by the physical therapist, prescribing exercises that take these problems into account. Often, at the start of treatment, patients are prone to accidents during weight-bearing physical activities such as jogging. Therefore, at the start of treatment, exercises like swimming and biking are preferred (Wills, 2004).

We recommend the following instruments for evaluation of the psychological aspects of childhood obesity:

1. The Eating Disorder Inventory (EDI) (Garner, Olmsted, & Polivy, 1983) is a self-assessment questionnaire that seeks to determine the psychological characteristics relating to anorexia and bulimia nervosa. The inventory has 64 items spread over eight subscales: drive for thinness (DT), bulimia (B), body dissatisfaction (BD), ineffectiveness (I), perfectionism (P), interpersonal distrust (ID), interoceptive awareness (IA), and maturity fears (MF). Williamson, Anderson, Jackman, and Jackson (1995) discuss the test and provide data on its reliability (test-retest reliability was greater than .80, with the exception of the MF subscale), internal consistency (coefficient alphas range from .65 to .93 in a group of 11- to 18-year-olds), and validity. Their conclusion was that the EDI is perfectly suited for screening risk groups in order to identify anorexia nervosa, bulimia, and binge eating in adults as well as adolescents.
2. The Dutch Eating Behavior Questionnaire (DEBQ) (Van Strien, Frijters, Bergers, & Defares, 1986) includes the screening of emotional eating (13 items), external eating (10 items), and restrained eating (10 items). A high score indicates a high degree of the eating behavior in question. The DEBQ was originally developed for assessing adults, but its use in children and adolescents (ages 7 to 17 years) was evaluated positively (Braet et al., 2003). The DEBQ scales have good internal consistency, satisfactory factorial validity, and dimensional stability (Williamson et al., 1995).
3. The Self-Perception Profile for Children (SPPC) (Harter, 1985) consists of 36 items and assesses the child's self-perceptions in five different areas of competence: academic competence, physical appearance, athletic competence, social acceptance, behavioral conduct, as well as global self-worth. The structured alternative answer format of this scale is purported to minimize the influence of social desirability on the child's responses. The reliability and validity of the two versions (child version, 7 to 12 years; adolescent version, 11 to 17 years) appear to be acceptable (alpha values range from .68 to .79).
4. The Eating Disorder Examination—Child Version (ChEDE) (Bryant-Waugh, Cooper, Taylor, & Lask, 1996) is based on the EDE for adults (see Fairburn & Wilson, 1993), a widely used diagnostic interview instrument to assess the core psychopathology of eating disorders and to generate eating disorder diagnoses. The EDE was modified for use

in children and adolescents (7 to 17 years) by experts in the field of eating disorders in youths, in collaboration with the authors of the original adult interview. Among other things, the interview assesses the presence and frequency of several forms of overeating and several compensatory behaviors over a 3-month time frame. As such, the ChEDE enables eating disorder diagnoses to be generated. To do so, we used the criteria for the assessment of binge eating disorder (BED) and bulimia nervosa (BN) as outlined in Fairburn and Wilson (1993). When a child reported binge eating episodes that did not occur frequently enough to justify a BED diagnosis, a diagnosis of subclinical binge eating was ascribed. If a child reported having experienced binge eating episodes and compensatory behavior that did not occur frequently enough to justify a diagnosis of BN, a diagnosis of eating disorder–not otherwise specified (ED-NOS) was ascribed. Psychometric evaluations of the ChEDE as a diagnostic tool are still ongoing. Concerning the assessment of overeating, Decaluwé and Braet (2004) found very good interrater and test-retest reliability for the objective bulimic episodes.

5. The Children's Depression Inventory (CDI) (Kovacs, 1992) assesses cognitive, affective, and behavioral symptoms of depression in youths (ages 7 to 17 years). The questionnaire has relatively high degrees of internal consistency, test-retest reliability, and predictive, convergent, discriminant, and construct validity. A cutoff score of 13 is needed to minimize false negatives and is recommended in a clinical sample; a higher cutoff score of 19 minimizes false positives and can be used in a nonclinical sample (Kovacs, 1992).

6. General psychopathology can be measured by asking parents to fill in the Child Behavior Checklist (CBCL) (Achenbach & Edelbrock, 1983). The CBCL is a 118 item scale that assesses an array of behavioral problems and social competencies in children between 3 and 18 years of age. The checklist provides scores on several factors or behavioral problem areas and identifies internalizing and externalizing problems. The scale has shown good reliability and validity. In cases where youngsters display a clinical score, a structured interview measuring psychiatric disorders is recommended.

Effectiveness of Inpatient Care Programs

At present, only a few services for severe obese children are available and little is known about their efficacy. Inpatient care is a very drastic intervention for obese children, but it is a treatment option that has to be evaluated. Most programs are, however, in an experimental phase. As described by Reinehr and Wabitsch (2003), only a minority of inpatient treatment institutions evaluate therapy success at the end of the treatment program. After consulting the Web of Science database, we found four articles reporting on inpatient care for children and adolescents. Besides two case reports, the two other studies offer evidence for a significant decrease in weight (Braet et al., 2003; Wabitisch et al., 1996).

The effects of our multidisciplinary 10-month inpatient treatment course have been analyzed, compared with subjects on a waiting list, and published (Braet et al., 2003). The primary outcome variable was weight loss, defined as the change between pretest and posttest overweight. Overweight before and after treatment was expressed as (1) adjusted BMI index expressed in percent, (2) in kg, and (3) in BMI. In this study, contrast analyses comparing pretest with posttest data revealed that the children lost a significant percentage of weight during their inpatient stay (49%, SD = 23; range 0 to 113%). At posttest, the children lost an average 21 kg and grew by 2 cm. Their BMI was reduced by 9, which is much more than what any outpatient treatment can offer (Epstein et al., 1990). We now know that this is also much more than what motivated children can reach if they are on a waiting list. The children on a 10-month waiting list continued to gain weight (Figure 12.1). At the end of the waiting period they weighed on average 97 kg and grew 2 cm. Analyses for gender revealed that boys and girls lost the same amount of overweight. No interaction effect was found. Further

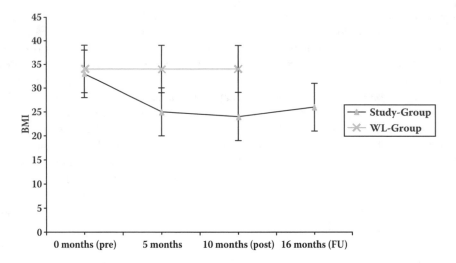

Figure 12.1 BMI trends in treated and untreated severely obese children.

analyses showed that at the end of the treatment, 25% of the children were still overweight by 35% or more, 23% were moderately overweight at 20% to 35%, and 52% had normalized their weight.

However, the weight evolution at the 6-month follow-up of these same children showed great variability among the subjects. Twenty-five percent continued to lose overweight, but others showed a weight regain that ranged from 1% to more than 23% of the weight lost. The weight regain was not totally unexpected. When children return to their home environment, the healthy lifestyle at home cannot be expected to be as "perfect" as it is at the center. Follow-up measurements up to 2 years after leaving the center are still positive for 77% of the subjects when success is defined as maintenance of a 10% weight loss (Braet et al., 2004). Comparing pretest with follow-up scores, contrast analyses reveal that the children still had lost a significant percentage of weight (32%; SD = 25; range –33% to 100%). Their BMIs were still reduced by 5. The amount of weight loss was 7 kg and the children had grown an average of 6 cm. But the children were still 44% overweight. The effect size of this result is estimated as $f = 1.3$. It is hypothesized that the amount of weight increase can be diminished if the treatment is followed by individual follow-up sessions in which the children learn maintenance strategies or relapse prevention techniques. Latner et al. (2000) argue that continuous care of indefinite duration may be necessary to achieve long-term treatment effects in most obese people. In our follow-up study it was found that the majority of the children (49%) spontaneously planned regular exercises via sports clubs or with the help of a physiotherapist. A smaller subgroup was monitored by a dietician (19%), a psychologist (17%), a medical doctor (12%), or through commercial programs (13%). At the 2-year follow-up, 35.4% of the subjects reported they were still in aftercare.

Weight reduction programs for children have been questioned in the past because of assumed side effects (Epstein et al., 1998). Variables that were used to measure eating behavior revealed no increase in eating psychopathology during either inpatient treatment studies (Braet et al., 2004) or outpatient treatment studies (Braet & Van Winckel, 2000; Epstein et al., 2001). It was also found that the children saw themselves as more capable of coping with external eating stimuli, as measured with a self-report questionnaire. An evaluation with self-report measures assessing psychopathology revealed a decrease in psychosocial problems during the treatment. Furthermore, the treatment succeeded in enhancing the poor self-esteem of obese children in important domains of the self: physical appearance, athletic competence, and social competence. Patients, often for the first time in years, were able to establish social contacts with their peers, and several of them had a friend of the opposite sex for the first time.

Identification of clinical markers associated with response to treatment can help us match treatments to clients. The idea of matching is appealing, as it acknowledges the heterogeneous nature of overweight individuals and the likelihood that people with different characteristics will respond differently to various treatments. A few important predictors of treatment success emerged in a recent study by Braet (2006). The baseline degree of overweight explained a substantial part of the variance in the weight loss. The greater the overweight of the child, the greater was the weight loss. The knowledge that even the most severely obese children can move toward a reasonable weight is a hopeful prospect. For children who are less overweight, a more modest weight loss prognosis is needed. It can be a frustrating experience that some children will lose more weight than others, even when adhering to the same program and putting in the same amount of effort. Therefore personalized and realistic weight loss goals need to be formulated for each child according to their initial weight. Furthermore, age emerges as another important predictor. At our center, older children (more than 12 years of age) were more successful, even after controlling for initial weight. It is assumed that long-term weight control requires self-control skills which older children are more able to summon.

With regard to the psychological outcome measures, baseline symptomatology emerged as the most important predictor of treatment changes for several outcome measures. As described in Braet (2006), regression analyses with change in psychopathology as the dependent variable described that baseline psychopathology was found as the only significant predictor. A separate regression analysis with change in self-worth as the dependent variable revealed that change was predicted by baseline self-worth and eating disordered symptoms. Finally, a change in eating disordered symptoms was predicted by baseline eating disordered symptoms and gender. A closer inspection of this finding revealed that girls had more eating disordered symptoms both at baseline and at follow-up; both boys and girls decreased in symptoms and no gender differences were found between their change scores. Finally, initial weight loss during the treatment can be identified as another important predictor of treatment success, after controlling for initial weight and age. Although this has not been the topic of purposive research in children, it is possible that children who lost a significant amount of weight had a greater motivation to continue their weight control program and had greater self-efficacy feelings, which may explain why they do better at continuing their weight control program.

Duration of the Treatment

Good results were found after an 8-week intervention (Gately et al., 2000). Inpatient treatment programs normally take 3 to 5 weeks (Jelalian & Saelens, 1999), however, some patients stayed for 21 months (Boeck et al., 1993). Health insurance will invariably recommend a reduction in the duration of residential care unless the effectiveness of a longer stay can be shown. In our study evaluating a 10-month stay, comparing the first 5 months with the next 5 months, it turned out that the children lost an enormous amount of weight in the first few months and continued to lose weight during the second leg of the program, but at a slower rate. Only 14% reached an acceptable weight within the first 5 months. It is therefore hypothesized that a longer inpatient treatment approach can help children toward a better integration of acquired healthy lifestyle skills which can keep their weight stable at a healthier level. Whether an ideal treatment duration for each child can be predicted remains to be seen.

Two things have to be considered as well: First, although a weight loss of 21 kg or more during treatment is spectacular for most obese children, at the end of the treatment the children are still moderately overweight. Therefore modest weight prognoses are advisable while continuing to develop greater self-acceptance (Wilson, 1996). Second, for those who question the feasibility of sustained inpatient treatment, adapted formats based on the same principles require further study. The lifestyle approach might be integrated in day care treatment programs. However, little is known about the children after they leave a treatment program. Therefore we question the long-lasting effects of short inpatient interventions or summer camps. Follow-up data on the weight evolution of obese children after a 10-day summer camp revealed that this produces no more weight loss than outpatient treatment (Braet & Van Winckel, 2000).

Some patients return home prematurely. In our study, four children left the program at their own request, but against the advice of the medical staff, two children were referred to a child psychiatry unit because of severe emotional problems, and one child had an accident. It is rather unusual for children ages 9 to 16 years to leave their home and family for 10 months. Therefore it is amazing to see how many children are interested in such long-term treatment programs (and all of them come voluntary; none of them can enter if they are not motivated). Perhaps the severity of their obesity is so problematic for these children that they reach a point where they feel they have nothing to lose. Also, in most cases it is their only remaining option. Even their hope for bariatric surgery or pharmacological treatment is questionable given recent statements that no acceptable evidence is available for children and adolescents to evaluate the effectiveness of surgical approaches for reducing overweight (U.S. Preventive Services Task Force, 2006) or for pharmacological treatment (Marcus, 2004b). Nevertheless, some children become homesick the first months of their stay at an inpatient center. Psychologists must be aware of this problem and should attempt to make the inpatient stay of the child as comfortable as possible.

In some cases, it takes considerable effort on the part of the family to ensure coverage of the costs, which are estimated at around $85/day, at least for European inpatient mental health services. In the United States, costs for inpatient mental health range between $500/day and $1500/day. Furthermore, health insurance companies sometimes refuse to refund the costs for this type of intensive inpatient treatment. This is quite remarkable, given the huge public health outlays to combat adult obesity, which was estimated to be around $117 billion in the United States in 2000. Obesity may soon replace smoking as the number one cause of preventable death. A system that transitions patients from less to more intensive treatment is already formulated for a variety of medical conditions, including hypertension. Therefore, applying a stepped care approach to the treatment of obesity remains a necessary condition for an efficient allocation of treatment resources.

REFERENCES

Achenbach, T. M., & Edelbrock, C. S. (1983). *Manual for the child behavior checklist and revised child behavior profile*. Burlington: University of Vermont, Department of Psychiatry.

American Psychiatric Association. (2000). *Diagnostic and statistical manual of mental disorders* (4th ed. – text revision). Washington, D.C.: American Psychiatric Association.

Barlow, S. E., & Dietz, W. H. (1998). Obesity evaluation and treatment: Expert Committee recommendations. *Pediatrics, 102,* E29.

Boeck, M., Lubin, K., Loy, I., Kasparin, D., Grebin, B., & Lombardi, N. (1993). Initial experience with long-term inpatient treatment for morbidly obese children in a rehabilitation facility. *New York Academy of Sciences, 699,* 257–259.

Braet, C. (1999). Treatment of obese children: a new rationale. *Clinical Child Psychology and Psychiatry, 4,* 579–591.

Braet, C. (2006). Patient characteristics as predictors of weight loss after an obesity treatment for children. *Obesity Research, 14,* 148–155.

Braet, C., Mervielde, I., & Vandereycken, W. (1997). Psychological aspects of childhood obesity: a controlled study in a clinical and non-clinical sample. *Journal of Pediatric Psychology, 22,* 59–71.

Braet, C., Tanghe, A., Decaluwé, V., Moens, E., & Rosseel, Y. (2004). Inpatient treatment for children with obesity: weight loss, psychosocial well being, and eating behavior. *Journal of Pediatric Psychology, 29,* 519–529.

Braet, C., & Van Winckel, M. (2000). Long-term follow-up of a cognitive behavioral treatment program for obese children. *Behavior Therapy, 31,* 55–74.

Braet, C., Van Winckel, M., Tanghe, A., de Bode, P., & Franckx, H. (2003). Inpatient treatment of obese children: a multicomponent program without stringent calorie restriction. *European Journal of Pediatrics, 162,* 391–396.

Brownell, K. D., & Wadden, T. A. (1991). The heterogeneity of obesity: fitting treatments to individuals. *Behaviour Therapy, 22,* 153–177.

Bryant-Waugh, R. J., Cooper, P. J., Taylor, C. L. & Lask, B. D. (1996). The use of the Eating Disorder Examination with children: a pilot study. *International Journal of Eating Disorders, 19,* 391–397.

Decaluwé, V., & Braet, C. (2004). Assessment of eating disorder psychopathology in obese children and adolescents: interview versus self-report questionnaire. *Behaviour Research and Therapy, 42,* 799–811.

Decaluwé V., Braet, C., & Fairburn, C. (2003). Binge eating in obese children and adolescents. *International Journal of Eating Disorders, 33,* 78–94.

Dietz, W. H. (1998). Health consequences of obesity in youth: childhood predictors of adult disease. *Pediatrics, 101,* 518–525.

Duffy, G., & Spence, S. H. (1993). The effectiveness of cognitive self-management as an adjunct to a behavioural intervention for childhood obesity: a research note. *Journal of Child Psychology and Psychiatry, 34,* 1043–1050.

Epstein, L. H., Myers, M. D., Raynor, H. A., & Saelens, B. E. (1998). Treatment of pediatric obesity. *Pediatrics, 101,* 554–570.

Epstein, L. H., Paluch, R.. A., Saelens, B. E., Ernst, M. M., & Wilfley, D. E. (2001). Changes in eating disorder symptoms with pediatric obesity treatment. *Journal of Pediatrics, 139,* 58–65.

Epstein, L. H., Valoski, A., Wing, R. R., & McCurley, J. (1990). Ten-year follow-up of behavioral family-based treatment for obese children. *JAMA, 264,* 2519–2523.

Epstein, L. H., Valoski, A., Wing, R. R., & McCurely, J. (1994). Ten-year outcomes of behavioral family-based treatment for childhood obesity. *Health Psychology, 13,* 373–383.

Fairburn, C. G., & Wilson, G. T. (Eds.). (1993). *Binge eating: nature, assessment and treatment.* New York: Guilford Press.

Fenning, S., & Fenning, S. (2006). Intensive therapy for severe paediatric morbid obesity. *European Eating Disorders Review, 14,* 118–124.

Garner, D. M., Olmsted, M. P., & Polivy, J. (1983). Development and validation of a multidimensional Eating Disorder Inventory for anorexia nervosa. *International Journal of Eating Disorders, 2,* 15–34.

Garner, D. M., & Wooley, S. C. (1991). Confronting the failure of behavioral and dietary treatments for obesity. *Clinical Psychological Review, 11,* 729–780.

Gately, P. J., Cooke, C. B., Butterly, R. J., Mackreth, P., & Carroll, S. (2000). The effects of a children's summer camp programme on weight loss, with a 10 month follow-up. *International Journal of Obesity, 24,* 1445–1452.

Gortmaker, S. L., Must, A., Perrin, J. M., Sobol, A. M., & Dietz, W. H. (1993). Social and economic consequences of overweight in adolescence and young adulthood. *New England Journal of Medicine, 329,* 1008–1012.

Harter, S. (1985). *Self-perception profile for children.* Denver, CO: University of Denver.

Jansen, A. (1998). A learning model of binge eating: cue reactivity and cue exposure. *Behaviour Research & Therapy, 36,* 257–272.

Jelalian, E., & Saelens, B. E. (1999). Empirically supported treatments in pediatric psychology: pediatric obesity. *Journal of Pediatric Psychology, 24,* 223–248.

Kovacs, M. (1992). *The Children's Depression Inventory (CDI) manual.* Toronto: Multi-Health Systems.

Latner, J. D., Stunkard, A. J., Wilson, G. T., Jackson, M. L., Zelitch, D. S., & Labouvie, E. (2000). Effective long-term treatment of obesity: a continuing care model. *International Journal of Obesity, 24,* 893–898.

Marcus, C. (2004a). Bariatric surgery. In: Kiess, W., Marcus, C., & Wabitsch, M. (Eds.), *Obesity in childhood and adolescence* (pp. 207–210). Basel: Karger.

Marcus, C. (2004b). Pharmacological treatment of childhood obesity. In: Kiess, W., Marcus, C., & Wabitsch, M. (Eds.), *Obesity in childhood and adolescence* (pp. 211–218). Basel: Karger.

Marcus, M. D., Wing, R. R., & Hopkins, J. (1988). Obese binge eaters: affect, cognitions, and response to behavioral weight control. *Journal of Consulting and Clinical Psychology, 56,* 433–439.

Mossberg, H. (1989). 40-Year follow-up of overweight children. *Lancet, 2,* 491–493.

Nuutinen, O., & Knip, M. (1992). Long-term weight control in obese children: persistence of treatment outcome and metabolic changes. *International Journal of Obesity, 16,* 279–287.

Reinehr, T., & Wabitsch, M. (2003). Structured survey of treatment programs for obese children and adolescents. Project of the Working Group on Obesity in Childhood and Adolescence. *Monatsschrift Kinderheilkunde, 151,* 757–760.

Roberts, C. K., & Barnard, R. J. (2005). Effects of exercise and diet on chronic disease. *Journal of Applied Physiology, 98,* 3–30.

Rössner, S. (1998). Childhood obesity and adult consequences. *Acta Paediatrica, 87,* 1–5.

Silber, T., Randolph, J., & Robbins, S. (1986). Long-term morbidity and mortality in morbidly obese adolescents after bypass. *Journal of Pediatrics, 108,* 318–322.

Torigoe, K., Numata, O., Matsunaga, M., Tanaka, Y., Imai, C., & Yamazaki, H. (1997). Effect of weight loss on body fat distribution in obese children. *Acta Paediatrica Japonica, 39,* 28–33.

U.S. Preventive Services Task Force. (2006). Screening and interventions for overweight in children and adolescents: recommendation statement. *Pediatrics, 116,* 205–209.

Van Strien, T., Frijters, J. E. R., Bergers, G. P. A., & Defares, P. B. (1986). The Dutch Eating Behavior Questionnaire for assessment of restrained, emotional and external eating behavior. *International Journal of Eating Disorders, 5,* 295–315.

Vila, G., Zipper, E., Dabbas, M., Bertrand, C., Robert, J., Ricour, C., & Mouren-Siméoni, M. (2004). Mental disorders in obese children and adolescents. *Psychosomatic Medicine, 66,* 387–394.

Wabitsch, M., Blum, W. F., Muche, R., Heinze, E., Haug, C., Mayer, H., & Teller, W. (1996). Insulin-like growth factors and their binding proteins before and after weight loss and their associations with hormonal and metabolic parameters in obese adolescent girls. *International Journal of Obesity, 20,* 1073–1080.

Whitaker, R. C., Wright, J. A., Pepe, M. S., Seidel, K. D., & Dietz, W. H. (1997). Predicting obesity in young adulthood from childhood and parental obesity. *New England Journal of Medicine, 337,* 869–873.

Williamson, D. A., Anderson, D. A., Jackman, L. P., & Jackson, S. R. (1995). Assessment of eating disordered thoughts, feelings and behaviors. In: Allison, D. B. (Ed.), *Handbook of assessment methods for eating behaviors and weight related problems.* Thousand Oaks, CA: Sage Publications.

Wills, M. (2004). Orthopedic complications of childhood obesity. *Pediatric Physical Therapy, 16,* 230–235.

Wilson, G. T. (1994). Behavioral treatment of obesity: thirty years and counting. *Advances in Behaviour Research and Therapy, 16,* 31–75.

Wilson, G. T. (1996). Acceptance and change in the treatment of eating disorders and obesity. *Behavior Therapy, 27,* 417–439.

World Health Organization. (1998). Obesity: preventing and managing the global epidemic. Report of a WHO consultation. *World Health Organization Technical Report Series, 894,* i–xii, 1–253.

Zametkin, A. J., Zoon, C. K., Klein, H. W., & Munson, S. B. (2004). Psychiatric aspects of child and adolescent obesity: a review of the past 10 years. *Journal of the American Academy of Child and Adolescent Psychiatry, 43,* 134–150.

13

Behavioral Approaches to Childhood Overweight Treatment

CRAIG A. JOHNSTON, CHERMAINE
TYLER, AND JOHN P. FOREYT

Approximately 17% of all school-age children in the United States are classified as overweight, and the prevalence of overweight has significantly increased over the past four decades (Ogden et al., 2006). Not only are more children becoming overweight, overweight children have consistently been getting heavier (Jolliffe, 2004). Similarly, more overweight has been seen in children at younger ages over the past two decades (Ogden et al., 2006). Overweight is not only a problem in the United States; it is estimated that more than 22 million children under the age of 5 years are overweight worldwide (Deckelbaum & Williams, 2001). In light of the incidence and prevalence of overweight in children (Ogden et al., 2006) and the impact it can have on their lives (Schwimmer, Burwinkle, & Varni, 2003; Zeller, Roehrig, Modi, Daniels, & Inge, 2006; Zeller, Saelens, Roehrig, Kirk, & Daniels, 2004), the need for prevention and treatment of this condition is clear.

In terms of treatment, an abundance of studies have examined weight management in children (Jelalian & Saelens, 1999). Most treatments take a multidisciplinary approach and include strategies for improving eating habits, increasing physical activity, and decreasing sedentary behavior. The greatest empirical support has been found for behaviorally based therapies (Summerbell et al., 2003). In fact, Robinson (1999) described behavioral treatments as the "state-of-the-art" approach for child weight management.

There are a number of behavioral strategies that are commonly used in weight management. Several specific behavioral components have been used successfully in a number of programs that have produced sustained weight loss over time (Epstein, Wing, Koeske, Drasik, & Ossip, 1981; Israel, 1999; McLean, Griffin, Toney, & Hardeman, 2003, Summerbell et al., 2003). Although "dismantling studies" (studies that determine the individual impact each single treatment component has on treatment outcomes) have not been conducted with children, the use of these strategies together to impact diet and physical activity has considerable empirical support (Epstein, 1996; Epstein, Wing, Koeske, & Valoski, 1984; Golan, Fainaru, & Weizman, 1998; Israel, Silverman, & Solotar, 1988).

BEHAVIORAL COMPONENTS

Self-Monitoring

Self-monitoring is the systematic observation and recording of specified target behaviors (Kanfer, 1970). The information that is provided allows the therapist to make specific recommendations for the future. Because self-monitoring can be inaccurate given it is a child or parent report, it is typically not used as a dependent variable (something used to measure change), but instead is used as an independent variable (something that impacts change). The simple observance of behavior can often have the effect of changing the target behavior in a desired direction.

Self-monitoring should take place with multiple target behaviors associated with the adoption of a healthier lifestyle (e.g., diet, physical activity, sedentary behavior). A "habit book" can be provided for maintaining records so the therapist can monitor participant progress across multiple behaviors. For example, older children can be taught to record dietary intake and the number of "junk" foods consumed (see Figure 13.1). Families can also be instructed to monitor the amount of time spent in physical and sedentary (e.g., television viewing) activities. A final dimension that should be monitored is the child's weight (see Figure 13.2). Several programs that have demonstrated successful weight loss and maintenance required the children to weigh themselves on a regular basis and chart their weights (Epstein et al., 1995; Israel, Guile, Baker, & Silverman, 1994). In addition, daily self-weighing has been associated with less weight regain in adults who were attempting to maintain weight loss (Wing, Tate, Gorin, Raynor, & Fava, 2006).

Although most children can be taught self-monitoring, this may prove too difficult for young children. In these cases, it may be beneficial for the parent to be responsible for completing self-monitoring records; however, depending on each child's ability, children should be given self-monitoring tasks to encourage active participation in their lifestyle change (Israel, Stolmaker, & Andrian, 1985a).

Stimulus Control

Stimulus control is a term that is used to describe the manipulation of one's environment to maximize the likelihood of behavior change. Another term often used for this concept is cue control. This involves families changing their home environment to remove cues that are associated with less healthy behaviors and to increase cues associated with more healthy behaviors. For example, parents may be instructed to remove less healthy foods from the home and increase the visibility of fruits and vegetables (Golan, Fainaru, & Weizman, 1998). Families should also be encouraged to decrease cues for sedentary behaviors, such as removing the television from the child's bedroom. In terms of increasing physical activity, families can be instructed to keep exercise clothing or bikes readily accessible.

In order to have children assist with stimulus control, they may help in packing a lunch for school. This active participation on the child's part facilitates learning to include healthy foods for meals and snacks and to prepare appropriate serving sizes to avoid overeating. Although children can begin to practice stimulus or cue control, parents are typically asked to implement this strategy because they are usually in charge of structuring the child's environment (e.g., buying groceries, permitting outside active play). It is important to note that the role of stimulus control in nutrition is to establish a healthy food environment without restricting the amount of food eaten. Restriction of food when attempting weight management with children has been associated with poor outcomes (Johnson & Birch, 1994).

Contingency Management

Contingency management refers to multiple strategies that change a behavior by modifying its consequences. One aspect of contingency management is positive reinforcement. Positive reinforcement involves providing the child with something preferred when a healthy behavior is exhibited. A

Grub Record

Name:_____   Date:_____

What did you eat today for:

Breakfast:

What	How much	When	Where

Snack:

What	How much	When	Where

Lunch:

What	How much	When	Where

Afternoon snack:

What	How much	When	Where

Dinner:

What	How much	When	Where

Night time snack:

What	How much	When	Where

Figure 13.1 Example food record for self-monitoring.

powerful form of positive reinforcement is social praise. For example, a parent provides praise (the child prefers positive attention from his or her parent) when the child eats vegetables (a healthful behavior is exhibited). Positive reinforcement can also include the use of rewards. A reward can be anything that the child prefers which he or she receives after accomplishing a target behavior. For example, the child gets to go to the store to pick out a toy after limiting television watching to 1 hr for the day. The use of rewards may be most appropriate when a child is having difficulty with a specific behavior. If the rewards being provided incur monetary cost, the cost should be kept to a minimum so that it does not become burdensome for the parents. The most appropriate rewards include parental attention, such as one-on-one parent time playing games or doing other child-chosen activities. Rewards can also be activities that promote further positive change, such as taking family bike rides, going to a park, or swimming.

Another form of contingency management is contracting. In making contracts, parents and children are taught how to administer specific rewards when particular behaviors are displayed.

Figure 13.2 Example weight chart for self-monitoring.

For example, parents agree to allow their child to have a friend come play at their home when the child successfully increases his or her vegetable consumption by an agreed upon amount. Reciprocal contracting may also be a beneficial strategy to use with families (Epstein, Valoski, Wing, & McCurley, 1990). In reciprocal contracting, the child and parent are instructed to provide mutually agreed upon reinforcers/rewards for each other when specified behavioral criteria are met. In this case, children provide rewards for specified parental behavior and parents reward child behavior. An example of parents being reinforced for providing vegetables at each meal would be allowing them to choose the music played during family chores.

An important factor in terms of using rewards and reinforcement successfully is individualizing them for each family. It is critical to determine each child's/family's individual preferences when determining appropriate reinforcers. The therapist may need to assist families in initially determining what rewards might be appropriate. The therapist needs to solicit both parent and child thoughts on those things that are motivating and that can be realistically provided by the parent and child. Based on this information, the therapist can assess the level of motivation of the family (Israel, Stolmaker, & Andrian, 1985b) and provide an individualized reward system for each family.

Modeling

Modeling can be defined as a way of learning in which individuals determine how to act based on observing others. Training parents to be role models for healthy behaviors is well supported in the literature (Epstein, Wing, Steranchak, Dickson, & Michelson, 1980; Golan & Crow, 2004a). Each of the target behaviors for child weight loss should also be target behaviors for parents. In this way, parents demonstrate healthy behaviors, encouraging the child to modify his or her actions accordingly. Some evidence suggests that children learn overeating patterns from parental modeling (Johnson & Birch, 1994), indicating that altering their eating and activity patterns may significantly impact treatment. To ensure that lifestyle changes are attainable for the child, it is vital to have parents participating in (i.e., modeling) healthy changes.

Social (Family) Support

Social support is essential for long-term maintenance of weight change (Jeffrey et al., 2000). Without others supporting the behavioral changes made during active treatment, it is likely that individuals will slowly return to the behaviors they engaged in before treatment. For children, family support is generally the focus. Including the parent has consistently been demonstrated as important for treatment success (Golan & Crow, 2004b; Israel, Solotar, & Zimand, 1990). In fact, some treatment programs have achieved child weight loss without having direct contact with the child, but instead by having parents learn the strategies for weight loss/maintenance to teach their children (Golan, Weizman, Apter, & Fainaru, 1998). However, the preponderance of empirical support for treating pediatric overweight is for family-based (including both the child and parent) interventions (McLean et al., 2003; Summerbell et al., 2003).

Goal Setting

Making a plan and determining realistic goals that can be met within a specified time frame are typically important parts of weight management programs for children. Goals are beneficial in that they give families a specific behavior on which to focus and provide structure for meetings. Discussing goals provides an opportunity for families to review the pros and cons of the previous week and strategize how to proceed in the future. The therapist uses this information to help the family establish new goals or methods for achieving unmet ones. In addition, goal setting encourages self-monitoring of behaviors, which is needed to determine if goals have been achieved.

Developmental Considerations

The most support for the behavioral treatment of pediatric overweight is provided for children between the ages of 8 and 12 years (Israel, 1999). Considerably less evidence exists for adolescents, and the behavioral treatments that have targeted adolescents have resulted in modest weight loss with a trend toward weight regain at follow-up (Mellin, Slinkard, & Irwin, 1987; Rocchini et al., 1988). One study addresses overweight treatment in adolescents (Jelalian, Mehlenbeck, Lloyd-Richardson, Birmaher, & Wing, 2006) using a peer-based "adventure therapy" component to make the treatment developmentally appropriate. Although participants who received the standard program as well as those who received the peer-based program lost weight, the older participants in the latter group lost significantly more weight. This finding demonstrates the importance of utilizing novel strategies for weight loss with older adolescents, but to date, there is little definitive evidence for the most effective method for achieving or maintaining weight loss with adolescents.

Literature on behavioral weight management with children under the age of 8 years is also lacking, with most studies focusing on prevention efforts with this age group. Multiple studies have been conducted with Head Start students or in a child care setting (Fitzgibbon et al., 2005; Stolley et al., 2003). However, these have limited long-term evidence to suggest that the interventions are effective. Furthermore, most of these programs have strong environmental, parental, or teacher components with less direct interaction with children.

CURRENT STATUS OF BEHAVIORAL APPROACHES

Although behavioral strategies have been used in a number of treatments not mentioned in this review, those presented have received the most empirical support or represent emerging areas of behavioral intervention. Although behavioral treatment in children has been supported for achieving weight loss, the use of behavioral strategies has not led to long-term weight maintenance (Summerbell et al., 2003). Quite some time ago, the state of behavioral obesity treatment with adults was summarized as follows:

> Although behavior therapy has advanced the treatment of obesity, its results are still of limited clinical significance. Weight losses have been modest and the variability in results large and unexplained. Even long-term maintenance of weight loss which, it was originally hoped, would be of particular benefit of the behavioral approach, has not yet been established. (Stunkard, 1978)

Sadly, this statement still reflects the state of behavioral weight management in children. Many of the children who have been successful in terms of weight loss continue to be overweight, and some significantly so (Epstein et al., 1990; Israel et al., 1985a). However, new methods and strategies for incorpo-rating other techniques into behavioral treatments are being developed, and continued study of these methodologies will likely hold the key to successful weight maintenance in children and adolescents.

Adjuncts to Behavioral Approaches

Internet-based programs may be useful in terms of sustaining healthy changes made during the course of an intense intervention. A study that examined the use of the Internet for decreasing body mass index (BMI), increasing fruit and vegetable consumption, and increasing physical activity showed that there was a trend in the expected direction for each of these variables (Baranowski et al., 2003). However, no statistical differences were found between the control and treatment groups in terms of BMI. Another study focused specifically on using the Internet for weight loss in African American girls and demonstrated a reduction in the percent body fat but not BMI (Williamson et al., 2005). Overall, little evidence exists for Internet-only interventions promoting weight loss, although there is a trend toward positive health outcomes. This mode of delivery may be used to bolster effects in standard treatments or to assist with maintenance upon completion of a treatment. However, this has yet to be empirically demonstrated.

Pharmacological treatments have been combined with behavioral methods and have resulted in successful weight loss for adolescents (Berkowitz et al., 2006). Given that the participants also demonstrated improved triglycerides, cholesterol, and insulin levels, additional studies combining pharmacological and behavioral methods are likely forthcoming. Although a discussion of phar-macological treatments of overweight in children is beyond the scope of this chapter, results appear promising. With the advent of safer, effective weight management drugs, multicomponent interven-tions that include behavior therapy should be further assessed and guidelines for using these treat-ments with adolescents developed.

LIMITATIONS TO BEHAVIORAL APPROACHES AND AREAS FOR FUTURE RESEARCH

Some of the most promising results discussed in the area of childhood overweight management have occurred with homogeneous samples (Stewart, Houghton, Hughes, Pearson, & Reilly, 2005). To date, little of the available literature addresses the use of behaviorally based therapy for weight management in minorities, children from low-income families, or significantly overweight chil-dren. Given the increased rates of overweight in minority children and low-income families (Gor-don-Larsen, Adair, & Popkin, 2003; Ogden et al., 2006) and the increased health and emotional problems for very overweight adolescents (Schwimmer et al., 2003; Tyler, Johnston, Fullerton, & Foreyt, 2007; Zeller et al., 2004), methods and strategies that are effective with these groups must be developed.

Given these increased risks (Gordon-Larsen et al., 2003; Hedley et al., 2004; Ogden et al., 2006), modifying behavioral strategies to address the specific needs of these families should be undertaken. Issues such as recruitment, adherence, and retention need to be better understood to increase the efficacy of interventions (Keller, Gonzales, & Fleuriet, 2005) for these groups. The use of meal replacements that meet the nutritional demands of children has been recommended as a means of overcoming economic limitations, especially given the effectiveness of this strategy as an adjunct to behavioral therapy with adults (Berkel, Poston, Reeves, & Foreyt, 2005). However, there is little evidence to support any particular strategy with this group. Overall, culturally and economically appropriate behaviorally based interventions are needed that meet the unique needs of these populations.

The paucity of data that exists for the treatment of very overweight children is also problematic. One behaviorally based program for children 160% or more above their ideal body weight demonstrated weight loss and improvement on several psychosocial variables (i.e., depression, anxiety, eating attitudes) for those participants who completed the program (Levine, Ringham, Kalarchian, Wisniewski, & Marcus, 2001). In addition, these children maintained this reduction in weight for up to 7 months after active treatment. However, approximately one-third of the families did not complete the treatment, and despite completers having maintained their weight loss, they remained significantly overweight. Currently treatments using weight loss medications (Chanoine, Hampl, Jensen, Boldrin, & Hauptman, 2005; McDuffie et al., 2002), bariatric surgery (Davis, Slish, Chao, & Cabana, 2006), and meal replacements (Ball et al., 2003) are being assessed for use with adolescents who are very overweight. Although these therapies are beyond the scope of this chapter, the importance of addressing the specific needs of very overweight children cannot be overstated.

CONCLUSION

A firm foundation for the behavioral treatment of pediatric overweight has been established. However, a great deal of work remains to be done in this area, given that children who receive treatment typically remain overweight and long-term maintenance of weight loss is not typically demonstrated. Furthermore, behavioral interventions have yet to demonstrate consistent positive results with very overweight children and economically and culturally diverse families. Despite these critiques, there is substantive evidence for the use of these interventions, with one behaviorally based intervention demonstrating 10-year improvements in weight for children (Epstein et al., 1990). Advances in the use of behavioral strategies will come as researchers and practitioners modify or enhance currently existing treatments for use with diverse groups and with new technologies.

ACKNOWLEDGMENTS

Preparation of this chapter was supported, in part, by a grant from the U.S. Department of Agriculture (USDA ARS 2533759358). The authors would also like to acknowledge the Peanut Institute for their support.

REFERENCES

Ball, S. D., Keller, K. R., Moyer-Mileur, L. J., Ding, Y., Donaldson, D., & Jackson, W. D. (2003). Prolongation of satiety after low versus moderately high glycemic index meals in obese adolescents. *Pediatrics, 111,* 488–494.

Baranowski, T., Baranowski, J. C., Cullen, K. W., Thompson, D. I., Nicklas, T., Zakeri, I. E., & Rochon, J. (2003). The Fun, Food, and Fitness Project (FFFP): the Baylor GEMS pilot study. *Ethnicity and Disease, 13*(suppl. 1), S30–S39.

Berkel, L. A., Poston, W. S. C., Reeves, R. S., & Foreyt, J. P. (2005). Behavioral interventions for obesity. *Journal of the American Dietetic Association, 105*(suppl. 1), S35-S43.

Berkowitz, R. I., Fujioka, K., Daniels, S. R., Hoppin, A. G., Owen, S., Perry, A. C., Sothern, M. S., Renz, C. L., Pirner, M. A., Walch, J. K., Jasinsky, O., Hewkin, A. C., Blakesley, V.A., & the Sibutramine Adolescent Study Group. (2006). Effects of sibutramine treatment in obese adolescents. *Annals of Internal Medicine, 145,* 81–90.

Chanoine, J., Hampl, S., Jensen, C., Boldrin, M., & Hauptman, J. (2005). Effect of orlistat on weight and body composition in obese adolescents: a randomized controlled trial. *JAMA, 293,* 2873–2883.

Davis, M. M., Slish, K., Chao, C., & Cabana, M. D. (2006). National trends in bariatric surgery, 1996–2002. *Archives of Surgery, 141,* 71–74.

Deckelbaum, R. J., & Williams, C. L. (2001). Childhood obesity: the health issue. *Obesity Research, 9*(suppl. 4), 239S–243S.

Epstein, L. H. (1996). Family-based behavioural intervention for obese children. *International Journal of Obesity, 20,* 14–21.

Epstein, L. H., Valoski, A., Vara, L. S., McCurley, J., Wisniewski, L., Kalarchian, M. A., Klein, K. R., & Shrager, L. R. (1995). Effects of decreasing sedentary behavior and increasing activity on weight change in obese children. *Health Psychology, 14,* 109–115.

Epstein, L. H., Valoski, A., Wing, R. R., & McCurley, J. (1990). Ten-year follow-up of behavioral, family-based treatment for obese children. *JAMA, 264,* 2519–2523.

Epstein, L. H., Wing, R. R., Koeske, R. R., & Valoski, A. (1984). Effects of diet plus exercise on weight change in parents and children. *Journal of Consulting and Clinical Psychology, 52,* 429–437.

Epstein, L. H., Wing, R. R., Koeske, R. R., Andrasik, F. & Ossip, D. (1981). Child and parent weight loss in family-based behavior modification programs. *Journal of Consulting and Clinical Psychology, 49,* 674–685.

Epstein, L. H., Wing, R. R., Steranchak, L., Dickson, B., & Michelson, J. (1980). Comparison of family-based behavior modification and nutrition education for childhood obesity. *Journal of Pediatric Psychology, 5,* 25–37.

Fitzgibbon, M. L., Stolley, M. R., Schiffer, L., Van Horn, L., KauferChristoffel, K., & Dyer, A. (2005). Two-year follow-up results for Hip-Hop to Health Jr.: a randomized controlled trial for overweight prevention in preschool minority children. *Journal of Pediatrics, 146,* 618–625.

Golan M., Fainaru, M., & Weizman, A. (1998). Role of behavior modification in the treatment of childhood obesity with the parents as the exclusive agents of change. *International Journal of Obesity and Related Metabolic Disorders, 22,* 1–8.

Golan, M., & Crow, S. (2004a). Parents are key players in the prevention and treatment of weight-related problems. *Nutrition Reviews, 62,* 39–50.

Golan, M., & Crow, S. (2004b). Targeting parents exclusively in the treatment of childhood obesity: long-term results. *Obesity Research, 12,* 357–361.

Golan, M., Fainaru, M., & Weizman, A. (1998). Role of behavior modification in the treatment of childhood obesity with the parents as the exclusive agents of change. *International Journal of Obesity, 22,* 1217–1224.

Golan, M., Weizman, A., Apter, A., & Fainaru, M. (1998). Parents as the exclusive agent of change in the treatment of childhood obesity. *American Journal of Nutrition, 67,* 1130–1135.

Gordon-Larsen, P., Adair, L. S., & Popkin, B. M. (2003). The relationship of ethnicity, socioeconomic factors, and overweight in U.S. adolescents. *Obesity Research, 11,* 121–129.

Hedley, A. A., Ogden, C. L., Johnson, C. L., Carroll, M. D., Curtin, L. R., & Flegal, K. M. (2004). Prevalence of overweight and obesity among U.S. children, adolescents, and adults, 1999–2002. *JAMA, 291,* 2847–2850.

Israel, A. C. (1999). Commentary. Empirically supported treatments for pediatric obesity: goals, outcome criteria, and the societal context. *Journal of Pediatric Psychology, 24,* 249–250.

Israel, A. C., Guile, C. A., Baker, J. E., & Silverman, W. K. (1994). An evaluation of enhanced self-regulation training in the treatment of childhood obesity. *Journal of Pediatric Psychology, 19,* 737–749.

Israel, A. C., Silverman, W. K., & Solotar, L. C. (1988). The relationship between adherence and weight loss in a behavioral treatment program for overweight children. *Behavior Therapy, 19,* 25–33.

Israel, A. C., Solotar, L. C., & Zimand, E. (1990). An investigation of two parental roles in the treatment of obese children. *International Journal of Eating Disorders, 9,* 557–564.

Israel, A. C., Stolmaker, L., & Andrian, C. A. (1985a). The effects of training parents in general child management skills on a behavioral weight loss program for children. *Behavior Therapy, 16,* 169–180.

Israel, A. C., Stolmaker, L., & Andrian, C. A. (1985b). Thoughts about food and their relationship to obesity and weight control. *International Journal of Eating Disorders, 4,* 549–558.

Jeffrey, R. W., Drewnowski, A., Epstein, L. H., Stunkard, A. J., Wilson, G. T., Wing, R. R., & Hill, D. R. (2000). Long-term maintenance of weight loss: current status. *Health Psychology, 19*(suppl.), 5–16.

Jelalian, E., Mehlenbeck, R., Lloyd-Richardson, E. E., Birmaher, V., & Wing, R. R. (2006). "Adventure therapy" combined with cognitive-behavioral treatment for overweight adolescents. *International Journal of Obesity, 30,* 31–39.

Jelalian, E., & Saelens, B. E. (1999). Empirically supported treatments in pediatric psychology: pediatric obesity. *Journal of Pediatric Psychology, 24,* 223–248.

Johnson, S. L., & Birch, L. L. (1994). Parents' and children's adiposity and eating style. *Pediatrics, 94,* 653–661.

Jolliffe, D. (2004). Extent of overweight among U.S. children and adolescents from 1971 to 2000. *International Journal of Obesity Related Metabolic Disorders, 28,* 4–9.

Kanfer, F. H. (1970). Self-monitoring: methodological limitations and clinical applications. *Journal of Consulting and Clinical Psychology, 35,* 148–152.

Keller, C. S., Gonzales, A., & Fleuriet, K. J. (2005). Retention of minority participants in clinical research studies. *Western Journal of Nursing Research, 27,* 292–306.

Levine, M. D., Ringham, R. M., Kalarchian, M. A., Wisniewski, L., & Marcus, M. D. (2001). Is family-based behavioral weight control appropriate for severe pediatric obesity? *International Journal of Eating Disorders, 30,* 318–328.

McDuffie, J. R., Calis, K. A., Uwaifo, G. I., Sebring, N G., Fallon, Hubbard, V. S., & Yanovski, J. A. (2002). Three-month tolerability of orlistat in adolescents with obesity-related comorbid conditions. *Obesity Research, 10,* 642–650.

McLean, N., Griffin, S., Toney, K., & Hardeman, W. (2003). Family involvement in weight control, weight maintenance and weight loss interventions: a systematic review of randomized trials. *International Journal of Obesity, 27,* 987–1005.

Mellin, L. M., Slinkard, L. A., & Irwin, C. E. (1987). Adolescent obesity intervention: validation of the SHAPEDOWN program. *Journal of the American Dietetic Association, 87,* 333–338.

Ogden, C. L., Carroll, M. D., Curtin, L. R., McDowell, M. A., Tabak, C. A., & Flegal, K. M. (2006). Prevalence of overweight and obesity in the United States, 1999–2004. *JAMA, 295,* 1549–1555.

Robinson, T. N. (1999). Behavioral treatment of childhood and adolescent obesity. *International Journal of Obesity, 23*(suppl. 2), S52–S57.

Rocchini, A. P., Katch, V., Anderson, J., Hinderlite, J., Becque, D., Martin, M., & Marks, C. (1988). Blood pressure in obese adolescents: effects on weight loss. *JAMA, 82,* 16–23.

Schwimmer, J. B., Burwinkle, T. M., & Varni, J. M. (2003). Health-related quality of life of severely overweight children and adolescents. *JAMA, 289,* 1813–1819.

Stewart, L., Houghton, J., Hughes, A. R., Pearson, D., & Reilly, J. J. (2005). Dietetic management of pediatric overweight and description of a practical and evidence-based approach. *Journal of the American Dietetic Association, 105,* 1810–1815.

Stolley, M. R., Fitzgibbon, M. L., Dyer, A., Van Horn, L., KauferChristoffel, K., & Schiffer, L. (2003). Hip-Hop to Health Jr., an obesity prevention program for minority preschool children: baseline characteristics of participants. *Preventive Medicine, 36,* 320–329.

Stunkard, A. J. (1978). Behavioral treatment of obesity: the current status. *International Journal of Obesity, 2,* 237–248.

Summerbell, C. D., Ashton, V., Campbell, K. J., Edmunds, L. D., Kelly, S., & Waters, E. (2003). Interventions for treating obesity in children. *Cochrane Review Database of Systematic Reviews, 3,* CD001872.

Tyler, C., Johnston, C. A., Fullerton, G., & Foreyt, J. P. (2007). Reduced quality of life in very overweight Mexican American adolescents. *Journal of Adolescent Health, 40,* 366–368.

Williamson, D. A., Martin, P. D., White, M. A., Newton, R., Walden, H., York-Crowe, E., Alfonso, A., Gordon, S., & Ryan, D. (2005). Efficacy of an internet-based behavioral weight loss program for overweight adolescent African-American girls. *Eating and Weight Disorders, 10,* 193–203.

Wing, R. R., Tate, D. F., Gorin, A. A., Raynor, H. A., & Fava, J. L. (2006). A self-regulation program for maintenance of weight loss. *New England Journal of Medicine, 355,* 1563–1571.

Zeller, M. H., Roehrig, H., Modi, A. C., Daniels, S. R., & Inge, T. H. (2006). Health-related quality of life and depressive symptoms in adolescents with extreme obesity presenting for bariatric surgery. *Pediatrics, 117,* 1155–1161.

Zeller, M. H., Saelens, B. E., Roehrig, H., Kirk, S., & Daniels, S. R. (2004). Psychological adjustment of obese youth presenting for weight management treatment. *Obesity Research, 12,* 1576–1586.

14

Examining Family-Based Treatments for Pediatric Overweight
A Review of the Literature and Conceptual Analysis

BRIE A. MOORE AND WILLIAM T. O'DONOHUE

Obesity is the most prevalent nutritional disease of children in this country (Dietz, 1998). Over the last 30 years, the percentage of children in the United States who are overweight has more than tripled (National Center for Health Statistics, 2001). Childhood obesity is not just limited to the United States. The prevalence of childhood obesity worldwide is rapidly accelerating (International Obesity Task Force, 2005) and is reaching global epidemic proportions (World Health Organization, 2005).

Assessment of overweight in children requires consideration of the child's age, height, weight, pubertal status, and growth patterns (Kirk, Scott, & Daniels, 2005). Overweight children are commonly defined as those ages 2 to 20 years with a body mass index (BMI) greater than the 95th percentile for age and sex. The determination of at-risk for overweight is made when a child's measured BMI falls within the 85th to 95th percentiles (Committee on Nutrition, 2004; Kuczmarski et al., 2002).

Childhood overweight is associated with significant health problems and is an important early risk factor for adult morbidity and mortality. Children who are inactive and overweight are more likely to have high blood pressure, abnormal insulin and cholesterol levels, and abnormal lipid profiles. In some populations, children who are overweight account for as much as 50% of patients with type 2 diabetes, a metabolic disorder historically rare in children (Fagot-Campagna et al., 2000). These changes increase the risk of early disability and death from heart disease, kidney disease, and other organ damage (Young-Hyman et al., 2001). Other medical complications include asthma, sleep apnea, skeletal and joint problems, liver disease, and gastrointestinal complications.

The psychological stress of social stigmatization imposed on children who are overweight may be as damaging as the medical morbidities. These commonly include poor self-esteem, body image disturbances, depression, social isolation, difficulty with peer relationships, and poor academic achievement (Schneider & Brill, 2005). Together, given its physical, psychosocial, and economic sequelae, childhood obesity poses an unprecedented burden in terms of children's health and future health care costs (Committee on Nutrition, 2003).

In this review we address the question of the extent to which the literature indicates that there are replicable treatments that produce clinically significant improvement in pediatric overweight. Some researchers have concluded that behavioral interventions involving the family as the unit of change represent the standard of care for the evidence-based treatment of childhood overweight (Kazdin & Weisz, 1998). Given that family-based programs have adopted the most rigorous methodology (i.e., randomized controlled trials) and have produced the best outcomes, we have chosen to concentrate this review on family-based treatment programs targeting child weight loss. This distinction allows the review to be of manageable size. In addition, most extant treatment outcome studies have adopted this distinction. Epstein (1998), and Jelalian and Saelens (1999) provide reviews of a broader scope.

Fifteen published studies from 1980 to 2005 were identified via (1) computer searches of databases such as PsychINFO and MEDLINE using keywords such as "pediatric," "child," "family," "overweight," and "obesity," and with limits for publication type (randomized controlled/clinical trial), age (child, 0–18), and language (English); (2) previous reviews of the literature; and (3) the reference sections of located studies. The random assignment of participants to conditions was judged the minimum necessary criterion for meaningful interpretation of data, particularly making causal inferences regarding efficacy. Studies that were excluded included pharmacotherapy or bariatric treatments, single group designs, and nonrandomized trials. Based on these criteria, a total of 15 studies were identified for review.

EVALUATION CRITERIA

The question motivating this review was: What evidence is there that there are replicable treatments that produce clinically significant and enduring improvement for pediatric overweight and obesity? Furthermore, to what extent has research been guided by the question: "What treatment, by whom, is most effective for this individual with that specific problem, under which set of circumstances?" (Paul, 1967, p. 111). For these questions to be answered, research needs to be designed and reported with several key considerations in mind. Specifically, to ensure a high-fidelity replication of an empirically validated treatment can be employed, clear articulation of the process of treatment development and evaluation is necessary. Furthermore, data measuring process variables and adherence are highly desirable to ascertain the extent to which hypothesized mechanisms thought to produce outcomes were actually engaged. To understand the potential clinical benefits of a given treatment and enhance its generalizability, participants and providers must be carefully selected and adequately described. Thus, in this review, we evaluated sample selection and description as well as key design elements such as process variables, protocol adherence, social validity, and dissemination.

Sample Selection and Description

The selection of the sample is critical because it determines the extent to which generalizations can be made to individuals not participating in the study. Samples must be described in terms of characteristics such as socioeconomic status, ethnicity, age, and degree of overweight to achieve meaningful interpretation of data. Family composition, history of weight control efforts, and motivation, as measured by stages of change (Miller & Rollnick, 2002; Prochaska & DiClemente, 1984), are important variables to include in a description of the sample.

Design Elements

Process Variables

To build upon established principles of behavior change, researchers must explicate the process variables thought to mediate treatment outcomes. The theoretical rationale and hypothesized causal chain (i.e., theory of change mechanisms) must be explicitly stated for these assumptions to be critically examined (Tracey & Tracey, 1999). For example, if a treatment involving educating families on the U.S. Food and Drug Administration's (FDA) Food Guide Pyramid (FGP) does not appear to result in significant improvement in the consumption of healthy foods, two interpretations are plausible: (1) the FGP was not adequately learned, or (2) the FGP was learned, but this learning did not significantly impact behavior. Measuring the extent to which knowledge changes provides treatment process information that can be used to choose between these alternative explanations.

Protocol Adherence

It is critical that studies include an adequate description of treatment components, therapist qualifications and training, and fidelity checks to ensure protocol adherence. These steps allow one to have a clear understanding of exactly what treatment consisted of and its consistent delivery across clients. Use of treatment manuals and fidelity checks is an essential design component (Pereplet-chikova & Kazdin, 2005).

Social Validity, Scalability, and Dissemination

In order to provide treatment programs that are widely used and clinically effective, behavioral health professionals must gain a better understanding of what consumers actually want (O'Donohue & Levensky, 2006). That is, treatments must be designed with the needs and constraints of families and providers in mind. Given the scope of the problem and limited social and economic resources, scalability and dissemination issues must be considered in effective and efficient treatment.

EFFECTIVENESS OF TREATMENT FOR PEDIATRIC OVERWEIGHT AND OBESITY

Review of Studies

Based on the review criteria mentioned above, 15 randomized controlled outcome studies are described below. It would have been advantageous to summarize results using the statistical techniques of meta-analysis, however, combining the results of the studies reviewed here was inappropriate because (1) the majority of studies included insufficient information about sample selection procedures, (2) the outcome measures differed across studies, (3) there were large differences in treatment procedures or the treatment procedures were inadequately described, and (4) there was large variability across studies in the length of follow-up periods. These factors made it difficult to determine the comparability of studies, which is a prerequisite for making the combination of their results meaningful.

Studies are presented according to the type of control condition employed. We aim to identify what treatment approaches outperform—(1) absence of intervention, (2) treatment as usual, and (3) novel treatment approaches (i.e., relative treatment efficacies)—in both the short and long term. Many studies utilize three group designs. Thus one study may provide information for several of these categories. Consistent with the goals of this review, these findings are discussed separately. A summary of the results of this review is provided in Table 14.1.

No Intervention Control

Kirschenbaum, Harris, and Tomarken (1984) randomly assigned forty 9- to 13-year-old children and their parents to one of three groups: (1) parent plus child behavioral treatment ($n = 16$), (2) child only behavioral treatment ($n = 15$), or (3) wait-list control ($n = 9$). Participants in both experimental

Table 14.1 Summary of the Evaluation of Pediatric Overweight Treatment Outcome Studies

	Sample Description		Design Elements and Findings			Social Validity		Dissemination
	Age (years)	Diversity: Minority, SES	Treatment Components	1-Year Outcome (% OW)	Process Variables and/or Adherence	Participant Acceptance	Clinical Significance	Scalability: Attending to Cost or Access
Epstein et al., 1984	8–12	NR	6 months; diet plus exercise	(10 year: −10%)	NR	NR	NR	NR
Epstein et al., 1985	5–8	NR, NR	6 months; **parent training**	−26%	NR	NR	NR	NR
Epstein, McKenzie et al., 1994	8–12	NR, middle class social strata IV	1 year; Traffic Light Diet + **mastery criteria** and **contingent reinforcement**	−26.5%	Program adherence data	Utility of program techniques rated	Large magnitude of change; 30% nonobese status	NR
Epstein et al., 1995	8–12	96% Caucasian, middle class	6 months; sedentary behavior	−18.7%	NR	NR	NR	NR
Epstein, Paluch, Gordy, Saelens et al., 2000	8–12	NR, NR	6 months; TAU	−1.4 (BMI z-score)	NR	NR	Total, internalizing behavioral problems; BMI	NR
Epstein, Paluch, Gordy, & Dorn, 2000	8–12	97% Caucasian, NR	6 months; **reinforce sedentary behavior or activity**	−25.5% (5 year: −38.4%)	NR	NR	NR (no normative data for body fat)	NR

Study	Age	Race, class	Treatment	Outcome			
Flodmark et al., 1993	10–11	NR, NR	14 to 18 months; family therapy	+1.4%	NR	NR	NR
Golan, Fainaru et al., 1998	6–11	NR, middle class	14 sessions; parents as sole agents of change	−14.7%	NR	35% nonobese status	NR
Golan, Weizman et al., 1998	6–11	NR, NR	14 sessions; parents as sole agents of change	−14.6%	NR	35% nonobese status	NR
Goldfield et al., 2001	8–12	100% Caucasian, middle class	13 sessions; mixed or group treatment	−8.04%	Described therapist qualifications	NR	Group only intervention cost effective
Graves et al., 1988	6–12	NR, NR	8 weeks; **problem solving**	(3 months **−24.3%**)	NR	NR	NR
Herrera et al., 2004	6–18, mean age 11.5	90% Caucasian, middle class	10 weeks; behavioral treatment	(10 weeks −9.51%)	Fidelity checks	NHANES I category: 40% behavioral; 12% cognitive	NR
Israel et al., 1985	8–12	NR, NR	8 weeks; TAU	−7.6%	NR	NR	NR
Israel et al., 1994	8–13	NR, NR	26 weeks; TAU	−5.8%	NR	NR	NR
Kirschenbaum et al., 1984	9–13	NR, NR	9 weeks; child only CBT	(9 weeks −7.1%)	NR	NR	NR

Note: NR = Not reported. All treatment outcomes are reported for 1 year posttest or follow-up evaluations unless otherwise stated in parentheses. Figures in bold represent best practices in terms of treatment components and outcomes.

groups received nutrition education, exercise information, and a 9-week cognitive behavioral treatment (CBT) program. CBT components included self-monitoring, stimulus control, self-reward, coping skills, assertiveness, and relaxation training. Demographic, adherence, process variables, social validity, clinical significance, and dissemination data were not reported. Immediately after treatment, children in the parent and child group (−6.3%) and in the child only group (−7.1%) demonstrated statistically greater reductions in the percentage of body weight than children in the control group (+0.6%), whose weight remained relatively stable.

Epstein, Wing, Koeske, and Valoski (1984) randomized fifty-three 8- to 12-year-old children to one of three groups: (1) diet and exercise intervention ($n = 15$), (2) diet only intervention ($n = 15$), or (3) a wait-list no treatment control group ($n = 14$). Participants in the experimental groups received the Traffic Light Diet (900 to 1200 kcal/day) and an exercise program consisting of energy expenditure of 2800 kcal/week. Intervention groups attended 15 education sessions. Demographic, adherence, process variables, social validity, clinical significance, and dissemination data were not reported. At 6 months, children in the treatment groups demonstrated significantly ($p < .01$) greater reductions in their percentage overweight than children in the control group (who demonstrated weight gain). At 6 months and 1 year, children in the treatment groups demonstrated statistically significant reductions in their percentage overweight from baseline ($p < .001$); no significant differences between groups were found. Although the statistical significance of these differences was reported, the percentage overweight at pretest, 6-month, and 1-year follow-up evaluations were not provided. At 10-year follow-up, children in the diet and lifestyle group (−10.0%) and the diet only group (−8.4%) demonstrated sustained reductions in their percentage overweight as compared to controls (Epstein, McKenzie, Valoski, Klein, & Wing, 1994).

Israel, Stolmaker, and Andrian (1985) randomized thirty-three 8- to 12-year-old children and their parents to one of three groups: (1) multicomponent behavioral weight reduction ($n = 12$), (2) weight reduction plus parent training ($n = 12$), or (3) a wait-list control group ($n = 9$). Families in both intervention groups received nutrition and exercise education. Parents in the weight reduction plus parent training group also received a short course in general child behavioral management skills. Demographic, adherence, process variables, social validity, clinical significance, and dissemination data were not reported. After completion of the 8-week program, children in the weight reduction (−11.6%) and parent training groups (−7.2%) demonstrated significantly greater weight reduction than controls (−0.9%).

Flodmark et al. (1993) randomized ninety-three 10- to 11-year-old children and their parents to one of three groups: (1) conventional treatment, (2) conventional treatment plus family therapy, or (3) a no intervention control group. Participants in both intervention groups received nutrition (i.e., 1500 to 1700 kcal/day diet; 30% fat intake per day) and exercise education. Conventional obesity treatment was defined as regular pediatrician visits, encouragement to exercise, and diet education provided by a nutritionist. Family therapy was administered as six family sessions and consisted of education about the importance of family support. Demographic, adherence, process variables, social validity, clinical significance, and dissemination data were not reported. Results indicated that children in the family therapy group (BMI +.03) had statistically less ($p < .04$) of an increase in BMI scores than children in either the standard treatment (BMI +.06) or control group (data not provided). At the 1-year follow-up ($p < .04$), this pattern of results persisted for children in the family therapy (BMI +1.1), standard treatment (BMI +1.6), and control groups (BMI +2.8). This intervention appears to have possibly prevented the exacerbation of, rather than actually treating, pediatric obesity.

Together, results suggest that early multicomponent interventions involving diet, exercise, and parent training, in conjunction with behavior modification skills, can be expected to result in minor decreases in the percentage overweight as compared to the relative stability observed in the absence of treatment. None of these studies included children younger than 8 years old, limiting the generalizability of these findings. Given the importance of early learning of healthy lifestyle behavior, early childhood may be a critical time to intervene. In addition, clinical information and data were not reported and are greatly needed. Conventional statistical comparisons between groups tell us very little about the benefits children derived from these treatments, their potencies, impacts on children and families, or ability to make a difference in the lives of children who are overweight (Jacobson & Truax, 1991). That is, it is unlikely that these minor reductions in percentage overweight resulted in a change from classification in the obese range to the nonobese range or substantial improvements in physiological and psychosocial functioning (percentage overweight at pretest was not presented). Given the findings of these studies, family-based behavioral treatment, compared to no-treatment control groups, appears to have limited efficacy.

Treatment as Usual

Treatment as usual (TAU) conditions may differ in their delivery, but most multicomponent, family-based programs include a combination of psychoeducation plus contingency management skills training. These approaches likely evaluate similar underlying processes.

Israel et al. (1985) compared the relative efficacies of (1) TAU and (2) TAU plus parent training. Results indicated that children in the TAU group (−11.6%) demonstrated statistically superior results to the parent training group (−7.2%) at 8 weeks posttest, but at the 1-year follow-up, children in the parent training group (+1.7%) showed better maintenance of outcomes than children in the TAU group (+4.0%). These long-term outcomes support the efficacy of general behavior management in weight control.

Graves et al. (1988) examined the differential efficacies of problem-solving training, behavioral TAU, and education. Forty 6- to 12-year-old children were randomly assigned to one of three groups: (1) behavioral TAU without problem solving, (2) parent problem-solving training, or (3) instruction only. TAU consisted of the Traffic Light Diet and exercise information (Epstein et al., 1984), self-monitoring, stimulus control, cognitive restructuring, family support, and weight loss maintenance strategies. Families in the problem-solving group received the same weight control information as the behavioral treatment group along with problem-solving skills training targeting improvements in child weight control. Participants in the instruction only group received diet and physical activity education. Demographic, adherence, process variables, social validity, clinical significance, and dissemination data were not reported. Results of the 8-week intervention indicate that at 3 months, problem-solving training (−24.3%) and TAU (−13.0%) both resulted in significant reductions in percentage overweight. Problem-solving training was found to be superior to both TAU and instruction alone (−10.3%). Statistically significant differences between groups were maintained at the 3- and 6-month follow-up evaluations. Although inconsistent with findings of other research teams (Epstein, Paluch, Gordy, Saelens, & Ernst, 2000), currently problem-solving (e.g., Graves et al., 1988) appears to result in the largest observed reductions in percentage overweight. However, limited sample sizes may reduce confidence in the generalizability of these findings.

Flodmark et al. (1993) compared (1) TAU and (2) TAU plus family therapy. The results indicated that TAU plus family therapy (BMI +.03) was statistically superior to TAU (BMI +.06) at posttest. Children in the family therapy group demonstrated statistically smaller gains in BMI over the course of treatment. At the 1-year follow-up, these results were maintained for the family therapy (BMI +1.1) and TAU groups (BMI +1.6).

Israel, Guile, Baker, and Silverman (1994) investigated the efficacy of enhanced child self-regulation training. Thirty-four 8- to 13-year-old children were randomized to one of two groups: (1) TAU or (2) enhanced child involvement (ECI). All participants received 26 weeks of multicomponent behavioral weight control treatment, including discussion and homework assignments regarding cue control, physical activity, food intake, and rewards. The TAU group emphasized parent responsibility for completion of homework and child motivation. Parents were also provided instruction on monitoring the child's food intake, promoting adherence to cue control rules, and rewarding appropriate behaviors. Behavioral parent training was supplemented with Patterson's (1976) text *Liv-*

ing with Children. The ECI group emphasized child management of weight loss efforts. Children were taught self-management skills, including goal setting, formulating and implementing behavior change plans, self-monitoring, self-reward, and problem-solving behaviors. Parents in this group were also to reward their children for engaging in self-management skills. Demographic, adherence, process variables, social validity, clinical significance, and dissemination data were not reported. Results indicated no significant between-group differences. The TAU (−15.6%) and ECI (−12.5%) intervention groups both demonstrated significant reductions in percentage overweight at posttest, 1-year (TAU +9.77%; ECI +11.72%), and 3 year (TAU +0.97%; ECI +7.2%) follow-up evaluations.

Epstein, Paluch, Gordy, Saelens, et al. (2000) investigated the differential effects of problem-solving training for parents and children. Sixty-seven 8- to 12-year-old children and their families were stratified by gender and degree of child and parent obesity and then randomized to one of three groups: (1) parent and child problem solving (*n* = 17), (2) child problem solving (*n* = 18), or (3) TAU (*n* = 17; 5 families decided not to participate at the outset, the remaining 10 families were noncompleters). All groups received the Traffic Light Diet and lifestyle physical activity education plus behavior change techniques. For families in the problem-solving group, didactic training, based on research by D'Zurilla and Goldfried (1971), was provided in group formats. Demographic, adherence, process variables, social validity, and dissemination data were not reported. Results indicated that TAU without problem solving (BMI z-score −1.5) resulted in clinically and statistically significant decreases in BMI z-scores than either the parent (BMI z-score −1.4) or parent-child (BMI z-score −1.3) weight control groups with problem solving. Although these decreases were similar at posttest (6 months), the TAU group (+0.1; +0.3) showed smaller increases in total weight at the 1- and 2-year follow-ups than either the parent-child (+0.2; +0.6) or the child problem-solving groups (+0.1; + 0.4). In addition, children demonstrated clinically significant reductions on measures of total behavior problems and internalizing behavior problems. The authors state that these findings may suggest that family-based intervention may implicitly teach child problem solving. Furthermore, the addition of problem-solving training may have impaired behavior changes needed for long-term success, as family resources may have been focused on problem solving rather than lifestyle changes.

Herrera, Johnston, and Steele (2004) compared cognitive and behavioral treatments to a TAU group consisting of nutritional education, exercise education, short- and long-term goal-setting instruction and evaluation, and components of the Traffic Light Diet (e.g., Epstein et al., 2001). Fifty children, ages 6 to 18 years old (mean age 11.5 years; 66.9% overweight), and their families were randomized to one of three groups: (1) cognitive obesity treatment, (2) behavioral obesity treatment, or (3) TAU. Participants were 90% Caucasian and predominately middle class. Across conditions, treatment was conducted with groups of five children and their parent(s) in 10 weekly 120-minute sessions. Treatment was provided by master's-level therapists supervised by doctorate-level licensed psychologists. Weekly multidisciplinary staff meetings were held to discuss treatment integrity. The results of the 10-week program indicated that participants in all conditions exhibited significant decreases in percentage over ideal BMI. Analyses of percentage overweight indicated that the behavioral group (−9.51%) was statistically superior to the comparison group (−4.67%), but that the cognitive group (−5.53%) and comparison group were not statistically different. Forty percent of participants in the behavioral group and 12% of children in the cognitive group achieved clinically significant reductions in overweight. Social validity and dissemination data were not presented.

In summary, multicomponent family-based treatment including nutrition education, increases in physical activity, and behavior modification skills training resulted in statistically greater short-term improvements in percentage overweight as compared to (1) cognitive therapy (Herrera et al., 2004), (2) TAU plus parent training (Israel et al., 1985), and (3) usual care at a for-profit weight loss facility (Herrera et al., 2004). At 1 year, parent training plus TAU provided better results. Data were mixed regarding the effectiveness of problem solving (Epstein, Paluch, Gordy, Saelens et al., 2000; Graves et al., 1988). These studies provide further evidence that multicomponent family-based interventions may result in modest reductions in the percentage overweight. However, without data supporting the clinical significance of these findings, the practical magnitude of these effects cannot be clearly discerned.

Novel Treatment Approaches (Investigating Relative Treatment Efficacies)

Kirschenbaum et al. (1984) investigated the relative efficacies of providing behavioral weight control treatment to (1) children and families, with an emphasis on collaboration; and (2) child only group weight control treatment. The results indicated that the parent-child (–6.3%) and child only (–7.1%) conditions produced similar results.

Epstein et al. (1984) compared the relative efficacies of a diet and exercise intervention and a diet only intervention. At 6 months and 1 year, children in the treatment groups demonstrated statistically significant reductions in the percentage overweight from baseline ($p < .001$), but no significant between-group differences were found. However, reductions in the percentage overweight at posttest were not provided. At the 10-year follow-up, children in the diet and lifestyle group (–10.0%) and the diet only group (–8.4%) demonstrated sustained reductions in the percentage overweight that were not significantly different between groups (Epstein, McKenzie et al., 1994).

Epstein et al. (1985) investigated the effect of adjunctive behavioral parent training in a comprehensive weight control program. Nineteen 5- to 8-year-old girls and their parents were randomized to one of two groups: (1) behavioral parent training plus TAU ($n = 8$) or (2) an equal attention weight management control group ($n = 11$). Families assigned to the parent training group received the Traffic Light Diet plus training in praise, modeling, self-monitoring, and contracting. Parents were provided with didactic training on management techniques and social learning principles. Participants in the control group received the Traffic Light Diet plus an equal amount of additional time with a behavior therapist. Demographic, adherence, process variables, social validity, clinical significance, and dissemination data were not reported. At the 1-year follow-up, children in the parent training group (–26%) demonstrated significant reductions in their percentage overweight as compared to children in the equal attention control group (–11.2%). Although the clinical significance of these findings was not reported, the 26% reduction in the percentage overweight presents a substantial improvement in outcomes from other reported studies. Similar outcomes were produced by Graves et al.'s (1988) adjunct problem-solving treatment (at 6 months) and by Epstein, McKenzie, et al.'s (1994) inclusion of mastery criteria and Epstein, Paluch, Gordy, Saelens, et al.'s (2000) contingent reinforcement of increases in physical activity and decreases in sedentary behavior (at 1 year).

Graves et al. (1988) examined the differential efficacies of (1) problem-solving training as an adjunct to TAU and (2) instruction alone. TAU consisted of the Traffic Light Diet and exercise information, self-monitoring, stimulus control, cognitive restructuring, family support, and weight loss maintenance strategies. Families in the problem-solving group received the same weight control information as the behavioral treatment group plus problem-solving skills training targeting improvements in child weight control. The results of the 8-week intervention revealed that at the 3-month follow-up, problem-solving training (–24.3%) resulted in significant reductions in the percentage overweight and was superior to instruction alone (–10.3%). Although problem-solving efficacy studies conducted by a different research group (Epstein et al., 2000) did not find a statistically significant advantage for problem solving as compared to TAU, the magnitude and possible clinical significance of the effects of this brief intervention appear promising.

Epstein et al. (1994) compared the effects of mastery criteria and contingent reinforcement to a linked TAU control. Forty 8- to 12-year-old children (average 59.6% over the 50th percentile for BMI) were randomized to one of two groups: (1) Traffic Light Diet plus mastery criteria and contingent reinforcement, or (2) Traffic Light Diet control group linked for presentation of behavior skills, information, and reinforcement. Participants were predominately middle class. Treatment was provided over 26 weekly meetings plus 6 monthly meetings. Weekly meetings were comprised of weight measurement and a didactic lecture focused on weight control or behavior change. In the experimental group, families progressed through five levels of treatment at their own rate based on mastery of information and behavioral skills. For parents, praise statements and stimulus control goals were also included. Staff members determined each week, via review of self-monitoring books and weight loss, if participants could progress to the next level and whether or not reinforcers were delivered. The control group was designed to control for paced introduction of educational material by linking progress in treatment and reinforcement to the progress of the experimental group. Although families reported strategy use (i.e., adherence) and the perceived utility of these strategies, these data were not presented. At the 1-year follow-up, children in the experimental group demonstrated a 26.5% decrease in their percentage overweight, whereas children in the linked control group showed significantly less weight reduction (−16.7%). Differences between the experimental and control groups were not maintained at the 2-year follow-up (−15.4% and −10.6%, respectively). The magnitude of the effects at 1 year were analyzed. A large magnitude of change was observed, with 30% of participants achieving nonobese status. A discussion of dissemination of these findings was not provided.

Epstein et al. (1995) evaluated the relative efficacies of diet and physical activity reinforcement programs. Sixty-one 8- to 12-year-old children (average 51.8% overweight) and their parents were randomized to one of three treatment groups: (1) reinforce reductions in sedentary behaviors, (2) reinforce increases in physical activity, or (3) reinforce decreases in sedentary and increases in physical activity. In addition to the unique treatment components, the 4-month treatment consisted of the Traffic Light Diet comprehensive weight control program. The sample was reportedly 96% Caucasian and predominately middle class. Adherence, process variables, social validity, clinical significance, and dissemination data were not reported. At 1 year, results indicated that children in the reinforce reductions in sedentary behavior group (−18.7%) demonstrated significant reductions in the percentage overweight as compared to children in the activity (−10.3%) and combined (−8.7%) groups.

Golan, Weizman, Apter, and Fainaru (1998) investigated the relative efficacy of a family-based approach in which parents serve as exclusive agents of change as compared to an approach in which children serve as agents of change. Sixty 6- to 11-year-old children (average 8.9 years old and 39.6% overweight) and their families were randomized to one of two groups: (1) parents as the sole agents of change, or (2) children as the sole agents of change. Parents in the experimental group were advised to take total responsibility for assisting their child in weight control. Demographic, adherence, process variables, social validity, and dissemination data were not reported. At 1 year, results of the 14-session treatment indicated that children with parents as the sole agents of change (−14.7%) demonstrated significantly greater reductions in their percentage overweight than did children in the control group (−8.1%). In a follow-up study utilizing the same methodology, these results were replicated (Golan, Fainaru, & Weizman, 1998). Children in the parents as agents of change group (−14.6%) showed significantly greater reductions in their percentage overweight than children in the child as agent of change group (−8.4%). These results were clinically significant, as 35% of children achieved nonobese status.

Epstein, Paluch, Gordy, and Dorn (2000) investigated the relative efficacies of decreasing sedentary behavior and increasing physical activity as part of a comprehensive pediatric obesity treatment program. Ninety 8- to 12-year-old children and their parents were stratified by gender and degree of obesity and then randomly assigned to four groups: (1) decrease sedentary, low dose; (2) decrease sedentary, high dose; (3) increase activity, low dose (10 miles/week); and (4) increase activity, high dose (20 miles/week). Participants were 97% Caucasian. Socioeconomic status, adherence, process variables, social validity, clinical significance, and dissemination data were not reported. Across groups, results indicated significant reductions in the percentage overweight from baseline to posttreatment (−25.5%) and through the 2-year follow-up (an additional −12.9%), representing a reduction of 38.4% from baseline. Although the clinical significance of these results was not provided, given the magnitude of these combined effects (−38.4%), the clinical efficacy of this approach warrants further investigation.

Goldfield, Epstein, Kilanowski, Paluch, and Kogut-Bossler (2001) evaluated the cost-effectiveness of a mixed (group and individualized) treatment format as compared to group only family-based treatment for pediatric obesity. Thirty-one 8- to 12-year-old children and their families were randomized to one of two groups: (1) mixed treatment, or (2) group only. Skilled master's-level therapists conducted separate parent and child groups. The entire sample was Caucasian and on average the sample was middle class. Highly skilled therapists utilized a mastery approach to teaching. Adherence, process variables, social validity, and clinical significance data were not reported. The results of the 13-session program indicated that there were no significant differences between interventions in changes in percentage overweight. Across groups, children demonstrated a reduction in their percentage overweight of −9.97% at 6 months and −8.04% at 1 year. The group only intervention was found to be significantly more cost effective than the mixed treatment. The systematic evaluation of cost and cost-effectiveness considerably strengthens the extent to which this intervention may be successfully disseminated.

Herrera, Johnston, and Steele (2004) examined the relative efficacies of cognitive and behavioral treatments. Results indicated that participation in the behavioral group (−9.51%) resulted in statistically greater reductions in the percentage overweight than did participation in the cognitive group (−5.53%). Follow-up data were not collected.

In summary, recent studies have identified treatment components that have increased the power of family-based treatment. These components include (1) reinforcing decreases in sedentary behavior and increases in physical activity (Epstein, Paluch, Gordy, Saelens et al., 2000), (2) mastery criteria and contingent reinforcement of treatment adherence behavior (Epstein, McKenzie et al., 1994), (3) parent training (Epstein et al., 1985), and (4) problem solving (Graves et al., 1988). Together, these studies demonstrate that at 1 year posttreatment, family-based behavioral weight control treatments may produce a wide range of outcomes, ranging from minor reductions for cognitively based treatments, to more significant reductions in the percentage overweight for comprehensive weight control programs involving behavioral parent training.

CONCLUSION

This chapter presents a review of randomized controlled trials evaluating the short- and long-term efficacy of family-based behavioral treatments for pediatric overweight. Studies were evaluated based on the degree to which they produced and maintained statistically and clinically significant changes in pediatric weight status. Based on this review, the following treatment components are useful in the effective treatment of pediatric obesity: (1) diet and nutrition education, (2) physical activity and contingency management, (3) mastery approaches to weight control education and behavior change, (4) behavioral parent training, and (5) problem solving. Across studies, at 1 year posttreatment, only modest reductions in the percentage overweight were found (range +1.4% to −26.5%). However, to better understand the practical implications of these outcomes for the diverse and widespread population of children coping with overweight, sample selection and description as well as key design elements, including protocol adherence, process variables, and social validity and dissemination, were also evaluated. Across studies, inadequate descriptions, exclusions, and other methodological weaknesses prevented a thorough analysis on all domains (see Table 14.1 for a summary of the findings).

Sample Selection and Description

In this review, 80% of the studies did not report both the ethnicity and socioeconomic status of the sample. At least one of these variables was reported by only 50% of the studies. Notably, however, of those reporting these data, samples were biased toward higher socioeconomic status, moderately overweight, preadolescent, and Caucasian children with few medical or psychological comorbidities (e.g., Epstein et al., 1995; Epstein, Paluch, Gordy, Saelens et al., 2000; Golan, Weizman et al., 1998). This is problematic, as some researchers have found that results from middle class, Caucasian families have not generalized to those from other groups—for example, families with diverse socioeconomic and ethnic backgrounds (Levine et al., 2001; Robinson et al., 2001). Given the higher prevalence of overweight in these diverse populations (Dietz, 2004), research efforts directed toward the effective prevention and treatment of overweight in disadvantaged and minority youth would be particularly valuable. Similarly, results obtained with preadolescent children may not generalize to a wider age range of children. Targeting early feeding dynamics may provide families with the skills to effectively prevent overweight and its sequelae (Satter, 2005). Although there currently are no data to support a firm assertion of a critical period for the development of healthy weight management behaviors, early childhood may represent an important window of opportunity for the identification and treatment of disrupted feeding and activity patterns (Birch & Fisher, 1998). These variables may provide unique subgroups to be considered in treatment development and evaluation.

Design Elements

Protocol Adherence

Both therapist adherence to treatment protocols and participant adherence to program recommendations are important variables to assess and report. In the studies reviewed, only one study included fidelity checks (Herrera, Johnston, & Steele, 2004) and only one other (Epstein, Valoski et al., 1994) collected data on the actual use of treatment techniques. Only one study described the qualifications of highly skilled therapists (Goldfield et al., 2001). No other studies reported protocol adherence, treatment fidelity, or therapist qualification data. Researchers were more likely to describe treatment components than to include manualized treatments or fidelity checks. Moreover, upon further investigation, treatment manuals were not published or publicly accessible (sometimes despite our efforts to acquire or purchase one from the primary investigator), compromising treatment replicability and dissemination. Although specific information on child adherence was not reported, treatment outcomes may be compromised if, for example, children are unable to successfully employ CBT techniques due to the difficulty of strategies or teaching method. We know from other literature that treatment adherence is a large problem and expect it to be no less of a problem here (O'Donohue & Levensky, 2006). Because of the lack of accessible treatment manuals and fidelity checks, little is known about provider training or supervision needs, and thus the cost of implementing existing treatments cannot be clearly ascertained. These limitations significantly compromise access to effective treatments and have profound implications for the successful management of childhood obesity at the population level. Given the essential nature of this design feature, future research would benefit from the inclusion of sound fidelity measures.

Social Validity

Research in the development and evaluation of pediatric obesity treatments has failed to consider issues of social validity. For example, two of the studies reviewed reported enrollment of less than 50% of interested participants (e.g., Epstein, Paluch, Gordy, & Dorn, 2000; Golan et al., 1998). Furthermore, only one study evaluated social validity via participant views of the utility of approaches (Epstein, McKenzie, et al., 1994). However, these data were not reported. Similarly, only 40% of studies reported clinical significance data. Thus the practical efficacy of these approaches for interested consumers is often unclear.

Scalability and Dissemination

Experts continue to struggle to develop effective strategies to treat childhood obesity because of a reliance on treatment approaches incongruent with the scope of the problem. Individual treatment approaches alone cannot effectively combat the rising prevalence of childhood obesity. Few investigators have examined the potential clinical and economic benefits of adopting a stepped care approach, including self-help, e-health, group, and community-based options. In this review, only one study (Goldfield et al., 2001) analyzed the cost and cost-effectiveness of multiple intervention approaches. No other studies included a discussion or analysis of the cost, cost-effectiveness, or accessibility of interventions. Future studies must examine the multiple layers of efficient and accessible treatment approaches possible in a stepped care model. Stepped care models aim to maximize the effectiveness and efficiency of the allocation of treatment resources (Fisher & O'Donohue, 2006). Stepped care models may be successful at bridging the gap between the current demand for effective childhood obesity treatments and the existing minimal supply.

The field would benefit from research investigating the clinical effectiveness and social validity of low-cost, accessible, and efficient stepped care approaches. A few progressive researchers are already addressing this notion (e.g., Harvey-Berino, Pintauro, Buzzell, & Gold, 2004; Saelens et al., 2002; Tate, Wing, & Winett, 2001). For example, Tate et al. (2001) showed that Internet-based behavioral treatment for adult weight loss produces superior outcomes to a Web-based information only condition. Harvey-Berino et al. (2004) found that an Internet-based weight management condition was equivalent to face-to-face maintenance strategies. Similarly, further research investigating the clinical efficacy of school-based nutrition programs (e.g., Simonetti D'Arca et al., 1986), community-based approaches (e.g., Coleman et al., 2005), and other novel interventions (e.g., video games, cartoons, etc.) is warranted. A review of population-based programs is beyond the scope of this chapter. Interested readers are referred to Fowler-Brown and Kahwati (2004). Pediatric obesity research must begin to look beyond efficacy and consider the criticism that existing programs have not yet been widely adopted in the applied realm (Barlow & Dietz, 2002). Treatment approaches that increase the number of children who can be successfully treated in a cost-effective manner will surely be welcomed in addressing the current epidemic.

In conclusion, several methodological advances could strengthen the extant literature. Future research may benefit from considering (1) early intervention and prevention, as the problems of young children may be less refractory; (2) cultural acceptability of treatment approaches; (3) measurement of process variables to see the extent to which hypothesized active ingredients have been instantiated; (4) research technologies that can be scaled (e.g., self-help books, e-health); and (5) consistent measurement and reporting of clinical significance (e.g., provide pre- and posttreatment deviation from maximum ideal weight). The adoption of these advances may improve the dissemination and effectiveness of current treatments.

REFERENCES

Barlow, S., & Dietz, W. (2002). Management of child and adolescent obesity: summary and recommendations based on reports from pediatricians, pediatric nurse practitioners and registered dieticians. *Pediatrics, 110,* 236–238.

Birch, L., & Fisher, J. (1998). Development of eating behaviors among children and adolescents. *Pediatrics, 101,* 539–549.

Coleman, K., Tiller, C., Sanchez, J., Heath, E, Sy, O., Milliken, G., & Dzewaltowski, D. (2005). Prevention of the epidemic increase in child risk of overweight in low income schools: the El Paso coordinated approach to child health. *Archives of Pediatric and Adolescent Medicine, 159,* 217–224.

Committee on Nutrition. (2003). Prevention of pediatric overweight and obesity. *Pediatrics, 112,* 424–430.

Dietz, W. H. (1998). Health consequences of obesity in youth: childhood predictors of adult disease. *Pediatrics, 101,* 554–570.

Dietz, W. H. (2004). Overweight in childhood and adolescence. *New England Journal of Medicine, 350,* 855–857.

D'Zurilla, T. J., & Goldfired, M. R. (1971). Problem solving and behavior modification. *Journal of Abnormal Psychology, 78*(1), 107–126.

Epstein, L. H., Gordy, C., Raynor, H., Beddome, M., Kilanowski, C., & Paluch, R. (2001). Increasing fruit and vegetable intake and decreasing fat and sugar intake in families at risk for childhood obesity. *Obesity Research, 9*(3), 171–178.

Epstein, L. H., Myers, M. D., Raynor, H .A., & Saelens, B. E. (1998). Treatment of pediatric obesity. *Pediatrics, 101*(3), 554–570.

Epstein, L. H., McKenzie, S., Valoski, A., Klein, R., & Wing, R. (1994). Effects of mastery criteria and contingent reinforcement for family-based child weight control. *Addictive Behaviors, 19,* 135–145.

Epstein, L. H., Paluch, R., Gordy, C., & Dorn, J. (2000). Decreasing sedentary behaviors in treating pediatric obesity. *Archives of Pediatric and Adolescent Medicine, 154,* 220–226.

Epstein, L. H., Paluch, R. A., Gordy, C., Saelens, B. E., & Ernst, M. M. (2000). Problem solving in the treatment of childhood obesity. *Journal of Consulting and Clinical Psychology, 68,* 717–721.

Epstein, L. H., Valoski, A., Vara, L., McCurley, J., Wisniewski, L., Kalarchian, M., Klein, K. R., & Shrager, L. R. (1995). Effects of decreasing sedentary behavior and increasing activity on weight change in obese children. *Health Psychology, 14,* 109–118.

Epstein, L. H., Valoski, A., Wing, R. R., & McCurley, J. (1994). Ten-year outcomes of behavioral family-based treatment for childhood obesity. *Health Psychology, 13,* 373–383.

Epstein, L. H., Wing, R., Koeske, R., & Valoski, A. (1984). Effects of diet plus exercise on weight change in parents and children. *Journal of Consulting and Clinical Psychology, 52,* 429–437.

Epstein, L. H., Wing, R., Woodall, K., Penner, B., Kress, M., & Koeske, R. (1985). Effects of family based behavioral treatment on obese 5- to 8-year-old children. *Behavior Therapy, 16,* 205–212.

Fagot-Campagna, A., Pettitt, D., Engelgan, M. Burrow, N., Geiss, L., Valdez, R., Beckles, G. L., Saaddine, J., Gregg, E. W., Williamson, D. F., & Narayan, K. M. (2000). Type 2 diabetes among North American children and adolescents: an epidemiologic review and a public health perspective. *Journal of Pediatrics, 136,* 664–672.

Fisher, J. E., & O'Donohue, W. T. (Eds.). (2006). *Practitioners guide to evidence-based psychotherapy.* New York: Springer.

Flodmark, C. E., Ohlsson, T., Ryden, O., & T. Sveger (1993). Prevention of progression to severe obesity in a group of obese schoolchildren treated with family therapy. *Pediatrics, 91*(5), 880–884.

Fowler-Brown, A., & Kahwati, L. (2004). Prevention and treatment of overweight in children and adolescents. *American Family Physician, 69,* 2591–2598.

Golan, M., Fainaru, M., & Weizman, A. (1998). Role of behavior modification in the treatment of childhood obesity with the parents as the exclusive agents of change. *International Journal of Obesity Related Metabolic Disorders, 22,* 1217–1224.

Golan, M., Weizman, A., Apter, A., & Fainaru, M. (1998). Parents as the exclusive agents of change in the treatment of childhood obesity. *American Journal of Clinical Nutrition, 67,* 1130–1135.

Goldfield, G., Epstein, L., Kilanowski, C., Paluch, R., & Kogut-Bossler, B. (2001). Cost-effectiveness of group and mixed family-based treatment for childhood obesity. *International Journal of Obesity and Related Metabolic Disorders, 25,* 1843–1849.

Graves, T., Meyers, A. W., & Clark, L. (1988). An evaluation of parental problem-solving training in the behavioral treatment of childhood obesity. *Journal of Consulting and Clinical Psychology, 56*(2), 246–250.

Harvey-Berino, J., Pintauro, S., Buzzell, P., & Gold, E. (2004). Effect of internet support on the long-term maintenance of weight loss. *Obesity Research, 12,* 320–329.

Herrera, E. A., Johnston, C. A., & Steele, R. G. (2004). A comparison of cognitive and behavioral treatments for pediatric obesity. *Children's Health Care, 33,* 151–167.

International Obesity Task Force. (2005). EU platform on diet, physical activity, and health. London: International Obesity Task Force. Available at www.iotf.org/media/euobesity3.pdf.

Israel, A. Guile, C., Baker, J., & Silverman, W. (1994). An evaluation of enhanced self-regulation training in the treatment of childhood obesity. *Journal of Pediatric Psychology, 19,* 737–749.

Israel, A., Stolmaker, L., & Andrian, C. (1985). The effects of training parents in general child management skills on a behavioral weight loss program for children. *Behavior Therapy, 16,* 169–180.

Jacobson, N., & Truax, P. (1991). Clinical significance: a statistical approach to defining meaningful change in psychotherapy research. *Journal of Consulting and Clinical Psychology, 59,* 12–19.

Jelalian, E., & Saelens, B. (1999). Empirically supported treatments in pediatric psychology: pediatric obesity. *Journal of Pediatric Psychology, 24,* 223–248.

Kazdin, A. E., & Weisz, J. R. (1998). Identifying and developing empirically supported child and adolescent treatments. *Journal of Consulting and Clinical Psychology, 66,* 19–36.

Kirk, S., Scott, B. J., & Daniels, S. (2005). Pediatric obesity epidemic: treatment options. *Journal of the American Dietetic Association, 105,* S44–S51.

Kirschenbaum, D. S., Harris, E. S., & Tomarken, A. J. (1984). Effects of parental involvement in behavioral weight loss therapy for preadolescents. *Behavior Therapy, 15,* 485–500.

Kuczmarski, R. J., Ogden, C. L., Guo, S. S., et al. (2002). CDC growth charts for the United States: methods and development. *Vital Health Statistics 11,* 246, 1–190.

Levine, M. D., Ringham, R. M., Kalarchian, M. A., Wisniewski, L., & Marcus, M. D. (2001). Is family-based behavioral weight control appropriate for severe pediatric obesity? *International Journal of Eating Disorders, 30*(3), 318–328.

Miller, W. R., & Rollnick, S. (2002). *Motivational interviewing: preparing people for change* (2nd ed.). New York: Guilford.

National Center for Health Statistics. (2001). Prevalence of overweight among children and adolescents: United States, 1999–2000. National Health and Nutrition Examination Survey (NHANES). Atlanta: Centers for Disease Control. Available at www.cdc.gov/nchs/products/pubs/pubd/hestats/overwght99.htm.

O'Donohue, W. T., & Levensky, E. R. (Eds.). (2006). *Promoting treatment adherence: a practical handbook for health care providers.* Thousand Oaks, CA: Sage Publications.

Patterson, G. R. (1976). *Living with children: new methods for parents and teachers* (revised ed.). Champaign, IL: Research Press.

Paul, G. L. (1967). Outcome research in psychotherapy. *Journal of Consulting Psychology, 31,* 109–118.

Perepletchikova, F., & Kazdin, A. E. (2005). Treatment integrity and therapeutic change: issues and research recommendations. *Clinical Psychology Science and Practice, 12,* 365–383.

Prochaska, J. O., & DiClemente, C. C. (1984). Self change processes, self efficacy and decisional balance across five stages of smoking cessation. *Progress in Clinical and Biological Research, 156,* 131–140.

Robinson, T. N., Chang, J. Y., Haydel, K. F., & Killen, J. D. (2001). Overweight concerns and body dissatisfaction among third-grade children: The impacts of ethnicity and socioeconomic status. *Journal of Pediatrics, 138*(2), 181–187.

Saelens, B., Sallis, J., Wilfley, D., Patrick K. Cella, J., & Buchta, R. (2002). Behavioral weight control for overweight adolescents initiated in primary care. *Obesity Research, 10,* 22–32.

Satter, E. (2005). *Your child's weight: helping without harming.* Madison, WI: Kelcy Press.

Schneider, M., & Brill, S. (2005). Obesity in children and adolescents. *Pediatrics in Review, 26,* 155–162.

Simonetti D'Arca, A., Tarsitani, G., Cairella, M., Siani, V., De Filippis, S., Mancinelli, S., Marazzi, M. C., & Palombi, L. (1986). Prevention of obesity in elementary and nursery school children. *Public Health, 100,* 166–173.

Tate, D., Wing, R., & Winett, R. (2001). Using Internet technology to deliver a behavioral weight loss program. *JAMA, 285,* 1172–1177.

Tracey, T., & Tracey, C. E. (1999). Integration of theory, research design, measurement, and analysis: toward a reasoned argument. *Counseling Psychologist, 27,* 299–324.

World Health Organization. (2005). Global strategy on diet, physical activity, and health: obesity and overweight. Geneva: World Health Organization. Available at www.who.int/dietphysicalactivity/publications/facts/obesity/en/

Young-Hyman, D., Schlundt, D.G., Herman, L., DeLuca, F., & Counts, D. (2001). Evaluation of the insulin resistance syndrome in 5- to 10-year old overweight/obese African-American children. *Diabetes Care, 24,* 1359–1364.

15

Behavioral Treatment of the Overweight Child and Families in Medical Settings

AMANDA N. ADAMS AND MARK A. ADAMS

Childhood obesity is now recognized as a major medical and public health problem. Overweight and obese children often become overweight and obese adults and obesity in adults is associated with many serious medical complications that impair the quality of life and lead to increased morbidity. As early as 10 years ago, evidence about an alarming increase in the number of overweight and obese adults and children across the United States and many other countries began to surface (Dietz, 1998). This trend has continued into the later half of the current decade (Dietz, 2004), and investigations into the effects of obesity on both adults and children reveal a variety of detrimental outcomes. There is little debate that overweight and obese adults and children are an at-risk population, and the number of adults and children in this category has now reached epidemic proportions.

It is the purpose of this chapter to provide a reader with a summary (not a comprehensive review) of some of the major trends and future directions of behavior treatments of overweight children and their families in medical and other settings. Given this title, medical treatments will not be the focus, but rather behavioral treatments that are appropriate or are in current use in medical settings. Also, in the interest of parsimony, we limited our search to two databases: PsychINFO and PubMed. The following terms and words were used to search each database: childhood obesity and behavioral treatment, obesity, family and child, and behavioral. The total number of articles found was 88 (52 on PsychINFO and 36 on PubMed). Upon further review of the abstracts, 53 peer-reviewed journal articles, book reviews, or book chapters seemed relevant to this chapter. Information from these sources is referenced below in response to the following: a summary of the best available scientific evidence bearing on behavioral treatment of the overweight child and family, recommendations for further research, and a discussion of practical implications of the current status of obesity and behavior treatments for children and families.

onto a placement. There is some incorporation of behavioral components, such as goal setting and reinforcement (handouts on reinforcement are included in the written materials), although the program's leaders, who are dieticians and pediatric endocrinologists, currently have not incorporated techniques such as self-monitoring, behavioral contracting, or education on prompting and stimulus control strategies. Outcomes of this program are not yet available, as it is a new initiative. Figures on the success and impact of this program will likely be available within the next year or two. While the focus in this chapter is on the behavioral components, the most commonly used diet and exercise components will be mentioned briefly.

There is some evidence that lifestyle exercise programs, which emphasize ways to incorporate less intense, but regular physical activity into daily activities versus intense or very programmed exercise programs, are more effective (Epstein et al., 1987; Johnson et al., 1997). Epstein's (1996) Traffic Light Diet is a diet that provides easy to understand guidelines for controlling food choices and intake, and is a commonly used approach for the dietary component in many studies that also use behavioral techniques. Many other dietary guidelines and programs are seen in the research and vary in their caloric restriction and fat versus protein intake, as well as other differences; however, all dietary components seek to educate the participant on good dietary choices and provide some method of assisting adherence to this end. While physical activity and diet are the behaviors to be changed in any weight loss intervention, the accomplishment of this change is the reason to develop a strategy based on behavioral techniques and principles. This is the "how-to" aspect of behavior change. That is, the behavioral components of an intervention program address not what to change, but the tools and methods of how to change.

Behavioral Interventions

Several behavioral strategies have accumulated over time considerable empirical support. The components that now comprise a state-of-the-art behavioral treatment package include reinforcement strategies, prompting, stimulus control, modeling, self-monitoring, contracting, and contingency management, and we add to this list problem-solving strategies (Epstein et al., 1990; Epstein & Wing, 1987; Epstein, Wing, Koeske, Andrasik, & Ossip, 1981; Graves et al., 1988). Arguably, the foremost researcher in behavioral treatment for childhood obesity is Leonard Epstein. With widely read published research dating back nearly three decades, it is nearly impossible to find research on behavioral interventions in obesity that has not involved or heavily referenced Epstein and his work. This acknowledgement is made here because this list of behavioral intervention components is, with only one exception, entirely derived from papers authored by Epstein and his colleagues. The exception, we will argue, is, in fact, appropriately grouped as a behavioral intervention, although it is not referred to as such by its authors. This exception is parental problem-solving training in the treatment of childhood obesity (Graves et al., 1988).

Problem Solving. Problem solving is described as a successful treatment that was run as a comparison to traditional behavioral treatment by Graves et al. (1988) and was shown to be more effective than treating the child alone with a traditional behavioral package. However, the technique of problem solving includes teaching parents, through skills training, to discriminate the preferred food choice, leading to a preferred behavioral outcome. This is nearly identical to many types of behavioral skills training procedures that appear in the behavioral literature, and the outcomes— effecting behavior change—are consistent with the goals of behavioral skills training. In the Graves et al. (1988) study, it may have been that the important distinction between the more effective parent problem-solving condition and the less effective child alone behavioral intervention condition was not the problem solving versus the behavioral treatment (as the authors concluded), but rather the inclusion of parental involvement over child alone, which has been shown in other studies to produce more favorable outcomes. We emphasize this point not to be contrary, but to make the case that although problem-solving training may not always be conceived of as a behavioral strategy, it actually is a very appropriate inclusion in this group of techniques. In the interest of addressing the goals of this chapter, we did not want to leave out problem solving, but also a rationale for its inclusion might be necessary for those readers familiar with Graves et al.'s research or other similar techniques. The question of what exactly constitutes a "behavioral" treatment will be addressed later in the chapter.

The other strategies in the list have a well-documented history in the literature on treatment for childhood obesity and are also rooted in a rich history of behavioral publications. Reinforcement, promoting, modeling, stimulus control, self-monitoring, and contracting have been extensively studied across disciplines and their effectiveness extends to many areas of behavior change. Each of these behavioral strategies will be described in terms of research recommendations and general application.

Reinforcement

Reinforcement may be the most generalizable behavioral principle and is a cornerstone of any effective behavioral change program. Reinforcement strategies have been administered as social praise between parents and children, as well as from therapists to parents and children, with perhaps the greatest impact on treatment being that from parents to children (Epstein et al., 1987). The principle of reinforcement is appropriately regarded as providing praise or another reward to the participant after a desirable behavior occurs. This basic type of parent-child interaction is the foundation of building a positive parent-child relationship that involves not only overt verbal reinforcement, but also an accompanying nonverbal or intrinsic reinforcer that increases in value as a parent continues to praise the child for a job well done. Both extrinsic/overt reinforcers and covert/intrinsic reinforcers are likely at work, but only the overt reinforcers are observable direct measures of treatment components.

Prompting and Stimulus Control

Prompting can take many forms, including textual prompts, as in written guidelines or leaflets, verbal prompts from therapists or from the parent to the child, and within-stimulus prompts that are inherently a part of many self-monitoring techniques. Each of these prompting techniques is effective and appropriate, and many times these go unmentioned because they are such a common part of intervention models, used most often in supplying instructions and information and in providing tools for program implementation. Stimulus control procedures can vary widely. These techniques can be in the form of instructions from a therapist, such as cleaning out the fridge and cupboard to removing unwanted food choices. However, stimulus control procedures may have a secondary unintended, but beneficial effect, as they are likely to become part of a successful participant's changing behavioral repertoire. Over time, an individual learns to incorporate new lifestyle habits into their existing behavioral repertoire, thus setting their own stimulus cues (having shoes and clothes laid out for a morning walk or arranging your schedule to include an exercise class without being explicitly told to do so).

Modeling

Modeling is another well-researched behavioral procedure that, in terms of childhood weight loss, has been shown to be most effective in terms of parents modeling preferred behaviors for their children. This has many implications. Modeling shows a strong effect for observational learners who wish to emulate the behavior of a trusted adult. In addition, if parents are modeling a preferred behavior (i.e., choosing a salad rather than pizza), not only is the child learning by observation, but may also have more favorable conditions in which to perform this alternative behavior. That is, the setting has changed. The response on the part of a child who is somewhat motivated to choose salad over pizza is greatly enhanced if an adult has not only modeled the response, but in so doing has provided the ingredients and the encouragement to do so. Compare that behavioral choice to a parent who models choosing pizza and expects the child to choose a salad. Not only has there been an opportunity for contrary or "unwanted" observational learning, the salad ingredients may not even be within sight, thus changing the setting as well as the model.

Self-Monitoring

Self-monitoring has been shown to have robust behavior change effects. Being aware of one's own behavior is sometimes all that is required for behavior changes along some dimension, such as frequency or intensity. Self-monitoring has been used for both adults and children, with the greatest effects being seen when children are responsible for recording food choices and exercise sessions. Self-monitoring can be done in many ways, from keeping a detailed journal (writing down all food consumed, as well as other habits such as water intake and physical activity) to recording behaviors and food choices on a simple checklist. The benefits of simplifying record keeping in self-monitoring for children are apparent. Self-monitoring intervention strategies should always be developed while considering the child's age and abilities. A younger child with fewer skills will need simple checklists, perhaps with stickers and pictures, to do effective self-monitoring, while an older child can use a planner or keep written checklists. Much like completing homework or practicing the piano is monitored by parents, self-monitoring systems should be used in conjunction with parental supervision and support.

Behavioral Contracts

Behavioral contracting involves a written document stating goals and the reward or other outcome for meeting (or failing to meet) the stated goals. Usually guidelines for goal writing include keeping the goal feasible or realistic, measurable, observable (recordable), and on a proposed timeline. The other part of the contract involves rewards for achieving the goals. These are sometimes facilitated by another party. Money has been included as a consequence in many behavioral contracts for weight loss. In many cases the consequence is the loss of money already put forth for this purpose by the participant. Contracts are a good general method in that they have inherent flexibility. They can be rewritten to state appropriate goals for any individual, with consequences that are individualized to incorporate meaningful outcomes for each participant. Contracts can be mediated by significant others, family members, parents, or professionals (trainers, therapists, etc.). Just as self-monitoring strategies are adjusted for a child's age and ability level, so a behavioral contract is written in language that is easily understood by a child and in such a way that the content is appealing. The reinforcers that are stated in a contract should be carefully determined by going over the child's preferences and negotiating what is reasonable and manageable for the parents while still being highly reinforcing to the child. For instance, money may appeal to older children, while a trip to the zoo or water park may appeal to younger children. This section of the behavioral contract must be highly individualized to be effective and is best done with a trained behavior analyst who is well versed in assessing reinforcers and related factors that may change the effectiveness of the chosen reinforcing item or activity.

Contingency Management

Contingency management is listed by Epstein et al. (1981) as the final component in their behavioral treatment package. Contingency management consists of an educational teaching module with quizzes to ensure that participants are actually learning what behavioral changes are expected of them (Epstein et al., 1981). In a more traditional behavior analytical description, contingency management, very broadly, consists of any number of antecedent and consequent strategies that are used to change the contingent relationship among variables in similar, recurring situations, such as eating behaviors. Investigating questions such as what are the stimuli that occasion "food-getting" behaviors, what foods are typically selected, and how much is selected can provide insight into important or controlling antecedent and consequent events that can shape and change food-getting behavior.

Contingencies for behavior can be conceptualized as the reasons why someone engages in a particular behavior. Managing the reasons why we behave is very important for self-control, self-monitoring, and other classes of behavior related to planning, monitoring, reinforcing, and punishing one's own behavior. Contingency management is also vitally important for the initial engagement in and the eventual lasting and sustaining changes in daily behavioral routines. A description of a typical contingency related to eating is provided below to help illustrate the role contingencies can play in the development of an overweight or obese person.

The typical contingency for the behavior of eating is as follows: antecedents to hunger, such as a growling stomach, are followed by the behavior of eating something, which is positively reinforced by removing the "feeling" of hunger and also positively reinforced if what is eaten is delicious and is associated with feeling good, fun, and pleasure. Foods that "taste good" and are usually most preferred are often those that are the most likely to create excess body fat because these foods include those that are high in fat and sugar and low in nutritional value—the so-called comfort foods. The reasons we fall into the habit of choosing less healthy food portions over less calorie dense options have to do with biologic systems developed for survival and a complex learning history consisting of receiving immediate reinforcement (taste, satiation, emotional state) when these easily available food options are consumed. In the United States and other developed countries, marketing, easy availability, and portion expansion are also issues deserving of mention; these are discussed more later in the chapter. This is an oversimplified analysis, but it begins to explain the complexities involved in developing a behavioral pattern of choosing unhealthy food options. However, this pattern can be relearned and changed.

Children and adults can learn to respond to the antecedents of hunger by eating healthy foods, and contingency management strategies grounded in the principles of behavior appear to be most effective in establishing contingencies for eating that promote healthy foods, appropriate portions, and other aspects of a healthy diet. In order to manage contingencies, one must engage first in education (why is this not a good choice, and what other choices are available) and then systematically create an environment in which engaging in the new preferred response is supported. This can be effectively accomplished through a combination of the following behavioral techniques: stimulus cues, prompting, modeling, reinforcement, problem solving, self-monitoring, and behavioral contracting.

RECOMMENDATIONS FOR FURTHER RESEARCH

The recommendations for further research are presented in two categories: conceptual and methodological. Conceptual issues are mentioned here as they relate to the basic assumptions guiding techniques and methods considered as treatment options for the phenomenon being analyzed, in this case obesity and overweight. Methodological issues are also only briefly discussed, in part because of the number of areas in need of future research.

Conceptual Issues

After reviewing the literature, three conceptual issues seem worth mentioning. First, there does not seem to be clear criteria for which a particular treatment would be considered behavioral. This is an important question because if determining factors of clear behavioral intervention can be described, then it may be possible to develop and implement behavioral intervention programs for this and other related health issues. Second, should we conceptualize overweight and obesity as a "disease"? This question is posed because the conceptualization of the problem has implications of whether it is treated with a medical model by drugs and medical procedures or conceptualized in a behavioral model as a set of behaviors appropriate for intervention by training new skills and developing new patterns of behavior. Third, and last, should we conceptualize overweight and obesity as an individual and family problem or as a societal problem that warrants contingency management strategies developed for large groups, such as communities or counties. The relevance of this issue is the assignment of responsibility and allocation of funding for the development and implementation of intervention approaches and also the nature of the intervention itself.

How to Determine if a Treatment Is Behavioral

The establishment of some basic evaluative questions for deciding if a treatment or treatment component should be considered a "behavioral" intervention is helpful in the conceptualization of the types of treatment procedures. While one researcher may consider any use of a behavioral principle or procedure to be a behavioral intervention, another may require more stringent criteria. For example, it can be argued that in order for a treatment to be considered behavioral, it must meet all of the following conditions: (1) must identify and demonstrate the use of a behavioral principle or technique, such as shaping or reinforcement; (2) must collect objective data prior to the implementation of treatment to establish baseline-dependent measures for treatment evaluation purposes; (3) must establish treatment goals related to baseline-dependent measures; and (4) must utilize data to guide treatment decisions. Some standards have been set within the field of applied behavioral analysis, including the treatment of childhood obesity, and would fit well within either framework provided by a cornerstone article by Baer, Wolf, and Risley (1968) and recently in a new publication, *How to Think Like a Behavior Analyst* (Bailey & Burch, 2005). The reader is referred to these publications for a more in-depth discussion of qualifiers for behavioral treatment.

Obesity: A Disease?

Insurance companies typically cover expenses related to medical conditions or "diseases" and are reluctant to cover expenses for the same services for conditions not categorized as diseases. For example, behavioral services for treating children diagnosed with autism are typically covered under insurance policies. However, behavioral services that are fundamentally the same are not covered when they are used as a treatment for children who are obese.

Until such a time that insurance will pay primary medical care providers for treating obese and overweight conditions, alternatives should be considered. For example, the lack of treatment providers presents an opportunity for another group or type of service provider to meet the need. Behavior analysts at the bachelor's and master's levels (BCABA and BCBA, respectively) are a potential group of service providers trained in the application of behavioral techniques, methods, and behavioral principles. Behavioral expertise is one aspect of a multifaceted approach that can be adopted within a medical setting. It is proposed that multidisciplinary teams within medical facilities include behaviorally trained and qualified personnel (i.e., board certified behavior analysts) to provide this specific expertise within the framework of developing appropriate individualized behavioral interventions within a medical setting. It is unlikely that insurance companies will cover behavioral interventions straight out. Services for obesity intervention or prevention are likely to be covered only if a person with behavioral expertise is working in conjunction with a physician who can bill the insurance company under his or her credentials. This may change in the future as the cost savings become more and more apparent.

Communitywide and Large-Scale Intervention Strategies

There are many health issues that are considered community or public health issues, even though they affect individual persons. When a health problem is common enough to affect many people within a population, it should be considered an issue worthy of public attention. The controversy of what is private and what is public becomes difficult to sort out. It can be argued that the fact that taxes go to pay for many societal health problems makes issues that seem entirely private (how one eats and exercises) actually become someone else's business. Agree or disagree, the American population is in a position with obesity that demands intervention not only on the individual level, but also on the community and societal levels.

Individuals, families, and small groups of people have clearly benefited from behavioral treatment of obesity and overweight. However, communities, cities, and states have less often been targeted for this type of effort. Although some excellent efforts have been researched and continue to be explored (including government programs like Healthy People 2010 and various American Heart Association programs), these large-scale interventions have not yet made large-scale impacts on the public. An excellent and comprehensive review of community-based health programs was published by Merzel and D'Afflitti (2003). They state that evidence from the past 20 years indicates that community-based programs have had only a modest impact overall (Merzel & D'Afflitti, 2003). Establishing feasible and attainable short- and long-term goals for communities and cities for reducing the number of children and adults who are obese or overweight, as well as decreasing the rates of other indicators such as the number of type 2 diabetes diagnoses, healthier lunch programs for schools, and generating corporate responsibility from companies that produce unhealthy food options, is critical to the types of societal changes necessary to significantly impact this epidemic in the future.

Many large companies have published data on the effectiveness of their worksite wellness programs (Erfurt, Foote, & Heirich, 1991a,b). Efforts to increase physical activity and increase the availability of healthy food choices have produced some very creative strategies, from group walking programs on the lunch hour to in-house fitness facilities. Insurance companies have noticed the financial impact and have offered price breaks for nonsmokers and people who are of normal BMI and blood pressure. Worksite programs have made a difference in the health of their employees, as evidenced by savings in their bottom line (Erfurt, Foote, & Heirich, 1991b). The hope now is that programs can be developed that will be appropriate for smaller companies and firms that may not be able to count the savings in the thousand's of dollars, but would produce significant quality of life changes for employees nonetheless. Rationale for worksite wellness programs includes the 40-plus hours a week people spend at their jobs (a significant amount of time) and the ability of the workplace to implement meaningful rewards. Health promotion in the workplace is an exciting and important area for continued research and application.

Providing program development and design assistance based on effective strategies demonstrated at the individual, family, and small group levels and applied to the masses is greatly needed. An agent for change within communities and large institutions, such as public education, must be identified and charged with this responsibility and then given appropriate support to begin the process of contingency management at the societal level. Input from a national council on the regulation of packed and processed food content, portion sizes, and other large-scale contingency management strategies for producers, suppliers, and stakeholders involved in food production and marketing may be a necessary control if the country is to effectively make a difference in the consumption habits of its population within a generation's time. Even a measure as dramatic as controlling food production standards is likely to have a modest effect on the goal of changing purchasing and consumption habits to the point that it changes actual weight, BMI, cholesterol, blood pressure, and other factors.

Another level of attack should come from the medical community. Although many large health and medical organizations have begun efforts of public health education, more can be done to help change the behaviors of those organizations and the general population. This is, of course, a very difficult goal to accomplish in a measurable way. The stimulus cues that carry the message of actual behavior change (i.e., "eat more fruits and veggies" or "take the stairs") are so embedded in the hundreds of other daily cues that they may either not be salient enough to discern effectively or are of too low an impact to effectively change behavior. It is a step in the right direction, however, and perhaps increasing the number, frequency, and saliency of the cues encountered from the medical community would pack more of a punch. For instance, it may send more of a message if general handouts in the front office of every medical office were followed up with a series of "tips" that patients would receive personally from their medical professional (physician, physician's assistant, or registered nurse) every time they saw him or her for any reason, (i.e., this month we are talking to patients about taking more steps throughout the day—here is a tip sheet on that topic).

Publicity Campaigns and Other Information Interventions

The amount of money necessary to mount these types of campaigns versus their utility in other areas, such as funding research efforts at the primary care level, in public school lunch programs, and in litigation that would restrict the kind of foods vendors can supply for children on campuses at all levels of education, including colleges and universities, would be another excellent area for future research.

Professionals with expertise in areas other than nutrition and medicine should be involved in any successful campaign. Marketing and advertising professionals, for instance, know strategies that nutritionists and physicians do not. Likewise, the qualifications of the individuals conducting the behavioral treatments should also be considered a research variable, as the most cost-effective strategies will most likely require large numbers of relatively inexperienced treatment practitioners from all walks of life, as this epidemic has reached virtually all populations of the United States and other countries worldwide (Speiser et al., 2005).

Methodological Considerations

Methodologically, behavioral components of treatment packages lack enough detailed information so that they can be replicated in a variety of settings for reliability and feasibility analyses. For example, Mellon's "ShapeDown" and the Dairy Council's "LifeSteps" are examples of programs that include guide manuals and participant materials that have been validated in controlled studies, can be implemented with novice instructors (that could be compensated at a more modest wage than a doctor would accept), and can be used for large numbers of participants (Mellin, Croughan-Mini-hane, & Dickey, 1997; Yen, Edington, McDonald, Hirschland, & Edington, 2001). These programs (as well as many others) also have accompanying Web sites that allow individuals to participate from home. The new modality of using the Internet for weight loss and health promotion has an enormous potential impact. Although we do not have the space to go into a discussion of it in this chapter, it should be noted that research evaluating Web-based intervention programs will be a huge area for public health promotion. Information is, as yet, incomplete, but Web-based programs are expected to grow extremely quickly.

What seems somewhat unresolved is specific descriptions of behavioral treatment packages and more careful analyses of the controlling variables in long-term behavior change. For example, we know many components that work (behavioral contracts, goal setting, education about making healthy choices), but the medical and health communities are not yet in agreement that certain components are vital to a behavioral treatment package. It seems that some medically oriented practices will continue to prescribe blood pressure medication before counseling a patient on lifestyle changes (i.e., behavior change). Perhaps this is because they do not believe the individual will engage in the change on their own, and perhaps it is because they still do not know what to tell them to do. "Eat right and exercise" has been shown to be an ineffective prescription. And despite the plentiful research, an agreement on the behavioral components that will make the jump from research to practice is still not apparent. To further illustrate the point, let us say (as a hypothetical example) that the leading behavioral intervention package turns out to include these elements: individual analysis of specific problem behaviors (eating late at night, exercising only once a week), followed by a behavioral contract stating specific goals related to the individual's issue and linked to meaningful outcomes or reinforcers for this individual. The development and implementation of the plan would be the job of a qualified BCBA working in conjunction with a physician in a medical setting. This would be accompanied by an education component offered at the facility or through an on-line self-education course. This package (in our fictitious example) was shown to be successful again and again, and was reported at medical conferences and began to be included in medical training programs such that it became adopted practice. The point being, that such adopted methodology still does not exist, and one reason may be that behavioral packages shown to have efficacy in the existing research have been varied, defined in general terms, and use a variety of personnel, leading to a general understanding that behavioral components are effective, but without specific information about what makes them work and why they work.

Targeting Specific Behaviors and Dependent Measures of Effectiveness

In most goal-setting programs, individuals are instructed to name a behavior they would like to change. "Loosing 15 pounds" or "achieving a 23 BMI" are not behaviors, they are outcomes. The actual behaviors needed to achieve those outcomes include things like walking 20 minutes every morning, not eating after 8:00 p.m., eating lean meat and vegetables for dinner, etc. Various dependent measures such as weight loss, BMI reduction, or changes in levels of adiposity are thus impacted by specific behavioral changes. Certain behavior change options and related measures of effectiveness will directly relate to the feasibility of primary care and other treatment provider attempts to reach the general population. A careful analysis of specific behaviors to target that generalize to the largest portion of the population could be extremely beneficial for treatment feasibility. Medical professionals may still focus on numbers and raw data (blood pressure too high, weight too high), leading their patients to believe that the goal should be to decrease the "number." While this is the desired outcome, leading a patient to the goal statement "I need to lose 15 pounds" is not as helpful as the goal statement "I need to exercise Monday through Thursday and eliminate fast food." The point is that the messages people get should not be "change the number," but rather a message specifying a behavior change and how to do it. In short, focus on the "how," not on the "what."

This has already begun with various public health messages such as "increase your number of steps per day," "eat 5 a day," and those in the U.S. Dietary Guidelines. But as mentioned earlier in this chapter, there may have more impact on actual behavior change if they are increased in frequency and type.

PRACTICAL IMPLICATIONS

Efficacy has been demonstrated with behavioral treatment of obese and overweight children and families. If treatment must be for a lifetime, as many would argue is the case for the prevention and lack of recurrence of certain diseases, then developing a treatment system that can accomplish this is necessary. Some argue that in order to move from efficacy to effectiveness, treatment of overweight and obese individuals must occur at the primary care level (Caprio, 2006). This does not appear to be on the agenda of major primary care providers, or at least their efforts are not reaching the literature contained in the PsychINFO and PubMed databases. This may be because currently there is no reimbursement for what is a time-intense treatment. It may also be due to a lack of education on the medical practitioners part. Just as physicians, physician's assistants, and nurses are not trained in marketing information, they are also not trained in the science of behavior change. A multidisciplinary approach is a simple and cost-effective solution. Just as nutritionists have been included in several medical practices to counsel patients about dietary choices, so too could BCBAs be included to develop effective behavior change programs.

CONCLUSION

A movie that captured the attention of many Americans, "Super-Size Me" brings to light some startling facts about the way food is presented to children and youth in our society (Spurlock, 2004). Another relevant popular reference is *Fast Food Nation* (Scholosser, 2001). From the bombardment of fast food ads and the availability of vending machines full of unhealthy choices to inadequate school lunch programs, a lack of funding for physical education, and minimal support for clean parks and walking trails, it should not be a surprise that the trend is toward growing numbers of overweight and obese children, which consequently results in the growing numbers of overweight and obese adults, with their additional physical and perhaps psychological complications.

Behavioral treatments for obese and overweight children and adults are perhaps the most promising options currently available. A strategic and concerted effort to bring these treatments into our culture needs to occur to treat this growing epidemic.

REFERENCES

Baer, D. M., Wolf, M. M., & Risley, T. R. (1968). Some current dimensions of behavior analysis. *Journal of Applied Behavior Analysis, 1,* 91–97.

Bailey, J. S., & Burch, M. (2005). *How to think like a behavior analyst.* Mahwah, NJ: Lawrence Erlbaum.

Braet, C., Tanghe, A., Decaluwé, V., Moens, E., & Rosseel, Y. (2004). Inpatient treatment for children with obesity: weight loss, psychological well-being and eating behavior. *Journal of Pediatric Psychology, 29,* 519–529.

Caprio, S. (2006). Treating child obesity and associated medical conditions. *Future of Children, 16,* 209–224.

Centers for Disease Control. (2007). BMI—body mass index. Atlanta: Centers for Disease Control. Available at www.phppo.cdc.gov/nccdphp/dnpa/bmi/index.htm.

Charney, M., Goodman, H. C., McBride, M., Lyon, B., & Pratt, R. (1976). Childhood antecedents on adult obesity: Do chubby infants become obese adults? *New England Journal of Medicine, 295,* 6–9.

Dietz, W. H. (1998). Health consequences of obesity in youth: childhood predictors of adult disease. *Pediatrics, 101,* 554–570.

Dietz, W. H. (2004). Overweight in childhood and adolescence. *New England Journal of Medicine, 350,* 855–857.

Devlin, M. J., Wilson, T. G., & Yanovski, S .Z. (2000). Obesity: What mental health professionals need to know. American Journal of Psychiatry, 157, 854–866.

Erfurt, J. C., Foote, A., & Heirich, M. A. (1991a). The cost-effectiveness of work-site wellness programs for hypertension control, weight loss and smoking cessation. *Journal of Occupational Medicine, 33,* 962–970.

Erfurt, J. C., Foote, A., & Heirich, M. A. (1991b). Worksite wellness programs: incremental comparison of screening and referral alone, health education, follow-up counseling, and plant organization. *American Journal of Health Promotion, 5,* 438–448.

Epstein, L. H., McCurley, J., Wing, R. R., & Valoski, A. (1990). Five-year follow-up of family-based behavioral treatments for childhood obesity. *Journal of Consulting and Clinical Psychology, 58,* 661–664.

Epstein, L. H., & Wing, R. R. (1987). Behavioral treatment of childhood obesity. *Psychological Bulletin, 101,* 331–342.

Epstein, L. H., Wing, R. R., Koeske, R., Andrasik, F., & Ossip, D. J. (1981). Child and parent weight loss in family-based behavior modification programs. *Journal of Consulting and Clinical Psychology, 49,* 674–685.

Epstein, L. H., Wing, R. R., Koeske, R., & Valoski, A. (1987). Long-term effects of family-based treatment of childhood obesity. *Journal of Consulting and Clinical Psychology, 55,* 91–95.

Epstein, L. H., Coleman, K. J., & Myers, M. D. (1996). Exercise in treating obesity in children and adolescents. *Medicine & Science in Sports & Exercise, 28* (4), 428–435.

Ferraro, K. F., Thorpe, R. J., & Wilkinson, J. A. (2003). The life course of severe obesity: Does childhood overweight matter? *Journals of Gerontology. Series B, Psychological Sciences and Social Sciences, 58,* S110–S119.

Garn, S. M., Clark, D. C., Lowe, C. U., Forbes, G., Garn, S., Owen, G. M., Smith, N. J., Weil, W. B., Jr., Nichaman, M. Z., Johansen, E., & Rowe, N. (1976). Trends in fatness and the origins of obesity. *Pediatrics, 57,* 433–456.

Graves, T., Meyers, A. W., & Clark, L. (1988). An evaluation of parental problem-solving training in the behavioral treatment of childhood obesity. *Journal of Consulting and Clinical Psychology, 56,* 246–250.

Guo, S. S., Roche, A. F., Chumlea, W. C., Gardner, J. D., & Siervogel, R. M. (1994). The predictive value of childhood body mass index values for overweight at age 35 y. *American Journal of Clinical Nutrition, 59,* 810–819.

Johnson, W., Hinkle, L., Carr, R., Anderson, D., Lemmon, C., Engler, L., & Bergeron, K. (1997). Dietary and exercise interventions for juvenile obesity: long-term effect of behavioral and public health models. *Obesity Research, 5,* 257–261.

Johnston, F. E., & Mack R.W. (1978). Obesity in urban black adolescents of high and low relative weight at 1 year of age. *American Journal of Disabled Children,132* (9), 862–864.

Mellin, L., Croughan-Minihane, M., & Dickey, L. (1997). The solution method: 2-year trends in weight, blood pressure, exercise, depression and functioning of adults trained in development skills. *Journal of the American Dietetic Association, 97,* 1133–1138.

Mei, Z., Grummer-Strawn, L. M., Pietrobelli, A., Goulding, A., Goran, M. I., & Dietz, W. H. (2002). Validity of body mass index compared with other body-composition screening indexes for the assessment of body fatness in children and adolescents. *American Journal of Clinical Nutrition, 75,* 978–985.

Merzel, C., & D'Afflitti, J. (2003). Reconsidering community-based health promotion: performance and potential. *American Journal of Public Health, 93,* 557–574.

Nemet, D., Barkan, S., Epstein, Y., Friedland, O., Kowen, G., & Eliakim, A. (2005). Short- and long-term beneficial effects of a combined dietary behavioral physical activity intervention for the treatment of childhood obesity. *Pediatrics, 115(4),* e443–e449. Available at http://pediatrics.aappublications.org/cgi/content/full/115/4/e443.

Ogden, C. L., Kuczmarski, R. J., Flegal, K. M., Mei Z., Guo, S., Wei, R., Grummer-Strawn, L. M., Curtin, L. R., Roche, A. F., & Johnson, C. L. (2002). Centers for Disease Control and Prevention 2000 growth charts for the United States: improvements to the 1977 National Center for Health Statistics version. *Pediatrics, 109,* 45–60.

Scholosser, E. (2001). *Fast-food nation: the dark side of the American meal.* New York: Houghton-Mifflin.

Speiser, P. W., Rudolf, M. C. J., Anhalt, H., Camacho-Hubner, C., Chiarelli, F., Eliakim, A., Freemark, M., Gruters, A., Hershkovitz, E., Iughetti, L., Krude, H., Latzer, Y., Lustig, R. H., Pescovitz, O. H., Pinhas-Hamiel, O., Rogol, A. D., Shalitin, S., Sultan, C., Stein, D., Vardi, P., Werther, G. A., Zadik, Z., Zuckerman-Levin, N., & Hochberg, Z., on behalf of the Obesity Consensus Working Group. (2005). Childhood obesity. *Journal of Clinical Endocrinology & Metabolism, 90,* 1871–1887.

Spurlock, M. (2004). *Supersize Me.* New York: Hart Sharp Video.

Whitaker, R. C., Wright, J. A., Pepe, M. S., Seidel, K. D., & Dietz, W. H. (1997). Predicting obesity in young adulthood from childhood and parental obesity. *New England Journal of Medicine, 337,* 869–873.

Wilson, T. G. (1994a). Behavioral treatment of childhood obesity: theoretical and practical implications. *Health Psychology, 13,* 371–372.

Wilson, T. G. (1994b). Behavioral treatment of obesity: thirty years and counting for a complete discussion. *Advances in Behavior Research and Therapy, 16,* 31–75.

Yen, L., Edington, M. P., McDonald, T., Hirschland, D., & Edington, D. W. (2001). Changes in health risks among the participants in the United Auto Workers–General Motors LifeSteps health promotion program. *American Journal of Health Promotion, 16,* 7–15.

16

School-Based Prevention of Child and Adolescent Obesity

MARY STORY AND KAREN M. KAPHINGST

INTRODUCTION

Schools have the potential to make valuable contributions to help improve children's eating and physical activity behaviors and thus to reduce child and adolescent obesity. More than 95% of American youth ages 5 to 17 years are enrolled in school, and no other institution has as much continuous and intensive contact with children during their first two decades of life. Four major components within schools provide a strong and viable forum for promoting good nutrition, physical activity, and healthy weights among youth: (1) the school food environment (e.g., healthy school meals and foods available in schools), (2) the school physical activity environment (e.g., physical education [PE], recess), (3) classroom health education, and (4) school health services. Because children eat a substantial portion of their daily energy at school, schools should provide an environment where children eat healthy foods and are exposed to and learn healthful eating patterns. PE classes and recess could be major resources for increasing energy expenditure in students. In addition, school facilities such as gyms and swimming pools could be open after school and on weekends and serve as community resources for students and families to increase physical activity. Classroom health education could help youth develop the knowledge, attitudes, and behavioral skills needed to establish and maintain healthy eating and a physically active lifestyle. Both primary and secondary prevention efforts are also feasible in school settings. Schools have access to school nurses and other health personnel who can provide screening, counseling, and a continuum of care. School-based health centers available in some schools provide health care and preventive services to students and thereby offer the potential for serving overweight youth. This chapter discusses these issues and the role of schools in obesity prevention and treatment efforts.

THE SCHOOL FOOD ENVIRONMENT

The school food environment can have a large impact on children's and adolescents' dietary intake because a substantial proportion of total daily energy is consumed at school. National data show that foods eaten at school comprise 19% to 50% of students' total daily energy intake (Gleason,

Suitor, & U.S. Food and Nutrition Service, 2001). Food is typically available for sale in schools in two ways: (1) formal school breakfast and lunch programs through the U.S. Department of Agriculture (USDA); and (2) "competitive foods," which are foods and beverages sold outside the federal school lunch and breakfast programs, such as from vending machines, a la carte offerings in the cafeteria, snack bars, school stores, and fundraisers (Trust for America's Health, 2006).

National School Breakfast and Lunch Programs

Today 99% of all public schools and 83% of total public and private schools participate in the National School Lunch Program (NSLP) (Fox, Hamilton, & Lin, 2004). The School Breakfast Program (SBP) is offered in about 78% of the schools that offer the NSLP (Fox et al., 2004). On an average school day, about 60% of children in schools that have the NSLP eat school lunch and about 37% of children in schools that participate in the SBP eat school breakfast. Meals served in the NSLP and SBP must meet federally defined nutrition standards in order for schools to be eligible for federal subsidies (cash reimbursements and donated commodities). Federal school lunches and breakfasts are required to provide approximately one-third of the recommended dietary allowances (RDAs) for lunch and one-fourth of the RDAs for breakfast for key nutrients. Since 1995, schools participating in the NSLP and SBP are required by the USDA to offer meals that meet the *Dietary Guidelines for Americans*, which include limits on total and saturated fat (no more than 30% of calories from fat and less than 10% of calories from saturated fat) (Fox, Hamilton, & Lin, 2004). While schools have made substantial improvements in reducing the average proportion of calories from fat in lunches, they still have significant progress to make (Fox, Crepinsek, Connor, & Battaglia, 2001; Gleason, Suitor, & U.S. Food and Nutrition Service, 2001). The majority (75%) of schools have not achieved lunches that meet the recommended 30% of calories from fat (Fox et al., 2001; Gleason et al., 2001). Elementary schools are doing better than high schools in meeting the dietary fat goals (Fox et al., 2001). So while progress in the nutritional profile of school meals has been made in the last 15 years, more efforts are needed to improve the nutrition quality of school meals.

School meal programs make an important contribution to school-age children's diets (Gleason et al., 2001). National data show that NSLP and SBP participation are associated with higher mean intakes of micronutrients compared to those who do not eat school meals. Further, the majority of participants (59%) eating school meals are low-income youth, and school meals provide a necessary safeguard against hunger (Food Research and Action Center, 2005). Participation in the NSLP declines drastically with age, with elementary students most likely to participate and high school students least likely (Gleason et al., 2001). Serving NSLP meals that are more tasty and appealing to the student population could encourage more students to participate in the school meal program. Some schools are hiring chefs and culinary experts to develop healthy, tasty meals and redesigning cafeterias to make them more youth friendly and cut down on long waiting lines.

A particularly important motivator for schools to address child nutrition is its link with academic performance. A recent review that examined the association between breakfast habits, nutritional status, body weight, and academic performance in children and adolescents found that breakfast consumption may improve cognitive function related to memory, test grades, and school attendance (Rampersaud, Pereira, Girard, Adams, & Metzl, 2005). Studies have also associated the federal SBP with increases in daily attendance, class participation, and academic test scores and decreases in tardiness (Action for Healthy Kids, 2004).

A major barrier to providing nutritious schools meals is budget pressures (General Accounting Office, 2003b). School food service programs, which were once regular line items in local school budgets, now must often be completely self-supporting (Department of Agriculture, 2001). Revenue from federal reimbursements and the sale of food are the principal sources of revenue for school food services. Options to enhance revenues include increasing the number of students who obtain federal meals at schools, expanding a la carte and catering sales, and increasing prices for full-price meals (General Accounting Office, 2003b). It is difficult to increase school meal participation when there are so many competing low-nutrition foods available throughout the school, and raising prices is difficult when students can purchase food at other school venues. To try to break even financially, many food service directors are compelled to sell popular, but nutritionally poor foods through a la carte (General Accounting Office, 2003b). Eliminating or restricting competitive foods may increase school meal participation.

Foods Sold Outside the National School Meal Programs (Competitive Foods)

The USDA defines competitive foods broadly to include all foods that are offered for sale at school, with the exception of meals served through the federal school meal program (General Accounting Office, 2004). Competitive foods include a la carte foods offered in the school cafeteria (individual foods and beverages sold separately from the school meal programs) and foods and beverages sold in snack bars, student stores, vending machines, and fundraisers (through which school-based organizations sell foods and beverages to raise money) (Food Research and Action Center, 2004).

The widespread availability of competitive foods in schools, which are primarily high-fat or high-sugar foods and energy-dense beverages, is well documented (French, Story, Fulkerson, & Gerlach, 2003; General Accounting Office, 2004; Harnack et al., 2000; Wechsler, Devereaux, Davis, & Collins, 2000; Wildey et al., 2000) and creates a school food environment that can contribute to excess energy intake and excess weight gain among students. A recent report on competitive foods found that nationally nearly 9 out of 10 schools offer competitive foods through a la carte cafeteria lines, vending machines, and school stores. High schools and middle schools were more likely to sell competitive foods than elementary schools (Government Accountability Office, 2005). The most common competitive foods are carbonated beverages, fruit drinks that are not 100% juice, salty snacks, and high-fat baked goods. Less than one-fifth (18%) of the foods available through vending machines, school stores, and snack bars were fruits or vegetables (Wechsler, Brener, Kuester, & Miller, 2001). In addition to these venues selling competitive foods on a daily basis, 40% of schools allow on-campus fundraisers to sell competitive foods such as chocolate bars and other candy (Government Accountability Office, 2005).

When the majority of schools provide ready access to foods of limited nutritional value through multiple venues it is difficult for students to make healthy choices. Several studies have related the availability of competitive foods to higher intakes of total calories, soft drinks, total fat, and saturated fat and lower intakes of key nutrients (e.g., calcium, vitamin A), fruits, vegetables, and milk (Cullen, Eagan, Baranowski, Owens, & de Moor, 2000; Cullen & Zakeri, 2004; Kubik, Lytle, Hannan, Perry, & Story, 2003; Templeton, Marlette, & Panemangalore, 2005). One longitudinal study among 594 fourth and fifth grade students showed that as students transitioned from elementary school to middle school and gained access to school snack bars at lunch they decreased their consumption of fruits by 33%, regular (not fried) vegetables by 42%, and milk by 35%. The study also found that students gaining access to snack bars increased their consumption of sweetened beverages (e.g., soft drinks) and high-fat vegetables (e.g., french fries and tater tots) (Cullen & Zakeri, 2004). Another study among seventh grade students in 16 Minnesota schools similarly found the availability of a la carte programs and snack food vending to be associated with lower intakes of fruits and vegetables. In addition, this study reported that a la carte availability was positively associated with intakes of total and saturated fat (Kubik et al., 2003).

Other research has further demonstrated the impact of school food policies and practices on students' food choices and weight status. A cross-sectional study among high school students from 20 schools observed that school food policies that limit access to foods high in fats and sugars are related to less frequent student purchases of these foods at school. For example, in schools where soft drink machines were turned off during the lunch period, students purchased 0.5 fewer soft drinks per week in comparison to student purchases in schools where soft drink machines were left on during lunch (Neumark-Sztainer, French, Hannan, Story, & Fulkerson, 2005). Researchers have also related the number of food practices (e.g., the use of food as incentives and rewards, classroom and schoolwide fundraising, students allowed to have food and beverages in the classroom) permitted by a school to higher body mass indexes (BMIs) in secondary students. In a study among eighth graders, student BMI increased by 0.10 BMI units for every additional food practice permitted in their school. The results of this study suggest that regular exposure to common school food practices increases the risk for excess weight gain among students (Kubik, Lytle, & Story, 2005).

School Food Policies

Federal requirements currently do little to limit the sale of competitive foods or to set school-wide nutrition standards, and USDA statutory authority to regulate competitive foods is extremely restricted. While reimbursable school meals must meet federal nutrition guidelines and comply with the *Dietary Guidelines for Americans*, competitive foods, which are widely available in schools, are not required to meet any such nutrition standards. Also, while the federal school meal programs set appropriate portion sizes, competitive foods are offered for sale without appropriate portion size guidelines. Strengthening the USDA's authority to set effective standards and limits on the availability and content of competitive foods throughout the entire school day in elementary and secondary schools could enhance children's nutrition and health.

State agencies can impose restrictions on the sale of foods and beverages at school for schools participating in federal school meal programs. In recent years, many states, local school districts, and individual schools have implemented competitive food policies that are more restrictive than USDA regulations, though they differ greatly in the type and extent of restrictions. Eleven states have taken legislative action to require higher nutritional standards on school meals than the "minimum" USDA requirements; 16 states have set nutrition standards on foods sold outside of school meal programs; and 20 states limit when and where foods that are not part of the school meal programs can be sold during school hours (Trust for America's Health, 2006).

In 2006, the Alliance for a Healthier Generation (www.healthiergeneration.org/), a partnership between the American Heart Association and the William J. Clinton Foundation, announced a collaboration with the American Beverage Association to eliminate sales of sugared soft drinks in schools. While this is a positive step, the guidelines are voluntary and depend upon compliance at the school level.

THE PHYSICAL ACTIVITY ENVIRONMENT

Schools have the unique potential to provide numerous opportunities to promote physical activity (Centers for Disease Control, 1997), increase energy expenditure, and thereby help reduce childhood obesity (Burgeson, 2004). A comprehensive school physical activity program should consist of PE; health education, including information about physical activity; recess time for elementary school students; intramural sports programs and physical activity clubs, and interscholastic sports for high school students (Burgeson, 2004). Other ways to increase physical activity and energy expenditure during the school day include incorporating brief periods of physical activity during classroom time, such as the Take 10! Program (International Life Sciences Institute (ILSI); www. take10.net), walking programs, and active commuting to school, such as walking or bicycling.

Physical Education Programs

Physical education is at the center of comprehensive school-based physical activity programs. PE has been defined as any formal school-based educational program that uses physical activity to achieve fitness, skills, health, or educational goals (Sallis, 2003). It is an important but undervalued curricular area that aims to help all students develop the knowledge, skills, and confidence needed to be physically active both in and out of school and throughout their lives (Burgeson, 2004).

Current physical activity guidelines are that children engage in at least 60 min of physical activity on most, and preferably all, days of the week (National Association for Sport and Physical

Education, 2004; Department of Health and Human Services & U.S. Department of Agriculture, 2005). The Institute of Medicine's (IOM) *Preventing Childhood Obesity: Health in the Balance* report (2005) recommended that at least 30 min, or half of the recommended daily physical activity time, be accrued during the school day. The National Association for Sport and Physical Education (NASPE) recommendations for K–12 PE are that instructional periods should total 150 minutes per week for elementary school children and 225 minutes per week for middle and secondary school children (National Association for Sport and Physical Education, 2004). Nationally only 8% of elementary schools and 6% of middle/junior and senior high schools meet these recommendations (Burgeson, Wechsler, Brener, Young, & Spain, 2001).

A recent national survey by the U.S. Department of Education found that while almost all public elementary schools (99%) reported that they scheduled PE for elementary grades, the percent of schools that provided daily PE ranged from 17% to 22% across elementary grades. The average number of days per week of scheduled PE for elementary schools was 2.5 (Parsad & Lewis, 2006). PE requirements in schools decline drastically as grade level increases. The percentage of schools requiring PE drops from around 50% for grades 1 through 5, to 25% in grade 8, to only 5% in grade 12 (Burgeson et al., 2001). Nationwide in 2005, only 54% of high school students went to a PE class on one or more days in an average school week and only 33% of students went to PE classes 5 days/week (Eaton et al., 2006). The quality of PE classes is also an essential consideration for potential impact of PE on child and adolescent overweight. Only a third of adolescents were physically active in PE class for more than 20 minutes 3 to 5 days/week (Department of Health and Human Services, 2000).

Significant barriers exist to increasing PE in schools. These include a low priority for PE compared to other academic subjects, large class sizes, and a lack of time throughout the school day due to requirements for standardized testing (Institute of Medicine, 2006). Research suggests that increased time devoted to PE does not lessen academic performance and achievement in other areas, and can in fact enhance students' readiness to learn and academic achievement (President's Council on Physical Fitness and Sports, 1999; Sallis et al., 1999; Shephard, 1997; Symons, Cinelli, James, & Groff, 1997).

Recess

For school children, recess is an important period of unstructured physical activity during the school day where children have choices, develop rules for play, release energy and stress, and practice and use skills developed in PE (National Association for Sport and Physical Education, 2001). Uninterrupted instructional time, ironically, may be an inefficient use of class time, as attention spans wane and children have difficulty concentrating on specific tasks in the classroom, are restless, and may be easily distracted. A study conducted with fourth grade students reported concentration problems among children on days when they did not participate in recess (Jarrett, 1998).

The 2000 School Health Policies and Programs Study (SHPPS) found that 29% of elementary schools did not provide regularly scheduled recess for students in kindergarten through fifth grade (Burgeson et al., 2001). The NASPE recommends that schools should provide supervised daily recess in grades prekindergarten through five or six; that recess should not be scheduled back to back with PE classes; students should not be denied recess as a form of punishment or to make up work; and recess should complement, not substitute for, structured PE (National Association for Sport and Physical Education, 2001).

Extracurricular Programs

Other important forms of physical activity in the school setting include interscholastic sports programs and intramural activities or physical activity clubs. Intramural sports and physical activity clubs offer opportunities for students with a wide range of abilities to engage in physical activity. Only half (49%) of schools offer intramural activities and physical activity clubs and only one-fifth (22%) of schools provide transportation home for students who participate in interscholastic sports, which is a barrier for lower income students who may need such transportation (Burgeson et al., 2001). To help prevent obesity, the IOM calls for a concerted effort in partnership development between schools and public and private sectors to enhance funding and opportunities for intramural team sports, nonteam sports, and other activities in school and after-school programs (Institute of Medicine, 2005).

School Physical Activity Policies

A recent analysis examined state statutes for school physical activity policies. All states except South Dakota have PE requirements for students (Trust for America's Health, 2006). However, the state requirements are often not enforced and often result in programs of poor quality. Reasons for the low enforcement include too many other mandated curriculum requirements, with PE being viewed as a lower priority compared to math, science, and reading given budgetary constraints. Further, states often allow schools exemptions from PE standards (Trust for America's Health, 2006). Some states have made improvements in PE requirements. For example, in 2005 North Carolina enacted a 30 min daily physical activity requirement for all students in grades K–8. Texas requires elementary school students to engage in 30 min/day of physical activity and middle/junior high students to have 135 min/week.

SCHOOL HEALTH EDUCATION

School health education that includes information about nutrition and physical activity is an important component of a coordinated school approach to improving dietary behavior and increasing physical activity (Centers for Disease Control, 2006). Key elements of health education include a documented, planned, and sequential program for students in grades K–12; behavioral skills development; a prescribed amount of instructional time at each grade level; instruction from qualified teachers who have been trained to teach health subjects; involvement of parents, health professionals, and other community members; and periodic curriculum evaluation and updating (Kann, Brener, & Allensworth, 2001; National Commission on the Role of the School and Community in Improving Adolescent Health, 1990). Research supports the effectiveness of behaviorally focused curricula in promoting healthful food choices and physical activity (Institute of Medicine, 2005). These curricula focus on skill-building activities and provide students with the opportunity to set goals, engage in the desired behaviors, self-monitor their efforts, receive feedback, and provide reinforcement of positive lifestyle changes (Institute of Medicine, 2006). Examples of behaviorally focused curricula include Planet Health (Gortmaker et al., 1999), Pathways (Caballero et al., 2003), and television reduction curricula (Robinson, 1999).

The 2004 School Health Profiles survey found that nearly all secondary schools in 25 states and 10 large urban school districts reported providing education to students on nutrition and physical activity topics through required health education courses. However, the specific content, duration, or effectiveness of the health education instruction was not assessed (Centers for Disease Control, 2006). Other studies have found that health education teachers in elementary, middle/junior high, and senior high schools spend an average of only about 5 hr/year teaching nutrition and dietary behavior and 4 hr/year on physical activity and fitness (Kann et al. 2001), which is not enough to impact children's behavior (Lytle & Achterberg, 1995). Barriers to providing more classroom nutrition and physical activity instruction include time demands, lack of resources, and the increased focus on meeting state academic standards (General Accounting Office, 2003a). Integrating nutrition and physical activity health education into the lesson plans of other school subjects such as math, science, and the language arts is one approach to overcome this barrier.

Only four states (Alaska, Colorado, Kansas, and South Dakota) do not require schools to provide health education (Trust for America's Health, 2006). However, in states that do require health education, few criteria have been set to ensure the quality of the health education curriculum or to establish a minimum credit requirement for graduating students (Trust for America's Health, 2006).

SCHOOL HEALTH SERVICES

School health services can play a central role in addressing obesity-related issues among students. School health clinics and other school-based health services have access to large numbers of students and health personnel to provide screening, health information, and referrals, although the extent and nature of services offered to students vary widely. Services and settings range from traditional, basic core services provided in schools to comprehensive primary care services provided in school-based health centers (SBHCs) or in other locations not on school property, such as school-linked health centers (Allensworth, 1994; Brener et al., 2001).

School-based health centers are defined as health centers on school property where enrolled students can receive primary care, including diagnostic and treatment services (Brener et al., 2001). The number of SBHCs has increased rapidly in the past 15 years, from approximately 200 in 1990 to about 1500 today (Center for Health and Health Care in Schools, 2005). A 2002 national survey of SBHCs found that 61% are in urban settings, 37% are in elementary schools, 36% are in high schools, and more than half of students in schools with SBHCs are African American or Hispanic (Center for Health and Health Care in Schools, 2003). SBHCs are typically open 29 hr/week and 39% are open during the summer. In the survey, nutrition was cited as the most important prevention-related topic for SBHCs (Center for Health and Health Care in Schools, 2003). SBHCs offer an untapped resource for obesity prevention efforts, especially since they serve a population at high risk of obesity and a group that tends to be underinsured and may not receive preventive or treatment services (Center for Health and Health Care in Schools, 2003).

Body Mass Index Screening

School health services provide a venue in which to collect height and weight or BMI information about children. Taking height and weight measures annually and converting them to an age- and gender-specific BMI percentile for each child allows for monitoring of individual children over time and the detection of changes, which provides an opportunity for early intervention. The IOM's (2005) report on preventing child obesity recommends that schools measure annually each student's weight, height, and gender- and age-specific BMI percentile and make this information available to parents and also to students when age appropriate. The IOM acknowledges the sensitivities and concerns surrounding BMI reporting and emphasizes the importance of data on students being collected and reported validly and appropriately, with particular attention to privacy concerns, and with information on referrals available if follow-up health services are needed.

A number of states have undertaken initiatives to screen students' BMI levels. The purpose of the screenings is to help identify schools, school districts, and student populations that may need interventions to help reduce the prevalence of overweight. Typically results are mailed to parents. Seven states—Arkansas, Illinois, Maine, New York, Pennsylvania, Tennessee, and West Virginia—have taken legislative action for schools to screen students' BMI levels (Trust for America's Health, 2006).

Coordinated School Health Programs

The Centers for Disease Control and Prevention (CDC) developed the coordinated school health program (CSHP) model, which creates an infrastructure for holistic health and consists of eight interactive components: healthy school environment, PE, nutrition services, health education, health services, counseling and social services, health promotion for staff, and family/community involvement (Centers for Disease Control, 2007). A CSHP provides a systematic approach for integrating and addressing physical activity and nutrition. A recent study found that fifth grade students from seven schools in Canada participating in a coordinated program incorporating aspects of the CDC recommendations for school-based healthy eating programs (e.g., nutrition education curriculum, integration of school food services and nutrition education, school policies) had lower rates of overweight and obesity, had healthier diets, and reported more physical activity compared to students from schools without nutrition programs (Veugelers & Fitzgerald, 2005). This study suggests the importance of comprehensive, multifaceted school programs that could be effective in preventing childhood obesity.

SCHOOL WELLNESS POLICIES

The most recent federal policy initiative for childhood obesity prevention efforts resulted from the federal Child Nutrition and WIC Reauthorization Act of 2004 (PL 108-265; June 30, 2004). This act contained a local school wellness policy provision to address obesity and promote healthy eating and physical activity through changes in the school environment. By the first day of the 2006–2007 school year, every school district that participated in the federal school meal program was required to enact a wellness policy that included goals for nutrition education and physical activity, nutrition guidelines for all foods available at school, and plans for evaluating implementation of the policy. Parents, students, school food service personnel, and school administrators were to be involved in the development of the local school wellness policy. However, no enforcement or monitoring efforts were required.

SCHOOL-BASED OBESITY INTERVENTION RESEARCH

School-based interventions for childhood obesity can be categorized as either primary or secondary prevention approaches. Primary prevention or population-wide efforts are targeted at all youth and aim to reduce obesity by changing eating and physical activity behaviors in all students. Secondary prevention or high-risk interventions target those children who are already overweight.

Primary Prevention Efforts

The rationale for a primary prevention approach is that even though overweight children represent a high-risk group, many people who are overweight as adults were not overweight as children. A population approach aims to modify environmental conditions or behavioral factors contributing to the development or maintenance of obesity in children.

Many school-based intervention studies have been conducted to promote healthful eating and physical activity behaviors among children and adolescents. However, relatively few school-based obesity prevention interventions have been conducted. Several comprehensive reviews have summarized the literature on school-based population-wide childhood obesity prevention interventions targeting nutrition and physical activity behaviors (Campbell, Waters, O'Meara, & Summerbell, 2001; French & Story, 2006; Institute of Medicine, 2005; Lobstein, Baur, & Uauy, 2004; Resnicow & Robinson, 1997; Story, 1999). Overall the results of school-based studies that targeted eating and physical activity behaviors have been positive. Consistent with these studies, school-based obesity prevention interventions have shown some success in changing eating and physical activity behaviors, but have been less successful in changing body weight or body fatness (Campbell et al., 2001).

Robinson (1999) found that a school-based intervention to decrease television and video viewing reduced the prevalence of obesity among third and fourth grade students. Planet Health, a school-based obesity prevention intervention for grades six to eight focused on decreasing television viewing and increasing physical activity and healthy eating among students, was successful in decreasing obesity among female students, but not among males (Gortmaker et al., 1999). Targeted interventions to reduce soft drink consumption have also showed intervention effects. James, Thomas, Cavan, and Kerr (2004) conducted a school-based study in England and found that a curriculum consisting of experiential lessons over the school year focused solely on reducing consumption of carbonated beverages was associated with a reduction in the number of overweight and obese children ages 7 to 11 years (James et al., 2004).

Several studies have been successful in implementing food environmental changes in schools, including reductions in the fat content of school lunches and modifying the prices of fruits and vegetables in the school cafeteria and in vending machines (French et al., 2001; French & Stables, 2003; French, Story, Fulkerson, & Hannan, 2004; French et al., 1997; Perry et al., 2004). The results of these studies have shown that the availability, promotion, and pricing of foods in schools can be changed to support more healthful food choices. Competitive pricing and promotions can lead to increases in student purchases of fruits, vegetables, and low-fat foods.

Physical activity environmental studies have also shown that school PE classes can be changed to make them much more active and increase the time spent in PE and in moderate to vigorous activity (Sallis et al., 1997, 2003). Datar and Sturm (2004) recently examined the effect of PE instruction time on BMI change in elementary school. Using data from a national survey of 9751 U.S. kindergartners followed for 2 years, they found that one additional hour of PE in the first grade compared with the time allowed for PE in kindergarten reduced the BMI among girls who were overweight or at risk for overweight in kindergarten. No effect was seen in boys. Environmental change interventions focused on increasing energy expenditure through increased physical activity and decreasing consumption of high-calorie, low-nutrition foods offer promising obesity prevention strategies.

Secondary Prevention Efforts

Relatively few research studies have targeted solely overweight youth in a school setting. Several controlled experimental obesity treatment studies were conducted in the mid-1960s through the mid-1980s in a group setting either during school or after school (Story, 1999). The results of the school-based interventions for the treatment of obesity were encouraging. In 10 of the 11 studies, the intervention group had a significantly greater reduction in overweight compared with the control group (Story, 1999). Overall, interventions aimed at younger children were more successful than those with adolescents. Treatment effects were also generally larger for the heavier children. Several methodologic issues were apparent, such as small sample sizes and short follow-up periods.

It should be noted that almost no studies on school-based treatment of obesity are found in the literature after 1985. The reasons for this are unclear, but perhaps concern for the potential harmful effects of obesity treatment studies in schools, such as labeling, stigma, or negative psychosocial impact, may have dampened enthusiasm for the programs (Story, 1999).

The issue of stigmatization, labeling, and other negative effects of school-based treatment interventions for overweight youth is important. In-depth interviews were conducted with 61 overweight adolescents, primarily white and African American, from inner-city public schools to determine their level of interest in participating in a school-based weight control program (Neumark-Sztainer & Story, 1997). The majority of overweight adolescents expressed interest in participating in a school-based weight control program, provided it was done in a supportive and respectful manner and was sensitive to the needs of overweight youth. Many students did not want others to know they were participating in a weight loss program for fear of being teased or embarrassed. Many felt the program should not be labeled as a weight control program for overweight youth, but rather as a nutrition or lifestyle program.

SCHOOL LINKAGES WITH THE COMMUNITY

Many efforts are under way at the district and school levels to link with the community to enhance schools' ability to provide healthful foods and greater physical activity opportunities for students. Efforts to enhance the availability of fresh fruits and vegetables have resulted in school linkages with local farmers. These programs not only provide high-quality local produce, but also provide economic support to the farmers and the state. Several schools have also developed school gardening programs in which students can participate in the cultivation of produce, including planting seeds, raising and tending plants, preparing meals with the food grown, and recycling waste back into the garden (Institute of Medicine, 2005). Classroom lessons incorporate hands-on activities in the garden and kitchen. Gardening programs have been shown to increase preferences for fruits and vegetables (Morris & Zidenberg-Cherr, 2002).

Schools can also be connected with communities to increase physical activity opportunities for youth by making their facilities available during after-school and weekend hours. Organized after-school programs could specifically target physical activity and nutrition behaviors, or incorporate them as components of existing programs whose primary focus involves other activities. Neighborhood programs to develop safe biking and walking paths to school are being initiated to encourage and support active commuting on the part of students. Active commuting programs that involve adult volunteers, such as a walking school bus (Pedestrian and Bicycle Information Center, 2007), which organizes neighborhood chaperones to supervise children as they walk to school, have the additional benefit of increasing physical activity among adults (Tudor-Locke, Ainsworth, Adair, & Popkin, 2003). Promoting walking and biking to school is one approach that schools and communities can take together to increase physical activity in young people.

Parent Involvement

To achieve maximal and sustained behavior change, parents and caregivers need to be involved in obesity prevention efforts. Reviews on family interventions and prevention of youth high-risk behaviors (e.g., school failure, aggressive behaviors, substance use) have found that combined school and family programs deliver more benefits than those managed in isolation from each other (Committee on Increasing High School Students' Engagement and Motivation to Learn, 2004; Greenberg et al., 2003; Kumpfer & Alvarado, 2003). Most obesity prevention programs have been "school-centric," in the sense that they focus almost exclusively on school programs. There are certainly challenges to actively involving parents. However, in other areas of youth prevention efforts, family recruitment efforts have been improved with the use of incentives, such as food, child care, transportation, and rewards for homework completion or attendance (Kumpfer & Alvarado, 2003). Community organizations and local resources can sometimes help schools connect with low-income and minority parents (Committee on Increasing High School Students' Engagement and Motivation to Learn, 2004). Given the importance of families in supporting and facilitating behavior change for healthy eating and physical activity, there is a need to find creative and effective ways to promote parent involvement.

RECOMMENDATIONS FOR SCHOOLS

Schools are important settings to combat the obesity epidemic in the United States. Health and school success are intertwined; schools cannot achieve their primary mission of education if students and staff are not healthy and fit physically, mentally, and socially. There are a number of action steps that schools can take to influence students' health behavior and create an environment conducive to healthy eating and physical activity. The CDC has summarized 10 key strategies schools can use to improve student nutrition and increase physical activity (Wechsler, McKenna, Lee, & Dietz, 2004).

Many schools throughout the country have made changes to improve the school food environment. *Making it Happen! School Nutrition Success Stories*, a joint project of the CDC and USDA Team Nutrition (Department of Agriculture, 2005), tells the stories of schools and school districts across the country that have implemented innovative strategies to improve the nutritional quality of foods and beverages sold in schools outside of the federally regulated meal programs. They describe six key approaches for improving the nutritional quality of competitive foods:

1. Establish nutrition standards for competitive foods.
2. Influence food and beverage contracts.
3. Make more healthful foods and beverages available.
4. Adopt marketing techniques to promote healthful choices.
5. Limit student access to competitive foods.
6. Use fundraising activities and rewards that support student health.

They also provide key lessons learned. These include

1. One champion, such as a parent, food service manager, or school principal, is usually the driving force behind the change.
2. Improving school nutrition involves multiple steps; teams with diverse skills and backgrounds are well positioned to undertake such change.
3. A useful starting point is to assess the current nutrition environment of the school to identify strengths and weaknesses.
4. Data are needed to document the impact and change.
5. Change is a destination and a process. Adopting a nutrition policy does not guarantee it will be implemented and requires ongoing attention.

There are other resources for school personnel, educators, parents, and health professionals. Action for Healthy Kids is a nonprofit organization formed specifically to address the epidemic of overweight by focusing on changes in schools. Their Web site (www.actionforhealthykids.org) provides a wealth of resources, including tools and materials to help schools take action to improve nutrition and physical activity in schools.

With national attention placed on the epidemic of child obesity and the need for the prevention and treatment of obesity, great care must be taken not to stigmatize overweight youth. Overweight youth are vulnerable to weight teasing. One study found that 63% of overweight (BMI greater than the 95th percentile) adolescent girls and 58% of overweight adolescent boys reported being teased by their peers. Weight teasing was associated with disordered eating behaviors among overweight students (Neumark-Sztainer et al., 2002). Another study found that teasing about body weight was consistently associated with low body satisfaction, low self-esteem, high depressive symptoms, and thinking about and attempting suicide, even after controlling for actual body weight. These associations held for adolescent boys and girls across racial, ethnic, and weight groups (Eisenberg, Neumark-Sztainer, & Story, 2003). Schools should increase awareness among staff members of weight-based teasing and mistreatment and the potentially harmful effects on students' emotional well-being. Obesity prevention interventions with youth should also incorporate education and messages related to treating everyone with respect. Weight-related teasing and bullying should not be tolerated in school settings and school polices should address this issue.

RECOMMENDATIONS FOR RESEARCH

The main conclusion that can be drawn from the school-based obesity prevention studies conducted to date is that interventions appear to hold promise, but further research is needed (French & Story, 2006). Future studies need to strengthen physical activity and healthy eating intervention components, use culturally appropriate approaches, and target different levels, such as the school environment, behavioral curricula, and parent involvement. Strengthening the intervention components might include expanding family involvement and home environmental modifications such as increasing the availability of healthful foods, including fruits and vegetables, and limiting the availability of energy-dense, low-nutrition foods. Strengthening the school environmental component includes more frequent, required PE classes, and schoolwide policies about food and beverage standards, availability, and sales (Wechsler et al., 2000). Research is also needed to identify the most potent behavioral targets for effective obesity prevention, such as reducing screen time, sugar-sweetened beverages, or portion sizes. Currently we do not know which specific behavior or combination of behaviors is the most effective to target for obesity interventions.

Research is also needed to examine whether certain types of interventions may be more successful with children of different age, gender, or racial/ethnic groups. For example, particular behaviors and settings might receive greater emphasis with different age groups. Interventions that target preschool and elementary school children might focus more on parents as agents of change; a greater emphasis might be placed on reducing television viewing among younger children and developing more structured and diverse PE opportunities among high school students; and school environmental changes might provide greater impact among high school versus elementary school students (e.g., changes in a la carte and vending machine food and beverage availability).

School-based obesity prevention research must also address the most appropriate study outcome variables. For example, is it reasonable to evaluate the success of school-based interventions primarily on changes in body mass or body composition, or are changes in behaviors related to energy balance the most appropriate evaluation outcome? Evaluating the effectiveness of obesity prevention programs, policies, and interventions is critical. The 2006 IOM report, *Progress in Preventing Childhood Obesity: How Do We Measure Up?*, concluded that a lack of systematic evaluation has hindered the ability to identify, apply, and disseminate promising childhood obesity prevention efforts. Strong evaluation components are needed to build a multifaceted evidence base upon which promising practices can be built.

Examples of school-based research topics needed to advance the field include (French & Story, 2006):

- Evaluate intervention components at different levels to determine the relative effectiveness of educational, environmental, and policy changes on students' BMI, eating and physical activity behaviors, and the school food and physical activity environment.
- Evaluate specific behavioral targets to determine the relative effectiveness of changes in specific behaviors on changes in body mass (e.g., decreases in television viewing, increases in PE class frequency, decreases in soft drink consumption).
- Evaluate strategies to increase parental involvement, parental behavior changes, and home environmental changes through school-based obesity prevention interventions.
- Evaluate interventions that link school-based obesity prevention efforts with other community settings such as primary care, youth groups, community centers, and after-school programs.
- Examine the effects of school, district, and state level policy changes regarding the school food environment on changes in student dietary outcomes or BMI changes.
- Develop more valid and accurate measures to assess the school food and physical activity environments as well as individual dietary intake and physical activity behaviors.

REFERENCES

Action for Healthy Kids. (2004). *The learning connection: the value of improving nutrition and physical activity in our schools.* Skokie, IL: Action for Healthy Kids. Available at www.actionforhealthykids. org/pdf/Learning%20Connection%20-%20Full%20Report%20011006.pdf.

Allensworth, D. D. (1994). School health services: issues and challenges. In P. Cortese & K. Middleton (Eds.), *The comprehensive school health challenge: promoting health through education,* vol. 1. Santa Cruz, CA: ETR Associates.

Brener, N. D., Burstein, G. R., DuShaw, M. L., Vernon, M. E., Wheeler, L., & Robinson, J. (2001). Health services: results from the School Health Policies and Programs Study 2000. *Journal of School Health, 71*, 294–304.

Burgeson, C. R. (2004). Physical education's critical role in educating the whole child and reducing childhood obesity. *The State Education Standard, 5*(2), 27–32.

Burgeson, C. R., Wechsler, H., Brener, N. D., Young, J. C., & Spain, C. G. (2001). Physical education and activity: results from the School Health Policies and Programs Study 2000. *Journal of School Health, 71*, 279–293.

Caballero, B., Clay, T., Davis, S. M., Ethelbah, B., Rock, B. H., Lohman, T., Norman, J., Story, M., Stone, E. J., Stephenson, L., & Stevens, J., for the Pathways Study Research Group. (2003). Pathways: a school-based, randomized controlled trial for the prevention of obesity in American Indian schoolchildren. *American Journal of Clinical Nutrition, 78*, 1030–1038.

Campbell, K., Waters, E., O'Meara, S., & Summerbell, C. (2001). Interventions for preventing obesity in childhood. A systematic review. *Obesity Reviews, 2*, 149–157.

Center for Health and Health Care in Schools. (2003). 2002 state survey of school-based health center initiatives. Washington, D.C.: Center for Health and Health Care in Schools. Available at www.healthinschools.org/sbhcs/2002rpt.asp.

Center for Health and Health Care in Schools. (2005). School-based health centers—background. Washington, D.C.: Center for Health and Health Care in Schools. Available at www.healthinschools.org/sbhcs/sbhc.asp.

Centers for Disease Control. (1997). Guidelines for school and community programs to promote lifelong physical activity among young people. *MMWR Morbidity and Mortality Weekly Report, 46*, 1–36.

Centers for Disease Control. (2006). Secondary school health education related to nutrition and physical activity—selected sites, United States, 2004. *MMWR Morbidity and Mortality Weekly Report, 55*, 821–824.

Centers for Disease Control. (2007). Coordinated school health program. Atlanta: Centers for Disease Control. Available at www.cdc.gov/HealthyYouth/CSHP/.

Committee on Increasing High School Students' Engagement and Motivation to Learn, National Research Council. (2004). *Engaging schools: fostering high school students' motivation to learn*. Washington, D.C.: National Academies Press.

Cullen, K. W., Eagan, J., Baranowski, T., Owens, E., & de Moor, C. (2000). Effect of a la carte and snack bar foods at school on children's lunchtime intake of fruits and vegetables. *Journal of the American Dietetic Association, 100*, 1482–1486.

Cullen, K. W., & Zakeri, I. (2004). Fruits, vegetables, milk, and sweetened beverages consumption and access to a la carte/snack bar meals at school. *American Journal of Public Health, 94*, 463–467.

Datar, A., & Sturm, R. (2004). Physical education in elementary school and body mass index: evidence from the early childhood longitudinal study. *American Journal of Public Health, 94*, 1501–1506.

Department of Agriculture. (2001). Foods sold in competition with USDA school meal programs: a report to Congress. Washington, D.C.: U.S. Government Printing Office.

Department of Agriculture. (2005). Making it happen! School nutrition success stories. FNS-374. Alexandria, VA: Food and Nutrition Service. Available at www.fns.usda.gov/tn/Resources/makingithappen.html.

Department of Health and Human Services. (2000). *Healthy people 2010: understanding and improving health* (2nd ed.). Washington, D.C.: U.S. Government Printing Office.

Department of Health and Human Services & U.S. Department of Agriculture. (2005). *Dietary Guidelines for Americans 2005*. Washington, D.C.: U.S. Government Printing Office.

Eaton, D. K., Kann, L., Kinchen, S., Ross, J., Hawkins, J., Harris, W. A., Lowry, R., McManus, T., Chyen, D., Shanklin, S., Lim, C., Grunbaum, J. A., & Wechsler, H. (2006). Youth risk behavior surveillance—United States, 2005. *MMWR Surveillance Summaries, 55*(5), 1–108.

Eisenberg, M. E., Neumark-Sztainer, D., & Story, M. (2003). Associations of weight-based teasing and emotional well-being among adolescents. *Archives of Pediatrics & Adolescent Medicine, 157*, 733–738.

Food Research and Action Center. (2004). Child nutrition policy brief. Competitive foods in schools. Washington, D.C.: Food Research and Action Center. Available at www.frac.org/pdf/cncompfoods.PDF.

Food Research and Action Center. (2005). State of the states: 2005: a profile of food and nutrition programs across the nation. Washington, D.C.: Food Research and Action Center. Available at www.frac.org/State_Of_States/2005/Report.pdf.

Fox, M. K., Crepinsek, P., Connor, P., & Battaglia, M. (2001). School nutrition dietary assessment study—II: summary of findings. Alexandria, VA: Food and Nutrition Service.

Fox, M. K., Hamilton, W., & Lin, B. H. (2004). Effects of food assistance and nutrition programs on health and nutrition: Vol. 3, Literature review. FANRR 19-3. Washington, D.C.: Economic Research Service. Available at www.ers.usda.gov/publications/FANRR19-3/.

French, S. A., Jeffery, R. W., Story, M., Breitlow, K. K., Baxter, J. S., Hannan, P., & Snyder, M. P. (2001). Pricing and promotion effects on low-fat vending snack purchases: the CHIPS study. *American Journal of Public Health, 91,* 112–117.

French, S. A., & Stables, G. (2003). Environmental interventions to promote vegetable and fruit consumption among youth in school settings. *Preventive Medicine, 37*(6 pt 1), 593–610.

French, S. A., & Story, M. (2006). Obesity prevention in schools. In M. I. Goran & M. S. Sothern (Eds.), *Handbook of pediatric obesity: etiology, pathophysiology, and prevention* (pp. 291–309). Boca Raton, FL: CRC Press.

French, S. A., Story, M., Fulkerson, J. A., & Gerlach, A. F. (2003). Food environment in secondary schools: a la carte, vending machines, and food policies and practices. *American Journal of Public Health, 93,* 1161–1167.

French, S. A., Story, M., Fulkerson, J. A., & Hannan, P. (2004). An environmental intervention to promote lower-fat food choices in secondary schools: outcomes of the TACOS study. *American Journal of Public Health, 94,* 1507–1512.

French, S. A., Story, M., Jeffery, R. W., Snyder, P., Eisenberg, M., Sidebottom, A., & Murray, D. (1997). Pricing strategy to promote fruit and vegetable purchase in high school cafeterias. *Journal of the American Dietetic Association, 97,* 1008–1010.

General Accounting Office. (2003a). School lunch program: efforts needed to improve nutrition and encourage healthy eating. GAO-03-506. Washington, D.C.: General Accounting Office.

General Accounting Office. (2003b). School meal programs: revenue and expense information from selected states. GAO-03-569. Washington, D.C.: General Accounting Office.

General Accounting Office. (2004). School meal programs: competitive foods are available in many schools; actions taken to restrict them differ by state and locality. GAO-04-673. Washington, D.C.: General Accounting Office.

Gleason, P., Suitor, C., & U.S. Food and Nutrition Service. (2001). Children's diets in the mid-1990s: dietary intake and its relationship with school meal participation. Alexandria, VA: Food and Nutrition Service.

Gortmaker, S. L., Peterson, K., Wiecha, J., Sobol, A. M., Dixit, S., Fox, M. K., & Laird, N. (1999). Reducing obesity via a school-based interdisciplinary intervention among youth: Planet Health. *Archives of Pediatric and Adolescent Medicine, 153,* 409–418.

Government Accountability Office. (2005). School meal programs: competitive foods are widely available and generate substantial revenues for schools. GAO-05-563. Washington, D.C.: Government Accountability Office.

Greenberg, M. T., Weissberg, R. P., O'Brien, M. U., Zins, J. E., Fredericks, L., Resnik, H., & Elias, M. J. (2003). Enhancing school-based prevention and youth development through coordinated social, emotional, and academic learning. *American Psychologist, 58*(6–7), 466–474.

Harnack, L., Snyder, P., Story, M., Holliday, R., Lytle, L., & Neumark-Sztainer, D. (2000). Availability of a la carte food items in junior and senior high schools: a needs assessment. *Journal of the American Dietetic Association, 100,* 701–703.

Institute of Medicine. (2005). *Preventing childhood obesity: health in the balance.* Washington, D.C.: National Academies Press.

Institute of Medicine. (2006). *Progress in preventing childhood obesity: How do we measure up?* Washington, D.C.: National Academies Press.

James, J., Thomas, P., Cavan, D., & Kerr, D. (2004). Preventing childhood obesity by reducing consumption of carbonated drinks: cluster randomised controlled trial. *BMJ, 328(7450),* 1237.

Jarrett, O. S. (1998). Effect of recess on classroom behavior: group effects and individual differences. *Journal of Education Research, 92,* 121–126.

Kann, L., Brener, N. D., & Allensworth, D. D. (2001). Health education: results from the School Health Policies and Programs Study 2000. *Journal of School Health, 71,* 266–278.

Kubik, M. Y., Lytle, L. A., Hannan, P. J., Perry, C. L., & Story, M. (2003). The association of the school food environment with dietary behaviors of young adolescents. *American Journal of Public Health, 93,* 1168–1173.

Kubik, M. Y., Lytle, L. A., & Story, M. (2005). Schoolwide food practices are associated with body mass index in middle school students. *Archives of Pediatric and Adolescent Medicine, 159,* 1111–1114.

Kumpfer, K. L., & Alvarado, R. (2003). Family-strengthening approaches for the prevention of youth problem behaviors. *American Psychologist, 58*(6–7), 457–465.

Lobstein, T., Baur, L., & Uauy, R. (2004). Obesity in children and young people: a crisis in public health. *Obesity Reviews, 5*(suppl. 1), 4–104.

Lytle, L. A., & Achterberg, C. (1995). Changing the diet of America's children: what works and why. *Journal of Nutrition Education, 27,* 250–260.

Morris, J. L., & Zidenberg-Cherr, S. (2002). Garden-enhanced nutrition curriculum improves fourth-grade school children's knowledge of nutrition and preferences for some vegetables. *Journal of the American Dietetic Association, 102,* 91–93.

National Association for Sport and Physical Education. (2001). Recess in elementary schools. Position paper. Reston, VA: National Association for Sport and Physical Education.

National Association for Sport and Physical Education. (2004). *Physical activity for children: a statement of guidelines for children 5–12* (2nd ed.). Reston, VA: National Association for Sport and Physical Education.

National Commission on the Role of the School and Community in Improving Adolescent Health. (1990). Code blue: uniting for healthier youth. Alexandria, VA: National Association of State Boards of Education.

Neumark-Sztainer, D., Falkner, N., Story, M., Perry, C., Hannan, P. J., & Mulert, S. (2002). Weight-teasing among adolescents: correlations with weight status and disordered eating behaviors. *International Journal of Obesity, 26,* 123–131.

Neumark-Sztainer, D., French, S. A., Hannan, P. J., Story, M., & Fulkerson, J. A. (2005). School lunch and snacking patterns among high school students: associations with school food environment and policies. *International Journal of Behavioral Nutrition and Physical Activity, 2(1),* 14.

Neumark-Sztainer, D., & Story, M. (1997). Recommendations from overweight youth regarding school-based weight control programs. *Journal of School Health, 67,* 428–433.

Parsad, B., & Lewis, L. (2006). Calories in, calories out: food and exercise in public elementary schools, 2005. NCES 2006-057. Washington, D.C.: National Center for Education Statistics.

Pedestrian and Bicycle Information Center. (2007). Starting a walking school bus. Chapel Hill, NC: Pedestrian and Bicycle Information Center. Available at www.walkingschoolbus.org/.

Perry, C. L., Bishop, D. B., Taylor, G. L., Davis, M., Story, M., Gray, C., Bishop, S. C., Mays, R. A., Lytle, L. A., & Harnack, L. (2004). A randomized school trial of environmental strategies to encourage fruit and vegetable consumption among children. *Health Education and Behavior, 31,* 65–76.

President's Council on Physical Fitness and Sports. (1999). Physical activity promotion and school physical education. *PCPFS Research Digests,* Sept. 1999. Available at www.fitness.gov/digest_sep1999.htm.

Rampersaud, G. C., Pereira, M. A., Girard, B. L., Adams, J., & Metzl, J. D. (2005). Breakfast habits, nutritional status, body weight, and academic performance in children and adolescents. *Journal of the American Dietetic Association, 105,* 743–760; quiz 761–742.

Resnicow, K., & Robinson, T. (1997). School-based cardiovascular disease prevention studies: review and synthesis. *Annals of Epidemiology, 7,* S14–S31.

Robinson, T. N. (1999). Reducing children's television viewing to prevent obesity: a randomized controlled trial. *JAMA, 282,* 1561–1156.

Sallis, J. F. (2003). Behavioral and environmental interventions to promote youth physical activity and prevent obesity. Available at www-rohan.sdsu.edu/faculty/sallis/Sallis_PA_interventions_for_Georgia_6.03.pdf.

Sallis, J. F., McKenzie, T. L., Alcaraz, J. E., Kolody, B., Faucette, N., & Hovell, M. F. (1997). The effects of a 2-year physical education program (SPARK) on physical activity and fitness in elementary school students. Sports, Play and Active Recreation for Kids. *American Journal of Public Health, 87,* 1328–1334.

Sallis, J. F., McKenzie, T. L., Conway, T. L., Elder, J. P., Prochaska, J. J., Brown, M. D., Zive, M. M., Marshall, S. J., & Alcaraz, J. E. (2003). Environmental interventions for eating and physical activity: a randomized controlled trial in middle schools. *American Journal of Preventive Medicine, 24,* 209–217.

Sallis, J. F., McKenzie, T. L., Kolody, B., Lewis, M., Marshall, S., & Rosengard, P. (1999). Effects of health-related physical education on academic achievement: project SPARK. *Research Quarterly for Exercise & Sport, 70*(2), 127–134.

Shephard, R. J. (1997). Curricular physical activity and academic performance. *Pediatric Exercise Science, 9,* 113–126.

Story, M. (1999). School-based approaches for preventing and treating obesity. *International Journal of Obesity and Related Metabolic Disorders, 23*(suppl. 2), S43–S51.

Symons, C. W., Cinelli, B., James, T. C., & Groff, P. (1997). Bridging student health risks and academic achievement through comprehensive school health programs. *Journal of School Health, 67,* 220–227.

Templeton, S. B., Marlette, M. A., & Panemangalore, M. (2005). Competitive foods increase the intake of energy and decrease the intake of certain nutrients by adolescents consuming school lunch. *Journal of the American Dietetic Association, 105,* 215–220.

Trust for America's Health. (2006). F as in fat: how obesity policies are failing in America 2006. Washington, D.C.: Trust for America's Health. Available at healthyamericans.org/reports/obesity2006/.

Tudor-Locke, C., Ainsworth, B. E., Adair, L. S., & Popkin, B. M. (2003). Objective physical activity of Filipino youth stratified for commuting mode to school. *Medicine and Science in Sports and Exercise, 35,* 465–471.

Veugelers, P. J., & Fitzgerald, A. L. (2005). Effectiveness of school programs in preventing childhood obesity: a multilevel comparison. *American Journal of Public Health, 95,* 432–435.

Wechsler, H., Brener, N. D., Kuester, S., & Miller, C. (2001). Food service and foods and beverages available at school: results from the School Health Policies and Programs Study 2000. *Journal of School Health, 71,* 313–324.

Wechsler, H., Devereaux, A. B., Davis, M., & Collins, J. L. (2000). Using the school environment to promote physical activity and healthy eating. *Preventive Medicine, 31*(suppl.), S121–S137.

Wechsler, H., McKenna, M. L., Lee, S. M., & Dietz, W. H. (2004). The role of schools in preventing childhood obesity. *The State Education Standard, 5,* 4–12.

Wildey, M. B., Pampalone, S. Z., Pelletier, R. L., Zive, M. M., Elder, J. P., & Sallis, J. F. (2000). Fat and sugar levels are high in snacks purchased from student stores in middle schools. *Journal of the American Dietetic Association, 100,* 319–322.

17

Public Health Approaches to the Control of Pediatric and Adolescent Obesity

DAVID L. KATZ AND ZUBAID FARIDI

INTRODUCTION

Obesity is arguably the gravest, and inarguably one of the least well-controlled, public health threats currently confronting the United States, and increasingly, the world. Obesity rates have been rising relentlessly among adults and children alike for decades in the United States, and similar patterns have now been established in most other countries. At the International Congress on Obesity held in Sydney, Australia, in September 2006, it was announced that for the first time in human history, there were more overfed than hungry persons on the planet (Caterson, 2006). Obesity is thus a public health crisis of the first magnitude. But it has been said that crises represent opportunities. By recognizing the dangers of epidemic obesity—particularly the dangers to children and adolescents—society is apt to become impassioned about the need to confront this threat, and therein lies opportunity.

This chapter briefly characterizes the dangers of obesity to children and adolescents, reviews proposed explanations regarding why epidemic obesity developed, and provides an overview of public health approaches to its containment, control, and prevention. The aim is to disclose the danger we all now face and illuminate the abundant opportunity attendant upon our collective insight and the requisite allotment of will.

WHAT IS THE DANGER?

Since the 1970s, the number of overweight children in the United States has increased dramatically (Ogden, Flegal, Carroll, & Johnson, 2002). Using the currently prevailing definition of overweight in children—an age- and sex-adjusted body mass index (BMI) at or above the 95th percentile (Flegal, Tabak, & Ogden, 2006; Hedley et al., 2004)—more than 15% of children (at least 9 million) ages 6 to 19 years in the United States are considered overweight (Hedley et al., 2004; Mokdad et al., 2001; Ogden et al., 2002, 2006). The prevalence of overweight among some ethnic minority groups is considerably higher: more than 23% of Mexican American children ages 6 to 19 years are overweight and approximately 20% of 6- to 11-year-old and 24% of 11- to 19-year-old non-Hispanic black children are overweight (Ogden et al., 2002). The prevalence of overweight among Native Americans has been estimated at 30% (Caballero et al., 2003). Overall, the number of children who are overweight has tripled over the past two decades (Ogden, Carroll, & Flegal, 2003; Ogden et al., 2002).

These numbers, troublesome as they are, nonetheless likely represent significant underestimates of the true prevalence of childhood and adolescent obesity. Just as the term "overweight" rather than "obese" is applied to children to minimize stigma (Cramer & Steinwert, 1998; Kraig & Keel, 2001; Latner & Stunkard, 2003), so too is the definition of overweight adjusted to that end. Obesity has long persisted as the last bastion of socially acceptable prejudice in our society (Puhl & Brownell, 2001). That consideration was factored into the development of a definition of overweight for children, with a goal of minimizing those burdened with the stigma. A definition more specific than sensitive resulted, risking false negatives to avoid false positives (Moran, 1999). Because of heightened concern about the potential number of false negatives, revision of the definition is currently under consideration. Cole, Bellizzi, Flegal, and Dietz (2000) recommend using an international standard for making international comparisons and monitoring the global epidemic of obesity. The authors attempt to develop an acceptable definition of obesity specifying the measurement, reference population, and age- and sex-specific cutoff points by analyzing data on BMI (weight/height) obtained from six large nationally representative cross-sectional surveys on growth from Brazil, Great Britain, Hong Kong, The Netherlands, Singapore, and the United States. A childhood obesity expert group convened by the American Medical Association, the Centers for Disease Control and Prevention (CDC), and the Health Resources and Services Administration suggests relating children's growth curves and cutoff points to the World Health Organization's (WHO) adult BMI criteria and reclassifying children who are currently called "at risk of overweight" and refer to them in the future as "overweight" (Chinn & Rona, 2002; Cole et al., 2000; Jebb & Prentice, 2001; Luciano, Bressan, Bolognani, Castellarin, & Zoppi, 2001).

Whatever the true rate of childhood obesity, its recent rapid rise and attendant consequences are undisputed, as are most of its grave consequences. Obesity in adulthood has been associated with an increased risk of cardiovascular disease (Burton, Chen, Schultz, & Edington, 1998; Harris, Launer, Madans, & Feldman, 1997; Willett et al., 1995), type 2 diabetes (Colditz, Willett, Rotnitzky, & Manson, 1995; Manson et al., 1992), and most cancers (Burton, Foster, Hirsch, & Van Itallie, 1985; Calle, Rodriguez, Walker-Thurmond, & Thun, 2003; Calle, Teras, & Thun, 2005a,b; Calle & Thun, 2004), to name only a few of the high-profile sequelae. Adults who were obese as children have increased mortality and morbidity independent of adult weight. Childhood and especially adolescent obesity predict adult obesity and its complications quite reliably for 18-year-olds with BMIs above the 60th percentile; the probability of overweight at age 35 years is 34% for men and 37% for women (Field, Cook, & Gillman, 2005; Guo & Chumlea, 1999; Jeffery & Utter, 2003; Mascie-Taylor & Karim, 2003; Tillotson, 2004).

The incidence of type 2 diabetes in the pediatric population parallels the increase in pediatric obesity (Aye & Levitsky, 2003). The CDC estimates that one in three children born in the year 2000 or after in the United States will develop diabetes in their lifetime, and for African Americans, that figure is one in two.

Mere mention of type 2 diabetes both highlights and obscures the gravity of epidemic childhood obesity. The rising prevalence of type 2 diabetes may be the single best gauge of the toll of obesity in children. Previously known as "non-insulin dependent diabetes mellitus" (NIDDM) or "maturity-onset/adult-onset diabetes," type 2 diabetes is the most common form of diabetes mellitus. It is primarily a disease of insulin insensitivity and is characterized by hyperinsulinemia, increased advanced glycosylation end product (AGE) production, and decreased longevity (Lee, Okumura, Davis, Herman, & Gurney, 2006; Liese et al., 2006). However, the name of the condition belies its history. Less than a generation ago, type 2 diabetes was called "adult-onset" diabetes, to distinguish it from "juvenile onset" diabetes. In the span of less than a generation, what was a chronic disease of midlife has become a rather routine pediatric diagnosis (Centers for Disease Control, 1999b; Fagot-Campagna et al., 2000; Pontiroli, 2004; Wiegand et al., 2004).

We might better recall the true hazards of obesity in children if we continue to refer to "adult-onset" diabetes even while diagnosing it in children. The name change may foster undue complacency about an alarming historical trend. Nor is adult-onset diabetes in childhood necessarily where this trend culminates. The Adult Treatment Panel of the National Cholesterol Education Program equates diabetes with established coronary disease in their guidance for cardiac risk factor management (Expert Panel on Detection, Evaluation, and Treatment of High Blood Cholesterol in Adults, 2001). With adult-onset diabetes increasingly common before age 10 years, we can anticipate a corresponding increase in cardiovascular disease in this population (Apedo, Sowers, & Banerji, 2002; Steinberger & Daniels, 2003). The effects of the increased prevalence of obesity at an ever younger age (Das, Gabriely, & Barzilai, 2004; Fontana, 2006; Masoro, 2005) may be tantamount to those of accelerated aging.

The psychological and social sequelae of childhood obesity are grave as well. Obesity severely diminishes children's quality of life to the level of children diagnosed with cancer (Schwimmer, Burwinkle, & Varni, 2003). Many have poor self-esteem (French, Jeffery, Klesges, & Forster, 1995; Hill, Draper, & Stack, 1994) and are subjected to teasing, discrimination, and victimization and may be socially excluded outside of the home (Schwartz & Puhl, 2003; Strauss & Pollack, 2003). In third grade girls, BMI was shown to be associated with depressive symptoms (Robinson, Haydel, & Killen, 2000). These psychological factors can effect children's ability to perform in school (Buhs & Ladd, 2001; Emslie, Mayes, Laptook, & Batt, 2003; Haney & Durlak, 1998).

Projections are uncertain, but include the prospect of our children living shorter lives as a direct consequence of epidemic obesity (Child Health Alert, 2005; Mann, 2005; Mizuno, Shu, Makimura, & Mobbs, 2004, Peeters et al., 2003; Pontiroli, 2004; Preston, 2005). More reliable are statistics suggesting that children growing up in the United States today will suffer more chronic disease and premature death from eating poorly and a lack of exercise than from exposure to tobacco, drugs, and alcohol combined (Department of Health and Human Services, 2003). Collectively these dangers indicate quite clearly that childhood obesity is indeed a public health crisis in urgent need of public health-based solutions.

WHY HAS CHILDHOOD OBESITY BECOME EPIDEMIC?

Elucidation of the gravity of childhood obesity tempts a headlong rush toward solutions. But that is the very mistake we have made in reality. The first, best recourse in solving most problems and meeting most challenges is to understand them. As a society, we have thus far failed to establish a widely accepted explanation for the advent of epidemic childhood obesity—and that is prerequisite to its remediation.

In children and adults alike, weight control is about calories in versus calories out. These, in turn, are dictated by behaviors we ostensibly have the capacity to control—eating and physical activity. Why would a putatively intelligent species eat itself into a state of epidemic obesity?

The succinct and yet largely sufficient answer to this question is, because we can. There are many explanations one might invoke, from the low cost of food, to its energy density, to stress, hectic schedules, technology, and advertising. But it all comes back to the most fundamental explanation of all. Animals—including the human animal—tend to get fat when circumstances allow. Circumstances have never so generously allowed for obesity as they now do.

One may reasonably contend that human beings, adapted to withstand exertion and the threat of starvation, have no native defenses against caloric excess. Human beings store body fat as a survival mechanism; it is a way of using excess calories available today as fuel tomorrow when calories may not be available. Since we now have an excess of calories available every day, we accumulate fat that is never burned as fuel. The result is obesity.

Some of the specific factors contributing to childhood obesity in the modern environment include a greater number of hours spent in sedentary pursuits (Dehghan, Akhtar-Danesh, & Merchant, 2005; Kaur, Hyder, & Poston, 2003; Philippas & Lo, 2005), a reduction in physical activity (Davison, Marshall, & Birch, 2006; Dencker et al., 2006; Patrick et al., 2004), increased energy intake, and intake of fat (Raynor & Maier, 2006; Sherry, 2005; Swinburn, Caterson, Seidell, & James, 2004). It has also been suggested that the increased consumption of sugar-laden soft drinks may be partly responsible for the increase in childhood obesity (Anderson, 2006; Ludwig et al., 2001; Pereira, 2006).

Children's diets are high in sugar and fat, particularly saturated and *trans* fat, and low in fruit and vegetables. *Trans* fats are fats that are artificially created through a chemical process of the hydrogenation of oils. This process solidifies the oil and limits the body's ability to regulate cholesterol. Research suggests a correlation between diets high in *trans* fats and diseases like atherosclerosis and coronary heart disease. Sixty-four percent of school-age children drink soda and a recent study has linked soft drink consumption with weight gain and obesity in children (Ludwig et al., 2001). Many eat less than the recommended five servings of fruits and vegetables a day and only 2% of school-age children meet the food guide pyramid's serving suggestions for the five major food groups (Gleason & Suitor, 2001). A recent analysis by the CDC (Block, 2004) suggests that fully one-third of the calories in the "typical" American diet come from so-called junk food.

Television watching has also been shown to be an independent factor in predicting a change in a child's BMI (Proctor et al., 2003). Television influences not only how much, but what types of food children eat. Total energy consumption, especially a high intake of fast food and junk food, is positively associated with the number of hours of television watched (Crespo et al., 2001; Muller, Koetringer, Mast, Languix, & Frunch, 1999). This comes as no surprise, as the food industry is, as yet, unregulated in their advertising techniques and children are bombarded with messages promoting the consumption of high-fat, high-sugar, and nutrient-empty products (Borzekowski & Robinson, 2001a; Taras & Gage, 1995). Because children's food selections are influenced by advertisements, even briefly, and they watch on average of 2.5 hr of television per day, this can have a large impact on their diet (Borzekowski & Robinson, 2001b). In the age of "advergaming," food marketing to children is ever more sophisticated, and in all probability, influential (Kelly, 2005; Lobstein & Dibb, 2005; McLellan, 2002; Nestle, 2006; Salinsky, 2006). Children are treated as consumers at an age where they are cognitively unable to decipher truth from fiction. Consequently children's food choices may be influenced in no small measure by advertising pitches that are misleading at best with regard to the nutritional and health-related properties of foods.

Many schools offer junk food via vending machines, school stores, and cafeteria selections—although recent trends in this area are promising (American Beverage Association, 2007; Shin, 2006). School lunches tend to exceed the national recommendations for fat, saturated fat, cholesterol, and sodium (Burghardt, Gordon, & Fraker, 1995; Devaney, Gordon, & Burghardt, 1993). Fast food and soda companies have also partnered with schools. With education funds being less than desirable, schools need to raise money for scholastic and sport programs, and advertisers are pleased to promote their product to a captive, impressionable audience 5 days a week. Recent efforts to curtail this practice are noteworthy. In October 2006, the Alliance for a Healthier Generation (a joint initiative of the American Heart Association and the William J. Clinton Foundation) announced an agreement with five major snack manufacturers to provide lower fat and lower calorie options for school vending machines. A similar agreement covering guidelines for beverages stocked in school vending machines was struck last year between the alliance and the American Beverage Association. Under the new guidelines, only lower calorie and nutritious beverages will be sold to schools. Cadbury Schweppes, Coca Cola, and PepsiCo have agreed to sell only water, unsweetened juice, and flavored and unflavored low-fat and fat-free milk to elementary and middle schools (Alliance for a Healthier Generation, 2006).

Finally, at a time of increasing childhood obesity, there is decreasing physical activity in the typical school day. This is due in part to the pressures of the No Child Left Behind Act of 2001 (Public Law 107-110), which links federal school subsidies to standardized test performance. Schools have jettisoned everything from physical education to recess to free more time for standardized test preparation.

Like their parents, our children are adrift in a literal flood of obesogenic factors. Their plight is unlikely to improve with each little thing that we do. Rather, we should expect to see meaningful improvements in these trends when, and only when, we have constructed an array of defenses commensurate with the flood they are intended to contain.

HOW CAN CURRENT TRENDS BE REVERSED?

In discussing the public health treatment, control, reversal, and prevention of childhood obesity, it is only fair to acknowledge up front that the case made is theoretical. We do not have a model of population-level success in obesity control in the real world. Thus a pure and strict evidence-based case for the prevention and control of childhood obesity would be a very succinct read. But a relative absence of evidence is not evidence of absence, and there is ample science to inform an assessment of what it would take to turn obesity trends around. The 2004 Institute of Medicine (IOM; Koplan, Liverman, & Kraak, 2005) report for the prevention of childhood obesity recommends immediate action to stem further increases in the prevalence of childhood obesity based on "the best available evidence rather than waiting for the best possible evidence."

This discussion presupposes that the best treatment of childhood and adolescent obesity at the population level is its prevention. For the most part, the public health strategies directed toward obesity prevention and control are confluent. Consideration of clinical interventions for established obesity once metabolic sequelae have developed or are imminent is beyond the scope of this chapter.

ACTIONS IN EVERY SETTING

The prevention and control of childhood obesity warrants a comprehensive, multifactorial response at both the individual and population levels. The IOM's report *Preventing Childhood Obesity: Health in the Balance* (Koplan, Liverman, & Kraak, 2005) underlies the importance of this approach. Key elements of a public health response to childhood obesity as outlined in the report include

- National leadership that emphasizes both personal and social responsibility to support healthy behaviors.
- Providing consumers with clear, effective messages enabling them to make informed choices related to their diet and physical activity.
- Monitoring existing trends in dietary and physical activity practices through surveillance programs and national surveys.
- Evaluating the effectiveness of existing nutrition and physical activity programs targeting children and adolescents.
- Identifying and addressing existing gaps in research.
- Synthesizing existing research findings to develop effective policies and programs
- Developing and disseminating evidence-based tools to assist communities and schools in implementing obesity prevention and control programs.

The operational framework for integrated action on obesity involves the creation of supportive environments, the promotion of positive behaviors, and mounting a clinical response. Environmental determinants of obesity must be addressed through public policies that promote the availability and

Table 17.1 Public Health Interventions to Control and Prevent Childhood and Adolescent Obesity, by Setting

Setting	Intervention/Strategy
Households/family	Education of parents about the fundamentals of healthful eating and physical activity, and the importance of a family-based approach. Engagement of parents in school-based initiatives to support healthful eating and physical activity.
Schools	Eliminate junk food, soda, and sports drinks. Provide only healthful foods in both the cafeteria and vending machines. Incorporate daily physical activity. Teach principles of good nutrition. Teach practical skills for achieving good nutrition. Develop programming that reaches into households. Develop programming that relies on youth leadership, peer teaching, and community engagement (e.g., supermarkets). Make fresh fruits and vegetables available daily, preferably for free. Incentivize out-of-school healthful eating and physical activity. Measure BMI in all children at the beginning and end of every school year.
Society/policy	Regulate food marketing to young children. Provide an objective measure of nutritional quality on all food labels. Subsidize fruits and vegetables. Disclose calorie content and nutrient composition on restaurant menus. Invest in walkable/bikeable neighborhoods. Develop social marketing campaigns to raise parental awareness of the importance of childhood obesity. Notify families of children's BMI and of local resources to help with weight management. Overcome cultural anachronisms (e.g., plate cleaning) by exposing them through social marketing.
Clinics	Enhance the training of providers to foster effective, compassionate counseling for family-wide weight management. Reimbursement of providers for preventive counseling related to weight control and health promotion. Online resources to supplement clinical counseling.
Worksites	Weight management/health promotion programs with family-wide relevance/reach. Provide incentive programs to encourage both employee and family health. Establish onsite physical activity facilities whenever possible.
Communities	Resources for healthful family recreation. Options for healthful and fun family dining. Physical activity facilities designed to accommodate families. Modify the built environment to foster physical activity. Dissemination of health messages.
Other	Innovative use of technology to foster weight control and health. Social marketing efforts to eliminate the stigma of obesity.

Note: This list is meant to be representative rather than comprehensive. See the text for discussion.

accessibility of a variety of low-fat, high-fiber foods and that provide safe places and opportunities for physical activity. Behavioral determinants of obesity must be addressed through the promotion of personal awareness, attitudes, beliefs, and skills that motivate and enable people to modify recently introduced unhealthy eating patterns; to restore, as much as possible, traditional methods of food preparation, processing, and preservation using locally grown products; and to increase physical activity, which has declined with modernization. The existing burden of obesity and its associated conditions needs control through clinical programs and staff training to ensure effective support for the maintenance or loss of weight among those already affected. Table 17.1 provides an overview of the key settings for obesity prevention and control efforts, and a representative list of strategies.

Households/Families

Often overlooked in efforts to combat childhood obesity is the fact that children generally live with adults and are influenced by them. Families are the basic functional units of our society. Thus efforts to prevent and control obesity in childhood must be directed toward sustainable behavior change for families (Birch & Davison, 2001; Lindsay, Sussner, Kim, & Gortmaker, 2006).

Programs should be made available through the Internet, clinics, colleges, faith-based organizations, and community centers to educate parents in both the importance of childhood obesity and family-based approaches to improving dietary and physical activity patterns. Parent-teacher organizations might be used as a particularly effective vehicle for conveying this message (Golan & Crow, 2004).

Families need education not only about what constitutes healthful eating, but about some largely covert influences that make applying what is known especially difficult. For example, sensory-specific satiety is the very well-researched tendency to become full faster when flavor varieties are limited and to stay hungry longer when flavors are available in greater variety at any one time (Raynor & Wing, 2006; Rolls, 2006).

The most universally familiar representation of this phenomenon is feeling stuffed at the end of a holiday meal, but still finding room for dessert. Rather than the proverbial hollow leg or extra stomach, this extra room actually is provided courtesy of the hypothalamus, where specialized cells respond to specific taste categories. When eating shifts from salty turkey to sweet pecan pie, a new appetite center is activated and hunger resumes.

This is of profound significance in a world awash in highly processed foods. First, a wide variety of foods is available almost constantly. Second, a variety of flavors is designed into individual foods, perhaps as a willful attempt by the food industry to manipulate appetite. Commercial breakfast cereals routinely contain nearly as much salt as salty snack items. Sauces, dressings, and condiments that taste salty routinely contain sugar in quantities to rival dessert items. And processed foods of every variety contain artificial flavor enhancers. Food industry exploitation of the responsiveness of the human appetite center to stimulation by diverse flavors was the subject of an expose in the *Chicago Tribune* in January 2006 (Callahan, Manier, & Alexander, 2006). *Tribune* examination of tobacco-lawsuit documents found that Kraft and Philip Morris explored the possibility of collaboration to see how foods and drinks can be "engineered to influence" a customer's mood or sense of fullness and sense of satiety. Critics contend that the documents suggest manipulation of food products by junk food manufacturers to make it harder for customers to stop eating them.

Many other food industry practices and cultural patterns that influence dietary intake are addressed in a recent book by nutritional science and marketing professor Brian Wansink (2006). He explores some of the psychological aspects of overeating to explain why we in fact consume more than we believe we do. He advocates weight-loss diets that cut calories by cutting overall consumption instead of strict elimination of intake. Wansink finds the greatest value in retraining one's mind and its perceptions by devices such as making sure one's plate contains at least half vegetables or salad. He suggests that a dieter will automatically eat less in social situations by being the last to start eating and the first to finish. He assesses the dangers of food shopping in bulk-sale stores, where customers are strongly encouraged to overconsume. Wansink's dual approach emphasizing food knowledge and self-knowledge offers a sensible route to permanent weight loss. Such information should be made widely available so that health-conscious children and parents are empowered to overcome weight-control obstacles intrinsic to the modern food supply.

School-based interventions for improving nutrition and physical activity (see below) should build in outreach to parents so that sustainable change for an entire household is fostered.

Schools

Schools have been a popular forum for implementation of childhood obesity control interventions, as they offer continuous and intensive contact with children. Several recent reviews of school-based childhood obesity control programs are available (Flynn et al., 2006; Glenny, O'Meara, Melville, Sheldon, & Wilson, 1997; Katz et al., 2005; Snethen, Broome, & Cashin, 2006; Summerbell et al., 2005).

In general, the following interventions have resulted in a modest positive change in weight-related measures in school children:

- Adding both nutrition and physical activity together in the school curriculum (Cole, Waldrop, D'Auria, & Garner, 2006; Dietz & Gortmaker, 2001; Edwards, 2005; Emslie et al.,

2003; Haney & Durlak, 1998; Sharma, 2006; Trost et al., 2002; Veugelers & Fitzgerald, 2005).

- Incorporating additional structured physical activity into the school day (Centers for Disease Control, 1997; 2007; Dowda, Ainsworth, Addy, Saunders, & Riner, 2001; Giugliano & Carneiro, 2004).
- Noncompetitive sports, such as dance (Centers for Disease Control and Prevention, 1997).
- Reducing sedentary activities (Centers for Disease Control, 1999a; French, Story, & Jeffery, 2001), especially television viewing.

When it comes to improving the eating behaviors of young people, though, school-based nutrition education has been shown to be effective (Contento, Manning, & Shannon, 1992; Lytle & Achterberg, 1995).

The American Dietetic Association (2006) reports that the most effective school-based strategies in changing children's eating behaviors involve using a clear message, multiple strategies that reinforce the message, family involvement, an increase in the amount of time and intensity of contact, and a theoretical framework. These principles must be reconciled with the competing demands on school officials for time during the school day; programs that are relatively unobtrusive are most likely to be applicable in real-world settings.

A number of programs, most requiring significant curricular overhaul, have shown some promise, although to date, no clear winner has emerged (CATCH [www.catchinfo.org/index.html]; Examining Negative Effects of Excess Television [http//notvstanford.edu]; PE4life [www.pe4life. org]; Planet Health [www.planethealth.com]; Take 10! [www.take10.net]; Way Planet [www.way-planet.com/]; We Can! [www.nhlbi.nih.gov/health/public/heart/obesity/wecan/index.htm). A CDC-funded systematic review and meta-analysis of school-based obesity control programs suggests the importance of interventions that address both nutrition and physical activity (Katz, O'Connell, Njike, Yeh, & Nawaz, 2007).

Among the more obvious priorities for schools are the elimination of junk food and soda, and the incorporation of daily physical activity. Progress has been made recently in the area of the former (Alliance for a Healthier Generation, 2006), whereas trends in the latter have generally been adverse. Physical activity during school has declined in part because of pressures attached to the No Child Left Behind Act of 2001 (Public Law 107-110). School and health officials fear that less and less time will be allotted for physical activity, and even recess, fueling the obesity epidemic in American children and teens. Some critics have taken to calling it "No Child Left Without a Big Behind" or "No Child Let Outside." While there are no specific trends or statistics proving a reduction in physical education programs, some experts say there are plenty of anecdotal reports of schools and districts cutting back on gym glasses to provide more time and money to focus on the act's mandates.

Resourcefulness can and should be used to reconcile the priorities for children's health with the demands made on educators. The rambunctiousness of youth warrants recess, not Ritalin, just as obesity is better addressed by regular physical activity rather than by bariatric surgery.

A program called ABC (activity bursts in the classroom) for Fitness (Katz, 2006b) exemplifies such reconciliation. The program begins by surveying teachers in an elementary or middle school to determine the amount of time squandered, on average, disciplining restless children during each session of the day. Teachers are then trained to convert that amount of time into structured aerobic activity right in the classroom. Such bouts may be as short as several minutes, but are run during each session of the day and thus can add 30 min or more of daily physical activity. Evidence to date suggests that physical activity during the school day tends to enhance rather than threaten academic achievement (Daley & Ryan, 2000; Sallis et al., 1999; Taras, 2005). Creative approaches to teaching can be superimposed so that productive teaching time actually increases with ABC for Fitness. The program is designed to enhance fitness, while improving the behavioral environment in the classroom, thus enhancing academic achievement. Evaluation of the program is on-going (Katz, 2006b).

Whereas many school-based nutrition education programs are expansive and thus require a considerable overhaul of the curriculum, there is the opportunity for streamlined approaches that may disseminate far more readily. The Nutrition Detectives program (Katz, 2006c) teaches the importance of healthful food choices and nutrition-label literacy to elementary school and middle school children. Because the goal of the program is to alter food selection patterns, parental engagement is essential and is achieved via assemblies, parent-teacher organization meetings, and memos sent home. The program requires as little as 2 hr of instruction over the course of an entire school year and appears to be amenable to a peer-teaching approach in which high school students act as instructors for younger students. The messages of the program can thus be delivered across a wide age range at virtually no cost to the school. The program has been adopted by schools in as many as a dozen states. Evaluation of the program is on-going (Superintendent, Independence, Missouri, personal communication, May 13, 2006).

The school cafeteria should function as a classroom, serving nutritious food and information about the importance of good nutrition at the same time. Approaches range from the engagement of children in growing their own food (Waters, 2006) to the simple packaging of nutritious items with entertaining educational materials.

In addition to physical activity during the school day, schools should find creative ways to provide incentives for at-home activity. A pedometer program might tally the steps per student; in the classroom this could be used to gauge progress across a map of the state or country. By involving parents to verify step counts submitted by the children, parental awareness of their children's activity level could be raised. Schools could send home suggestions for family activities to raise the students' step counts. Schools and even school districts could compete on the basis of aggregated step counts, with awards for those reaching specific "destinations" first.

The above approaches offer the distinct benefit of minimal cost in money and resources. Strategies aimed at reducing television viewing show promise, but may require technology for monitoring television viewing time (Jago, Baranowski, Baranowski, Thompson, & Greaves, 2005; Salmon, Hume, Ball, Booth, & Crawford, 2006; Viner & Cole, 2005). Providing fresh produce throughout the school day increases consumption, but comes at a cost (Harkin, 2004a). Physical education can and should be made more intensive, however, the best programs tend to be somewhat labor and resource intensive (PE4life; www.pe4life.org/). The tailoring of physical activity instruction to match preference and to provide noncompetitive exertion, such as dance, shows promise (Robinson & Sirard, 2005).

The systematic assessment of BMI in all public school students at the beginning and end of every school year would be a boon to researchers, who could then test interventions without needing to first broach this often sensitive issue (Ikeda & Crawford, 2000; Katz et al., 2005). If such assessments were entirely systematic, any associated stigma would be much alleviated. Providing BMI data to parents, along with compassionate guidance on how to respond productively to the information, shows promise, as evidenced by the experience to date in Arkansas (Ryan, Card-Higginson, McCarthy, Justus, & Thompson, 2006). School health policies are rapidly evolving nationwide (Center for Science in the Public Interest, 2005; Centers for Disease Control, 2005) and a number of promising programs are emerging (Gortmaker et. al, 1999a,b; Katz, 2004; National Association of School Psychologists, 1998; Veugelers & Fitzgerald, 2005).

Society/Policy

A variety of society-wide innovations are warranted to accelerate the control and reversal of childhood obesity trends. The Institute of Medicine recently issued a report on food marketing to children (Committee on Food Marketing and the Diets of Children and Youth, 2006) suggesting the need for reforms. These suggestions should be legislated and food marketing to children regulated by the government; industry oversight, the standard at present, leaves the fox guarding the henhouse.

Food packages should come with a clear indication of overall nutritional quality accessible at a glance; health-conscious parents should not need to overcome both marketing hype and fine print to make good choices for their families. Systems for measuring nutritiousness objectively are proliferating (Department of Agriculture, 2007; Drewnowski, 2005; Hansen, Wyse, & Sorenson, 1979; Kant, 1996; Mojduszka & Caswell, 2000; Moorman, 1998; Padberg, Kubena, Ozuna, Kim, & Osborn, 1993); the FDA should identify the best of these and apply it to the entire food supply. Portion sizes should be adjusted downward, and standardized, with FDA oversight. Results from a number of studies indicate that providing subjects with larger portions in a laboratory setting leads to increased energy intake. Studies in natural settings confirm these findings (Kral, Meengs, Wall, Roe, & Rolls, 2003; Rolls, Morris, & Roe, 2002; Rolls, Roe, Kral, Meengs, & Wall, 2004a; Rolls, Roe, Meengs, & Wall, 2004b). The FDA (2004) report "Calories Count" recommends that foods be labeled as single serving if they can be consumed at one sitting. The report also encouraged food manufacturers to use appropriate comparative labeling statements and urged the restaurant industry to provide point-of-purchase information. The FDA is also considering pilot testing providing their logo on menus and advertisements as an incentive to restaurants and food manufacturers to provide a greater range of portion sizes and to make smaller portions more appealing. This would also encourage restaurants and food retailers to provide consumers with voluntary point-of-purchase information (Food and Drug Administration, 2004; Seligson, 2003).

Suburban sprawl is convincingly associated with obesity risk (Cummins & Jackson, 2001; Hood, 2005; Perdue, Stone, & Gostin, 2003; Sturm, 2005; Sturm & Cohen, 2004). As neighborhoods are built, expanded, or renovated, a premium should be placed on ensuring walkability, bikeability, and the provision of recreational facilities.

Governmental subsidies that favor the production of energy-dense, highly processed foods should give way to subsidies for fruit and vegetable consumption. Economic forces should incentivize healthful eating rather than conspire against it. Possible options include subsidies for store overheads; selective subsidies for healthy food; reduction in prices differentially by applying different reductions to different categories of food items; provide some foods free of charge to at-risk groups; offer freight subsidies to address the "tyranny of distance" in remote or rural communities; and positive discrimination in terms of provision of grants and funding to local industry in favor of healthy foods, providing participants in the food stamp program with incentives to purchase healthy foods and taxation of unhealthy foods such as potato chips and snack items. Senator Harkin (D-IA) recently introduced legislation to create a National Health Promotion Trust Fund to pay for marketing of healthy foods to children using penalties on tobacco companies that fail to cut smoking rates among children (Harkin, 2004b).

Social marketing is the use of marketing principles and techniques to influence a target audience to voluntarily accept, reject, modify, or abandon a behavior for the benefit of individuals, groups, or society as a whole. Commercial marketing methods should be used to raise awareness among parents and children alike about what may be called "cultural anachronisms." No red-blooded American can resist the bargain of an "all-you-can-eat" buffet or a super-sized fast-food meal. But in an age of epidemic obesity, these "bargains" often mean a chance to get fat at no extra charge and then spend a fortune trying to lose the weight gained. A family-based approach to weight control requires a heightened awareness of culture-bound practices—from plate cleaning to bake sales—that once made sense, but no longer do.

Clinics

By adopting a prevention-oriented, proactive approach to weight management, clinicians have another role to play in the public health response to epidemic obesity along with the more strictly clinical role of treating the metabolic consequences of established obesity. Health care providers have long been discouraged from offering weight management counseling by a lack of knowledge, limited time, and a lack of reimbursement (Whitlock, Orleans, Pender, & Allan, 2002), among other factors. New strategies to empower providers with streamlined counseling techniques, such as Web-based instruction offering continuing medical education credits, can be employed to redress deficiencies of knowledge and time. Third-party payers can be engaged to reimburse for counseling provided by trained providers; the same online system that offers instruction could be used to establish a database of trained providers, accessible by insurers (Katz, 2006a). Web-based training systems could further provide quality control indicators to be used in chart audits. Such instruction should foster complementary message delivery by providers to children, and their parents, so that household-wide commitment to health-promoting weight control strategies is fostered.

A variety of systemic changes to the health care delivery system are warranted to support obesity control. An overview of such approaches has been published recently (Katz & Faridi, 2007). The authors recommend developing and refining existing strategies for the delivery of clinical counseling that allow health care providers to serve as more effective agents of behavioral change, adjustments to the resources and operations applied in clinical practice based on evolving models of chronic disease care, the application of novel technologies that facilitate information exchange and coaching between clinical encounters, and coordination and synergy between clinical and school settings for primary and secondary prevention of obesity.

Worksites

Mention of worksites in a discussion of settings relevant to the control of childhood obesity may suggest rampant violation of child labor laws, but that is not the implication. Rather, worksites provide access to the parents of children and adolescents as schools provide access to the children and adolescents themselves. These should be used to cultivate healthful lifestyle practices that translate to the home setting. Just as school-based programs can deliver information home to parents, so might worksite wellness programs deliver information and resources home to family members, children in particular. Examples include worksite nutrition programs that provide demonstrations of and recipes for family-friendly meals (Engbers, van Poppel, Chin, & van Mechelen, 2005; Pelletier, 2001) or even prepared meals to take home, open access for families to worksite exercise facilities, employer-based incentives for family health goals, and educational programs for employees that promote awareness of the importance of nutrition and physical activity to the well-being of children.

Communities

Facilities for physical recreation are available for adults (e.g., Curves, Bally's) and children (e.g., Discovery Zone, Gymboree) in some communities, but they tend to be separate. The development of facilities that offer side-by-side physical activity programming to adults and children would help cultivate a family-oriented view of health promotion. Communities should pass zoning ordinances that prioritize walkability and bikeability (Frank, Andresen, & Schmid, 2004; King et al., 2006; Nelson, Gordon-Larsen, Song, & Popkin, 2006).

Schools should be placed to allow for walking and cycling routes. Building codes should make stairwells prominent and attractive, and signage should encourage their use. Health-conscious communities should use chambers of commerce to incentivize the establishment of family-friendly restaurants that offer healthful nutrition and full disclosure of calorie and nutrient content. Wellness committees should be convened by community leaders and work to disseminate consistent health messages in venues from supermarkets to faith-based organizations.

Other

Technology has contributed to the problem of epidemic childhood obesity by displacing the work of muscles with sedentary pursuits such as television viewing and video games. Technology can also contribute to the solution, as suggested by such innovations as the "Dance, Dance Revolution" program. Cell phone use by adolescents is widespread, and could serve as a system for delivery of health information, including point-of-purchase guidance based on global positioning system (GPS) information. Creative use of the Internet can help empower families seeking to navigate safely through the challenges of the modern nutritional landscape; an example of such assistance is found at the Healthy Dining Finder Web site (www.healthydiningfinder.com/site/). Social marketing messages, delivered via print and screen media, should encourage awareness of the obesity problem, mitigate the stigma associated with obesity, and propagate awareness of obesity-control resources.

COST-EFFECTIVENESS OF CHILDHOOD OBESITY AND CONTROL INTERVENTIONS

The cost-effectiveness of childhood obesity prevention efforts is not well documented. Results of the "Assessing Cost-Effectiveness of Obesity Interventions in Children" (ACE Obesity) report (Department of Human Services, 2006) represent an important effort in documenting the evidence and value of a number of public health interventions designed to reduce childhood obesity. From a list of 30 interventions, a total of 13 were selected for this detailed study. The overall benefit of the interventions was determined using two measures: disability adjusted life years (DALY) and incremental cost-effectiveness ratio (ICER). Results indicate that interventions with the greatest impact on health also scored well in terms of affordability and cost-effectiveness. Interventions and policies designed to reduce television advertising for children, targeting children who are already in the obese category, and interventions aimed at reducing consumption of sugar-sweetened beverages among school children were deemed cost effective. The use of pharmaceutical and surgical interventions, such as orlistat and gastric banding, was also cost effective. The report provides policy makers with important guidance on efficiency, impact, and acceptability for a wide range of obesity interventions (Department of Human Services, 2006).

PRACTICAL IMPLICATIONS FOR PREVENTION AND CONTROL OF CHILDHOOD OBESITY

Childhood obesity prevention and control requires a review of available facts, an element of risk that the evidence is inadequate, and a negotiation of proposed programs and policies in the context of competing economic and political interests. This process of risk, review, and negotiation is outlined by Lobstein (2006).

A review conducted by Flynn et al. (2006) found that out of a total of 13,000 reports and articles on childhood obesity programs, only 500 gave sufficient information on their methods to allow for identification of good practices. This indicates that a number of potentially useful interventions are taking place that do not provide sufficient information to be evaluated. More importantly, while anti-obesity programs may meet the criteria for methodological rigor, they did not identify best practices and policies to be of practical use. Most interventions deal with small populations in school, community, or clinical settings and fail to address the upstream population health questions or population-level inequalities. The author notes the lack of interventions at midstream (community and sector level) and upstream (Department of Human Services, 2006; Haby et al., 2006). None of the studies looked at the effect of population-wide policy-related issues, such as food marketing, pricing, transport, or planning controls. Social interventions that will help children and parents counter the subtle influences of the obesogenic environment are needed that permit the development of a "social policy approach to healthy lifestyles rather than a current healthy lifestyle approach to policy."

Lobstein (2006) delineates a logical process to assist practitioners in developing and implementing programs addressing childhood obesity within a societal context. This involves a scoping exercise summarizing known risk factors within the target population, incorporating expert opinion and best practices, and looking at the potential harm of proposed programs. The scoping exercise leads to a risk assessment process in which upstream and downstream relationships are analyzed and participants' values are incorporated. Stakeholder participation is an important component of this step and requires consensus building for which upstream factors need to be addressed. The process can be structured by using the ANGELO (Analysis Grid for Environments/Elements Leading to Obesity) model proposed by Egger and Swinburn (1997) or the STEFANI (Strategies for Effective Food and Nutrition Initiatives) matrix developed for government use (Robertson, 2004). The issue of who will pay for these programs can be addressed by employing the approach suggested by Swinburn, Gill, and Kumanyika (2005), which evaluates interventions on predicted effectiveness and population impact. The last step involves implementation and evaluation. The author gives examples of several antiobesity efforts currently under way that were not the result of randomized controlled trials, but were introduced in response to political pressure or voluntary action by local communities and schools. Practical and sustainable childhood obesity interventions have to be large in scale and must address a broad spectrum of social, commercial, cultural, and political factors. Use of structured frameworks and participatory approaches are essential in the design of pragmatic solutions to childhood obesity (Kumanyika, 2001; Orleans, 2000).

OF POLICY AND PERSPECTIVE

There are, for the first time in history, more overfed than hungry *Homo sapiens* on the planet. The implications for obesity management are both clear and compelling. A universal preventive approach is warranted, as the entire population—indeed the species—is in the at-risk group.

The challenge of obesity control is not about what, it is about how. How can we enable an increasingly overweight population to resist the obesogenic forces conspiring against it?

There are two reasonable approaches. One is to reengineer the modern environment so that its obesogenicity is attenuated. The second is to better exploit our native intelligence and resourcefulness, and empower individuals and families with the knowledge, skills, and strategies necessary to resist fixed obesogenic elements of the modern landscape. These approaches are both achievable to some degree, and likely both will be required. There is a limit to how far either can go alone. Some environmental reforms seem much more plausible than others. We may, for example, construct sidewalks more consistently in neighborhoods of the future. It seems improbable that having devised snow blowers, leaf blowers, and tractors, we will ever renounce them and return to rakes, shovels, and plows.

How much can be achieved through a focus on the environment and how much through empowering individuals is a matter worthy of dedicated attention. To strike the right balance will require recognition that the approaches are complementary rather than competitive. Current opinion tends to be divisive and polarized, with some proponents of "personal responsibility" and others of "environmental determinism." We would be well served by measures that tell us who is sufficiently empowered to take control of their weight and who is not. If responsibility comes with power (Hassed, 2004; Minkler, 1999; Mittelmark, 2001), the corollary is that empowerment is prerequisite to taking responsibility. Divisive rhetoric all too often conceals the middle path of reasoned consensus from all concerned.

While simple to explain, epidemic obesity will be anything but easy to fix. We must overcome the propensity of our genes, the propulsive force of culture, and some 6 million years of gathering momentum. To hold back the flood waters, you need an entire dam; no single sandbag, brick, or branch will make any discernible difference at all. But every dam begins with a first sandbag, brick, or branch, and could not accomplish its intended purpose without them.

The remedy to epidemic obesity—in children and adults alike—may appear as daunting as holding back the surge of a restless sea. But the only alternative is an increasing number of victims drowning in the flood. Prevention in this case is weighty, but far less so than the cure.

Nothing done to date has convincingly altered adverse childhood obesity trends at the population level. But this is neither because we lack promising and effective programs, nor because we lack knowledge and insight about what is required. Rather it is because we have not yet done enough. Our efforts going forward should be informed by both the available evidence and judgment; absence of evidence is not evidence of absence. Ultimately anything that serves to reduce calorie intake, or increase energy expenditure, will help curtail obesity. Research efforts should assess the cumulative effects of multiple conjoined programs; should be sensitive to improvements in intervening variables such as dietary pattern, activity level, and even knowledge and attitude; and should encompass the evaluation of programs developed outside of academia.

Any single intervention for obesity control is like a single sandbag for flood control. No matter how robust the intervention, or sandbag, it simply cannot exert a meaningful effect in isolation. The aggregation of sandbags can establish a levee or dam sufficient to contain the flood. This approach must be applied to the containment, control, and prevention of childhood obesity as well. A barricade against a deluge of obesogenic factors will need to be built from everything we can think of. If and when we commit to bending our backs and building such a barrier, better health and weight control for our children will surely come.

ACKNOWLEDGMENT

The insight Meghan O'Connell, MPH, and the technical assistance of Dr. Yuka Yazaki are greatly appreciated.

REFERENCES

Alliance for a Healthier Generation. (2006). Statement from the Centers for Disease Control and prevention concerning agreement by five U.S. Food companies to meet nutritional guidelines for food sold in schools. New York: Alliance for a Healthier Generation. Available at www.healthiergeneration.org/uploadedFiles/For_Schools/CDC-Snack%20foods%20Statement.pdf.

American Beverage Association. (2007). School beverage guidelines. Washington, D.C.: American Beverage Association. Available at from www.ameribev.org/industry-issues/beverages-in-schools/school-beverage-guidelines/index.aspx.

American Dietetic Association. (2006). Individual-, family-, school-, and community-based interventions for pediatric overweight. *Journal of the American Dietetic Association, 106,* 925–945.

Anderson, G. H. (2006). Sugars-containing beverages and post-prandial satiety and food intake. *International Journal of Obesity (London), 30*(suppl. 3), S52–S59.

Apedo, M. T., Sowers, J. R., & Banerji, M. A. (2002). Cardiovascular disease in adolescents with type 2 diabetes mellitus. *Journal of Pediatric Endocrinology & Metabolism, 15*(suppl. 1), 519–523.

Aye, T., & Levitsky, L. L. (2003). Type 2 diabetes: an epidemic disease in childhood. *Current Opinions in Pediatrics, 15,* 411–415.

Birch, L. L., & Davison, K. K. (2001). Family environmental factors influencing the developing behavioral controls of food intake and childhood overweight. *Pediatric Clinics of North America, 48*(4), 893–907.

Block, G. (2004). Foods contributing to energy intake in the U.S.: data from NHANES III and NHANES 1999–2000. *Journal of Food Composition and Analysis, 17,* 439–447.

Borzekowski, D. L., & Robinson, T. N. (2001a). The 30-second effect: an experiment revealing the impact of television commercials on food preferences of preschoolers. *Journal of the American Dietetic Association, 101,* 42–46.

Borzekowski, D. L., & Robinson, T. N. (2001b). Pitching to preschoolers: the impact of televised food commercials on a sample of Head Start children. *Journal of the American Dietetic Association, 101,* 42–46.

Buhs, E. S., & Ladd, G. W. (2001). Peer rejection as an antecedent of young children's school adjustment: an examination of the mediating processes. *Developmental Psychology, 37,* 550–560.

Burghardt, J. A., Gordon, A. R., & Fraker, T. M. (1995). Meals offered in the national school lunch program and the school breakfast program. *American Journal of Clinical Nutrition, 61*(suppl.), 187S–198S.

Burton, B. T., Foster, W. R., Hirsch, J., & Van Itallie, T. B. (1985). Health implications of obesity: An NIH consensus development conference. *International Journal of Obesity, 9*(3), 155–170 [published erratum appears in *International Journal of Obesity* 1986;10(1):79].

Burton, W. N., Chen, C., Schultz, A. B., & Edington, D. W. (1998). The economic costs associated with body mass index in the workplace. *Journal of Occupational and Environmental Medicine, 40*, 786–792.

Caballero, A. E., Saouaf, R., Lim, S. C., Hamdy, O., Abou-Elenin, K., O'Connor, C., Logerfo, F. W., Horton, E. S., & Veves, A. (2003). The effects of troglitazone, an insulin-sensitizing agent, on the endothelial function in early and late type 2 diabetes: a placebo-controlled randomized clinical trial. *Metabolism, 52*, 173–180.

Callahan, P., Manier, J., & Alexander, D. (2006). Where there's smoke, there might be food research, too. *Chicago Tribune,* January 29. Available at www.chicagotribune.com/business/chi-060129054jan29,1,3082179. story.

Calle, E. E., Rodriguez, C., Walker-Thurmond, K., & Thun, M. J. (2003). Overweight, obesity, and mortality from cancer in a prospectively studied cohort of U.S. Adults. *New England Journal of Medicine, 348*, 1625–1638.

Calle, E. E., Teras, L. R., & Thun, M. J. (2005a). Adiposity and physical activity as predictors of mortality. *New England Journal of Medicine, 352*, 1381–1384; author reply 1381–1384.

Calle, E. E., Teras, L. R., & Thun, M. J. (2005b). Obesity and mortality. *New England Journal of Medicine, 353*, 2197–2199.

Calle, E. E., & Thun, M. J. (2004). Obesity and cancer. *Oncogene, 23*(38), 6365–6378.

Caterson, I. (2006). Keynote address. 10th International Congress of Obesity, Sydney, Australia, 3–8 September.

Center for Science in the Public Interest. (2005). Policy options: improve school food. Washington, D.C.: Center for Science in the Public Interest. Available at www.cspinet.org/schoolfood/.

Centers for Disease Control and Prevention (1997). Guidelines for school and community programs to promote lifelong physical activity among young people. *Morbidity & Mortality Weekly Report, 46*(RR-6), 1–36.

Centers for Disease Control. (1999a). SHPPS: School Health Policies and Programs Study. Atlanta: Centers for Disease Control. Available at www.cdc.gov/HealthyYouth/shpps/index.htm.

Centers for Disease Control. (1999b). Diabetes threat on the rise among U.S. children, specialists say. *Chronic Disease Notes & Reports, 12*(2), 1, 10–12.

Centers for Disease Control. (2005). U.S. physical activity statistics: state legislative information. Atlanta: Centers for Disease Control. Available at apps.nccd.cdc.gov/DNPALeg/.

Centers for Disease Control. (2007). Overweight and obesity: contributing factors. Atlanta: Centers for Disease Control. Available at www.cdc.gov/nccdphp/dnpa/obesity/contributing_factors.htm.

Child Health Alert. (2005). Obesity in children—What might be its impact on life expectancy? *Child Health Alert, 23*, 1–2.

Chinn, S., & Rona, R. J. (2002). International definitions of overweight and obesity for children: A lasting solution? *Annals of Human Biology, 29*, 306–313.

Colditz, G. A., Willett, W. C., Rotnitzky, A., & Manson, J. E. (1995). Weight gain as a risk factor for clinical diabetes mellitus in women [see comments]. *Annals of Internal Medicine, 122*, 481–486.

Cole, K., Waldrop, J., D'Auria, J., & Garner, H. (2006). An integrative research review: effective school-based childhood overweight interventions. *Journal of Specialists in Pediatric Nursing, 11*(3), 166–177.

Cole, T. J., Bellizzi, M. C., Flegal, K. M., & Dietz, W. H. (2000). Establishing a standard definition for child overweight and obesity worldwide: international survey. *BMJ, 320*(7244), 1240–1243.

Committee on Food Marketing and the Diets of Children and Youth. (2006). *Food marketing to children and youth: Threat or opportunity?* Washington, D.C.: National Academies Press.

Contento, I. R., Manning, A. D., & Shannon, B. (1992). Research perspective on school-based nutrition education. *Journal of Nutrition Education, 24*, 247–260.

Cramer, P., & Steinwert, T. (1998). Thin is good, fat is bad: How early does it begin? *Journal of Applied Developmental Psychology, 19*, 429–451.

Crespo, C. J., Smit, E., Troiano, R. P., Bartlett, S. J., Macera, C. A., & Andersen, R. E. (2001). Television watching, energy intake, and obesity in U.S. children: results from the third National Health and Nutrition Examination Survey, 1988–1994. *Archives of Pediatric and Adolescent Medicine, 155*, 360–365.

Cummins, S. K., & Jackson, R. J. (2001). The built environment and children's health. *Pediatric Clinics of North America, 48*, 1241–1252, x.

Daley, A. J., & Ryan, J. (2000). Academic performance and participation in physical activity by secondary school adolescents. *Perceptual & Motor Skills, 91,* 531–534.

Das, M., Gabriely, I., & Barzilai, N. (2004). Caloric restriction, body fat and ageing in experimental models. *Obesity Reviews, 5,* 13–19.

Davison, K. K., Marshall, S. J., & Birch, L. L. (2006). Cross-sectional and longitudinal associations between TV viewing and girls' body mass index, overweight status, and percentage of body fat. *Journal of Pediatrics, 149,* 32–37.

Dehghan, M., Akhtar-Danesh, N., & Merchant, A. T. (2005). Childhood obesity, prevalence and prevention. *Nutrition Journal, 4,* 24.

Dencker, M., Thorsson, O., Karlsson, M. K., Linden, C., Eiberg, S., Wollmer, P., & Andersen, L. B. (2006). Daily physical activity related to body fat in children aged 8–11 years. *Journal of Pediatrics, 149,* 38–42.

Department of Agriculture. (2007). The healthy eating index. Washington, D.C.: Department of Agriculture. Available at www.cnpp.usda.gov/HealthyEatingIndex.htm.

Department of Health and Human Services. (2003). Summary health statistics for U.S. children: National Health Interview Survey, 2001. Washington, D.C.: Department of Health and Human Services. Available at www.cdc.gov/nchs/nhis.htm.

Department of Human Services. (2006). Assessing cost-effectiveness of obesity interventions in children: summary of results. Melbourne: Department of Human Services, Victoria.

Devaney, B., Gordon, A., & Burghardt, J. (1993). *The school nutrition dietary assessment study: dietary intakes of program participants and nonparticipants.* Hyattsville, MD: Department of Agriculture.

Dietz, W. H., & Gortmaker, S. L. (2001). Preventing obesity in children and adolescents. *Annual Review of Public Health, 22,* 337–353.

Dowda, M., Ainsworth, B. E., Addy, C. L., Saunders, R., & Riner, W. (2001). Environmental influences, physical activity, and weight status in 8- to 16-year-olds. *Archives of Pediatric and Adolescent Medicine, 155,* 711–717.

Drewnowski, A. (2005). Concept of a nutritious food: Toward a nutrient density score. *American Journal of Clinical Nutrition, 82,* 721–732.

Edwards, B. (2005). Childhood obesity: a school-based approach to increase nutritional knowledge and activity levels. *Nursing Clinics of North America, 40,* 661–669, viii–ix.

Egger, G., & Swinburn, B. (1997). An "ecological" approach to the obesity pandemic. *BMJ, 315*(7106), 477–480.

Emslie, G. J., Mayes, T. L., Laptook, R. S., & Batt, M. (2003). Predictors of response to treatment in children and adolescents with mood disorders. *Psychiatric Clinics of North America, 26,* 435–456.

Engbers, L. H., van Poppel, M. N., Chin, A. P. M. J., & van Mechelen, W. (2005). Worksite health promotion programs with environmental changes: a systematic review. *American Journal of Preventive Medicine, 29,* 61–70.

Expert Panel on Detection, Evaluation, and Treatment of High Blood Cholesterol in Adults. (2001). Executive summary of the third report of the National Cholesterol Education Program (NCEP) Expert Panel on Detection, Evaluation, and Treatment of High Blood Cholesterol in Adults (Adult Treatment Panel III). *JAMA, 285,* 2486–2497.

Fagot-Campagna, A., Pettitt, D. J., Engelgau, M. M., Burrows, N. R., Geiss, L. S., Valdez, R., Beckles, G. L., Saaddine, J., Gregg, E. W., Williamson, D. F., & Narayan, K. M. (2000). Type 2 diabetes among North American children and adolescents: an epidemiologic review and a public health perspective. *Journal of Pediatrics, 136,* 664–672.

Field, A. E., Cook, N. R., & Gillman, M. W. (2005). Weight status in childhood as a predictor of becoming overweight or hypertensive in early adulthood. *Obesity Research, 13,* 163–169.

Flegal, K. M., Tabak, C. J., & Ogden, C. L. (2006). Overweight in children: definitions and interpretation. *Health Education Research, 21,* 755–760.

Flynn, M. A., McNeil, D. A., Maloff, B., Mutasingwa, D., Wu, M., Ford, C., & Tough, F. C. (2006). Reducing obesity and related chronic disease risk in children and youth: A synthesis of evidence with "best practice" recommendations. *Obesity Reviews, 7*(suppl. 1), 7–66.

Food and Drug Administration. (2004). Calories count: report of the Working Group on Obesity. Washington, D.C.: Food and Drug Administration. Available at www.cfsan.fda.gov/~dms/owg-toc.html.

Fontana, L. (2006). Excessive adiposity, calorie restriction, and aging. *JAMA, 295,* 1577–1578.

Frank, L. D., Andresen, M. A., & Schmid, T. L. (2004). Obesity relationships with community design, physical activity, and time spent in cars. *American Journal of Preventive Medicine, 27,* 87–96.

French, S., Jeffery, R., Klesges, L., & Forster, J. (1995). Weight concerns and change in smoking behavior over two years in working population. *American Journal of Public Health, 85,* 720–722.

French, S. A., Story, M., & Jeffery, R. W. (2001). Environmental influences on eating and physical activity. *Annual Review of Public Health, 22,* 309–335.

Giugliano, R., & Carneiro, E. C. (2004). Factors associated with obesity in school children. *Jornal de Pediatria, 80,* 17–22.

Gleason, P., & Suitor, C. (2001). *Changes in children's diets: 1989–1991 to 1994–1996.* CN-01-CD2. Alexandria, VA: Food Nutrition Service.

Glenny, A. M., O'Meara, S., Melville, A., Sheldon, T. A., & Wilson, C. (1997). The treatment and prevention of obesity: a systematic review of the literature. *International Journal of Obesity and Related Metabolic Disorders, 21,* 715–737.

Golan, M., & Crow, S. (2004). Parents are key players in the prevention and treatment of weight-related problems. *Nutrition Review, 62,* 39–50.

Gortmaker, S. L., Cheung, L. W. Y., Peterson, K. E., Chomitz, G., Cradle, J. H., Dart, H., Fox, M. K., Bullock, R. B., Sobol, A. M., Colditz, G., Field, A. E., & Laird, N. (1999a). Impact of a school-based interdisciplinary intervention on diet and physical activity among urban primary school children: eat well and keep moving. *Archives of Pediatrics and Adolescent Medicine, 153,* 975–983.

Gortmaker, S. L., Peterson, K., Wiecha, J., Sobol, A. M., Dixit, S., Fox, M. K., & Laird, N. (1999b). Reducing obesity via a school-based interdisciplinary intervention among youth: Planet Health. *Archives of Pediatrics and Adolescent Medicine, 153,* 409–418.

Guo, S. S., & Chumlea, W. C. (1999). Tracking of body mass index in children in relation to overweight in adulthood. *American Journal of Clinical Nutrition, 70,* 145S–148S.

Haby, M. M., Vos, T., Carter, R., Moodie, M., Markwick, A., Magnus, A., et al. (2006). A new approach to assessing the health benefit from obesity interventions in children and adolescents: The assessing cost-effectiveness in obesity project. *International Journal of Obesity, 30*(10), 1463–1475.

Haney, P., & Durlak, J. A. (1998). Changing self-esteem in children and adolescents: a meta-analytic review. *Journal of Clinical Child Psychology, 27,* 423–433.

Hansen, R. G., Wyse, B. W., & Sorenson, A. W. (1979). *Nutrition quality index of food.* Westport, CT: AVI Publishing.

Harkin, T. (2004a). Harkin announces 28 new Iowa schools to participate in the fruit and vegetable program. Available at http://harkin.senate.gov/press/print-release.cfm?id=227983.

Harkin, T. (2004b). Health care, not sick care. *American Journal of Health Promotion, 19*(1), 1–11.

Harris, T. B., Launer, L. J., Madans, J., & Feldman, J. J. (1997). Cohort study of effect of being overweight and change in weight on risk of coronary heart disease in old age. *BMJ, 314*(7097), 1791–1794.

Hassed, C. (2004). Taking personal responsibility for our health. Nectar or a poisoned chalice? *Australian Family Physician, 33*(1–2), 74–75.

Hedley, A. A., Ogden, C. L., Johnson, C. L., Carroll, M. D., Curtin, L. R., & Flegal, K. M. (2004). Prevalence of overweight and obesity among U.S. children, adolescents, and adults, 1999–2002. *JAMA, 291,* 2847–2850.

Hill, A. J., Draper, E., & Stack, J. (1994). A weight on children's minds: body shape dissatisfactions at 9 years old. *International Journal of Obesity and Related Metabolic Disorders, 18,* 383–389.

Hood, E. (2005). Sharing solutions for childhood obesity. *Environmental Health Perspectives, 113*(8), A520–A522.

Ikeda, J. P., & Crawford, P. (2000). Guidelines for collecting heights and weights on children and adolescents in school settings. Berkeley: University of California. Available at www.cnr.berkeley.edu/cwh/PDFs/bw_weighing.pdf.

Jago, R., Baranowski, T., Baranowski, J. C., Thompson, D., & Greaves, K. A. (2005). BMI from 3–6 y of age is predicted by TV viewing and physical activity, not diet. *International Journal of Obesity (London), 29,* 557–564.

Jebb, S. A., & Prentice, A. M. (2001). Single definition of overweight and obesity should be used. *BMJ, 323*(7319), 999.

Jeffery, R. W., & Utter, J. (2003). The changing environment and population obesity in the United States. *Obesity Research, 11,* 12S–22S.

Kant, A. K. (1996). Indexes of overall diet quality: a review. *Journal of the American Dietetic Association, 96,* 785–791.

Katz, D. (2004). The way to eat. Available at www.thewaytoeat.net.

Katz, D. (2006a). The NECON initiative as a case study in collaborative obesity control. Available at www.davidkatzmd.com/media/NOAF.Katz.6-5-06.ppt.

Katz, D. (2006b). School nutrition programs: ABC for Fitness. Available at www.davidkatzmd.com/abcforfitness.aspx.

Katz, D. (2006c). School nutrition programs: Nutrition Detectives. Available at www.davidkatzmd.com/nutritiondetectives.aspx.

Katz, D., O'Connell, M., Njike, V. N., Yeh, M., & Nawaz, H. (in press). Strategies for the prevention and control of obesity in the school setting: systematic review and meta-analysis. *International Journal of Obesity.*

Katz, D. L., & Faridi, Z. (2007). Health care system approaches to obesity prevention and control. In *Obesity, epidemiology, and prevention* (chap. 15). New York: Springer.

Katz, D. L., O'Connell, M., Yeh, M. C., Nawaz, H., Njike, V., Anderson, L. M., Cory, S., & Dietz, W. (2005). Public health strategies for preventing and controlling overweight and obesity in school and worksite settings: a report on recommendations of the Task Force on Community Preventive Services. *MMWR Morbidity and Mortality Weekly Report, 54*(RR-10), 1–12.

Kaur, H., Hyder, M. L., & Poston, W. S. (2003). Childhood overweight: an expanding problem. *Treatments in Endocrinology, 2,* 375–388.

Kelly, B. (2005). To quell obesity, who should regulate food marketing to children? *Global Health, 1,* 9.

King, A. C., Toobert, D., Ahn, D., Resnicow, K., Coday, M., Riebe, D., Garber, C. E., Hurtz, S., Morton, J., & Sallis, J. F. (2006). Perceived environments as physical activity correlates and moderators of intervention in five studies. *American Journal of Health Promotion, 21,* 24–35.

Koplan, J. P., Liverman, C. T., and Kraak, V. A. (Eds.). (2005). *Preventing childhood obesity: health in the balance.* Washington, D.C.: National Academies Press.

Kraig, K. A., & Keel, P. K. (2001). Weight-based stigmatization in children. *International Journal of Obesity and Related Metabolic Disorders, 25,* 1661–1666.

Kral, T. V. E., Meengs, J. S., Wall, D. E., Roe, L. S., & Rolls, B. J. (2003). Effect on food intake of increasing the portion size of all foods over two consecutive days. *FASEB Journal, 17,* A809.

Kumanyika, S. K. (2001). Minisymposium on obesity: overview and some strategic considerations. *Annual Review of Public Health, 22,* 293–308.

Latner, J. D., & Stunkard, A. J. (2003). Getting worse: the stigmatization of obese children. *Obesity Research, 11,* 452–456.

Lee, J. M., Okumura, M. J., Davis, M. M., Herman, W. H., & Gurney, J. G. (2006). Prevalence and determinants of insulin resistance among U.S. adolescents: a population-based study. *Diabetes Care, 29,* 2427–2432.

Liese, A. D., D'Agostino, R. B., Jr., Hamman, R. F., Kilgo, P. D., Lawrence, J. M., Liu, L. L., Loots, B., Linder, B., Marcovina, S., Rodriguez, B., Standiford, D., & Williams, D. E. (2006). The burden of diabetes mellitus among us youth: Prevalence estimates from the search for diabetes in youth study. *Pediatrics, 118,* 1510–1518.

Lindsay, A. C., Sussner, K. M., Kim, J., & Gortmaker, S. (2006). The role of parents in preventing childhood obesity. *Future of Children, 16*(1), 169–186.

Lobstein, T. (2006). Comment: preventing child obesity—an art and a science. *Obesity Reviews, 7*(suppl. 1), 1–5.

Lobstein, T., & Dibb, S. (2005). Evidence of a possible link between obesogenic food advertising and child overweight. *Obesity Reviews, 6,* 203–208.

Luciano, A., Bressan, F., Bolognani, M., Castellarin, A., & Zoppi, G. (2001). Childhood obesity: different definition criteria, different prevalence rate. *Minerva Pediatrica, 53,* 537–541.

Ludwig, D. S., Peterson, K. E., & Gortmaker, S. L. (2001). Relation between consumption of sugar-sweetened drinks and childhood obesity: a prospective, observational analysis. *Lancet, 357,* 505–508.

Lytle, L., & Achterberg, C. (1995). Changing the diet of America's children: What works and why? *Journal of Nutrition Education, 27,* 250–260.

Mann, C. C. (2005). Public health. Provocative study says obesity may reduce U.S. life expectancy. *Science, 307*(5716), 1716–1717.

Manson, J. E., Nathan, D. M., Krolewski, A. S., Stampfer, M. J., Willett, W. C., & Hennekens, C. H. (1992). A prospective study of exercise and incidence of diabetes among us male physicians. *JAMA, 268,* 63–67.

Mascie-Taylor, C. G., & Karim, E. (2003). The burden of chronic disease. *Science, 302,* 1921–1922.

Masoro, E. J. (2005). Overview of caloric restriction and ageing. *Mechanisms of Ageing and Development, 126,* 913–922.

McLellan, F. (2002). Marketing and advertising: harmful to children's health. *Lancet, 360*(9338), 1001.

Minkler, M. (1999). Personal responsibility for health? A review of the arguments and the evidence at century's end. *Health Education and Behavior, 26,* 121–140.

Mittelmark, M. B. (2001). Promoting social responsibility for health: health impact assessment and healthy public policy at the community level. *Health Promotion International, 16,* 269–274.

Mizuno, T., Shu, I. W., Makimura, H., & Mobbs, C. (2004). Obesity over the life course. *Science of Aging Knowledge Environment, 2004*(24), re4.

Mojduszka, E. M., & Caswell, J. A. (2000). A test of nutritional quality signaling in food markets prior to implementation of mandatory labeling. *American Journal of Agricultural Economics, 82,* 298–309.

Mokdad, A. H., Bowman, B. A., Ford, E. S., Vinicor, F., Marks, J. S., & Koplan, J. P. (2001). The continuing epidemics of obesity and diabetes in the United States. *JAMA, 286,* 1195–1200.

Moorman, C. (1998). Market-level effects of information: competitive responses and consumer dynamics. *Journal of Marketing Research, 2,* 82–98.

Moran, R. (1999). Evaluation and treatment of childhood obesity. *American Family Physician, 59,* 758, 761–762.

Muller, M. J., Koetringer, I., Mast, M., Languix, K., & Frunch, A. (1999). Physical activity and diet in 5 to 7 year old children. *Public Health Nutrition, 2,* 443–444.

National Association of School Psychologists. (1998). Obesity in children: helping children at home and at school. Bethesda, MD: National Association of School Psychologists. Available at www.nasponline.org/families/index.aspx.

Nelson, M. C., Gordon-Larsen, P., Song, Y., & Popkin, B. M. (2006). Built and social environments associations with adolescent overweight and activity. *American Journal of Preventive Medicine, 31,* 109–117.

Nestle, M. (2006). Food marketing and childhood obesity—a matter of policy. *New England Journal of Medicine, 354,* 2527–2529.

Ogden, C. L., Carroll, M. D., Curtin, L. R., McDowell, M. A., Tabak, C. J., & Flegal, K. M. (2006). Prevalence of overweight and obesity in the United States, 1999–2004. *JAMA, 295,* 1549–1555.

Ogden, C. L., Carroll, M. D., & Flegal, K. M. (2003). Epidemiologic trends in overweight and obesity. *Endocrinology and Metabolism Clinics of North America, 32,* 741–760.

Ogden, C. L., Flegal, K. M., Carroll, M. D., & Johnson, C. L. (2002). Prevalence and trends in overweight among U.S. children and adolescents, 1999–2000. *JAMA, 288,* 1728–1732.

Orleans, C. T. (2000). Promoting the maintenance of health behavior change: recommendations for the next generation of research and practice. *Health Psychology, 19*(1 suppl.), 76–83.

Padberg, D. I., Kubena, K. S., Ozuna, T., Kim, H., & Osborn, L. (1993). *The nutritional quality index: an instrument for communicating nutrition information to consumers.* College Station: Agricultural and Food Policy Center, Texas A&M University.

Patrick, K., Norman, G. J., Calfas, K. J., Sallis, J. F., Zabinski, M. F., Rupp, J., & Cella, J. (2004). Diet, physical activity, and sedentary behaviors as risk factors for overweight in adolescence. *Archives of Pediatric and Adolescent Medicine, 158,* 385–390.

Peeters, A., Barendregt, J. J., Willekens, F., Mackenbach, J. P., Al Mamun, A., & Bonneux, L. (2003). Obesity in adulthood and its consequences for life expectancy: a life-table analysis. *Annals of Internal Medicine, 138,* 24–32.

Pelletier, K. R. (2001). A review and analysis of the clinical and cost-effectiveness studies of comprehensive health promotion and disease management programs at the worksite: 1998–2000 update. *American Journal of Health Promotion, 16,* 107–116.

Perdue, W. C., Stone, L. A., & Gostin, L. O. (2003). The built environment and its relationship to the public's health: the legal framework. *American Journal of Public Health, 93,* 1390–1394.

Pereira, M. A. (2006). The possible role of sugar-sweetened beverages in obesity etiology: a review of the evidence. *International Journal of Obesity (London), 30*(suppl. 3), S28–S36.

Philippas, N. G., & Lo, C. W. (2005). Childhood obesity: etiology, prevention, and treatment. *Nutrition in Clinical Care, 8*(2), 77–88.

Pontiroli, A. E. (2004). Type 2 diabetes mellitus is becoming the most common type of diabetes in school children. *Acta Diabetologica, 41*(3), 85–90.

Preston, S. H. (2005). Deadweight?—the influence of obesity on longevity. *New England Journal of Medicine, 352,* 1135–1137.

Proctor, M. H., Moore, L. L., Gao, D., Cupples, L A., Bradlee, M L., Hood, M Y., & Ellison, R C. (2003). Television viewing and change in body fat from preschool to early adolescence: the Framingham Children's Study. *International Journal of Obesity and Related Metabolic Disorders, 27,* 827–833.

Puhl, R., & Brownell, K. D. (2001). Bias, discrimination, and obesity. *Obesity Research, 9,* 788–805.

Raynor, H., & Maier, D. (2006). The childhood obesity epidemic: key eating and activity behaviors to address in treatment. *Medicine and Health Rhode Island, 89*(7), 241–243, 246.

Raynor, H. A., & Wing, R. R. (2006). Effect of limiting snack food variety across days on hedonics and consumption. *Appetite, 46,* 168–176.

Robertson, A. (Ed.). (2004). *Food and health in Europe: a new basis for action.* Geneva: World Health Organization.

Robinson, T., Haydel, F., & Killen, J. (2000). Are overweight children unhappy? *Archives of Pediatric and Adolescent Medicine, 154,* 931–935.

Robinson, T. N., & Sirard, J. R. (2005). Preventing childhood obesity: a solution-oriented research paradigm. *American Journal of Preventive Medicine, 28*(2 suppl. 2), 194–201.

Rolls, B. J., Morris, E. L., & Roe, L. S. (2002). Portion size of food affects energy intake in normal-weight and overweight men and women. *American Journal of Clinical Nutrition, 76,* 1207–1213.

Rolls, B. J., Roe, L. S., Kral, T. V., Meengs, J. S., & Wall, D. E. (2004a). Increasing the portion size of a packaged snack increases energy intake in men and women. *Appetite, 42,* 63–69.

Rolls, B. J., Roe, L. S., Meengs, J. S., & Wall, D. E. (2004b). Increasing the portion size of a sandwich increases energy intake. *Journal of the American Dietetic Association, 104,* 367–372.

Rolls, E. T. (2006). Brain mechanisms underlying flavour and appetite. *Philosophical Transactions of the Royal Society of London. Series B, Biological Sciences, 361*(1471), 1123–1136.

Ryan, K. W., Card-Higginson, P., McCarthy, S. G., Justus, M. B., & Thompson, J. W. (2006). Arkansas fights fat: translating research into policy to combat childhood and adolescent obesity. *Health Affairs (Millwood), 25,* 992–1004.

Salinsky, E. (2006). Effects of food marketing to kids: I'm lovin' it? *Issue Brief (George Washington University National Health Policy Forum), Aug 15*(814), 1–16.

Sallis, J. F., McKenzie, T. L., Kolody, B., Lewis, M., Marshall, S., & Rosengard, P. (1999). Effects of health-related physical education on academic achievement: Project spark. *Research Quarterly for Exercise and Sport, 70,* 127–134.

Salmon, J., Hume, C., Ball, K., Booth, M., & Crawford, D. (2006). Individual, social and home environment determinants of change in children's television viewing: the switch-play intervention. *Journal of Science and Medicine in Sport, 9,* 378–387.

Schwartz, M., & Puhl, R. (2003). Childhood obesity: a societal problem to solve. *Obesity Reviews, 4,* 57–71.

Schwimmer, J. B., Burwinkle, T. M., & Varni, J. W. (2003). Health-related quality of life of severely obese children and adolescents. *JAMA, 289,* 1851–1853.

Seligson, F. H. (2003). Serving size standards: Can they be harmonized? *Nutrition Today, 38,* 247–253.

Sharma, M. (2006). School-based interventions for childhood and adolescent obesity. *Obesity Reviews, 7,* 261–269.

Sherry, B. (2005). Food behaviors and other strategies to prevent and treat pediatric overweight. *International Journal of Obesity (London), 29*(suppl 2), S116–S126.

Shin, A. (2006). Snack makers strike deal to alter school offerings. *Washington Post,* October 7, p. D01.

Snethen, J. A., Broome, M. E., & Cashin, S. E. (2006). Effective weight loss for overweight children: a meta-analysis of intervention studies. *Journal of Pediatric Nursing, 21,* 45–56.

Steinberger, J., & Daniels, S. R. (2003). Obesity, insulin resistance, diabetes, and cardiovascular risk in children: an American Heart Association scientific statement from the Atherosclerosis, Hypertension, and Obesity in the Young Committee (Council on Cardiovascular Disease in the Young) and the Diabetes Committee (Council on Nutrition, Physical Activity, and Metabolism). *Circulation, 107,* 1448–1453.

Strauss, R. S., & Pollack, H. A. (2003). Social marginalization of overweight children. *Archives of Pediatric and Adolescent Medicine, 157,* 746–752.

Sturm, R. (2005). Childhood obesity—what we can learn from existing data on societal trends, part 2. *Preventing Chronic Diseases, 2*(2), A20.

Sturm, R., & Cohen, D. A. (2004). Suburban sprawl and physical and mental health. *Public Health, 118,* 488–496.

Summerbell, C. D., Waters, E., Edmunds, L. D., Kelly, S., Brown, T., & Campbell, K. J. (2005). Interventions for preventing obesity in children. *Cochrane Database of Systematic Reviews, July 20*(3), CD001871.

Swinburn, B., Gill, T., & Kumanyika, S. (2005). Obesity prevention: a proposed framework for translating evidence into action. *Obesity Reviews, 6,* 23–33.

Swinburn, B. A., Caterson, I., Seidell, J. C., & James, W. P. (2004). Diet, nutrition and the prevention of excess weight gain and obesity. *Public Health Nutrition, 7*(1A), 123–146.

Taras, H. (2005). Physical activity and student performance at school. *Journal of School Health, 75*(6), 214–218.

Taras, H., & Gage, M. (1995). Advertised foods on children's television. *Archives of Pediatric and Adolescent Medicine, 149,* 649–652.

Tillotson, J. E. (2004). Pandemic obesity: What is the solution? *Nutrition Today, 39,* 6–9.

Trost, S., Pate, R., Sallis, J., Freedson, P., Taylor, W., Dowda, M., Sirard, J. (2002). Age and gender differences in objectively measured physical activity in youth. *Medicine and Science in Sports and Exercise, 34,* 350–355.

Veugelers, P. J., & Fitzgerald, A. L. (2005). Effectiveness of school programs in preventing childhood obesity: a multilevel comparison. *American Journal of Public Health, 95,* 432–435.

Viner, R. M., & Cole, T. J. (2005). Television viewing in early childhood predicts adult body mass index. *Journal of Pediatrics, 147,* 429–435.

Wansink B. (2006). *Mindless eating: why we eat more than we think*. New York: Bantam Books.

Waters, A. (2006). Eating for credit. *New York Times,* February 24. www.healthyschoolscampaign.org/news/media/food/2006-2007_eating-for-credit.php.

Whitlock, E. P., Orleans, C. T., Pender, N., & Allan, J. (2002). Evaluating primary care behavioral counseling interventions: an evidence-based approach. *American Journal of Preventive Medicine, 22,* 267–284.

Wiegand, S., Maikowski, U., Blankenstein, O., Biebermann, H., Tarnow, P., & Gruters, A. (2004). Type 2 diabetes and impaired glucose tolerance in European children and adolescents with obesity—a problem that is no longer restricted to minority groups. *European Journal of Endocrinology, 151,* 199–206.

Willett, W. C., Manson, J. E., Stampfer, M. J., Colditz, G. A., Rosner, B., Speizer, F. E., & Hennekens, C. H. (1995). Weight, weight change, and coronary heart disease in women. Risk within the "normal" weight range [see comments]. *JAMA, 273,* 461–465.

Part IV
NUTRITIONAL APPROACHES

18

Nutrition Education Basics
Navigating the Food Environment

MADELEINE SIGMAN-GRANT

INTRODUCTION

Throughout this book, strategies related to addressing behavior change within the context of the psychosocial issues of child overweight have been presented. This chapter describes the synthesis into practice of nutrient and energy requirements within the context of the environment while simultaneously addressing psychosocial issues. It first discusses general dietary guidance (the U.S. Dietary Guidelines; Department of Health and Human Services, 2005) and the interpretation of this guidance into action steps (MyPyramid and the Nutrition Facts Panel on the food label). Following this is a brief overview of nutrition education, along with evaluations of current nutrition strategies to treat childhood overweight. The bulk of this chapter focuses on how those working with overweight children and their families can assist them in navigating through an environment that promotes unhealthy eating and physical inactivity. The concluding section delineates nutrition education resources readily available to health professionals, clinicians, and families.

TRANSLATING NUTRIENT NEEDS INTO ACTIONABLE PRACTICES

Throughout the 20th century, various governmental agencies (specifically, the U.S. Departments of Agriculture and Health) established federal nutrition policy based on the nutrient needs of specific population groups. In recent years, these have been issued as the U.S. Dietary Guidelines (Davis and Saltos, 1996). The latest version of this guidance is the Dietary Guidelines for Americans 2005, which includes messages about physical activity and food safety as well as nutrient needs (Department of Health and Human Services, 2005). The adult version also includes a section on alcohol. Likewise, various professional and governmental groups have designed materials to help American families translate established guidelines into practice. MyPyramid, the latest interpretation, is available for both adults and children (Figure 18.1).

MyPyramid suggests (1) choosing foods from five food groups (grains, vegetables, fruits, milk, and meats and beans) in appropriate amounts over a day, (2) balancing food and fun (a reference

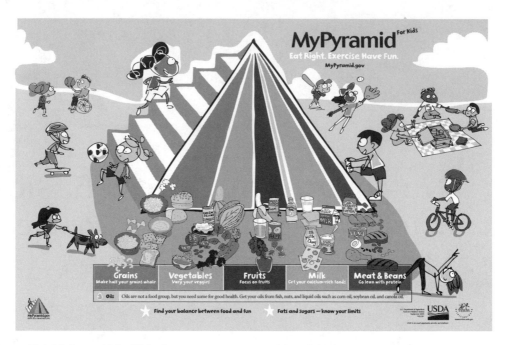

Figure 18.1 MyPyramid for Kids (Source: www.mypyramid.gov/kids/).

to physical activity), and (3) learning limits on fats and sugars (Yamini, Juan, Marcoe, & Britten, 2006). In the past, the number of daily servings and portion sizes were specified. However, MyPyramid has moved away from this approach and replaced it with total daily amounts needed from each of the food groups ("food intake patterns") (Britten et al., 2006). This allows for personalization in meal patterns and food choices (Table 18.1), while accommodating individual energy needs based on estimated energy requirements for gender, growth rate, age, and activity levels as set by the Institute of Medicine (IOM). Key dietary recommendations, incorporating both the dietary guidelines and MyPyramid for children, appear in Table 18.2.

While these generic recommendations are a base for families to choose healthful foods, without readily available specific information (e.g., the nutrient and energy content in foods) they are inadequate. Hence the U.S. Food and Drug Administration (FDA) issued requirements to food companies to provide consumers with specific nutrient information (see Figure 18.2). Currently no such requirements are in place for restaurants and other food establishments, making eating out difficult. As to how to prepare healthful foods, information is easily accessible in magazines, newspapers, books, and via the Internet.

CHALLENGES TO NUTRITION EDUCATION

Armed with all these materials, nutrition educators and clinicians should be able to simply discuss the dietary guidelines, dispense information, and demonstrate how to use MyPyramid and food labels. Armed with all this information, families should be able to march into a store and make healthful food selections.

Unfortunately, nutrition information alone is not useful unless it is presented in the context of a family's lifestyle. Food choice, initially an adult responsibility, is actually a parental decision. As children begin to choose their own foods, parental responsibility shifts to assisting the child with decision making. Thus, for families, nutrition education must be woven into discussions of parenting responsibilities, role modeling, and decision making.

Table 18.1 Food Intake Patterns for Children, Ages 2 Years and Older

Calorie Level	Daily Amount of Food from Each Group											
	1000	1200	1400	1600	1800	2000	2200	2400	2600	2800	3000	3200
Fruits	1 cup	1 cup	1.5 cups	1.5 cups	1.5 cups	2 cups	2 cups	2 cups	2 cups	2.5 cups	2.5 cups	2.5 cups
Vegetables	1 cup	1.5 cups	1.5 cups	2 cups	2.5 cups	2.5 cups	3 cups	3 cups	3.5 cups	3.5 cups	4 cups	4 cups
Grains	3 oz eq.	4 oz eq.	5 oz eq.	5 oz eq.	6 oz eq.	6 oz eq.	7 oz eq.	8 oz eq.	9 oz eq.	10 oz eq.	10 oz eq.	10 oz eq.
Meat and beans	2 oz eq.	3 oz eq.	4 oz eq.	5 oz eq.	5 oz eq.	5.5 oz eq.	6 oz eq.	6.5 oz eq.	6.5 oz eq.	7 oz eq.	7 oz eq.	7 oz eq.
Milk	2 cups	2 cups	2 cups	3 cups	3 cups	3 cups	3 cups	3 cups	3 cups	3 cups	3 cups	3 cups
Oils	3 tsp	4 tsp	4 tsp	5 tsp	5 tsp	6 tsp	6 tsp	7 tsp	8 tsp	8 tsp	10 tsp	11 tsp
Discretionary calorie allowance	165	171	171	132	195	267	290	362	410	426	512	648

Note: eq., equivalents.
Source: USDA (2005). Available at http://www.mypyramid.gov/downloads/MyPyramidFoodIntakePatterns.pdf.

Table 18.2 Key Dietary Recommendations for Children, Ages 2 and Older

Adequate Nutrients within Calorie Needs

Balance calorie intake from foods and beverages with calories expended.

Food Groups to Encourage

Make at least half of the total grains eaten whole grains.

Eat recommended amounts of vegetables and choose a variety of vegetables each day.

Eat recommended amounts of fruit and choose a variety of fruits each day.

Consume recommended amounts of fat-free or low-fat (1%) milk, or an equivalent amount of low-fat yogurt or cheese per day.

Make choices that are low fat or lean when selecting meats and poultry.

Fats and Oils

Choose most fats from sources of monounsaturated and polyunsaturated fatty acids, such as fish, nuts, seeds, and vegetable oils.

Carbohydrates

Choose and prepare foods and beverages with little added sugars or caloric sweeteners.

Sodium and Potassium

Choose and prepare foods with little salt.

Source: Department of Health and Human Services (2005).

Figure 18.2 Sample Nutrition Facts panel (Source: U.S. Food and Drug Administration, 2004).

As with any behavior, food choice is complex and has determinants in the biological, psychosocial, economic and political environments (Wetter et al., 2001) (Figure 18.3). Furthermore, increasing evidence suggests expecting behavior change by simply delivering information is not effective when it involves behaviors related to overall health and well-being or when it relates to practices with strong economic and cultural implications (Buchanan, 2000), such as food choice. The underlying assumption that once people know what is good or right they will change their behaviors does not automatically occur, even with the most well-meaning, well-funded, and science-based interventions (Nestle and Jacobson, 2000). This is especially true in relation to weight reduction programs, where more than 90% of those who lose weight regain the lost weight (Wing and Hill, 2001).

While some consumers select food for health reasons, frequently food selections are driven by issues unrelated to health, such as availability, convenience, access, and cost (Berkel, Poston, Reeves, & Foreyt, 2005; Bisogni, Connors Devine, & Sobal, 2002; Galef, 1996; Kendall, Olson, & Fronqillo, 1996; Nestle et al., 1998; Sigman-Grant, 2003; Wethington, 2005; Whitaker, 2004; Sharkey, 2006). In addition, children's food choices are contingent upon familial selections (Borah-Giddens and Falciglia, 1993; Golan & Crow, 2004; Pliner, 1983; Ritchey & Olson, 1983; Rozin, Fallon, & Mandel, 1984) and that of their peers (Birch, 1980). However, ultimately what children (and

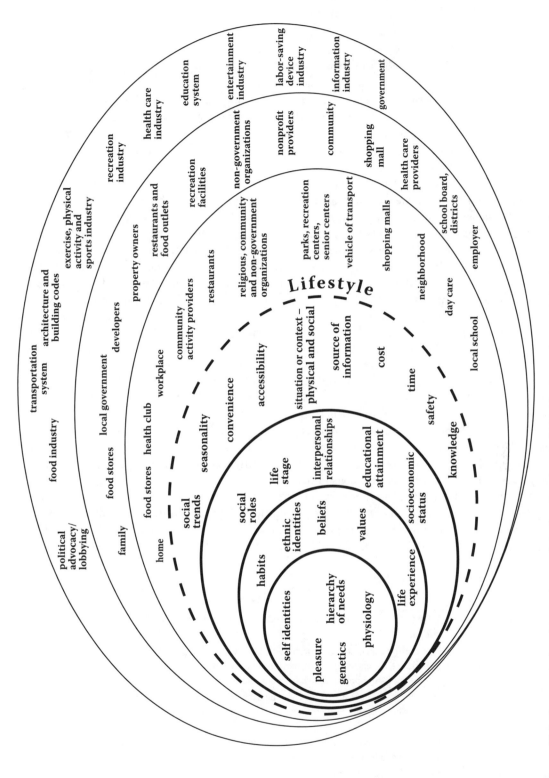

Figure 18.3 The complexity of determinants of obesity. (Booth et al., 2001. Reprinted with permission from the International Life Sciences Institute.)

Table 18.3 Environmental Factors Associated with the Obesogenic Environment

Easy access to inexpensive, high-energy dense foods.

Reduced energy demands of daily life activities.

Increase sedentary leisure time.

Reduced physical education in school.

Limited opportunities for recreational physical activity.

Marketing and media messages promoting eating and sedentary behavior.

Overall family influences.

Source: Wadden, Brownell, & Foster (2002); Woodward-Lopez et al. (2006).

adults) choose to eat is dependent upon taste (Drewnowski, 1997; Glanz, Basil, Maibach, Goldberg, & Snyder, 1998). Children are born with an innate preference for sweet (Birch 1998; Mennella, Jagnow, & Beauchamp, 2001; Mennella, Turnbull, Ziegler, & Martinez, 2005). Preferences for fat and salt begin to develop in infancy (Birch, 1992, 1999; Cowart and Beauchamp, 1986; Engell, Bordi, Borja, Lambert, & Rolls, 1998; Fisher and Birch, 1995; Johnson, McPhee, & Birch, 1991; Ricketts, 1997; Sullivan and Birch, 1990). Acceptance of bitter (alkaloid) flavors associated with many plants is acquired more slowly and appears to be dependent on frequent exposure (Birch and Marlin, 1982; Birch, McPhee, Shoba, Pirok, & Steinberg, 1987; Rozin, 1989; Rozin, Fallon, & Augustoni-Ziskind, 1986). While adults may accept less flavor to gain other attributes (e.g., less fat or sugar), those working with children must acknowledge taste as the driving force of food choice.

Similar to other educators, those attempting to deliver nutrition education face the challenge of selecting a theoretical framework upon which to base their interventions. More than 50 different theories serve as frameworks for nutrition education interventions (Achterberg and Trenkner, 1990). Such theoretical variety is guided by the multifactorial nature of food selection and demonstrates the difficulty of changing food choice behavior.

Another challenge to nutrition education is providing meaningful information within the context of the current environment, which has been labeled "obesogenic" (Table 18.3). Not only is food everywhere (Table 18.4), but most Americans are physically inactive, although they lead extremely busy lives and face tremendous time constraints.

Whether at school, home, play, or work, children and adolescents are exposed to food. Generally this food is affordable but can be of varying nutritional quality. Moreover, more families are dining away from home, where the potential exists for consuming foods of higher energy and fat content (Stewart, Blisard, & Jolliffe, 2006). This trend is expected to continue, and hence strategies

Table 18.4 The Ubiquity of Food in America

Classification	Examples
In the home	At the table; in the cupboards; in the garden; in front of the television; as part of nonmealtime activities
Traditional food and beverage stores	Supercenters, supermarkets; groceries; convenience stores; specialty stores (e.g., meat market, fish market, bakery, etc.); snack and nonalcoholic beverage bars (e.g., ice cream, donuts, coffee, juice); "mom-and-pop" stores; beer, wine, and liquor stores
Other outlets	Gas stations; discount stores; roadside stands; mobile food service; vending machines in schools; farmer's markets; microenterprises (e.g., food stands secondary to nonfood business or residence)
Out-of-home dining	Full-service restaurants; fast-food establishments; taverns; cafeterias and buffets; school cafeterias and lunchrooms; churches
Recreational outlets	Parks; ballparks; movie theaters; arcades

Table 18.5 Portion Distortion and Serving Size

	20 Years Ago			Today	
	Portion	**Calories**		**Portion**	**Calories**
Bagel	3 in. diameter	140	Bagel	6 in. diameter	350
Cheeseburger	1	333	Cheeseburger	1	590
Spaghetti with meatballs	1 cup sauce and 3 small meatballs	500	Spaghetti with meatballs	2 cups sauce and 3 large meatballs	1020
Soda	6.5 oz	85	Soda	20 oz	250
Blueberry muffin	1.5 oz	210	Blueberry muffin	5 oz	500

Source: National Heart, Lung, and Blood Institute (http://hp2010.nhlbihin.net/portion/).

for dining out must be specifically addressed. Advertising techniques further intensify the ubiquitous nature of food and its influence on childhood weight. Strategies focused on children are particularly troublesome (Committee on Food Marketing and the Diets of Children and Youth, 2006), as television and printed advertisements stress high-energy, low-nutrient, energy-dense foods. In addition, the food manufacturing and eating establishment industries attempt to influence children with premium offers, tie-ins of licensed characters and movies on food packages, free toys with child-size meals, and foods designed specifically for children. These marketing techniques attempt to influence children to pressure parents with requests, setting up family conflicts (Aktas, 2006; Bagley, Salmon, & Crawford, 2006; Roberts, Blinkhorn, & Duxbury, 2003).

Another challenge to educating families about nutrition is portion size. Portion sizes of most foods have steadily increased over several decades (Smiciklas-Wright, Mitchell, Mickle, Goldman, & Cook, 2003; Young & Nestle, 2002). Given the strong American value of getting the most for the money, families seek out food buys in both the market (e.g., large packaging) and when dining out (value meals and super-sizing). Hence educating about portion distortion has become a familiar nutrition education message (Table 18.5).

Furthermore, while most people recognize when they are hungry, they are less able to identify the signs of satiation. Children can be "socialized" into eating large portions (through coaxing and bribery) (Birch, Marlin, & Rotter, 1984; Birch, McPhee, Shoba, Steinberg, & Krehbiel, 1987) or simply from being overfed (Birch, Fisher, & Davison, 2003; Fisher, Rolls, & Birch, 2003; McConahy, Smiciklas-Wright, Birch, Mitchell, & Picciano, 2002; Rolls, Engell, & Birch, 2000). It is essential that children be taught to stop eating when their body signals fullness (e.g., stomach distention, hunger pangs and growling noises cease, etc.).

PREVIOUS NUTRITION INTERVENTIONS SPECIFIC TO CHILD OVERWEIGHT

The above discussion highlights the complexity of providing meaningful nutrition education to families with overweight children and the need for individualization for it to be effective. Over the last two decades, specific strategies based on addressing the many antecedents of childhood overweight have been used in interventions (Table 18.6) (Brown, 2006). Interestingly, evaluations reveal limited effectiveness for each strategy (American Dietetic Association, 2006; Gill, King, & Caterson, 2005; Woodward-Lopez, Ritchie, Gerstein, & Crawford, 2006). Furthermore, although there is a paucity of evidence demonstrating the effectiveness of educating families about each of these behaviors singularly, nutrition counseling that focuses on the entire food selection process does appear promising (American Dietetic Association, 2006), as is the family approach rather than teaching either the parents or the child alone (Epstein, Valoski, Wing, & McCurley, 1990; St. Jeor, Perumean-Chaney, Sigman-Grant, Williams, & Foreyt, 2002).

Table 18.6 Targeted Behaviors for Child Overweight Interventions and Level of Evidence

Targeted Behaviors	Evidence Grades[a]
Decrease intake of sweetened beverages	II–III; probable
Monitor portion sizes	III; possible
Moderate choices when eating out	III; possible
Make sensible snacking selections	II; NA
Avoid skipping breakfast	II; NA
Reduce intake of high-energy, low-nutrient foods	II; convincing
Increase intake of fruits, vegetables, high-fiber foods	III; convincing for fiber
Practice an authoritative parental feeding style (including avoiding parental restriction)	III; possible

[a] ADA evidence grades (I = good/strong; II = fair; III = limited/weak; IV = expert opinion only; V = grade not assignable); Gill evidence grades: convincing, probable, possible and not available.

Source: American Dietetic Association (2006); Gill et al. (2005); Woodward-Lopez et al. (2006).

Some of the observed ineffectiveness of previous interventions may lie in the outcome measurement chosen—changes to the child's BMI. Using BMI as the sole outcome criteria negates the impact of genetic propensity to body size: some children are born to be large, whereas some are born to be small, no matter what (Friedman, 2004). However, all children can make healthful food choices and be provided with healthful foods and opportunities for physical activity.

NAVIGATING THE FOOD ENVIRONMENT

Clinicians working with families of overweight children are in an excellent position to assist with delivering basic nutrition information. They are uniquely familiar with the family's values, the interrelationships of the family members, the parenting styles, and the child's temperament. They often understand or can assess the dynamics of the family's socioeconomic situation. They can motivate families into action to increase physical activity and decrease sedentary behavior. Their style of interacting with the family allows clinicians to ask open-ended questions that challenge the family members' assumptions regarding what, and how much, their child should be eating. This is particularly relevant with families who appear to be adopting food selections whereby they are eliminating a nutrient (e.g., fats or sugars) or food group (such as red meats or dairy products). Although parents may mean well in taking this approach, this practice can severely retard normal growth and development. In addition, such elimination sends a distorted message to the child.

Oftentimes, families know basic nutrition, having obtained information from their health care providers. The clinician's role is to help the family take this information and create a healthful eating environment. Working with the family and separately with each family member will be beneficial in identifying supportive and sabotaging relationships in terms of food and physical activity behaviors. Clinicians can increase the awareness of the negative impact of television viewing (Bagley et al., 2006; Gable, Chang, & Krull, 2007; Matheson, Killen, Wang, Varady, & Robinson, 2004; Proctor et al., 2003; Robinson, 2001) and the positive impact of family mealtimes (Da Ros and Duff, 1995; Gable et al., 2007; Koivisto, Fellenius, & Sjöden, 1994) as part of an overall strategy to improve family dynamics in domains other than eating.

One relatively simple approach to food choice is the GO, SLOW, and WHOA foods plan, sometimes called the stoplight approach (Green, Yellow, Red) (Epstein and Squires, 1988; Epstein et al., 1990; CATCH: Coordinated Approach to Child Health, 2006). GO foods are those that can be eaten almost anytime. SLOW foods are foods that are eaten, at the most, several times a week. WHOA foods are those that are eaten only occasionally as treats or on special occasions. Combining the food intake patterns (Table 18.1) with the GO, SLOW, and WHOA foods list (Table 18.7) helps families consider not only which foods to select, but how these foods should be prepared (Table 18.8). Children quickly learn the terms and become engaged in the "game." This approach also allows for great flexibility in food choices, including accommodating eating inside or out of the house. Children can apply the technique when at school or when grocery shopping with the family.

The clinician can challenge family members to find ways to enhance the taste of GO foods (with the use of seasonings and spices), moderate the SLOW foods, and negotiate when to incorporate the WHOA foods. By making this a family activity, the clinician can observe relationships and dynamics focused around foods and make strategic suggestions.

In addition, clinicians can support an authoritative approach to food choice (Baumrind, 1991; Drucker, Hammer, Agras, & Bryson, 1999; Hughes, Power, Orlet Fisher, Mueller, & Nicklas, 2005; Satter, 1996, 2005; Smetana, 1995) and help adults recognize, and correct, restrictive behavior patterns (Birch et al., 2003; Faith and Kerns, 2005; Fisher and Birch, 1999, 2000; Gill et al., 2005; Polivy, 1996). Parental restriction in relation to food selection occurs when a child is not allowed access to a particular food when that food is already in the home. Restriction also occurs when an overweight child is denied food that a normal weight or thin child (or parent) is allowed to eat (e.g., letting the other members of the family eat french fries in front of the overweight child). Restrictive behaviors appear to increase weight (Ballard-Barbash, Graubard, Krebs-Smith, Schatzkin, Thompson, 1998; Birch et al., 2003; Faith and Kerns, 2005; Fisher and Birch, 2000) and can set up cravings for the forbidden food (Polivy, 1996).

Thus the questions remain: What basic information is necessary for selecting healthful foods? What do clinicians relate about nutrition to overweight children and their families? How can clinicians make nutrition information meaningful, relevant, and useful? Table 18.9 presents a partial list detailing how clinicians can provide basic nutrition information, interwoven with basic clinical issues, in ways that are meaningful to families and integrating nutrition into the context of family life.

PRACTICAL NUTRITION RESOURCES

It is imperative for those working with overweight children and their families to familiarize themselves with readily available materials. There are many reputable resources available on the Internet, a short selection of which can be found in Table 18.10. In addition to containing basic food and nutrition guidance, information on food selection, shopping, label reading, and cooking are provided.

Community resources are also available for families. For example, the Cooperative Extension System provides up-to-date information to families and health professionals about food, nutrition, and health issues at county offices across the United States. Local extension offices are listed in the telephone book or Internet directories. Other local sources of free or low-cost materials include public health offices, school district food service departments, and health organizations such as the American Heart Association.

CONCLUSION

The task of educating families about nutrition is overwhelmingly complex. Basic nutrition knowledge continues to expand and the food supply is ever changing. Educating about nutrition is further complicated by lifestyles where families need to balance work, play, finances, and time. Therefore incorporation of basic nutrition information into other weight management behavioral strategies will provide the context needed to make the nutrition information immediately relevant and useful.

Table 18.7 GO, SLOW, and WHOA Food List

Food Group	GO (Almost Anytime Foods)	SLOW (Sometimes Foods)	WHOA (Once in a While Foods)
	Nutrient-Dense		**Calorie-Dense**
Vegetables	Almost all fresh, frozen, and canned vegetables without added fat and sauces	All vegetables with added fat and sauces; oven-baked french fries; avocado	Fried potatoes, like french fries or hash browns; other deep-fried vegetables
Fruits	All fresh, frozen, canned (in juice)	100% fruit juice; fruits canned in light syrup; dried fruits	Fruits canned in heavy syrup
Breads and cereals	Whole-grain breads, pita bread; tortillas and pasta; brown rice; hot and cold unsweetened whole-grain breakfast cereals	White refined-flour bread, rice, and pasta; French toast; taco shells; cornbread; biscuits; granola; waffles and pancakes	Croissants; muffins; doughnuts; sweet rolls; crackers made with *trans* fats; sweetened breakfast cereals
Milk and milk products	Fat-free or 1% reduced-fat milk; fat-free or low-fat yogurt; part skim, reduced fat, and fat-free cheese; low-fat or fat-free cottage cheese	2% low-fat milk; processed cheese spread	Whole milk; full-fat American, cheddar, Colby, Swiss, cream cheese; whole-milk yogurt
Meats, poultry, fish, eggs, beans, and nuts	Trimmed beef and pork; extra lean ground beef; chicken and turkey without skin; tuna canned in water; baked, broiled, steamed, grilled fish and shellfish; beans, split peas, lentils, tofu; egg whites and egg substitutes	Lean ground beef, broiled hamburgers; ham, Canadian bacon; chicken and turkey with skin; low-fat hot dogs; tuna canned in oil; peanut butter; nuts; whole eggs cooked without added fat	Untrimmed beef and pork; regular ground beef; fried hamburgers; ribs; bacon; fried chicken, chicken nuggets; hot dogs, lunch meats, pepperoni, sausage; fried fish and shellfish; whole eggs cooked with fat
Sweets and snacks	Ice milk bars; frozen fruit juice bars; low-fat frozen yogurt and ice cream; fig bars, ginger snaps, baked chips; low-fat microwave popcorn; pretzels		Cookies and cakes; pies; cheese cake; ice cream; chocolate; candy; chips; buttered microwave popcorn
Fats and condiments	Vinegar; ketchup; mustard; fat-free creamy salad dressing; fat-free mayonnaise; fat-free sour cream; vegetable oil, olive oil, and oil-based salad dressing	Low-fat creamy salad dressing; low-fat mayonnaise; low-fat sour cream	Butter, margarine; lard; salt pork; gravy; regular creamy salad dressing; mayonnaise; tartar sauce; sour cream; cheese sauce; cream sauce; cream cheese dips
Beverages	Water; fat-free milk or 1% reduced-fat milk; diet soda; diet iced tea and lemonade	2% low-fat milk; 100% fruit juice; sports drinks	Whole milk; regular soda; sweetened iced tea and lemonade; fruit drinks with less than 100% fruit juice

Source: www.nhlbi.nih.gov/health/public/heart/obesity/wecan/downloads/gswtips.pdf (accessed January 4, 2007). Adapted from CATCH: Coordinated Approach to Child Health (2006).

Table 18.8 Examples of Preparation of GO, SLOW, and WHOA Foods

	GO	SLOW	WHOA
Vegetable	Plain baked potato	Baked potato with 1 tsp butter and 1 tsp sour cream	French fries
Bread	Slice of toast	Slice of French toast	Doughnut
Meat	Skinless chicken breast	Chicken with skin	Fried chicken

Source: www.nhlbi.nih.gov/health/public/heart/obesity/wecan/downloads/gswtips.pdf (accessed January 4, 2007). Adapted from CATCH: Coordinated Approach to Child Health (2006).

Table 18.9 Inclusion of Nutrition Information within a Clinical Session

Family Togetherness

While stressing the importance of family times as an overall strategy for improving family interactions, clinicians can inquire about mealtimes. The clinician can inquire about what foods are typically served at the meal. This affords the opportunity to present the concepts of the dietary guidelines and the MyPyramid for Kids.

Decrease Television Viewing

If discussions arise about the impact of television viewing, clinicians can inform the family about opportunities to use this time to increase physical activity. If families wish to play games instead of watch television, clinicians can suggest appropriate interactive Web sites where the "games" revolve around food selection.

Authoritative Parenting

While discussing issues of guidance, clinicians can address the problems with food restriction. It is also an opportune time to discuss portion sizes, the food intake plan, and WHOA, SLOW, and GO foods.

Children's Independence

During discussions about the need for children to make their own choices, clinicians can review the WHOA, SLOW, and GO foods with the child.

Table 18.10 Selected Interactive Web Sites Containing Games and Materials Providing Basic Food Choice and Nutrition Information

Web Site	Source	Type of Materials
www.mypyramid.gov/kids/index	U.S. Department of Agriculture	Games and information for children 6 to 18 years
www.mypyramid.gov/kids/	U.S. Department of Agriculture	Information for caregivers of children 2 to 6 years
www.nhlbi.nih.gov/health/public/heart/obesity/wecan/downloads/gswtips.pdf	National Institutes of Health	We Can! (Ways to Enhance Children's Activity and Nutrition), a national program for 8- to 13-year-old children in helping support a healthy weight
www.nhlbi.nih.gov/health/public/heart/obesity/wecan/live-it/go-slow-whoa.htm	National Institutes of Health	GO, SLOW, and WHOA foods list
www.nhlbi.nih.gov/health/public/heart/obesity/wecan/learn-it/distortion.htm	National Institutes of Health	Portion distortion (portion size)
www.kidnetic.com/	International Food Information Council	Games and materials
www.teamnutrition.usda.gov/parents.html	U.S. Department of Agriculture	Information, games, materials
www.fns.usda.gov/tn/Resources/power_of_choice.html	Department of Health and Human Services and Department of Agriculture	Video, song, materials
www.dole5aday.com/	Dole Foods	Songs, video, materials
www.cfsan.fda.gov/~dms/foodlab.html	Food and Drug Administration	Food label
www.cfsan.fda.gov/~dms/transfat.html	Food and Drug Administration	Food label
www.americanheart.org/presenter.jhtml?identifier=531	American Heart Association	Dining out

REFERENCES

Achterberg, C., & Trenkner, L. L. (1990). Developing a working philosophy of nutrition education. *Journal of Nutrition Education, 22,* 189–193.

Aktas, A. (2006). The effects of television food advertisement on children's food purchasing requests. *Pediatrics International, 48,* 138–145.

American Dietetic Association. (2006). Childhood Overweight Evidence Analysis Project. Chicago: American Dietetic Association. Available at www.adaevidencelibrary.com/topic.cfm?cat=1046.

Bagley, S., Salmon, J., & Crawford, D. (2006). Family structure and children's television viewing and physical activity. *Medicine and Science in Sports and Exercise, 38,* 910–918.

Ballard-Barbash, R., Graubard, I., Krebs-Smith, S. M., Schatzkin, A., & Thompson, F. E. (1998). Contribution of dieting to the inverse association between energy intake and body mass index. *European Journal of Clinical Nutrition, 50,* 98–106.

Baumrind, D. (1991). The influence of parenting style on adolescent competence and substance use. *Journal of Early Adolescence, 11,* 56–95.

Berkel, L. A., Poston, W. S., Reeves, R. S., & Foreyt, J. P. (2005). Behavioral interventions for obesity. *Journal of the American Dietetic Association, 105,* 35–43.

Birch, L. L. (1980). Effects of peer models' food choices and eating behaviors on preschoolers' food preferences. *Child Development, 51,* 489–496.

Birch, L. L. (1992). Children's preferences for high-fat foods. *Nutrition Reviews, 50*(9), 249–255.

Birch, L. L. (1998). Development of food acceptance patterns in the first years of life. *Proceedings of the Nutrition Society, 57,* 617–624.

Birch, L. L. (1999). Development of food preferences. *Annual Review of Nutrition, 19,* 41–62.

Birch, L. L., Fisher, J. O., & Davison, K. K. (2003). Learning to overeat: maternal use of restrictive feeding practices promotes girls' eating in the absence of hunger. *American Journal of Clinical Nutrition, 78,* 215–220.

Birch, L. L., & Marlin, D. W. (1982). I don't like it; I never tried it: effects of exposure on two-year-old children's food preferences. *Appetite, 3,* 353–360.

Birch, L. L., Marlin, D. W., & Rotter, J. (1984). Eating as the "means" activity in a contingency: effects on young children's food preference. *Child Development, 55,* 431–439.

Birch, L. L., McPhee, L., Shoba, B. C., Pirok, E., & Steinberg, L. (1987). What kind of exposure reduces children's food neophobia: looking versus tasting. *Appetite, 9,* 171–178.

Birch, L. L., McPhee, L., Shoba, B. C., Steinberg, L., & Krehbiel, R. (1987). "Clean up your plate": effects of child feeding practices on the conditioning of meal size. *Learning and Motivation, 18,* 301–317.

Bisogni, C. A., Connors, M., Devine, C. M., & Sobal, J. (2002). Who we are and how we eat: a qualitative study of identities in food choice. *Journal of Nutrition Education and Behavior, 34,* 128–139.

Booth, S. L., Sallis, J. F., Ritenbaugh, C., Hill, J. O., Birch, L. L., Frank, L. D., Glanz, K., Himmelgreen, D. A., Mudd, M., Popkin, B. M., Rickard, K. A., St. Jeor, S., & Hays, N. P. (2001). Environmental and societal factors affect food choice and physical activity: rationale, influences, and leverage points. *Nutrition Reviews, 59*(3 pt 2), S21–S39.

Borah-Giddens, J., & Falciglia, G. A. (1993). A meta-analysis of the relationship in food preferences between parents and children. *Journal of Nutrition Education, 25,* 102–107.

Britten, P., Lyon, J., Weaver, C., Kris-Etherton, P., Nicklas, T., Weber, J., & Davis, C. (2006). MyPyramid food intake pattern modeling for the Dietary Guidelines Advisory Committee. *Journal of Nutrition Education and Behavior, 38*(suppl. 2), S143–S152.

Brown, M. (2006). Childhood obesity prevention literature review—2006. Newark: University of Delaware Cooperative Extension. Available at http://ag.udel.edu/extension/fam/obesity/ObLitRevS.pdf.

Buchanan, D. R. (2000). *An ethic for health promotion: rethinking the sources of human well-being.* New York: Oxford University Press.

CATCH: Coordinated Approach to Child Health. (2006). GO, SLOW and WHOA food list. Berkeley: Center for Weight and Health. Available at www.catchinfo.org/CATCHNEWTEST/newweb/Document_Content/PDF/GO-SLOW-WHOA%20List_Color.pdf.

Committee on Food Marketing and the Diets of Children and Youth. (2006). *Food marketing to children and youth: Threat or opportunity?* Washington, D.C.: National Academies Press.

Cowart, B. J., & Beauchamp, G. K. (1986). The importance of sensory context of young children's acceptance of salty tastes. *Child Development, 57,* 1034–1039.

Da Ros, D., & Duff, R. E. (1995). The benefits of family style meals. *Dimensions of Early Childhood, Winter,* 17–20.

Davis, C. A., & Saltos, E. A. (1996). The dietary guidelines for Americans—past, present, future. *Family Economics and Nutrition Review, 9*(2), 4–13.

Department of Health and Human Services (2005). Dietary guidelines for Americans 2005. Washington, D.C.: Department of Health and Human Services. Available at www.health.gov/dietaryguidelines/dga2005/document/.

Drewnowski, A. (1997). Taste preferences and food intake. *Annual Review of Nutrition, 17,* 237–253.

Drucker, R. R., Hammer, L. D., Agras, W. S., & Bryson, S. (1999). Can mothers influence their child's eating behavior? *Journal of Developmental and Behavioral Pediatrics, 20,* 88–92.

Engell, D., Bordi, P., Borja, M., Lambert, C., & Rolls, B. (1998). Effects of information about fat content on food preferences in pre-adolescent children. *Appetite, 30,* 269–282.

Epstein, L., & Squires, S. (1988). *The stoplight diet for children: an eight-week program for parents and children.* Boston: Little, Brown.

Epstein, L. H., Valoski, A., Wing, R. R., & McCurley, J. (1990). Ten-year follow-up of behavioral family-based treatment for obese children. *JAMA, 264,* 2591–2523.

Faith, M., & Kerns, J. (2005). Infant and child feeding practices and childhood overweight: the role of restriction. *Maternal and Child Nutrition, 1,* 164–168.

Fisher, J. O., & Birch, L. L. (1995). Fat preferences and fat consumption of 3- to 5-year-old children are related to parental adiposity. *Journal of the American Dietetic Association, 95,* 759–764.

Fisher, J. O., & Birch, L. L. (1999). Restricting access to foods and children's eating. *Appetite, 32,* 405–419.

Fisher, J. O. & Birch, L. L. (2000). Parents' restrictive feeding practices are associated with young girls' negative self-evaluation of eating. *Journal of the American Dietetic Association, 100,* 1341–1346.

Fisher, J. O., Rolls, B. J., & Birch, L. L. (2003). Children's bite size and intake of an entree are greater with large portion than with age-appropriate or self-selected portions. *American Journal of Clinical Nutrition, 77,* 1164–1170.

Friedman, J. (2004). Modern science versus the stigma of obesity. *Nature Medicine, 10,* 563–569.

Gable, S., Chang, Y., & Krull, J. (2007). Television viewing and frequency of family meals are predictive of overweight onset and persistence in a national sample of school-aged children. *Journal of the American Dietetic Association, 107,* 53–61.

Galef, B. G., Jr. (1996). Food selection: problems in understanding how we choose foods to eat. *Neuroscience and Biobehavioral Reviews, 20,* 67–73.

Gill, T., King, L., & Caterson, I. (2005). Obesity prevention: necessary and possible. A structured approach for effective planning. *Proceedings of the Nutrition Society, 64,* 255–261.

Glanz, K., Basil, M., Maibach, E., Goldberg, J., & Snyder, D. (1998). Why Americans eat what they do: taste, nutrition, cost, convenience, and weight control concerns as influences on food consumption. *Journal of the American Dietetic Association, 98,* 1118–1126.

Golan, M., & Crow, S. (2004). Parents are key players in the prevention and treatment of weight-related problems. *Nutrition Reviews, 62,* 39–50.

Hughes, S., Power, T. G., Orlet Fisher, J., Mueller, S., & Nicklas, T. A. (2005). Revisiting a neglected construct: parenting styles in a child-feeding context. *Appetite, 44,* 83–92.

Johnson, S. L., McPhee, L., & Birch, L. L. (1991). Conditioned preferences: young children prefer flavors associated with high dietary fat. *Physiology and Behavior, 50,* 1245–1251.

Kendall, A., Olson, C. M., & Fronqillo, E. A. (1996). Relationship of hunger and food insecurity to food availability and consumption. *Journal of the American Dietetic Association, 96,* 1019–1024.

Koivisto, U. K., Fellenius, J., & Sjöden, P. O. (1994). Relations between parental mealtime practices and children's food intake. *Appetite, 22,* 245–257.

Matheson, D. M., Killen, J. D., Wang, Y., Varady, A., & Robinson, T. N. (2004). Children's food consumption during television viewing. *American Journal of Clinical Nutrition, 79,* 1088–1094.

McConahy, K., Smiciklas-Wright, H., Birch, L. L., Mitchell, D. C., & Picciano, M. F. (2002). Food portions are positively related to energy intake and body weight in early childhood. *Journal of Pediatrics, 140,* 34–37.

Mennella, J., Jagnow, C., & Beauchamp, G. K. (2001). Prenatal and postnatal flavor learning by human infants. *Pediatrics, 107*(6), E88.

Mennella, J. A., Turnbull, B., Ziegler, P. J., & Martinez, H. (2005). Infant feeding practices and early flavor experiences in Mexican infants: an intra-cultural study. *Journal of the American Dietetic Association, 105,* 908–915.

Nestle, M., & Jacobson, M. F. (2000). Halting the obesity epidemic: a public health policy approach. *Public Health Reports, 115,* 12–24.

Nestle, M., Wing, R., Birch, L., DiSogra, L., Drewnowski, A., Middleton, S., Sigman-Grant, M., Sobal, J., Winston, M., & Economos, C. (1998). Behavioral and social influences on food choice. *Nutrition Reviews, 56,* S50–S64.

Pliner, P. (1983). Family resemblance in food preference. *Journal of Nutrition Education, 15*(4), 137–139.

Polivy, J. (1996). Psychological consequences of food restriction. *Journal of the American Dietetic Association, 96,* 589–592.

Proctor, M., Moore, L., Gao, L., Cupples, L. A., Bradlee, M. L., Hood, M. Y., & Ellison, R. C. (2003). Television viewing and change in body fat from preschool to early adolescence: the Framingham Children's Study. *International Journal of Obesity and Related Metabolic Disorders, 27,* 827–33.

Ricketts, C. D. (1997). Fat preferences, dietary fat intake and body composition in children. *European Journal of Clinical Nutrition, 61,* 778–781.

Ritchey, N., & Olson, C. (1983). Relationships between family variables and children's preference for and consumption of sweet foods. *Ecology of Food and Nutrition, 13,* 257–266.

Roberts, B., Blinkhorn, A. S., & Duxbury, J. T. (2003). The power of children over adults when obtaining sweet snacks. *International Journal of Paediatric Dentistry, 13*(2), 76–84.

Robinson, T. (2001). Television viewing and childhood obesity. *Pediatric Clinics of North America, 48,* 1017–1025.

Rolls, B. J., Engell, D., & Birch, L. L. (2000). Serving portion size influences 5-year-old but not 3-year-old children's food intakes. *Journal of the American Dietetic Association, 100,* 232–234.

Rozin, P. (1989). The role of learning in the acquisition of food preferences by humans (pp. 205–227). In R. Shepherd (Ed.), *Handbook of the psychophysiology of human eating.* Chichester: John Wiley & Sons.

Rozin, P., Fallon, A., & Augustoni-Ziskind, M. L. (1986). The child's conception of food: the development of categories of acceptable and rejected substances. *Journal of Nutrition Education, 18*(2), 75–81.

Rozin, P., Fallon, A.,. &. Mandell, R. (1984). Family resemblance in attitudes to foods. *Developmental Psychology, 20,* 309–314.

Satter, E. (1996). Internal regulation and the evolution of normal growth as the basis for prevention of obesity in childhood. *Journal of the American Dietetic Association, 96,* 860–864.

Satter, E. (2005). *Your child's weight: helping without harming; birth through adolescence.* Madison, WI: Kelcy Press.

Sharkey, J. (2006). Food accessibility and concentrated deprivation in rural areas. College Station: Texas A&M University.

Sigman-Grant, M. (2003). Hungry and overweight: the paradox of food insecurity in America. *Pediatric Basics, 103,* 12–28.

Smetana, J. (1995). Parenting styles and conceptions of parental authority during adolescence. *Child Development, 66,* 299–316.

Smiciklas-Wright, H., Mitchell, D. C., Mickle, S. J., Goldman, J. D., & Cook, A. (2003). Foods commonly eaten in the United States, 1989–1991 and 1994–1996: Are portion sizes changing? *Journal of the American Dietetic Association, 103,* 39–40.

St. Jeor, S., Perumean-Chaney, S., Sigman-Grant, M., Williams, C., & Foreyt, J. (2002). Family-based interventions for the treatment of childhood obesity. *Journal of the American Dietetic Association, 102,* 640–644).

Stewart, H., Blisard, N., & Jolliffe, D. (2006). Let's eat out. Washington, D.C.: USDA Economic Research Service.

Sullivan, S. A., & Birch, L. L. (1990). Pass the sugar, pass the salt: experience dictates preference. *Developmental Psychology, 26,* 546–551.

U.S. Department of Agriculture (2005). Available at: http://www.mypyramid.gov/downloads/MyPyramid-FoodIntakePatterns.pdf.

Wadden, T. A., Brownell, K. D., & Foster, G. D. (2002). Obesity: responding to the global epidemic. *Journal of Consulting and Clinical Psychology, 70,* 510–525.

Wethington, E. (2005). A life course perspective on health behavior. *Journal of Nutrition Education and Behavior, 37,* 114–119.

Wetter, A., Goldberg, J., King, A. C., Sigman-Grant, M., Baer, R., Crayton, E., Devine, C., Drewnowski, A., Dunn, A., Johnson, G., Pronk, N., Saelens, B., Snyder, D., Novelli, P., Walsh, K., & Warland, R. (2001). How and why do individuals make food and physical activity choices? *Nutrition Reviews, 59*(3 pt 2), S11–S20.

Whitaker, R. C. (2004). A review of household behaviors for preventing obesity in children. Princeton, NJ: Mathematica Policy Research, Inc.

Wing, R., & Hill, J. (2001). Successful weight loss maintenance. *Annual Review of Nutrition, 21,* 323–341.

Woodward-Lopez, G., Ritchie, L. D., Gerstein, D. E., & Crawford, P. B. (2006). Obesity: dietary and developmental influences. Boca Raton, FL: Taylor & Francis.

Yamini, S., Juan, W., Marcoe, K., & Britten, P. (2006). Impact of using updated food consumption and composition data on selected MyPyramid food group nutrient profiles. *Journal of Nutrition Education and Behavior, 38*(suppl. 2), S136–S142.

Young, L., & Nestle, M. (2002). The contribution of expanding portion sizes to the U.S. obesity epidemic. *American Journal of Public Health, 92,* 246–249.

19

The Satter Feeding Dynamics Model of Child Overweight Definition, Prevention, and Intervention

ELLYN SATTER

The Satter Feeding Dynamics Model recommends optimizing feeding and parenting and supporting each child in growing in the way that is genetically and metabolically appropriate at any weight level. According to the Feeding Dynamics Model of child overweight definition, prevention, and treatment, the underlying cause of today's trends toward increasing child overweight is disruption in the feeding relationship and in parenting overall (Satter, 1996, 2005b). The conventional approach of diagnosing overweight, managing energy balance, and striving for weight maintenance or weight loss (Centers for Disease Control, 2000b) exacerbates those distortions in feeding and parenting.

The fundamental principle of the Feeding Dynamics Model is that, provided parents guide the feeding process based on information coming from the child and are reasonably skillful with feeding, children eat as much or as little as they need based on their internal processes of hunger, appetite, and satiety (Adair, 1984; Fomon, Filer, Thomas, Anderson, & Nelson, 1975) and grow predictably (Hamill et al., 1979; Zack, Harlan, Leaverton, & Cornoni-Huntley, 1979) in accordance with their genetic endowment (Garn & Clark, 1976; Pietilanen et al., 2001).

Effective feeding is based on a division of responsibility (Satter, 1986). For the infant, the parent does the *what* of feeding, the infant does everything else: how often, how much, at what tempo, and what level of skill. Beyond infancy, the parent is responsible for the *what*, *when*, and *where* of feeding and the child is responsible for the *how much* and *whether* of eating. Adolescents gradually learn to manage the *what*, *when*, and *where* for themselves, but they continue to depend on parents to take leadership with feeding and maintain the structure of family meals.

The division of responsibility in feeding is based on research in child nutrition and energy balance (Davis, 1928; Fomon, 1993; Fomon et al., 1975; Gesell & Ilg, 1937), child oral-motor (Morris & Klein, 2000) and psychosocial (Greenspan & Lourie, 1981) development, feeding (Ainsworth & Bell, 1969; Birch & Fisher, 1995; Birch, Johnson, & Fisher, 1995; Eisenberg, Olson, Neumark-Sztainer, Story, & Bearinger, 2004), and parenting (Baumrind, 1971; Maccoby & Martin, 1983).

The division of responsibility is an authoritative model (Baumrind, 1971; Maccoby et al., 1983) defining the parents' role as both taking leadership with feeding and giving the child autonomy with eating. According to Rhee, Lumeng, Appugliese, Kaciroti, and Bradley (2006), authoritative parenting correlates with the lowest incidence of overweight in first-grade children (3.9%) followed in overweight incidence by permissive (9.8%), neglectful (9.9%), and authoritarian parenting (17.1%). Distinctions lie in the ways parents combine the elements of leadership and autonomy. Authoritative parents balance the two, neglectful and permissive parents give autonomy without taking leadership, and authoritarian parents take leadership but do not give autonomy.

The Satter Feeding Dynamics Model as it applies to child overweight prevention and management is outlined in Figure 19.1. The Feeding Dynamics Model is competency based. It is grounded on well-supported evidence that children have a powerful and resilient ability to maintain energy balance and grow in a predictable fashion (Centers for Disease Control, 2000a; Donnelly et al., 1996; Fomon et al., 1975; Pietilanen et al., 2001; Rose & Mayer, 1968). However, for the child to maintain appropriate energy intake, the feeding relationship must be responsive and supportive (Birch et al., 1995; Crow, Fawcett, & Wright, 1980; Neumark-Sztainer, Wall, Story, & Fulkerson, 2004).

Based on this assumption of competency with energy regulation and growth, the feeding dynamics definition of child overweight is not high weight per se, but weight acceleration: abnormal upward weight divergence for the individual child. The principle of conservation of growth, which provides the theoretical basis for growth charts, indicates that most children, most of the time, grow along a particular growth trajectory (Centers for Disease Control, 2000a; Fomon et al., 1975; Hamill et al., 1979; Legler & Rose, 1998; Pietilanen et al., 2001; Zack et al., 1979). That trajectory may be low, in the middle, or high—even above the 95th body mass index (BMI) percentile defined as the cutoff point for child overweight. Thus, consistent growth at any trajectory is normal. Abrupt, rapid, and ongoing acceleration (crossing upward across percentiles) is not (Legler & Rose, 1998). This perspective avoids labeling as overweight the child whose weight/height, or BMI, is above a certain percentile but who is growing consistently. It also identifies for early intervention the child whose measurements fall closer to the mean, but whose weight is nonetheless diverging from his previously established growth pattern (Centers for Disease Control, 2000a; Committee on Nutrition, 2003; Legler & Rose, 1998).

NORMAL GROWTH AND DEVELOPMENT

From the feeding dynamics perspective, to prevent child overweight from birth, feed optimally, support normal growth and development, and avoid disruptive influences. For the infant and young child, and to a lesser extent for older children, nourishing is synonymous with nurturing. Symbolically, in terms of actual time spent, and in terms of consequences to normal growth and development, feeding is of primary importance during a child's early life. Appropriate feeding supports the child in achieving developmental tasks at every stage as well as instills positive eating attitudes and behaviors. Problems with feeding can impair normal growth and development, but on a more profound level, they can reflect distortions in parent-child interaction that interfere with the child's positive psychosocial development.

Feeding is parenting, and appropriate feeding allows children to achieve developmental tasks at every stage (Satter, 1995). Health care professionals who understand the principles and practices of optimal, stage-related feeding (Satter, 2000a) can concretely teach good parenting within the feeding context. Good parenting with feeding is observing a division of responsibility in feeding, guiding the feeding process based on information coming from the child with respect to inclinations for eating and physical abilities, and accepting the child's constitutionally endowed growth (even when that growth exceeds standard cutoff points) (Satter, 2006).

Satter Feeding Dynamics Model
of Child Overweight Prevention and Treatment[i,ii]
Ellyn Satter, MS, RD, LCSW, BCD

Many of today's children are getting too heavy. This is clearly indicated by population-wide surveys showing increasing percentages of children whose BMI plots in excess of diagnostic cutoff percentiles. Those trends indicate that environmental influences are disrupting children's ability to regulate energy balance and grow consistently.

1. *Perspective*: The feeding dynamics model of child overweight is competency-based. It is grounded on well-supported evidence that children have a powerful and resilient ability to maintain energy balance and grow in a predictable fashion, *provided* the feeding relationship is appropriate.

2. *Definition*: The feeding dynamics definition of child overweight is not high weight *per se*, but weight *acceleration*: Abnormal upward weight divergence for the *individual* child. The child is compared only to *himself*, not to statistical cutoff points established for the purpose of population-wide evaluation.

3. *Exploring causation*: The feeding dynamics model considers medical and psychosocial issues, food selection, parenting, the feeding relationship, and child development. In identifying causes of weight acceleration, the feeding dynamics question is:
   a. *Not*, how do we get this child to lose weight?
   b. *But rather*, what is happening in this child's environment to undermine his considerable ability to regulate energy balance and grow predictably?

4. *Typical causes*: Clinically and from an examination of the research literature, it emerges that there are four typical causes, alone or in combination, for a child's weight acceleration:
   a. Misinterpretation of normal growth.
   b. Restrained feeding and circumstances that mimic restrained feeding.
   c. Poor feeding practices.
   d. Stress.

5. *Prevention*: Preventing weight acceleration mandates supporting normal growth and development *and* avoiding disruptive influence by:
   a. Optimizing feeding from birth and throughout the growing-up years by maintaining a division of responsibility in feeding.
   b. Maintaining a division of responsibility in *activity*.
   c. Supporting parents in accepting consistent weight, even if that weight is at or above levels defined as "overweight" or "at risk of overweight."

6. *Treatment*: Treatment of child overweight from feeding dynamics perspective involves:
   a. Careful assessment *of the individual child* to identify causes of weight acceleration.
   b. Constructing and enacting a treatment plan to correct those causes, supporting patents in optimizing feeding and activity and holding steady with feeding during their child's transition to internally regulated eating.
   c. Letting the child's weight establish its own level in response to a. and b. Depending on the child's metabolic patterns, this weight trajectory may stabilize at the current level or gradually decrease.

---

[i] For more information, see Ellyn Satter's *Your Child's Weight: Helping without Harming.*
[ii] To find references, further information and handouts, go to www.EllynSatter.com and click on *Child Overweight.*

Figure 19.1

Homeostasis and Attachment: Infancy

Encourage parents to feed on demand, based on information coming from the infant with respect to timing, tempo, amount, and level of skill. Feeding in this tuned-in, responsive fashion allows the infant to eat as much or as little as he needs, provides the experience of eating as being pleasant and rewarding, supports the infant's ability to calm and organize himself, gives him a sense of being loved, and provides the experience of autonomy—of being respected as an individual.

Separation-Individuation: Toddler Years

Separation-individuation begins toward the end of the first year as the child begins to make the transition from the demand feeding of an infant to the meals-plus-snacks routine of an older child. The infant who has started this transition cares deeply about feeding himself. The toddler who is well into separation-individuation is skeptical of new food and tests limits by begging for food handouts between meals. Include the toddler in family meals and sit-down snacks at predictable times, allow him to eat what and how much he wants from what grownups provide, but do not let him panhandle for food between meals. Provide meals that are considerate of the child's limitations and capabilities without catering to his likes and dislikes or limiting the menu to foods the child readily accepts. Feeding in this authoritative fashion gives security, as it supports the toddler's experience of being a separate person and continues to make eating rewarding by avoiding introducing conflict and anxiety around eating. It also supports the toddler's task of somatopsychological differentiation: of learning to sort out his feelings and sensations and apply the proper solution.

Initiative and Industry: Preschool and School-Age Child

Continuing to give the preschooler or school-age child both structure and autonomy allows him to follow his own inclinations with eating at the same times as he pleases his parents. Teach parents to maintain the structure of family meals and sit-down snacks. To avoid precipitating heightened interest in "forbidden food" (Fisher & Birch, 2002), encourage parents to include a variety of food, including high-fat, high-sugar food. When the child enters the upper grades, support his eating competence by gradually teaching him to manage the timing and choosing of his own after-school snack.

Identity: Adolescent

The feeding dynamics goal is to gradually teach the adolescent to manage the what, when, and where of feeding, equipping her to manage food after she leaves home. However, this teaching is within the context of parents continuing to take primary responsibility for family food management. This responsibility includes having regular family meals and laying out the expectation that the adolescent will participate in those meals.

CAUSES OF WEIGHT ACCELERATION

Application of the Feeding Dynamics Model encourages providers and parents to avoid treating the symptom of weight acceleration with food restriction. Instead, it stresses asking the fundamental question: What is interfering with this child's normal ability to eat as much as he or she needs to grow in a consistent fashion? That is, what is disrupting this individual child's energy homeostasis and distorting his normal growth trajectory? To answer this question, the Feeding Dynamics Model considers medical and psychosocial issues, food selection, parenting, the feeding relationship, and child development (Davies et al., 2006; Satter, 1996, 2005a). Clinically, and from an examination of the research literature, it emerges that there are four typical causes, alone or in combination, for a child's weight acceleration.

1. Misinterpretation of Normal Growth

Clinical observations indicate that in many, if not most, cases the child's "weight problem" is in the eyes of the beholder: health professionals, parents or even extended families, neighbors, and society in general. Sometimes the child is not even large, but is simply the child of heavy parents and therefore perceived as being "at risk" of becoming overweight. The often casual labeling of the child as overweight sets off a chain of events, including food restriction and struggles around feeding, undermines the child's ability to regulate food intake, and creates the very problem the overweight "diagnosis" is intended to address.

However, clinical observations must be considered hypothetical until they are tested by research. Research, in fact, confirms these observations. Diagnosing overweight appears to distort feeding and growth. Irrespective of actual weight status, the weight of infants (Burdette, Whitaker, Hall, & Daniels, 2006) and children (Faith et al., 2004) tends to accelerate when parents perceive them as overweight and are concerned about it. Also irrespective of actual weight status, when children perceive themselves as overweight, even 5-year-olds try to restrict their food intake and their weight accelerates (Shunk & Birch, 2004). Associations among girls' weight concerns, body dissatisfaction, and weight status increase with age (Davison, Markey, & Birch, 2003). In a group of similar-size children, the ones who perceived themselves as overweight felt flawed in every way: not smart, not physically capable, and not good about themselves (Davison & Birch, 2001).

Despite the fact that no cure exists, early diagnosis of child overweight is emphasized (Committee on Nutrition, 2003) and clinicians decry parental refusal to accept the overweight diagnosis (Jain et al., 2001). According to expert committee consensus, at risk of overweight for children ages 2 to 20 years is a BMI for age between the 85th and 95th percentiles and overweight is a BMI for age at or above the 95th percentile. According to the expert committee, "An appropriate final goal for all children and adolescents who are overweight or at risk for overweight is a BMI for age below the 85th percentile" (Barlow & Dietz, 1998). A child is also considered at risk for overweight if one or both parents has a BMI of 30 or greater (Expert Panel on the Identification, Evaluation, and Treatment of Overweight and Obesity in Adults, 1998). A currently convened expert committee is considering reclassifying children whose BMI is at or above the 85th percentile from "at risk of overweight" to "overweight" (Moynihan, 2006).

Arbitrary BMI cutoffs deliver false positives. While statistical cutoff points are appropriate for the purpose of population-wide evaluation, they are not appropriate for the diagnosis of individual children. According to the Feeding Dynamics Model, that diagnosis can only be made on the basis of longitudinal growth tracking and identification of weight acceleration. Children growing at the 85th and 95th percentiles are unusual, but not necessarily abnormal (Hamill et al., 1979). Five percent of a given population of children normally plot at the 95th percentile or above and 15% plot at the 85th percentile or above. According to 2003–2004 National Health and Examination Survey (NHANES) data, 18% of children currently have a BMI at the 95th percentile or above (Ogden et al., 2006). The reality is that 5% of children belong statistically in that category, reducing the actual incidence of disproportionately high BMI to 13%, a figure that is still concerning.

Body mass index cutoffs deliver false positives for physically dense children as well. Since BMI measures body density, not body fat, lean children with relatively heavy bones or high muscle mass may plot in diagnostic ranges. This is particularly evident in certain ethnic groups. Hispanic children are short, broad, and solidly built, and as a result, their median BMI falls at roughly the 85th percentile of Centers for Disease Control (CDC) growth charts (Ryan, Roche, & Kuczmarski, 1999). The same applies to Navaho children (Eisenmann et al., 2000). Peruvian children have low body fat, but high weight/height because of their short stature, high muscle mass, and a resultant high percentage of body water (Boutton et al., 1987). As Wright, Parker, Lamont, and Craft (2001) found in the Thousand Families longitudinal study, while BMI—that is, body density—tracks from childhood to adulthood, body fatness does not.

Concern about tendencies for "overweight" infants (defined as weight/length in the 95th percentile or greater) to become overweight adults (BMI 25 or greater) is based on similar flaws in statistical logic, as well as misunderstanding of normal growth processes. Body weight tends to be transmitted genetically (Bouchard et al., 1990; Garn & Clark, 1976; Pietilanen et al., 2001; Stunkard, Harris, Pedersen, & McClearn, 1990). Given genetic transmissibility, it is logical for large infants and children of large parents to grow fast and become large adults. Such patterns, rather than being a warning sign of impending adult obesity (Stettler, Kumanyika, Katz, Zemel, & Stallings, 2003; Stettler et al., 2005; Stettler, Zemel, Kumanyika, & Stallings, 2002), simply describe normal growth. (The logical likelihood that an "overweight" child would become an "overweight" or "obese" adult becomes particularly apparent when cutoff points for both child and adult "overweight" are expressed in similar, nonpejorative terms. The 95th percentile is roughly two standard deviations above the mean. The current cutoff point for the diagnosis of adult overweight is set at the mean: a BMI of 25. Little wonder then that a child whose BMI is +2 SD would grow up to be an adult whose BMI is above the mean!

While large parents tend to have large children, growth also tends to diverge toward the mean. Relatively small infants become larger later in childhood, and relatively large infants become smaller (Garn, Pilkington, & Lavelle, 1984). Unless the process is disrupted by food restriction, the tendency in childhood is toward slimming. Less than 25% of infants who plot in the 95th percentile weight/length plot in that same percentile as young adults. The percentages of overweight retained into adulthood among preschool children was 26% to 41%, and among 9- to 15-year-olds was 42% to 63% (Serdula et al., 1993; Whitlock, Williams, Gold, Smith, & Shipman, 2005). Conversely, there is no basis for the assumption that a person who leaves childhood slim will be slim for life. More than 79% of obese 36-year-olds first became obese in early adult life. Individuals who became obese at between 11 and 36 years of age were often not the most overweight in childhood (Braddon, Rodgers, Wadsworth, & Davies, 1986).

2. Restrained Feeding and Circumstances That Mimic Restrained Feeding

Clinical observations show that the onset of a child's weight acceleration often coincides with the institution or exacerbation of food restriction. Children whose food intake is restricted become preoccupied with food and are prone to overeat when they get the opportunity. Even during infancy, parents who perceive their child as being overweight are at risk of restricting food intake (and being given advice to restrict), thereby creating the very condition that they fear. Children are a captive audience with respect to food access. Children become afraid of going hungry when their food intake is restricted for the purpose of weight management, because of erratic or unreliable feeding, or when economic circumstances limit the parents' ability to provide. Parents who are chronic dieters and overconcerned about their own weight or health are particularly prone to restrict a child's food intake, either consciously or unconsciously.

When distortions in feeding and parenting are corrected and stay corrected, children change and stay changed. Children recover their sensitivity to their internal regulators of food intake when parents restore a division of responsibility in feeding, provided parents extinguish all efforts, direct and indirect, to manage the amount and type of food the child eats. Once children experience parents as being trustworthy, they rediscover their internal regulators of hunger, appetite, and satiety. How long that takes depends on the child's age. Toddlers, preschoolers, and young school-age children take 2 to 4 weeks. Older school-age children take 6 to 8 weeks and benefit from being in sessions with their parents so together they can work out the kinks in establishing the division of responsibility in feeding. Adolescents take 10 to 12 weeks and do best when parents and children are seen separately from one another. Parents address feeding and parenting; the child learns to internally regulate within the context of the parents' supportive limits.

Research verifies these clinical observations. Restrained eating and feeding—the chronic tendency to eat and provide less food or less-appealing food than desired—has become normative in our culture, with 64% of men and 78% of women attempting to lose or maintain weight at any one time (Serdula et al., 1999). While food restriction may be normative, it hardly represents "competent" eating. Competent eating is providing regular and reliable access to ample and rewarding food and eating enough to be satisfied, both aesthetically and calorically, based on the utility of biopsychosocial processes: hunger and the need to survive, appetite and the desire for subjective reward, and the biological tendency to maintain a preferred and stable body weight (Satter, 2007).

Food restriction with respect to either amount (Faith, Scanlon, Birch, Francis, & Sherry, 2004) or type (Fisher & Birch, 2002) of food precipitates a counterregulatory effect and the child's weight accelerates. Girls who were classified as at risk for overweight at age 5 years reported significantly higher levels of restraint, disinhibition, weight concern, and body dissatisfaction by age 9 years (Shunk & Birch, 2004). The Eating in the Absence of Hunger (EAH) protocol measures disinhibition with eating by giving children a standard lunch, then giving free access to snack foods. In EAH trials, young girls (ages 5 to 7 years) whose access to "palatable" foods (high-sugar, high-fat snack foods) was restricted by parents were more likely to eat those foods—and feel badly about it—than girls who were not restricted. Negative feelings were associated not with the amount eaten, but with the feeling that parents did not want them eating those foods (Fisher & Birch, 2000). Restricted girls were also more likely to be overweight than unrestricted girls (Birch & Fisher, 2000). Being overweight at age 5 years potentiated parents' tendency to restrict and children's tendency to eat in the absence of hunger at 7 and 9 years of age (Birch, Fisher, & Davison, 2003). Food restriction, in turn, increases the tendency in adults and children to use food for emotional reasons (Herman, Polivy, & Esses, 1987). Interpersonal stress increases snacking in children whose food intake has been restricted, but decreases it in unrestrained children (Roemmich, Wright, & Epstein, 2002).

The counterregulatory impact of food restriction on body weight is particularly evident in preadolescents and adolescents. The BMI of 12- to 14-year-old girls was significantly correlated with the degree of dietary restraint: as restraint went up, so did BMI (Hill, Rogers, & Blundell, 1989). In the 4 years of high school, girls who identified themselves during their freshman year as using dietary restraint, self-labeled dieting, exercise for weight-control purposes, and appetite suppressant/ laxative abuse were at increased risk for obesity onset (Stice, Cameron, Killen, Hayward, & Taylor, 1999). Thirteen- to 16-year-olds who restricted themselves became heavier, whether their weight reduction efforts were healthful (more fruits, vegetables, and whole grains, less fat, more activity) or unhealthful (extreme food restriction, diuretics, laxatives, diet pills, vomiting) (Neumark-Sztainer et al., 2006). Sixteen- to 19-year-olds who were told by their doctor that they were overweight were more likely to initiate food restriction (Kant & Miner, 2007). Professionally administered weight management programs appear to have similar limitations with respect to achieving target eating and weight outcomes. Among children 8 to 13 years of age, intensive, generally family-based, short-term (1 year or less) behavioral approaches produced modest to no changes in BMI. Extensive reviews of weight management interventions found, at most, a 10% decrease in participant BMI values, a decrease that was rarely maintained for more than 1 year (Epstein, Myers, Raynor, & Saelens, 1998; Whitlock et al., 2005). To arrive at these generalizations about weight loss, all reported outcomes were converted to reduction in BMI. For instance, a reported 17% reduction in percent overweight converts to a 10% reduction in BMI.

For a child, any feeding practice that fails to reassure the child of getting enough to eat mimics restrained feeding and precipitates a counterregulatory effect. Erratic or inconsistent family meals correlate with increased rates of child overweight (Taveras et al., 2005). Food-insecure children— those whose parents cannot feed them reliably—also display food preoccupation and tendencies to weight gain (Alaimo, Olson, & Frongillo, 2001). Food insecurity growing out of poverty correlates with increased child overweight in 15- to 17-year-olds, but not 12- to 14-year-olds (Miech et al., 2006). In low-income children, tendencies to overweight are neutralized by access to food assistance programs, such as food stamps, school nutrition, and Women, Infants, and Children (WIC) (Jones, Jahns, Laraia, & Haughton, 2003).

Parents' own eating attitudes and behaviors impact children's eating and body weight. In the Framingham Children's longitudinal study, parents who displayed high levels of disinhibited eating, especially when coupled with high dietary restraint, appeared to foster the development of excess body fat in their children. Children whose parents had particularly high scores on both restraint and disinhibition had particularly large increases in BMI (Hood et al., 2000). Overweight mothers felt responsible and were likely to monitor the amounts and types of food their children ate. Mothers' bulimia correlated with controlling feeding practices in daughters and fathers' body dissatisfaction correlated with monitoring of sons' food intake (Blissett, Meyer, & Haycraft, 2006). Infants (Burdette et al., 2006) and children (Spruijt-Metz, Lindquist, Birch, Fisher, & Goran, 2002) of mothers who had high concern about their child's overeating or becoming overweight produced children with greater fat mass than did those mothers who did not have high concern.

3. Poor Feeding Practices

Poor feeding practices cross the lines of division of responsibility in feeding and, in the process, undermine children's eating capability, including their ability to regulate food intake and grow appropriately. Based on clinical observations, children react to poor feeding practices by becoming upset—anxious, angry, rebellious—and their emotional arousal precipitates errors in food regulation. Once internal regulatory processes have been undermined, the child is vulnerable to errors in food regulation and may undereat or overeat. Uncorrected, these errors persist into adolescent and adult life.

Certainly, restricting a child's food intake is a poor feeding practice. There are others. Failing to feed in a developmentally appropriate way is a poor feeding practice: giving solid foods too early, failing to wean when the child is developmentally ready, letting the toddler graze for food, or failing to maintain the structure of meals and snacks for the older child or adolescent. Poor parenting with feeding is another. Parents may be permissive or neglectful with feeding on the one hand, or authoritarian with feeding on the other. A toddler who is allowed to graze for food may overeat and gain too much weight, undereat and grow poorly, or be such a good regulator that he grows consistently. A headstrong toddler is likely to undereat and grow poorly when his drive for autonomy is thwarted by overbearing feeding tactics. He becomes so anxious and angry that he simply cannot sense that he is hungry. In contrast, a compliant toddler in a similar feeding situation may deny his drive for autonomy, overeat, and gain too much weight.

Parents may do poorly with feeding because they do poorly with their own eating, because they do not know appropriate feeding practices or are getting inaccurate advice, because they react to a child's illness or poor appetite by urging food, or because they are characterologically or situationally too controlling or too chaotic to maintain the division of responsibility in feeding. Failure to provide the structure of family meals and sit-down snacks is an increasingly common and particularly destructive poor feeding practice.

The research substantiates these clinical observations. An estimated 25% to 45% of typically developing children and up to 80% of developmentally disabled children present with feeding problems. Problems include food refusal, difficulty in accepting various food textures, disruptive mealtime behavior, rigid and bizarre food preferences, less-than-optimal growth, and delays in self-feeding (Linscheid, Budd, & Rasnake, 2003). From birth, relatively small but healthy children attract more feeding pressure from their parents and grow less well as a result (Crow et al., 1980). Some toddlers eat more when they are urged by their parents (Crow et al., 1980; Klesges, Malott, Boschee, & Weber, 1986), others eat less (Chatoor et al., 2004). Preschoolers who have difficulty regulating food intake have parents who are controlling of their food intake (Johnson & Birch, 1994). In a study of almost 200 children followed in detail from age 6 months to 16½ years, children who later became fat compared with children who remained slim ate no more calories and no more low nutrient-density or sweet foods, were no more likely to have been bottle fed, were started no earlier on solid foods, were no more likely to have been given high-fat milk, and were no more likely to have been raised in single-parent families. However, the risk of later obesity increased with toddler lack of feeding-time structure, with increased incidence of toddler feeding problems, and with increased parental concern about obesity (Crawford & Shapiro, 1991).

Failure to provide family meals is a particularly pervasive feeding problem. Currently, one-quarter of surveyed adolescents report two or fewer family meals a week, half report four or fewer (Eisenberg et al., 2004), and the incidence decreases as children progress through adolescence (Center on Addiction and Substance Abuse, 2005). Children with regular family meals do better nutritionally (Gillman et al., 2000), socially, emotionally, academically (Eisenberg et al., 2004; Center on Addiction and Substance Abuse, 2005; Council of Economic Advisors, 2000), and with respect to resistance to overweight (Taveras et al., 2005), drug and alcohol abuse, and early sexual behavior (Center on Addiction and Substance Abuse, 2005; Council of Economic Advisors, 2000). Meal time is far more powerful in predicting positive outcomes for adolescents than time spent in school, studying, church, sports, and art activities, irrespective of parents' race and ethnicity, education and age, family structure and employment, income, and family size (Hofferth, 2001).

Adolescents who have been exposed to poor feeding practices are vulnerable to weight reduction dieting as a way of managing their own food intake, and in fact, 65% of girls and 70% of boys reported dieting to lose weight. Extreme dieting methods were employed by 31% (Neumark-Sztainer, Hannan, Story, & Perry, 2004; Neumark-Sztainer, Wall, et al., 2004). As reported earlier, adolescents who diet using either moderate or extreme methods are heavier 5 years later than those who do not diet (Neumark-Sztainer et al., 2006). On the other hand, adolescents appeared to be protected from weight control behaviors when they feel their parents assign a high priority to structured family meals and maintain a positive atmosphere at family meals (Neumark-Sztainer, Wall, et al., 2004).

Parents' own eating attitudes and behaviors as well as their ability to take appropriate leadership with parenting is reflected in their ability to maintain the structure of family meals. As noted earlier, the division of responsibility in feeding is authoritative parenting, which in turn correlates with the lowest incidence of overweight in first-grade children (Rhee et al., 2006). Parents have trouble giving children appropriate autonomy with eating when they have their own limitations in eating competence. Heavier mothers and mothers with disinhibited eating have greater concern for their children's future health and weight independent of the children's current weight status (Saelens, Ernst, & Epstein, 2000). Maternal body dissatisfaction, internalization of the thin ideal, dieting, bulimic symptoms, and maternal and paternal body mass prospectively predict the emergence of childhood eating disturbances (Stice, Agras, & Hammer, 1999). Parents who have heightened concern about food selection tend to put pressure on their children to eat vegetables or restrict fat, pressure that produces the opposite results of those intended (Galloway, Fiorito, Lee, & Birch, 2005; Lee, Mitchell, Smiciklas-Wright, & Birch, 2001).

4. Stress

Clinical experience indicates that stress can cause excessive weight gain, provided the individual has previously learned to misuse food for emotional reasons. It is normal to use eating as one of a variety of ways of coping. We all eat to celebrate, soothe ourselves, or find pleasure. However, eating is misused when it is done reflexively in an attempt to address or avoid emotional arousal, especially when the individual depends on eating as virtually the only means of coping.

Eating for emotional reasons is most powerfully instilled in childhood. For stress to cause weight acceleration, children must have learned to substitute food demands and eating for what they actually feel, want, and need. That learning grows out of distortion in the feeding relationship. Most often that distortion is restrained feeding, but other poor feeding practices can teach stress-related eating as well, such as indiscriminately feeding a fussy infant, giving constant food handouts to a fractious toddler, or failing to provide older children the security and support of rewarding family meals.

For a child whose food intake is restricted, hunger is the constant and pervasive reality. Chronic hunger profoundly disrupts the child's social and emotional development and undermines parent-child relationships. The hungry child has great difficulty achieving developmental tasks at every stage, and parents who feel obligated to make their child go hungry are handicapped in meeting their child's needs. The hungry and chronically dissatisfied infant cannot achieve homeostasis, become attached, or build trust in herself and other people because what she most wants and needs is the very thing that parents are reluctant to give her: enough to eat. The hungry, clingy, and demanding toddler cannot gain autonomy because exploring and defying carries the risk of alienating the people who control the food supply. The hungry, self-preoccupied older child has trouble with initiative, industry, and identity because she is caught in a dilemma: does she comply with parents, gain their approval, and continue to go hungry, or defy, risk shame and punishment, and get enough to eat?

Research verifies the connection between stress and excessive child weight gain. In previously normal weight 8- to 11-year-old children, clinically meaningful behavior problems were independently associated with an increased risk of becoming overweight (Lumeng, Gannon, Cabral, Frank, & Zuckerman, 2003). Compared with children who gained weight at an appropriate rate, 7- to 13-year-old children who gained weight at an accelerated rate experienced elevated levels of psychosocial stress. The association between stress and weight gain was particularly marked for children between 10 and 13 years of age (Mellbin & Vuille, 1989). Compared with children who had no psychiatric disorder, BMI was two points higher after 10 to 15 years in children who had been diagnosed with major depression at age 6 to 17 years (Pine, Goldstein, Wolk, & Weissman, 2001).

Less-than-optimal parenting stresses children, which in turn correlates with increased child overweight. As noted elsewhere, authoritative parenting tends to produce fewer overweight children than permissive, neglectful, and authoritarian parenting (Rhee et al., 2006). Repeated parent interviews as children aged from 6 to 22 years revealed both obese boys and girls were four to five times more likely to have been exposed earlier in life to low parental education, physical neglect, and poverty. Among girls only, additional early adversities were harsh maternal punishment and loud arguments between parents. Poor parental maintenance of the home appeared to be particularly obesogenic for girls (Johnson, Cohen, Kasen, & Brook, 2002). Compared with mothers of nonobese children, mothers of obese children ages 8 to 16 years reported significantly greater psychological distress and greater family conflict. Both mothers and fathers reported negative mealtime interactions (Zeller et al., 2007).

Indirect measures of child stress correlate with higher levels of child overweight. Those indirect measures include disturbance in children's sleep patterns (Beebe et al., 2007), school children's dirty and ragged clothing (Lissau & Sorensen, 1994), child constipation (Pashankar & Loening-Baucke, 2005), and parents not knowing about children's sweets intake (Lissau, Breum, & Sorensen, 1993).

Hunger creates impairment in all ways—physically, emotionally and socially (Keys, Brozek, Henschel, Mickelsen, & Taylor, 1950)—and directly increases stress on food-insecure parents and children. According to data from NHANES, 86% of low-income parents and 14% of middle-income parents describe themselves as being food insufficient (Alaimo, Olson, Frongillo, & Briefel, 2001). With increasing food insecurity, a greater percentage of mothers experienced major depressive episodes or generalized anxiety disorders. The percentage of children with a behavior problem also increased with increasing food insecurity, even after adjustment for maternal mental health issues (Wang & Zhang, 2006). Irrespective of family income level, U.S. adolescents show a strong association between food insufficiency and depressive disorder and suicidal symptoms (Alaimo, Olson, & Frongillo, 2002). As noted earlier, younger but not older adolescents appear to be protected against poverty-related overweight (Miech et al., 2006), perhaps because parents give younger but not older children preferential access to limited family food supplies. Ironically, for more than two-thirds of adolescents, hunger is a chronic reality as the result of self-imposed food restriction in the pursuit of weight loss (Neumark-Sztainer, Hannan, et al., 2004).

THREE CASE EXAMPLES OF DISTORTED FEEDING DYNAMICS

Case 1. Mary: Misinterpretation of Normal Growth, Restrained Feeding, Poor Feeding Practices, Stress

Nineteen-year-old Mary was referred by her psychotherapist for treatment of her bulimia and over-weight. As indicated in Figure 19.2, Mary's current weight for age plotted at the 97th percentile. (Weight for age is used instead of weight/length or BMI because lengths and heights were not taken according to prescribed practice.) From her longitudinal pattern, it appeared that her weight problem had begun with a rapid gain when she was 10 years old. Mary could explain her weight

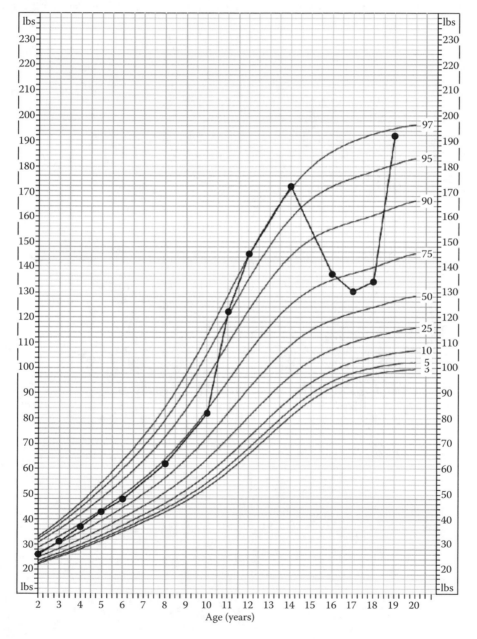

Figure 19.2

inconsistencies after age 14 years: she joined Weight Watchers and lost almost 50 pounds by age 17 years. Then, as Mary put it, "the minute I hit bottom I started eating again and gained it all back and more besides. Then I started throwing up." But explaining what had happened before age 14 years was more complicated.

Retrieving Mary's growth records from birth and reconstructing the story from her medical records filled in the missing pieces. As indicated in Figure 19.3, for her first 5 months Mary's weight and weight/length (which is not shown; while they are based on faulty length and height data, the weight/length and BMI values indicate that Mary was relatively heavy; had Mary been tall as well as heavy, her weight/length or BMI would have plotted closer to the 50th percentile) plotted just above the 97th percentile. At age 5 months, according to the family's story, Mary's doctor warned her

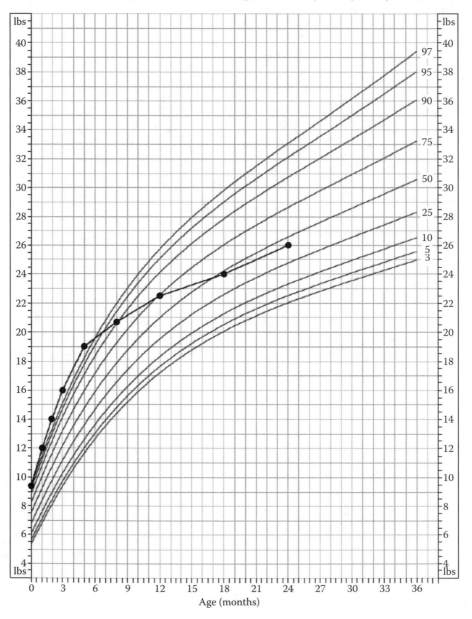

Figure 19.3

mother, "if you let her stay obese, she will develop too many fat cells and she will be fat for life." The doctor was talking about Hirsch's fat cell theory of obesity, popular in the late 1970s and periodically revived since. Hirsch may have been right about "fat cells," but he was wrong about people. Fat babies have no greater risk of growing up fat than thin ones (Crawford et al., 1991; Serdula et al., 1993).) From then on, Mary's parents restricted her food intake, forcing her weight down to the 50th percentile by the time she was 18 months old and keeping it between the 50th and the 75th percentile until she was 10 years old. At that point, a crisis so serious erupted between her parents that Mary's father left the family. Mary's mother became so depressed and overwhelmed that she not only stopped restricting Mary, she stopped feeding her as well. It was disastrous for Mary emotionally, and disastrous for her weight. After years of food restriction, Mary had long since lost touch with her internal regulators of hunger, appetite, and satiety. Without her mother's external controls, she was left with no controls at all. Her weight climbed rapidly, then leveled off back where she started—just above the 97th percentile. Could that have been where her weight belonged all along?

On the other hand, most relatively fat infants and toddlers slim down as they get older (Whitlock et al., 2005). Restricting Mary's food intake may have deprived her of that natural slimming process.

Causes of Mary's Weight Acceleration.

Misinterpretation of Normal Growth. Despite 5 months of consistent growth, and therefore evidence of her ability to maintain energy homeostasis, Mary's doctor and mother colluded in interpreting her high body weight as overweight.

Restrained Feeding. In response to this misinterpretation, Mary's food intake was restricted beginning at age 5 months and persisting until age 10 years. In the process, she lost track of her internal regulators of hunger, appetite, and satiety. When her mother stopped controlling her eating, Mary unsuccessfully tried to restrict herself.

Poor Feeding Practices. When Mary was 10 years old, feeding changed from deprivation to neglect. Her mother stopped feeding her at all, the ultimate in poor feeding practices, and Mary was left to fend for herself. Years of restrained feeding taught Mary that the way to manage food intake was with food restriction. However, she lacked the skills and determination to deprive herself the way her mother had deprived her and she rapidly gained weight.

Stress. At age 10 years, Mary's loss and anxiety were extreme, past and present food restriction exacerbated her tendency to eat for emotional reasons, and she showed stress-related eating and weight gain. Mary's father was gone, her mother was incapacitated, and Mary was on her own emotionally. She turned to eating to try to ease her misery and anxiety.

Intervention with Mary's Eating and Weight

The assessment helped Mary to understand what had happened to her with respect to her eating and weight and to forgive herself for her weight gain. From the feeding dynamics perspective, here were the recommendations for intervention:

Avoid Food Restriction and Striving for Weight Loss. Food restriction would represent more of the same with respect to Mary's eating and weight. Further dieting would likely exacerbate her pattern of reactive overeating and weight gain. Focusing on dieting would also divert Mary's emotional energy from psychotherapy.

Address Psychosocial Issues. In psychotherapy, Mary was addressing her lack of trust in other people, low emotional self-awareness, and low self-confidence. However, psychotherapy could not correct the distortion in her eating attitudes and behaviors.

Address Eating Attitudes and Behaviors. To address Mary's conflict and anxiety about eating, as well as help her learn internally regulated eating, Mary was coached in regulating her food intake based on hunger, appetite, and satiety.

Address Activity. Mary pursued activity at a high level when she dieted, then suspended activity when she stopped dieting. The task was to help Mary find rewarding, realistic, and therefore sustainable ways of being active.

Let Weight Find Its Own Level. Rather than striving for a particular weight outcome, let Mary's weight find its own level in response to competent eating and sustainable activity. Only time would tell what that weight level would be. However, in view of Mary's past history, weight would likely remain at or near where it was when she presented for assessment.

Outcome with Mary

Mary chose to address her eating and activity and let her weight do what it would in response to her changes in behavior. It would not have been surprising had she chosen to reject the assessment and recommendations and try still again to lose weight. She was young and slimness had been an ideal for as long as she could remember. But in psychotherapy she was learning to replace her hope for weight loss with hope for what mattered more and what she could achieve—feeling good about herself, discovering her capabilities, and having rewarding relationships with other people.

Mary worked hard and successfully achieved internally regulated eating. She learned to make feeding herself a priority, developed the ability to eat what and as much as she wanted without going out of control, and she found rewarding ways of moving her body. Her weight remained about the same as it had been at the assessment, and she came to terms with that. Her physical self-esteem had improved somewhat as a result of the eating intervention, but the major improvement came as a result of psychotherapy. Clinical experience demonstrates that physical self-esteem is closely related to self-esteem overall, and self-esteem can only change through corrective life experience or psychotherapy.

Case 2. Wellington: Poor Feeding Practices, Restrained Feeding, Misinterpretation of Normal Growth, Stress

According to the weight-for-age plottings in Figure 19.4, 6½-year-old Wellington's weight was accelerating rapidly from the 97th percentile. Wellington's growth record from birth (Figure 19.5) shows that he grew appropriately from birth until age 12 months, then his weight began to accelerate.

While growth chart plottings outside the percentile curves are graphically impressive, they tell nothing about the magnitude and pattern of growth. To get an accurate longitudinal picture of his growth pattern, Wellington's weight-for-age values were calibrated by converting them into z-scores, or standard deviations above the mean. Then z-scores were plotted against his age, as in Figure 19.6 (Krick, 1986). To compare z-scores with growth records, consider that the 50th percentile is the median, or 0 SD, the 85th percentile is close to 1 SD, the 95th percentile is 1.6 SD, and the 97th percentile is 1.8 SD above the median (Krick, 1986). Figure 19.6 shows that Wellington's weight remained around the median for the first year, then rapidly accelerated to more than +4 SD by age 2 years. His weight stayed at that level for a year, then gradually decreased until, at age 6½ years, it plotted at +3.3 SD. In contrast to the apparent continuing weight gain conveyed by weight/height plottings in Figure 19.4, Wellington's weight was gradually decreasing. His major weight acceleration was between ages 1 and 2 years.

Wellington was breast fed on demand for the first 3 years. Breast-feeding was conducted appropriately for the first year. He regulated well during the time he was exclusively breast fed, when semisolid food was introduced, and when he started eating from the family table. But he was inap-

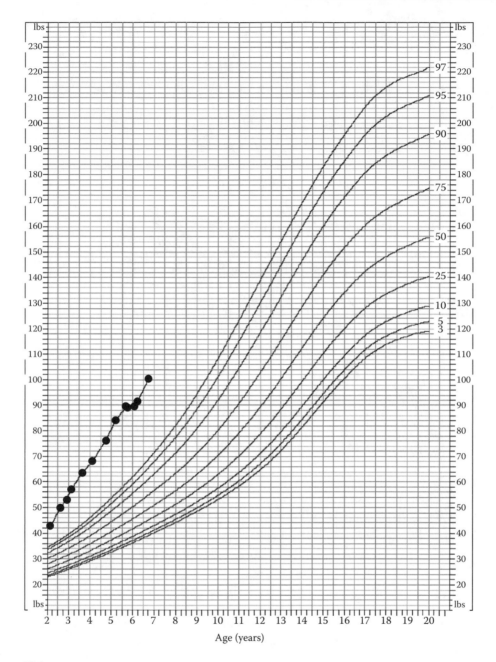

Figure 19.4

propriately fed as a toddler, and he regulated poorly. His mother continued to breast feed him on demand. She fed Wellington for nourishment, to calm him down, to distract and entertain him, and to keep him company. As a consequence, Wellington failed to achieve his toddler tasks of separation-individuation and somatopsychological differentiation.

Wellington's behavior in the family interview revealed his lack of earlier developmental mastery as well as the manner in which his lack of mastery served his parents. An overly talkative, highly active child who constantly sought attention, Wellington made an effective lighting rod for his parents' unexpressed conflict and anxiety. Wellington's father was impatient and critical with

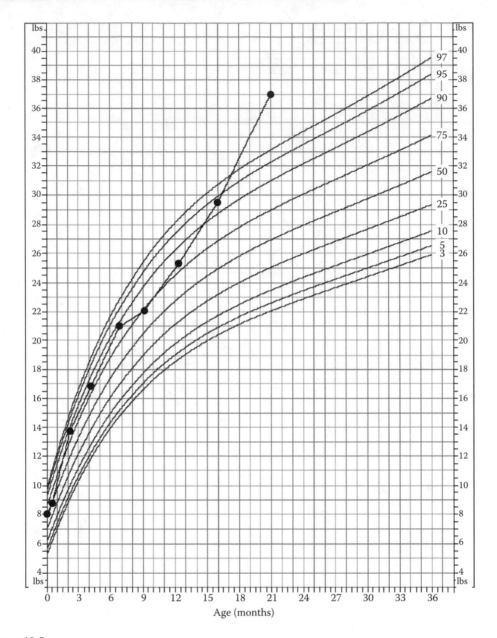

Figure 19.5

him; his mother protected him. Wellington appeared to be trying to define himself through his commotion, but got little traction because his parents' conflict left him with lax limits, low expectations, and excessive criticism.

Videotapes of family meals revealed only modest distortions in feeding dynamics. Wellington's parents provided meals at set times and they did not appear to restrict Wellington's food intake. But they filled his plate for him and made him wait at the table until everyone finished eating. Meals were tense. Wellington talked and talked, his father shushed and scolded and his mother placated. Food availability and stress could have promoted Wellington's eating more than he wanted. In addition, the babysitter reportedly ignored the parents' snacking guidelines and let Wellington graze for food.

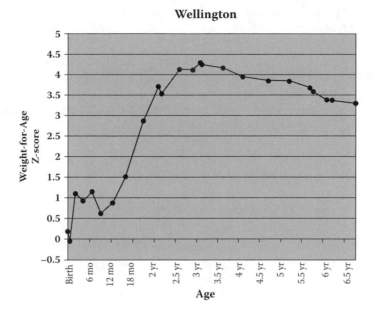

Figure 19.6

Individual, couple, and family interviews revealed Wellington's parents to be incapable of directly addressing or resolving their conflicts. Instead, they routed their feelings through Wellington by being overinvolved and overprotective. They appeared to have replicated the conditions defined as instrumental in developing and maintaining severe psychosomatic problems in children: (1) family organization that encourages somatization (enmeshed, rigid, overprotective), (2) involvement of the child in parental conflict, and (3) physiological vulnerability (Minuchin et al., 1975).

Causes of Wellington's Growth Acceleration
    Poor Feeding Practices. Demand breast-feeding throughout the toddler period interfered with Wellington's achieving separation-individuation as well as his ability to regulate his food intake and grow appropriately. For his part, Wellington submitted to being overfed and allowed himself to be placated rather than insisting on being independent and maintaining his drive to explore.

    Stress. Wellington was stressed by his involvement in the conflict between his parents as well as by his own immaturity. Poor feeding practices and lack of somatopsychological differentiation taught Wellington to use food to cope with stress.

    Restrained Feeding. Indirect and relatively mild restriction of food intake contributed to slowing his weight loss.

    Misinterpretation of Normal Growth. Assessment of Wellington was an afterthought to the assessment of his sister, who attracted most of the parents' concern. Wellington was actually heavier and had more pronounced behavioral limitations. Costanzo and Woody (1984) found a similar pattern, with parents focusing concern on daughters, even though sons showed distorted patterns with respect to weight and behavior.

Intervention with Wellington's Weight Issues
    Avoid Food Restriction and Striving for Weight Loss. Food restriction would undermine Wellington's current energy homeostasis and gradual weight loss. At age 6½ years, he has a better

than even chance of continuing to slim down. Restricting his food intake would arrest and likely reverse that normal slimming.

Address Psychosocial Issues. Seek family therapy to address the parents' individual patterns of emotional functioning, relationship with each other, and involvement of Wellington in their relationship. Support Wellington's autonomy by setting clear limits, giving firm expectations, and following through. Help Wellington develop positive social skills. Relatively large children, like other unusual children, need better-than-average social skills in order to do well.

Address Feeding. Emphasize family meals and structured snacks, being meticulous about maintaining a division of responsibility in feeding. Serve food in dishes, and let Wellington serve himself and decide what and how much to eat from what is on the table and on his plate. Include preferred food—chips, sweets, etc., in meals and snacks. Excuse Wellington when he asks, do not let him come back for food handouts, and expect and enforce his entertaining himself after he leaves. Be firm with the babysitter about providing Wellington with one sit-down after-school snack at a time that the parents indicate.

Address Activity. Limit television viewing, offer a variety of rewarding activities, then let Wellington pick and choose, being as active or inactive as he chooses. Stop trying to entertain Wellington. Instead, be firm about not allowing him to pester. Let him get bored enough to find his own entertainment.

Let Weight Find Its Own Level. Rather than striving for a particular weight outcome, let Wellington's weight find its own level in response to these positive patterns. Only time will tell what that weight level will be. Wellington's weight could continue its pattern of gradually diverging downward. On the other hand, his weight could equilibrate at its current level.

What Happened with Wellington

Wellington's parents took the assessment and recommendations back to their home community. They seemed accepting of the findings, but given their facility for avoiding conflict, it is unlikely they would indicate otherwise. It remains to be seen whether they will be able to institute the recommended changes. It is asking a lot of parents who for their whole lives have been afraid of their own feelings and indirect about dealing with their issues to tackle such significant change on behalf of their child. But Wellington's parents love him and want the best for him, so maybe they will be able to pull it off.

On the other hand, it would be easy enough for Wellington's parents to find someone to help them decide that the problem is really his weight and that what he needs is weight reduction. Restricting Wellington's food intake would make him even more of a lightening rod for his parents' unexpressed issues. Children who are put on diets constantly agitate for food or become food sneaks. Given Wellington's energy and drive to keep himself the center of attention, he could take them for quite a ride.

Case 3. Marcus: Poor Feeding Practices, Stress, Restrained Feeding, Misinterpretation of Normal Growth

Fifteen-year-old Marcus came for assessment on the instigation of his foster mother, who was concerned about his food preoccupation and overeating. Marcus was placed in foster care on the grounds that his biological mother failed to restrict his food intake and get his weight down. After 1½ years of careful food restriction in foster care, Marcus lost 150 lb. But recently he had begun eating voraciously. He sneaked food at home, stole food in grocery stores, and even ate out of garbage cans. At 150 lb below his previous weight, Marcus's biological pressure to eat and restore his usual weight had become extreme.

Determined digging through Marcus's voluminous records produced enough data to make the z-score graph in Figure 19.7. After growing consistently during his first year, Marcus's weight accelerated rapidly. By age 2 years, Marcus weighed 44 lb; age 4 years, 78 lb; age 6½ years, 152 lb; age 10 years, 367 lb. At age 13 years, he topped out at 447 lb. At age 13½ he was placed in foster care, and food restriction brought his weight down to 406 lb at age 14 years and 297 lb at age 15 years.

While Marcus's preadolescent and adolescent weights are extreme, Figure 19.7 gives evidence that disruptive forces began when he was between 1 and 2 years of age. What went on back then? His mother's reports were vague and contradictory. She claimed that Marcus had always been a voracious eater with out-of-control weight, but that was refuted by his consistent growth from birth to 1 year. His z-score remained high from age 2 to 6 years. His mother said he "didn't give any trouble" and was "independent and good at occupying his time," and that starting at about age 4 years he took care of his infant brother. Weight data were missing for ages 7, 8, and 9 years, and at age 10 to 11 years Marcus's weight dropped. At that time, social service workers were making regular visits to the home.

When Marcus was 8 years old, the accumulating school, medical, and social services reports showed him to be in a world of trouble. He was frequently tardy for or absent from school, poorly groomed, tired and sleepy, explosive, impulsive, and demanding too much attention. Marcus suffered from poor hygiene—dirty, ripped clothing and fecal odor. He often had no lunch money, and when his mother was contacted—with difficulty—she urged school personnel to pay for his lunch. Child protective services noted in home visits that Marcus and his younger brother were frequently left alone at night, that his mother was abusing alcohol, and that the house was filthy. Marcus's mother was jailed for failure to pay driving-while-intoxicated tickets and Marcus and his brother were briefly placed in a residential treatment facility. Marcus was enrolled in a specialized obesity management program, which his mother did not attend. Medical reports diagnosed Marcus's overweight and described unsuccessful attempts to find endocrine or genetic reasons for his high body weight.

From age 8 years, every assessment gave ample evidence that Marcus was neglected and that he was trying to do what was expected of him with little or no support from home. Every assessment summed up by blaming his problems on his weight. In reality, Marcus's weight was the least of his problems. Rather than being provided for, he had been given adult responsibilities from the time he was a preschooler.

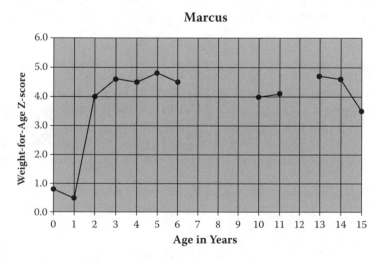

Marcus

Figure 19.7

Rather than being helped by the people who were supposed to protect and support him, Marcus's teachers, principal, social workers, and health personnel blamed him for his problems: he was too fat. Ironically, when Marcus was finally placed in a foster home where he could be provided for, it was on the grounds that "efforts to have his mother supervise his food intake have not worked."

What happened? Are schools and other agencies feeling so much pressure about child obesity that they overlook basic child welfare issues? Was Marcus's mother so formidable that no one wanted to take her on? Whatever the flaw in the process, Marcus was the one who paid the price.

Causes of Marcus's Weight Acceleration

Poor Feeding Practices. Marcus's consistent growth during his first year indicated that he got enough to eat, that he was capable of regulating his food intake, and that he may have achieved homeostasis and attachment. Feeding and parenting apparently deteriorated after that. Rather than being fed in a reliable and structured fashion, Marcus likely had to beg for food handouts. Beginning when he was a preschooler, Marcus was made responsible for feeding himself and his little brother. In foster care, food restriction mimicked the food insecurity from which he had suffered his whole life.

Stress. Beyond infancy, neglect and chaos in his home made it impossible for Marcus to achieve developmental tasks. His rapid weight gain between 1 and 2 years of age indicates extreme food panhandling and failure of separation-individuation. Marcus learned to use food for emotional reasons and undoubtedly continued to use food to assuage his fear of hunger and sense of abandonment. Marcus's z-score dip at ages 10 and 11 years, coinciding with child protective services involvement and presumed improvement in the family situation, supports the stress hypothesis. When life got better, Marcus slimmed down.

Restrained Feeding. Marcus experienced profound food insecurity growing out of erratic food availability and infrequent family meals, as well as frequent lack of access to food at home and at school. In addition, Marcus's mother, as well as health and school personnel, continually criticized his weight and tried to stop him from eating so much. Marcus was also periodically enrolled in weight-loss interventions.

Misinterpretation of Normal Growth. Marcus's growth was hardly normal, but it was still misinterpreted. Rather than getting heavier and heavier, Marcus's weight stabilized at a high level. He was regulating his energy balance and body weight, the same as he had during his first year.

Treatment Plan

Extreme weight gain grows out of extreme conditions. It does not call for extreme solutions.

Avoid Food Restriction and Striving for Weight Loss. Marcus's current food restriction and weight loss disrupted his energy and weight homeostasis and will likely precipitate regain to an even higher level. At presentation, Marcus's still high, but lower than usual weight meant that he was in a starved state. As much as he wanted to please his foster mother and stay on his diet, he was so hungry that he could not help eating whatever he could get, whenever he could get it.

Address Psychosocial Issues. In foster care, emphasize providing Marcus with a good home and good parenting. Provide Marcus with counseling to help him deal with anxiety and feelings of worthlessness.

Address Feeding. Stop restricting Marcus's food intake and optimize feeding. Emphasize structure: provide substantial and filling meals and sit-down snacks, include foods that Marcus finds rewarding, and reassure him that he can have as much as he wants at those scheduled times. Be firm about not allowing him to graze between meals. Provide Marcus with short-term treatment to help him get back in touch with his internal regulators of hunger, appetite, and satiety.

Let Weight Find Its Own Level. For a while Marcus will eat a lot and he may regain a considerable amount of weight, but eventually his hunger will not drive him so hard, he will begin to trust that he will be fed and provided for, and his weight will equilibrate. One cannot predict where this will be—it could be the same as or lower than before, or he could regain to an even higher level. Avoid trying to manage his weight gain; further food restriction will exacerbate his fear of going without and his tendency to reactively overeat.

What Happened with Marcus

Before the treatment plan could be enacted, the courts gave in to Marcus's mother's pressure and sent him back to live with her. Nothing had changed at home—it was the same chaotic, neglectful environment as ever. The message to Marcus was, "now your weight is down, we do not care what happens to you." Being back in that stressful environment will exacerbate his weight regain, but as from the time he was very young, Marcus's weight will be the least of his problems. Marcus will have a difficult time, but it will be because of his upbringing, not his weight. Not having learned what he needed to make his way, life will be overwhelming for Marcus and he will get by as best he can.

PREVENTION OF CHILD OVERWEIGHT

These three complicated cases grew out of missed opportunities. In Mary's case, the opportunity was to do no harm. The spurious age 5 months obesity diagnosis set off long-term food restriction and eventual weight rebound and destroyed her chances of slimming down as she got older. What to do instead? Teach parents appropriate stage-related feeding and support them in accepting high body weight.

The missed opportunity with Wellington was failure to do informed health supervision. Wellington's rapid weight gain at the 18 month and 24 month checkups clearly indicated that something was amiss. Asking feeding questions at those points would have revealed his mother's errors with feeding and provided openings for teaching appropriate toddler feeding, thereby correcting those errors. Breast-feeding a toddler is fine, but breast-feeding a toddler on demand is not developmentally appropriate. What to do instead? Stop the grazing. Include Wellington in family meals, let him drink from a cup, and do not breast feed at mealtime. Structure breast-feeding by offering it morning and evening and as a sit-down snack at set times between meals.

Toddlers need structured meals and sit-down snacks between times. Letting them graze for food and beverage handouts (except for water) is a common feeding error that can cause weight acceleration. Toddlers whose food intake is restricted when they were infants are particularly likely to graze relentlessly and gain too much weight. Whether the toddler's weight increases, like Wellington's, or remains low, like Mary's, depends on whether the toddler or the parent is tougher and more persistent. Wellington got the upper hand; Mary did not.

There were lots of missed opportunities with Marcus. By age 2 years his weight had accelerated more than enough to prompt questions, and those questions should have continued as he got older. What to do instead? Assume, based on his rapid weight gain, his continuing high body weight and his mother's evasive answers that something is badly amiss. Remember Marcus's consistent growth during his first year and reject his mother's facile explanation that he has no "off" button. With the possible exception of children who have Prader-Willi syndrome, children are excellent and resilient at regulating their food intake and growing appropriately. At every stage, avoid striving for weight reduction and instead stress optimizing feeding and parenting. Emphasize having three meals a day, sit-down snacks, and no food or beverages between meals except for water. That is a doable intervention, even for a parent who is situationally challenged.

If feeding and parenting continue to be so negative that the child is endangered, consider a referral to child protective services. Be clear, however, that the referral is on the grounds of neglect and for the purposes of protecting and supporting the child, not for getting his weight down.

ADDRESSING ESTABLISHED PROBLEMS IN A PRIMARY CARE SETTING

Primary care providers who have a good understanding of feeding dynamics are well prepared to prevent childhood weight acceleration or to promptly correct disruptions before they morph into entrenched, complicated problems with long-term weight acceleration. On the other hand, once eating and weight problems are well established, fully addressing them calls for services typically not readily available in a primary care setting. Those services include multidisciplinary assessment and referrals to specialists for feeding dynamics intervention, family therapy, or individual counseling. Unfortunately it is sometimes necessary to refer to child protective services.

In the absence of such services, stick with solid primary intervention, stressing authoritative, stage-appropriate feeding. Establishing a structured meals plus snacks routine can take months or even years. Help parents resist the temptation to impose food restriction and weight loss, keeping in mind that food restriction increases the likelihood that in the long run children will be fatter, not thinner. Parents who cannot provide meals will do poorly with the far more difficult task of restricting a child's food intake. Not only that, but imposing the threat of hunger on poorly parented, already-stressed children stresses them further.

Be prepared to support parents in riding out eating extremes when they restore a division of responsibility in feeding. At first, restricted children eat a lot and continue hounding their parents for food handouts. After a few weeks, the child will settle into eating like any other child of a given developmental stage, provided parents truly apply and sustain a division of responsibility in feeding. Use of the Feeding Dynamics Model challenges providers and parents to set aside agendas and focus primarily on good parenting over the long haul. If a parent has a weight agenda for the child, that agenda will continue to distort feeding and parenting, undermine the child's ability to develop and maintain internal regulation of food intake, and in the long run, promote weight gain. To avoid instituting such an agenda, do not promise weight loss or make predictions about weight. If a child's weight has been following a consistent trajectory, it is reasonable to expect that it will continue to do so. One can always hope that a child will slim down, but trying to make it happen will distort feeding and parenting, promote weight gain, and ultimately be demoralizing for both parents and child.

The story of Erica (Figure 19.8) provides an example of a positive outcome using this model. Despite the fact that she was born big, Erica still showed rapid early catch-up growth—possibly exacerbated by her parents' tendencies to be controlling with feeding. Beginning when she was 7 months old, Erica's parents began deliberately restricting her food intake. After an initial dip, Erica's weight climbed to an even higher level and her parents complained that ignoring her pleas for food and fending off her raids on the kitchen was becoming increasingly difficult. When Erica was 3 years old her parents discovered the division of responsibility in feeding after reading *Child of Mine* (Satter, 2000a). They stopped restricting her food intake, emphasized meals and sit-down-snacks, and reassured Erica she could eat as much as she wanted at those structured and predictable times.

Initially Erica confirmed their worst fears by eating great quantities of food. However, after 2 or 3 weeks, her eating moderated and she began to eat like a normal toddler—a lot some times, hardly anything another, ravenous for snack one time, barely interested another. Over the next 3 years, Erica's weight for age dropped to the 97th percentile, where it leveled off. Her parents are content with her growth and capable of holding themselves steady with respect to accepting her stocky build and relatively high body weight.

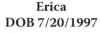

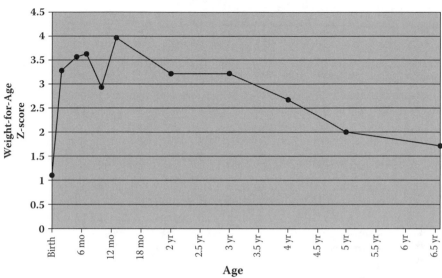

Figure 19.8

Primary intervention handouts that address child overweight can be downloaded from www. EllynSatter.com.

DOES THE FEEDING DYNAMICS MODEL WORK?

Whether or not the Feeding Dynamics Model works depends on what is meant by the question. Does the Feeding Dynamics Model work to get children to conform to arbitrary guidelines of size and shape? No, it does not. Defined weight outcome is absolutely contradictory to the model. Does the Feeding Dynamics Model work to support normal growth and development, including the development of self-esteem? Yes, it does. Feeding principles are based on child development principles. Studies and data presented in this chapter correlate positive feeding with predictable growth. Moreover, the Feeding Dynamics Model accepts children as they are and supports their capabilities, which in turn supports self-esteem.

On the other hand, what about the conventional approach of restricting food intake and increasing activity to achieve weight loss? Does the conventional approach work to get children to conform to arbitrary guidelines of size and shape? It does not. As noted earlier, there is insufficient evidence that screening and conventional interventions work, and even ambitious, multidisciplinary programs produce little or no lasting weight loss.

Does the conventional approach work to support normal growth and development, including self-esteem? No, it does not. As noted earlier, identifying children as overweight and instituting restrained feeding undermines self-esteem and distorts growth, whether children restrict themselves or are restricted by their parents. Children of all ages who diet become fatter, not thinner.

FURTHER RESEARCH

This chapter presents ample evidence correlating distortions in feeding dynamics—misinterpretation of normal growth, restrained feeding, poor feeding practices, and stress—with children's weight acceleration. The piece that remains to be demonstrated is the positive one: that optimum feeding, as defined by the Satter Feeding Dynamics Model, prevents child overweight from the perspective of supporting each child's growth in weight along a predictable, constitutionally determined trajectory.

REFERENCES

Adair, L. S. (1984). The infant's ability to self-regulate caloric intake: a case study. *Journal of the American Dietetic Association, 84,* 543–546.

Alaimo, K., Olson, C. M., & Frongillo, E. A. (2002). Family food insufficiency, but not low family income, is positively associated with dysthymia and suicide symptoms in adolescents. *Journal of Nutrition, 132,* 719–725.

Alaimo, K., Olson, C. M., & Frongillo, E. A., Jr. (2001). Low family income and food insufficiency in relation to overweight in US children: is there a paradox? *Archives of Pediatric and Adolescent Medicine, 155,* 1161–1167.

Alaimo, K., Olson, C. M., Frongillo, E. A., Jr., & Briefel, R.R. (2001). Food insufficiency, family income, and health in US preschool and school-aged children. *American Journal of Public Health, 91,* 781–786.

Barlow, S. E., & Dietz, W. H. (1998). Obesity evaluation and treatment: Expert Committee recommendations. *Pediatrics, 102*(3), e29.

Baumrind, D. (1971). Current patterns of parental authority. *Developmental Psychology Monograph, 4*(1 pt 2), 1–103.

Beebe, D. W., Lewin, D., Zeller, M., McCabe, M., MacLeod, K., Daniels, S. R., & Amin, R. (2007). Sleep in overweight adolescents: shorter sleep, poorer sleep quality, sleepiness, and sleep-disordered breathing. *Journal of Pediatric Psychology, 32,* 69–79.

Birch, L. L., & Fisher, J. O. (1995). Appetite and eating behavior in children. *Pediatric Clinics of North America, 42,* 931–953.

Birch, L. L., & Fisher, J. O. (2000). Mothers' child-feeding practices influence daughters' eating and weight. *American Journal of Clinical Nutrition, 71,* 1054–1061.

Birch, L. L., Fisher, J. O., & Davison, K. K. (2003). Learning to overeat: maternal use of restrictive feeding practices promotes girls' eating in the absence of hunger. *American Journal of Clinical Nutrition, 78,* 215–220.

Birch, L. L., Johnson, S. L., & Fisher, J. O. (1995). Children's eating: the development of food-acceptance patterns. *Young Children, 50*(2), 71–78.

Blissett, J., Meyer, C., & Haycraft, E. (2006). Maternal and paternal controlling feeding practices with male and female children. *Appetite, 47,* 212–219.

Bouchard, C., Tremblay, A., Despres, J. P., Nadeau, A., Lupien, P. J., Theriault, G., Dussault, J., Moorjani, S., Pinault, S., & Fournier, G. (1990). The response to long-term overfeeding in identical twins. *New England Journal of Medicine, 322,* 1477–1482.

Boutton, T. W., Trowbridge, F. L., Nelson, M. M., Wills, C. A., Smith, E. O., Lopez de Romana, G., Madrid, S., Marks, J. S., & Klein, P. D. (1987). Body composition of Peruvian children with short stature and high weight-for-height. I. Total body-water measurements and their prediction from anthropometric values. *American Journal of Clinical Nutrition, 45,* 513–525.

Braddon, F. E. M., Rodgers, B., Wadsworth, M. E. J., & Davies, J. M. C. (1986). Onset of obesity in a 36 year birth cohort study. *British Medical Journal, 293,* 299–303.

Burdette, H. L., Whitaker, R. C., Hall, W. C., & Daniels, S. R. (2006). Maternal infant-feeding style and children's adiposity at 5 years of age. *Archives of Pediatric and Adolescent Medicine, 160,* 513–520.

Center on Addiction and Substance Abuse. (2005). The importance of family dinners II. New York: Center on Addiction and Substance Abuse.

Centers for Disease Control. (2000a). CDC growth charts: United States. Atlanta: Centers for Disease Control. Available at www.cdc.gov/growthcharts/.

Centers for Disease Control. (2000b). Overweight children and adolescents: screen, assess and manage. Atlanta: Centers for Disease Control. Available at www.cdc.gov/nccdphp/dnpa/growthcharts/training/modules/module3/text/page1b.htm.

Chatoor, I., Surles, J., Ganiban, J., Beker, L., Paez, L. M., & Kerzner, B. (2004). Failure to thrive and cognitive development in toddlers with infantile anorexia. *Pediatrics, 113*(5), e440–e447.

Committee on Nutrition. (2003). Prevention of pediatric overweight and obesity. *Pediatrics, 112*, 424–430.

Costanzo, P. R., & Woody, E. Z. (1984). Parental perspectives on obesity in children: the importance of sex differences. *Journal of Social and Clinical Psychology, 2*, 305–313.

Council of Economic Advisors. (2000). Teens and their parents in the 21st century: an examination of trends in teen behavior and the role of parental involvement. Washington, D.C.: Council of Economic Advisors. Available at http://clinton3.nara.gov/WH/EOP/CEA/html/Teens_Paper_Final.pdf.

Crow, R. A., Fawcett, J. N., & Wright, P. (1980). Maternal behavior during breast- and bottle-feeding. *Journal of Behavioral Medicine, 3*, 259–277.

Davies, W. H., Satter, E., Berlin, K. S., Sato, A. F., Silverman, A. H., Fischer, E. A., Arvedson, J. C., & Rudolph, C. D. (2006). Reconceptualizing feeding and feeding disorders in interpersonal context: the case for a relational disorder. *Journal of Family Psychology, 20*, 409–417.

Davis, C. M. (1928). Self selection of diet by newly weaned infants: an experimental study. *American Journal of Diseases of Children, 36*, 651–679.

Davison, K. K., & Birch, L. L. (2001). Weight status, parent reaction, and self-concept in five-year-old girls. *Pediatrics, 107*, 46–53.

Davison, K. K., Markey, C. N., & Birch, L. L. (2003). A longitudinal examination of patterns in girls' weight concerns and body dissatisfaction from ages 5 to 9 years. *International Journal of Eating Disorders, 33*, 320–332.

Donnelly, J. E., Jacobsen, D. J., Whatley, J. E., Hill, J. O., Swift, L. L., Cherrington, A. C., Polk, B., Tran, Z. V., & Reed, G. (1996). Nutrition and physical activity program to attenuate obesity and promote physical and metabolic fitness in elementary school children. *Obesity Research, 4*, 229–243.

Eisenberg, M. E., Olson, R. E., Neumark-Sztainer, D., Story, M., & Bearinger, L. H. (2004). Correlations between family meals and psychosocial well-being among adolescents. *Archives of Pediatric and Adolescent Medicine, 158*, 792–796.

Eisenmann, J. C., Katzmarzyk, P. T., Arnall, D. A., Kanuho, V., Interpreter, C., & Malina, R. M. (2000). Growth and overweight of Navajo youth: secular changes from 1955 to 1997. *International Journal of Obesity, 24*, 211–218.

Epstein L. H., Myers, M. D., Raynor, H. A., & Saelens, B. E. (1998). Treatment of pediatric obesity. *Pediatrics, 101*, 554–570.

Expert Panel on the Identification, Evaluation, and Treatment of Overweight and Obesity in Adults. (1998). *Clinical guidelines on the identification, evaluation, and treatment of overweight and obesity in adults: the evidence report.* NIH publication 98-4083. Bethesda, MD: National Institutes of Health. Available at www.nhlbi.nih.gov/guidelines/obesity/ob_gdlns.pdf.

Faith, M. S., Berkowitz, R. I., Stallings, V. A., Kerns, J., Storey, M., & Stunkard, A. J. (2004). Parental feeding attitudes and styles and child body mass index: prospective analysis of a gene-environment interaction. *Pediatrics, 114*(4), e429–e436.

Faith, M. S., Scanlon, K. S., Birch, L. L., Francis, L. A., & Sherry, B. (2004). Parent-child feeding strategies and their relationships to child eating and weight status. *Obesity Research, 12*, 1711–1722.

Fisher, J. O., & Birch, L. L. (2000). Parents' restrictive feeding practices are associated with young girls' negative self-evaluation of eating. *Journal of the American Dietetic Association, 100*, 1341–1346.

Fisher, J. O., & Birch, L. L. (2002). Eating in the absence of hunger and overweight in girls from 5 to 7 y of age. *American Journal of Clinical Nutrition, 76*, 226–231.

Fomon, S. J. (1993). *Nutrition of normal infants* (pp. 455–458). St. Louis, MO: Mosby-Year Book.

Fomon, S. J., Filer, L. J., Jr., Thomas, L. N., Anderson, T. A., & Nelson, S. E. (1975). Influence of formula concentration on caloric intake and growth of normal infants. *Acta Paediatrica Scandanavica, 64*, 172–181.

Galloway, A. T., Fiorito, L., Lee, Y., & Birch, L. L. (2005). Parental pressure, dietary patterns, and weight status among girls who are "picky eaters." *Journal of the American Dietetic Association, 105*, 541–548.

Garn, S. M., & Clark, D. C. (1976). Trends in fatness and the origins of obesity. *Pediatrics, 57*, 443–456.

Garn, S. M., Pilkington, J. J., & Lavelle, M. (1984). Relationship between initial fatness level and long-term fatness change [abstract]. *Ecology of Food and Nutrition, 14*, 85–92.

Gesell, A., & Ilg, F. L. (1937). *Feeding behavior of infants.* Philadelphia: J.B. Lippincott.

Gillman, M. W., Rifas-Shiman, S. L., Frazier, A. L., Rockett, H. R., Camargo, C. A., Field, A. E., Berkey, C. S., & Colditz, G. A. (2000). Family dinner and diet quality among older children and adolescents. *Archives of Family Medicine, 9,* 235–240.

Greenspan, S., & Lourie, R. S. (1981). Developmental structuralist approach to the classification of adaptive and pathological personality organizations: Infancy and early childhood. *American Journal of Psychiatry, 138,* 725–735.

Hamill, P. V. V., Drizd, T. A., Johnson, C. L., Reed, R. B., Roche, A. F., & Moore, W. M. (1979). Physical growth: National Center for Health Statistics percentiles. *American Journal of Clinical Nutrition, 32,* 607–629.

Herman, C. P., Polivy, J., & Esses, V. M. (1987). The illusion of counter-regulation. *Appetite, 9,* 161–169.

Hill, A. J., Rogers, P. J., & Blundell, J. E. (1989). Dietary restraint in young adolescent girls: a functional analysis. *British Journal of Clinical Psychology, 28,* 165–176.

Hofferth, S. L. (2001). How American children spend their time. *Journal of Marriage and the Family , 63,* 295–308.

Hood, M. Y., Moore, L. L., Sundarajan-Ramamurti, A., Singer, M., Cupples, L. A., & Ellison, R. C. (2000). Parental eating attitudes and the development of obesity in children: the Framingham Children's Study. *International Journal of Obesity, 24,* 1319–1325.

Jain, A., Sherman, S. N., Chamberlin, L. A., Carter, Y., Powers, S. W., & Whitaker, R. C. (2001). Why don't low-income mothers worry about their preschoolers being overweight? *Pediatrics, 107,* 1138–1146.

Johnson, J. G., Cohen, P., Kasen, S., & Brook, J. S. (2002). Childhood adversities associated with risk for eating disorders or weight problems during adolescence or early adulthood. *American Journal of Psychiatry, 159,* 394–400.

Johnson, S. L., & Birch, L. L. (1994). Parents' and children's adiposity and eating style. *Pediatrics, 94,* 653–661.

Jones, S. J., Jahns, L., Laraia, B. A., & Haughton, B. (2003). lower risk of overweight in school-aged food insecure girls who participate in food assistance: results from the Panel Study of Income Dynamics child development supplement. *Archives of Pediatrics and Adolescent Medicine, 157,* 780–784.

Kant, A. K., & Miner, P. (2007). Physician advice about being overweight: association with self-reported weight loss, dietary, and physical activity behaviors of U.S. adolescents in the National Health and Nutrition Examination Survey, 1999–2002. *Pediatrics, 119*(1), e142–e147.

Keys, A., Brozek, J., Henschel, A., Mickelsen, O., & Taylor, H. (1950). *The biology of human starvation.* Minneapolis: University of Minnesota Press.

Klesges, R. C., Malott, J. M., Boschee, P. F., & Weber, J. M. (1986). The effects of parental influences on children's food intake, physical activity and relative weight. *International Journal of Eating Disorders, 5,* 335–346.

Krick, J. (1986). Using the Z score as a descriptor of discrete changes in growth. *Nutritional Support Services, 6*(8), 14–21.

Lee, Y., Mitchell, D. C., Smiciklas-Wright, H., & Birch, L. L. (2001). Diet quality, nutrient intake, weight status, and feeding environments of girls meeting or exceeding recommendations for total dietary fat of the American Academy of Pediatrics. *Pediatrics, 107,* e95.

Legler, J. D., & Rose, L. C. (1998). Assessment of abnormal growth curves. *American Family Physician, 58,* 158–168.

Lissau, I., Breum, L., & Sorensen, T. I. (1993). Maternal attitude to sweet eating habits and risk of overweight in offspring: a ten-year prospective population study. *International Journal of Obesity, 17,* 125–129.

Lissau, I., & Sorensen, T. I. (1994). Parental neglect during childhood and increased risk of obesity in young adulthood. *Lancet, 343,* 324–327.

Lumeng, J. C., Gannon, K., Cabral, H. J., Frank, D. A., & Zuckerman, B. (2003). Association between clinically meaningful behavior problems and overweight in children. *Pediatrics, 112,* 1138–1145.

Mellbin, T., & Vuille, J.-C. (1989). Rapidly developing overweight in school children as an indicator of psychosocial stress. *Acta Paediatrica Scandinavica, 78,* 568–575.

Miech, R. A., Kumanyika, S. K., Stettler, N., Link, B. G., Phelan, J. C., & Chang, V. W. (2006). Trends in the association of poverty with overweight among U.S. adolescents, 1971–2004. *JAMA, 295,* 2385–2393.

Minuchin, S., Baker, L., Rosman, B. L., Liebman, R., Milman, L., & Todd, T. C. (1975). A conceptual model of psychosomatic illness in children. *Archives of General Psychiatry, 32,* 1031–1038.

Morris, S. E. & Klein, M. D. (2000). *Pre-feeding skills: a comprehensive resource for mealtime development* (pp. 59–95). San Antonio, TX: Therapy Skill Builders/Harcourt.

Moynihan, R. (2006). Expanding definitions of obesity may harm children. *BMJ, 332*(7555), 1412.

Neumark-Sztainer, D., Hannan, P., Story, M., & Perry, C. (2004). Weight-control behaviors among adolescent girls and boys: implications for dietary intake. *Journal of the American Dietetic Association, 104,* 913–920.

Neumark-Sztainer, D., Wall, M., Guo, J., Story, M., Haines, J., & Eisenberg, M. (2006). Obesity, disordered eating, and eating disorders in a longitudinal study of adolescents: How do dieters fare 5 years later? *Journal of the American Dietetic Association, 106,* 559–568.

Neumark-Sztainer, D., Wall, M., Story, M., & Fulkerson, J. A. (2004). Are family meal patterns associated with disordered eating behaviors among adolescents? *Journal of Adolescent Health, 35,* 350–359.

Ogden, C. L., Carroll, M. D., Curtin, L. R., McDowell, M. A., Tabak, C. J., & Flegal, K. M. (2006). Prevalence of overweight and obesity in the United States, 1999–2004. *JAMA, 295,* 1549–1555.

Pashankar, D. S., & Loening-Baucke, V. (2005). Increased prevalence of obesity in children with functional constipation evaluated in an academic medical center. *Pediatrics, 116*(3), e377–e380.

Pietilanen, K. H., Kaprio, J., Rasanen, M., Winter, T., Rissanen, A., & Rose, R. J. (2001). Tracking body size from birth to late adolescence: contributions of birth length, birth weight, duration of gestation, parents' body size, and twinship. *American Journal of Epidemiology, 154,* 21–29.

Pine, D. S., Goldstein, R. B., Wolk, S., & Weissman, M. M. (2001). The association between childhood depression and adulthood body mass index. *Pediatrics, 107,* 1049–1056.

Rhee, K. E., Lumeng, J. C., Appugliese, D. P., Kaciroti, N., & Bradley, R. H. (2006). Parenting styles and overweight status in first grade. *Pediatrics, 117,* 2047–2054.

Roemmich, J. N., Wright, S. M., & Epstein, L. H. (2002). Dietary restraint and stress-induced snacking in youth. *Obesity Research, 10,* 1120–1126.

Rose, H. E., & Mayer, J. (1968). Activity, calorie intake, fat storage, and the energy balance of infants. *Pediatrics, 41,* 18–29.

Ryan, A. S., Roche, A. F., & Kuczmarski, R. J. (1999). Weight, stature, and body mass index data for Mexican Americans from the Third National Health and Nutrition Examination Survey (NHANES III, 1988–1994). *American Journal of Human Biology, 11,* 673–686.

Saelens, B. E., Ernst, M. M., & Epstein, L. H. (2000). Maternal child feeding practices and obesity: a discordant sibling analysis. *International Journal of Eating Disorders, 27,* 459–463.

Satter, E. M. (1986). The feeding relationship. *Journal of the American Dietetic Association, 86,* 352–356.

Satter, E. M. (1995). Feeding dynamics: helping children to eat well. *Journal of Pediatric Health Care, 9,* 178–184.

Satter, E. M. (1996). Internal regulation and the evolution of normal growth as the basis for prevention of obesity in childhood. *Journal of the American Dietetic Association, 96,* 860–864.

Satter, E. M. (2000a). *Child of mine: feeding with love and good sense.* Palo Alto, CA: Bull Publishing.

Satter, E. M. (2000b). Your child knows how to eat and grow (pp. 31–76). In *Child of mine: feeding with love and good sense.* Palo Alto, CA: Bull Publishing.

Satter, E. M. (2005a). Appendix E: assessment of feeding/growth problems (pp. 396–402). In E. M. Satter, *Your child's weight: helping without harming.* Madison, WI: Kelcy Press.

Satter, E. M. (2005b). Help without harming (pp. 3–22). In E. M. Satter, *Your child's weight: helping without harming.* Madison, WI: Kelcy Press.

Satter, E. M. (2007). Eating competence: definition and evidence for the Satter Eating Competence Model. *Journal of Nutrition Education and Behavior, 39*(suppl.). (In press.)

Serdula, M. K., Ivery, D., Coates, R. J., Freedman, D. S., Williamson, D. F., & Byers, T. (1993). Do obese children become obese adults? A review of the literature. *Preventive Medicine, 22,* 167–177.

Serdula, M. K., Mokdad, A. H., Williamson, D. F., Galuska, D. A., Mendlein, J. M., & Heath, G. W. (1999). Prevalence of attempting weight loss and strategies for controlling weight. *JAMA, 282,* 1353–1358.

Shunk, J. A., & Birch, L. L. (2004). Girls at risk for overweight at age 5 are at risk for dietary restraint, disinhibited overeating, weight concerns, and greater weight gain from 5 to 9 years. *Journal of the American Dietetic Association, 104,* 1120–1126.

Spruijt-Metz, D., Lindquist, C. H., Birch, L. L., Fisher, J. O., & Goran, M. I. (2002). Relation between mothers' child-feeding practices and children's adiposity. *American Journal of Clinical Nutrition, 75,* 581–586.

Stettler, N., Kumanyika, S. K., Katz, S. H., Zemel, B. S., & Stallings, V. A. (2003). Rapid weight gain during infancy and obesity in young adulthood in a cohort of African Americans. *American Journal of Clinical Nutrition, 77,* 1374.

Stettler, N., Stallings, V. A., Troxel, A. B., Zhao, J., Schinnar, R., Nelson, S. E., Ziegler, E. E., & Strom, B. L. (2005). Weight gain in the first week of life and overweight in adulthood: a cohort study of European American subjects fed infant formula. *Circulation, 111,* 1897–1903.

Stettler, N., Zemel, B. S., Kumanyika, S., & Stallings, V. A. (2002). Infant weight gain and childhood overweight status in a multicenter, cohort study. *Pediatrics, 109,* 194–199.

Stice, E., Agras, W. S., & Hammer, L. D. (1999). Risk factors for the emergence of childhood eating disturbances: a five-year prospective study. *International Journal of Eating Disorders, 25,* 375–387.

Stice, E., Cameron, R. P., Killen, J. D., Hayward, C., & Taylor, C. B. (1999). Naturalistic weight-reduction efforts prospectively predict growth in relative weight and onset of obesity among female adolescents. *Journal of Consulting and Clinical Psychology, 67,* 967–974.

Stunkard, A. J., Harris, J. R., Pedersen, N. L., & McClearn, G. E. (1990). The body-mass of twins who have been reared apart. *New England Journal of Medicine, 322,* 1483–1487.

Taveras, E. M., Rifas-Shiman, S. L., Berkey, C. S., Rockett, H. R. H., Field, A. E., Frazier, A. L., Colditz, G. A., & Gillman, M. W. (2005). Family dinner and adolescent overweight. *Obesity Research, 13,* 900–906.

Wang, Y., & Zhang, Q. (2006). Are American children and adolescents of low socioeconomic status at increased risk of obesity? Changes in the association between overweight and family income between 1971 and 2002. *American Journal of Clinical Nutrition, 84,* 707–716.

Whitlock, E. P., Williams, S. B., Gold, R., Smith, P. R., & Shipman, S. A. (2005). Screening and interventions for childhood overweight: a summary of evidence for the U.S. Preventive Services Task Force. *Pediatrics, 116,* e125–e144.

Wright, C. M., Parker, L., Lamont, D., & Craft, A. W. (2001). Implications of childhood obesity for adult health: findings from thousand families cohort study. *British Medical Journal, 323*(7324), 1280–1284.

Zack, P. M., Harlan, W. R., Leaverton, P. E., & Cornoni-Huntley, J. (1979). A longitudinal study of body fatness in childhood and adolescence. *Journal of Pediatrics, 95,* 126–130.

Zeller, M. H., Reiter-Purtill, J., Modi, A. C., Gutzwiller, J., Vannatta, K., & Davies, W. H. (2007). Controlled study of critical parent and family factors in the obesigenic environment. *Obesity, 15,* 126–136.

20

Protecting Growth and Maintaining Optimal Nutrition

BARBARA J. SCOTT

As we strive to find new strategies to combat the problems associated with pediatric obesity, it is important to never lose sight of the ultimate goal—to help children grow up to be healthy, happy adults—embodied in the two primary goals of the Healthy People 2010 initiative (www.healthy-people.gov): (1) help individuals of all ages increase their quality and years of healthy life; and (2) eliminate health disparities among different segments of the population. We must be vigilant to ensure that our attempts to help children and families deal with issues of overweight do not unintentionally do harm by compromising their nutrition or their growth or by labeling or treating them in such a way as to limit or narrow their life possibilities. Our job as practitioners (health care providers, counselors, therapists, etc.) is to learn as much as we can about the outside forces and secular trends that are causing many children to be heavier than they were meant to be and provide guidance and treatment recommendations to combat these forces while also optimizing each child's physical and mental health and development. The goals of this chapter are to provide some basic guidance for what constitutes normal growth and good nutrition for children at different ages and to offer practical examples, recommended reading, and useful references.

GROWTH

Under typical conditions, human growth proceeds in a very orderly progression, encompassing increases in both cell number (hyperplasia) and cell size (hypertrophy), with genetics playing the central role in determining the rate and pattern of growth. Yet it also results in a fascinating variety of individual and diverse patterns—short, tall, round, and thin. With our increasing emphasis on the alarming increase in the number of children who are overweight, we must resist the tendency to subscribe to the "one size fits all" mentality and remember that it is natural to have this grand "smorgasbord" of human typologies. We can learn to trust that a child is growing normally if they are growing steadily, even if their growth falls outside the usual boundaries (i.e., below the 3rd or above the 97th percentiles). We must understand when it is inappropriate to label a child as being too small or too large and resist the initiation of treatment intended to modify their natural body size.

However, it is true that both poor growth (wasting and stunting) as well as excessive growth (obesity) continue to pose problems for the children of the world (Iyengar & Nair, 2000; James,

2005). It is important to tackle these problems, remembering that one problem should not be overlooked at the expense of the other. Thus routine monitoring of both height and weight is needed to provide critical information about the health of an individual child in particular and of the children in a population in general, often providing early information about subtle, but sometimes catastrophic problems. Growth tends to be most vulnerable to changes in nutrition during times of the most rapid growth: in utero, during infancy, and during the peak pubertal growth spurt. Evidence is emerging that indicates that prolonged over- or undernutrition during different phases of growth can both affect final size and weight status and possibly disease or health status in later life (Ekelund et al., 2006; Ong, 2006; Regan, Cutfield, Jefferies, Robinson, & Hofman, 2006). In general, undernutrition tends to impact weight first, but if prolonged and severe, linear growth can also be permanently affected (Allen, 1994). Overnutrition, with rapid early (0 to 5 months) weight gain in normal weight infants and early in childhood, can cause children to become obese and to be taller during childhood (but not after puberty) than their nonobese counterparts (de Simone et al., 1995; Dubois & Girard, 2006; Papadimitriou, Gousi, Giannouli, & Nicolaidou, 2006; Toschke, Beyerlein, & von Kries, 2005). Paradoxically, low infant birth weight or early infant malnutrition followed by rapid "catch-up" growth may also be associated with greater risk of obesity, diabetes, hypertension, cardiovascular disease, and osteopenia in later life (Weaver, 2006). It appears that primitive adaptive recovery mechanisms may be triggered that would be beneficial for survival if conditions of malnutrition were to continue, but which become detrimental when nutrition is abundant (Demmelmair, von Rosen, & Koletzko, 2006; Desai & Hales, 1997; Ong, Ahmed, Emmett, Preece, & Dunger, 2000).

Because of this complexity of growth patterns and influences, practitioners working in the field of pediatric obesity need a good understanding of the typical pattern and range of variability that constitute normal growth in order to identify when outside factors have caused it to "go wrong." It is neither desirable nor practical for everyone working in pediatric overweight to be doing the actual measuring and plotting of an overweight child's growth, as this is most often best left to the primary care (medical) provider or perhaps to a public health nurse or WIC program dietitian. (The mission of the Special Supplemental Nutrition Program for Women, Infants, and Children (WIC) is to safeguard the health of low-income women, infants, and children up to age 5 years who are at nutritional risk by providing nutritious foods to supplement diets, nutrition education, growth monitoring, and referrals to health care and other social services. WIC is based on the premise that early intervention programs during critical times of growth and development can help prevent medical and developmental problems. WIC is one of the central components of the nation's food assistance and nutrition system, serving about 8 million participants per month, including almost half of all infants born in the United States.) However, anyone providing obesity treatment must be familiar with how to use and interpret growth charts. For each client/child, it is important to request copies of their growth charts from health care providers, using information about the child's height and weight over time to understand the child's individual current and past growth patterns.

The growth charts (eight for boys and eight for girls) most commonly used in the United States were developed by the National Center for Health Statistics (NCHS) in 1977 and recently (2000) updated by the Centers for Disease Control (CDC) using U.S. pediatric data from the National Health and Nutrition Examination Survey (NHANES). The charts, which depict percentile curves (3rd, 5th, 10th, 25th, 50th, 75th, 90th, 95th, 97th) based on gender and age distribution of length (zero to 36 months) or height (2 to 20 years), weight, head circumference (up to 36 months), and body mass index (BMI; 2 to 20 years), can be accessed at www.cdc.gov/growthcharts along with complete information as to their development, use, and interpretation (see Figure 20.1). EpiInfo, a software package developed by the CDC for use by public health and medical professionals, includes a nutrition module (NutStat) that can be downloaded at no cost (www.cdc.gov/epiinfo) to calculate and plot growth percentiles and z-scores using the NCHS growth reference standards.

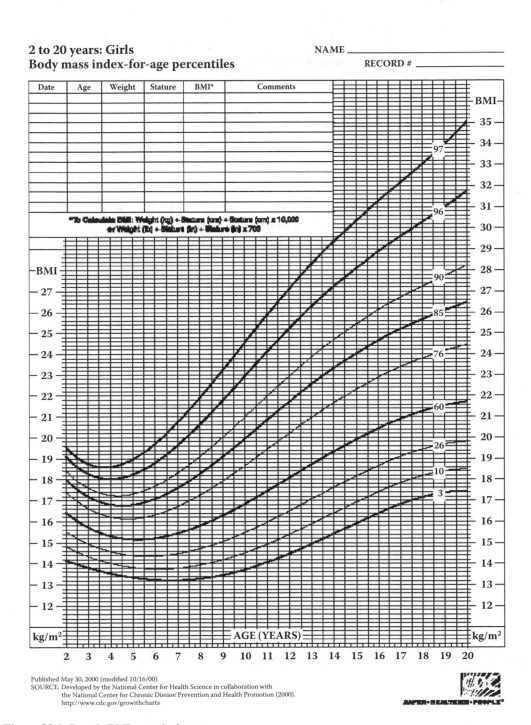

Figure 20.1 Sample BMI growth chart.

Recently (April 2006) the World Health Organization (WHO) released a new set of growth standards and corresponding growth curves suitable for assessing the growth and nutritional status of population groups and individual children from birth to 5 years of age in response to challenges to the suitability of the U.S.-based NCHS reference standards (which have been used internationally as well as nationally). The NCHS standards are based primarily on retrospective observations on the growth of U.S. infants, the majority of whom were fed artificially (formula fed) and who tend to be heavier and grow differently than healthy, breast-fed infants. Thus it may be wise for U.S. practitioners to begin to use these new WHO standards which are based on a prospective, international sample of breast-fed infants selected to represent optimum growth (de Onis, Garza, Onyango, & Borghi, 2007; de Onis, Onyango, Borghi, Garza, Yang, & WHO Multicentre Growth Reference Study Group, 2006) for the assessment and growth of U.S. children from birth to 5 years. These new charts (weight for age, weight for length or height, and BMI for age) can be downloaded and printed from the WHO website (www.who.int/childgrowth/standards).

Body mass index is a clinically valid measure that correlates well with measures of body fatness (Pietrobelli et al., 1998) and is used to screen for overweight in children ages 2 years and older (95th percentile or greater indicates overweight, and 85th to 95th percentiles indicate at risk for overweight) (Committee on Nutrition, 2003; Department of Health and Human Services, 2001; Himes & Dietz, 1994). BMI measures in childhood track moderately well to adulthood, and particularly well for children over 13 years of age who are overweight (BMI 95th percentile or greater) and who have one or two overweight parents (BMI greater than 30 kg/m^2) (Whitlock, Williams, Gold, Smith, & Shipman, 2005). BMI percentile can also be used to screen for underweight or short stature, and although there is no clear consensus as to screening guidelines, the 5th percentile or less is a typical indicator for both of these. It is important to remember that while these growth curves representing mathematical averages based on large numbers of children can be very useful, informed interpretation is required for each individual child. For example, it might appear from the charts that growth proceeds in a smooth, continuous process, yet observations of daily growth indicate that this is more of a stepwise process with periods of gain, no gain, and gain. This is especially true in the first year of life, when many infants shift percentiles in their linear growth (also referred to as rechanneling). In one classic study of 90 healthy, full-term infants (Smith et al., 1976), 63% crossed one, 23% crossed two, and 9% crossed three percentile lines on the growth chart, illustrating the breadth of individual variability.

Body composition changes markedly during infancy, childhood, and adolescence and is affected by many variables: genetic, dietary, environmental, hormonal, nutritional, behavioral (Rigo, 2006; Veldhuis et al., 2005; Ziegler, 2006). Thus assessment and monitoring of body composition may be of particular interest when considering the weight status of an individual child. Specific information about the relative amounts and distribution of body fat and about lean body mass and bony structures cannot be derived from the BMI, so body composition information may give clues to the type, cause, and severity of overweight and help to identify underlying metabolic disturbances. Until recently, measurement of body composition, particularly in children, has been challenging, but recent advances in safe, noninvasive measurement technologies are making it more practical to learn about the distribution and amount of adiposity in an overweight child (Shen, Lui, Punyanitya, Shen, & Heymsfield, 2005; Wells & Fewtrell, 2006).

NUTRITION

Parents and children are likely to encounter a variety of different health care professionals over time—pediatricians, family practice doctors, school nurses, school counselors, psychologists, family therapists. They may also seek the services of a dietitian or nutritionist if overweight is a problem, but it is otherwise relatively rare that families have the chance to speak directly with a nutrition professional. Therefore it is important that all health care professionals be educated about some of the basic principles of good nutrition, including the recommended child feeding/parenting practices outlined in this section. If families and children receive consistent messages about good nutrition from all of their health care providers, it may make it easier to follow through and implement healthy practices for healthy weight. However, because nutrition is such a "hot topic" these days, nutrition advice, especially that related to weight loss, tends to come from all directions—television, the Internet, magazines, neighbors, product promotions—and not all of it is accurate or appropriate for children. Therefore nonnutrition professionals should critically evaluate the source and accuracy of nutrition information before passing it on to families or seek guidance from a registered dietitian to be sure they are delivering accurate, appropriate nutrition information.

The first years of life are characterized by rapid changes in a baby's ability to digest and utilize different foods and a transition from total dependence on adult caregivers to increasing independence and individuation. Recognition for and support of a baby's natural ability to regulate energy intake to meet needs and enjoy healthy eating habits during this time is the best means of obesity prevention possible. Breast milk is ideally suited to the needs of the healthy, full-term infant and has been associated in both resource-poor and affluent societies with a multitude of benefits (health, nutritional, cognitive, environmental, economic, immunologic, developmental, social, and psychological) for infants and mothers, families, and societies (Work Group on Breastfeeding, 2005; Kramer et al., 2001; Schack-Nielsen & Michaelsen, 2006). Thus exclusive breast-feeding (water, infant formula, other liquids, and solid foods are excluded) for the first 6 months of life is universally recommended as the best source of nutrition for the majority of healthy, full-term infants, with continued breast-feeding for up to 2 years and beyond (Work Group on Breastfeeding, 2005; Health Canada, 2004; Kramer & Kakuma, 2002; United Nations Children's Fund, 1999; World Health Organization, 2002).

Advances in our understanding about these benefits, enhanced training of pediatric health care providers, and the increased availability of certified lactation consultants have greatly enhanced the encouragement, support, and education available to women desiring to breast feed their infants. Implementation of the Baby Friendly Hospital Initiative (BFHI), based on the WHO's Ten Steps to Successful Breast-Feeding, a program that summarizes the practices that maternity wards need to adopt to support breast-feeding (World Health Organization, 1989, 1998), has resulted in higher rates of extended and exclusive breast-feeding (Braun et al., 2003; Merten, Dratva, & Ackermann-Liebrich, 2005). Many different studies have now demonstrated benefits of breastfeeding associated with prevention of child overweight. It appears that this protective effect is due in part to early "programming" of growth in the first year of life, with breast-fed infants growing more slowly than formula-fed infants. However, many questions remain about the degree of risk reduction (Sherry, 2005) and about the relative contribution of specific "protective" properties of human milk (Agostoni et al., 2005; Miralles, Sanchez, Palou, & Pico, 2006; von Kries, Koletzko, Sauerwald, & von Mutius, 2000; Zeigler, 2006), the importance of the duration (Burke et al., 2005) and exclusivity of breast-feeding, the contribution of other confounding factors such as maternal/parental weight (Li et al., 2005) and smoking status (Owen et al., 2005), the timing and quality of the introduction of first foods, whether the influence of an "obesogenic" environment can cancel out this protection (Goldfield et al., 2006; Nelson, Gordon-Larsen, & Adair, 2005), and whether this protective effect lasts only through early childhood or into adolescence (Gillman et al., 2006; Shields, O'Callaghan, Williams, Najman, & Bor, 2006).

Health care practitioners can do much to prevent child overweight by educating and supporting parents to recognize and reinforce their infant's natural ability to regulate energy intake to meet energy needs. This begins with parents learning to read their baby's cues for hunger and satiety. Signs of hunger include rooting, bringing fist to mouth, lip smacking, and eye movements, and feeding should be initiated before crying begins, as this is actually a late signal for hunger. Signs of fullness include spitting out or playing with the nipple, falling asleep, and losing interest in feeding. Infants and young babies must be fed on demand (as often as the child wants, day and night), and it is normal for the intervals between their "requests" for feeding to vary from every 1½ hr to every 3 hr. At about 6 months of age, neither breast milk nor formula is sufficient to meet all of an infant's nutritional needs, and the baby is developmentally ready with a maturing digestive system, good coordination of sucking-swallowing-breathing, greater head and neck control, increased trunk strength, diminishing tongue protrusion and beginning lateralization of tongue movement, greater ability to interact with care providers, early tooth eruption, evolving pincer grasp, etc., to begin complementary foods. Complementary foods are added to the diet to supplement nutrient intake and to provide opportunities to foster normal gross and fine motor development by slowly increasing the nutritional and physical complexity of the foods offered.

Nutritionists recommend that the first complementary food be iron-fortified infant cereal, a simple carbohydrate-based grain with low potential for allergic reaction, mixed to a thin consistency with breast milk or formula and fed from a spoon. Recommendations vary somewhat about which foods to introduce next, fruits or vegetables, but often it is suggested that starting with vegetables first may help infants become accustomed to their flavors without first being "biased" by the sweetness of fruit. These foods are nutritionally easy to digest, add important nutrients such as vitamins A and C, folic acid, and fiber, introduce the infant to a wide variety of colors, smells, and flavors, and can be progressed in texture (pureed, mashed, finely chopped, sliced) as the infant is ready. The next foods include pureed or finely chopped meats and beans, and mixed dishes like soups or stews of appropriate consistency.

It's helpful to remind parents that eating habits are established very early in life. Encourage the parents to sit with their child during feeding, introducing a wide variety of healthy foods, modeling healthy eating habits, trusting their child's ability to self-regulate their calorie intake—allowing them to eat when they are hungry and stop when they are full—and not getting discouraged if the infant does not readily accept new foods, as it may take many exposures before a baby accepts a new food. Excellent and practical information for parents on feeding and nutrition for infants and children, along with links to downloadable, peer-reviewed, evidence-based nutrition education materials (often in Spanish and English and sometimes other languages) can be found on the "WIC Works" Web site (www.nal.usda.gov/wicworks/Topics/index.html). (A complete list of recommended nutrition education resources is included in Chapter 18, Nutrition Education Basics: Navigating the Food Environment.)

The toddler and preschool years are characterized by increasing assertion of independence and individuation, increased physical skills and fine and gross motor coordination, and decreased growth velocity. With respect to feeding, this can be a concerning time for many parents who may worry when their child's appetite diminishes and the child rejects foods that are offered. This is an excellent time to reassure parents that it is normal for appetite to drop off at this age and for children to want more autonomy with respect to food choices. Once parents understand that children of this age feel most secure when caregivers abide by clear, fair, and consistent structure, they can feel confident in continuing to offer healthy food choices every 2 to 3 hr in a relaxed, quiet atmosphere. They can reject the temptation to prepare multiple meals or give in to child demands for "goodies" and instead trust their child to eat when they are hungry and stop when they are full. Tactics such as bribing, catering, tricking, or forcing children to eat are not helpful and are to be avoided. Young children should be offered three meals and two to three snacks, and while the amount they eat (or do not eat) can vary widely from day to day, a typical portion size for a toddler is about one-fourth of an appropriate adult serving. "Picky" eating is normal for toddlers, and giving them mealtime "jobs" to do that are appropriate for their developmental level, like washing the lettuce in a bowl, stirring the macaroni, or putting the napkins on the table, can make them feel important and valued and may increase their interest in eating.

As children enter school their exposure to new foods, some of which parents would prefer that they not have, increases. Parents can continue to offer healthy choices at home and encourage healthy choices at school, understanding that they cannot control everything about their child's environment. As children are ready, nutrition concepts can be taught in a real-world context. For example, parents can sit with their child and critique television junk food ads targeted to young children, thus helping their children begin to learn to separate fact from fiction (Committee on Communications, 2006). School menus can be used to discuss and teach good nutrition, and children can be encouraged to add healthful foods to the family grocery list and to look through cookbooks or magazines to find new recipes to try.

It is critical that parents not confuse the concept of a healthy diet for their young child with a low-fat or calorie-restricted diet. Up until at least 2 years of age, children need to get half of their calories from fat, much more than the 30% of calories from fat recommended for adults. After that, the amount of fat can gradually be reduced with healthy, lower fat food choices. Parents can use tools like MyPyramid for Kids (www.mypyramid.gov/kids) for guidance in offering a wide range of healthy foods, and they can continue to model healthy eating behavior. It is also critical that they provide their child with ample opportunities for physical activity and even consider getting involved with advocacy efforts to increase the amount of structured daily physical activity provided as part of the regular school program (Zahner et al., 2006).

As in early infancy, it appears that an energy-restricted diet (particularly fat restricted) and possibly a high protein diet during early childhood may program a type of thrifty metabolism that can lead to obesity and other adverse consequences, especially if the child is exposed to overnutrition later in life (Rolland-Cachera, Deheeger, Maillot, & Bellisle, 2006). Indeed, the ages between 4 and 7 years have been identified as a time of "adiposity rebound," when BMI reaches a nadir and then begins to increase throughout the rest of childhood, adolescence, and young adulthood. Body composition studies provide evidence that this acceleration in BMI is associated with increased levels of fatness and not with increased lean mass or with any slowing of height velocity (Taylor, Williams, & Goulding, 2004). Children who have an early adiposity rebound (occuring before 5 years of age) have been shown to be at greater risk for overweight and associated chronic diseases such as type II diabetes, hypertension, and cardiovascular disease in later life than children with later adiposity rebound (occuring after 7 years of age) (Cameron & Demerath, 2002; Taylor, Grant, Goulding, & Williams, 2005), highlighting this period as a critical one for obesity prevention efforts.

The school years are often ones when families seem overwhelmed with other priorities, and good nutrition can suffer, taking a back seat to jobs, after-school activities, homework, etc. Indeed, this modern frantic pace of life is often cited as one of the main causes of the rising problem of pediatric overweight, with healthful foods being replaced with fast foods, skipping meals, eating on the run, and increased use of processed, packaged foods. Health care professionals can be instrumental in helping families reexamine priorities during these busy years and in identifying solutions to reinstate healthful eating. Examples include preparing lunches the night before, doing shopping and cooking on the weekend as a family activity, storing food for meals during the week, purchasing healthy snack options for children to select from after school, and using cooking and meal preparation as a family creative activity and a time for "checking in" and "quality time"—something many families desire and need.

Adolescence can be a particularly challenging time for maintaining good nutritional habits. Adolescents, food choices tend to be higher in fat and lower in fruits, vegetables, and calcium-rich foods than recommended by dietary guidelines (Story, Neumark-Sztainer, & French, 2002), putting them at some nutritional risk during a period of peak nutrient needs (Jenkins & Horner, 2005). By this time, most teens have clear food likes and dislikes, and peer influence is paramount, and parents may feel that they no longer have any control over what their teen eats. However, whether they show it or not, adolescents still depend on their parents for structure and constancy. Nutrient needs are very high during the adolescent growth spurt, and it is still very important that a healthful, balanced diet be available at home and that parents continue to model and encourage healthful eating (Larson, Story, Wall, & Neumark-Sztainer, 2006) and physical activity and enforce rules that teens eat at least some meals at home with their family (Fulkerson et al., 2006; Neumark-Sztainer,

Hannan, Story, Croll, & Perry, 2003). Having easy to prepare, quick to eat foods on hand like whole-wheat bagels or crackers, whole-grain cereals, mozzarella cheese sticks, rice cakes, fresh fruit, hard boiled eggs, yogurt, fruit cups, nuts, and dried fruit can help provide a teenager with good food "on the run." Developmentally teens are "now oriented," so emphasizing the benefits of healthful eating for energy and appearance are likely to be more motivating than discussions of disease prevention in later life. Unfortunately this is also the time that eating disorders can surface as body image develops (Croll, Neumark-Sztainer, Story, & Ireland, 2002), so discussions about what is normal (diversity in size and shape) versus what is marketed to teens (one size, thin) may be comforting and helpful.

Many parents have questions about the specific nutrient needs for their child: "How many calories should she have every day?" or "How will I know if he is getting enough calcium?" Clinicians can do a complete health and growth check to rule out or diagnose any nutritional problems. They can also provide guidance for recommended calorie and nutrient intake, being careful to remind parents that it is not typically possible to ensure that their child eats a nutritionally prefect diet every day. Supporting parents to fulfill their responsibility to provide foods to meet nutrient needs, to model healthful eating, and to trust their child to make selections from foods offered provides reassurance that they are doing a good job in caring for their child's nutritional needs and helps them resist the temptation to try to control their child's intake. The energy needs of infants, children, and adolescents can vary widely depending on size, metabolism, growth rate, and activity level, as can be seen in Table 20.1 (Kleinman, 2004). Pediatric Dietary Reference Intakes and selected nutrients (Food and Nutrition Information Center, 2002–2007) for children are included in Table 20.2. Tolerable upper limits (TULs), the maximum levels of intake of nutrients likely to pose no risk of adverse effects, are included where this information is available. This TUL information can be particularly useful when advising clients regarding safe levels of vitamins and supplement products to give to

Table 20.1 Estimated Energy Requirements

Age	Mean Weight (kg)	Mean Height (cm)	Calories/Day (Mean and Range)	Calories/kg of Body Weight	Calories/cm of Height
Infant (months)					
0–2.9	4.5	55	500 (400–700)	110	9.1
3–5.9	6.6	64	650 (500–850)	100	10.2
6–8.9	7.9	69	750 (600–1000)	95	10.9
9–11.9	9.0	73	900 (700–1200)	100	12.3
Children					
(years)	11	82	1200 (900–1600)	105	14.0
1–1.9	14	96	1400 (1100–1900)	10	14.6
2–3.9	18	109	1700 (1300–2300)	92	15.6
4–5.9	22	121	1800 (1400–2400)	83	14.9
6–7.9	28	132	1900 (1400–2500)	69	14.4
8–9.9					
Females (years)					
10–14.9	44	155	2200 (1700–2900)	50	14.2
15–17.9	56	162	2300 (1700–3000)	41	14.2
18–24.9	58	163	2300 (1900–2700)	39	14.1
Males (years)					
10–14.9	36	143	2200 (1700–2900)	61	15.4
15–17.9	57	169	2700 (2000–3600)	47	16.0
18–24.9	70	177	2800 (2400–3200)	40	15.8

Source: Kleinman (2004).

Table 20.2 Pediatric Dietary Reference Intakes (DRIs): Recommended Daily Intakes (and Tolerable Upper Intake Levels) for Individuals

Nutrient	Infants		Children		Females		Males	
	0–6 Months	7–12 Months	1–3 Years	4–8 Years	9–13 Years	14–18 Years	9–13 Years	14–18 Years
Total water (l)	0.7	0.8	1.3	1.7	2.1	2.3	2.4	3.3
Protein (g)	9.1	11.0	13	19	34	46	34	52
Carbohydrate (g)	60	95	130	130	130	130	130	130
Fiber (g)	ND	ND	19	25	26	26	31	38
Vitamin A (μg)	400 (600)	500 (600)	300 (600)	400 (900)	600 (1700)	700 (2800)	600 (1700)	900 (2800)
Vitamin C (mg)	40	50	15 (400)	25 (650)	45 (1200)	65 (1800)	45 (1200)	75 (1800)
Folate (μg)	65	80	150 (300)	200 (400)	300 (600)	400 (800)	300 (600)	400 (800)
Calcium (mg)	210	270	500 (2500)	800 (2500)	1300 (2500)	1300 (2500)	1300 (2500)	1300 (2500)
Iron (mg)	0.27 (40)	11 (40)	7 (40)	10 (40)	8 (40)	15 (45)	8 (40)	11 (45)
Zinc (mg)	2 (4)	3 (5)	3 (7)	5 (12)	8 (23)	9 (34)	8 (23)	11 (34)
Sodium (mg)	120	370	1000 (2300)	1200 (2900)	1500 (3400)	1500 (3600)	1500 (3400)	1500 (3600)

Source: Food and Nutrition Information Center (2002–2007).

their children. Parents can also be referred to the many excellent resources available on the Internet and to use the information on the Nutrition Facts label to make more informed choices.

CONCLUSION

The problem of child overweight will only be successfully addressed through the coordinated efforts of parents and health care providers in partnership with policy makers, schools, the media, food producers, and public health agencies (Flynn et al., 2006). This is a serious problem that affects and involves all of society, yet it is the welfare of each individual overweight child that must be of primary concern as we consider what actions to take. Best practice guidelines require practitioners to provide interventions and treatment strategies that support overweight children to achieve their healthy weight through the development of healthful eating habits while also protecting their normal growth and development. This is not an easy task given the often conflicting nutrition advice and ever-changing food environment. However, reliance on basic principles of sound nutrition—balance, variety, and moderation—coupled with an understanding of normal child development and good parenting skills provide the foundation for application of effective intervention and treatment strategies.

RECOMMENDED READING

W. H. Dietz & L. Stern. (1999). *The Official, Complete Home Reference Guide to Your Child's Nutrition*. Elk Grove Village, IL: American Academy of Pediatrics. An authoritative, comprehensive resource for parents, this book provides useful tips on how to feed children well without turning into the "food police." Subjects cover all ages and include instructions for breast- and bottle-feeding, introducing semisolids and solids, toddler meals and resistance, school lunches, adolescent/parent food struggles, eating disorders, parental influence, peer pressure, television, food safety, alternative diets, and allergies.

S. Hassink (Ed.). (2006). *A Parent's Guide to Childhood Obesity: A Road Map to Health*. Elk Grove Village, IL: American Academy of Pediatrics. This book provides research-based evidence for understanding and treating childhood obesity. Medical, emotional, and psychological factors and normal pediatric nutrition are addressed, and practical guidelines are offered to help parents create balanced meals, encourage physical activity, deal with setbacks, and address such challenges as sneaking food, snacking and grazing, and eating during the holidays.

E. Satter. (2005). *Your Child's Weight: Helping Without Harming.* Madison, WI: Kelcy Press. Written by a registered dietitian, licensed clinical social worker, and mother, this book combines excellent practical and compassionate information about parenting and feeding and presents the overweight child issue in a new way. Conventional thinking about treatment (having overweight children eat less and exercise more) is challenged and two-way trust and respect in feeding is emphasized.

M. Story, K. Holt, & D. Sofka (Eds.). (2002). *Bright Futures in Practice: Nutrition,* 2nd ed. Arlington, VA: National Center for Maternal and Child Health. This book is written specifically for health care professionals, policy makers, and educators working with children and families in a variety of community and clinical settings. It is organized by age and developmental stages and includes basic nutrition information, guidance for interview questions, recommendations for screening and assessment, and suggestions for counseling and anticipatory guidance.

B. Swinney. (1999). *Healthy Food for Healthy Kids: A Practical and Tasty Guide to Your Child's Nutrition.* New York: Simon and Schuster. Written by a registered dietitian and mother, this book includes good basic nutrition information, practical and realistic suggestions for parents to help their young children develop good attitudes about healthy eating, and many nutritious, easy to prepare recipes.

REFERENCES

Agostoni, C., Scaglioni, S., Ghisleni, D., Verduci, E., Giovannini, M., & Riva, E. (2005). How much protein is safe? *International Journal of Obesity, 29*(suppl. 2), S8–S13.

Allen, L. H. (1994). Nutritional influences on linear growth: a general review. *European Journal of Clinical Nutrition, 48*(suppl. 1), S75–S89.

Braun, M. L., Giugliani, E. R., Mattos-Soares, M. E., Giugliani, C., de Oliveira, A. P., & Machado Danleon, C. M. (2003). Evaluation of the impact of the baby-friendly hospital initiative on rates of breastfeeding. *American Journal of Public Health, 93,* 1277–1279.

Burke, V., Beilin, L. J., Simmer, K., Oddy W. H., Blake, K. V., Doherty, D., Kendall, G. E., Newnham, J. P., Landau, L. I., & Stanley, F. J. (2005) Breastfeeding and overweight: longitudinal analysis in an Australian birth cohort. *Journal of Pediatrics, 147,* 56–61.

Cameron, N., & Demerath, E. W. (2002). Critical periods in human growth and their relationship to diseases of aging. *American Journal of Physical Anthropology, 35,* 159–184.

Committee on Communications. (2006). Children, adolescents and advertising. *Pediatrics, 118,* 2563–2569.

Committee on Nutrition. (2003) Prevention of pediatric overweight and obesity. *Pediatrics, 112,* 424–430.

Croll, J., Neumark-Sztainer, D., Story, M., & Ireland, M. (2002). Prevalence and risk and protective factors related to disordered eating behaviours among adolescents: relationship to gender and ethnicity. *Journal of Adolescent Health, 31,* 166–175.

Demmelmair, H., von Rosen, J., & Koletzko, B. (2006). Long-term consequences of early nutrition. *Early Human Development, 82,* 567–574.

de Onis, M., Garza, C., Onyango, A. W., & Borghi, E. (2007). Comparison of the WHO child growth standards and the CDC 2000 growth charts. *Journal of Nutrition, 137,* 144–148.

de Onis, M., Onyango, A. W., Borghi, E., Garza, C., Yang, H., & WHO Multicentre Growth Reference Study Group. (2006). Comparison of the World Health Organization (WHO) child growth standards and the National Center for Health Statistics/WHO international growth reference: implications for child health programmes. *Public Health Nutrition, 9,* 942–947.

Department of Health and Human Services. (2001). The Surgeon General's Call to Action to Prevent and Decrease Overweight and Obesity. Rockville, MD: Department of Health and Human Services, Public Health Service, Office of the Surgeon General. Available at www.surgeongeneral.gov/topics/obesity/calltoaction/CalltoAction.pdf.

Desai, M., & Hales, C. N. (1997). Role of fetal and infant growth in programming metabolism in later life. *Biological Reviews of the Cambridge Philosophical Society, 72,* 329–348.

de Simone, M., Farello, G., Palumbo, M., Gentile, T., Ciuffreda, M., Oliso, P., Cinque, M., & de Matteis, F. (1995). Growth charts, growth velocity and bone development in childhood obesity. *International Journal of Obesity and Related Metabolic Disorders, 19,* 851–857.

Dubois, L., & Girard, M. (2006). Early determinants of overweight at 4.5 years in a population-based longitudinal study. *International Journal of Obesity, 30,* 610–617.

Ekelund, U., Ong, K., Linne, Y., Neovius, M., Grage, S., Dunger, D. B., Wareham, N. J., & Rössner, S. (2006). Upward weight percentile crossing in infancy and early childhood independently predicts fat mass in young adults: the Stockholm Weight Development Study (SWEDES). *American Journal of Clinical Nutrition, 83,* 324–330.

Flynn, M. A., NcNeil, D. A., Maloff, B., Mutasingwa, D., Wu, M., Ford, C., & Tough, S. C. (2006). Reducing obesity and related chronic disease risk in children and youth: a synthesis of evidence with "best practice" recommendations. *Obesity Reviews, 7*(suppl. 1), 7–66.

Food and Nutrition Information Center. (2002–2007). Dietary guidance. Available at http://fnic.nal.usda.gov/nal_display/index.php?info_center=4&tax_level=1&tax_subject=256.

Fulkerson, J. A., Story, M., Mellin, A., Leffert, N., Neumark-Sztainer, D., & French, S. A. (2006). Family dinner meal frequency and adolescent development: relationships with developmental assets and high-risk behaviors. *Journal of Adolescent Health, 39,* 337–345.

Gillman, M. W., Rifas-Shiman, S. L., Berkey, C. S., Farzier, A. L., Rocket, H. R., Camargo, C. A., Jr., Field, A. E., & Colditz, G. A. (2006). Breast-feeding and overweight in adolescence. *Epidemiology, 17,* 112–114.

Goldfield, G. S., Paluch, R., Keniray, K., Hadjuyannakis, S., Lumb, A. B., & Adamo, K. (2006). Effects of breastfeeding on weight changes in family-based pediatric obesity treatment. *Journal of Developmental and Behavioral Pediatrics, 27,* 93–97.

Health Canada (2004). Exclusive Breastfeeding Duration—2004 Health Canada Recommendation. Her Majesty the Queen in Right of Canada. Accessed from http://www.hc-sc.gc.ca/fn-an/nutrition/child-enfant/infant-nourisson/excl_bf_dur-dur_am_excl_e.html

Himes, J. H., & Dietz, W. H. (1994). Guidelines for overweight in adolescent prevention services: recommendations from an expert committee. *American Journal of Clinical Nutrition, 59,* 307–316.

Iyengar, G. V., & Nair, P. P. (2000). Global outlook on nutrition and the environment: meeting the challenges of the next millennium. *Science of the Total Environment, 249,* 331–346.

James, W. P. (2005). The policy challenge of coexisting undernutrition and nutrition-related chronic diseases. *Maternal and Child Nutrition, 1,* 197–203.

Jenkins, S., & Horner, S. D. (2005). Barriers that influence eating behaviors in adolescents. *Journal of Pediatric Nursing, 20,* 258–267.

Kleinman, R. E. (Ed.). (2004). *Pediatric nutrition handbook*, 5th ed. Elk Grove Village, IL: American Academy of Pediatrics.

Kramer, M. S., Chalmers, B., Hodnett, E. D., Sevkovskaya, Z., Dzikovich, I., Shapiro, S., Collet, J. P., Vanilovich, I., Mezen, I., Ducruet, T., Shishko, G., Zubovich, V., Mknuik. D., Gluchanina, E., Dombrovskiy, V., Ustinovitch, A., Kot, T., Bogdanovich, N., Ovchinikova, L., Helsing, E., & PROBIT Study Group (Promotion of Breastfeeding Intervention Trial (2001). Promotion of Breastfeeding Intervention Trial (PROBIT): a randomized trial in the Republic of Belarus. *JAMA, 285,* 413–420.

Kramer, M. S., & Kakuma, R. (2002). The optimal duration of exclusive breastfeeding: a systematic review. Geneva: World Health Organization. Available at www.who.int/nutrition/publications/optimal_duration_of_exc_bfeeding_review_eng.pdf.

Larson, N. I., Story, M., Wall, M., & Neumark-Sztainer, D. (2006). Calcium and dairy intakes of adolescents are associated with their home environment, taste preferences, personal health beliefs, and meal patterns. *Journal of the American Dietetic Association, 106,* 1816–1824.

Li, C., Kaur, H., Choi, W. S., Huang, T. T., Lee, R. E., & Ahluwalia, J. S. (2005). Additive interactions of maternal prepregnancy BMI and breast-feeding on childhood overweight. *Obesity Research, 13,* 362–371.

Merten, S., Dratva, J., & Ackermann-Liebrich, U. (2005). Do baby-friendly hospitals influence breastfeeding duration on a national level? *Pediatrics, 116,* e702–e708.

Miralles, O., Sanchez, J., Palou, A., & Pico, C. (2006). A physiological role of breast milk leptin in body weight control in developing infants. *Obesity, 14,* 1371–1377.

Nelson, M. C., Gordon-Larsen, P., & Adair, L. S. (2005). Are adolescents who were breast-fed less likely to be overweight? Analysis of sibling pairs to reduce confounding. *Epidemiology, 16,* 247–253.

Neumark-Sztainer, D., Hannan, P. J., Story, M., Croll, J., & Perry, C. (2003). Family meal patterns: associations with sociodemographic characteristics and improved dietary intake among adolescents. *Journal of the American Dietetic Association, 103,* 317–322.

Ong, K. K. (2006). Size at birth, postnatal growth and risk of obesity. *Hormone Research, 65*(suppl. 3), 65–69.

Ong, K. K., Ahmed, M. L., Emmett, P. M., Preece, M. A., & Dunger, D. B. (2000). Association between postnatal catch-up growth and obesity in childhood: prospective cohort study. *BMJ, 320,* 967–971.

Owen, C. G., Martin, R. M., Whincup, P. H., Davey-Smith, G., Gillman, M. W., & Cook, D. G. (2005). The effect of breastfeeding on mean body mass index throughout life; a quantitative review of published and unpublished observational evidence. *American Journal of Clinical Nutrition, 82,* 1298–1307.

Papadimitriou, A., Gousi, T., Giannouli, O., & Nicolaidou, P. (2006). The growth of children in relation to the timing of obesity development. *Obesity, 14,* 2173–2176.

Pietrobelli, A., Faith, M. S., Allison, D. B., Gallagher, D., Chiumello, G., & Heymsfield, S. B. (1998). Body mass index as a measure of adiposity among children and adolescents: a validation study. *Journal of Pediatrics, 132,* 204–210.

Regan, F. M., Cutfield, W. S., Jefferies, C., Robinson, E., & Hofman, P. L. (2006). The impact of early nutrition in premature infants on later childhood insulin sensitivity and growth. *Pediatrics, 118,* 1943–1949.

Rigo, J. (2006). Body composition during the first year of life. *Nestlé Nutrition Workshop Series. Paediatric Programme, 58,* 65–76.

Rolland-Cachera, M. F., Deheeger, M., Maillot, M., & Bellisle, F. (2006). Early adiposity rebound: causes and consequences for obesity in children and adults. *International Journal of Obesity, 30*(suppl. 4), S11–S17.

Schack-Nielsen, L., & Michaelsen, K. F. (2006). Breast feeding and future health. *Current Opinion in Clinical Nutrition and Metabolic Care, 9,* 289–296.

Shen, W., Lui, H., Punyanitya, M., Shen, J., & Heymsfield, S. B. (2005). Pediatric obesity phenotyping by magnetic resonance methods. *Current Opinion in Clinical Nutrition and Metabolic Care, 8,* 595–601.

Sherry, B. (2005). Food behaviors and other strategies to prevent and treat pediatric overweight. *International Journal of Obesity, 29*(suppl. 2), S116–S126.

Shields, L., O'Callaghan, M., Williams, G. M., Najman, J. M., & Bor, W. (2006). Breastfeeding and obesity at 14 years: a cohort study. *Journal of Paediatrics and Child Health, 42,* 289–296.

Smith, D. W., Truog, W., Rogers, J. E., Greitzer, L. J., Skinner, A. L., McCann, J. J., & Harvey, M. A. (1976). Shifting linear growth during infancy: illustration of genetic factors in growth from fetal life through infancy. *Journal of Pediatrics, 89,* 225–230.

Story, M., Neumark-Sztainer, D., & French, S. (2002). Individual and environmental influences on adolescent eating behaviors. *Journal of the American Dietetic Association, 102*(3 suppl.), S40–S51.

Taylor, R. W., Grant, A. M., Goulding, A., & Williams, S. M. (2005). Early adiposity rebound: review of papers linking this to subsequent obesity in children and adults. *Current Opinion in Clinical Nutrition and Metabolic Care, 8,* 607–612.

Taylor, R. W., Williams, S. M., & Goulding, A. (2004). Girls undergoing early adiposity rebound gain fat at a faster rate than girls with a later rebound. *Asia Pacific Journal of Clinical Nutrition, 13*(suppl.), S43.

Toschke, A. M., Beyerlein, A., & von Kries, R. (2005). Children at high risk for overweight: a classification and regression tree analysis approach. *Obesity Research, 13,* 1270–1274.

United Nations Children's Fund. (1999). *Breastfeeding: foundation for a healthy future.* New York: United Nations Children's Fund.

von Kries. R., Koletzko. B., Sauerwald, T., & von Mutius, E. (2000). Does breast-feeding protect against childhood obesity? *Advances in Experimental Medicine and Biology, 478,* 29–39.

Veldhuis, J. D., Roemmich, J. N., Richmond, E. J., Rogol, A. D., Lovejoy, J. C., Sheffield-Moore, M., Mauras, N., & Bowers, C. Y. (2005). Endocrine control of body composition in infancy, childhood, and puberty. *Endocrine Reviews, 26,* 114–146.

Weaver, L. T. (2006). Rapid growth in infancy: balancing the interests of the child. *Journal of Pediatric Gastroenterology and Nutrition, 43,* 428–432.

Wells, J. C. K., & Fewtrell, M. S. (2006). Measuring body composition. *Archives of Disease in Childhood, 91,* 612–617.

Whitlock, E. P., Williams, S. B., Gold, R., Smith, P. R., & Shipman, S. A. (2005). Screening and interventions for childhood overweight: a summary of evidence for the U.S. Preventive Services Task Force. *Pediatrics, 116,* e125–e144.

Work Group on Breastfeeding. (2005). Breastfeeding and the use of human milk. *Pediatrics, 115,* 496–506.

World Health Organization. (1989). *Protecting, promoting, and supporting breastfeeding: the special role of maternity services.* Geneva: World Health Organization.

World Health Organization. (1998). *Evidence for the ten steps to successful breastfeeding.* Geneva: World Health Organization.

World Health Organization (2002). Nutrition: Infant and young child: exclusive breastfeeding. Accessed from http://www.who.int/child-adolescent-health/NUTRITION/infant_exclusive.htm

Zahner, L., Puder, J. J., Roth, R., Schmid. M., Guldimann, R., Puhse, U., Knopfli, M., Braun-Fahrlander, C., Marti, B., & Kriemler, S. (2006). A school-based physical activity program to improve health and fitness in children aged 6–13 years ("Kinder-Sportstudie KISS"): study design of a randomized controlled trial [ISRCTN15360785]. *BMC Public Health, 6,* 147.

Zeigler, E. E. (2006). Growth of breast-fed and formula-fed infants. *Nestlé Nutrition Workshop Series. Paediatric Programme, 58,* 51–59.

Index